P9-AZW-707

The Complete Guide To Acupuncture And Acupressure

THE COMPLETE GUIDE TO ACUPUNCTURE AND ACUPRESSURE

Two Volumes In One

MASARU TOGUCHI
AND
FRANK Z. WARREN, M.D.

GRAMERCY PUBLISHING COMPANY
NEW YORK

Publisher's Note: This book is not intended as a substitute for the medical advice of physicians. The reader should consult his or her physician in matters relating to his or her health, and particularly with respect to any procedures or techniques that may be described in this book.

This 1985 edition is published by Gramercy Publishing Company, distributed by Crown Publishers, Inc. by arrangement with Frederick Fell.

Printed and bound in the United States of America

Library of Congress Cataloging-in-Publication Data

Toguchi, Masaru.
The complete guide to acupuncture and acupressure.

Includes index.
1. Acupuncture. 2. Acupressure. I. Warren, Frank Z., 1916- . II. Title. [DNLM: 1. Acupuncture. WB 369 T645c]
RM184.T584 1985 615.8'92 85-15494

ISBN: 0-517-47316X

h g f e d c b a

Contents

Part I
Acupuncture

Part I
Acupuncture

Preface

If modern medicine were infallible and could cure all illnesses, I would not have learned the Chinese science of acupuncture and moxacautery* from my grandfather. I would not have written this book if there had not been individuals dissatisfied with modern medicine or patients who had come to have a deep faith in Chinese acupuncture and moxacautery after having been disillusioned by modern medical remedies, as well as people who were not inclined to use that science to improve their health.

Many doctors think acupuncture and moxacautery are unscientific medical skills, and such practices are not recognized by American medicine. Nevertheless, the medical techniques of acupuncture and moxacautery are clinically the most effective techniques available, with qualities which make them superior to modern medicine. I really wish that people in medical and political fields could recognize this fact.

Acupuncture and moxacautery treatment methods are attracting public attention these days despite remarkable progress in modern medicine. The reason is not only that the former have the power to cure illnesses by using a different approach from that of modern medicine, but also because the treatment is natural, so that the patient need not worry about harmful and poisonous aftereffects as in modern medical treatment. However, the general trend of public opinion shows that people are still far from understanding acupuncture and moxacautery.

Furthermore, few people know the advantages and disadvan-

*"Moxa" comes from the Japanese *moe kusa* (burning herb), a combustible material applied to the skin and ignited for the purpose of producing as eschar or counterirritant.

tages of acupuncture and moxacautery versus modern medicine. Some consider acupuncture and moxacautery treatments to be a moldering and musty medical art of the distant past, and they conclude that they are the superstitious activities of barbarians, somewhat akin to magic.

Acupuncture and moxacautery are hardly unscientific. They do have some unavoidable disadvantages, however. For example, moxacautery leaves a dirty-looking burn scar on the skin. This is mainly why many people dislike moxacautery.

Acupuncture and moxacautery give the impression of being a type of folk remedy that somehow has remained in existence after parting company with modern medicine. Not only do acupuncture and moxacautery grow out of a long tradition of medical science in the Orient. In addition, outstanding results using these treatments have been observed by doctors of modern medicine and, after much experimentation and observation, such treatments are being elucidated and substantiated by new scientific theories. Moreover, I think you will be able to understand the scar from moxacautery burns after reading this book.

However, theory is not the issue. The fact is that some diseases which are hard to cure through modern medicine can be cured easily by means of acupuncture and moxacautery treatments. And there is nothing more compelling than this.

A person can ultimately do only what he himself can do. Only the person who has full knowledge of his own temperament and abilities can accomplish anything because he can do one thing well.

Perhaps those of you who have bought this book might find something of value in acupuncture and moxacautery. Still, you may not be able to fully understand these sciences just by reading this book. But I hope you will gain a new interest in this unique aspect of medical treatment as you learn about the science of acupuncture and moxacautery.

CHAPTER I

The True Value of Acupuncture and Moxacautery as Medical Science

THE SCIENCE OF ACUPUNCTURE AND MOXACAUTERY IS STILL not accorded its proper value. This is especially true in the American medical field. The reason that medical doctors in the United States are very cold and indifferent toward the medical science of acupuncture and moxacautery is their fascination with the grandeur of Western medicine and a preoccupation with false notions of true medical science existing only in the West.

Although some medical doctors have recently begun to show an interest in the science of acupuncture and moxacautery, the degree of interest is quite limited. Actually, it is still largely ignored. However, history moves onward. While American medicine looks the other way, studies have been started in France, Germany, China, and Russia. Year after year, such research grows and flourishes. This is especially true in China today, where there is a national acupuncture and moxacautery research center; in addition, they are also practiced in general hospitals. The departments of acupuncture and moxacautery and Chinese herb medicine are equal to and accorded the dignity of the other departments of modern medicine. Also, due to

Chinese influence, acupuncture and moxacautery research centers have been built in Russia and the results from such research are continually being reported.

Science is a reality because of the efforts of men who acknowledge truth. This fact should not be overlooked. The science of acupuncture and moxacautery must be acknowledged and evaluated justly. Medical doctors in America need to discard their old prejudices and confront the medical truth to be found in acupuncture and moxacautery medical science, with the calm and open mind of the scientist who seeks the truth. The science of acupuncture and moxacautery and the techniques used at present contain many mysterious elements which must still be investigated. Therefore they may seem primitive to the person knowledgeable in modern medical science. But judging from clinical evidence, the fact is clear that acupuncture and moxacautery are surprisingly effective.

The proper attitude for a true scientist should be to accept this fact and to try to find the truth concealed in it. In this sense, the science of acupuncture and moxacautery can be said to be a medical treatment science with many aspects still to be discovered.

It is my belief that if we use modern medicine together with acupuncture and moxacautery, the blind spots of modern medical science can not only be filled in, but it can also be vastly improved.

CHAPTER II

The Trend in France, Germany, and China

HERBERT SCHMIDT, M.D., CAME FROM GERMANY TO JAPAN TO study acupuncture and moxacautery in April, 1953, and gave lectures in various places throughout Japan during his one year of study. He stated: "Although acupuncture and moxacautery may be relics of ancient medical science in Japan and China, they have a new and promising future in Europe."

Indeed, according to Dr. Schmidt, acupuncture and moxacautery are highly valued in France and Germany. Three thousand doctors in France and several hundred in Germany use them in general medical treatment, and many people have been helped through such treatment.

In China, acupuncture and moxacautery have flourished vigorously since the establishment of the new Chinese Communist government. Chairman Mao Tse-tung had an influence in Chinese medicine because he treated as equals both Western doctors and Chinese doctors who practiced Chinese herb medicine and acupuncture and moxacautery. He appealed to them all to teach one another their medical specialties and help one another to cure or prevent suffering. Premier Chou En-lai made a similar appeal as well at a people's conference. As a result, a national acupuncture and moxacautery research center was built. Each hospital contains Chinese medicine and acupuncture and moxacautery departments, and these doctors perform medical treatment in close cooperation with doctors of Western medicine.

In addition, China has established a Chinese medical research institute as a training center. University professors and Western medical doctors are encouraged to attend this institute and initiate research on Chinese medicine. At the same time, there are even specialized schools for Chinese medicine.

We surmise that the progress of acupuncture and moxacautery in Communist China will take on striking dimensions in the future.

CHAPTER III

Why Are Acupuncture and Moxacautery Effective?

TREATMENT BY ACUPUNCTURE ATTEMPTS TO CURE ILLNESS BY inserting extremely thin gold or silver needles into the skin and subcutaneous tissues. Medicines are not injected with the needles. Moxacautery medical treatment attempts to cure illness by putting a small amount of moxa on the skin and burning it.

A question that everyone asks is how and why such simple treatment can cure disease. That is not an easy question to answer. Many more questions still remain unsolved. Such questions will eventually be resolved, one by one, as research flourishes, concurrently with progress in medical science. If this is so, are the principles of these curative effects understood at all? To a considerable extent, they are.

While we know that many illnesses are cured by treatments of acupuncture and moxacautery, there are still some who scorn such treatment as unscientific; this is so because its theory is not well known.

The principles of cure of "acupuncture and moxcautery" are already clarified experimentally in the specialized field of scores of medical doctors. We apply these principles at the clinic, actually proving them and attaining successful results day after day. Nonetheless, the theory is complex. Captain Wiseman of the U.S. Medical Corps said of acupuncture and moxacautery, "This is the oldest medical science, but its theory cannot be explained without the most advanced medical science of today." Let me point out some of the important points as to what the cure theory is.

Action due to Autonomic Nervous System

Relationship between skin and intestinal organs: Autonomic nerves control all the functions of the intestinal organs; these nerves constitute a system in which messages from the brain are delivered to the intestinal organs. Conversely, there is a system that stimulates the cerebro-spinal system from the body surface and reflexively adjusts the functioning of the intestinal organs. The system was discovered by Dr. Hidetsurumaru Ishikawa, honorary professor at Kyoto University, and later the study was carried on by Professor Kyugo Sasagawa of Kyoto University. This is the basic theory of acupuncture and moxacautery: When acupuncture and moxacautery are performed on the body, depending on the location and technique, all the functions of the intestinal organs can be adjusted.

Head's Band

When there is an ailment in the intestinal organ, a sensitive area appears on a certain part of the skin; this area is called "Head's band." When acupuncture and moxacautery are performed on the Head's band, according to the study of Dr. Michio Goto, the pain in the organ and the subjective symptoms diminish. This phenomenon is explainable by the same theory as the autonomic nervous system theory.

Application: When the above theory is applied in the clinic, a wide range of illnesses can be effectively treated by acupuncture and moxacautery. Some of the important ones are: laryngitis, pleuritis, gastritis, gastric ulcer, enteritis, diarrhea, constipation, hemorrhoids, hepatitis, cholecystitis, nephritis, neurasthenia, menstrual pain, and many others.

Pharmaceutical Action

Free Amino Acid and Histotoxin: According to the study by Dr. Bunjiro Terada, professor at Nippon University, when acupuncture is given to a mouse whose kidney has been removed, it can stay alive for a long period of time (it dies soon without acupuncture); the number of leucocytes increases and the number of lymphocytes decreases; it controls the action of hyaluronidase (rheumatism causes scatter of pigments, but acupuncture controls it); it develops anti-allergy, and a similar change occurs when cortisone is injected; it also shows results similar to injections of salicylic acid, a painkiller; it has been found that the effect lasts longer when acupuncture is applied than when injections are used. Hence, it has been proven that acupuncture is especially effective against rheumatism and neuralgia.

Dr. Masaru Osawa, professor at Kyoto University, researched the fact that histotoxin is produced as the result of moxacautery. He observed that this histotoxin produced unexpectedly good results for neuralgia and rheumatism.

According to my clinical observations, the same good results were observed, and such treatment showed superior results for neuralgia and rheumatism.

Application: It is clear that from the standpoint of pharmaceutical reactions, acupuncture and moxacautery are effective for treatment of the following illnesses:

Rheumatism, neuralgia, headache (headache on one side), hip pain, toothache.

Anti-allergic characteristic

When the parasympathetic nervous system (often called the vagus, which activates the function of stomach and intestines) becomes overactive, it causes asthma, hives, and gastric ulcer. In this case, acetylcholine is increased in the blood stream. According to the study by Professor Terada, however, when acupuncture is given, choline-esterase, which neutralizes acetylcholine, increases and these illnesses are known to be cured. Consequently, acupuncture is especially effective against allergy-type ailments, and also when acupuncture is applied to the neck, attacks of asthma and stomach pains are immediately eased. With moxacautery, the same effect is achieved.

Application: The above studies have shown that acupuncture is extremely suitable for the following allergy-type ailments: Rheumatism, asthma, hives, gastric ulcer, duodenal ulcer, conjunctivitis, hoshime [white speck in the eye], nephritis, cystitis.

Histotoxin and Yushi*

According to the study by Professor Osawa, histotoxin, which is produced when moxacautery is given, has the power to prevent arteriosclerosis. Furthermore, experiments show that a patient who already has arteriosclerosis can also be cured by moxacautery.

*Derived from the name of the famous ancient Chinese physician, Yu.

When the acupuncture is applied in the manner of Yushi to the spine, according to Haruto Kinoshita, Director of Academic Science of Tokyo Acupuncture and Moxacautery Association, high blood pressure can be dramatically lowered.

Moreover, the histotoxin produced by application of moxacautery is found to bring about natural biological sleepiness; also, when acupuncture is applied on the neck or shoulder, sleep can be improved by the effect of the acupuncture which is transmitted to the interbrain section via the autonomic nerves.

Application: High blood pressure, arteriosclerosis, tinnitus aurium, dizziness, neurasthenia, hysteria, insomnia.

Effect on Intestinal Organs

This effect may be regarded as caused by the joint result of autonomic nerves and pharmaceutical action.

Subsidence of Stomachache

Dr. Kinnosuke Miura, honorary professor at Tokyo University, states that acupuncture acts as a kind of anesthesia which slows down the excitation of the intestinal motor nerve function; slows the blood circulation and influences muscular contraction.

Application: Based on the explanation given above, acupuncture is known to be capable of stopping the distress of stomachache, abdominal pain, cholecystitis, chololithiasis.

Intestinal Movement (peristalsis)

Dr. Jujiro Kashida experimented on the decrease of intestinal movement induced by moxacautery on the stomach, and also Dr. Hideji Fujii experimented on the decrease of the small-intestine movement induced by acupuncture. According to my own experiment, when acupuncture called "sesshi" is applied on the hip, diarrhea is effectively cured.

Application: It is understandable that good results are obtained if we can slow down the intestinal movement against diarrhea caused by indigestion and food poisoning.

Expansion of Blood Vessels

According to Dr. Jujiro Kashida, blood vessels can be contracted in a very short time by applying moxacautery. It is then observed that blood vessels are expanded and blood circulation becomes active.

Dr. Michio Goto experimented on increasing the amount of blood after expanding the blood vessels in the hands and feet by giving moxacautery on the back. When acupuncture and moxacautery are applied, the blood circulation increases and paralytic contraction of muscles recover successfully; I have also noticed that due to expansion of the blood vessels, pain caused by neuralgia is eased.

Dr. Kashida constructed a fatigue curve by letting the muscle get tired, and when he applied moxacautery on the skin he found that the fatigue had been overcome.

Application: Based on these results, we realize that acupuncture and moxacautery give excellent results for the following ailments: Hemiplegia, infantile paralysis, paralysis of muscular movement, neuralgia, stiff-shoulder, and exhaustion.

Effect on Constituent Parts of Blood

LEUCOCYTES

According to Drs. Jujiro Kashida, Shigeo Harada, Keoru Tokicda, Masaaki Aochi, and Shimetaro Hara, after moxacautery is applied, the number of leucocytes increase twofold within one to two hours and continue to maintain this level for four to five days.

Again, according to Dr. Seikichi Yamashita, leucocytes increase the wandering function (wandering speed) within the system; they start the leftward metastasis of the nuclei and increase their ability to devour bacteria. An experiment by Dr.

Masaaki Aochi showed that after moxacautery was given, the opsonin* increased the activity of the leucocytes.

Application: From these results, we can say that the following ailments can be cured or lessened and the treatments can become useful in preventive medicine: Tonsilitis, rhinitis, colds, otitis media, tuburculosis, pleurisy, caries, hemorrhoids.

ERYTHROCYTES

According to research by Dr. Shimetaro Hara, if moxacautery is continuously performed for one month, the number of erythrocytes is increased and especially the amount of hemoglobin (blood pigment) that transports oxygen brought in by breathing is greatly increased and promotes metabolism.

Application: Anemia, fatigue and exhaustion.

Infantile Acupuncture and Alkalosis

When a large amount of sugar is consumed, the blood turns to acidosis (turns to acid and becomes harmful), but if moxacautery is applied, the blood becomes alkaline and is beneficial) and improves the growth of bones, according to a study by Dr. Hisashi Kurosumi; a similar change was noted with application of acupuncture by Dr. Shigemoto Mizuno.

Dr. Hideji Fujii also found that if a skin acupuncture is performed on a child, the treatment becomes a kind of variational treatment and promotes vital functions; this method is said to be an ideal stimulating treatment for children.

Furthermore, according to the study of skin acupuncture which is used on a child without pain, rabbits may be raised without sunlight by means of acupuncture and the growth result is just as equal to that in rabbits raised in sunlight.

So for city children who play under little sunshine or who consume a large amount of sugar which causes acidosis, we

*Opsonin occurs normally in the blood serum and prepares for the destruction of bacteria.

apply skin acupuncture (infantile acupuncture) two or three times a month. The results are surprisingly good.

Incidentally, infantile acupuncture can be performed on a child after one month of its birth.

Application: Night crying, temper, loss of appetite, under-development.

Antibodies

According to the studies by Dr. Kaoru Tokieda and Dr. Masaki Aochi, agglutinine, hemolysin, precipitin and complement body volume are increased by use of acupuncture and moxacautery and their immunoreactions become stronger. The use of such treatment is important in preventive medicine, and also increases the number of leucocytes.

Application: Rejuvenation, promotion of health, longevity, increase of resistance against virus due to contageous diseases.

On Kyoraku

Ancient medical books, such as *Naikyo* and *Nankyo*, are old references written two or three thousand years ago in China, which were imported to Japan about 1400 years ago (Asuka Era) and were studied widely during the Edo Era. These books were passed on to us today with the addition of some of the unique Japanese methods. *Kyoraku* is the principal concept of diagnosis and treatment by acupuncture and moxacautery.

Adjustment of the 14 Kyoraku

With the exception of a portion of *kyoraku*, most of the other parts of the theory of *kyoraku* have not been explained by modern medical science; however, as Dr. Takehiro Itakura has said, the principal *kyoketsu (tsubo)* are joined by hypothetical conjunction lines called *kyoraku;* there is a system of 14 kyoraku over the body. As long as these lines are in balance by equal forces, a person is healthy; however, once a person becomes ill, unequal strengths are created somewhere in the system. In such a case, we can make a diagnosis if we examine the pulse, stomach, and the face. And in order to adjust the unbalanced strengths of the system, we check the reactions of *kyoketsu (tsubo)* of the hands and feet and treat them. This becomes the principal philosophy of Oriental medicine (which states that we treat according to the symptom). There are, therefore, some people in the business of acupuncture and moxacautery who perform moxacautery only on the stomach if the stomach requires it or who perform acupuncture only on the hip if the hip is in pain, but such a treatment is called local treatment and is not a true treatment; even if the ailment is cured, it can easily recur.

Function of Warm Moxacautery

Warm moxacautery is a method used without directly burning the skin. (The kind sold in stores which uses incense sticks in porcelain to give warmth and is similar to a pocket heater cannot be classified as warm moxacautery.)

The function of warm moxacautery is to expand the blood vessels and to increase blood circulation, and thus promote the function of the organs and improve digestion and absorption; hence, the function of the liver is improved and secretion of the digestive fluid is increased.

Therefore, warm moxacautery is extremely effective against loss of appetite, diarrhea, and constipation, which are all caused by gastroenteric disorder; physical stamina is increased and the body puts on weight; sexual drive becomes stronger; a person is rejuvenated and sterility is overcome.

When warm moxacautery is performed, the stomach and intestines as well as the liver are vigorously activated and they begin to function properly. Consequently, more food than usual should be consumed during the main meals, increasing protein, fatty foods, and fruits. Empty stomach and intestines due to small food intake is not good.

Also, in most cases of gastroenteric disorders, the ailment has become chronic over many years; in order to cure the disorder, the treatment must start from improvement of the physical constitution. Hence, the treatment must be started with 100 treatments as a unit basis. It is important that treatment must be performed every day; if treatment is given every other day, the effectiveness drops by more than half.

While there are people who blindly believe in medicines and injections, they question the effectiveness of acupuncture and moxacautery; however, their effectiveness cannot be stated in one word, because various fields are covered.

Many people are afraid of the pain and burning due to their lack of experience with acupuncture and moxacantery; acupuncture can be painless, depending on skill. Moxacautery, also, is not so hot since the size is smaller than a grain of rice. As one becomes accustomed to it, he feels very comfortable. After the treatment, the body and soul feel wonderfully pleasant. Ordinary medical treatment cannot give such a feeling.

Summary of Treatments by Our Clinics in Japan

Rejuvenation, aphrodisiac, potent hormone treatment (treatment by gold needle.)

Neuralgia, rheumatism, hemiplegia, shoulder pain, hip pain, recovery from fatigue, stiff shoulder, sprain, bruise, malfunction of the stomach and intestines, jaundice, beriberi, diabetes, hemorrhoids, closure of urinary tract due to enlargement of prostate, chronic appendicitis, cold, tonsillitis, high blood pressure, anemia, insomnia, chronic otitis media, cystitis, menstruation difficulty, bed wetting at night, menopause disorder, etc.

CHAPTER IV

Localized Treatment and Overall Treatment

LOCALIZED TREATMENT ACHIEVES ITS EFFECT THROUGH THE application of acupuncture or moxacautery at selected Vital Points near the affected part of the body. On the other hand, overall treatment involves the examination of the patient in general and the adjustment of the all-around imbalance in the functioning of the whole body. Localized treatment is usually more effective in cases of acute illness and is simple for the layman to use and understand.

In order to cure an illness completely, one must always try to apply overall treatment. For treatment of a chronic illness, the necessity for overall treatment is stressed. If you cannot discover a name for the illness, even though the patient exhibits a variety of symptoms, apply overall treatment consistently. This sometimes produces an unexpectedly favorable reaction. Therefore, if you suspect that the condition is complicated, overall treatment is recommended.

In some cases, you may have surprising results through such treatment at the Vital Points. Sometimes, though, you may not get such effective results. Even so, and actual cases appear to be insufficient, it is not necessarily the acupuncture or moxacautery treatment that is at fault. There are many conceivable causes for this; for example, one might not discover the proper point of treatment, or choose the wrong treatment point, or lack the necessary skill.

It is inevitable for the differences in results—which are subject to the skill of the practitioner—to be pointed out since it is the nature of acupuncture and moxacautery treatment to vary according to ability. Even a nonprofessional can obtain very good results.

CHAPTER V

Relationship to Other Types of Medical Treatment

IF ACUPUNCTURE AND MOXACAUTERY TREATMENT ARE DONE properly, very good results can be obtained. The patient may not require any other treatment. However, you must keep in mind the relationship of acupuncture and moxacautery to other types of treatment and be mindful of this at all times. This is because in many cases a person may use acupuncture and moxacautery in combination with other types of treatment after various of treatments have been tried.

The essence of Oriental medical science is the idea that the most desirable treatment is the use of acupuncture and moxacautery in combination with general Chinese herb treatment because they are based on the same philosophy. However, there are limitations common to both Chinese herb medicine and acupuncture and moxacautery. Therefore, in some cases, using these treatments alone may not be enough to resolve the matter. For example, there are some illnesses which cannot possibly be cured without emergency methods such as surgery, and some symptoms that can be relieved more safely and quickly through the use of antibiotics.

Although the method may be taken from either modern medicine or Oriental medicine, if the results are generally effective, then the combined use of these methods would be desirable in achieving better results. And in many cases the combination of two types of treatment would not be expected to cause negative results.

However, even though a particular medicine is supposed to be good for a particular illness, medicine that is not very effective may be continually given to a patient in a careless way. For example, the patient should not continually use customary remedies just because an injection can relieve neuralgia or just because a drug can relieve asthma. It is probably futile for such a person to hope for favorable results, and it is obvious that only harmful side effects can be expected. Favorable results cannot be expected in these particular cases, even if acupuncture and moxacautery are used in combination with that treatment.

One should avoid such medicines which have well-known side effects or offer only temporary relief, for they are apt to aggravate the body disorders, whereas acupuncture and moxacautery help to adjust body disorders.

CHAPTER VI

Method of Treatment for General Effect

SENSATIONS OF STIMULATION ARE GENERALLY PREDICTABLE side effects with application of acupuncture and moxacautery, and will be obtained from whatever part of the body treatment is aimed. However, if gentle applications are given evenly throughout the body, a certain definite general stimulating effect can be expected. In the case of acupuncture, treatment for the general well-being of the body will involve, in effect, the insertion of countless needles all over the body.

CHAPTER VII

The Patients' Complaints

COMPLAINTS OF PAIN OR DISCOMFORT MUST NOT BE IGNORED. Anywhere the patient complains of pain or paralysis becomes a matter for observation and treatment.

In Western medicine, the complaints of the patients are not always ignored, but only main points are considered, as the term "major complaint" indicates. The patients' sensations and emotional complaints were not given much attention since there is an admonition, "Don't pay attention to what the patient says." But in dermatology, hypersensitivity or numbness of the skin sense cannot be discovered through the principles and evidence of physics and chemistry alone.

Therefore the practice of listening to the complaints of the patient should be adopted as standard procedure. Even the first examination should lead to a correct understanding of the location of the paralysis.

CHAPTER VIII

The Four Methods of Diagnosis

GENERALLY SPEAKING, THERE SHOULD BE NO TREATMENT without diagnosis. The science of acupuncture and moxacautery has its own methods of diagnosis. These diagnostic methods do not involve the mere examining of a person to name an illness, as in modern medicine. Rather, they are examinations into the nature of the illness itself—that is, treatment-oriented diagnosis. From ancient times, four kinds of diagnosis have been used: observing, listening, questioning, and treatment.

CHAPTER IX

Remedial Medicine and Acupuncture and Moxacautery

THE HUMAN BODY MAINTAINS ITS HEALTH IN PHASES WHICH shift and flow according to ceaseless changes in the internal and external environment. When the body cannot sustain its constant balance and cannot return to its proper track, it is in an abnormal state, i.e., a condition of sickness. Because of this, the body falls into a state of susceptibility to illness, depending on various factors.

At this state, the condition cannot yet be adjudged definitely to be an illness. The patient feels bad and ill at ease because his nerves and blood vessels are in an abnormal state. The doctor will perform various types of examination, but he may not be able to find anything wrong, and merely say, "You must be tired. There is nothing wrong with your body." But the patient is not satisfied with the doctor's conclusions, and he goes home still feeling ill.

Suppose the patient then consults a doctor of acupuncture and moxacautery. This doctor can usually discover the abnormal condition of the body by means of examination used in the science of acupuncture and moxacautery. He can detect signs of disorder in the body by examining the pulse and the color of the skin, or by palpation. The most conclusive method in these cases is by palpation of the Vital Points, or by using mechanical testing measurements of the electricity on the skin. Thus, the acupuncture and moxacautery practitioner may discover areas of tenderness or induration through palpation of the Vital Points, which will indicate the location of abnormalities.

Using the neurometer, he can judge the location of abnormal internal organs or diseased portions of the body according to the distribution of the electrical voltage measuring points. Thus, treatment for such a case can be applied, depending upon the observed reactions at these Vital Points, even though the illness may not have been diagnosed yet.

Sometimes the patient may be restored to health without ever knowing the name of the illness. Thus, it is possible to prevent an illness if it is caught at the early stages of susceptibility to illness, and if treatment is promptly applied.

This is an extremely important matter in terms of medical treatment. It is the best method from the modern medical standpoint of "early medical treatment."

I call this application of medical treatment "remedial medicine." I consider acupuncture and moxacautery to be the best among those sciences which function as "remedial medicine."

It is said that tools will keep a long time without major damage if they are taken care of. It is the same with houses. And also with the human body. A person who treasures his watch takes care of it from time to time. He has his watch cleaned and oiled regularly, even if there is no sign of defect. The watch will then keep good time and remain in good condition.

Recently it has become popular to get treatment at clinics. That is fine, but a simpler diagnosis can be obtained through frequent application of treatments of acupuncture and moxacautery than by taking exaggerated measures such as those clinics do. Not only diagnosis but also remedial treatment is possible.

Remedial medicine is necessary. And the treatment by acupuncture and moxacautery can fill a major function in remedial medicine.

Gerontology belongs to remedial medicine as well. It is like caring for an old house. As the years pass after a house has been built, it becomes old and deteriorates. If you neglect its repair and upkeep, it will get completely run down and become unfit for use. The older it gets, the more it becomes necessary to repair it.

In recent times, the need for gerontology has been much discussed. That is very good. But treatment for illnesses of the aged by means of acupuncture and moxacautery is a special field, reaching beyond modern medicine.

High blood pressure, arteriosclerosis, the aftereffects of a cerebral hemorrhage, and encephalomacia are illnesses of the aged. This is the very field in which acupuncture and moxacautery as remedial medicine are especially effective. The various types of neuralgia, such as deformities of the lumbar discs, deformities of the joints, "fifty-year-old back," and low back pains occur as a part of the aging process. These illnesses of the aged are effectively treated by acupuncture and moxacautery.

One cannot expect complete cures through remedial medicine. Relative relief, although not a complete cure, is sufficient. It is enough to repair the body so that life may be extended.

CHAPTER X

Disorders of the Autonomic Nervous System and the Use of the Neurometer

AFTER MIDDLE AGE, PEOPLE BEGIN TO EXPERIENCE TROUBLE in various parts of the body. The family doctor may diagnose the case as a disorder of the autonomic nervous system. However, there may be no improvement, so the patient comes to depend upon acupuncture and moxacautery and Chinese herb medicine. Yoshio Nakatani, M.D., of Osaka Medical University, vice president of the Japan Association for Adjustment and Cure of the Autonomic Nervous System, explains the disorders of the autonomic nervous system in simple terms:

When the body is exposed to a cold wind, the blood vessels contract as a reflex action to protect the body. During meals, the body secretes saliva and gastric fluid to digest and absorb the food and to excrete the waste products. Further, if an organ becomes ill, the body takes action to cure it. The nerves which adjust bodily functions according to the circumstance independent of a person's will are called the autonomic nerves.

They are also called Vital Nerves because they control such internal organs and their structure as the heart, stomach, intestines, and kidneys. They are also related to the water, salt, protein, and carbohydrates in the body; hormonal and digestive secretions; blood formation; perspiration; and muscle tension. For these reasons, doctors diagnose many cases as disorders of the autonomic nervous system in the course of the aging process.

The Relationship of the Autonomic Nervous System to Illnesses

What is the relationship between disorders of the autonomic nervous system and illnesses?

Since the autonomic nerves can not be stimulated or restrained voluntarily, abnormalities in their functions may develop due to unfavorable external conditions such as weather, stress, mental and emotional state, intake of food and drink, or from poisoning. These abnormalities are what can constitute an illness.

For illnesses caused by bacteria, such as appendicitis, if the constitution of the affected region is strong enough, bacteria cannot be propagated. Therefore, the basic treatment for cure requires not only killing the bacteria but also strengthening the constitution of that part of the body. In other words, it is necessary to adjust the autonomic nerves to a point of order and allow normal functioning of the body.

Another example is the case in which hormonal secretion has decreased. The most desirable treatment for this would be to strengthen the autonomic nerve center, which controls the organs that secrete the hormone.

The majority of the more difficult illnesses to cure such as bronchial asthma, stomach ulcers, constipation, neuralgia, and rheumatism are especially connected with the autonomic nerves. Thus, returning the autonomic nerves to order is very important in curing these illnesses.

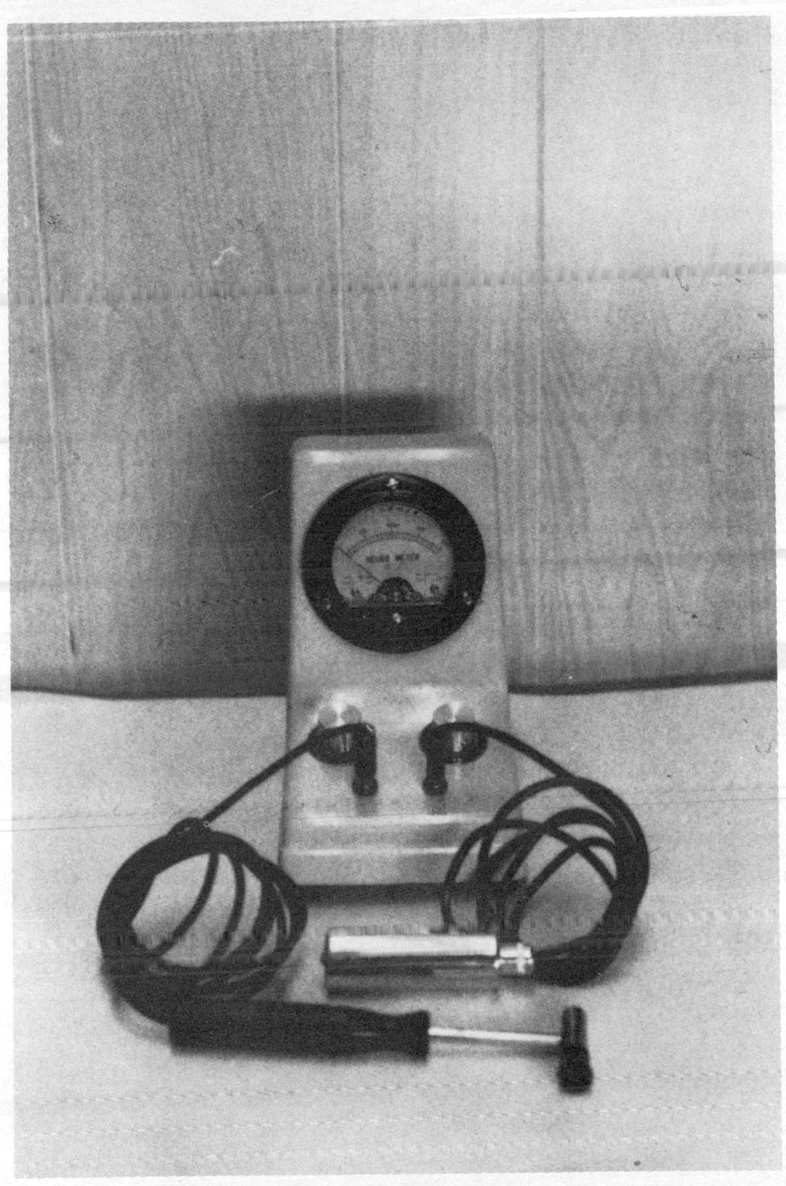

The portable neurometer

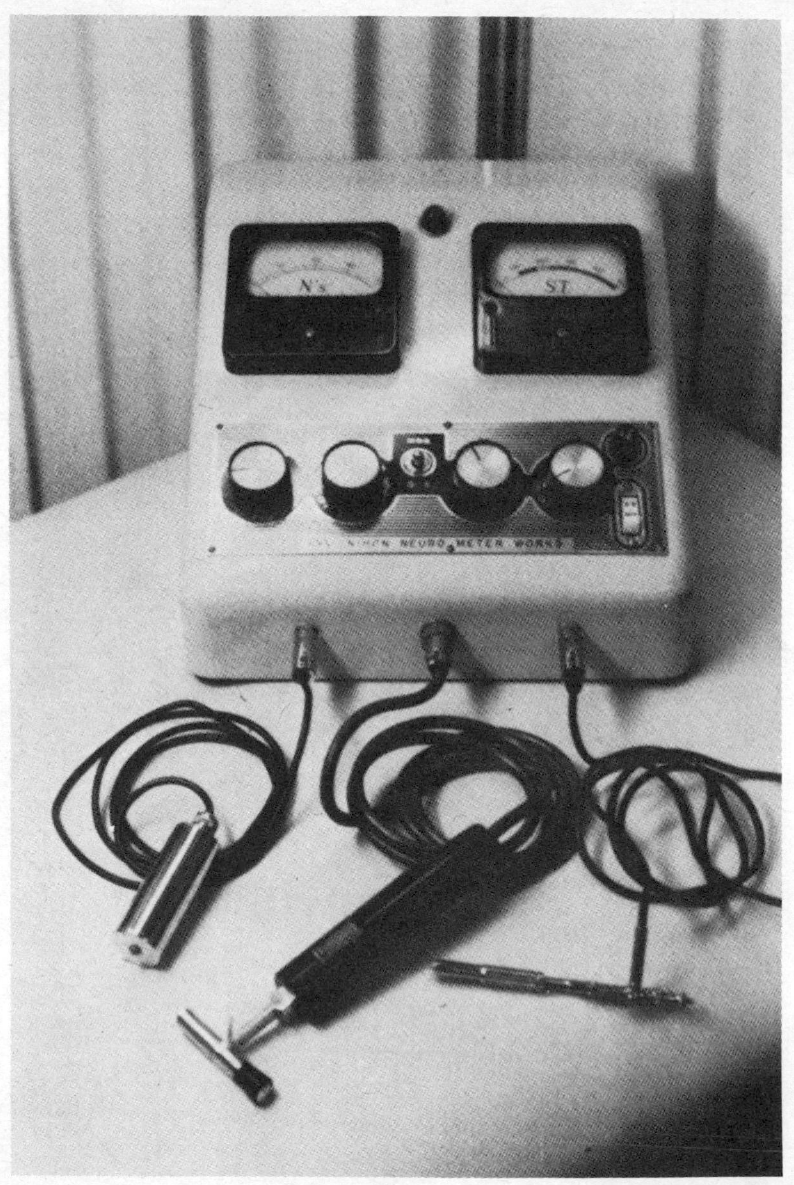

The neurometer for office

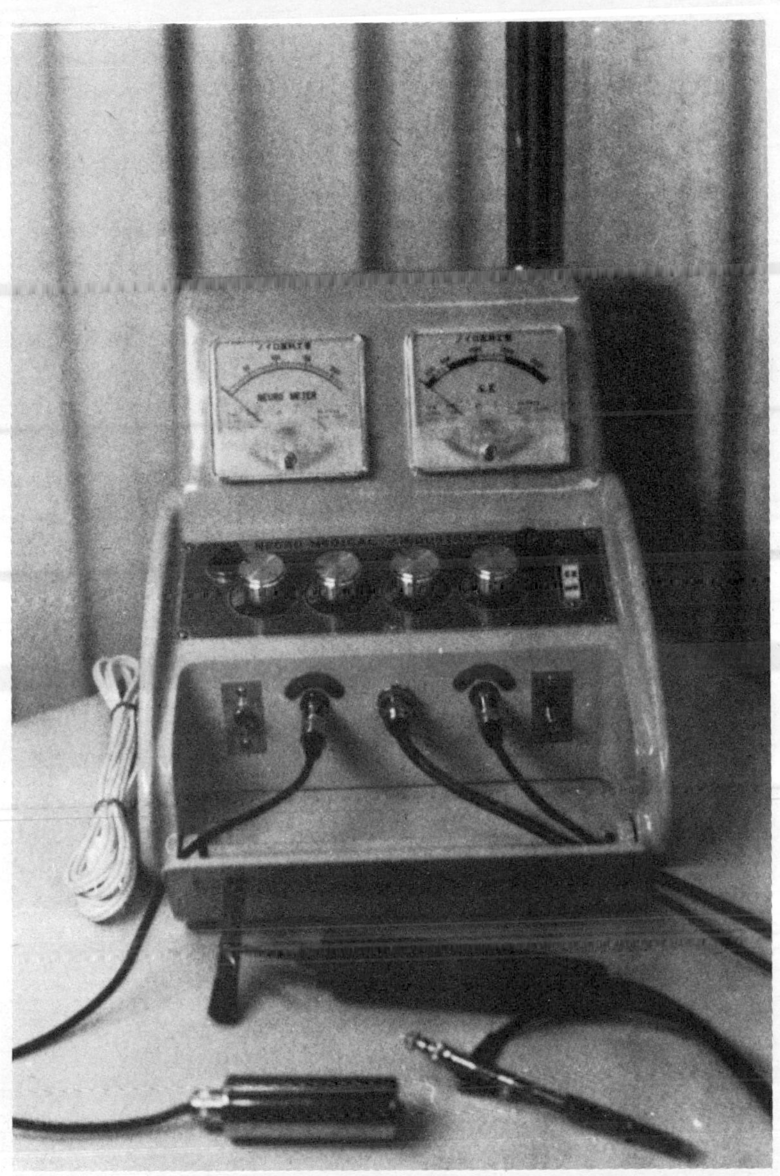

To measure H6 (LI) by the neurometer

Examination with the Neurometer

The neurometer, an autonomic nerve-function measuring device (invented by Dr. Nakatani in 1950), can indicate the exact location of disorders in a patient. It is a very simple device that measures the amperage on the surface of the skin at certain points of the wrist and ankle.

For example, the average amperage of the part of the autonomic nervous system which governs the liver is from 50–75 amperes in a 41-year-old woman. If the neurometer registers 80 amperes for a woman of this age group, however, it is an indication that her liver function is overaccelerated. On the other hand, if her kidney function registers 40 amperes, it means that her kidney function is overly inhibited. In both cases some trouble in those organs is indicated. In fact, this woman has an ailment involving pain in the digestive system and suffers from such symptoms of the aging process as lumbago and stiff shoulders.

Treatment of the **Ryodo-raku (Electric Permeable Point)**

Women are susceptible to symptoms of stiff shoulders, lumbago, and muscle pain. Is massage or are acupuncture and moxacautery effective in treating these symptoms? It can relax the muscles and stimulate the Vital Points, but it is not sufficient to treat only painful areas. In the human body, the meridians through which electric currents flow easily are called Ryodo-raku. In stomach illness, treatment is not complete unless it involves stimulation on the stomach Ryodo-raku and the reaction points on that Ryodo-raku.

Fourteen Ryodo-raku have been found on both the left and right sides of the body; six going to the hands, another six going to the feet, one down the center of the front, and one down the center of the back. The six Ryodo-raku going to the hands are termed the H_1 through H_6; Ryodo-raku for the "H" from "Hand" and the six Ryodo-raku going to the feet are termed the F_1 through F_6; Ryodo-raku for the "F" from "Foot." The front center Ryodo-raku is the VM Ryodo-raku, and the back center Ryodo-raku is the HM Ryodo-raku.

A new method of treatment which testifies to the scientific validity of acupuncture and moxacautery has recently become popular. This method involves the stimulation of the meridians of the Ryodo-raku using an electrified needle relative to the conditions of the normal state of the Ryodo-raku, thus returning the autonomic nervous system to its normal level of functioning.

Measuring the function of the internal organs on the neurometer, we can know the symptoms of the patient and, even though the name of the illness may not be known, we can treat the Ryodo-raku. As a result, we can cure illnesses by maintaining the normal condition of the autonomic nervous system. Further, treatment with drugs may also be necessary for the illness.

Although it was stated in the beginning of this chapter that the autonomic nervous system is not controlled by the will, it must be added that this system can be changed by the emotions. From ancient times, it was felt that each of the internal organs were affected by various emotions; for example, worry was thought to have an effect on the lungs, fear on the kidneys, and anger on the liver. Man can control negative emotions through his will.

A middle-aged woman on the one hand faces deteriorating health and, on the other, has increasing worries and concerns for her children and husband. Negative emotions such as stress accumulate. She should take care of her health by trying to keep calm and by consciously exercising control of feeling in daily living.

CHAPTER XI

Ryodo-raku Treatment

IN 1950, DR. NAKATANI MEASURED THE LEVEL OF ELECTRICAL resistance of the skin on the leg of a patient suffering from kidney trouble. He found a certain meridian through which electrical resistance was low (the voltage increases). The spot that he found was the *Jin-Kei,* described in the Chinese classics. He named this meridian *"Ryodo-raku."* He subsequently found many more points which have low electrical resistance *(Ryodo-ten)* on this *Ryodo-raku.* After this he was able to prove in the same way the existence of twelve similar *Ryodo-raku* which relate to various illnesses.

Following this, Dr. Nakatani performed statistical calculations for the *"tsubo,"* traditional points for acupuncture and moxacautery. Among the *tsubo,* he found that those electrical currents similar to the average electric current of the major tsubo of the four limbs *(Gogyoketsu)* were the *"Genketsu"* described in the Chinese classics. He defined them as the representative measurement points of each *Ryodo-raku.*

The Utilization of These Points in Clinical Treatment

(1) Measure the electrical resistance of the representative measurement points (there are in all 24 on both sides of the body) using the neurometer. Then transfer the measurements

to a personal graph chart and look for the measurements with marked discrepancies between right and left corresponding values, or wide variation from the average electrical current among all the representative measurement points.

(2) If abnormal *Ryodo-raku* are found in this way, apply acupuncture and moxacautery to adjust their balance. The purpose of this treatment is mainly to stimulate the points of tonification of the *Ryodo-raku* (equivalent to the "Mother-point" of the *Gogyoketsu*) in the *Ryodo-raku* of low voltage and the points of sedation (equivalent to the "Son-point") in the *Ryodo-raku* of high voltage.

(3) For localized treatment, measure the electrical resistance on the *Ryodo* point of the affected part of the body. Apply acupuncture and moxacautery treatment mainly in the region at which the voltage is abnormally high.

Relationship of the internal organs and viscera with the *Ryodo-raku*:

H1	*Ryodo-raku*	Lung
H2	"	Blood vessel, pericard
H3	"	Heart
H4	"	Small intestine
H5	"	Lymph duct
H6	"	Large intestine
F1	"	Spleen (digestion)
F2	"	Liver (genital organs)
F3	"	Kidney
F4	"	Bladder
F5	"	Gallbladder
F6	"	Stomach

Ryodo-raku measuring points—feet

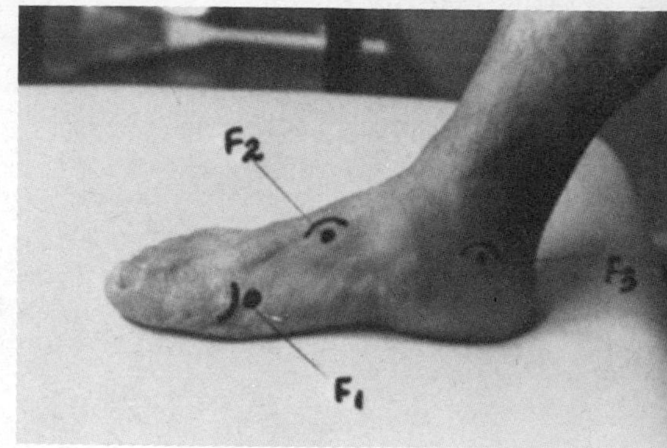

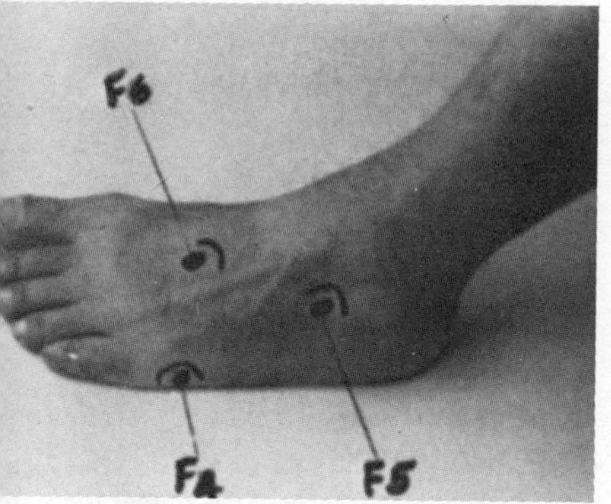

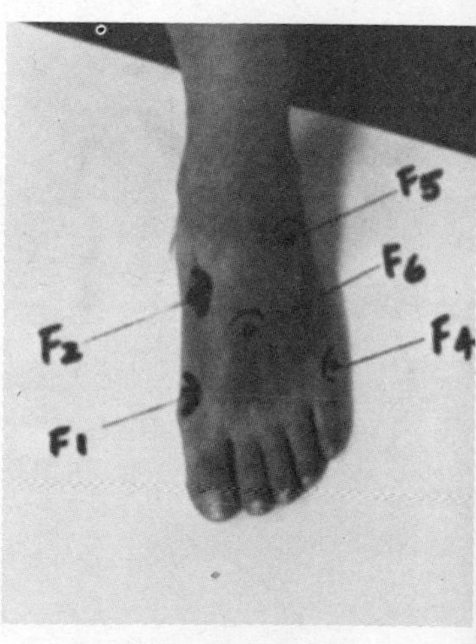

Ryodo-raku measuring points—hands

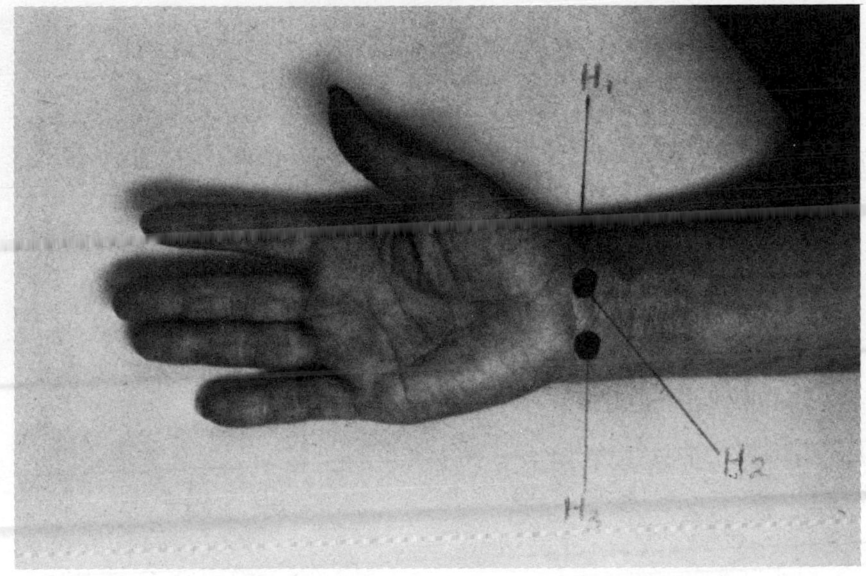

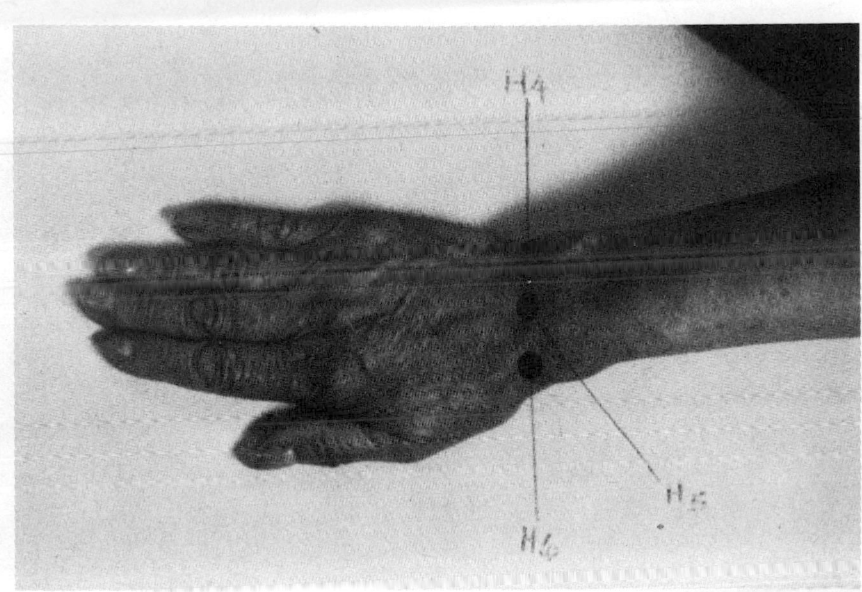

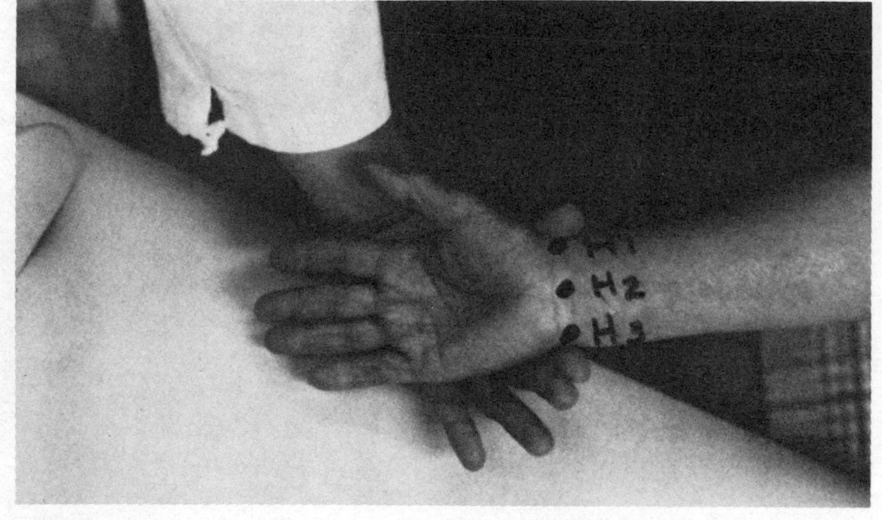

Locating Ryodo-raku points on hands

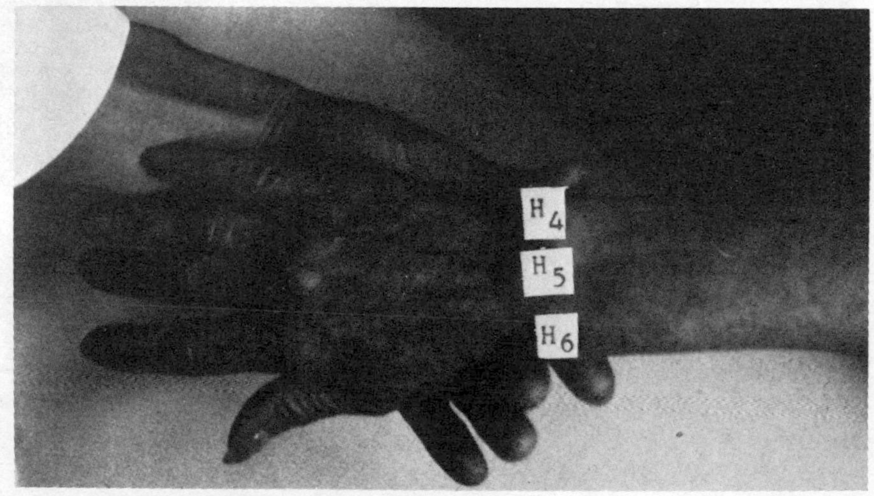

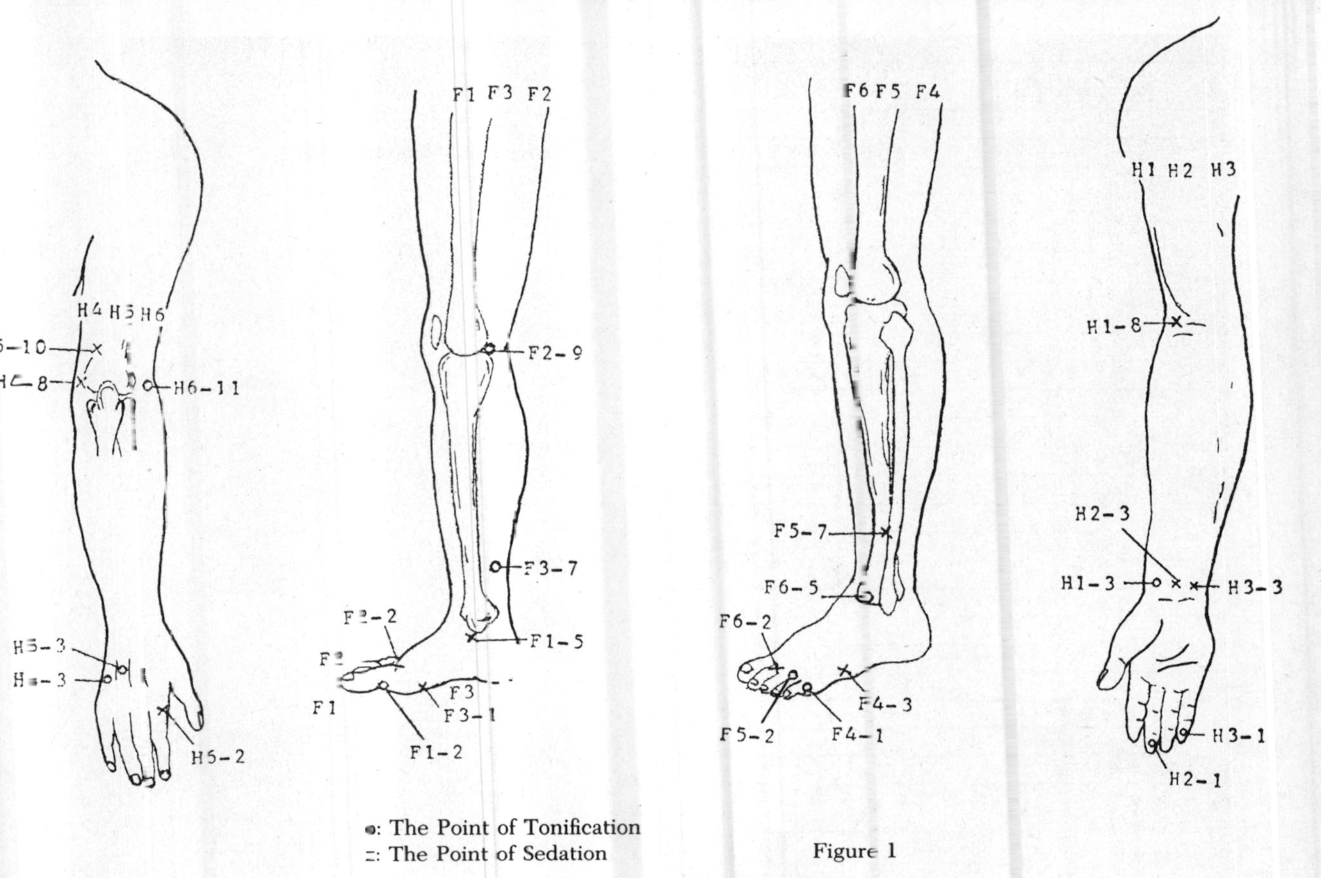

o: The Point of Tonification
x: The Point of Sedation

Figure 1

Personal Graph Chart

平均値	H1		H2		H3		H4		H5		H6		F1		F2		F3		F4		F5		F6		平均値
	左	右	左	右	左	右	左	右	左	右	左	右	左	右	左	右	左	右	左	右	左	右	左	右	
160 150 140 130 120 110 100 90 80 70 60 50 40 30 20 15 10 5	190 180 170 160 150 140 130 120 110 100 90 80 70 60 50 40 30 20 15 10 5		170 160 150 140 130 120 110 100 90 80 70 60 50 40 30 20 15 10 5		140 130 120 110 100 90 80 70 60 50 40 30 20 15 10 5		170 160 150 140 130 120 110 100 90 80 70 60 50 40 30 20 15 10 5		200 190 180 170 160 150 140 130 120 110 100 90 80 70 60 50 40 30 20 15 10 5		200 190 180 170 160 150 140 130 120 110 100 90 80 70 60 50 40 30 20 15 10 5		160 150 140 130 120 110 100 90 80 70 60 50 40 30 20 15 10 5		130 120 110 100 90 80 70 60 50 40 30 20 15 10 5		160 150 140 130 120 110 100 90 80 70 60 50 40 30 20 15 10 5		150 140 130 120 110 100 90 80 70 60 50 40 30 20 15 10 5		130 120 110 100 90 80 70 60 50 40 30 20 15 10 5		150 140 130 120 110 100 90 80 70 60 50 40 30 20 15 10 5		160 150 140 130 120 110 100 90 80 70 60 50 40 30 20 15 10 5

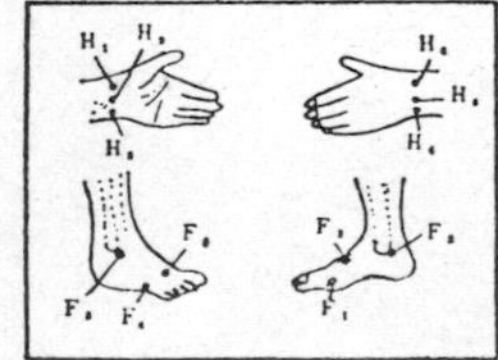

The Point of Tonification is over from area
The Point of Sedation is under from area

Figure 2

CHAPTER XII

Monshin *(Diagnosis by Questioning)*

Chills and Cold

Chills means a person feels chilly even after he warms himself. Cold means a person feels unpleasantly different only when he is out in the wind or when he faces the outside air. In both cases, it is a symptom of Hyo sho. Therefore it is important to ask the patient about these symptoms in order to determine the symptom of Hyo-sho. On the other hand, it is not always true that the patient has Hyo-sho simply because of a chill.

Chill and fever is designated by the existence of a chill and fever simultaneously, and is a sign of Hyo-sho. If the chill disappears but the fever goes up, it is called Alternating Cold and Fever and is a type of fever which belongs to Shoyobyo (Little Yang Illness).

When there is no fever but just a chill, it is Yin sho, caused by a chill.

Kantaiyobyo (Perspiration of Big Yang Illness). Hyo-sho causes natural sweating without the use of sweat medicine and is indicative of Hyokyo. However, even if it is Hyokyo, there is a period in which the patient does not sweat. In this case the differentiation must be made by taking the pulse.

In the case of Hyokyo, the pulse is weak. In the case of Hyo-jitsu, no natural sweating occurs and the pulse is strong.

Basically, Inbyo (Yin Illness) is not accompanied by sweating. If sweat pours out, it is called Dakken (profuse sweating) and is indicative of a serious illness.

Fever

In Chinese herbs, fever does not always imply a rise in body temperature. A feverish feeling is also considered to be a fever and is defined as a feverish feeling on the body surface and is felt to be feverish to the touch of others.

By the fever alone, it can't be distinguished whether it is Hyo-sho or Ri-sho; if a chill occurs simultaneously, then it is Hyo-sho.

In general Alternating Cold and Fever means cold and fever alternately; when the chill stops, the fever increases and when the fever stops, the chill takes over. This is a type of fever that belongs to Shoyobyo (Little Yang Illness).

Chonetsu (tide fever) means that when the fever appears, it spreads all over the body and is not accompanied by a chill or coldness; at the same time the patient perspires from the top of his head to the tips of his fingers and toes. If his feet get cold or if perspiration develops on his head only, it can not be designated as Chonetsu. Chonetsu is a type of fever related to Yomeibyo.

Shinnetsu (body fever) is similar to Chonetsu in that the whole body becomes feverish; however, there is no perspiring of the whole body. Shinnetsu is also a type of fever related to Yomeibyo.

In the case of Shusokuhannetsu (fever of hands and feet), the hands and feet feel hot and the patient prefers to leave them uncovered and likes to touch cool objects.

Stool

Those with hard stool and who are constipated are in most cases Jitsu-sho. Those who have diarrhea or soft bowel movements are Kyo-sho, although there are exceptions in this case.

There are those who are Kyo-sho but who get constipated. Even if a person feels congestion in his stomach and is constipated his pulse may be weak with no strength to his abdomen.

If a person is constipated due to a fever and has a weak pulse, then he is Kyo-sho.

If a person has diarrhea but the area below the heart remains hard and is painful, it is Jitsu-sho. If the diarrhea is severe and repetitious, then it is Jitsu-sho.

When the stool is black, it may be caused by Oketsu (stagnated blood). If the stool has a bad odor and is viscous, it is generally Jitsu-sho. If the stool is bluish or pale without viscosity, of the diarrhea type, without the ordinary odor, then it is Kyo-sho.

Urination

Shobenfuri means a small amount of urination. Shobenjiri means excessive urination. Shobennan means difficult urination.

Shobenfuri has distinctions such as Kyo and Jitsu. Due to perspiration, diarrhea, bleeding, vomiting, etc., body fluids are reduced and Shobenfuri can develop. In such a case, nothing in particular to increase urination is necessary.

As an early symptom of Osoku or Fushu, Shobenfuri may occur. In such a case, Kokatsu (dryness in the mouth) develops. If on the other hand there is no swelling but body fluids are maldistributed, then Shobenfuri can develop.

Those who have Shobenjiri are generally Yin-sho and Kyo-sho. There is also Shobenfuri which can occur due to Oketsu (blood stagnation).

Kokatsu

Kokatsu is defined as thirst; a person needs water. When the thirst is severe, it is called Hankatsuin. Persons who complain of Kokatsu may be divided into those who have dry lips as well as dry tongue and those who have moist tongue. Also, there are those who prefer hot water and others who prefer cold water. Furthermore, there are those who have dry mouths and little saliva and who want to wet their mouth but do not wish to drink water. This symptom is called Kokan and is distinguished from Kokatsu.

Hankatsuinin may be either Yang-sho or Yin-sho. To distinguish between these two, we look for Myaku-sho (pulse) or other references and make a diagnosis.

When a person prefers hot water, we call it Yin-sho, and when he prefers cold water, we call it Yan-sho. This is just what some people say. We may use this as a reference point but that is all. We should not separate the sho as Yang or Yin. Even a Yin-sho at its most extreme would cause a person to wish to drink cold water as if it had been changed into Yang-sho. The Yang-sho, too, at its extremes will cause a preference for hot water.

Kokatsu has no Jitsu-sho but only Kyo-sho. However, Kokan may be brought on due to Oketsu (blood stagnation). It is imperative that the sho be clearly understood by comparing it with other sho. With the exception of Oketsu, heat-giving and nutritional medications are applied depending on the sho.

For example, a seriously ill person or an old person may wake up after a nap with such a thirst that he can hardly move his tongue unless he drinks water.

Kokan caused by taking chemical drugs must be carefully distinguished.

Coughs

When a person coughs, we need to find out if he also wheezes or not, if it is a dry cough or a wet cough, if the phlegm is easy or difficult to cough up, and if the quantity of phlegm is great or little. It is also necessary to find out if he has to cough until his face becomes red, if he feels dry deep inside of his throat, if he coughs more often when he uses a heater, if he coughs badly at night, or if he coughs more frequently in the morning. A dry cough has no phlegm.

If the coughing is accompanied by Hyo-sho, we can stop the coughing by treating for Hyo-sho. However, if the coughing continues after Hyo-sho has left, then the treatment must be given according to the sho.

Headaches

There are also different kinds of headaches due to Yin, Yang, Kyo and Jitsu. If a person has a headache, fever, and chill with a strong pulse, he has a headache which is Taiyobyo (Big Yang Illness) and indicates a sho. This is called a Hyo-sho headache.

If the headache is so severe that a person vomits, his hands and feet turn cold, he becomes irritable, and his pulse becomes slow and subdued, this headache is also part of Shoinbyo.

Those who have Kyokyokuman (distressing fullness in the hypochondrium region) or Shingehiko (hardness in the region below the heart) often complain of symptoms of heavy-headedness and headaches. In Oriental medicine, this is called Zutsu (heavy-headedness).

Dizziness

Sometimes, it is called eye-dizziness or head-dizziness. They are all types of dizziness.

A patient with dizziness usually has stiff-shoulders at the same time. These stiff-shoulders are generally caused by Kyokyokuman, Shingemanshin (fullness in the region below the heart), or Shingehiko.

Sesshin

Sesshin means that the hands are used directly to make contact with the patient's body in order to make a diagnosis. Among these types of contact, the important ones are Myakushin and Fukushin.

Myakushin

Among the diagnostic skills in Chinese medicine, the one which is considered of greatest importance and has developed independently of the others is the method of pulse diagnosis. Modern medicine also describes the pulse in great detail. However, the pulse is understood to be related mostly to the conditions involving the circulatory system. There has been little thought given to finding clues for judging the state of the internal organs through pulse diagnosis as there has been in Oriental studies of medical diagnosis. Modern medicine does admit to some relationship between the body and the pulse. An obviously feeble pulse in a patient with head bruises is an indication of high cerebrospinal fluid pressure, and a slow pulse may be the result of an empty stomach.

Oriental medicine can diagnose the functioning of the liver, kidneys, organs of digestion and various others through the pulse for the presence of conditions such as pregnancy, constipation, diarrhea. It has become the very foundation for treatment. This point is very difficult for doctors of Western medicine to understand; many of them regard this practice as superstition.

The location for pulse diagnosis in acupuncture and moxacautery is the same as in modern medicine. Use the middle finger, index finger, and ring finger to palpate the pulse. The pulse at this position is called the Pulse of Sunko. The Pulse of Sunko is further divided into three: the "sunko" (the pulse closest to the hand), the "kanjo" (the middle pulse), and the "shakuchu" (the pulse closest to the arm). The Meridians of the Six Fu (Hollow) Organs (the Large Intestine Meridian running through the arm, the Stomach Meridian through to the legs, the Triple Warmer Meridian through the arms, the Small Intestine Meridian through the arms, the Gallbladder Meridian through to the legs, the Bladder Meridian through the legs) and the Meridians of the Six Tsang (Solid) Organs (the Lung Meridian through the arms, the Spleen Meridian through the legs, the Circulation

Meridian through the arms, the Heart Meridian through the arms, the Liver Meridian through the legs, the Kidney Meridian through the legs) are designated positions on these three parts of the pulse. Through pulse diagnosis, one can determine hyperactivity or hypoactivity in each of the meridians. Treatment by tonification or sedation (Pu-Hsieh) can be applied accordingly to each meridian.

This examination will show the condition of the pulse at which each of the meridians appears. After diagnosis of the points of hyper- and hypoactivity, it is possible to determine the degree of Pu and Hsieh necessary for each respective meridian.

There are two methods of examination at each of the three parts of the pulse: superficial and deep. Keep in mind that the deep pulse on the left hand corresponds to the heart, the liver and the kidneys while the deep pulse in the right hand corresponds to the lungs, the spleen and the "gateway of life" (an important Vital Point on the spine which is related to fertility, vitality, and the origin of the body's power or Qi).

The small intestines correspond to the superficial pulse on the Sunko of the left hand and the heart to the deep pulse of the Sunko on the left hand. The gallbladder corresponds to the superficial pulse on the Kanjo of the left hand, and the liver to the deep pulse on the same spot. The bladder corresponds to the superficial pulse on the Shakuchu of the left hand and the kidneys to the deep pulse of that spot.

In the same way, the large intestines correspond to the superficial pulse on the sunko of the right hand; the lungs to the deep pulse on that spot. The stomach corresponds to the superficial pulse on the Kanjo of the right hand, and the spleen to the deep pulse on the same spot. The Triple Warmer (function of nervous energy and warmth) corresponds to the superficial pulse of the right hand, and Circulation (also translated as the function of heart-constrictor and circulation-sex; more aptly called the function of control of the bodily organs) to the deep pulse on the same spot.

The interval between the fingers while taking the pulse is such that all three fingers touch each other lightly. If the patient has a long forearm, spread the fingers a little; if he has a short arm, close the fingers a little.

THE PURPOSE OF *MYAKUSHIN*

The purpose of Myakushin is to know the location of the illness, to know the Yin, Yang, Kyo and Jitsu, to know how cold or feverish the person is, to identify the *sho*, to know the condition of the illness before and after, and to know the physiological condition of the patient.

TYPES OF *MYAKU* (PULSES)

1. Fu—a pulse that seems to float on the surface (indicates location of illness is close to the surface)
2. Chin—a pulse detected by pressing down hard (indicates location of illness is internal)
3. Su—fast pulse (indicates fever within)
4. Chi—slow pulse (indicates Yin and Kyo)
5. Gen—strong pulse like the snapping of a bowstring (the pulse of Sho-yobyo—Little Yang Illness)
6. Kin—delicate but strong pulse (indicates Jitsu, pain, or cold)
7. Katsu—smooth pulse (indicates a fever or Jitsu)
8. Shoku or Ju—a hesitant pulse (indicates Kyo)
9. Bi—barely detectable pulse (indicates loss of vitality)
10. Ko or Dai—thick pulse (indicates fever)
11. Ko—hollow pulse like the leaves of an onion (indicates an atrophied condition after loss of blood)
12. Fun—deep, internal pulse (indicates Jitsu)
13. Jyaku or Nan—weak pulse (indicates Kyo)
14. Sai or Sho—thin pulse (indicates Yin or Kyo)
15. Kan—slow and mild pulse (indicates a slight illness or delicateness)
16. Soku—fast but irregular pulse (indicates Yang)

17. Kettai—slow and halting pulse (indicates Yang or Kyo, also irregular pulses)
18. Cho—long pulse (indicates Jitsu)
19. Tan—short pulse (indicates Kyo)
20. Kan—pulse that is neither fast nor slow and indicates a calm, medium pulse; so when a Kan pulse is detected in various illnesses, the illness is not serious and recovery is on its way.

CHAPTER XIII

Fukushin

The Fukushin Method

Make the patient lie down on his back, extend the legs, and either place his hands at his side or join his hands over his chest. Make him feel relaxed so that he does not tighten up his stomach muscles before examination.

If the patient tightens up his stomach muscles, it will not only lead the diagnosis to be mistakenly made as Kyokyokuman (distressing fullness in the hypochondrium region) or Rikyo of Fukuchokkin (tight stretching, straight muscles of abdomen), but also will often make it impossible to hear the sloshing water noises below the heart. It is therefore necessary to carry out Fukushin with the patient's legs stretched out and then to repeat Fukushin with his legs bent at the knees so that the straight muscles of the abdomen are relaxed.

Right				Left		
Superficial	Deep	The five elements		Superficial	Deep	The five elements
Large intestine	Lung	metal	Sun	Small intestine	Heart	Fire–1
Stomach	Spleen	Earth	Kan	Gall bladder	Liver	Wood
Triple Warmer	Circulation	Fire–2	Shaku	Bladder	Kidney	Water

Pulse of the internal viscera with the five elements.

	Kyo-Syo	Jitsu-Syo
First weakest pulse	•	⊕
Second weakest pulse	○	○
First strongest pulse	○	○
Second strongest pulse	○	○
Kyo pulse	●	
Jitsu pulse		●

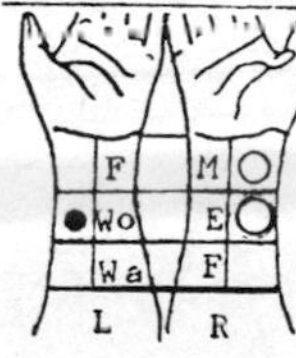

The type of liver Kyo-sho

Wood overcomes earth; in this case,
if it is Kyo-sho, earth pulse feels strong.

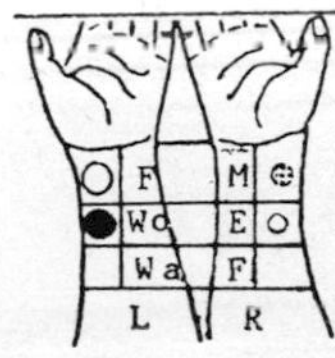

The type of liver Jitsu-sho

Wood engenders fire; in this case,
if it is Jitsu-Syo, fire pulse feels strong.

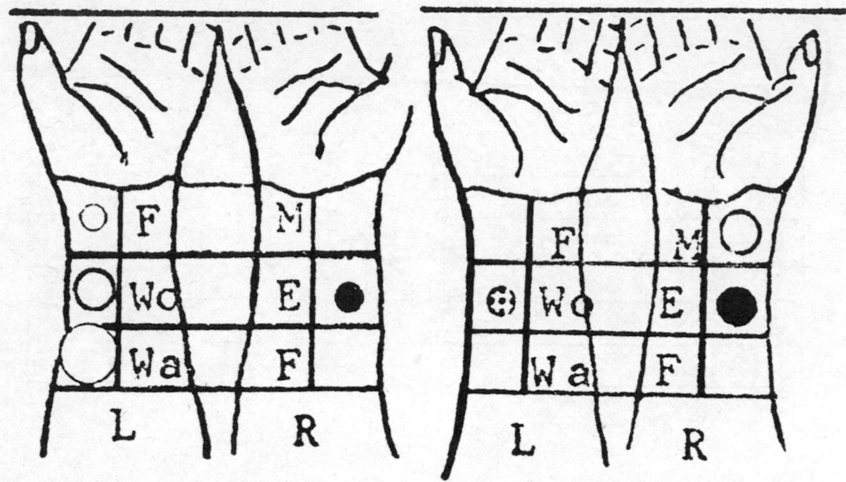

The type of spleen Kyo-sho *The type of spleen Jitsu-sho*

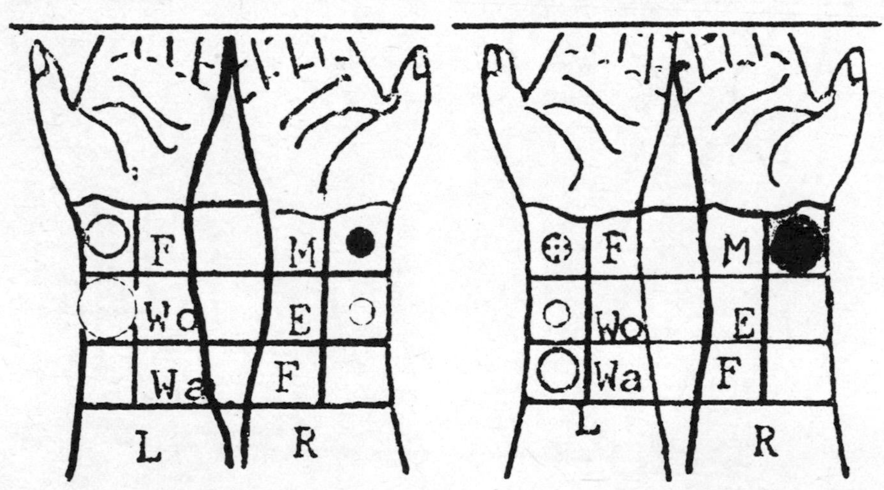

The type of lung Kyo-sho *The type of lung Jitsu-sho*

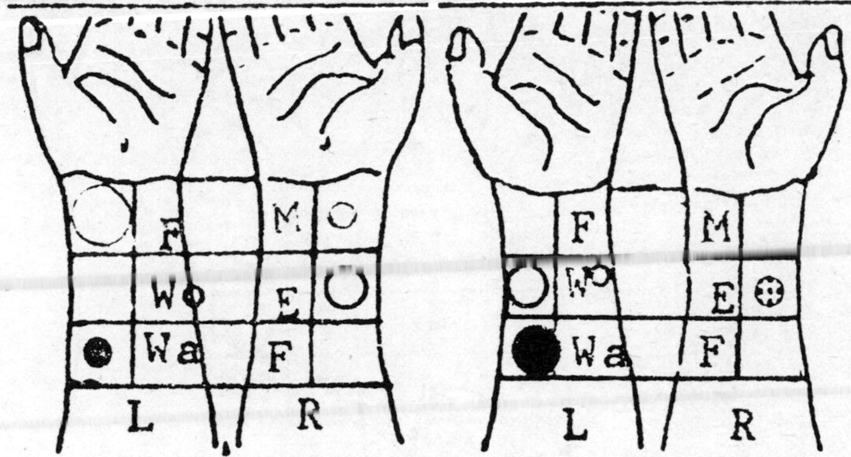

The type of kidney Kyo-sho

The type of kidney Jitsu-sho

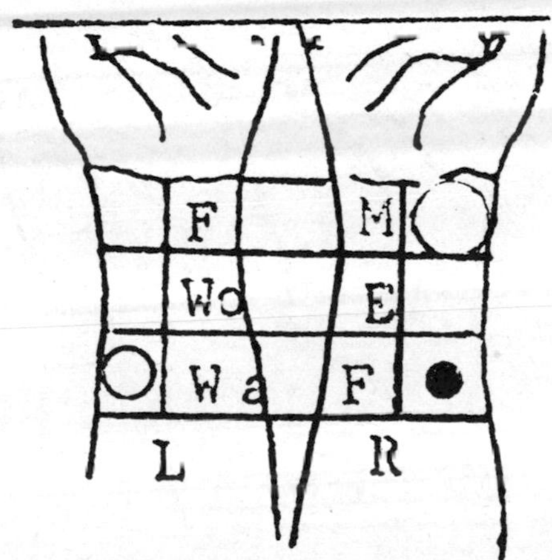

The type of fire–2 Kyo-sho

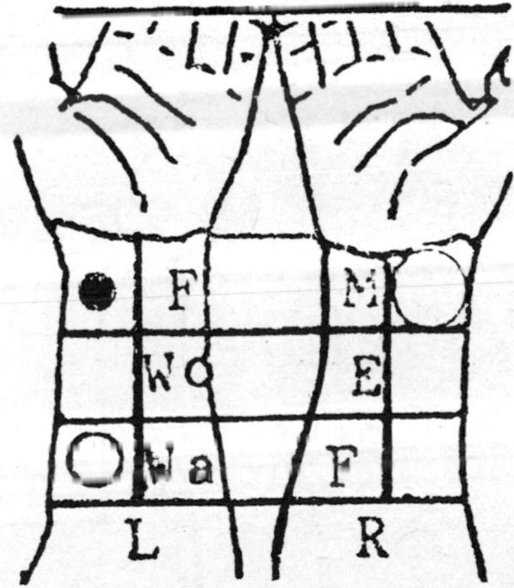

The type of heart Kyo-sho

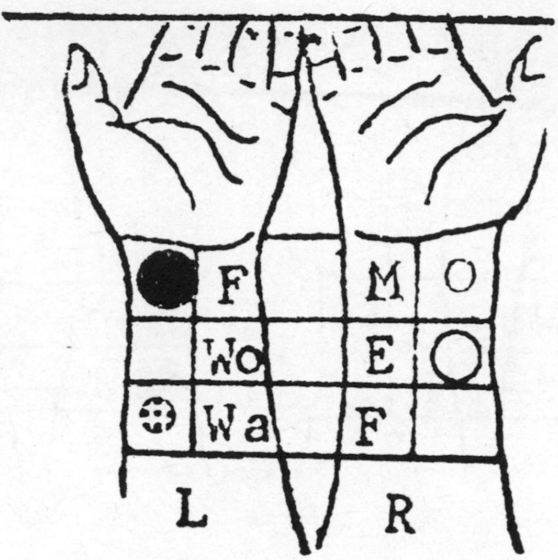

The type of heart Jitsu-sho

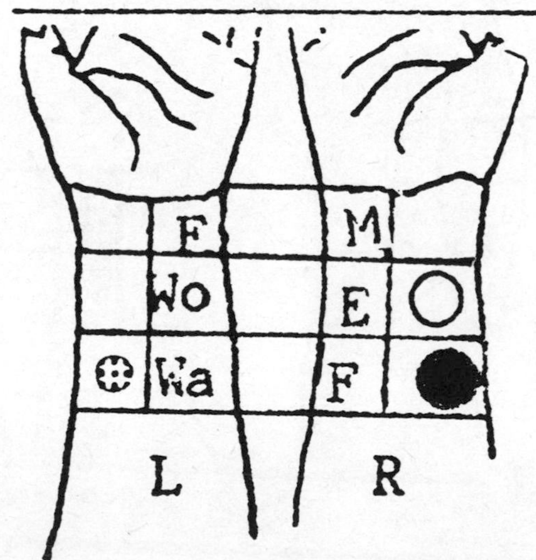

The type of fire–2 Jitsu-sho

The Purpose of Fukushin

The purpose of Fukushin in Chinese herbs is to find out about Kyo and Jitsu. However, if the determination of Kyo and Jitsu is done through Fukushin alone, there is the possibility of making a faulty diagnosis. It is therefore necessary to refer to Myakushin and other symptoms and to make overall observations.

Fuku-sho

If a person has an overall softness to his stomach with no strength or resilience, a weak and subdued pulse, and if his hands and feet are cold, it is Rikyo-sho. In this case, even if there is a sloshing noise, it is still Rikyo-sho.

When the stomach is soft and weak, the intestines have peristaltic irregularity, and through the abdominal wall the peristaltic motion of the intestines can be felt.

When the stomach is soft but feels strong, it is Jitsu-sho. If a person is constipated, the pulse is subdued but strong, it is also Jitsu-sho.

Fukuman (Fullness of the Abdomen)

Fukuman is also either Kyo-sho or Jitsu-sho. There is more Jitsu-sho among those people with Fukuman and constipation. If a person has Fukuman with Kyo-sho, his stomach has no strength and sags.

When a person purges his bowel and yet feels that his stomach is bloated, it is Kyo-sho. Also, after a loss of body fluids, if a person develops Fukuman, it is Kyo-sho. A person who has Fukuman and yet the area of his abdomen has a basic strength, and who may be constipated and yet have a strong pulse, is Jitsu-sho.

When a person has Fukuman but the surface of the stomach is hard with no basic strength in the area of the abdomen and if his pulse is weak, then it is Kyo-sho.

A patient with gastroptosis (prolapse) or gastric atony often has the symptom of sloshing water noises in the region below the heart. That patient is, in most cases, Hyo-sho.

Shingehiko

This symptom can be defined as a feeling of pressure due to a fullness in the region below the heart. Hi (from Shingehiko) means pressure.

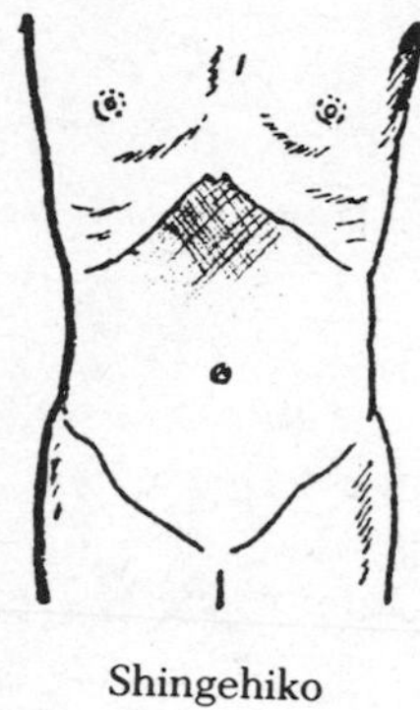
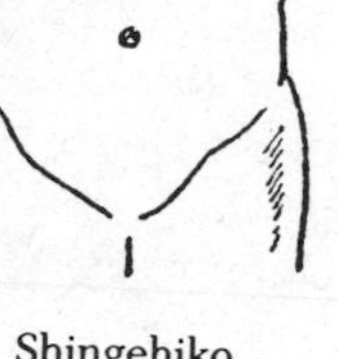

Shingehiko

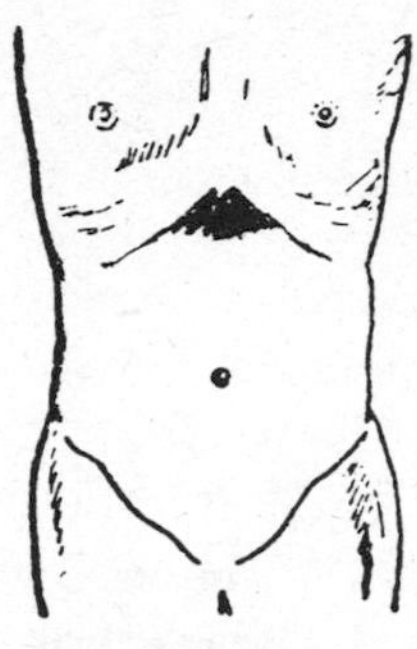

Shingehi

Shingehi

Shingehi is a symptom commonly described as a feeling of something pushing out from the pit of the stomach. There is no sign of resistance or oppressive pain in this region detectable by others. A person with Shingehi often hears a sloshing water noise. In most cases, Shingehi appears as Kyo-sho.

Kyokyokuman

There is a congested feeling at the hypochondrium and it is distressing. The pressure and pain when pressed in this area can be sensed clearly by others. Kyokyokuman appears on both sides, but it also appears on one side (left or right) only.

This is a congested hardening below the hypochondrium. In many cases, it occurs simultaneously with Kyokyokuman.

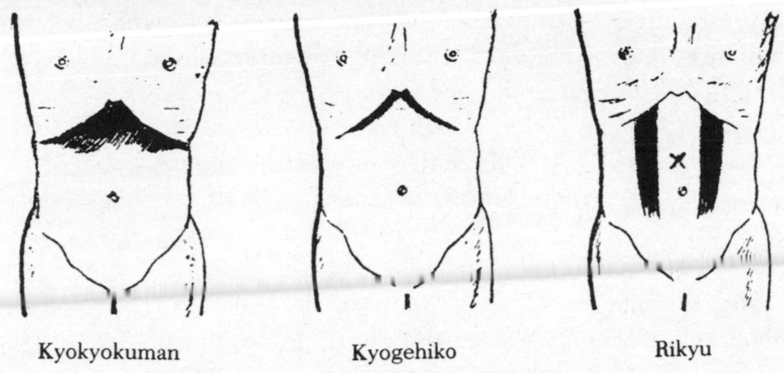

Kyokyokuman Kyogehiko Rikyu

Rikyu

Rikyu means a feeling of contraction underneath the abdominal skin. Contractions of Fukuchokkin (tight stretching, straight muscles of abdomen) are also included in this definition. Furthermore, the feeling of the stomach being full and stretched without the contraction of Fukuchokkin is also included in this definition. Rikyu occurs among Kyo-sho patients.

Shofukukokyu

Shofuku means lower abdomen. Shofukukokyu means that the lower abdomen is in a contracted condition. In this case, Fukuchokkin is contracted from the navel down to the pubic bone. This is frequently observed when Kyo of Kasho develops. In other words, this is Fuku-sho, due to kidney trouble.

Shofukukyuketsu

Shofukukyuketsu is the Fuku-sho for Togakujokito; that is, it is Fuku-sho due to Oketsu (blood stagnation). Fuku-sho seldom appears on the right side. When light pressure is applied to the iliac cavity on the left side, a funicular object the size of a pencil or finger, which gives increasing pain, is probed for. In order to examine this Fuku-sho, it is necessary to have the patient stretch out both his legs before examination. As the tips of the fingers touch the abdominal wall lightly, move them quickly as if rubbing from the navel diagonally toward the node of the left ilium. In this case, if Shofukukyuketsu exists, the patient will suddenly bend his knees and complain of severe pain. This Fuku-sho exists more among women than men.

Shofukuman, Shofukukoman

Shofukuman means the expansion of the lower abdomen. Shofukukoman means after the lower abdomen expands, pressure exists. This Fukusho often appears as Oketsu-sho (stagnated blood) but it also appears as Tanin-sho (body fluids). Furthermore, the abdomen is hard, and Shobenfuri occurs; this is called bloodlessness. When Shobenjiri occurs, it is called Ketsu-sho (blood).

Shinki, Shinkaki, Saikaki

Shinki means palpitation of the heart. When we say that the motion of Kyori accelerates, it means palpitation of the heart. When we speak of the motion that is taking place among Shinkaki, Saikaki, moisture, and kidneys, we mean that we can observe externally the abdominal pulsation of the main artery and

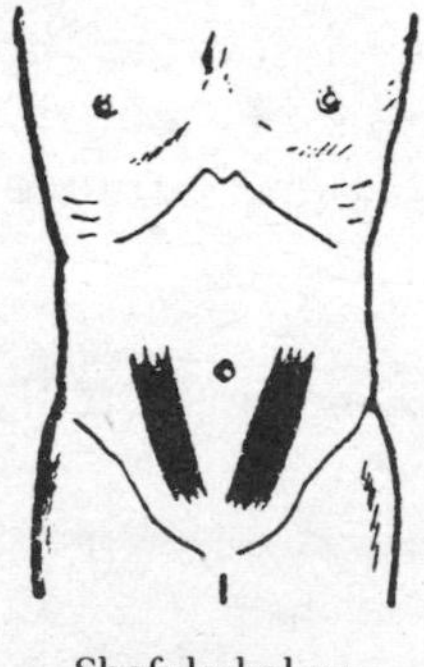

Shofukukokyu

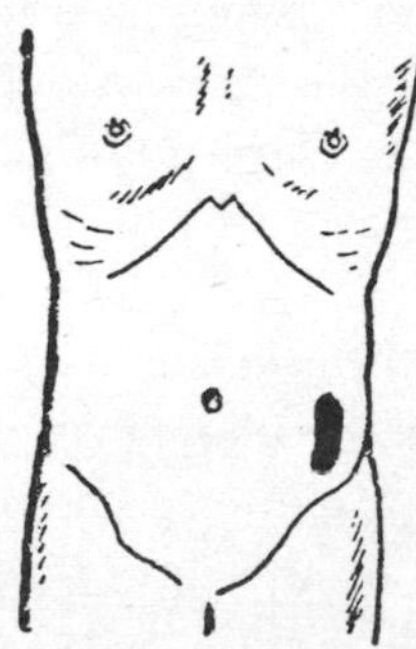

Shofukukyuketsu

also that we are able to feel it easily with our hands.

When the palpitation accelerates in these regions, they are all Kyo-sho, and therefore perspiration, purging, and vomiting must be avoided.

Shofukuman &
Shofukukoman

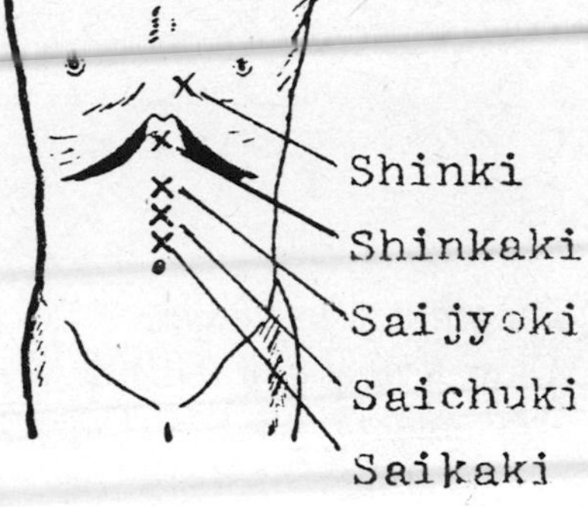

CHAPTER XIV

Three Yins—Three Yangs

GENERAL UNSPECIFIED ILLNESSES ARE CLASSIFIED AS YIN, Yang, Kyo, and Jitsu in order to be treated. However, it is more convenient to use the Three Yins–Three Yangs classification for the treatment of Shokan, that is, acute fever. According to the Shokan theory, the Three Yins–Three Yangs classification is used for an illness depending on how far it has progressed.

Taiyobyo

At the early stages of a fever, there are many illnesses that start with the symptoms of Taiyobyo (Big Yang illness). Therefore, from the Shokan theory, the following can generally be stated: Taiyobyo consists of Fumyaku (floating-on-the-surface pulse), headaches, severe pain, and chill.

These four symptoms as listed here characterize Taiyobyo. So if all four symptoms are present, regardless of the name of the illness, it is called Taiyobyo. Then, if it is called Taiyobyo, is it always necessary to have all four symptoms present? Not always. Here are a couple of examples. The most important one among the symptoms of Taiyobyo is Fumyaku. However, just because the pulse is Fu does not necessarily mean that it is Taiyobyo. The reason is that although it rarely occurs, Shoyobyo (Little Yang illness), Yomeibyo (Yang Ming illness), Taiyobyo

(Big Yin illness), and Shoinbyo (Little Yin illness) can also have Fumyaku. Therefore, in addition to Fumyaku, there must be related symptoms that characterize Taiyobyo. Otherwise, we can not define it as Taiyobyo.

Although headaches are also characteristic of the symptoms of Taiyobyo, with such symptoms alone it cannot be called Taiyobyo. A similar argument can also be used for severe pain and chill.

Then it becomes apparent that Taiyobyo is determined depending on which symptoms are combined with the others.

If the pulse is Fu and there is a fever and chill, then it is Taiyobyo. If the pulse is Fu together with a fever, cold, and headache, then it is Taiyobyo.

If the pulse is Fu together with a fever, headache, chill, and pain in the joints, then it is Taiyobyo.

Symptoms of Taiyobyo appear on the surface of the body, and therefore they coincide with the symptoms of Hyo sho.

Shoyobyo

When an illness starts out as Taiyobyo but after three or four days changes to Shoyobyo, then the following symptoms occur:

The characteristics of Shoyobyo are a bitterness inside the mouth, a dryness in the throat, and a dizziness in the eyes.

Here, bitterness in the mouth, dryness of the throat, and dizziness, which are listed as characteristics of Shoyobyo, are all subjective symptoms and only by Monshin (diagnosis by questioning) can they be detected. The symptom of bitterness in the mouth is caused by the fever and the mouth tends to become sticky at the same time.

There is no symptom of bitterness in the mouth for Taiyobyo and The Three Yin illnesses. However, Yomeibyo (Yang Ming illness) may cause bitterness in mouth. Hence, with such a symptom alone, it is difficult to differentiate between Yomeibyo and Shoyobyo. In order to distinguish between these illnesses, we need to consider the Fuku-sho (Abdomen) and other symptoms. Inkan means a feeling of dryness in the throat, but this symptom does not mean that water is needed to quench the thirst. Mokugen means dizziness. Dizziness as well as dryness of the mouth is caused by fever. Shoyobyo is a Netsu-sho (Fever) somewhere in between Hyo and Ri and is also called Hangai-Hanri-sho. In addition to the symptoms mentioned above, it has the symptoms of Kyo-mankyotsushinhan (pain from feeling of pressure in the chest), coughing, palpitation of the heart, fast breathing (difficulty in breathing), nausea, vomiting, and a lack of appetite.

Yomeibyo

When Shoyobyo turns into Ri, it becomes Yomeibyo (Yang Ming illness). In the Shokan theory, Yomeibyo is explained as, a congestion of the stomach and intestines.

Therefore, Yomeibyo tends to be associated with constipation and Fukuman (fullness of the abdomen). Using Fukushin (diagnosis of abdomen), a feeling of fullness in the abdomen can be proved. However, even if a patient has constipation and Fukuman, he may not feel congestion in the abdomen. That is, he has Fukuman due to Kyoman or Fukuman due to water in the abdomen. For example, Fukuman due to cancer, hardening of the liver, and tubercular peritonitis do not generally belong to Yomeibyo.

While Taiyobyo is Hyo-sho, this Yomeibyo is Ri-sho.

Taiinbyo

In the Shokan theory, Taiinbyo (Big Yang illness) is explained as follows: The symptoms of Taiinbyo are Fukuman, vomiting, a lack of purging of the bowels, heavy urination, and sometimes pains in the stomach. If purging of the bowels is attempted, it always ends up with a hardening under the chest.

Fukuman caused by Taiinbyo is Kyo and is different from Jitsu due to Yomeibyo: in addition, Taiinbyo causes vomiting and diarrhea and at times causes stomachache. When this happens, the pulse is weak and there is no vitality. If this Kyo is misjudged as Jitsu, the region below the heart hardens.

A person who has a weak stomach and intestines originally may show symptoms of Taiinbyo in the early stages of the illness.

Shoinbyo

A person with a delicate constitution or an old person is likely to show Shoinbyo-sho (Little Yin illness) from the early stages. Shoinbyo is either Hyo or Ri of Kan-sho (cold), and in the Shokan theory, it is explained as follows: Shoinbyo accompanies a weak pulse and the desire to lie down constantly.

Shoinbyo does not cause pain particularly, but stamina is gone; and it makes a person want to lie down all the time. The pulse is also weak; it indicates a deterioration of vitality. In addition, even if the body temperature rises in the case of Shoinbyo, his urine is thin, his appetite is good, and his appetite does not change in many cases. When he is Hyokan-sho, his body aches, he has a headache and chill, and his feet become cold. When he is Rikan-sho, he has a stomachache, diarrhea, constipation, pressure in the chest, and profuse urination.

Ketsuinbyo

Ketsuinbyo ("Ketsu" Yin illness) means an illness that causes a fever in the upper half of the body and a chill in the lower half. Therefore, the upper half of the body feels cold. In the Shokan theory, it is explained as follows: Ketsuinbyo causes Shokatsu (severe thirst), ki rises, the mind is affected, there is pain and fever in the heart, and hunger without appetite. If the patient eats, he vomits worms; if he tries to purge the worms, his urination does not stop.

Here, Shokatsu does not mean diabetes but the condition of severe thirst in the mouth; Kai means intestinal worms. However, it is said that Shokatsu and Kai were not in the original Shokan theory but rather the interpretation was inserted in the main theory at a later time. Consequently, today this portion has been excluded from the theory and so the principle of Ketsuinbyo is defined without it.

CHAPTER XV

Tenzoku, Tennyu, Heibyo, Gobyo

SHO IS NOT UNCHANGEABLE; RATHER, THEY TEND TO CHANGE. Taiyobyo at the beginning might become Shoyobyo, and, again, become Yomeibyo. In some cases, Taiyobyo may become Ketsuinbyo.

Tenzoku means, for example, when Taiyobyo turns into Yomeibyo, it does not change into Yomeibyo completely but some of the symptoms of Taiyobyo remain.

If it changes completely into Yomeibyo, then it is Tennyu. Therefore, when Tenzoku occurs, it is Heibyo (Parallel illness). For example when Tenzoku occurs between Taiyobyo and Yomeibyo, it becomes the Heibyo of Taiyobyo and Yomeibyo. In this case, Taiyobyo is treated first and then treat Yomeibyo.

Gobyo is different from Heibyo in that a person can become ill with two yangs or even three yangs at the same time; for instance, Taiyobyo and Shoyobyo or Taiyobyo and Yomeibyo or Taiyobyo, Shoyobyo and Yomeibyo.*

*For treatment, in the case of Gobyo with Taiyobyo and Shoyobyo, treat for Shoyobyo; in the case of Gobyo with Taiyobyo and Yomeibyo, treat for Taiyobyo; in the case of Gobyo, with the Three Yangs.

CHAPTER XVI

Kaibyo

DUE TO THE WRONG KIND OF TREATMENT AND FOR OTHER reasons, sho breaks down and can no longer be called the correct sho; this situation is called Kaibyo. Because of excessive perspiration, even before Taiyobyohyo-sho can be cured, it has already partially become Yin sho. Although it is no longer Taiyobyo, it cannot yet be called Shoinbyo either, since the sho has not completely become Yin-sho. Hence it is called Kaibyo.

TRANSLATOR'S NOTE: Taiyobyo and Taiinbyo should be written as Daiyobyo and Daiinbyo but for phonetic consistency within this translation the former spelling was used. Also, words ending in "tsu" in combination with the ending "sho" normally are contracted to the combined form "-ssho", but again for consistency the words were not combined according to this rule for this translation (e.g., "Jitsu-sho instead of contracted form "Jissho").

CHAPTER XVII

The Theory of Meridians

THE *Nei Ching* [*"Ko-Tei-Dai-Kyo-So-Mon"*], A RECORD OF research in the preservation of health and the healing of diseases, was written by Huang Ti, the "Yellow Emperor," and his subjects. It is the oldest existing book on Oriental medicine. In addition to this, there are reports of other such books, the *Rei-Kyu*, the *Ko-Tei-Mei-Do-Kyu-Kyo*, and the *Ko-Tei-Shin-Kyu-Ko-Hi-Kyo*. Huang Ti is said to have been the first Emperor of China, in part a legend and in part an actual person, and he stands as a symbol of the sovereigns of his era, about 2000 B.C.

Long after this, about six hundred years ago, during the Yuan Dynasty, Po Jen, a famous and skillful physician, wrote a book entitled, "The Exposition of the Fourteen Meridians," in which he unified the ancient records and books, systematized their study, and added illustrations and explanatory notes. The book is commonly called "The Fourteen Meridians" and the methods of acupuncture and moxacautery for years after centered on the concepts found in this book.

The meridians and the Vital Points form the basis for the medical techniques of acupuncture and moxacautery. Their study is what constitutes the sciences of physiology and pathology in acupuncture and moxacautery. In addition, they are, simultaneously, the foundations for diagnoses and for treatment.

There are three Yin pulses and three Yang pulses or "meridians" in each of the arms and legs of the body. The three Yin meridians of the arm are the Lung Meridian (Yin Maximum), the Heart Meridian (Yin Minimum), and the Circulation Meridian (also translated as Heart Constrictor Meridian and as Meridian of Circulation-Sex; more aptly called Controller Meridian of the Body Organs) (Yin in equilibrium). Each of these meridians begins from an internal organ and runs down the arm through the palms clear to the tips of the fingers. The three Yang meridians of the arm are the Large Intestine Meridian (Yang in equilibrium), the Small Intestine Meridian (Yang maximum), and the Triple Warmer Meridian (Yang minimum). Each of these starts from the tips of the fingers and runs through the back of the hand and up the arm to the side of the neck and to the head.

The three Yin meridians of the leg are the Spleen Meridian (Yin maximum), the Kidney Meridian (Yin minimum), and the Liver Meridian (Yin in equilibrium). The former two start from the toes and go up the leg to the abdomen and chest. The latter, the Liver Meridian (Yin in equilibrium), extends further up to the crown of the head. The three Yang meridians of the legs are the Stomach meridian (Yang in equilibrium), the Bladder Meridian (Yang maximum), and the Gallbladder Meridian (Yang minimum). These descend from the head and end at the feet.

The above-mentioned twelve meridians are not independent. Not only, of course, do they cross each other, but they exist in a complex interrelationship. Each of the strategic points on the meridians has been given a name. In addition to these twelve meridians, there are two others: the Meridian of the Governing Vessel and the Meridian of the Vessel of Conception. Thus, the total is fourteen meridians.

The Vital Points in acupuncture and moxacautery are taken from "The Theory of the Meridians," the major body of doctrine in Oriental medicine. It is very difficult to understand because it contains such philosophical concepts as Yin and Yang and the Five Elements.

The fact of human life is defined as meaning that "Qi" is circulating all through the body along certain roads. These roads are interconnected through the various meridians from the tips of the fingers to the regions of each of the internal organs. Twelve main roads and two other subsidiary roads—fourteen roads altogether—run throughout the body. These roads are connected by crossroads. It is "the flow of Qi" that is always running and circulating along these roads. If the flow of Qi can circulate smoothly, the body is in perfect health.

However, if a "traffic accident" or obstruction were to occur on the road for some reason, this flow of Qi would become congested. This congestion is what constitutes illness. Stations are set up at important points along the roads to function as observation post, road office, and police station to control the traffic. These "stations" correspond to the Vital Points. Therefore, when "traffic congestion," that is to say, an illness, occurs in the internal organs or elsewhere in the body, we should bring the issue to the attention of these offices, the Vital Points, by means of stimulation so that the flow will return to normal.

CHAPTER XVIII

Abnormalities of the Meridians

ONCE ONE KNOWS WHICH MERIDIAN HAS BECOME SICK, HE can decide on the proper method of treatment. It then becomes easy to determine the effectiveness of such treatment. One can gain a general understanding of the body's condition through Pressing or Touching Diagnoses alone. However, in order to make a positive diagnosis, it is recommended that judgment be arrived at from a synthesis of several diagnostic techniques. Methods such as Pressing Diagnosis and Touching Diagnosis are part of the technique of "Sesshin" ("Close Diagnosis") (examination by palpation) in Oriental medicine. Together with Pulse Diagnosis and Abdominal Diagnosis, they are called "Sekkei" ("Close Measurement").

In addition to Sesshin, that is, diagnosis by direct palpation of the body, Oriental medicine also includes other methods of diagnosis: Boshin (diagnosis by observation), Monshin (diagnosis by asking questions), and Bunshin (diagnosis by auscultation). Together, they are called the Four Methods of Diagnosis. Each of them is significant for the understanding of disorders of the meridians. That is to say, the four methods help the practitioner perceive the disorders of the internal organs.

For example, the use of Monshin checks the patient's taste preference (the Five Flavors), the nature of his secretions (the

Five Fluids), and his emotional fluctuation (the Five Emotions), etc. Furthermore, Monshin not only involves auscultation, but also Shushin (diagnosis by smelling). Also, the state of disease can be observed by the nature of the patient's voice (the Five Sounds) and the odor of his body (the Five Odors).

These facts relating to the Solid (Tsang) and Hollow (Fu Organs are useful in judging abnormalities in the corresponding meridians).

All these relationships have been set up based on the Law of the Five Elements. All are arranged in five categories. Subsequently, the organs have been defined as the Five Solid Organs and Five Hollow Organs (Usually there are said to be Five Solid and Six Hollow Organs, but when matched to corresponding meridians, there are Six Solid Organs and Hollow Organs.) (See the chapter on The Law of Yin-Yang and the Five Elements.)

CHAPTER XIX

The Meridian Treatment Principles

THE TECHNIQUES OF ACUPUNCTURE AND MOXACAUTERY would never have developed as a method of medical treatment if the meridians and the Vital Points had been ignored. Treatment of the meridians means treatment of the symptoms derived from the meridians and Vital Points.

Treatment of the meridians regards disharmony in mind and body, i.e., sickness, as being imbalances in the meridians. The technique of treatment of the meridians involves the removal of the disharmony in the body by discovering the imbalances in the meridians and adjusting them by means of acupuncture or moxacautery, thus aiding the natural curative powers of the body in overcoming illnesses.

We regard the imbalances in the meridians as being hyperactivity or hypoactivity. To regulate the imbalances requires adjusting this condition and restoring equilibrium by using the Pu-Hsieh method (Tonification and Sedation).

CHAPTER XX

Methods of Symptomatic Treatment

SYMPTOMATIC TREATMENT IS THE BASIS FOR THE SYSTEM of medical treatment in the Orient. Treatment by Chinese herb medicine as well as by acupuncture and moxacautery techniques subscribe to this school of symptomatic treatment methods.

In comparison with modern medicine, this method is historically the product of ancient times. This fact, however, does not mean that symptomatic treatment is therefore old and useless in comparison with modern medicine; rather, it has been historically in existence long before modern medicine.

Modern medicine has shown surprising progress in the area of medical science fundamentals. From this standpoint, the methods of symptomatic treatment may appear extremely crude, unauthentic, and even unrealistic. However, as a system of clinical medicine, the methods of symptomatic treatment contain aspects superior to those of modern medicine in terms of how an illness is grasped structurally, systematically and dialectically. It is necessary to be able to name the patient's illness in the method of treating it.

Symptomatic treatment is a method in which so-called Major Symptoms are distinguished from the various body symptoms that appear due to the disharmony of mind and body and for which the application of appropriate treatment is involved. Symptoms are: mind and body disorders such as headaches, chills, fevers, diarrhea, vomiting, insomnia, lumbago, and unusually frequent or infrequent urination.

Major Symptoms comprise the group of symptoms distinctive to disorders of the meridians. They are not simply the mathematical sum of the symptoms. Symptoms are the phenomena of an illness. Through these phenomena, the Major Symptoms, the essence, can be understood theoretically and abstractly. Symptoms are phenomena; the Major Symptoms are the essence. There is, however, no relationship of cause and effect.

The reason the phenomena occur, appearing as symptoms, may not be understood at first. However, Major Symptoms are defined as symptoms of hyper- and hypoactivity of meridians and can be discovered through the Four Methods of Diagnosis (observation, questioning, auscultation, and palpation). It then becomes clear that the symptoms, the phenomena, which could not be understood at first, are an indication of the Major Symptoms, the essence. When this fact becomes clear, the Major Symptoms can be dealt with as the object of treatment.

For example, if hypoactivity in the Lung Meridian and the Spleen Meridian and hyperactivity in the Liver Meridian and the Heart Meridian are found in the course of diagnosis, the condition can be recognized as a symptom of lung hypoactivity. Therefore, these symptoms are understood as phenomena of lung hypoactivity, and appropriate treatment can be applied for Major Symptoms of lung hypoactivity.

In short, the Major Symptoms are an indicator for treatment. Since each of the symptoms is related to one of the meridians, they will always correspond to the imbalance of the related meridian. However, the method of symptomatic treatment, treating each symptom individually, cannot be expected to produce perfect results. The type of treatment needs to be appropriate for the Major Symptoms, and one needs to understand the relationship between the meridians and the symptoms.

CHAPTER XXI

Treatment of Essence and Treatment of Phenomena

IN TREATING THE MERIDIANS, PERFECT RESULTS CAN BE expected with the use of Treatment of Essence (method aimed at cure) together with Treatment of Phenomena (method for relief of symptoms). Treatment of Essence adjusts imbalances of the meridians by treating Principal Vital Points of the four limbs (arms and legs) which correspond to the Major Symptoms revealed in diagnosis. Concurrently, Treatment of Phenomena utilizes Pu-Hsieh (tonification and sedation) directly on imbalances of the response points, i.e., Vital Points, for treatment of symptoms, taking into consideration their relationship to the meridians.

Sometimes the symptoms disappear after use of Treatment of Essence alone. When this happens, there is no need for Treatment of Phenomena. Usually, however, both treatments should be applied simultaneously. Treatment of Phenomena is directed at the symptoms, and Treatment of Essence is directed at the essence, the Major Symptoms. However, one cannot conclude that Treatment of Essence is primary and Treatment of Phenomena is secondary; rather, the value of both is the same. One cannot expect perfection in treatment using only symptomatic methods of Treatment of Phenomenon while excluding Treatment of Essence. Both methods should be applied at the same time and be given equal value.

The Principal Vital Points

The Principal Vital Points are those of the Five Elements: the I-ketsu, Ei-ketsu, Yu-ketsu, Kyo-ketsu, and Go-Ketsu of the arms and legs; the Kyo-ketsu, To-ketsu, and Gen-ketsu of the arms and legs; the Yu-ketsu of the lower back; the Bo-ketsu on the side of the chest and the abdomen; the Kai-ketsu; and so on.

When there is disharmony of mind and body and an imbalance of the meridians occurs, the Principal Vital Points appear from the beginning as distinctive and responsive Vital Points. Subsequently, these Principal Vital Points are very important for diagnosis in the "Sekkei" ("Close Measurement") method of Pulse Diagnosis by pointing out in which meridians an imbalance has occurred. These Principal Vital Points are, at the same time, points of treatment.

I-ketsu (I–points)

The I-ketsu control bloating in the area beneath the heart. This condition constitutes an illness of the liver (wood-element); in other words, disorders in the functioning of the Liver Meridian. The area above the stomach becomes full and hard. (Li–1, H–9, Sp–1, Lu–11, K–1, C–9, GB–43, SI–1, S–45, Li–1, B–63, T–1.)

Ei-ketsu (Ei-points)

The Ei-ketsu control body temperature. This condition constitutes an illness of the heart (fire-element); or disorders in the functioning of the Heart Meridian. Fever results from a rising body temperature. Despite the rise in temperature, however, the patient sometimes may feel chills. This produces a glowing sensation all over the body. (Li–2, H–8, Sp–2, L–10, K–2, C–8, GB–43, SI–2, S–44, Li–2, B–62, T–2.)

Yu-ketsu (Yu-points)

The Yu-ketsu control the sensations of Torpor-Aching Joints. This condition constitutes an illness of the spleen (earth-element); or disorders in the functioning of the Spleen Meridian. Torpor-Aching Joints is the state in which the body feels languid and fatigued with the joints aching when moved. (Li–3, H–7, Sp–3, Lu–9, K–3, C–7, GB–40, SI–3, S–43, B–61, T–3.)

The Yu-ketsu mainly appear in cases of chronic illness. Indeed, they are like a window on the Five Solid and Six Hollow Organs and whenever some illness occurs in these organs, these Yu-ketsu on the back show an obvious response. These Vital Points reveal hyperactivity and hypoactivity just as they are in relation to the hyper- and hypoactivity of the Solid Organs, Hollow Organs, and the meridians. One can therefore perceive this condition of the organs and meridians through analysis by means of Sekkei Diagnosis of the Yu-ketsu.

Kyo-ketsu (Kyo-points)

The Kyo-ketsu control asthma, coughing, chills and fever. This condition constitutes an illness of the lungs (metal-element); or disorders in the functioning of the Lung Meridian. Asthma is a continuous, wheezing coughing, sometimes accompanied by phlegm or a dry cough. Chills and fever are commonly called fluctuations of chills and fever and are an indication of illness on the surface of the skin. (Li–4, H–4, Sp–5, Lu–8, K–7, C–5, GB–37, SI–5, S–41, Li–5, B–56, T–6.)

Go-ketsu (Go-points)

The Go-ketsu control reverses in the flow of Qi as well as uncontrollable excretion. This constitutes an illness of the kidneys (water-element); or disorders in the functioning of the Kidney Meridian. A reverse in the flow of Qi is a laxity of the bowels, that is, acute diarrhea. (Li–8, H–3, Sp–9, Lu–5, K–10, C–3, GB–33, SI–8, S–36, Li–11, B–36, T–10.)

Gen-ketsu (Gen-points)

The Gen-ketsu are the Vital Points related to the fire element. They are the points where the original Qi, that is, the Qi of the life-force, most likely resides. Whenever the Five Solid or Six Hollow Organs becomes sick, a response will appear unfailingly at the Gen-ketsu. Therefore, it is possible to adjust the disorders of the body, curing them by observing the responses of the Gen-ketsu. (L–9, H–7, LI–3, Sp–3, K–3, C–7, LI–4, SI–4, GB–39, S–42, B–60, T–4.)

Geki-ketsu (Geki-points)

The To-ketsu are the points at which noxious Qi accumulates in great quantities. They are the Vital Points which appear as the reaction points in cases of Yang Qi, acute symptoms, and disorders and agitation of an external and noxious nature. In treatment, these Vital Points are used to bring to a halt symptoms such as acute diarrhea and stomach cramps. Once the acute symptoms have been halted, the use of these Vital Points must be stopped immediately. Regardless of whether the symptoms are acute or chronic, these Vital Points also appear as distinctive Response Points in the event of an invasion of noxious Qi. (L–6, H–6, Li–6, Sp–8, K–6, C–4, LI–7, Si–6, GB–35, S–43, B–59, T–7.)

Ryaku-ketsu (Ryaku-points)

The Ryaku-ketsu are junctions at which the meridians intersect each other. These Vital Points are frequently the response points of an illness which appear long after external noxious invasions have entered the body. In other words, they appear in response in the event that the invasion of noxious Qi strikes internally, or in the presence of chronic symptoms. For example, they appear in response to neuralgia, rheumatic pain of the joints, pleurisy, hyperactivity due to overenergetic Qi, etc. (when one meridian becomes hypoactive, the counter-meridian becomes hypoactive due to overabundant Qi) and, in the case of hypoactivity, they appear both internally and superficially.

In cases of hyperactivity, the response points appear as points of stiffness or oppressive pain. They appear as sunken points of the body in the case of hypoactivity. These Vital Points are where hypoactivity and hyperactivity appear as distinctive points.

Also, because these Vital Points are apt to move very easily, it is important when performing Sekkei to examine the meridians in all directions before deciding on the location of the point. These meridians deserve special attention because a Vital Point will frequently appear with Yang symptoms. This frequently occurs when the symptoms belong to the Yang even if the symptoms occur within the Yin meridians. (L–7, H–5, Li–5, Sp–4, K–4, C–6, LI–6, SI–7, GB–36, S–40, B–54, T–5.)

Bo-ketsu and Yu-ketsu

The Bo-ketsu of the Five Solid Organs reside in the Yin and the Yu-ketsu reside in the Yang. Illnesses of the Yang go to the Yin and illnesses of the Yin go to the Yang. The Bo-ketsu reside in the areas of the Yin, i.e., in the area of the chest and abdomen; the Yu-ketsu reside in areas of the Yang, i.e., in the area of the back. Illnesses of the Yin (illnesses of the Solid Organs) go to the Yang-Yu (the Yu-ketsu in the area of the back), and illnesses of the Yang (illnesses of the Hollow Organs) go to the Yin-Bo (the Bo-ketsu in the area of the chest and abdomen).

Bo-ketsu

The Bo-ketsu are the points at which the Qi of the meridians accumulates. These Vital Points are important as the response points for most acute symptoms of Yang illnesses of an external noxious nature and for Abdominal Diagnosis and Sekkei Diagnosis. They are, of course, important in treatment as well. (L–i, VC–14, Li–12, GB–25, VC–17, S–25, VC–4, G–B–24, VC–3, VC–5.)

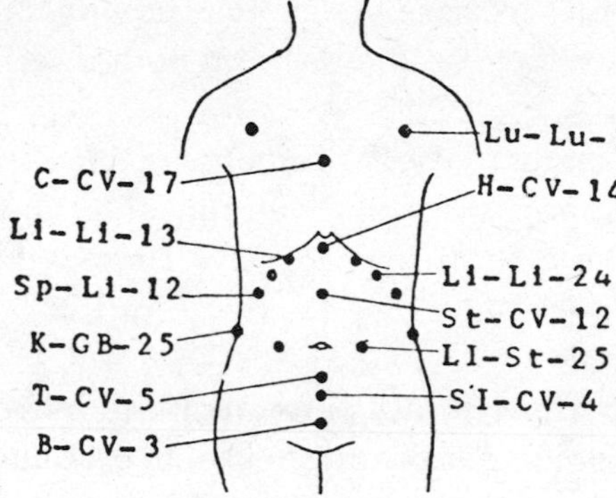

Bo-Ketsu (Bo-points)

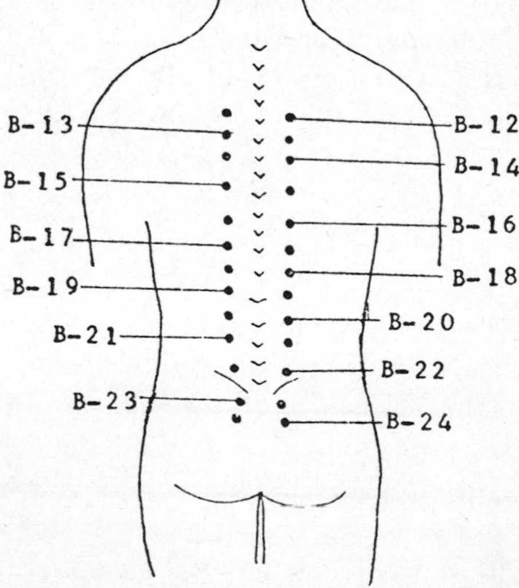

Yu-Ketsu (Yu-points)

CHAPTER XXII

The Law of Yin-Yang and the Five Elements

IT IS THOUGHT TO HAVE BEEN 2000 YEARS AGO DURING THE Chin and Han Dynasties that the *So-Mon-Rei-Kyu,* the most esteemed classic on Oriental medical science, and other such works were compiled. Since the Law of Yin-Yang and the Five Elements were the philosophy of nature in ancient China at this time, these concepts were utilized in theoretical explanations in the classics on Oriental medical science. For example, the classics tried to fix the number of Vital Points, the points of response, of diagnosis and of treatment for disharmony of the body, at 365, in order to be in agreement with the number of days in the year. This follows from the concepts regarding the human body as the Microcosm. The rules which govern the movement of the heavenly bodies also govern the Microcosm, the human body, to the same degree.

In terms of the Five Senses, spring is the season of the liver, summer is the season of the heart, midsummer of the spleen, autumn of the lungs, and winter of the kidneys.

In terms of the directions, east is the liver, south is the heart, the center is the spleen, west is the lungs, and north is the kidneys.

Compared with the Five Planets, Jupiter is the liver, Mars is the heart, Saturn is the spleen, Venus is the lungs, and Mercury is the kidneys.

Thus, everything between heaven and earth was regarded as something to be measured by the Five Elements of wood, fire, earth, metal, and water.

The Five Colors are considered to be the colors of the Five Solid Organs: the liver is blue, the heart red, the spleen yellow, the lungs white, and the kidneys black. By discerning the patient's skin color, one can diagnose in which of the Solid Organs the disharmony has occurred. Clinically, this is a useful method of diagnosis.

As a note of caution, one should keep in mind that the concept of the Five Solid Organs, i.e., the liver, the heart, the spleen, the lungs, and the kidneys, differs from the concept of these organs as they are referred to in modern medicine. They take on special meanings in Oriental medical science. Therefore, the terminology as used by modern medical science and by Oriental medical science should not be intermixed.

The Five Smells indicate body odor or bad breath emanating from each of the Solid Organs. For example, the liver is rancid, the heart scorched, the spleen fragrant, the lungs fleshy, and the kidneys rotted.

The Five Tastes are the preferred food tastes of each of the Five Solid Organs, and the taste which each of the organs requires. For example, the liver likes tart food, the heart bitter, the spleen sweet, the lungs hot, and the kidneys salty. The proper amount of each of these will benefit the Qi of that corresponding organ. However, excessive consumption of any of the Five Flavors will harm the corresponding organ.

The Five Evils are the conditions of the external Qi which each of the Solid Organs dislikes. The liver is said to dislike wind, the heart to dislike heat, the spleen to dislike wetness, the lungs to dislike dryness, and the kidneys to dislike the cold.

The Five Emotions are the emotions to which each of the Solid Organs belongs. For example, anger is an illness of the liver, and excessive anger will harm the liver. Laughter is an illness of the heart, and excess laughter will harm the leart. Worrying is an illness of the spleen, and excessive brooding will harm the spleen. Sorrow is an illness of the lungs, and excessive sorrow will harm the lungs. Fear is an illness of the kidneys, and excessive fear may harm the kidneys.

The Five Spirits are the spirits which each of the Five Solid Organs govern. The liver controls the soul, the heart divinity, the spleen the mind and knowledge, the lungs spirit, and the kidneys vitality and will.

The Five Fluids are secretions controlled by each of the Organs: the liver controls tears, the heart sweat, the spleen saliva, the lungs nasal mucus, and the kidneys spittle.

The Five Changes are symptoms of illness of each of the Five Solid Organs. Clenched fists result from illnesses of the liver, anxiety from illnesses of the heart, hiccoughs from illnesses of the spleen, coughing from illnesses of the lungs, and trembling from illnesses of the kidneys.

The Five Bases belong to the five sensory organs and are related to the Five Solid Organs: the eyes are governed by the liver, the tongue by the heart, the lips and mouth by the spleen, the nose by the lungs, and the ears by the kidneys.

The Five Primary Objects are the structures which supply nutrition to each of the Solid Organs: muscles to the liver, blood to the heart, flesh to the spleen, skin to the lungs, and bones to the kidneys.

The Five Supports reveal where the vitality, the Qi, of the Five Organs appears: in the nails for the liver, in the body hair for the heart, in the breasts for the spleen, in the breath for the lungs, and in the hair of the head for the kidneys.

The Law of Generation and Subjugation Among the Five Elements (–A)

The Relationship of Mutual Generation is also called the Relationship of Mother and Child. The Five Elements show the following relationship among wood, fire, earth, metal, and water. Wood engenders fire, fire engenders earth, earth engenders metal, metal engenders water, and water engenders wood. Therefore, wood is the Mother to fire, and fire is the Child to wood. The same can be said about the relationships between fire and earth, earth and metal, and water and wood. In other words, the generating element is "the Mother" and the engendered element is "the Child."

The Relationship of Conquest is also called the Relationship of Mutual Subjugation. In contrast to the Relationship of Mutual Generation called the "Mother-Child Relationship," the Relationship of Conquest is called the "Husband-Wife Relationship." This defines a relationship of opposition among the Five Elements. The relationship between metal and wood is such that metal overcomes wood, i.e., conquers wood, and wood is defeated by metal. Also, wood overcomes (conquers) earth, earth overcomes water, water overcomes fire, and fire overcomes metal.

The Relationship of Reflected Conquest is the relationship in which the Child Element overcomes that which has overcome the Mother. That is, the Child, on behalf of the Mother, takes revenge on the latter's conqueror. For example, water conquers fire. Earth, the Child of fire, overcomes water on behalf of fire—the Mother of earth.

We have defined three rules governing relationships among the Five Elements. The first, the Relationship of Mutual Generation, is the relationship between the engendering and the engendered elements; the second, the Relationship of Conquest (Mutual Subjugation), is the relationship of opposition and contention; and the third, the Relationship of Reflected Conquest, is the relationship of the resolution of opposition and contention.

The Law of Generation and Subjugation Among the Five Elements (–B)

The Law of the Five Elements defines the five fundamental attributes of all things in heaven and on earth, and attempts to explain, in terms of these attributes, all phenomena of mutuality. Also, the Relationship of Mutual Generation, the Relationship of Conquest, etc., are defined with this law in mind. The Five Elements, wood, fire, earth, metal, and water, have a relationship in which each element submits to the element preceding it in the above order. These relationships are called the Relationships of Mutual Generation, or the Relationships of Mother-Child. Namely, wood engenders fire, fire engenders earth, earth metal, metal water (and water wood); the elements are mutually generated from each other. Wood is the Mother of fire, fire the Mother of earth, earth the Mother of metal, and metal the Mother of water (and water the Mother of wood). In other words fire is the Child of wood, earth the Child of fire, metal the Child of earth, and water the Child of metal (and wood the Child of water); that is, they are in a Mother-Child Relationship. This is a natural (lucky) relationship and is called the Relationship of Mutual Harmony (from the Child to the Mother).

Furthermore, each of the elements, wood, fire, earth, metal, and water, have the tendency to subdue the second following element in the chain. This is called the Relationship of Mutual Subjugation (meaning conquest). This is to say, wood overcomes earth, earth overcomes water, water fire, and fire metal. This is an unnatural (unlucky) relationship and is also called the Relationship of Mutual Fear. These two relationships are two versions of the cyclical method of logic.

The third mutual relationship is derived from the Relationship of Engendering and Overcoming and is called the Relationship of Reflected Conquest (Overcoming the Conquerer). For example, if wood tends to overcome earth (earth to be overcome by wood), metal, the Child of earth, having a Mother-Child relationship with earth, will overcome wood, subduing the power of wood. At the same time, metal will reduce the power of wood in controlling earth, and will try to maintain a balance. That is, this Relationship of Reflected Conquest indicates phenomena which are mutually related.

The following is an explanation of the Relationship of Mutual Generation:

Wood engenders Fire	=	fire is generated, using wood as fuel
Fire engenders Earth	=	burned out fire becomes ashes and earth
Earth engenders Metal	=	metal is generated inside the earth
Metal engenders Water	=	water is often found in land with much metal ore
Water engenders Wood	=	wood is from trees which absorb water from the soil

Also, the Relationship of Subjugation can be explained as follows:

Wood overcomes Earth	=	wood, as trees, absorbs nourishment from earth
Earth overcomes Water	=	water can be dammed by earth or be absorbed into it
Water overcomes Fire	=	water extinguishes fire
Fire overcomes Metal	=	fire melts metal
Metal overcomes Wood	=	wood can be cut by tools made of metal

CHAPTER XXIII

The Fourteen Meridians and their Disorders

WHEN THE LUNG MERIDIAN BECOMES HYPERACTIVE, THE lungs swell and there are coughing fits and pain in certain of the Vital Points. In extreme cases, the left or right hand will become numb, stiff, and painful. This will be accompanied by stiff shoulders, chills and fever, swelling, pain in the throat, and cold hands and feet. Sometimes, bleeding from hemorrhoids may occur.

When the Lung Meridian becomes hypoactive, the patient experiences chills, pain in the shoulders and back, difficulty in breathing, and dry throat. The hands and feet become cold and sometimes numb. There is pain in the skin. The urine color may change and sometimes the patient will become incontinent.

When the Large Intestine Meridian becomes hyperactive, stiff shoulder, toothache, swelling in the cheeks, fits of wheezing, coughing, nosebleeds, and bloating of the abdomen will sometimes occur.

When the Large Intestine Meridian becomes hypoactive, the patient suffers fits of chills and never feels warm. His intestines, mouth and lips become dry and he suffers from diarrhea.

When the Stomach Meridian becomes hyperactive, the abdomen becomes bloated, the breasts become swollen, the mouth and lips feel dry, and there is pain in the joints. Sometimes chills become unbearable.

When the Stomach Meridian becomes hypoactive, the patient experiences loss of appetite, swelling in the face, and anxiety and depression.

When the Spleen Meridian becomes hyperactive, the abdomen becomes bloated. The patient experiences loss of appetite and oppressive pain in the chest. He finds it difficult to lie still. The condition also causes nausea and diarrhea.

When the Spleen Meridian becomes hypoactive, the patient experiences physical fatigue (languor) and a strong desire to lie down. He also yawns, and has urinary difficulties. Insomnia, nausea, oppressive pain of the chest, and jaundice result from disorders of the Spleen Meridian.

When the Heart Meridian becomes hyperactive, the patient experiences fever and pain in the area of the heart, and a desire for food and drink. There is bloating of the stomach and difficulty in defecation in some cases.

When the Heart Meridian becomes hypoactive, pain in the side, heart palpitations, and anxiety result. The patient's eyes are tinged with yellow, and he may sometimes lose consciousness.

When the Small Intestine Meridian becomes hyperactive, there is high fever and oppressive chest pain. Cold sores may appear in the mouth. The patient's throat becomes swollen and painful, and he is unable to move his neck.

When the Small Intestine Meridian becomes hypoactive, the patient's eyes are tinged with yellow, his cheeks swell, he suffers pain behind the ears, and sometimes he becomes hard of hearing and suffers from migraines.

When the Bladder Meridian becomes hyperactive, piercing pain through the head (headache), eye pains, shoulder pains, lumbago, leg pains, and nosebleed may occur. Epilepsy and madness may result from disorders of the Bladder Meridian.

When the Bladder Meridian becomes hypoactive, pain in the back of the head, hemorrhoids, lumbago, leg pains, and stiffness of the shoulders will occur.

When the Kidney Meridian becomes hyperactive, there is nausea, hemoptysis, bloody discharges from the bowels, fits of wheezing and cough, swollen throat, pain in the area of the heart, slight abdominal bloating, and feverish sensations on the bottoms of the feet.

When the Kidney Meridian becomes hypoactive, the patient experiences chills and heaviness of the entire body, and the color of his urine is reddish yellow. Forgetfulness, ringing in the ears, dizziness, numbness of the arms and legs, loss of sexual desire, and insomnia may occur. It furthermore becomes impossible for the patient to eat even though he may have a good appetite, and he may suffer from either diarrhea or constipation.

When the Circulation Meridian becomes hyperactive, the patient's face becomes flushed and he experiences heart palpitations. The armpit swells and becomes painful.

When the Circulation Meridian becomes hypoactive, oppressive sensations in the chest and pain in the area of the heart occur. The shoulder and elbow become painful and cramped.

When the Triple Warmer Meridian becomes hyperactive, the patient's face becomes flushed, and he perspires excessively. The throat becomes swollen and painful. The outer corner of the eyes becomes painful.

When the Triple Warmer Meridian becomes hypoactive, the abdomen feels cold, and there is difficulty in breathing and urination.

When the Gallbladder Meridian becomes hyperactive, there are headaches, a bitter taste in the mouth, and chills. There may be also pain in the left side of the body.

When the Gallbladder Meridian becomes hypoactive, the patient's eyes become yellowish, his arms and legs feel warm, his face becomes oily and his skin dry. He sighs heavily.

When the Liver Meridian becomes hyperactive, lumbago and eye diseases will result. The patient's armpits become stiff. He suffers fits of chills and fever, and bloating of the abdomen. Women will suffer leukorrhea.

When the Liver Meridian becomes hypoactive, a decrease in sexual desire, menstrual irregularity, stiffness in the area below the heart, loss of vitality, fatigue in the arms and legs, decrease in eyesight, and difficulty in urination may result.

CHAPTER XXIV

Acupuncture of the Carotid Sinus and Its Practical Application

Concerning Carotid Sinus Acupuncture (St–9)

Carotid Sinus Acupuncture is a new method of acupuncture to effect treatment by stimulation at a junction of the carotid artery, i.e., the carotid sinus, in order to stimulate the afferent nerve fibers of the autonomic nervous system in that area. This method was discovered and first used in the field of Japanese acupuncture and moxacautery after World War II. In 1948, Dr. Bunshi Shiroda and Dr. Shiro Hosono devised this scheme, and then built up its theoretical basis and, through clinical studies, substantiated and generalized the method of Carotid Sinus Acupuncture. Since then, supplementary studies have been made by many people, and the validity of this method has been gaining in acceptance. In 1963, Dr. Bunshi Shirota delivered a long-overdue report on the subject "A Clinical Study of Carotid Sinus Acupuncture" before the general meeting of the Japan Acupuncture and Moxacautery Medical Treatment Society. Since this report, clinical research on Carotid Sinus Acupuncture has been able to produce some general conclusions.

A totally new field has been developed in acupuncture and moxacautery treatment, and a path has now been opened for the scientific development of acupuncture and moxacautery. This concept of acupuncture incorporates scientific principles of Western medical science concerning the structure of the sinus areas with acupuncture techniques of Oriental medical science, in a dialectic synthesis.

At any rate, due to the discovery of Carotid Sinus Acupuncture and its clinical applications, the range of treatment by acupuncture and moxacautery has been expanded. The discovery has led to the achievement of better results than ever before for those diseases treatable by acupuncture and moxacautery.

The Technique of Carotid Sinus Acupuncture and the Point of Application

"The point": "The carotid sinus is located at the intersection of the carotid artery and a horizontal line drawn just above the larynx. It is located slightly higher in persons with a short neck than in those with longer necks." (From *Clinical Applied Anatomy* by Dr. Mori.)

First, the patient must lie in a supine position without a pillow. The lower jaw is raised to expose the carotid sinus. The point at which acupuncture is applied is on the front edge of the sternomastoid muscle, about 2.5 cm outward from the upper edge of the protuberance of the larynx, and on the carotid artery at the point at which the pulse appears the most strong to the touch.

The needle: Use No. 2 or No. 3 silver or steel needles. No. 3

is easier to use. The recommended length of the needle is three inches. Insert the needle using the special acupuncture guide-tube. If a long, thin needle is used, it will be difficult to judge during the insertion whether the needle has hit the carotid artery or not, as the shaft may bend when it is released from the hand.

Insertion: Insert the needle vertically into the specified point. When you sense that the point of the needle has hit the carotid artery, release the shaft of the needle and observe its oscillations. If it moves at the same speed as the pulse, the needle has struck home. The depth of the needle to the sinus should be about 0.5–1.5 cm. The depth will be slightly deeper in fat persons and slightly shallower in thin persons, and in patients with arteriosclerosis.

Length of time: Generally five to ten seconds are sufficient. It is said that 30 seconds is the most suitable length of time for stimulation in a person with high blood pressure. In the event of an asthma attack, it is better to insert the needle gradually and withdraw it quickly. If the needle remains inserted for a long period of time, it may, on the contrary, cause an attack. (Dr. Shiro Hosono.)

The simple insertion technique is often sufficient. There is generally no need for the "Pecking Sparrow" technique of repeated insertion-withdrawal. If there is no effect after the needle has been inserted once, it is best to withdraw it and attempt again at another point.

Points of Caution on the Application of Acupuncture

1. Apply when the patient is in a supine position. Insertion with the patient in a seated position is very dangerous, as he may develop cerebral anemia.

2. Insert the needle slowly. Rapid insertion of the needle produces too strong a stimulation and may give rise to too strong a reaction in the sinus and lead to cerebral anemia, headache, and fainting.

3. Do not insert the needle too deeply. Insertion whereby the point of the needle barely touches or penetrates the wall of the carotid sinus is sufficient. The needle does not need to pass through the artery. It is mentioned in the classics that inserting the needle more than about 1.5 cm should be avoided.

4. Check for any subcutaneous veins in the area around the point of acupuncture. If any veins are found, insertion of the needle into them should be carefully avoided. If a vein is pierced by mistake, internal hemorrhaging may occur and act as a pressure stimulation, causing lowering of the blood pressure, difficulty in breathing, and irregular pulse, cerebral anemia, and fainting. None of these conditions may result, but still the internal hemorrhage is disfiguring, because it occurs on an exposed part of the body.

5. It should go without saying that the acupuncture practitioner should thoroughly cleanse the point of insertion and his fingers as well.

6. Usually there is no pain at the time of insertion. There are some, however, who experience slight pain. In addition, the needle may on occasion transmit a vibration to the larynx and ears. A few patients will be refreshed from head to toe.

Learning Acupuncture and Moxacautery

This section discusses the main points on learning acupuncture and moxacautery and is included for the benefit of those who will be practicing in the future.

The three steps to learning are as follows: (1) Learning how to apply moxa and how to insert the acupuncture needles in actual practice; (2) learning how to detect the treatment points; (3) learning to judge the proper points for treatment according to each individual patient and the symptoms of his illness.

One can gain a basic knowledge from books. As they say, however, "Seeing is believing," and one should at least learn the practical techniques through frequent observations of actual procedures. It would be ideal to receive rudimentary instructions directly from a good teacher. One should first practice applying acupuncture and moxacautery on the general treatment points such as LI 10 (upper limb) and St 36 (lower limb).

It is impossible to obtain enough skill to deal with any and all diseases from the very beginning. One should therefore limit himself at first only to some symptoms and to consult books about the use of common combinations of treatment points. One should further take every opportunity to carry out supplementary examinations to discover the actual effectiveness of the treatment.

Yet at the same time, it is also important to try to master only a few limited treatment points. Even limited treatment points, if properly selected and adapted, can be applied to many symptoms.

For example, acupuncture and moxacautery only on LI 10 (upper limb) and St 36 (lower limb) can cure to some extent. However, if one depends only on these, he will necessarily come to a deadlock before long. Then it will be necessary to proceed step by step, consulting books, being innovative, and pursing new methods.

It is normal to perform acupuncture and moxacautery at first as a technique in imitation, and then to break open gradually into one's own individual path.

The Types of Needles

The needle mainly used at present is about 1.98 cm long, with a thin, rounded gold or silver shaft and a sharp tip. The length of the needles ranges from about 1.6–10 cm, but the commonly used ones range from 1 to 6 cm in length. Various kinds are preferred, depending on the object of its use and the practitioner's taste. The most commonly used lengths, however, are from 4.3 to 5.3 cm long. The thicknesses are usually graded by number, from 1 to 10.

No. 1 about 0.17 mm in diameter
No. 2 about 0.185 mm in diameter
No. 3 about 0.20 mm in diameter
No. 4 about 0.22 mm in diameter
No. 5 about 0.235 mm in diameter
No. 6 about 0.26 mm in diameter
No. 7 about 0.28 mm in diameter
No. 8 about 0.30 mm in diameter
No. 9 about 0.31 mm in diameter
No. 10 about 0.33 mm in diameter

Among these, the No. 3 through No. 5 needles are most widely used. Thin needles are generally used for light stimulation. A "Super Needle" has come to be frequently used recently. It is smooth, flexible, and does not break or bend. It penetrates well, is durable and very simple to use. Gold needles are used to produce gentle stimulation. For strong stimulations, the Super Needle should be used.

The Method of Applying Acupuncture

THE GUIDE-TUBE METHOD

This method was invented by Kengyo Kazuichi Sugiyama in the Tokugawa (1624–1867) period of Japan. The use of the guide-tube has made penetration of the skin easier, and thus greatly promoted the spread of acupuncture techniques.

An outline of the method is as follows:

The needle is placed in the guide-tube and held with the right hand in a manner that the tip of the needle does not protrude from the guide-tube. The end of the guide-tube containing the tip of the needle is held between the fingers of the left hand pressing against the skin and is settled firmly in place on the skin surface. Next, the head of the needle protruding from the top of the guide-tube is tapped (lightly struck with the fingertip) once or twice with the index finger of the right hand. In this manner, the head of the needle begins to sink down into

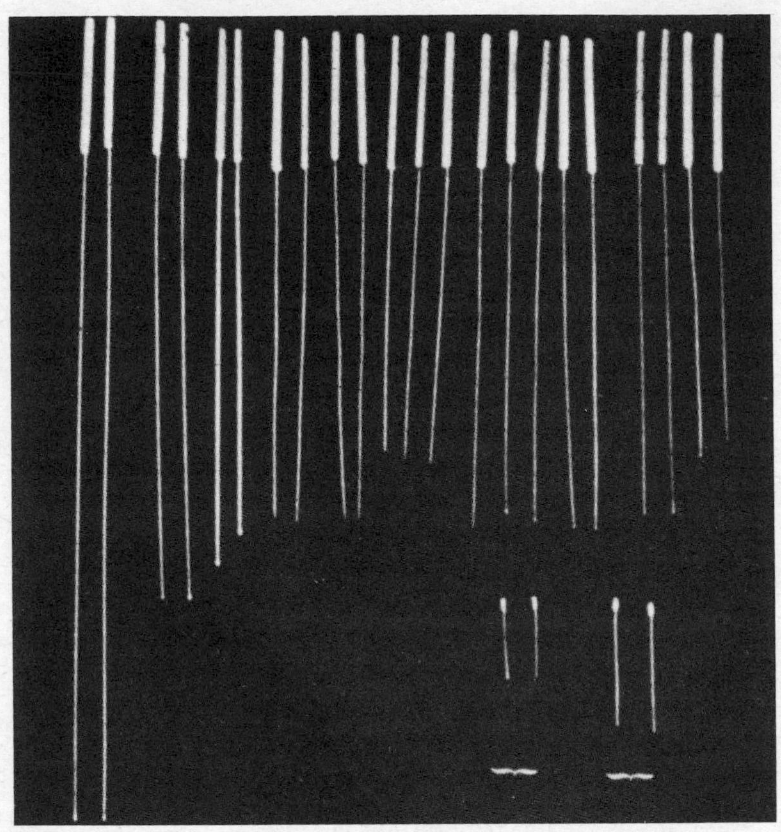

Various types of needles

Method of applying acupuncture

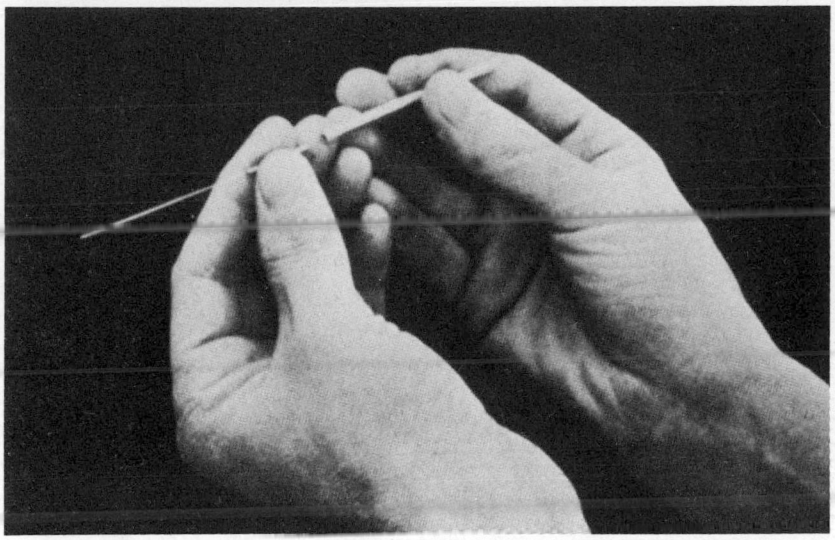

Insert the needle into the guide tube with both hands Fig. I-A

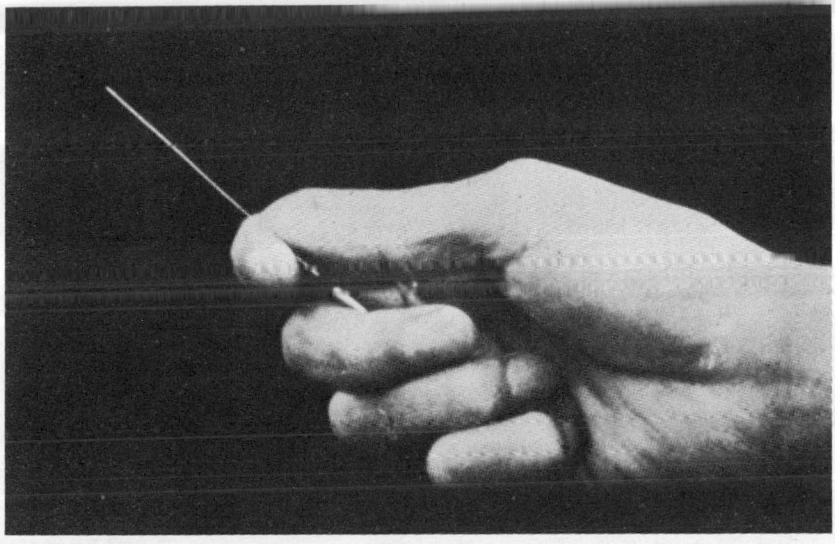

Insert the needle into the guide tube with one hand Fig. I-B

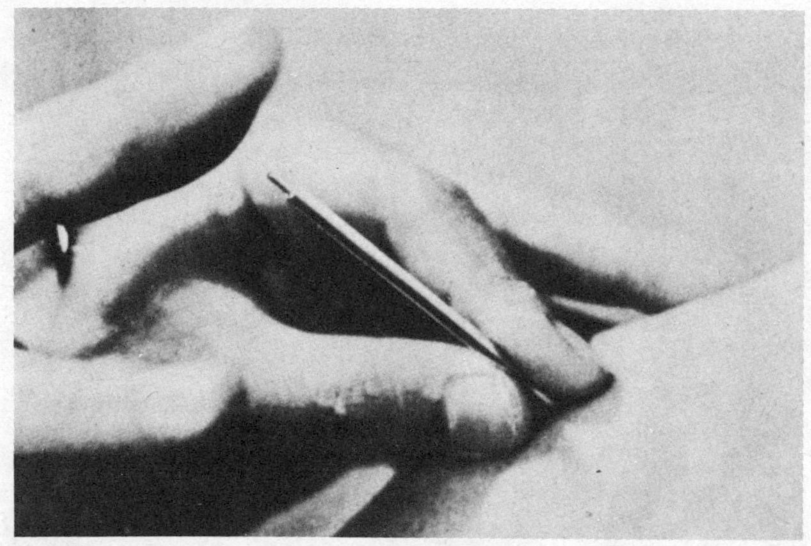

Inserting needle on vital points - A Fig. III

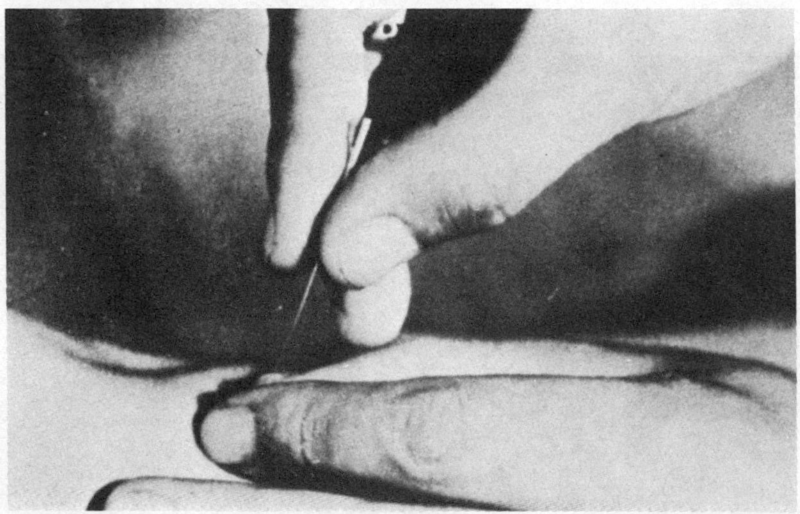

Inserting needle on vital points - B Fig. IV

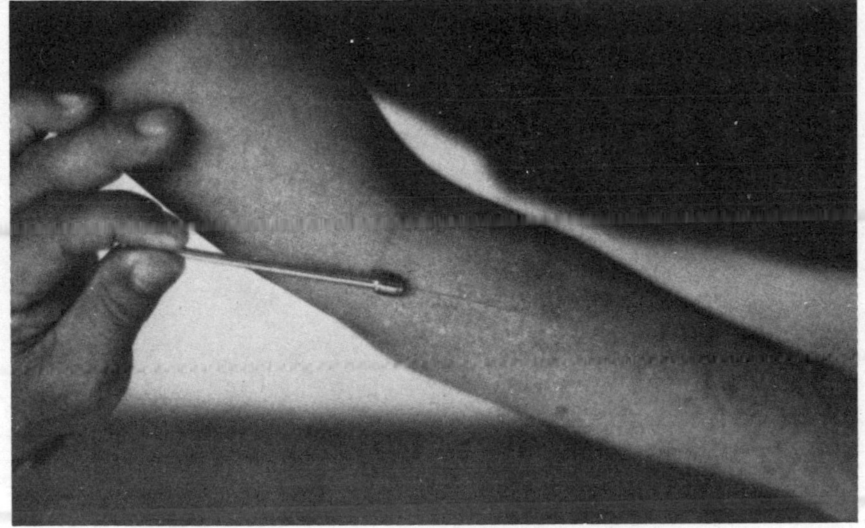

Electric Needle

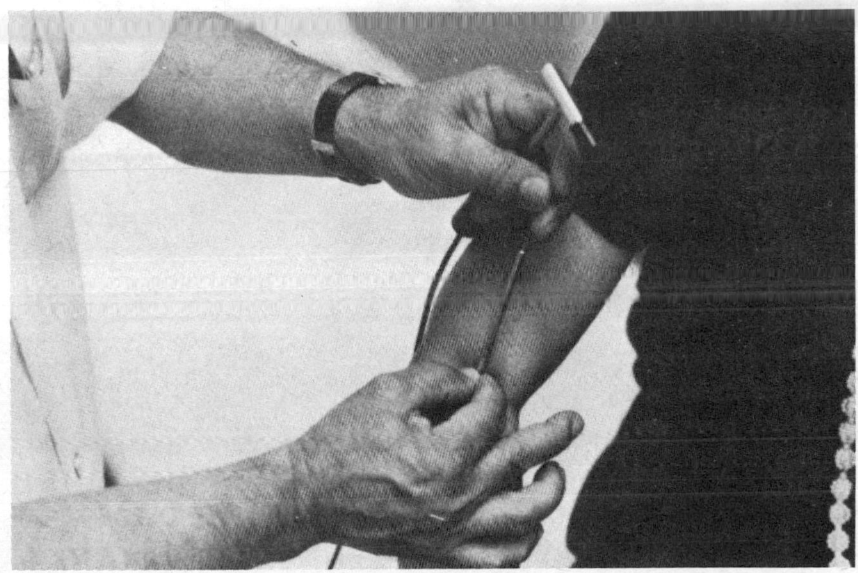

Preparing insertion of *Electric Needle* into skin.

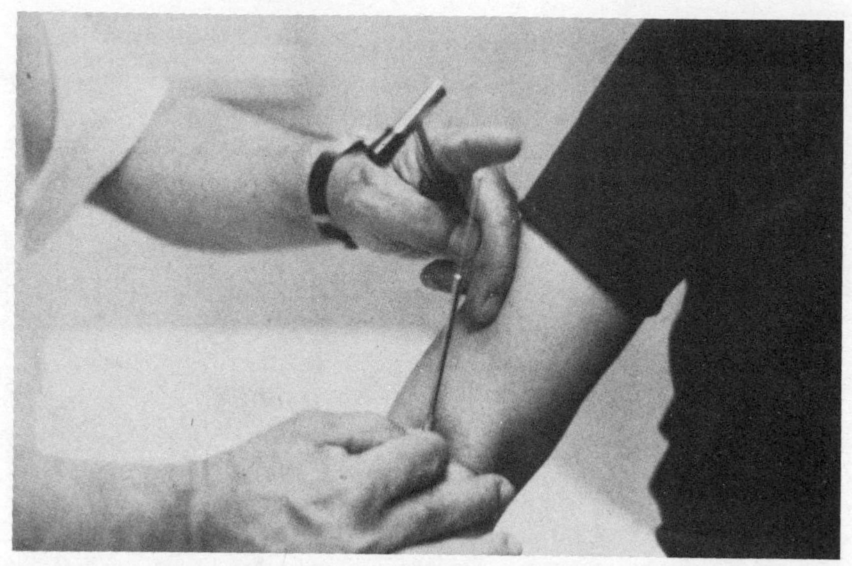

Electric Needle ready for "Pecking."

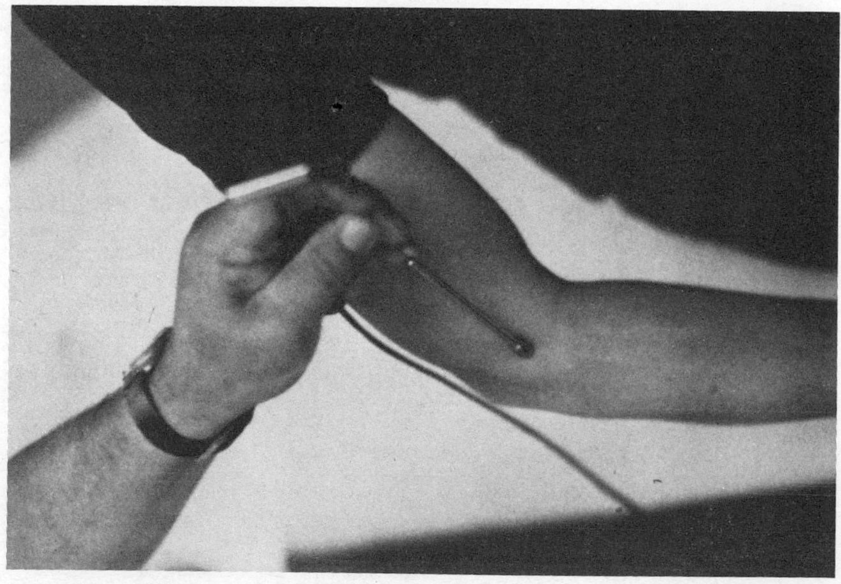

Electric Needle injected.

the guide-tube, indicating penetration of the skin. The guide-tube is then gently removed. The needle is inserted by turning the shaft with the right hand, holding the section near the tip with the left.

The Technique of Acupuncture

There are several techniques used in the application of acupuncture. One controls the strength or weakness of stimulation through the hands.

The Technique of Simple Insertion

This is the technique of inserting the needle straight in, without turning, to the intended depth, and withdrawing it gently. This is the most basic technique. If the needle is gently inserted and withdrawn, it will produce a light stimulation.

The Technique of "the Pecking Sparrow"

This hand technique involves inserting the needle to the intended depth and moving it up and down, in the manner of a sparrow bobbing his head while pecking at food. Also, in this manner, the technique of inserting the needle to the right and left and to the front and back of the point, and turning it as it is being inserted, is called Random Acupuncture Technique. Both methods are used in producing strong stimulations.

The Technique of Leaving the Needle in Place

For this technique, the needle is left in place after having reached the intended depth, usually 20 to 30 seconds for relatively short treatment, and 20 to 30 minutes for longer treatments.

Another technique combines the "Pecking Sparrow" technique with the Leaving in Place technique. In this case, several needles are inserted and left in place for a length of time and then alternately withdrawn and reinserted.

The Leaving in Place technique produces a slight and lasting stimulation and is used to cure chills caused by irregular blood circulation and to reduce mental or physical activity.

The Encircling Technique

This technique involves the insertion of many needles in a small area around the affected part of the body, in the area of oppressive pain, induration, or muscle strain. Special points are not defined for this treatment. The encircling technique is used to cure still shoulders, lumbago, arthritis, and other ailments.

Difficulty in Withdrawing Acupuncture Needles

There are some occasions in which withdrawal of a needle is not possible due to sudden muscle contractions during the insertion. In most cases, this occurs because the needle is bent underneath the skin. Therefore, if the needle is withdrawn forcefully, it may break. This will tend to happen especially when acupuncture is applied in the area of the lower back. In such a case, leave the needle quietly as it is for thirty seconds or a minute without trying to force it out. Then withdraw it gently when the muscle tension decreases. Another method of withdrawing the needle involves leaving the resisting needle and first relieving the muscle tension by inserting other needles in the area around it. After this measure, the needle can be withdrawn.

The Problem of Broken Needles

Since the needles are extremely thin, they are quite flexible and hard to break, although they may be bent, even becoming zigzag in shape. However, if the needle is even slightly scratched, there is the possibility that the tip of the needle may be wrenched off due to sudden muscular contractions, which occur reflexively when the needles are inserted. The portion of the needle which remains in the body may sometimes be moved by the movements of the muscles. In many cases, however, it will remain for a long time in the position of least obstruction to muscle movement. There may be some pain around that area for ten days or more during times of activity, but after that, there will be no sensation at all and usually no interference with everyday activity. If there is severe pain or inflammation in the area of the broken needle, it will be necessary to operate to remove it. However, if there are no problems, there is little fear of serious consequences from leaving it as is.

CHAPTER XXV

Moxa (Artemisia moxa)

MOXA IS MADE FROM WILD MUGWORT (WORMWOOD). THE leaves of wormwood are picked in April or May. They are exposed to the heat of the sun, dried completely over summer, and then pounded with a tile mortar and softened during winter. The powder (the short fibers and the dried substance from the surface of the leaves) is sifted out. The remains are pounded again to soften certain large fibers, which become just like cotton. This is called "moxa." Moxa is indispensable to moxacautery. Without moxa, moxacautery could not be applied. Moxacautery involves placing a small amount of moxa on the skin and burning it with a stick of incense.

Since the procedure of moxacautery involves burning the moxa directly onto the skin, scars will remain to some degree. However, for those people who hate to have lasting scars, an indirect type of moxacautery called shielded moxacautery has been developed. That is, almost no scars will be formed on the skin if the appropriate dosage of moxa is placed on a piece of ginger or garlic at the moxacautery point and then burned. This procedure is called warm (not hot) moxacautery.

There is even an instrument which can achieve the goals of moxacautery without leaving scars at all nor requiring burning of moxa on the skin. Instead of moxacautery, a new field is developing. An electrical moxacautery instrument has been produced by Horikoshi. Especially important are the recently established developments from the Ryodo-raku theory of Dr. Nakatani of Osaka, i.e., the searching method of finding the moxacautery points by using the neurometer, instruments which measure low electric current, and new methods of measuring and treatment in acupuncture and moxacautery. Also, so-called silver particles are used instead of moxacautery.

Stimulation of the Skin by Medicine

"Sheetless soft"* rubbed into a painful region provides relief by properly stimulating the painful part. It is even more effective to cover the skin into which "sheetless soft" is rubbed with a thin sheet of paper.

Silver Particle

"Silver Particle" is a new anodyne, developed after years of study and research in "Magnetic Medicine" by the Japanese pharmacists. There are various soothing methods developed by both Chinese and Western medical people in the past. The "Silver Particle" is composed of micromagnetic balls made of a special alloy. Through direct contact of the steel balls to the sore spot on the human body, it will produce a strikingly soothing effect through ionization of the ball alloy.

*Sheetless soft—CMC ointment.

Warning: Remove it at an early stage in treatment for persons with especially sensitive skin if the stimulation is unbearably strong.

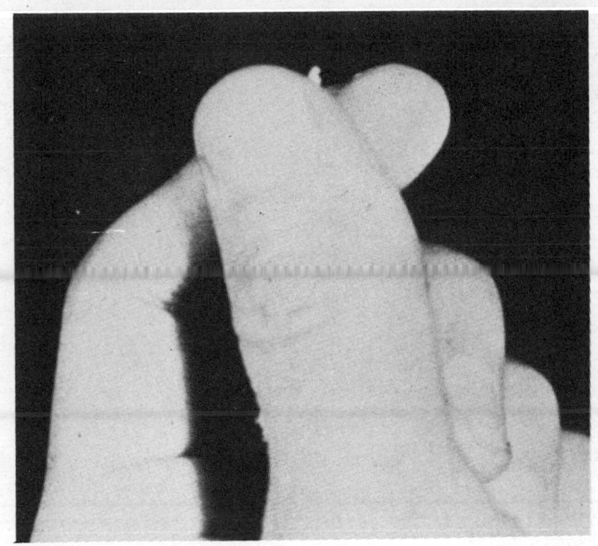

Breaking Moxa 1

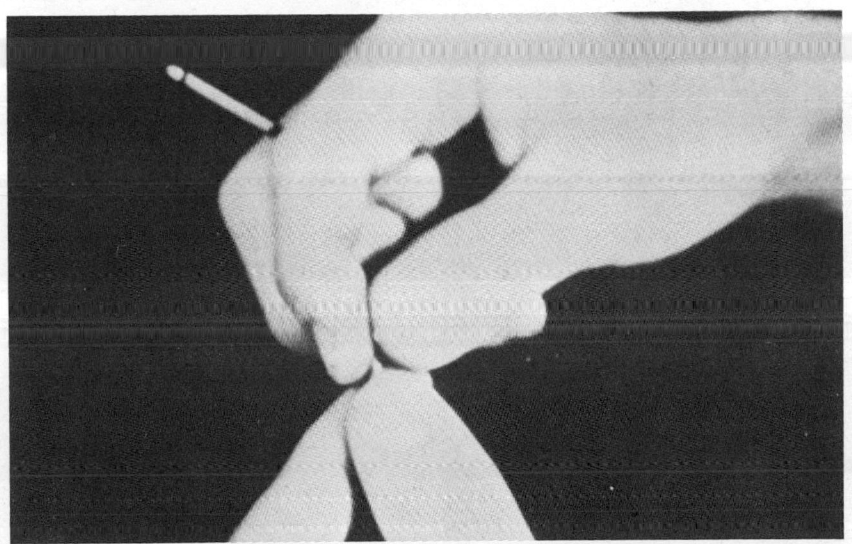

Breaking Moxa - 2

Practical Techniques of Moxacautery

With the exception of certain special methods of moxacautery, the materials for general moxacautery are moxa and joss sticks.

Although there are several dozen qualities of moxa, the highest possible should be used in those types of moxacautery treatment which leave scars. Superior, well-manufactured moxa has thin fibers. It is soft and light to the touch with a light yellow color, and has a fragrance. In contrast, inferior moxa is rough to the touch, heavy, slightly dirty in color, and not as fragrant. High quality moxa stretches easily, ignites quickly, and produces a comfortable, penetrating heat. Keep moxa away from humidity.

Joss Sticks

The most suitable joss sticks have the thickness and rigidity of a matchstick. Joss sticks longer than 15 cm are inconvenient to use. They should be broken into proper lengths before use. Avoid strong-smelling incense sticks because they are adhesive and, during treatment, the pieces of moxa are apt to be lifted away with the joss stick.

Dosage

Generally the proper dose of moxa for moxacautery is smaller than a grain of rice. If possible, moxa half the size of a grain of rice (about 0.2 mg) or one third the size (about 0.1 mg) is preferable. It is a mistake and in fact rather harmful to think that the more moxa used, the better the effect. If too much moxa is applied, the heat becomes unbearably painful, the scars that remain are apt to be large, and blister and pus-filled scars are apt to form. Therefore, moxacautery should be carefully applied using the smallest pieces of moxa possible. On some occasions tiny, fine doses of moxa resembling thread are used, especially for children.

Breaking Moxa

Lightly hold a small amount of moxa in the left hand and roll it until it is as fine as a piece of incense, gently twisting and stretching it with thumb and forefinger. Next, gently tear off a dose with a twisting motion of the thumb and forefinger of the right hand, and form it into a cone-shaped dose. With skill, one can make about thirty doses of the same weight, hardness, and size in a minute. It is difficult for the beginner to twist out the moxa with the left hand, so the following methods are advisable.

The first method involves placing a small amount of moxa on a straw mat, holding it down with the edge of a fan and moving the fan at right angles to the woven grain of the mat. The other method involves placing a piece of moxa between two sheets of cardboard and moving the boards gently. With both methods, the moxa should be stretched into the shape of a joss stick. Cut it into 1 to 2 cm pieces, twist these pieces between the thumb and forefinger of the left hand and break them in half with the thumb and forefinger of the right hand.

Applying Moxa

Use a piece of moxa torn off by the thumb and forefinger of the right hand and form into a well-shaped, elongated cone. Dampen the bottom of it with sterilized cotton and set it upright on the moxacautery point. The moxacautery point may also be dampened. In this manner, when the moxa is placed on the skin and pressed into place by hand, the pieces of moxa will not adhere to the fingers when it is released by the hand.

Since burned out cinders will remain once moxa has been burnt, pieces of moxa can be set directly on the treatment point from the second treatment. The skin will not especially need to be wet because the moxa will stick to the cinder. Since moxa is likely to stick to the fingers because of perspiration in summer, ashes or similar substances should first be dusted on the fingers.

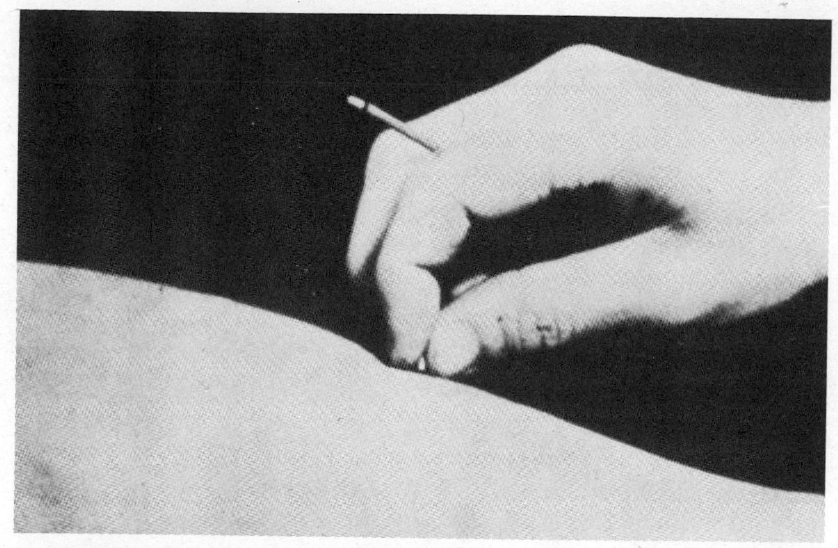

Applying Moxa

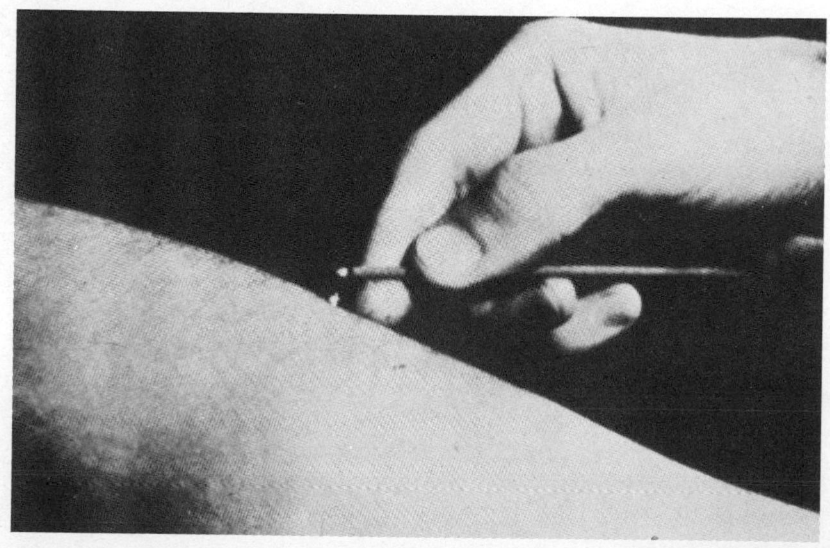

Lighting the Moxa

Lighting the Moxa

Hold the joss stick with the thumb, forefinger and middle finger at an angle about one centimeter from the ember. Remove any ash completely and light the piece of moxa, touching the ember very lightly to the top of the moxa. Propping the forefinger against the skin, control of the treatment can be effected quite safely despite any body movement. If the ember of the joss stick touches the moxa for too long a time, the dose may adhere to the joss stick. Therefore, touch the dose of moxa with the ember only slightly, then lift it up again with a twist in order to ignite it right. Also, if the ember is left near the skin too long, the patient will experience painful heat. Therefore, treatment should be completed as quickly as possible.

After moxacautery has been performed two or three times, cinders collect. Cover the cinders with fresh moxa and gingerly lift them off the skin without dirtying the fingers nor enlarging the moxacautery points. If the cinders smear on the skin, the center of the moxacautery point will be indiscernible and the moxacautery point will be enlarged.

Methods of Tonification and Sedation

The method of tonification produces a comfortable, warm heat as the moxa burns itself out. For that purpose, good quality moxa should be dried, twisted softly and set lightly on the skin. Do not remove old cinders; rather, the moxacautery should be performed on them. The piece of moxa should be small, elongated, and narrow at the bottom.

Application of the Sedation Method of Moxacautery

The method of sedation aims at stinging and sensations of intense heat by blowing on the piece of moxa when it is about to burn out. High quality moxa is not necessary. For this purpose, moxa is twisted lightly and set on the skin. A new piece of moxa is set on the point after the cinder has been removed.

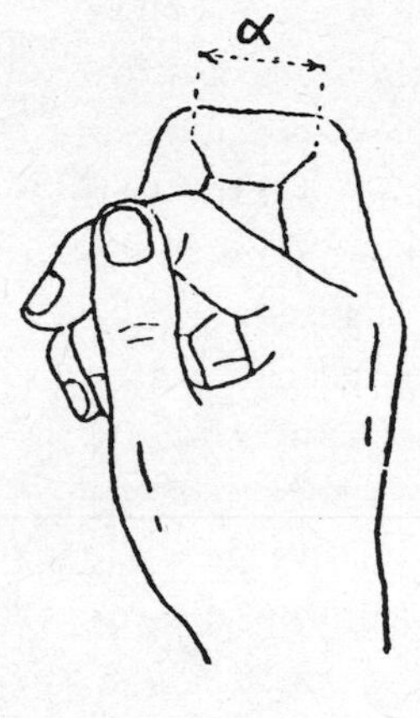

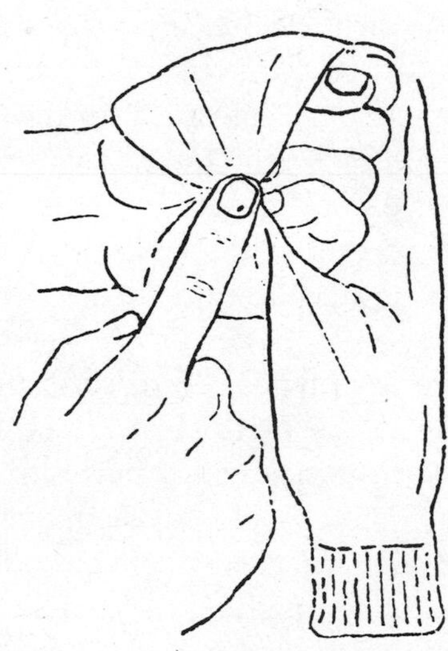

All you need is to make a fist, wrap the sock once around the widest part of your fist. If the toe of the sock and the heel meet exactly, the sock will fit.

The dose of moxa should be large, squat, and wide on the bottom.

Position of the Patient During Moxacautery Treatment

Moxacautery must be applied with the patient in the same position as the position of diagnosis in which the doctor determined the point of treatment. For example, if the position of diagnosis of the patient was lying in a prone position and moxacautery is performed with the patient in a seated position, the moxacautery point will shift from its proper place and the expected result can not be achieved. In general, the following postures are preferred.

Chest and abdominal region—supine position
Back, shoulders, neck, head—seated posture
Lower back, hips, back of legs—prone posture
Arms and legs—extended forward

These suggestions do not need to be followed persistently, depending on the symptoms of the patient; however, it would be better, once the position for treatment has been decided, to maintain it consistently through the course of treatment.

Measurements in Acupuncture and Moxacautery

One alpha (α) is the distance in length between the first and second knuckles of the patient's crooked middle finger, as shown in Figure 1. 1.5 α means one and one-half times this length, and 3 α means three times this length. This was invented because the height of a person has a precise relationship to the distances between the joints of his fingers.

Determining the Location of the Vital Points

The Vital Points of the center of the back are systematically aligned so that they generally fall along seven vertical lines.

Visualizing the vertical lines of the chest and abdomen is the basis for determining the position of Vital Points, and therefore it is important to measure exactly.

First, imagine the center line running straight through the navel. This is Line A (Figure 1). Next, draw Line B 0.5 α on either side of Line A (Figure 2). Next draw Line D through the nipples of the left and right breasts (Figure 3). Finally draw Line C halfway between Lines A and D (Figure 4). Now you have the seven basic lines: Line A, Line B (two lines), Line C (two lines), and Line D (two lines) (Figure 5).

Drawing the Imaginary Lines of the Back

First draw Line A down the center of the back (Figure 1). Then draw Line B about 1.5 α on either side of Line A (Figure 2). In the same manner, draw Line C 1.5 α outwards from Line B (Figure 3). Now you have the five basic lines: Line A, Line B (two lines), Line C (two lines). Remember that each of the Vital Points of the arms and legs are in the same position on both the left and right sides of the body, and not only on one side alone.

Advice Concerning Moxacautery

The moxa dosage can be determined as the sum of the patient's moxacautery points, the number of times treatment is repeated, and the "size of the moxa." The dosage must be determined with care, considering the condition of the illness, the patient's constitution, age, sex, past experiences with moxacautery, and so on. It will generally be safer to start with small doses at first and gradually increase the dosage from there.

Correction of the Moxacautery Points

Generally the moxacautery points are apt to shift depending on changes in the condition of the illness and the person's constitution. Sometimes the moxacautery points will also shift because of the unskillful application of moxacautery. Therefore, it is necessary to check on these points again, once every seven to ten days, in cases of long-term moxacautery treatment. Care must be taken to use only the proper moxacautery points at all times, omitting unnecessary points for treatment and adding

The lines of the back

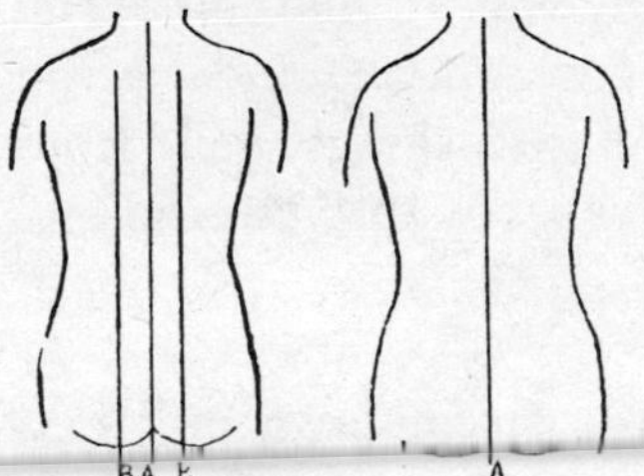

Figure 2 Figure 1

The lines of the chest and abdomen

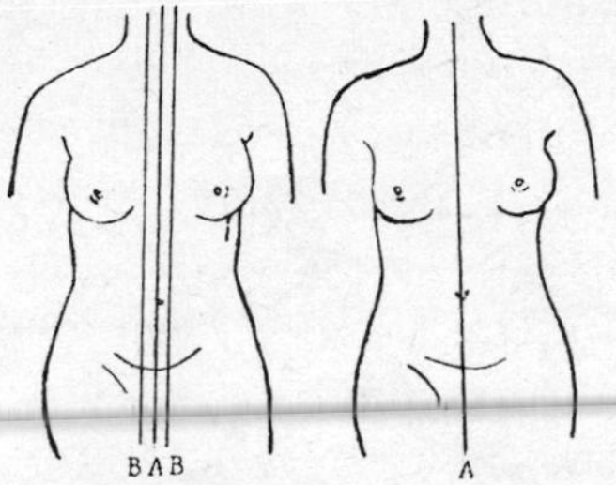

Figure 2 Figure 1

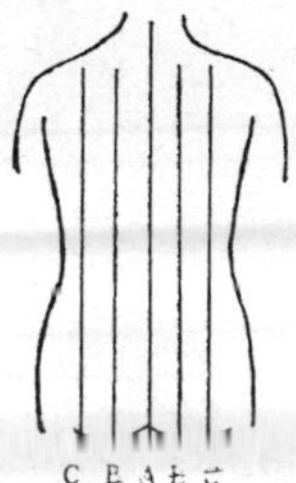

Figure 3

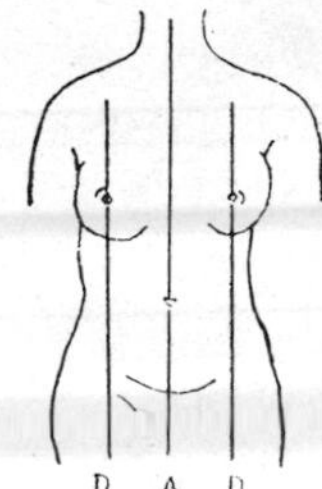

Figure 3

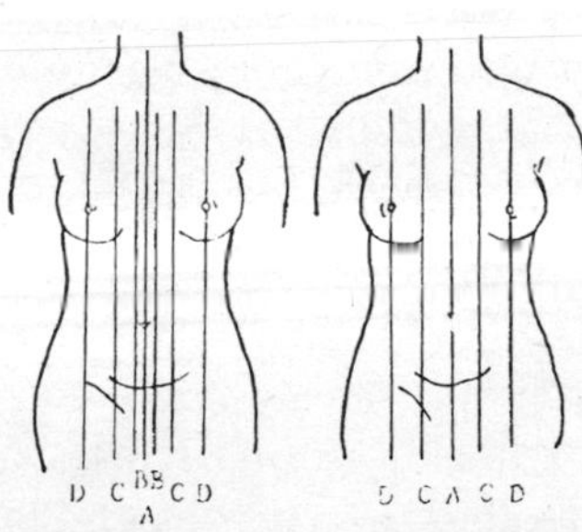

Figure 5 Figure 4

new ones that are necessary. If this is neglected, effective treatment can not be attained and sometimes the condition of the illness may even be worsened. For convenience and ease in distinguishing moxacautery points that are no longer valid from those that are valid is to cover the former with plaster.

The Duration of Treatment

Acute illnesses and mild symptoms generally can be cured with one to three applications of moxacautery, but treatment for chronic illnesses may need to be continued for several weeks, months, or even years. There are many cases in which supposedly incurable illnesses have been cured through patient continuation of moxacautery treatment to improve the person's constitution. Therefore, for chronic illnesses, it is best not to judge the effectiveness of moxacautery until after six weeks of continuous treatment.

Moxacautery can be applied at any time during the day. However, from ancient times morning has been regarded as the ideal time. This indicates that it is preferable to perform moxacautery before the patient has become tired.

Bathing: It is best to bathe thirty minutes to one hour before or after treatment by moxacautery. In addition, it is best to avoid bathing on the day of the first moxacautery treatment because the moxacautery point may become indiscernible.

Menstruation and Pregnancy: Women who become especially sensitive to moxacautery during the menstrual period should not continue treatment during this time. If there are no abnormalities, treatment can be continued. As a rule, moxacautery can be continued even during pregnancy up until the time of birth. However, it will be difficult to perform moxacautery on the lower back or the abdomen during the latter part of pregnancy.

Drinking: Moxacautery should not be performed on a patient who has been drinking. If one dares to apply treatment, the patient will generally feel a burning pain.

Uncomfortable Phenomena of Moxacautery

Sometimes the patient's whole body will feel very tired the day after or for several days after moxacautery treatment. Sometimes the patient suffers from a fever and dullness in the head, with frequent yawning. In addition he may experience a high fever, diarrhea, and loss of appetite. These phenomena are called Rejection of Moxacautery or Defeat of Moxacautery.

In any case, these phenomena are mostly temporary and will disappear soon even if moxacautery is continued. However, if the symptoms continue to be serious and remain for a long time, it is best to stop moxacautery treatment for a while and observe the patient's progress. Since these phenomena in many cases are caused by excessive doses, it may be possible to continue treatment with an adjusted dosage.

Blisters and Scabs

Sometimes blisters form at the point of moxacautery after treatment. Small blisters will be absorbed and soon disappear, but large blisters should be pierced once with a sterile needle and the liquid allowed to drain out. In both cases moxacautery treatment can still be continued.

When moxacautery is being performed, a scab soon forms. Too large a dose of moxa or an improper method of attaching moxa to the skin will cause the scab to grow larger. Usually the patient does not feel the heat of moxacautery applied on the scab. However, the mark from moxacautery will disappear sooner in the future if treatment is performed without tearing the scab off the wound each time. The smaller the scab, the smaller the mark of moxacautery will be. Hardly any scar should be left after several months.

Suppuration of the Mark of Moxacautery

The mark of moxacautery may sometimes suppurate. This will often happen to persons with a tendency for suppuration but will also occur in cases in which the dose of moxa was too large or in the event the patient may have scratched off the scab. Temporarily cease moxacautery treatment on the suppurating point, wipe the area clean, and apply mercurochrome or dermatol. The pus must not be allowed to come in contact with other moxacautery points.

There is even a technique in moxacautery called Pus-inducing Moxacautery with the goal of producing suppuration. Actually, suppuration may sometimes increase the effectiveness of the treatment. On the other hand, suppuration tends to produce permanent scars on the point of moxacautery, and so it is better to try to prevent suppuration as much as possible.

Pain Caused by the Heat

Nervous, oversensitive people or small children or persons undergoing moxacautery for the first time often cannot bear the painful heat. In this case, remove the dose of moxa quickly before it has burned out for the first four or five doses at this stage and allow the patient to grow accustomed to the stimulation of warmth.

One method for relief is to wash the moxacautery point with a strong saline solution.

If moxacautery is applied by pressing the skin around the moxacautery point with the fingers, the pain from the heat can be lessened. However, this procedure may cause the point to shift. Therefore, it should be avoided.

CHAPTER XXVI

Treatment and Location of Vital Points in Acupuncture and Moxacautery

THE FOURTEEN MERIDIANS AND THEIR IDENTIFICATION WHEN the vital points are located for treatment with acupuncture or moxacautery, are as follows:

1. Lung	Lu	Lu–1	to	Lu–11
2. Large Intestine	L I	LI–1	to	LI–20
3. Stomach	St	St–1	to	St–45
4. Spleen	Sp	Sp–1	to	Sp–21
5. Heart	H	H–1	to	H–9
6. Small Intestine	S I	SI–1	to	SI–19
7. Bladder	B	B–1	to	B–63
8. Kidney	K	K–1	to	K–27
9. Circulation	C	C–1	to	C–29
10. Triple Warmer	T	T–1	to	T–23
11. Gallbladder	G B	GB–1	to	GB–43
12. Liver	Li	Li–1	to	Li–13
13. Governing Vessel	G V	GV–1	to	GV–27
14. Vessel of conception	C V	CV–1	to	CV–24

CHAPTER XXVII

Respiratory Diseases

The Cold

The ailment generally referred to as the common cold has many varied symptoms; such as nasal inflammation, pharyngitis, and the early stages of tonsillitis. Furthermore, common symptoms are headache, chills, running nose, sore throat, and sneezing. In many cases the cold may develop into such diseases as bronchitis, or be accompanied with gastroenteric disorders, lower back pain, and pain in the joints.

Treatment: Moxacautery: Apply repeated applications of moxacautery at GV–13 (back), GV–11 (back), and B–11 (back).

In the early stages of the cold, the performance of moxacautery at these locations often is sufficient to effect cure.

Acupuncture: Shallow insertion technique, and rapid insertion and withdrawal technique are effective along B–11 (back), GV–13 (back), B–12 (back) and L1–11 (upper limb).

For sneezing, acupuncture at B–2 (face) and L1–20 (face) is effective.

For sore throat, apply at Lu–5 (upper limb), T–17 (neck), and VC–22 (neck).

For persistent coughing, moxacautery at K–26 (chest) and Lu–5 (upper limb) should be tried.

LOCATION OF VITAL POINTS IN ACUPUNCTURE AND MOXACAUTERY TREATMENT

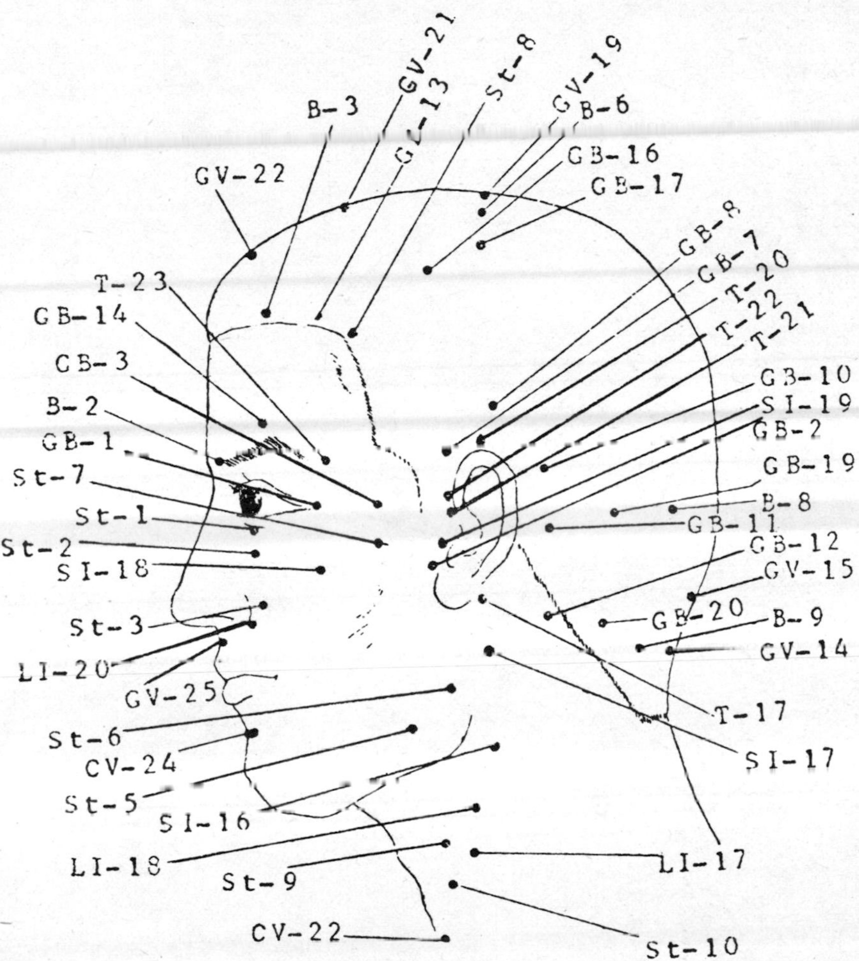

Side view of the face, neck and head section

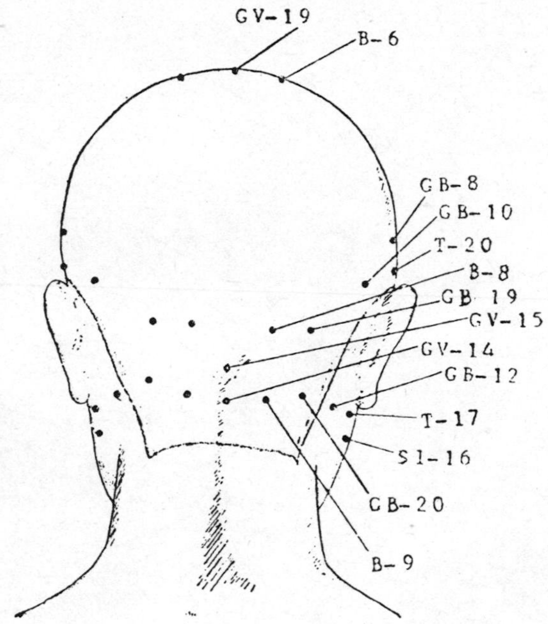

Back view of the head and neck

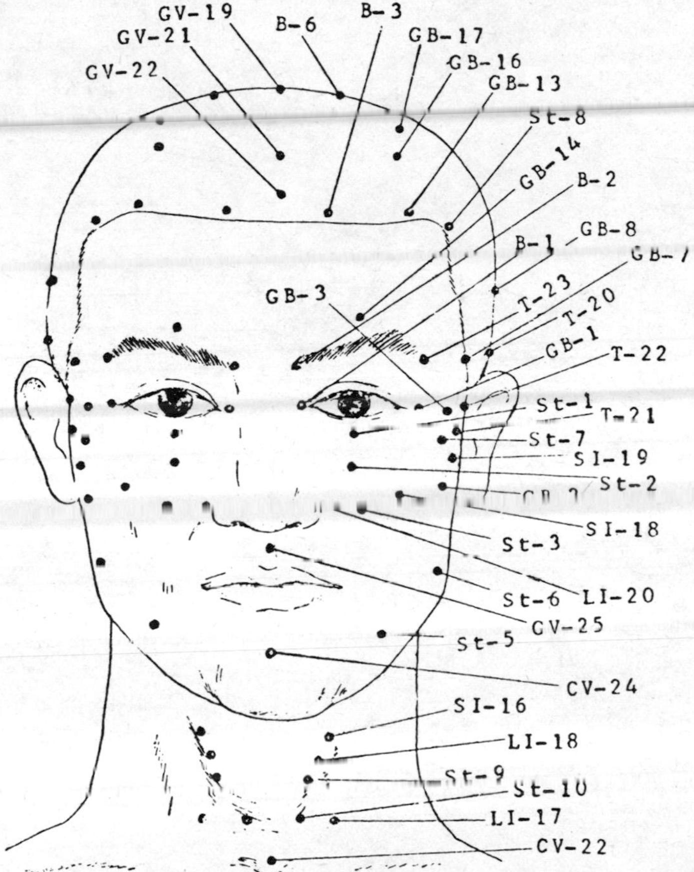

Front section of the head, face and neck

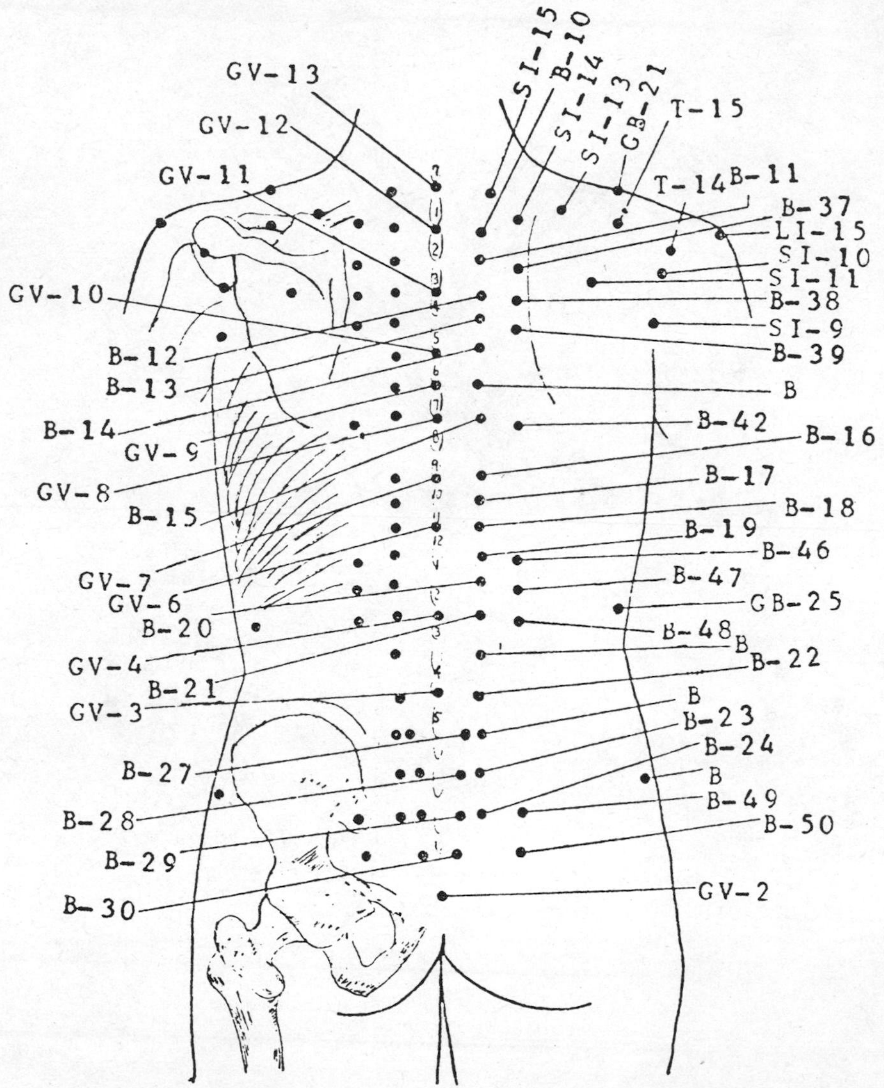

The Back and Lower Trunk

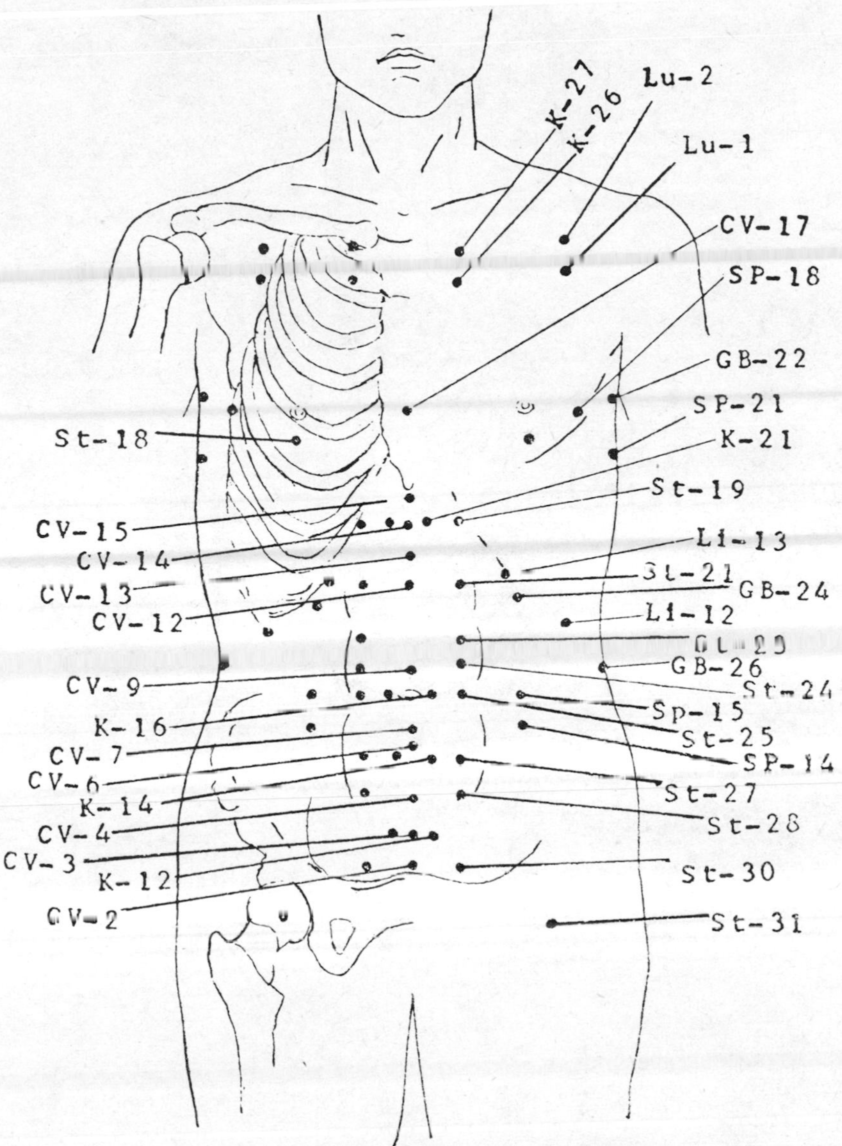

The Front: Chest and Abdomen

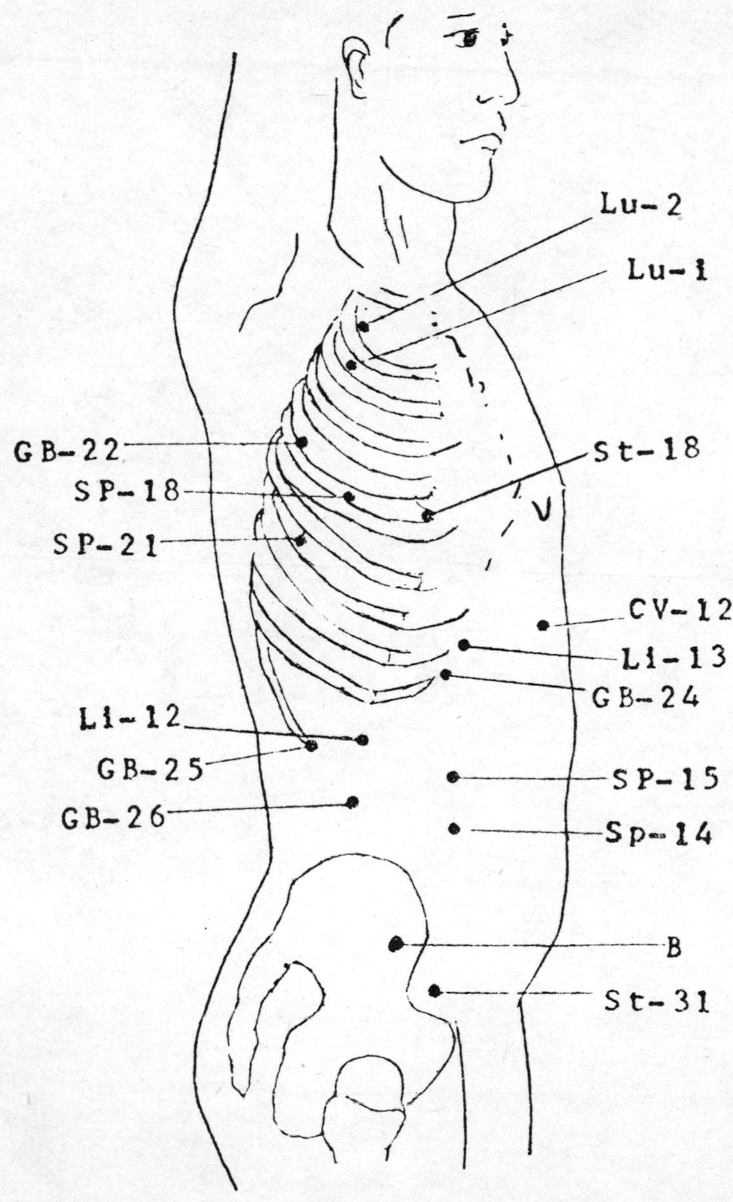

Side view of Chest and Abdomen

THE UPPER LIMBS

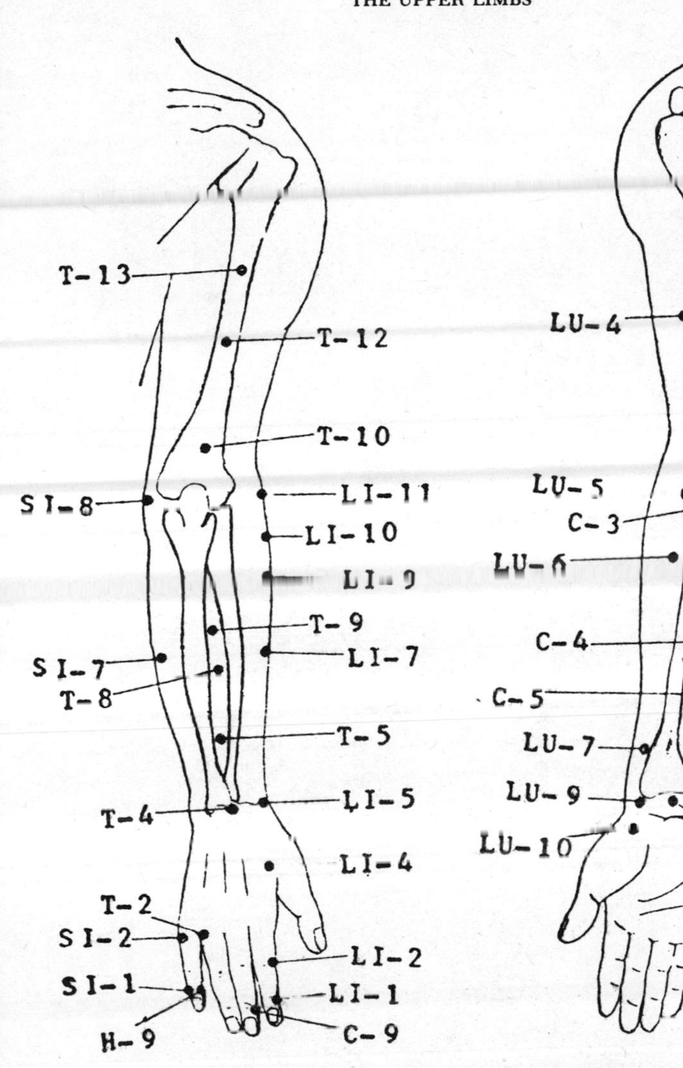

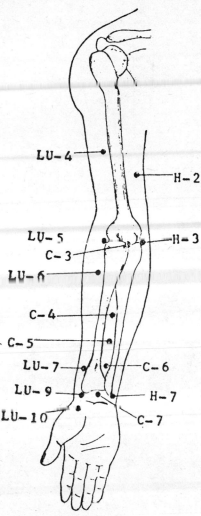

Back section of upper limbs

Front section of upper limbs

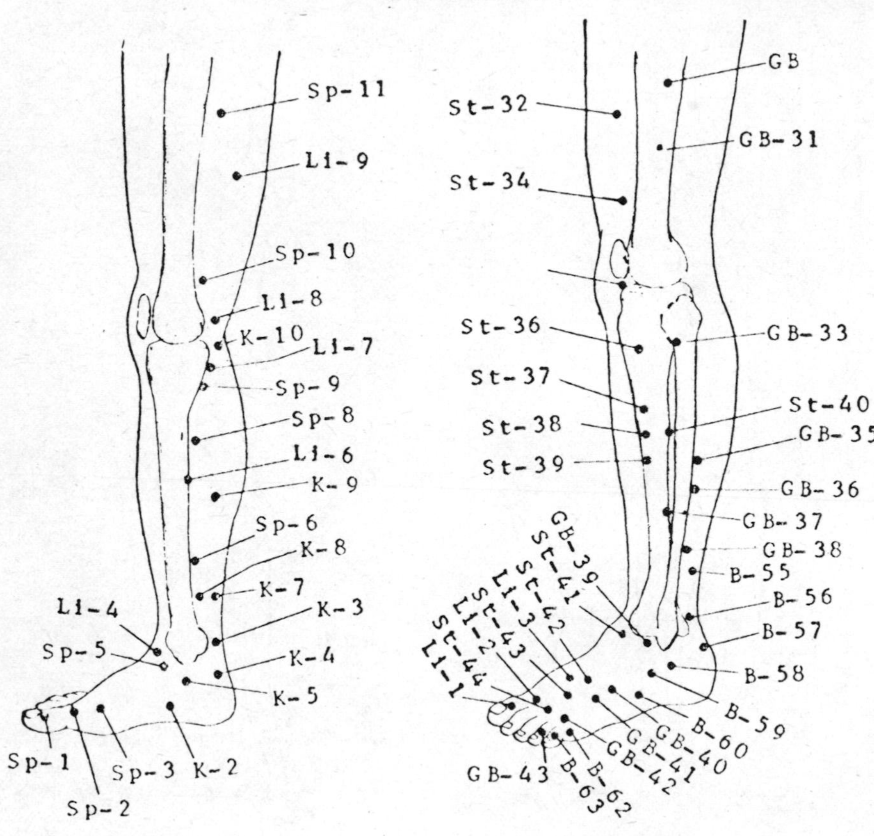

The inside view of leg

The outside view of leg

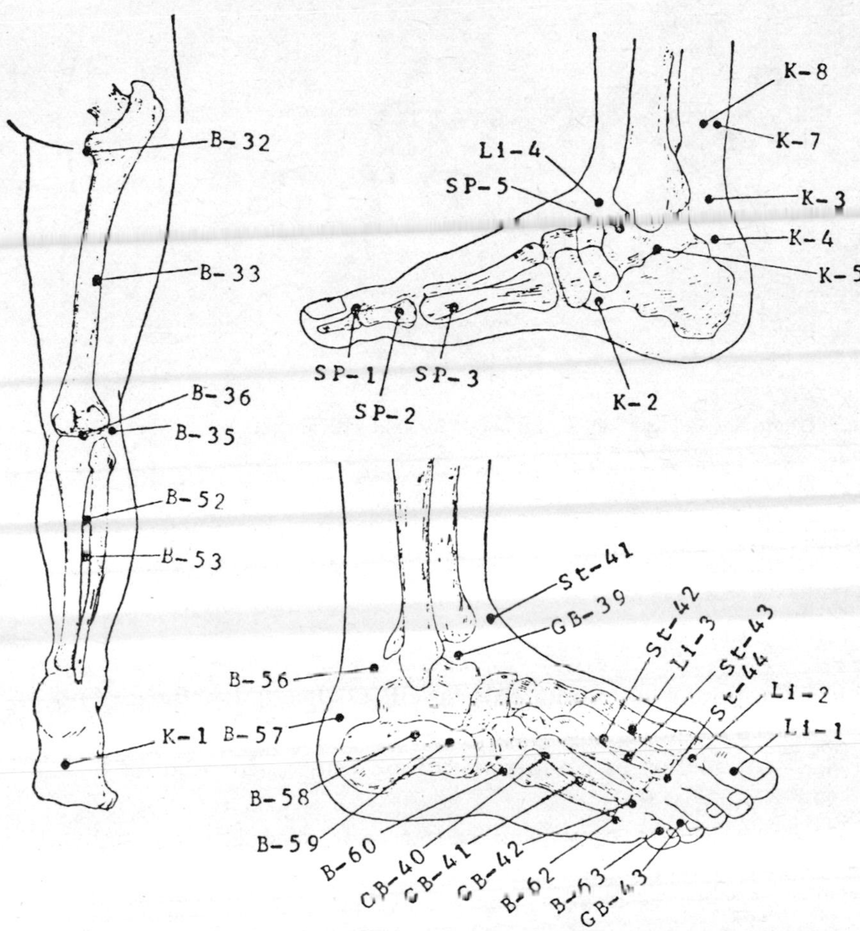

Back section of leg

Inside and outside view of the Foot

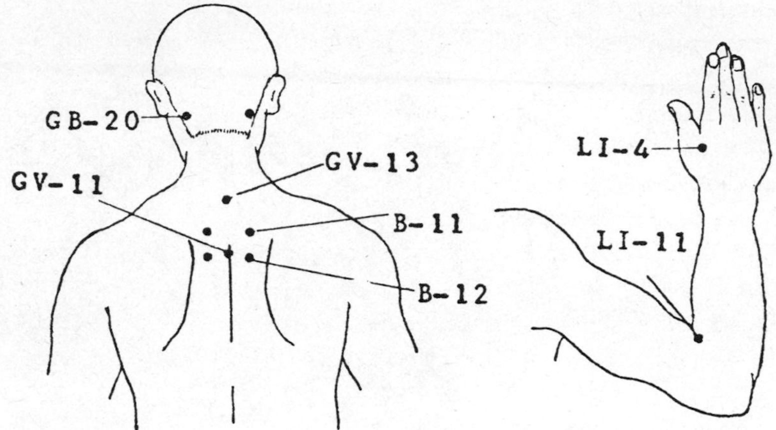

Treatment and location of vital points for cold with acupuncture and moxacautery

For headache, acupuncture at GB–20 (head), B–9 (head), and GV–19 (head) is effective.

Acupuncture is preferred to moxacautery in treating high fever over 100.5°F.

Acupuncture: Apply shallow but strong stimulatory acupuncture at LI–11 (upper limb), LI–4 (upper limb), St–41 (lower limb) and B–56 (lower limb).

Furthermore, apply encircling technique of acupuncture [technique of applying several acupuntures encircling the affected area, not necessarily at any vital points] at various sections of the body such as the shoulder, back, and the upper chest. When the muscles along both sides of the spinal column seem to be tense, then apply acupuncture to relieve the tension.

Acute Bronchitis

In many cases, a cold will develop into acute bronchitis. Coughing is the main symptom; accompanied in severe cases by pain in the chest. The patient's phlegm, initially in mucous state, later changes to a pus-like phlegm which sometimes includes blood.

Treatment: Acupuncture: Application in the cavity of a sinus St–9 (neck) and such acupuncture as at GV–11 (back), B–11 (back), B–12 (back), B–15 (back), B–16 (back), GV–9 (back), LU–5 (upper limb), CV–22 (neck), Lu–1 (chest),K–26 (chest), Li–13 (abdomen),GB–21 (back) and CV–14 (abdomen).

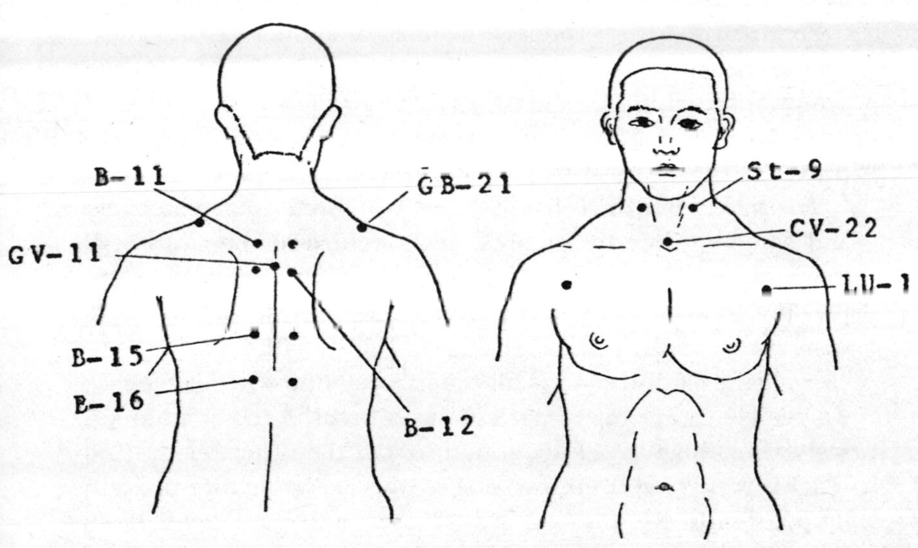

The vital points of treatment for Acute Bronchitis

Chronic Bronchitis

In the case of chronic bronchitis, use acupuncture as well as moxacautery. It will also be beneficial to follow the treatment described for acute bronchitis although the patient will require many repeated treatments.

Treatment: Apply acupuncture and moxacautery at GV–11 (back), B–11 (back), GV–9 (back), B–15 (back), CV–12 (abdomen), CV–14 (abdomen), K–27 (chest), Li–13 (abdomen), Lu–5 (upper limb), and K–3 (lower limb).

Bronchial Asthma

There are two ways to treat bronchial asthma. One is to use a temporary measure to stop the seizure. The other is to treat the basic cause with Chinese herb medicine on a continuing basis over a long period of time, regardless of seizures. In Chinese medicine, the latter path is stressed more than the first. In deciding which method to use for treatment of bronchial asthma, it is necessary first to examine the patient's stomach.

For treatment of bronchial asthma, acupuncture and moxacautery are both very effective. They stop the seizure, ease the symptoms, begin the healing process, and are also capable of preventing seizures as the patient's physical condition improves.

Treatment: For the relief of difficulty in breathing, wheezing, and coughing due to seizures, acupuncture of the sinus St–9 (neck) is an extremely effective measure. The method of application is insertion at the region of the carotid sinus; and as soon as the needle reaches the carotid sinus withdraw immediately. If the carotid sinus is hit too hard, symptoms will become worse. There are many patients who breathe easier immediately after this type of acupuncture. On the other hand, if no relief is witnessed from the seizure, then acupuncture of Lu–5 (upper limb), K–27 (chest), B–11 (back), B–12 (back), B–46 (back), and B–9 (neck) should be performed.

Moxacautery of K–27 (chest), Lu–1 (chest), CV–14 (abdomen),

GV–12 (abdomen), GV–11 (back), B–11 (back), GV–9 (back), Lu–5 (upper limb) K–3 (lower limb), and GB–33 (lower limb) is effective.

Coughing

Coughing is caused by the stimulation of the bronchial tube or by reflex action to remove secretions or harmful materials (such as phlegm). Coughing often accompanies respiratory diseases in many cases, but it may also be caused by nervousness or stimulations from other than the respiratory organs.

Treatment: Acupuncture and moxacautery: Apply at GB–20 (neck), GB–21 (back), B–12 (back), B–39 (back), Lu 1 (chest), CV–14 (abdomen), CV–12 (abdomen) and Lu–5 (upper limb).

If a patient has difficulty in clearing his throat of phlegm, apply acupuncture at CV–22 (neck). When dry coughing is caused by an uncomfortable feeling in the throat, apply acupuncture at St–10 (neck), St–9 (neck), and T 17 (neck).

For coughing accompanied by pain in the hypochondrium, apply acupuncture at B–18 (back), B–46 (back), B–19 (back), CV–14 (abdomen), Li–13 (abdomen), and Sp–12 (abdomen).

Emphysema

Emphysema is the condition in which the lungs are continuously and abnormally swollen. It often occurs to people past middle age. Contraction of the lungs is hindered, causing difficulty in breathing and interfering with blood circulation in the lungs. Recognizable symptoms are coughing and an oppressed feeling in the chest. The patient's chest may be expanded to a round shape until it resembles a beer keg. Emphysema is apt to be complicated by bronchitis and may lead to seizures similar to asthma.

Treatment: Acupuncture and moxacautery: Apply at B–12 (back), B–39 (back), B–15 (back), Lu–1 (chest), St–19 (abdomen), Lu–5 (upper limb), Lu–9 (upper limb), LI–10 (upper limb) and K–3 (lower limb).

Apply properly selected treatment points for such diseases as bronchitis, bronchial asthma, etc.

Difficulty in Breathing

This is caused by various respiratory diseases and also by diseases of the nose and throat, by heart ailments, poisoning, or seizures of hysteria, etc.

Treatment: Acupuncture and moxacautery: Apply at B–10 (back), B–12 (back), B–5 (back) located between B–14 (back) and B–15 (back), Lu–5 (upper limb), K–26 (chest), Lu–1 (chest), Li–13 (abdomen), CV–13 (abdomen) and in the cavity of a sinus St–9 (neck). One method worth trying is the encircling technique of acupuncture for stiffening of the chest.

For difficulty of breathing caused by hysterical seizures apply, in addition, acupuncture at GB–20 (neck), B–16 (back), and GB–33 (lower limb).

Hemoptysis

Hemoptysis refers to the condition in which a patient's phlegm is mixed with blood. This may occur due to pulmonary tuberculosis and also expansion of the bronchial tubes, bronchitis, lung necrosis, pulmonary abscess, pneumonia, parasitism of the lungs, and congestion of blood in the lungs. It may also occur in a person who bleeds easily or in a woman as compensatory bleeding.

Treatment: Acupuncture: Apply acupuncture at K–7 (lower limb) and Lu–6 (upper limb) in addition to the K–10 (lower limb) and K–3 (lower limb).

Night Sweating (Perspiration in Sleep)

A person may persire while he sleeps; this affliction is called night sweating or perspiration in sleep. It can occur in persons of weak constitution, or persons who are overexhausted. Night sweating is thought to be caused by abnormal tension of the autonomic nervous system.

Treatment: Acupuncture and moxacautery: Apply at B–14 (back), B–21 (lower trunk), Lu–5 (upper limb), K–7 (lower limb), B–10 (back), B–12 (back), CV–6 (abdomen), and St–36 (lower limb).

Chest Pain

In most cases, chest pain occurs due to stimulation of the pleura as in cases of pleurisy, tuberculosis, and pneumonia. It may also be due to muscular rheumatism or intercostal neuralgia pain. In many cases, the pain runs from the left side of the back to the lower part of the breast. Characteristic pain develops along the ribs.

Treatment: Acupuncture and moxacautery: Apply at B–14 (back), B–15 (back), SI–11 (back), B–39 (back), Sp–21 (chest), Li–13 (abdomen), CV–17 (chest), GB–33 (lower limb), and in addition, at C–4 (upper limb) and H–7 (upper limb) of the affected side.

For breast pain, moxacautery of L–1 (chest) and CV–17 (chest) is effective.

CHAPTER XXVIII

Circulatory Diseases

Valvular Diseases of the Heart (Heart Failure)

Sometimes, this disease is caused by inherent abnormal development of the heart, but in many cases it occurs with the acute inflammation of the lining membrane of the heart.

The patient's pulse becomes recognizably abnormal, accompanied by noticeably unpleasant palpitations of the heart, difficulty in breathing, and dizziness.

The valves of the heart close imperfectly and the mouth of the valve becomes narrowed; consequently, blood circulation is obstructed. As a result the functioning of the heart is impaired. This is sometimes accompanied by various types of blood congestion, gastroenteric disorders, bronchitis, cardiac asthma, and other disorders. Acupuncture and moxacautery are effective in relief of these symptoms.

Treatment: Acupuncture and moxacautery: Apply at CV–12 (abdomen), Li–13 (abdomen), K–27 (chest), GV–11 (back), T–15 (back), GV–8 (back), SI–11 (back), C–4 (upper limb), H–7 (upper limb), St–36 (lower limb), GB–33 (lower limb), and K–5 (lower limb). When a patient is bothered by dizziness, ringing in the ears, or vomiting, apply acupuncture at GV–19 (head).

Cardiac Nerve Disorders

This disease gives rise to symptoms similar to those for heart ailments but shows no particular change in the heart. It is a form

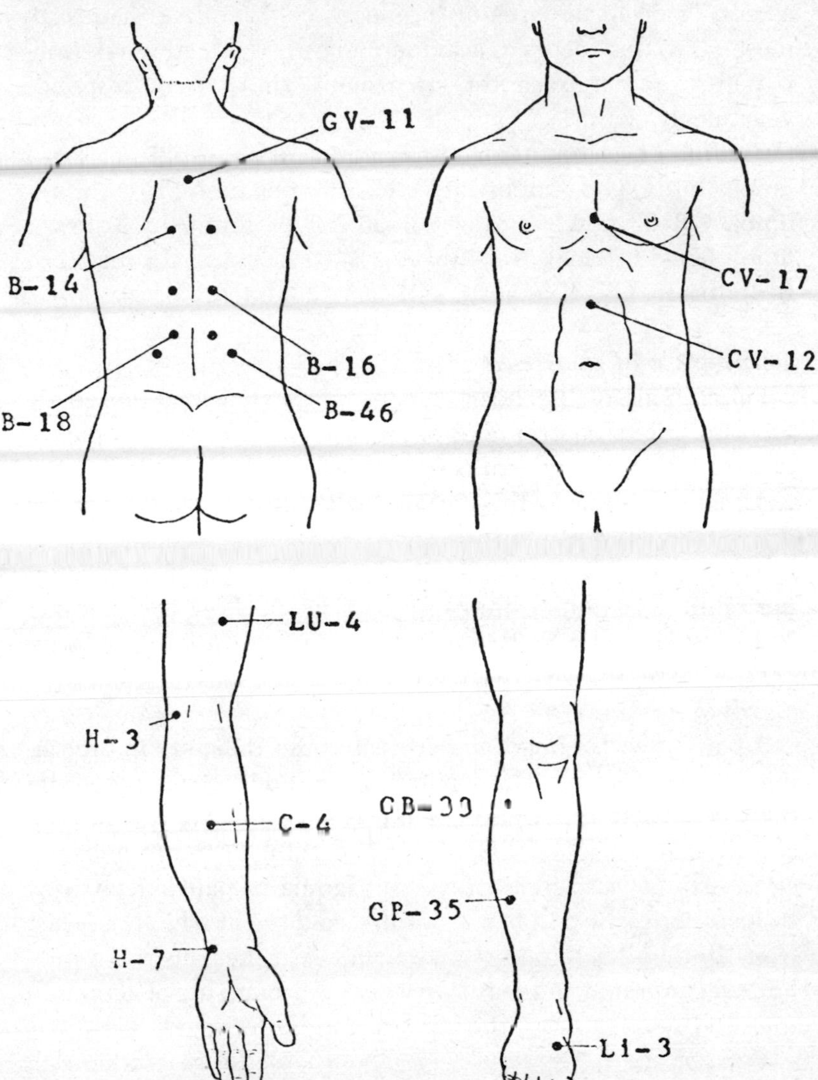

The vital points of treatment for Cardiac Nerve Disorders

of neurosis, sometimes called a nervous disorder of the cardiac blood vessels. The general symptoms are: palpitation of the heart, an oppressive feeling in the chest, difficulty in breathing, anxiety, pain in the area of the heart, cold feet and hands. In most cases, this occurs as a sudden seizure. With adequate acupuncture and moxacautery treatment, the patient responds very nicely.

Treatment: Acupuncture and moxacautery: Apply at Lu–4 (upper limb), C–4 (upper limb), H–3 (upper limb), H–7 (upper limb), GB–33 (lower limb), GB–35 (lower limb), Li–3 (lower limb), GV–11 (back), B–14 (back), B–16 (back), B–18 (back) or B–46 (back), CV–17 (chest), and CV–12 (abdomen).

Palpitation of the Heart

Palpitations of the heart can be physiologically caused by surprise, fright, or strenuous physical activity. However, pathologically, this usually results from heart ailments, among other causes. In many cases, this nervous palpitation of the heart is the major complaint of neurosis.

Treatment: Acupuncture and moxacautery: Apply at C–4 (upper limb), SI–8 (upper limb), CV–17 (chest), CV–14 (abdomen), B–14 (back), and GV–21 (head).

Cardiac Asthma

A patient with a heart ailment will suffer difficulty in breathing during a seizure. The seizure may not only strike when the body is in motion but also when it is at rest at night. Not only will the patient suffer difficulty in breathing at the time of the seizure, but he also complains about agonizing pain and anxiety. In many cases, he will break out in a cold sweat which may last from 20 minutes to one or two hours. At times, his pulse may be weak but rapid and may skip a beat. Through use of acupuncture and moxacautery, the seizure can be lessened.

Treatment: Apply at CV–12 (abdomen), Li–13 (abdomen), K–27 (chest), Lu–1 (chest), GV–11 (back), B–11 (back) or T–15 (back), B–14 (back), GV–9 (back), LI–11 (neck) or Lu–5 (upper limb), C–4 (upper limb) or Lu–6 (upper limb) or SI–8 (upper limb), St–36 (lower limb), K–5 (lower limb) or K–2 (lower limb) and St–6 (lower limb).

Apply acupuncture near the tip of the small finger SI-1 (upper limb) and draw out blood. As an emergency treatment during seizures, apply acupuncture of St–9 (neck).

Heart Attack (Angina Pectoris or Stenocardia)

Angina pectoris is a seizure which attacks with severe pain as if the patient's chest were being tightly squeezed. In most cases it results from disorders of the coronary arteries. The patient feels spasmodic pain at the heart and certain specific areas of the body, and at the same time is struck with extreme anxiety and severe anguish. The pain mostly runs along the heart meridian (Yin minimum) and is spread around to the intraclavicular region, the chest, neck, shoulder, and ulna of the left arm; sometimes, it is accompanied by difficulty of breathing or develops into cardiac asthma. The period of an attack may last somewhere from several seconds to 20 or 30 minutes; in rare occasions it can last for almost an hour.

Treatment: During the seizure: Apply acupuncture at St–9 (neck), draw out blood from SI–1 (upper limb), and apply a rather strong acupuncture at SI–8 (upper limb), H–7 (upper limb), SI–6 (upper limb), C–1 (upper limb), etc., as well as moxacautery of these areas. In addition, apply acupuncture and moxacautery at St–36 (lower limb) and GB–33 (lower limb) once every day for prevention of seizures and for relief of angina pectoris.

Treat with acupuncture and moxacautery at CV–12 (abdomen), CV–14 (abdomen), CV–17 (chest), Lu–1 (chest), B–21 (lower trunk), B–18 (back), B–28 (lower trunk), GV–11 (back), T–15 (back), SI–11 (back), GV–18 (back) or GV–7 (back), LI–11 (upper limb), SI–8 (upper limb), H–7 (upper limb), GB–33 (lower limb), K–5 (lower limb), and GV–19 (head).

Arteriosclerosis (Hardening of the Arteries)

Arteriosclerosis is considered to be a sign of aging. The patient may complain of throbbing pain or oppressiveness in the chest, of fearful feelings or difficulty in breathing. The pulse is hard and strained and will become rapid. Blood pressure rises continuously.

Arteriosclerosis causes such diseases as angina pectoris, cardiac asthma, atrophy of the kidney, intermittent stomachache, and cerebral hemorrhage, as well.

Treatment: Apply acupuncture and moxacautery at the GV–19 (head), GV–11 (back), T–15 (back), GV–9 (back), LI–4 (upper limb), CV–12 (abdomen), CV–9 (abdomen), B–14 (back), B–16 (back), B–21 (lower trunk), B–28 (lower trunk), LI–11 (upper limb), and GB–33 (lower limb).

For insomnia, heavy headedness, headache, or dizziness, apply acupuncture and moxacautery at GB–20 (neck), GB–12 (head), B–9 (neck) and B–6 (head).

For cerebral arteriosclerosis, or for impairment of the mind, or speech, apply acupuncture and moxacautery at GV–14 (head), and GB–12 (head).

For throbbing pain or oppressiveness in the chest, apply acupuncture and moxacautery at St–11 (back) and CV–17 (chest) or B–3 (back), B–16 (back), CV–17 (chest), CV–14 (abdomen), Lu–5 (upper limb), and C–4 (upper limb).

For the problem of frequent nocturnal urination due to atrophy of the kidney apply acupuncture or moxacautery at CV–3 (abdomen) and LI–8 (lower limb).

For trembling hand, apply treatment at LI–10 (upper limb) or LI–4 (upper limb).

For diminishing eyesight, apply at T–22 (face) or GB–5 (head).

For paresthesia (tingling sensation) of the fingertips, apply acupuncture using the Sanryoshin [scalpel-like needle] near the nail at the tip of the finger which has lost the most sensation and draw out blood.

As arteriosclerosis of the lower limbs worsens, the patient develops what is called an intermittent lameness and walking becomes difficult. As the patient walks, his legs feel heavy and cramped to the extent that he cannot lift them to walk.

No matter how heavy and cramped his legs feel, he can walk again if he rests a little. After a while the same symptoms will return; this is characteristic of the disease.

For this illness apply treatment at S* (lower trunk), B-33 (lower limb), S (lower limb), B–53 (lower limb), St–36 (lower limb), and GB–40 (lower limb).

For slight pain in the stomach and the cecum, apply at Sp–14 (abdomen) and B–19 (back).

High Blood Pressure

In the early stages, high blood pressure appears in the form of renal or instinctive high blood pressure; but later on it may be accompanied by arteriosclerosis. We categorize high blood pressure into three levels: severe, medium, and light; and describe each of their standard Vital Points for treatment.

Severe high blood pressure: Maximum blood pressure over 200 mm; minimum blood pressure over 100 mm. As arteriosclerosis develops in the aorta, the minimum blood pressure will be about 70 mm or 80 mm in many cases.

The method of treatment follows the following steps: Acupuncture at CV–12 (abdomen), CV–9 (abdomen), B–28 (lower trunk), CV–11 (back), T–15 (back), K–2 (lower limb), and CV–19 (head).

For stiffness in the back of the neck accompanied by headache, heavy headedness, ringing in the ears, and dizziness apply acupuncture using the Sanryoshin [scalpel-needle] at CV–19 (head) and B–9 (neck) or GB–20 (neck), or B–9 (neck) and draw out blood.

For extreme stiffness of the upper back, apply acupuncture

*Special points found in Japanese acupuncture.

at B–11 (back) or GB–21 (back) and draw out blood. The stiffness will be immediately relieved.

For high blood pressure of medium degree (maximum pressure of 170 mm to 200 mm) add treatment at the following Vital Points to those used for the severe type of high blood pressure: Acupuncture at GV–8 (back) or GV–9 (back), and LI–11 (upper limb).

For high blood pressure of light degree (maximum pressure from 150 mm to 170 mm), apply treatment at the Vital Points used for the medium case, and in addition, selected treatment spots of those for arteriosclerosis can be used. After treatment with acupuncture or moxacautery the overwhelming majority of high blood pressure cases turn for the better. In applying acupuncture or moxacautery, the aim is not only to lower the blood pressure by force. We always try to let the blood pressure return to normal by itself by adjusting the total functioning of the body in a rational manner. However, high blood pressure can be considered a kind of aging process which stems from the environmental complexity of life. Therefore, it is difficult to expect improvement in the condition of a patient unless the patient can take care of his everyday living situation in such matters as clothing, food, and shelter.

Low Blood Pressure

Low blood pressure is defined as that in which the maximum blood pressure is low, less than 100 mm, from no specific cause. The patient lacks vitality and tires easily. He complains of headache, dizziness, heart palpitation and cold hands and feet.

Treatment: Apply acupuncture at CV–12 (abdomen), St–21 (abdomen), GV–11 (back), T–13 (back), B–15 (back), B–18 (back), B–21 (lower trunk), B–9 (neck), LI–11 (upper limb), Sp–36 (lower limb), and K–5 (lower limb).

One of the common complaints from a patient with low blood pressure is an unpleasant stiffness from the top of the neck to the back of the head. For this case, try acupuncture of B–9 (neck) and draw out a small amount of blood.

For diminishing eyesight and insomnia, apply acupuncture at GB–5 (head), GB–12 (head), and GB–20 (neck).

For cold hands and feet, apply treatment at B–21 (lower trunk), B–28 (lower trunk), CV–4 (abdomen), K–9 (lower limb), K–3 (lower limb), and K–5 (lower limb).

CHAPTER XXIX

Diseases of the Digestive System

Stomatitis (inflammation of the soft tissues of the mouth)

Moxacautery is applicable to stomatitis, but acupuncture yields better results. This disease is generally caused by stomach fever. Consequently, it is necessary to focus treatment on the stomach; it is also important to improve the blood circulation on the inside of the mouth and to relieve tight shoulders and neck.

To lower stomach fever, apply acupuncture at CV–12 (abdomen), CV–14 (abdomen), St–21 (abdomen), B–18 (back), B–19 (back), and St–36 (lower limb).

For relief of stiffness in the shoulders and neck, apply acupuncture at B–11 (back), T–13 (back), B–9 (back), and LI–10 (upper limb).

For the area of the mouth, apply acupuncture at LI–20 (face), St–4 (face), St–5 (face), and St–7 (face).

If moxacautery is desired, apply at GV–11 (back), B–11 (back), GB–21 (back), LI–10 (upper limb), St–36 (lower limb), CV–12 (abdomen), and B–19 (back).

Esophagostenosis (Stricture of the Esophagus)

Esophagostenosis is caused either by neurosis and other nervous disorders or by cancer. In the former case, acupuncture and moxacautery are effective, but for the latter, treatment by either method can merely work to lessen the pain symptoms but not to cure the disease.

Acupuncture and moxacautery: B–10 (back), B–14 (back), B–15 (back), K–26 (chest), CV–14 (abdomen), and T–17 (neck).

In addition, for the neurosis-caused esophagostenosis, apply acupuncture or moxacautery at CV–17 (chest), B–9 (back), GV–21 (head), CV–12 (abdomen), and B–18 (back).

Acute Gastritis (Inflamation of the Stomach)

Generally, this illness is caused by immoderate or excessive eating habits. There are also cases in which the disease occurs

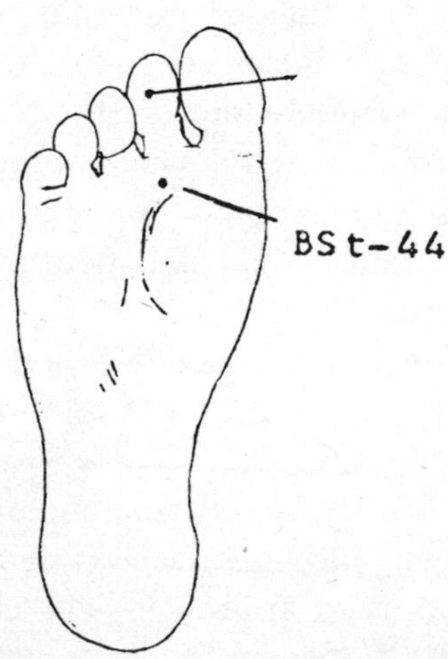

Vital point of treatment for food poisoning

diarrhea and constipation, accompanied by coated tongue, bad breath, dry mouth, headache, dizziness and fatigue.

For a patient with such symptoms apply moxacautery at BSt–44 (lower limb) to see if he is suffering from food poisoning. If he does not feel heat from the moxacautery, then the diagnosis generally is food poisoning. Repeat applications of moxacautery until he feels the heat. His stomach should feel better after such treatment. In some cases, the patient will vomit and then feel much better.

Treatment: Acupuncture and moxacautery: Apply at CV–12 (back), CV–13 (abdomen), B–18 (back), B–46 (back), B–15 (back), GV–11 (back), St–34 (lower limb), and St–36 (lower limb).

Effective for stomach pain are acupuncture and moxacautery at St–34 (lower leg) and B–46 (back).

Chronic Gastritis

In the case of chronic gastritis, the patient will not suffer fever but his stomach will feel uncomfortably bloated and oppressed; he will suffer from bad breath, heartburn, yawning, lack of appetite, and dry mouth. In general he will be nervous and

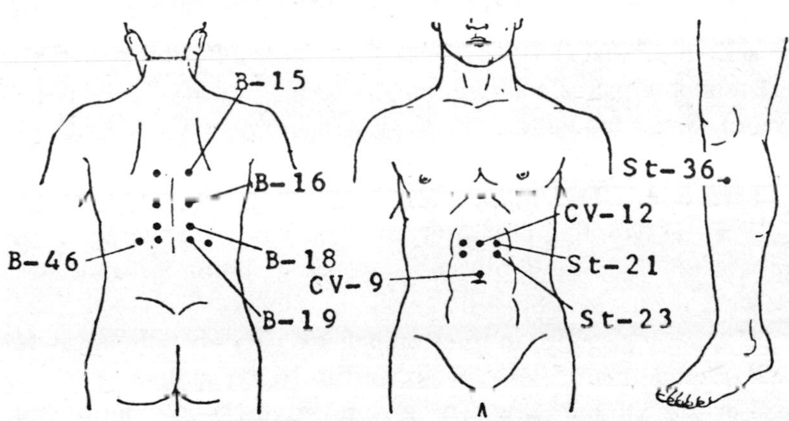

Vital points of treatment for Chronic Gastritis

complain of heavy-headedness, dizziness and insomnia.

Treatment: Apply acupuncture or moxacautery at CV–9 (abdomen), CV–12 (abdomen), St–21 (abdomen), St–23 (abdomen), B–19 (back), B–18 (back), B–46 (back), B–15 (back), B–16 (back), LI–11 (upper limb), and St–36 (lower limb).

For constipation, apply acupuncture and moxacautery at H–7 (upper limb), and Sp–14 (abdomen).

For diarrhea, add treatments at B–28 (lower trunk) and St–27 (abdomen).

If symptoms are accompanied by feelings of heavy-headedness, apply at GV–19 (head) and GV–20 (head).

Atony of the Stomach (Muscle Weakness)

This disease is caused by the loss of muscle tension of the stomach. It is an indication that the person's constitution is basically low and that he tends to suffer from gastraptosis.

The stomach apparently makes splashing sounds and feels bloated and oppressed. The patient also yawns very much. These symptoms are accompanied by headache, dizziness, and lack of appetite. A nervous person is especially liable to suffer from this disease.

Treatment: Acupuncture and moxacautery: Apply at B–12 (back), B–15 (back), B–16 (back), B–18 (back), B–19 (back), CV–12 (abdomen), St–24 (abdomen), St–25 (abdomen), K–16 (abdomen), St–19 (abdomen) St–36 (lower limb) or GB–33 (lower limb), Sp–6 (lower limb), B–9 (neck). K–21 (abdomen) and T–5 (upper limb) LI–11 (upper limb)

For the symptom of an uncomfortably bloated stomach, apply at St–37 (lower limb) or St–40 (lower limb), Sp–6 (chest), GV–21 (head), and Sp–3 (lower limb).

If splashing sounds in the stomach are very obvious, apply at CV–9 (abdomen), GV–8 (back), and B–15 (back).

For the symptom of yawning, apply at Sp-8 (lower limb) and St–42 (lower limb).

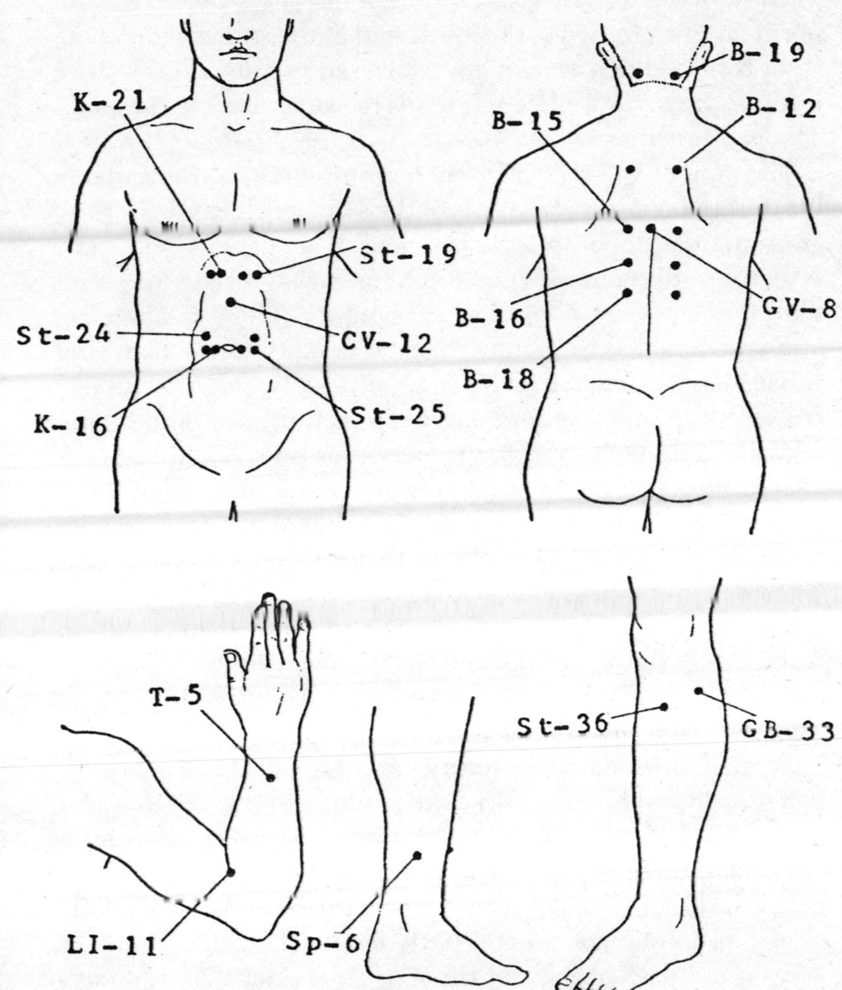

Vital points of treatment for Atony of the Stomach

Gastroptosis (Prolapse of the Stomach)

This disease causes various physical disorders due to the abnormally low position of the lower end of the stomach. In many cases this condition accompanies lowered positions of the other internal organs as well. It also tends to cause atony of the stomach and gastritis.

The patient will recognize such symptoms as uncomfortably bloated and oppressed feelings of the stomach, lower back pain, an abnormal appetite, and yawning. The patient will show symptoms of neurasthenia, such as heavy-headedness, insomnia, melancholia, and loss of memory. These feelings are also accompanied by feelings of total debility of the body and exhaustion. Since most of the cases of this diseases are chronic, treatment by moxacautery and acupuncture must also be unfailingly continued over a long period of time.

Treatment: Moxacautery: Apply at CV–12 (abdomen), CV–9 (abdómen), CV–6 (abdomen), St–27 (abdomen), Li–12 (abdomen), B–18 (back), B–19 (back), B–15 (back), GV–11 (back), GB–33 (lower limb), B–21 (lower trunk), and GV–19 (head).

Especially effective is acupuncture of B–19 (back), B–46 (back), B–20 (lower trunk), and St–36 (lower limb).

Hyperacidity and Hypoacidity

Acupuncture and moxacautery are extemely effective against hyperacidity and hypoacidity. The patient, after meals, feels his stomach to be uncomfortably bloated and suffers heartburn. For one to three hours after a meal he feels uncomfortable; he belches and complains of pain. This condition occurs frequently after consumption of sweet or fatty foods. The pain sometimes spreads out to the back and the scapular region. The patient's appetite increases in spite of the illness and he tends to become constipated.

Treatment: Acupuncture and moxacautery: Apply at CV–13 (abdomen), Li–13 (abdomen), CV–12 (abdomen), B–39 (back), GV–8 (back), B–15 (back), B–16 (back), B–17 (back), B–46 (back),

Sp–8 (lower limb), GB–33 (lower limb), and B–9 (neck).

When the pain spreads out to the back, apply acupuncture of the encircling technique at B–12 (back), B–38 (back), B–39 (back), SI–14 (back), and SI–11 (back).

In many cases, the patient will suffer from constipation. In this event, apply acupuncture and moxacautery at H–7 (upper limb) and Sp–14 (abdomen).

Cancer of the Stomach

This disease starts with symptoms similar to those of chronic gastritis, such as loss of appetite, uncomfortable bloating and oppressiveness of the stomach after eating, yawning, and constipation. The patient loses weight rapidly, begins to avoid eating meat, develops pain in his stomach, and vomits after meals.

As the condition worsens, he can feel lumps on his body. The contents of his vomit resembles coffee grounds. As the cancer spreads to other organs, cachectic and anemic edema begin to appear; his facial color turns yellowish brown.

Treatment by acupuncture and moxacautery is not applicable to cancer of the stomach. However, for those cancers which respond to surgery and for those which recur following surgery, acupuncture and moxacautery can be used effectively as an allopatric means for lessening pain and prolonging life. In general, the method of treatment is the same as that for gastritis.

Ulcer (Gastric Ulcer)

This disease is thought to be caused by impeded blood circulation of the stomach wall mainly from disorders of the central autonomic nervous system, also by mental fatigue and exhaustion. There is a burning, piercing, or convulsive pain just before or just after meals. The pain may be dispersed to the back and the scapula, etc. There is oppressive pain specifically in the epigastrium and the back. The pain in the stomach produces vomiting of blood as well as the stomach contents. The stool resembles tar due to the blood discharged with it. For the pa-

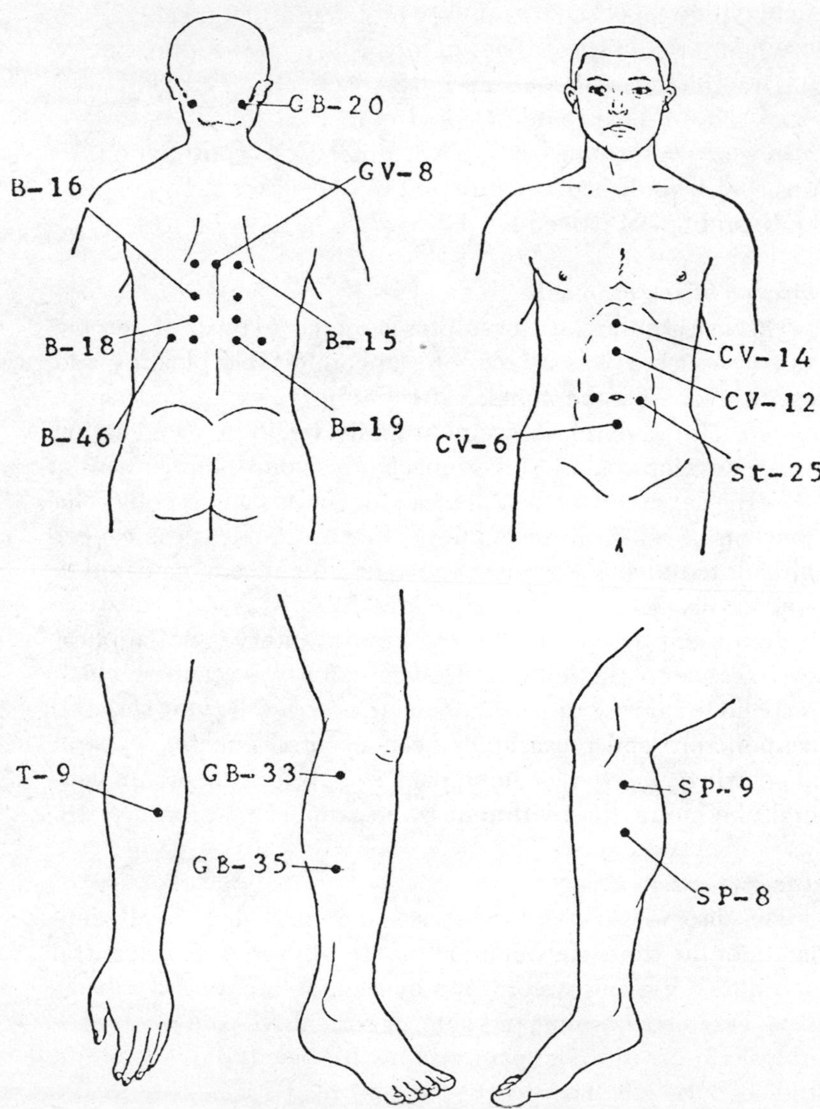

Vital points of treatment for Ulcer

tient with the potential for hemorrhage, acupuncture and moxacautery may be applied from the start.

There is a spot which is a special vital point (S) located 3 to 4 cm below the perimeter of the center of the crista iliac. Firmly press this spot with a finger tip to see if there is a reaction felt from below the knee to the tip of the toe. About 60 percent of the people indicating such a response suffer from ulcer of the stomach or the duodenum. This is a useful point to keep in mind for diagnosis and for observation of the process of recovery. In other words, as the reaction to this pressure test decreases, the patient indicates gradual recovery from the disease.

Treatment: Apply at CV–12 (abdomen), CV–14 (abdomen), CV–6 (abdomen), St–25 (abdomen), B–16 (back), B–18 (back), B–19 (back), B–46 (back), S (lower trunk), B–15 (back), GV–8 (back), GB–20 (head), T–9 (upper limb), GB–35 (lower limb), GB–33 (lower limb), and Sp–9 (lower limb) Sp–8 (lower limb)

Acute Enteritis (Intestinal Catarrh) and Chronic Enteritis

These diseases are caused by immoderate or excessive intake of food and other reasons. They produce nausea, vomiting, abdominal pain, and diarrhea with grumbling noises in the abdomen. The stool will resemble gruel, mud, or liquid (like water). It is yellow in color, sometimes mixed with mucus or blood, and may contain gas with a bad odor. Inflammation of the small intestines sometimes does not result in diarrhea. High fever may be caused by contagious or bacterio-toxic intestinal inflammation. In serious cases, the patient can be debilitated within a few days; his hands and feet become cold and his pulse weak. Small children and aged people are more seriously affected by this disease and their condition can turn abruptly worse.

When the inflammation is limited to the small intestines, the patient may not necessarily suffer diarrhea. However, his stool is soft, indicating poor digestion, and is yellowish or greenish and mixed with mucous fluid or blood. There are grumbling

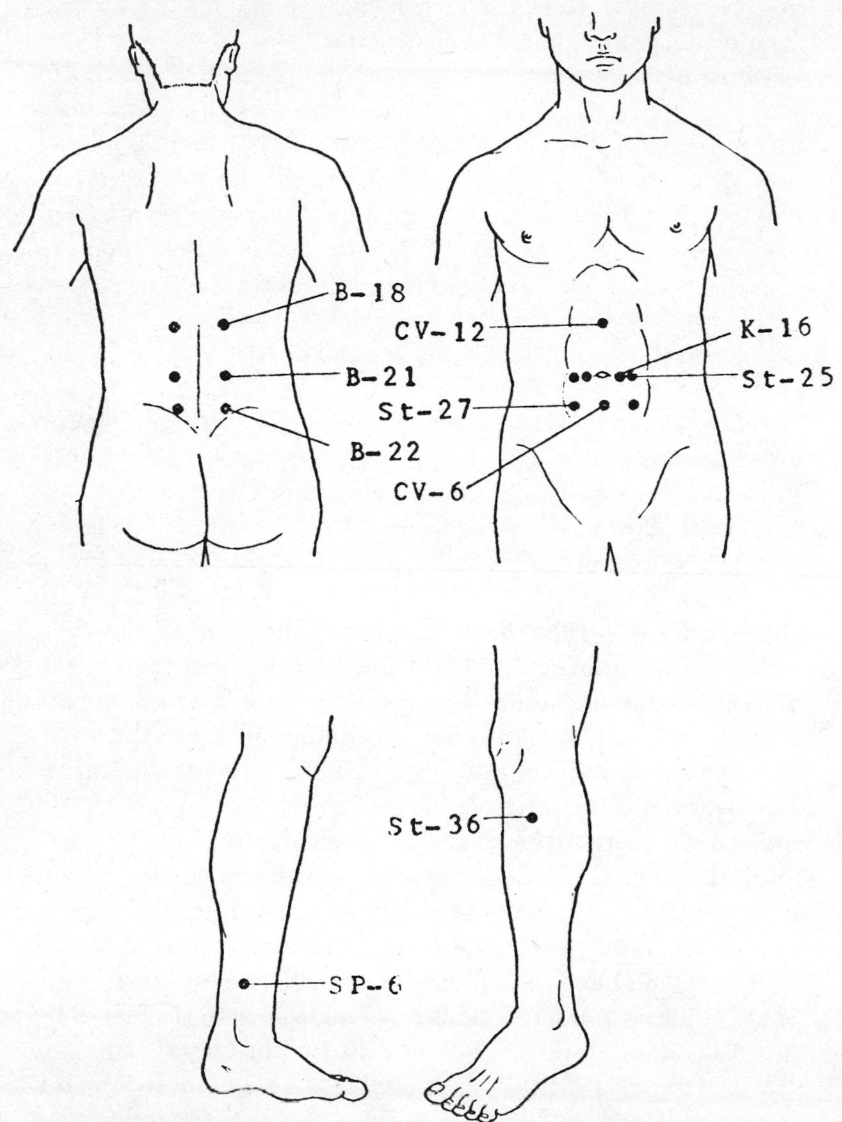

Vital points of treatment for Acute Enteritis and Chronic Enteritis

noises from the intestines, the abdomen feels bloated, and the patient complains of abdominal pain.

When the colon is the part mainly affected; the patient suffers abdominal pain and diarrhea with gripes producing slow and uncomfortable evacuation.

When the rectum is affected, the patient feels urgent need for evacuation; however, very little is excreted during his frequent visits to the toilet. The patient suffers loss of appetite, feels nauseous, and vomits. He feels thirsty and his tongue is coated a white or brown color. Sometimes his abdomen is bloated and filled with gas.

In chronic cases, the patient usually complains of discomfort of the abdomen; an uncomfortable, bloated feeling; pain; grumbling noises in the abdomen; and diarrhea. When gas accumulates in the large intestines, the phrenic diaphragm is pushed up and presses against the heart and lungs, so that the patient's heart throbs noticeably and he experiences difficulty in breathing. If the disease is prolonged, the body becomes debilitated and the patient feels extremely sensitive, complaining of headache, dizziness, insomnia, and lack of vitality.

Apply at CV–12 (abdomen), CV–9 (abdomen), K–16 (abdomen), St–25 (abdomen), St–27 (abdomen), B–18 (back), B–21 (lower trunk), B–22 (lower trunk), B–29 (lower trunk), St–36 (lower limb), Sp–6 (lower limb) and LI–10 (upper limb).

For frequent diarrhea, apply repeated doses of moxacautery at CV–9 (abdomen), CV–6 (abdomen), and St–27 (abdomen). If this is to no avail, add moxacautery of K–16 (abdomen).

For tenesmus (feeling need for evacuation remains despite repeated visits to the toilet), accompanied by acute proctitis (inflammation of the rectum), apply acupuncture or moxacautery at B–29 (lower trunk). When acupuncture at B–29 (lower trunk) is precisely applied, the cranial nerve may occasionally become overstimulated. In that event, apply moxacautery at GV–19 (head). Then, the described ailment generally is halted.

For chronic cases, follow the same treatment as that described for acute cases.

Abdominal Pain

Abdominal pain is caused by irregularity within the abdominal organs. If the pain is in the stomach, it will be specifically localized in the upper abdominal region; however, if it is caused by the intestines, the pain remains in the lower half of the abdomen. The pain is often caused by peristaltic action of the intestines and by stimulation of the peritoneum. Pain caused by appendicitis is limited to the right lower abdominal region. In addition, abdominal pain can be caused by diseases of the kidney, pancreas, and female reproductive organs; also by neurotic hysteria during menopause. Careful distinction should be made among such pains as those caused by calculi, peritonitis, and ileus.

Treatment: First apply deep, stimulating acupuncture or repeated doses of moxacautery at the treatment points on the lower limb; and only if the pain persists, apply treatment in the abdomen and the back.

Acupuncture: Apply at St–44 (lower limb), Li–2 (lower limb), B–56 (lower limb), and St–36 (lower limb).

Moxacautery: Apply at B–34 (lower limb) and Sp–6 (lower limb).

For upper abdominal pain, apply at B–16 (back) and B–19 (back).

For lower abdominal pain, apply deep acupuncture of B–20 (lower trunk) and CV–6 (abdomen) or repeated doses of moxacautery at the same locations. Apply acupuncture first of all at St–9 (carotid sinus).

Constipation

Constipation usually is caused by intestinal stricture or oppression from the surrounding area; sometimes, however it can occur with no special change in the intestinal tract.

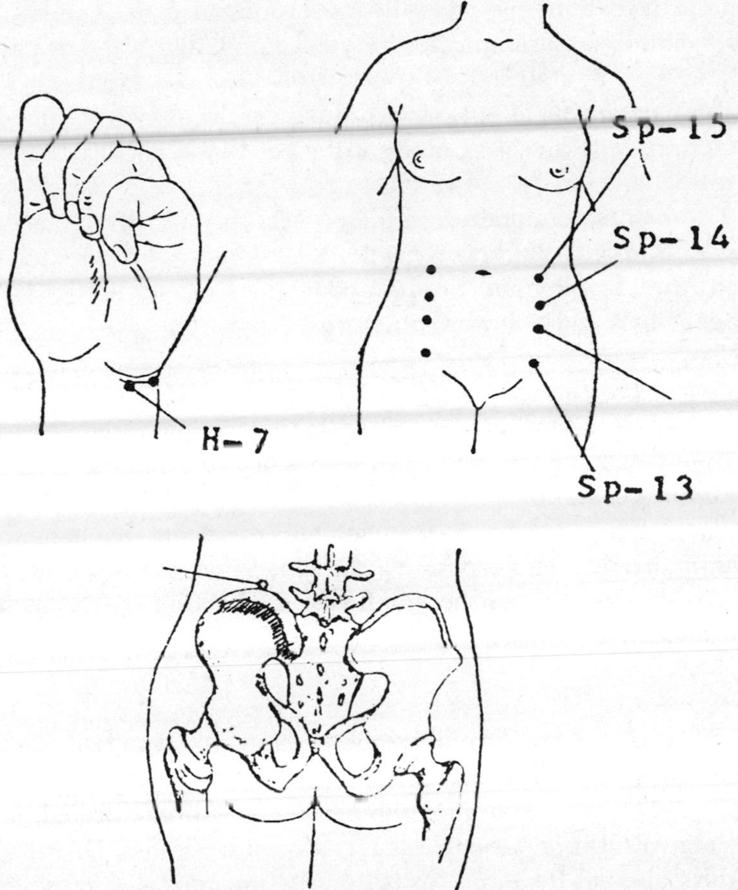

Vital points of treatment for Constipation

Habitual constipation may occur due to looseness, paralysis, or spasm of the intestines because of malfunction of the intestinal muscles.

Besides the oppressive and bloated feeling in the abdominal region, the patient may suffer headache, dizziness, fatigue, nausea, vomiting or insomnia. He may develop lethargy, heart palpitations, or neuralgia.

Examination of patients who complain of the above described symptoms will reveal in many instances that they also suffer constipation.

Treatment: Acupuncture and moxacautery: Apply at B–20 (lower trunk), B–22 (lower trunk), S (abdomen), Sp–13 (abdomen), Sp–14 (abdomen), Sp–15 (abdomen), S (upper limb), H–7 (upper limb) and S (lower spine area).

Blood in the Feces

In the case of hemorrhoids, the color of the stool is red. Blood stains either the periphery of the feces or the toilet tissue due to rupture of the pile.

For bloody feces due to stomach and duodenal ulcers or to griping diarrhea and tenesmus, the blood may be mixed with mucus. (See section on hemorrhoids; see section on stomach and duodenal ulcers; see section on enteritis.)

Hepatitis

Hepatitis is a very troublesome disease. An American microbiologist who conducted a research study among a tribe on the island of Maui, Hawaii, announced a new breakthrough in dealing with this disease. He is Dr. Steven Collestad, Director of the Collestad Research Institute in Minneapolis, Minnesota. He said, "We have found a new test which is 90 percent effective in diagnosing this disease prior to the appearance of symptoms of hepatitis."

Since the middle of October, 1970, Dr. Collestad has been engaged in a research study with a tribe on Maui where large numbers of the population were infected by hepatitis.

Dr. Collestad said, "We have discovered a hepatitis virus in an individual who had not yet shown any symptoms of hepatitis. We think this is an epoch-making discovery because this person has remained in health." UPI, Friday, January 8, 1971, Rafu Shimpo, No. 20253.

A Chinese herb doctor will examine his patient's pulse, tongue, abdomen, and back and may then tell him, "Your liver functioning is weak." The patient usually will answer, "The doctor at the hospital took a blood test, urine test, and X-ray and told me there is nothing wrong with me. The doctor said, 'It is just fatigue and nervous tension, so don't worry.' "

As long as 80 percent of its cells are unaffected, the liver does not indicate its malfunction. It is difficult to diagnose malfunction even if 20 to 30 percent of the liver is affected. Even if 50 percent of the liver is affected, it may appear to be functioning normally. As such is the case, it is very difficult to diagnose latent hepatitis. On the other hand, there are increasing numbers of liver ailments. They result from excessive eating, drinking, and smoking; also to excessive consumption of artificial coloring, chemical medicines, and the new medicines.

Points about Chinese Herb Medicine

When the abdomen of a patient suffering from hepatitis is examined, he complains of the feeling of heaviness, pain, and stuffiness from the chest to the sides of his abdomen, and around his upper abdomen. When these areas are palpated, the patient complains of pain and the examiner feels hard resistance. This symptom is called pain from tight chest and sides in Chinese herb medicine.

Underneath the area in which this pain appears, there are important internal organs such as the liver, lungs, heart, stomach, gallbladder, pancreas, and kidneys. When trouble occurs with these organs, the rectus abdominus becomes tense for protection. This tension is due to the reflex action of the somatic layer of the internal organs and is the cause of tight chest and side pain.

The important point in treating hepatitis is to remove the symptom of pain from tight chest and sides. The medicine to remove this pain involves *Bupleurum* as its main ingredient. *Bupleurum* (a genus of 65 species of herbs belonging to the carrot family) adjusts the functioning of the liver continuously. It is an excellent medicine which adjusts the metabolism of sugar, protein, fat, and water content and also acts as an antidote, antipyretic, and an antiphlogistic agent. Furthermore, it acts with the suprarenal body hormones to increase vitality. Once the pain from tight chest and sides is relieved by *Bupleurum,* the liver function can adjust itself to normal. There is no way to diagnose the pain from tight chest and sides through modern Western medical science; also there is no medicinal equivalent to *Bupleurum* in the West. Consequently, it is natural that Western medical doctors can only suggest rest and diet as treatment for hepatitis.

Treatment with Chinese herbs

Bupleurum—increases liver function. Chinese herb medicine prescribes medicines using *Bupleurum* as a main ingredient in order to readjust the liver function, and secondly, prescribes diet treatment. The following lists some typical herb medicines.

Shosaikoto—This medicine is frequently prescribed for many kinds of hepatitis such as epidemic hepatitis, serum hepatitis, drug hepatitis, and latent hepatitis. This medicine is extremely effective especially in the case of epidemic hepatitis with high fever, loss of appetite, nausea, and vomiting.

For cirrhosis of the liver, combine Goreisan with Shoshikoto.

This medicine is prescribed for the medium built patient with light degree of tight chest and sides.

Daisaikoto—This prescription can be applied to the more corpulent patient than the patient who uses Shoshikoto. This person is better nourished and his facial color is better. He has a bulky physique, the so-called executive type; due to social drinking and over indulging, fat has accumulated in his subcutaneous tissue. He suffers a more severe pain from tight chest and sides with stiff shoulders, ringing in the ears, insomnia, constipation, and high blood pressure.

Intokoto—Apply this prescription for a patient who feels bloated in the upper abdomen, feels obstruction and oppression in the chest, thirsty, excretes little urine and feces, and finally develops jaundice. This treatment is used in many cases of serum hepatitis and is often combined with Shosaikoto or Daisaikoto.

Intogoreisan—This prescription is used for the patient who urinates little and feels thirsty after being treated with Intokoto and Daisaikoto. Generally this prescription is used to cure serum hepatitis.

Acute Hepatitis (Catarrhal Jaundice)

Acupuncture and moxacautery: Apply at GV–8 (back), B–15 (back), B–16 (back), B–17 (back), B–18 (back), St–19 (abdomen), St–21 (abdomen), Li–13 (abdomen), CV–12 (abdomen), K–16 (abdomen), Li–8 (lower limb), St–36 (lower limb), Sp–6 (lower limb), and GB–20 (neck).

For acute hepatitis accompanied by headache and fatigue, apply acupuncture at B–9 (neck), GB–20 (neck), GB–21 (back), Sp–8 (lower limb), and St–40 (lower limb).

For acute hepatitis accompanied by gastrointestinal disorders refer to sections dealing with each disorder and apply appropriate treatment.

Chronic Hepatitis (Troubles of Liver Function)

Treatment: The patient may follow the treatments described in the case of acute hepatitis. The following are some of the important treatments.

Acupuncture and moxacautery: Apply at B–15 (back), B–16

(back), CV–12 (abdomen), Li–13 (abdomen), Li–8 (lower limb), and Sp–6 (lower limb).

Cholecystitis

The disease often occurs in combination with cholangitis and cholelithiasis. The patient feels oppression and bloated in the stomach as well as a spontaneous illness and oppressive pain of the right hypochondriac region. The disease is accompanied with light fever, nausea, vomiting, loss of appetite, and sometimes jaundice. When the pain is severe in the gall bladder region, it spreads out to the right scapular region.

The treatment follows in general that for cholelithiasis (gallstones).

Cholelithiasis (Gallstones)

This disease usually effects people past middle age. In some cases the disease shows no obvious symptoms despite the formation of gallstones in the gallbladder or bile duct. The foremost symptom is an oppressive feeling in the right hypochondriac region and apt to be accompanied by symptoms of stomach trouble as well. When a stone moves from the gallbladder into the gall duct and irritates the mucous membrane of the duct, the muscle layer reacts with reflexive spasmodic contractions and causes an attack of colic. Pain sometimes is scattered to such regions as the chest, the back, the right scapular region, the upper extremities, and the groin.

Treatment: Acupuncture: In the case of colic attack, first apply in the cavity of a carotid sinus St–9 (neck) only on the right side. For relief of symptoms of a colic attack, apply at B–16 (back), B–17 (back), B–15 (back) B–6 (back) between B–14 (back) and B–15 (back), Li–13 (abdomen), St–21 (abdomen), B–46 (back), B–18 (back), GB–33 (lower limb), and Sp–1 (lower limb).

During a colic attack fever may develop. In such case, apply acupuncture at B–9 (neck) and B–10 (back).

For general treatment of gallstone cases which do not involve colic attacks, use moxacautery and acupuncture in combination. Apply at CV–12 (abdomen), CV–14 (abdomen), Li–13 (abdomen), St–21 (abdomen), St–27 (abdomen), B–18 (back), B–17 (back), B–46 (back), GV–11 (back), SI–11 (back), Lu–6 (upper limb), GB–33 (lower limb), and GB–40 (lower limb).

CHAPTER XXX

Urinary Diseases

Nephrosis

This is a disease of the kidney which starts at the epithelial cells of the kidney (urethral capillaries). The main symptoms are the presence of albuminuria and edema. Also, the amount of urine excreted diminishes, facial color turns pale, swelling occurs, and the patient complains of total exhaustion.

In this case, apply moxacautery for the main treatment with acupuncture as a supplement. Begin applications by repeating the moxacautery treatment twice at first and increase to five times.

Moxacautery: Apply at B–18 (back), B–21 (lower trunk), GV–3 (lower trunk), CV–9 (abdomen), K–16 (abdomen), St–25 (abdomen) CV–6 (abdomen) or CV–4 (abdomen), CV–12 (abdomen), K–7 (lower limb), and K–1 (lower limb).

Acupuncture: Apply at K–21 (lower trunk), B–48 (lower trunk), B–28 (lower trunk), CV–12 (abdomen), CV–6 (abdomen), Lu–5 or LI–11 (upper limb), and Sp–6 (lower limb).

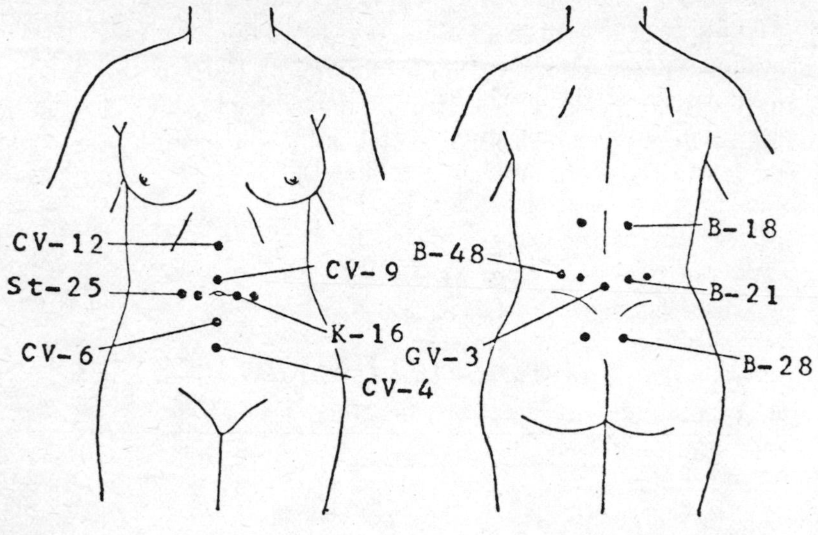

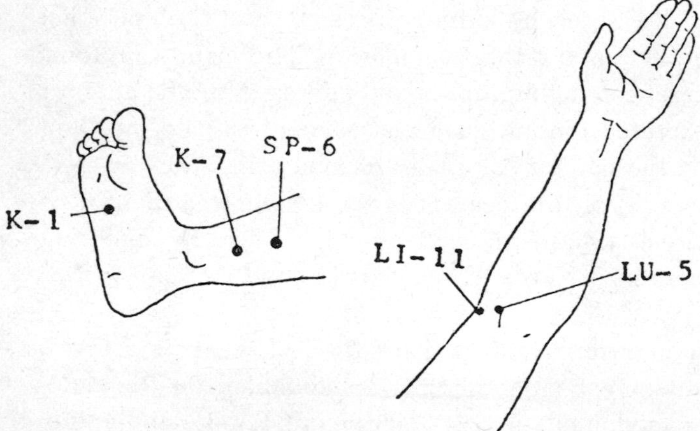

Vital points of treatment for Nephrosis

Nephritis

This kidney disease starts at the glomerulus in the kidney and is called glomerulonephritis. It is accompanied by symptoms of swelling and albuminuria and also by hematuria. In severe cases, the patient complains of pain in the area of the kidneys and high fever; breathing may become difficult. In particular, blood pressure increases. The amount of urine excreted decreases; edema begins in the face and spreads out over the whole body. In some cases however, there may be no swelling. This disease tends to become chronic and cause uremia, cardiac weakness, and cerebral hemorrhage.

Treatment: Treatment follows that described in the section on treatment for nephrosis. However, some of the principal treatment points are listed below.

Acupuncture and moxacautery: Apply at K–21 (lower trunk), GV–4 (lower trunk), K–48 (lower trunk), K–20 (lower trunk), CV–6 (abdomen) or CV–4 (abdomen), B–36 (lower limb), K–10 (lower limb), and St–36 (lower limb).

For diminishing results of urination, apply acupuncture deeply and leave it inserted for a time at B–5 (lower trunk), B–32 (lower limb), and B–35 (lower limb).

For difficulty in breathing, apply acupuncture at B–12 (back) and B–18 (back).

For cardiac weakness apply moxacautery three times, repeatedly, at C–4 (upper limb).

Edema (Swelling)

Acupuncture and moxacautery should be applied depending on the symptoms indicated. For example, if swelling is caused by heart disease, consult treatment application described for disease of the heart valves; if swelling is caused by liver diseases, follow the application described for gallstone or hepatitis treatment. For edema stemming from kidney disorders, follow application described for nephritis treatment. For swelling caused by nutritional disorders, follow the application described for treatment of gastroptosis.

Atrophy of the Kidney

Atrophy of the kidney is caused by the destruction of the structure of the kidneys so that the entire kidney withers. It follows after conditions of high blood pressure or chronic nephritis. The patient also complains of headache, stiff shoulders, ringing in the ears, dizziness, insomnia, and agonizing pain inside the chest. He tends to bleed easily, has frequent urination at night, and also suffers lower back pain, edema, and numbness of the lower limbs.

Treatment: Moxacautery: Apply at GB–20 (head), GB–21 (back), B–16 (back), B–21 (lower trunk), B–29 (lower trunk), St–36 (lower limb), and K–5 (lower limb).

Acupuncture: Apply at B–21 (lower trunk), B–22 (lower trunk), CV–12 (abdomen), CV–4 (abdomen), St–36 (lower limb), K–7 (lower limb), and K–1 (lower limb).

For frequent urination at night, apply moxacautery at B–60 (lower limb).

For ringing in the ears, apply acupuncture and moxacautery at GB–12 (head).

For dizziness and insomnia, apply moxacautery and acupuncture at CV–19 (head), GB–20 (neck), CV–11 (back), and B–12 (back).

Pyelitis

This disease is caused by an inflammation of the part of the kidney where urine is temporarily stored. It is frequently caused by other diseases in the body if the patient's physical condition is such that urine tends to stagnate. The quantity of the urination diminishes and urination becomes frequent. The urine is mixed with mucus, pus, or blood and becomes cloudy. The patient develops fever over the entire body, headache, exhaustion, and loss of appetite. In chronic cases, the changes in the urine are not constant.

Treatment: Acupuncture and moxacautery: Apply at CV–12 (abdomen), CV–9 (abdomen), CV–3 (abdomen), K–12 (abdomen), K–21 (back), K–18 (back), Sp–25 (lower trunk), K–28 (lower trunk), CV–11 (back), K–16 (back), LI–11 (upper limb), Lu–6 (upper limb), St–36 (lower limb), S (lower limb), and Sp–6 (lower limb).

For such symptoms as headache, vomiting, exhaustion, insomnia, and loss of appetite, apply at the GV–19 (head) and B–9 (neck).

For rapid decrease in the quantity of the urination, apply at K–27 (lower trunk), K–28 (lower trunk), and Sp–11 (lower limb).

Renal Tuberculosis and Tuberculosis of the Bladder

This disease is the result of disorders of the kidney tubules. There is pain in the area of the kidney which spreads out to the urinary bladder region. The patient notes blood in his urine, frequent and painful urination. He generally develops cystitis.

Usually the patient suffers a slight fever although at times this fever can be high. He tends to be anemic, has little appetite, and loses weight.

Acupuncture and moxacautery: Apply at CV–12 (abdomen), CV–9 (abdomen), CV–3 (abdomen), K–12 (abdomen), B–21 (back), B–18 (back), Sp–25 (lower trunk), B–28 (lower trunk), GV–11 (back), B–15 (back), LI 11 (upper limb), Lu 5 (upper limb) or Lu–6 (upper limb), St–36 (lower limb), Li–8 (lower limb), Sp–8 (lower limb) or Sp–6 (lower limb), K–5 (lower limb) or K–1 (lower limb).

For relief of frequent desire for urination or difficult urination, apply acupuncture at B–23 (lower trunk), B–27 (lower trunk), B–28 (lower trunk), B–30 (lower trunk), B–50 (lower trunk), CV–3 (lower trunk), CV–2 (lower trunk), and K–12 (lower trunk). Such treatment is very effective.

Renal Calculi (Kidney Stones) and Vesical Calculi (Bladder Stones)

Although he has a kidney stone, a patient may sometimes be unaware of symptoms. Occasionally the stone is excreted, but if it becomes lodged in the urethra, the patient suffers severe pain. The pain attacks suddenly along the urethra and spreads out from the bladder to the genital area, anus, and often toward the back. The patient has a fever; the quantity of his urine decreases; he urinates frequently; and sometimes his urine is mixed with blood (he develops hematuria).

Treatment: Acupuncture and moxacautery: Apply strong stimulatory acupuncture at B–12 (back), B–18 (lower trunk), B–21 (lower trunk), S (lower trunk), Sp–26 (abdomen), Li–8 (lower limb), K–7 (lower limb), and K–3 (lower limb).

Moxacautery: Apply repeated doses of moxacautery at B–21 (lower trunk), B–24 (lower trunk), CV–3 (abdomen), CV–12 (abdomen), K–16 (abdomen), K–9 (lower limb), and Lu–5 (upper limb).

Cystitis

The disease may be chronic or acute. In either case, it is caused by inflammation of the mucous membrane of the bladder due to bacterial infection.

The disease develops as the result of bacterial infection with such secondary causes as overstimulation of the bladder by withholding of urine, bladder stones, foreign matter, or tumors. The patient feels pressure and pain in the bladder region. He feels a strong urge to urinate frequently but very little is excreted. The urine has a cloudy color, and there is severe pain during urination. In chronic cases, the symptoms are not as strong as in acute cases. Whether the case is chronic or acute, treatment by moxacautery or acupuncture is almost the same. Application of treatment on the vital points follows that described for renal tuberculosis and tuberculosis of the bladder.

For relief of the frequent urge to urinate, painful urination,

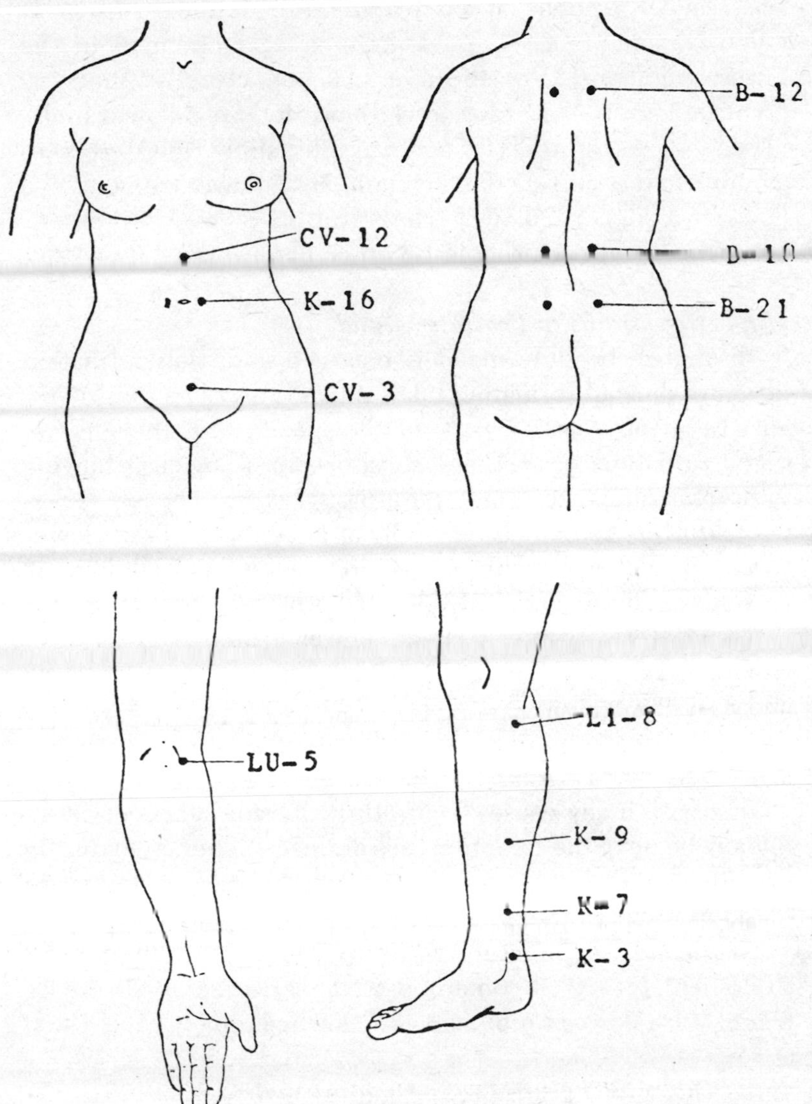

Vital point of treatment for Renal Calculi and Vesical Calculi

and bladder trouble, apply acupuncture or moxacautery at CV–3 (abdomen), CV–2 (abdomen), K–12 (abdomen) in the lower abdomen. Also, effective is acupuncture at the vital points of loins such as Li–8 (lower limb) and Sp–6 (lower limb).

For severe symptoms for acute cystitis, apply repeated doses of moxacautery at B–28 (lower trunk), B–29 (lower trunk), GV–3 (lower trunk), GV–2 (lower trunk), and Li–8 (lower limb), etc. After this, symptoms should be immediately arrested.

Hypertrophy of the Prostate Gland

The entire prostate gland is enlarged and, thus, urination becomes difficult (urination takes much time). The disease occurs frequently in men past middle age. At first, there is frequent urination. Then the dysuria becomes obvious, showing symptoms similar to those of anuria.

Treatment: Acupuncture: Apply at B–16 (back), B–21 (lower trunk), B–28 (lower trunk), CV–4 (abdomen), CV–2 (abdomen), Li–8 (lower limb), and K–10 (lower limb).

Moxacautery: Apply at B–21 (lower trunk), B–28 (lower trunk), K–12 (abdomen), CV–3 (abdomen), Sp–10 (lower limb), and K–4 (lower limb).

Urethritis

There are many causes for urethritis besides gonococcal infection. Some of the symptoms are drainage of pus, pain during urination, and turbid urine. Some of the lighter symptoms are cured in a short time, but others may take a long time.

Treatment: Acupuncture and moxacautery: Apply at K–12 (abdomen), CV–12 (abdomen), B–22 (lower trunk), B–28 (lower trunk), Li–8 (lower limb), and K–7 (lower limb).

Impotence and Pollution (Spermatorrhea)

Impotence is defined as a condition in which sexual intercourse becomes impossible due to the loss of erection from organic defects of the nervous system, diabetes, nephritis, or defects of hormonal functionings. When ejaculation occurs without erection, sexual intercourse becomes practically impossible.

Treatment: Acupuncture: Apply at B–21 (lower trunk), GV–3 (lower trunk), B–28 (lower trunk), CV–4 (abdomen), CV–3 (abdomen), St–30 (abdomen), Li–5 (lower limb), Sp–6 (lower limb), and Li–3 (lower limb).

Moxacautery: Apply at GV–10 (head), B–10 (back), B–29 (lower trunk), S–27 (abdomen), CV–2 (abdomen), and Sp–6 (lower limb).

CHAPTER XXXI

Metabolic Diseases

Anemia

Anemia is generally caused by abnormal decrease in the quantity of hemoglobin and the number of red blood cells (erythrocytes) in the blood. Anemia can also result from loss of blood due to bleeding, intestinal parasites, or cancer. The skin, conjunctiva of the eyes, and the mucous membrane of the lips of an anemic patient turn pale. The patient experiences fatigue and exhaustion and decrease in mental ability. These symptoms are accompanied by headache, dizziness, ringing in the ears, stiffness in the shoulder, and disturbed vision.

In addition, he is apt to suffer from increasingly rapid hard breathing, heart palpitations, and shortness of breath. Furthermore, his hands and feet may become cold and the quantity of urine increased.

Treatment: The treatment is primarily based on moxacautery. Acupuncture is supplementary. It is necessary to continue treatment over a period of time.

Moxacautery: Apply at B–15 (back), B–16 (back), B–21 (lower trunk), GV–4 (lower trunk), CV–12 (abdomen), Li–13 (abdomen), T–5 (upper limb), and St–36 (lower limb).

Acupuncture: Apply at B–14 (back), B–16 (back), B–21 (lower trunk), B–48 (lower trunk), CV–12 (abdomen), CV–6 (abdomen), St–36 (lower limb), and Li–8 (lower limb).

Exophthalmic Goiter

This disease is caused by the accelerating secretion of hormones from the thyroid gland. The main symptoms are heart palpitations, swollen thyroid glands, and bulging eyeballs. In general, the patient is easily excited or tired; his fingers and eyelids quiver; he also suffers from headaches and insomnia, etc. On the other hand, his appetite for food and drink increases and he feels dryness in the throat; he tends to perspire and to lose weight. Female patients have irregular menstrual periods and male patients experience a decrease in sexual desire.

Treatment: Acupuncture: Apply at GB–20 (neck), B–11 (back), GV–11 (back) B–16 (back), B–21 (lower trunk), Li–13 (abdomen), CV–4 (abdomen), LI–11 (upper limb), T–8 (upper limb), St–36 (lower limb), K–7 (lower limb), St–9 (neck), and CV–22 (neck).

Moxacautery: Apply at GV–13 (back), B–14 (back), B–16 (back), LI–11 (upper limb), and GB–33 (lower limb).

When this disease is accompanied by headache and insomnia, apply moxacautery at GV–19 (head), GB–12 (head), and B–9 (neck).

For twitching eyelids, apply acupuncture at B–1 (face) and T–23 (face).

Diabetes

This disease is caused by a problem in the internal secretion from the islets of Langerhans in the pancreas. Some of the symptoms of diabetes are fatigued feeling, glycosuria, thirst, and overeating. In severe cases, the patient may suddenly experience vomiting, headache or abdominal pain, or go into a coma. The disease can easily be accompanied by other diseases such as pulmonary tuberculosis, arteriosclerosis and nephritis. The skin feels itchy and will tend to suppurate. The patient tends to develop sciatica and cataracts, and male patients decrease in sexual desire.

Treatment: Acupuncture and moxacautery: Apply at CV–12 (abdomen), St–19 (abdomen), B–16 (back), B–18 (back), B–20 (lower trunk), GV–19 (head), B–9 (neck), LI–11 (upper limb), St–36 (lower limb), Sp–8 (lower limb) or Sp–5 (lower limb).

Patients with this disease tend to suffer suppurating skin, therefore it is best not to apply moxacautery in the areas where hair grows, such as the head and neck regions.

Beriberi

Beriberi is caused by a deficiency of thiamine (vitamin B_1). The general symptoms are dulling of sensation (numbness), difficulty in mobility of the arms and legs (beginning with feelings of lassitude in the lower limbs), heart palpitations, and edema. There are four types of beriberi symptoms. One involves primarily the sensation of oppressiveness and lassitude of the lower limbs. A second type involves difficulty in mobility due to the atrophy of the arms and legs. The third type results in swelling. The fourth type involves primarily such symptoms as heart palpitations, agonizing pain inside of the chest, rapid breathing, and vomiting.

Treatment: Moxacautery: Apply at B–16 (back), B–18 (back), CV–12 (abdomen), CV–7 (abdomen), St–36 (lower limb), Sp–6 (lower limb), GB–28 (lower limb) and LI–11 (upper limb).

Acupuncture: Apply at B–18 (back), B–20 (lower trunk), B–22

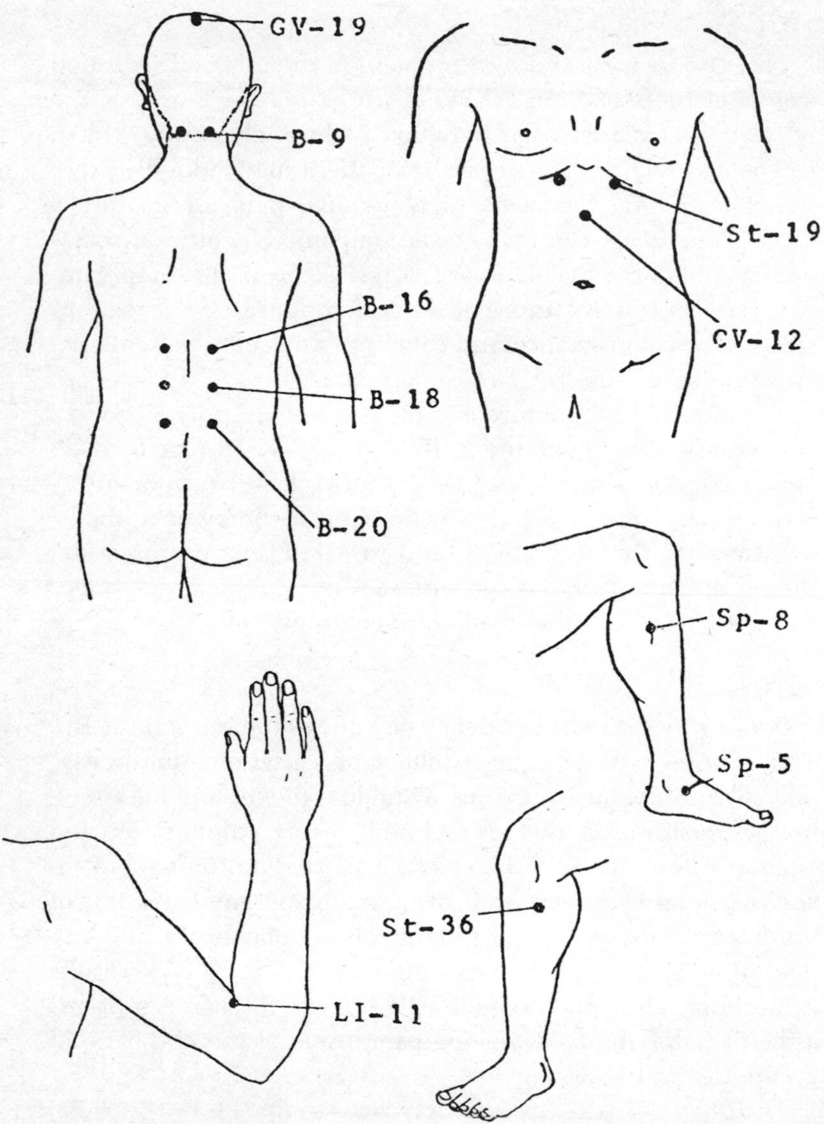

Vital points of treatment for Diabetes

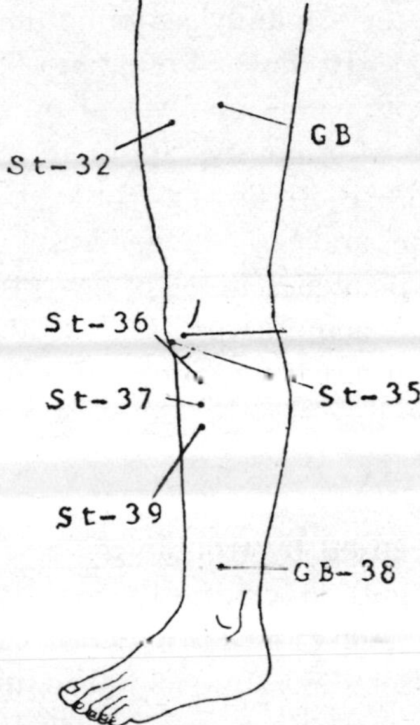

Vital points of treatment for beriberi

This treatment for beriberi has been used for many centuries and it is still being used today.

(lower trunk), CV–12 (abdomen), St–25 (abdomen), LI–10 (upper limb), GB–S (lower limb), GB–33 (abdomen), and Sp–8 (lower limb).

For the first type, whose main symptoms are sensation of lassitude and oppressiveness of the legs, apply acupuncture and moxacautery at B–18 (back), B–20 (lower trunk), CV–12 (abdomen), St–36 (lower limb), and Sp–8 (lower limb).

For the second type, which involves swelling, apply acupuncture and moxacautery (mainly acupuncture) at B–19 (back), S–36 (lower limb), K–10 (lower limb), and Sp–8 (lower limb).

For the third type, which involves atrophy of the arms and legs and difficulty of mobility, apply moxacautery at B–16 (back), GB–7 (back), B–21 (lower trunk), GB–S (lower limb), GB–35 (lower limb), and Sp–6 (lower limb).

For the fourth type, which involves heart trouble and breathing difficulties apply acupuncture at B–13 (back), B–16 (back), and GB–33 (lower limb) and moxacautery at C–4 (upper limb) and H–7 (upper limb).

Addison's Disease

This disease is caused by trouble in the functioning of the suprarenal glands and affects mostly middle-aged males. The patient tires easily, suffers lack of vitality, loss of memory, and sleepiness. Brown pigment appears in the mucous membranes and the skin. Also, the patient suffers lack of appetite, nausea, stomach pain, constipation or diarrhea, and weight loss. Blood pressure decreases and sexual desire diminishes.

Treatment: Acupuncture and moxacautery: Apply at GV–11 (back), B–15 (back), B–18 (back), B–18 (lower trunk), B–48 (lower trunk), B–28 (lower trunk), B–9 (neck), CV–12 (abdomen), CV–6 (abdomen), K–16 (abdomen), and St–36 (lower limb) or Sp–8 (lower limb) or K–3 (lower limb).

CHAPTER XXXII

Diseases of the Locomotor Organs

Arthritis

In addition to the relatively common rheumatoid arthritis, this category of illness includes, relative to their causes, such ailments as gonorrheal arthritis, syphilitic arthritis, and tubercular arthritis (knee and hip joint areas). In addition, there is arthritis deformans which affects aged people (occurring at such areas as the knees, thighs, arms, legs, elbows, shoulders, and spinal joints). Furthermore, due to sprains, metastatic arthritis may develop as fluids ooze out and accumulate in the joints. Suppurative arthritis also may develop from infections due to pyogenic bacteria. This occurs mostly in the knee joints.

Treatment: The following is the location of the overall treatment points.

Moxacautery: Apply at B–12 (back), B–16 (back), CV–12 (abdomen), LI–10 (upper limb), GB–33 (lower limb), St–36 (lower limb), Sp–6 (lower limb).

Acupuncture: GB–20 (neck), B–14 (back), B–16 (back), B–21 (back), CV–12 (abdomen), CV–6 (abdomen), St–36 (lower limb), Sp–6 (lower limb).

Localized Treatment: For the back-shoulder area: Apply at GV–11 (back), T–16 (back), and SI–11 (back).

For the lower back and loin area: Apply at GV–3 (lower

trunk). B–22 (lower trunk), B–23 (lower trunk), B–28 (lower trunk) and S (lower trunk).

For the shoulder joint area: Apply at LI–15 (back), and SI–10 (back).

For the elbow joint area: Apply at LI–11 (upper limb), SI–8 (upper limb), and Lu–5 (upper limb).

For the arm joint area: Apply at C–4 (upper limb), SI–6 (upper limb), C–7 (upper limb), H–7 (upper limb), and LI–4 (upper limb).

For the knee joint area: Apply at St–34 (lower limb), Sp–10 (lower limb), LI–7 (lower limb), St–36 (lower limb), GB–33 (lower limb), and B–36 (lower limb).

In the ankle joint area: Apply at K–5 (lower limb), K–2 (lower limb), GB–39 (lower limb), and B–56 (lower limb).

Peripheral Inflammation of the Shoulder Joint ("Fifty-year-old Shoulders")

This disease is seen in aged men and women and is sometimes called "Fifty-year-old arms" or "Fifty-year-old shoulders" (arm or shoulder pain of people in their fifties). The major symptoms of this disease are troubles in the scapular region and in the shoulder joint.

There are several bursas around the periphery of the shoulder joint among which the bursas below the deltoids, the membranes of the bursas below the acromion, and the bursas below the scapula are easily affected by illness. In the area of these inflamed bursas, there is oppressive pain, but no pain in the overall area of the joint. The pain in the joint persists only when the arm is moved in a certain direction; for example, pain may develop when the arm is raised or moved around the back, thus making it difficult to comb one's hair.

Treatment: Acupuncture and moxacautery: Apply at GB–21 (back), LI–16 (back), SI–13 (back), SI–10 (back), LI–15 (back), T–14 (back), T–9 (upper limb), LI–11 (upper limb), LU–2 (chest), H–3 (upper limb), T–3 (back) B–21 (lower trunk) on the side of

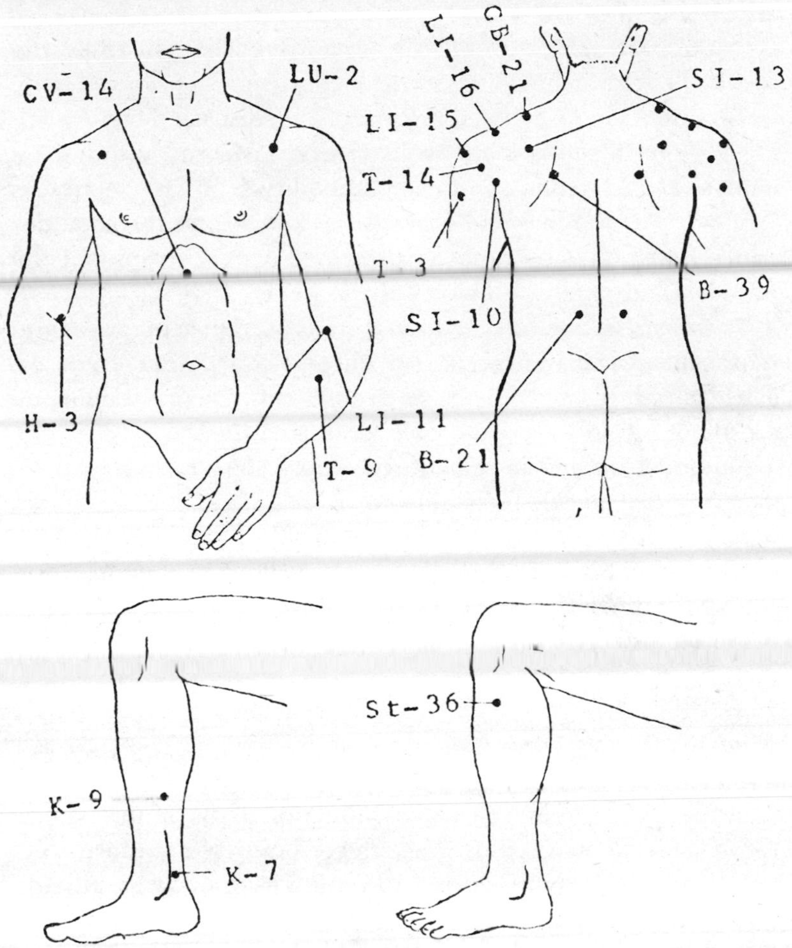

Vital points of treatment for Peripheral Inflammation of the Shoulder Joint

the body affected, and B–39 (back). In addition, combine with applications at CV–14 (abdomen) and St–36 (lower limb). K–9 (lower limb) K–7 (lower limb)

Rheumatism of the Joint

In the past, the cause of this disease was thought to be the toxins of bacteria; however, more recently it is considered to be caused by a virus. The acute form of this disease develops following tonsillitis; the joint swells up and turns red and there is pain, a feverish feeling and loss of mobility. The disease attacks such areas as the toes and fingers, the knees, and the shoulder joints. Later on it becomes chronic and causes atrophy of the muscles, and finally, ankylosis of the joint.

Treatment: Generally, acupuncture is used in acute cases and moxacautery is mainly applied in chronic cases. Acute cases are easily cured, but chronic cases are difficult to cure. Following are the locations of points for overall treatment.

Acupuncture and moxacautery: Apply at B–12 (back), B–14 (back), B–18 (back), B–21 (lower trunk), B–48 (lower trunk), B–23 (lower trunk), CV–12 (abdomen), CV–6 (abdomen), St–36 (lower limb), Sp–6 (lower limb), and in the cavity of a carotid sinus St–9 (neck).

For localized treatment, follow the instructions given in the section on arthritis.

Myositis (Inflammation of the muscle)

Contusion or overexhaustion makes an individual more susceptible to this disease. However, infection of pyogenic bacteria is the cause in many cases. The affected muscle area turns red, painful, swollen, and feverish. The muscle then turns stiff and hard and the oppressed pain becomes unbearable. Convulsive spasms and conglutination of the muscle often result, sometimes interfering with mobility.

Treatment: Apply either acupuncture or moxacautery at the Vital Points of the affected muscle area. When acupuncture is used, apply it wherever there is pain regardless of the specified area of the Vital Points. The result is extremely effective.

CHAPTER XXXIII

Diseases of the Nervous System

Cerebral Hemorrhage

This disease is caused by hemorrhage due to rupture of the branches of the cerebral artery as a result of such conditions as an increase in blood pressure or engorgement in the flow of blood. At the same time as the hemorrhage occurs, the patient has a stroke (apoplexy). In mild cases of apoplexy, the patient may feel headache and dizziness, but in severe cases the patient may fall into a coma and lose his mobility and his five senses. The patient's neck is twisted toward the paralyzed side and, sometimes, he suffers from incontinence. In rare cases, his arms and legs develop spasms. If the patient does not take a turn for the worse and die, he will be gradually restored to his functional abilities although hemiplegia and other symptoms of the disease will remain.

Prior to an attack, the patient may indicate premonitory symptoms such as heavy-headedness, headache, dizziness, ringing in the ears, slow speech, agitation, and impeded sensation and mobility in one half of the body.

For treatment, refer to the section on high blood pressure.

Encephalomalacia

This disease is caused by embolism or thrombosis of the flow of blood of the cerebral artery which results in malacia of the cerebral parenchyma beyond the point of the blockage. In many cases, the attack due to an embolism is similar to the attack from cerebral hemorrhage and the patient often suffers fits resembling those of epilepsy. In the case of cerebral thrombosis, the patient gradually develops hemiplegia or other cessation of bodily functions. The cessation of bodily functions due to encephalomalacia are mainly such symptoms as hemiplegia (gradual loss of sensation in half of the body) and aphasia.

For treatment in the case of embolism caused by cardiac troubles, refer to the section on the valvular diseases of the heart. The following Vital Points should be added especially in the area of treatment of hemiplegia.

Apply at the affected side of GB–5 (chest), Lu–1 (chest), S (lower trunk), B–S (lower trunk), SI–11 (back), SI–9 (back) or SI–10 (back), T–9 (upper limb), T–5 (upper limb), LI–4 (upper limb), and C–8 (upper limb).

Apply at the points on the leg of the affected side such as CB–33 (lower limb) or GB–35 (lower limb, GB–39 (lower limb) or GB–40 (lower limb) and Sp–1 (lower limb).

For aphasia, apply at GV–14 (head) or GV–15 (head).

Cerebral Anemia

This disease results from emotional excitement which causes contraction of the cerebral blood vessels or obstruction of the cardiac functions and, consequently, impedes circulation of blood to the brain. The patient's face turns pale, the extremities become cold, and he experiences cold sweat, hearing difficulties, ringing in the ears, loss of vision, dizzy spells, nausea, and vomiting, etc. Eventually, the patient may suffer fainting fits and lose consciousness. This tends to happen to a person suffering continuously from diarrhea or to a woman during her menstrual periods.

Treatment: Acupuncture: Apply at B–9 (neck), GV–25 (face) or CV–14 (abdomen), CV–6 (abdomen), St–36 (lower limb), Li–1 (lower limb), and SI–1 (upper limb).

Moxacuatery: CV–12 (abdomen), CV–6 (abdomen), B–16 (back), B–18 (back), St–36 (lower limb), and Li–2 (lower limb).

Cerebral Hyperemia

This may be caused by overexhaustion and other reasons, but it generally afflicts persons of sanguine temperament. The patient experiences during the fit a sudden feverish rush of warmth at the head and the face and feels throbbing at the temple. His face turns red, he suffers headache and dizziness. His mind sometimes becomes confused.

Treatment: Acupuncture: Apply at B–9 (neck, GB–21 (back), SI–14 (back), B–39 (back), LI–10 (upper limb), LI–4 (upper limb), St–37 (lower limb) or St–36 (lower limb), St–41 (lower limb), and Sp–9 (lower limb).

Moxacautery: Apply at GB–21 (back), B–16 (back), LI–10 (upper limb), and St–36 (lower limb).

Epilepsy

This disease attacks with loss of consciousness and repeated fits accompanied by spasms over the entire body. There is no particular change to the brain. The cause may be mental or physical overexhaustion, or external injury to the head, or as a reflection of other diseases. Epilepsy may be also caused by brain tumors or encephalomalacia. There are mild cases in which a patient may experience a spasm, only losing consciousness, or may suffer only fits of dizziness. There are instances in which these fits are also accompanied by premonitory symptoms such as heavy-headedness, headache, anxiety, and others.

Treatment: Acupuncture and moxacautery: Apply at B–10 (back), GV–11 (back), B–39 (back), GV–10 (back), GV–7 (back), B–16 (back), B–21 (lower trunk), CV–12 (abdomen), T–8 (upper limb), SI–1 (upper limb), GB–33 (lower limb), and Li–1 (lower limb).

Parkinson's Disease (Paralysis Agitans)

In the beginning, the patient's hand shakes; then this trembling spreads to the arm and leg on the same side of the body and from there spreads to the limbs of the opposite side. Eventually, the trembling extends over the entire body, and the muscle tension increases. The patient suffers loss of facial expression, maintains a peculiar posture, and his walk takes on a characteristic style. By acupuncture and moxacautery treatments, the symptoms sometimes are lessened.

Treatment: Acupuncture: Apply at GB–13 (head), LI–15 (back), B–16 (back), B–17 (back), Li–10 (upper limb), T–5 (upper limb), C–4 (upper limb), B–21 (lower trunk), B–S (lower trunk), GB–S (lower limb), St–36 (lower limb), GB–33 (lower limb) and K–9 (lower limb).

Moxacautery: GV–19 (head), GV–11 (back), GV–7 (back), B–37 (back) GV–4 (lower trunk), B–22 (lower trunk), LI–11 (upper limb), LI–4 (upper limb), St–36 (lower limb), GB–35 (lower limb), and Sp–6 (lower limb).

Myelitis

This disease is caused by changes in the parenchyma of the spinal cord. At the beginning, the symptoms are an oversensitivity of the spinal cord, sensation of constriction about the waist, and the abnormal sensitivity of the lower limbs. Later this disease will lead to paralysis of the legs. However, depending on the location of the primary site of the disease on the spine, the symptoms will vary; the patient may suffer from trouble with his bladder or rectum; his skin in the area over the affected part of the spine will change; the muscles governed by the affected portion of the spinal column atrophy and degenerate.

Treatment: Acupuncture and moxacautery: Apply at GV–11 (back), B–40 (back), GV–7 (back), B–16 (back) GV–4 (lower trunk), B–22 (lower trunk), LI–11 (upper limb), H–7 (upper limb), St–38 (lower limb) or GB–36 (lower limb), and K–3 (lower limb).

For paralysis of the lower limbs, apply at GB–S (lower limb), GB–31 (lower limb), GB–35 (lower limb), St–36 (lower limb), St–39 (lower limb), Sp–6 (lower limb), and Li–3 (lower limb).

If accompanied by problems of the bladder and rectum: Apply acupuncture and moxcautery at B–2 (lower trunk), B–24 (lower trunk), CV–4 (abdomen), CV–2 (abdomen), Lu–5 (upper limb), K–10 (lower limb), K–9 (lower limb), and B–60 (lower limb).

Hypersensitivity of Spinal Cord

Patients suffering from this disease develop pain in protuberances of the spine. This usually occurs in young females. The most sensitive areas are the protuberances of the fifth and sixth dorsal vertebrae. The skin becomes hypersensitive to feeling and to pain.

Treatment: Acupuncture: Apply at GV–12 (back), GV–11 (back), GV–10 (back), GV–8 (back), GV–7 (back), and also apply encircling acupuncture to areas that react, regardless of vital points. Apply at B–2 (lower trunk), SI–8 (upper limb), T–8 (upper limb) or GB–33 (lower limb), and K–7 (lower limb).

Moxacautery: Apply at GV–19 (head), B–12 (back), GV–19 (back), B–15 (back), B–16 (back), GB–33 (lower limb), GB–39 (lower limb), and K–1 (lower limb).

Psychoneurosis

Usually disorders which present symptoms with no organic changes are generally called neuroses. Among the different types of neuroses, psychopathic neurosis is a general term denoting such symptoms as nervous prostration, neurasthenia, hysteria, and neurotic compulsiveness. Frequently, this occurs in so-called nervous persons, caused by mental and emotional stresses such as dissatisfaction, discontent, anxiety, worry, anger, fright, fear, sadness, agonizing pain.

The patient experiences such symptoms as vomiting, heart palpitations, difficulty in breathing, and a tendency towards cerebral anemia. He suffers afflux of blood in the head or cold hands and feet. He becomes overemotional, weak, and constantly complaining, and tends to worry excessively.

Treatment: Acupuncture: Apply at GV–21 (head), GB–20 (neck), GB–21 (back), B–14 (back), B–16 (back) or B–17 (back), B–39 (back), B–21 (lower trunk), B–28 (lower trunk), CV–14 (abdomen), CV–12 (abdomen), Li–13 (abdomen), LI–10 (upper limb), C–6 (upper limb), SI–1 (upper limb), GB–33 (lower limb), and GB–41 (lower limb).

Moxacautery: Apply at B–9 (neck), GV–11 (back), GV–10 (back), B–15 (back), B–16 (back), B–21 (lower trunk), GB–33 (lower limb), and K–3 (lower limb).

Neurasthenia

The patient suffering from neurasthenia will complain of insomnia, tire easily, experience anxiety, and becomes distressful, forgetful, and indecisive, and generally his mental capacity decreases.

He often suffers frequent headaches, dizzy spells and heart palpitations. He may become very sensitive to pain in various parts of the body, feel uncomfortable, and suffer paresthesia (tingling sensation). He loses his appetite, and his eyelids and tongue tremble. In addition, he suffers frequent desire to urinate, and may also be troubled with constipation or dry mouth.

Treatment: Treatment for neurasthenia is the same as that described for psychoneurosis. However, if the disorder is accompanied by gastrointestinal troubles, efforts should be concentrated on treatment of the latter at the following points.

Acupuncture and moxacautery: Apply at B–18 (back), CV–12 (abdomen), St–21 (abdomen), CV–6 (abdomen), and St–36 (lower limb).

Hysteria

This is a symptom of the disorder of the so-called hysteric person as a result of emotional causes. Psychological symptoms are rapid changes of ideas and emotions. The patient responds readily to suggestion and has a highly developed imagination. The physical symptoms involve paresthesia, obstructed sensation and mobility, and also various other symptoms or problems of the internal organs arise. The patient suffers attacks of characteristic spasmodic hysteria and loss of clarity of consciousness.

Treatment: Acupuncture and moxacautery: Apply at GV–19 (head), GB–20 (neck), B–9 (neck), GV–11 (back), B–16 (back), B–21 (lower trunk), B–23 (lower trunk), B–28 (lower trunk), CV–17 (chest), CV–12 (abdomen), CV–6 (abdomen), C–3 (upper limb), H–7 (upper limb), Li–8 (lower limb), GB–33 (lower limb), Sp–6 (lower limb), and Li–3 (lower limb) or GB–40 (lower limb).

For spasmodic seizures, apply acupuncture at GV–19 (head), Li–1 (lower limb), and SI–1 (upper limb).

Headaches and Migraine Headaches

Headaches appear among the symptoms of many types of illnesses. There are various kinds of headaches such as the pain inside the skull, pain on the surface of the skin, pain of the forehead, of the occipital region, or the left half of the head; also, dull, heavy pain, throbbing pain, pain in fits, pain in the morning after awakening, severe pain at night.

Migraine headaches usually affect the left side of the head, although they may sometimes occur on the right side. In addition, pain may be felt on both sides of the head at the same time. The characteristic symptom is a sudden attack of severe pain with sparks flying before the eyes and vomiting.

Treatment: Acupuncture: Apply at St–8 (head), GV–19 (head), GB–19 (head), GB–20 (neck), GV–15 (neck), B–9 (neck), CV–13 (back), B–12 (back), B–14 (back), B–17 (back), St–36 (lower limb), B–56 (lower limb), LI–4 (upper limb), and SI–1 (upper limb).

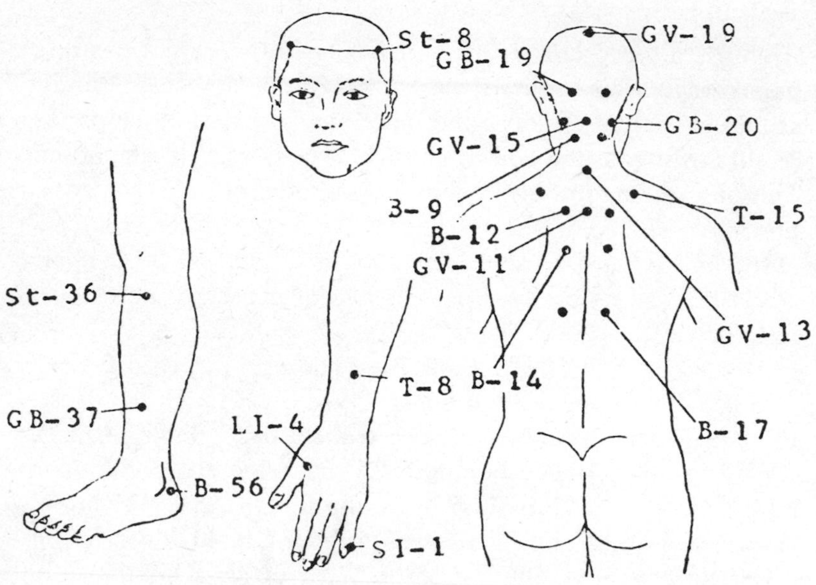

Vital points of treatment for Headaches

Moxacautery: Apply at GV–19 (head), B–9 (neck), T–15 (back), GV–11 (back), B–17 (back), T–8 (upper limb), and GB–37 (lower limb).

Pain in the occipital region indicates bladder disease in many cases.

Acupuncture: Apply at B–7 (head), B–8 (head), B–9 (neck), B–12 (back), B–21 (lower trunk), K–9 (lower limb), and B–56 (lower limb).

Moxacautery: Apply at GV–19 (head), B–9 (neck), GV–11 (back), and B–21 (lower trunk).

Pain in the forehead in many cases indicates troubles of the stomach or the lungs.

Acupuncture and moxacautery: Apply at GV–23 (head), GB–15 (head), St–8 (head), GV–21 (head), GB–20 (neck), B–9 (neck), B–19 (back), St–36 (lower limb), St–38 (lower limb), and Sp–2 (lower limb).

Pain in one side of the head usually indicates troubles in the gallbladder.

Acupuncture and moxacautery: Apply at GB–20 (neck), B–9 (neck), B–21 (back), B–17 (back), and GB–33 (lower limb).

Stiff Back and Shoulders

The main symptom of stiff back is tension and pain in the trapezius muscle. In fact, it also involves the tension and pain in other muscles in the scapular region. The causes may stem from local ailments at the shoulders and back, disorders directly affecting the governing nerves of the scapular region, and from other disorders such as that of the chest; however, in general this ailment is considered a subsidiary symptom of various diseases all over the body, and especially of chronic diseases. In many cases, it is caused by muscle fatigue and by mental and physical exhaustion.

Treatment: Acupuncture and moxacautery: Apply at B–15 (back), B–18 (back), B–21 (lower trunk), CV–12 (abdomen), St–25 (abdomen), LI–11 (upper limb), St–36 (lower limb), and Sp–6 (lower limb).

Localized Treatment: Acupuncture and moxacautery: Apply at GB–20 (neck), B–9 (neck), GB–21 (back), SI–14 (back), B–12 (back), and B–39 (back).

Dizziness

Dizziness is caused by obstruction in the organs which maintain equilibrium in the body, such as the labyrinth of the inner ear and the cerebellum or by obstruction in the pathway which connects them to the cerebrum. Dizziness accompanies auricular diseases, brain diseases, diseases of the organs of circulation, and various other chronic diseases. This symptom frequently accompanies such other symptoms as heavy-headedness, ringing in the ears, and nausea. In severe cases, the patient feels like fainting.

Treatment: Acupuncture: Apply at GV–21 (head) or GV–22

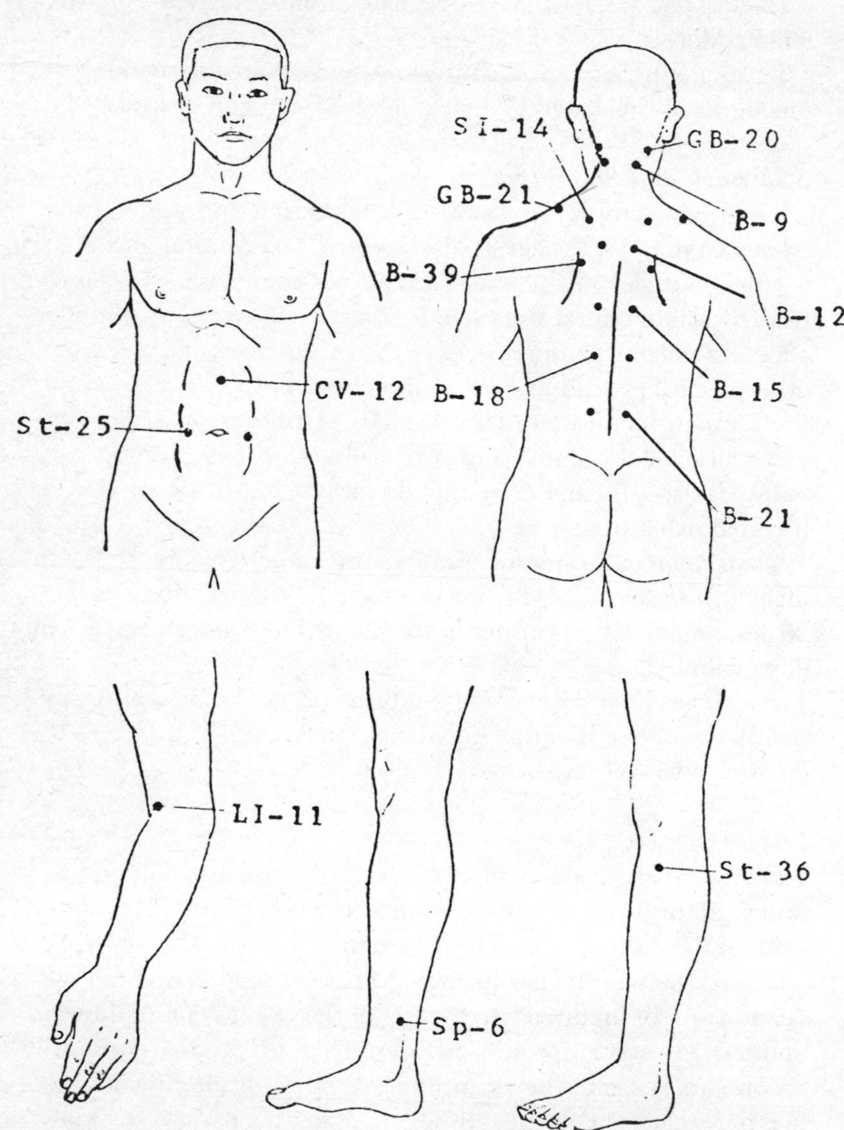

Vital points of treatment for Stiff Back and Shoulders

(head), GB–12 (head), B–9 (neck), GV–11 (back), B–16 (back), T–5 (upper limb), K–7 (lower limb), GB–42 (lower limb) and in the region of shoulders and upper back.

Moxacautery: Apply at GV–19 (head), GB–12 (head), B–9 (neck), GV–11 (back), B–15 (back), T–4 (upper limb), and GB–33 (lower limb).

Insomnia

Sleep can be stifled by pain, itching, coughing, and difficulty in breathing. The object of treatment discussed here, however, is that for neural insomnia which stems from neurosis, neurasthenia, and hysteria.

The patient suffering from neural insomnia does not become sleepy, cannot fall asleep, sleeps very lightly, dreams and awakes easily, and feels tired the following day.

Treatment: Acupuncture: Apply at GB–20 (neck), GV–15 (head), GB–3 (face), B–14 (back), B–15 (back), B–16 (back), B–17 (back), GB–35 (lower limb), and K–9 (lower limb).

Moxacautery: GB–20 (neck), B–13 (back), B–15 (back), CV–14 (abdomen), St–36 (lower limb), and K–3 (lower limb).

Neuralgia

Neuralgia is one of the symptoms of other diseases. Only in rare cases do the causes of neuralgia remain unknown. Neuralgia in most cases can be clearly traced to its cause. Consequently, there is no doubt that the first step in treating neuralgia is to treat the original disease. However, regardless of the cause of the neuralgia the pain from most of the different types can be relieved by moxacautery and acupuncture and so we consider these treatments to be suitable for all forms of neuralgia.

Where neuralgia is caused by or accompanies neuritis, it is often difficult to distinguish between the two from the standpoint of clinical diagnosis. It is difficult to expect a recovery from neuralgia in combination with neuritis after only a short-term treatment with moxacautery and acupuncture. Furthermore, neuritis leaves traces of neural paralysis to some degree after recovery. Typically, a portion of muscle will become thin or a stubborn numbness will remain as a result of the neuritis. There are various kinds of neuralgia distinguished by the manner in which the pain appears. Treatment of acupuncture and moxacautery can be given for the following typical types of neuralgia which are most frequently encountered. In addition, the course of treatment for neuralgia combined with neuritis is the same as that for simple neuralgia. No special treatment is indicated.

Trigeminal Neuralgia (Facial Neuralgia)

Trigeminal neuralgia may affect only the first branch of the trigeminal nerve, but in many cases it may also strike the second or the third branches as well. In any case, this type of neuralgia is persistent. Mild cases can undergo relief and cure after four or five treatments. In serious cases, the patient should

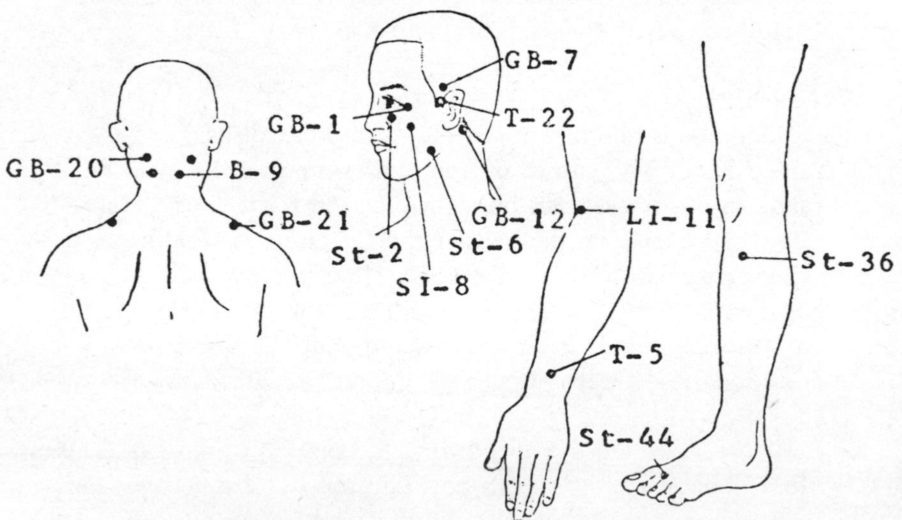

Vital points of treatment for Trigeminal Neuralgia

experience relief to some extent but may never be completely cured. This is the most difficult of all the types of neuralgia to cure.

Treatment: The aim of acupuncture and moxacautery treatment in cases of facial neuralgia is the adjustment of the function of the entire body.

Acupuncture and moxacautery: Apply in combination at CV-12 (abdomen), B-21 (back), GV-11 (back), T-5 (upper limb), LI-11 (upper limb), St-36 (lower limb).

For neuralgia of the first branch of the trigeminal nerve, the opthalmic nerve (pain of the temple, the eyes, and forehead): Apply acupuncture and moxacautery of the affected half of the body at GB-16 (head), T-20 (head), GB-5 (head), T-22 (face), GB-1 (face) or T-12 (neck), and LI-4 (upper limb).

Acupuncture of the affected side: GB-14 (face), B-2 (face), T-23 (face), with No. 3 needle to the depth of 0.5 to 1.5 cm. Acupuncture is also lightly applied on the unaffected side.

For neuralgia of the second branch of the trigeminal nerve, the superior maxillary nerve (pain ranges from the lower eyelid to the upper lip and the upper teeth), apply acupuncture and moxacautery of the affected side at B-9 (neck), GB-12 (head), T-22 (face), GB-5 (head), and LI-4 (upper limb).

Acupuncture of the affected side: The acupuncture includes that of St-7 (face), SI-18 (face) and LI-20 (face).

For neuralgia of the third branch of the trigeminal nerve: For mandibular neuralgia (pain in the entire region of the lower jaw, tongue, and the lower teeth), apply acupuncture and moxacautery of the affected side at GB-20 (neck), GB-21 (back), GB-7 (head) or T-17 (neck), SI-19 (face), and LI-4 (upper limb).

Acupuncture of the affected side includes that of St-2 (face), St-6 (face), Si 8 (face), and St-44 (lower limb), outside of the lower alveolaris. Single insertion with No. 3 needle applied to the depth of 0.5 to 1.5 cm. Acupuncture of the unaffected side yields stronger stimulation than that of the affected side and may well be worth experimenting.

Occipital Neuralgia

Pain is felt at the occipital region of the head or the area from the hairline on the neck to the occipital region and to behind the ears. In some cases, merely touching the ends of the hair can produce severe pain. However, most cases can be easily cured in a short time by treatment of acupuncture and moxacautery.

For adjustment of the entire body the same Vital Points are followed as described in the section on treatment of the trigeminal neuralgia.

For localized treatment: Apply acupuncture and moxacautery at B–9 (neck) and GB–20 (neck). Insert the needle diagonally to a depth of 0.5 to 2 cm to produce good stimulation.

Brachial Neuralgia

Brachial neuralgia develops in many cases as the result of engaging in unaccustomed labor, of exposure to severe cold, or from accumulation of fatigue after heavy labor.

The patient has free mobility in contrast to the ailments "Forty-year-old Shoulders" and "Fifty-year-old Arms," which will be described later. Severe pain, however, persists even during times of rest in many cases.

For the adjustment of the entire body, the same treatment is followed as is described in the previous section on neuralgia.

Treatment: Acupuncture and moxacautery of the affected side: Apply at St–11 (back), St–9 (back), St–10 (back), and Lu–4 (upper limb).

For *gyo* pain (the side of the arm containing the radius and the thumb), apply acupuncture and moxacautery at T–9 (upper limb), LI–12 (upper limb), LI–7 (upper limb), T–4 (upper limb), SI–6 (upper limb), and LI–4 (upper limb).

For *shaku* pain (on the side of the arm containing the ulna and the little finger), apply acupuncture and moxacautery at H–3 (upper limb), C–13 (upper limb), and H–6 (upper limb). Insert needle diagonally to a depth of 1.0 to 2.5 cm.

Intercostal Neuralgia

Intercostal neuralgia produces severe pain in the chest region. Frequently, the pain shoots mainly from the left side of the back to the area below the nipple. The pain characteristically runs along the region of the ribs.

It is often difficult to distinguish this disease from such others such as angina pectoris or pleurisy.

Most cases can be cured after one or more treatments of acupuncture and moxacautery. For adjustment of the entire body, follow the same treatment as described in the section on trigeminal neuralgia.

Treatment: Acupuncture and moxacautery of the affected side: Apply at B–13 (back) B–14 (back) or B–15 (back), B–16 (back), SI–11 (back), B–39 (back), St–24 (abdomen) Sp–21 (chest), Li–13 (abdomen) or Li–12 (abdomen) St–27 (abdomen) GB–22 (abdomen) CV–17 (chest), H–7 (upper limb, and C–4 (upper limb).

For breast pain, as a specific type of intercostal neuralgia,

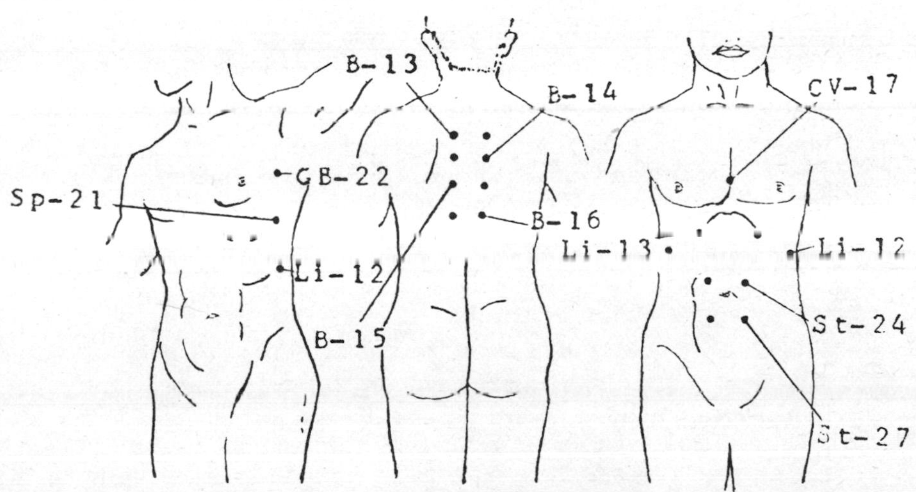

Vital points of treatment for Intercostal neuralgia

apply moxacautery at CV–17 (chest) and Lu–1 (chest).

Special attention in acupuncture treatment for intercostal neuralgia is required in order to avoid inserting the needle too deeply. All the muscles of the chest are tender and thus needles are apt to slide in too deep without meeting any resistance before the doctor realizes it, and so may wound the pleura. As a result of this wound the patient may develop spontaneous pneumothorax and will probably suffer from severe pain. Therefore ample caution is needed. The depth of the needle insertion should be restricted to 2 to 3 cm in the back and 1 to 2 cm in the chest.

Lumbar Neuralgia

There are many varied causes of lumbar neuralgia. The most frequent and severe case is called "cricked back" which develops into the vertebral hernia.

Neuralgia of the chorda spermatica produces pain in the area from the lower back to the lower abdomen, the groin, and the genital region. It is commonly called Senki (lumbago) or Subako. The pain is especially severe in the genital area. Not too many people, however, suffer from this disease.

Treatment: For adjustment of the entire body follow the same treatment as described in the section on trigeminal neuralgia.

Acupuncture and moxacautery: Apply at the affected side at GB–26 (abdomen), St–27 (abdomen) GB–28 (abdomen), K–12 (abdomen), B–18 (back), B–45 (back), B–46 (back), GB–25 (lower trunk), B–48 (lower trunk), B–27 (lower trunk), B–28 (lower trunk), and B–50 (lower trunk).

In contrast to acupuncture of the chest, there is no danger in this case of too deep insertion even if the insertion depth reaches from 5 cm to 7 cm.

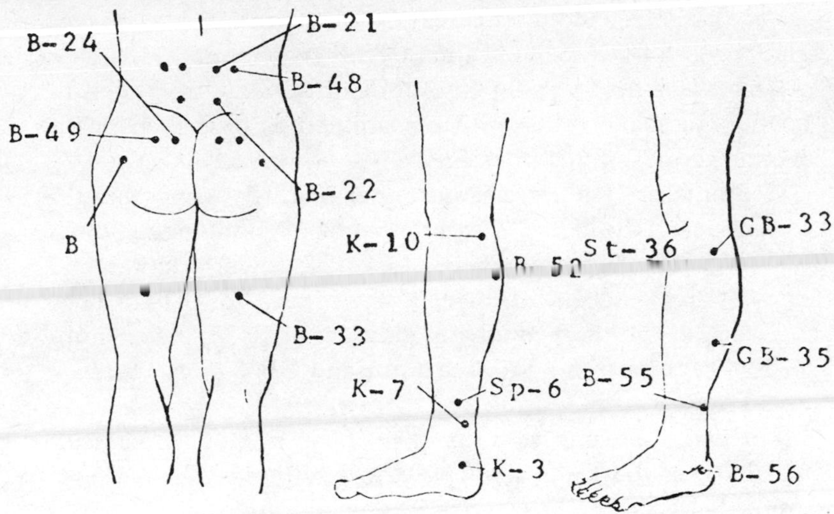

Vital points of treatment for Sciatica

Sciatica

Of all the types of neuralgia, sciatica occurs the most frequently. Sciatica produces pain running from the lower back down to the buttocks and to the back of the thigh and lower legs, also down the outside of the leg to the tip of the toe. The pain may become severe during the day or night, even while the patient is in a calm state. Even the slightest movement may cause him to scream in pain. He cannot stand up, sit down, nor walk, and suffers such severe pain especially at night that he cannot fall asleep at all. There are various types of pain characterized by the areas in which it is most severe, such as the pain in the area of the buttocks, the area of the thigh, in the lower leg and even pain that runs throughout the entire length of the sciatic nerve. The area of pain may shift. The nature of the pain is also varied, for example burning pain, cutting pain, and unpleasant sensations of numbness and painful cramps. They cannot be grouped into one category. This disease, however, is one of those for which treatment by acupuncture and moxacautery is very effective, and most cases of sciatica are quickly relieved and cured following application of this treatment.

Treatment: For adjustment of the entire body, treatment by acupuncture and moxacautery is applied as described in the section on trigeminal neuralgia.

Acupuncture and moxacautery: For pain that runs from the lower back to the kidney area, apply at St–27 (abdomen), GB–25 (lower trunk), B–24 (lower trunk), B–21 (lower trunk), B–22 (lower trunk) and B–48 or B–49 (lower trunk). For pain through the back of the thigh, apply in addition, at B–33 (lower limb), B–52 (lower limb), Sp–6 (lower limb), and GB–5 (lower limb) or St–36 (lower limb).

For pain that runs from the back of the thigh to the outside and back of the lower leg, apply, in addition, at B–36 (lower limb), B–35 (lower limb), GB–32 (lower limb), GB–33 (lower limb), GB–35 (lower limb), K–3 (lower limb) or B–55 (lower limb), B–56 (lower limb) or K–10 (lower limb). Probe lightly the above areas and apply treatment especially at those areas at which there is much oppressive pain.

Lumbago

Lumbago is a general term for pains which include muscle (rheumatic) neuralgia of the lower back as well as ailments of the fascia and vertebral joints of the spinal column. Lumbago may be caused by external injury or various other ailments, but it is believed that lumbago will also develop in persons whose constitution is conducive to atony.

Treatment: Applying a slightly stronger stimulation than normal to the localized area for treatment generally is recommended. On the other hand, it is better to apply a light stimulation to persons of weak constitution.

Acupuncture: Apply at B–18 (back), B–21 (lower trunk), B–48 (lower trunk), B–22 (lower trunk), B–27 (lower trunk), GB–5 (lower limb) B–36 (lower limb), B–35 (lower limb), B–56 (lower limb), and Sp–6 (lower limb).

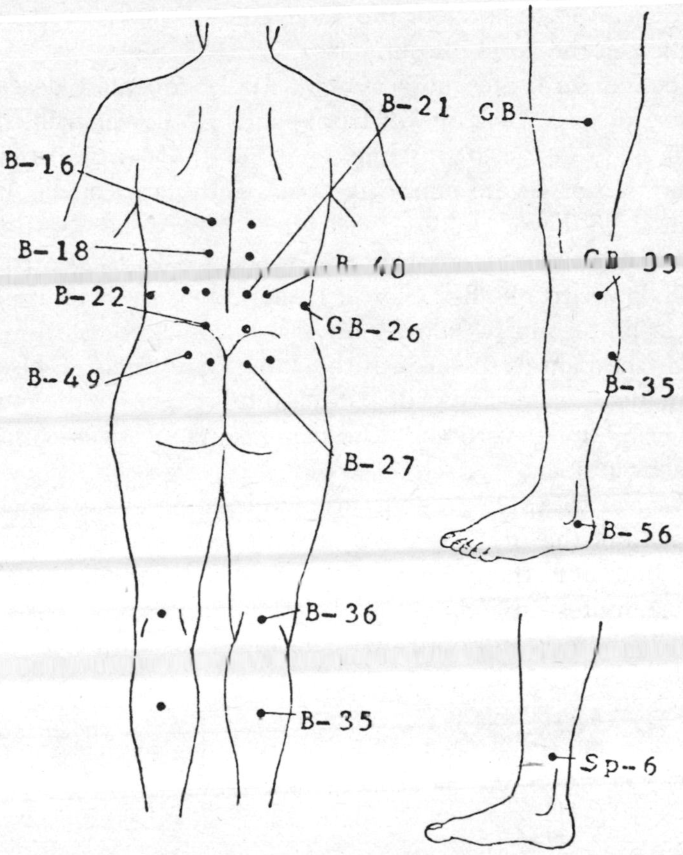

Vital points of treatment for Lumbago

Moxacautery: Apply at B–16 (back), B–21 (lower trunk), B–27 (lower trunk), B–49 (lower trunk), GB–26 (abdomen), GB–33 (lower limb), and B–53 (lower limb).

For pain in the area of the Vital Point *Jin Yu* (mainly centered in the kidney area):

Acupuncture and moxacautery: Apply at B–21 (lower trunk), B–48 (lower trunk), B–S (lower trunk), CV–4 (abdomen), St–27 (abdomen), B–53 (lower limb), and B–56 (lower limb).

For pain in the area of the Vital Point *Daichyoyu* (mainly existing in the large intestine area):

Acupuncture and moxacautery: Apply repeated doses of moxacautery at B–22 (lower trunk) and B–S (lower trunk)

For pain in the area of the Vital Point *Shishitsu* (obvious induration or severe oppressive pain in the area of the Vital Point B–48 (lower trunk):

Acupuncture and moxacautery: Apply at B–21 (lower trunk), B–48 (lower trunk), B–23 (lower trunk), Li–8 (lower limb), K–7 (lower limb), and K–9 (lower limb).

For the pain in the area of the Vital Point *Sagai.* (This is a spontaneous pain at the side of the protuberances of the fourth and fifth lumbar vertibrae. The pain occurs mostly with spontaneous lumbago.)

Treatment: Apply acupuncture at a location about 1 inch to the side of the protuberances of the fourth and fifth lumbar vertebrae until there is a response. Leave the needle inserted for 5 minutes. In addition, apply repeated doses of moxacautery. If there is an oppressive pain in the B–53 (lower limb), apply both acupuncture and moxacautery.

CHAPTER XXXIV

Surgical Disorders

Contusion and Sprain

Both acupuncture and moxacautery are applicable and very effective in cases of contusion regardless of the location on the body. In the case of sprains as distinct from contusions, acupuncture and moxacautery treatment are equally good. For contusion, apply acupuncture at the area of the contusion. With contusion, there is usually periostal pain in the bone beneath. In such event, it is necessary in acupuncture treatment to insert the needle to the depth that it reaches the periosteum. If there is internal hemorrhage, apply acupuncture at one or two spots in the hemorrhaging area and draw out blood. After that, the pain will be quickly relieved. In the application of moxacautery, locate the area of the most pain and apply at one or two spots on that area. For example, contusion in the chest produces pain in the back, then apply acupuncture and moxacautery at the location of the pain on the back.

In the case of sprains, apply acupuncture and moxacautery in the region of the sprained joint. Acupuncture applied between the joints is very effective. In the event of internal hemorrhage, the treatment is the same as that described above.

Furuncles, Carbuncles of the Face, and Anthrax

These diseases are caused by an eruption of pyogenic bacteria in the hair follicles or the sebaceous glands of the skin. If the infection results in folliculitis, the symptoms will be nothing worse than the formation of small pustules. On the other hand, the infections which develop into furuncles cause the skin surrounding the affected area to redden, swell, and stiffen. The furuncles are painful and eventually swell and develop a core of pus at the center. Sometimes many furuncles develop in one place after another. This occurs frequently in diabetics. In general furuncles tend to develop on the nape of the neck, the face, back, and the buttocks. Among these, furuncles which develop on the face are called facial carbuncles. Carbuncles that develop especially in the vicinity of the upper lip will cause the entire face to swell and produce fever. In time this condition may become dangerous.

Treatment: For these infections occurring on the upper half of the body, apply repeated doses of moxacautery at LI–11 (upper limb), LI–10 (upper limb), LI–4 (upper limb), and B–14 (back).

For the infections occurring on the lower half of the body, apply repeated doses of moxacautery at LI–11 (upper limb), St–36 (lower limb), B–56 (lower limb), B–14 (back), and B–21 (back).

For facial carbuncles, it is necessary to apply repeated doses of moxacautery at LI–4.

If the patient cannot feel heat from the beginning of treatment, continue the treatment until he does. If the patient can feel the heat from the beginning, apply the treatment continuously until he no longer does.

Tubercular Inflammation of the Lymphatic Glands

This disease is an inflammation of lymphatic glands due to tubercle bacilli. The bacilli generally attack the lymphatic glands in the neck. This is commonly called "Ruiraki" (scrofula).

In some cases, this symptom appears in other regions of the body such as the armpits, thighs, the glands in the elbows, and abdominal cavity. If the case is benign, there will be a single lymphatic swelling or two or three at the most. The swellings are small, hard, and easy to treat. If the case is malignant, the swellings of the lymphatic glands increase in number and finally grow together and become abscessed. Eventually, the abscess breaks open by itself and forms a fistula. After this happens, the task of healing becomes difficult.

Treatment: Acupuncture: Apply at B–12 (back), B–18 (back), Lu–5 (upper limb), LI–10 (upper limb), CV–12 (abdomen), CV–4 (abdomen), St–36 (lower limb), and Sp–8 (lower limb).

Moxacautery: Apply at B–11 (back), GV–11 (back), B–18 (back), LI–11 (upper limb), and St–36 (lower limb).

Tuberculosis of the Bone (Caries)

This is the most frequently occurring among chronic bone diseases, and affects the backbone, arms and legs. (So-called caries of the ribs occurs following pleurisy and has its own particular characteristics.)

At the beginning, there are no symptoms of disease, but gradually the periosteum becomes infected and tumors appear. Cold sores form and eventually break out through the skin. Then, at last, the patient finally realizes his illness. In the vicinity of the joints swelling, functional interruption, and pain develop. In the case of spinal caries, there may be spontaneous pain, striking and oppressive pain, external disfigurement, movement restriction, etc., in the localized area; and, in some cases, the patient may also suffer neuralgic paralysis.

Treatment: Acupuncture and moxacuatery: Apply at B–12 (back), B–21 (back), CV–12 (abdomen), St–25 (abdomen), LI–11 (upper limb), St–36 (lower limb), and Sp–6 (lower limb).

Localized Treatment

Apply tap-stimulatory acupuncture in the surrounding area of oppressive pain above the affected bone.

Apply three to five doses of moxacautery, each about half the size of a grain of rice, at about four spots in the surrounding area at which oppressive pain or swelling appears.

For spinal caries, apply 3 to 5 doses of moxacautery at 4 points in a circle around the painful area with the protuberance of the affected vertebra at the center.

Refer to the respective sections if these symptoms are combined with neuralgia; for example, neuralgic paralysis.

Hemorrhoids (Blind Piles)

Hemorrhoids are caused by localized congestion of blood due to varicose enlargement of the veins located in the area around the anus and lower section of the rectum. In the beginning, there are oppressive and burning sensations in the localized area and bleeding. Gradually, nodules (hemorrhoids) form inside and outside the anus. When the internal hemorrhoids prolapse outside the anus, the pain becomes severe. In addition, external hemorrhoids tend to develop inflammation due to stimulation and the pain is apt to follow.

Treatment: Primarily, moxacautery is used and acupuncture becomes supplementary.

Moxacautery: Apply at GV–19 (head) B–11 (back) or B–12 (back), B–21 (lower trunk), B–22 (lower trunk), B–30 (lower trunk), GV–2 (lower trunk), St–25 (abdomen), St–37 (lower limb) Lu–6 (upper limb), and LI–10 (upper limb).

Acupuncture: Apply at B–12 (back), B–21 (lower trunk), B–22 (lower trunk), B–29 (lower trunk), B–30 (lower trunk), Sp–6 (lower limb) St–36 (lower limb) and LI–11 (upper limb).

When there is bleeding, apply acupuncture and moxacautery at Lu–6 (upper limb) or GB–33 (lower limb).

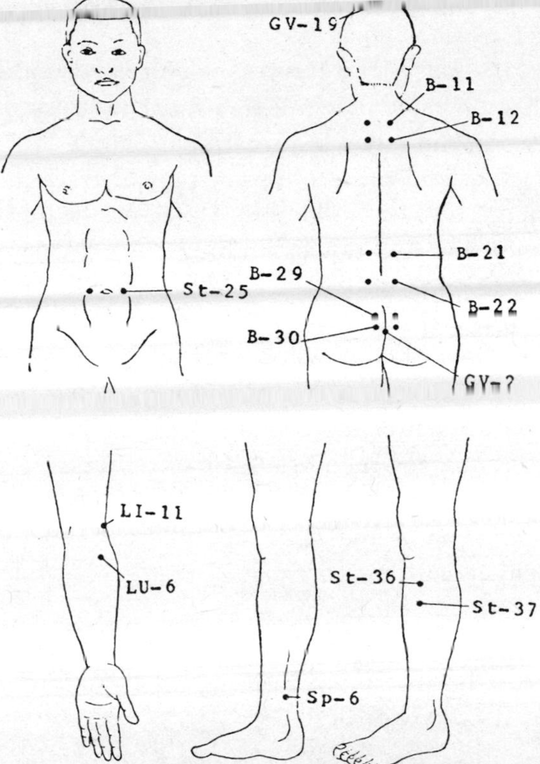

Vital points of treatment for Hemorrhoids

Anal Fistula

This disease can be caused by a ruptured abscess in the area of the anus or rectum or by a chronic fistula formed around the anus after an operation. It is often tubercular in nature. External anal fistulas have an orifice on the skin. Internal anal fistulas have orifices on the mucous membrane. Fistulas with orifices on both surfaces are called complete anal fistulas. If the orifice of a fistula becomes closed for a while, severe pain and fever may develop.

Treatment: Follow the treatment described under the section for hemorrhoids. Overall treatment is stressed, and particularly select the following treatment points.

Acupuncture and moxacautery: Apply at B–12 (back), B–21 (lower trunk), CV–12 (abdomen), Lu–5 (upper limb) or Lu–6 (upper limb), and K–7 (lower limb).

Prolapse of the Rectum

This is the condition in which a part of the rectum protrudes from the anus. This often happens during defecation.

When the return of the rectum through the anus becomes difficult, the mucous membrane turns red and swells; severe pain is likely to result.

Treatment: Follow the same treatment as described in the section dealing with hemorrhoids. In particular, select the following treatment points.

Moxacautery: Apply at the GV–19 (head), GV–11 (lower trunk), B–21 (lower trunk), B–49 (lower trunk), CV–12 (abdomen), and B–53 (lower limb).

Inflammation at the End of Finger or Toe (Whitlow)

This disease may be caused by an infection of pyogenic bacteria in a small wound of a finger.

When the symptoms are mild, only superficial pustules form. However, there have been cases in which whitlow has spread to the region of the tendons and periosteum and eventually led to death.

For light symptoms: Acupuncture and moxacautery treatments are applicable only for mild symptoms.

Treatment: Moxacautery is primarily used and acupuncture is supplementary.

Moxacautery: When the hand is infected by this disease, apply repeated dosages of moxacautery at Lu–10 (upper limb) and LI–4 (upper limb) and small dosage at SI–2 (upper limb). When the foot is infected, apply large dosages at St–36 (lower limb), GB–33 (lower limb), and a small dosage at B–62 (lower limb).

When inflammation is localized at the tip of a finger, apply a large dosage of moxacautery about 2 to 3 mm to left and right of both corners of the nail. This will relieve the pain considerably.

CHAPTER XXXV

Gynecology

Menstrual Abnormalities

Menstruation normally occurs once a month and lasts about 5 days. A variation of 10 days more or less is considered physiologically normal. Oligomenorrhea is the condition in which the interval between the menstrual periods is abnormally long. Hypomenorrhea is the condition of menstruation with a small amount of menstrual flow. These disorders are caused by hypogenitalismus, ovarian hypofunction, blockage of internal secretions, and by various other diseases of the body.

Treatment: Acupuncture: Apply at GB–21 (back), LI–4 (lower limb), B–21 (lower trunk), B–23 (lower trunk), B–28 (lower trunk), B–29 (lower trunk), Sp–10 (lower limb), and Sp–6 (lower limb).

Moxacautery: Apply at B–16 (back), B–21 (lower trunk), B–28 (lower trunk), St–27 (abdomen), CV–3 (abdomen), Li–8 (lower trunk), Sp–6 (lower limb), and K–5 (lower limb).

Amenorrhea

Amenorrhea refers to the condition of the stoppage of menstrual periods with the exception of that stoppage which occurs during the period of pregnancy and lactation.

This generally occurs as a result of extreme hypomenorrhea or from emotional shock. There may be periodic bleeding from the nose, stomach, intestines, or lungs. It can lead to epistaxis, hematemesis, bloody stool, and hemoptysis.

Treatment: Acupuncture and moxacautery treatments are the same as those described in the section of menstrual abnormalities.

Polymenorrhea and Hypermenorrhea

Polymenorrhea is a disorder in which the interval between the menstrual periods has become abnormally short.

Hypermenorrhea is a disorder in which the amount of menstrual bleeding is unusually large.

These disorders may be caused by uterine tumors, obstructed circulation inside the pelvis, incomplete contractions of the uterine muscles (myometrium), or by hormone obstructions.

Treatment: Acupuncture and moxacautery: Apply at B–21 (lower trunk), B–23 (lower trunk), B–28 (lower trunk), St–27 (abdomen) or CV–4 (abdomen), Lu–5 (upper limb), St–36 (lower limb), K–10 (lower limb), and K–7 (lower limb) or K–3 (lower limb).

Dysmenorrhea

This is the condition of abnormally severe menstrual pain accompanied by nausea, vomiting, headache, and diarrhea. This disorder may be caused by hypoplasia or inflammation of the uterus or possibly neurologically.

Treatment: Acupuncture: Apply at B–21 (lower trunk), B–48 (lower trunk), B–S (lower trunk), St–28 (abdomen), CV–4 (abdomen), Lu–6 (upper limb) or Lu–5 (upper limb), K–9 (lower limb) or Sp–6 (lower limb), K–7 (lower limb), K–9 (lower limb) and B–9 (neck).

Moxacautery: Apply at B–16 (lower trunk), B–21 (lower trunk), B–48 (lower trunk), B–28 (lower trunk), CV–12 (abdomen), CV–4 (abdomen), Sp–6 (lower trunk), and K–3 (lower limb), K–5 (lower limb).

Leukorrhea ("Whites")

This is sometimes called "whites" or "discharges of the uterus."

Genital secretions increase and make the external genitals moist and uncomfortable. It is caused by inflammation of the uterine cavity, cervical canal, or the uterine body. There are two types of leukorrhea; one is the ordinary "whites" and the other is the type with blood in it.

Treatment: Acupuncture: Apply at B–16 (back), B–21 (lower trunk), B–28 (lower trunk), GB–26 (abdomen), St–27 (abdomen), Lu–5 (upper limb), K–10 (lower limb), K–7 (lower limb), Li–8 (lower limb), and St–30 (lower limb).

Moxacautery: Apply at B–21 (lower trunk), B–29 (lower trunk), CV–4 (abdomen) or CV–2 (abdomen), St–36 (lower trunk), Sp–6 (lower limb) or K–3 (lower limb).

Retroflexion of the Womb

This may be congenital in nature or occur as a result of poor hygiene after childbirth. The uterine body is bent backward at an angle with the position of the cervix. Sometimes there are

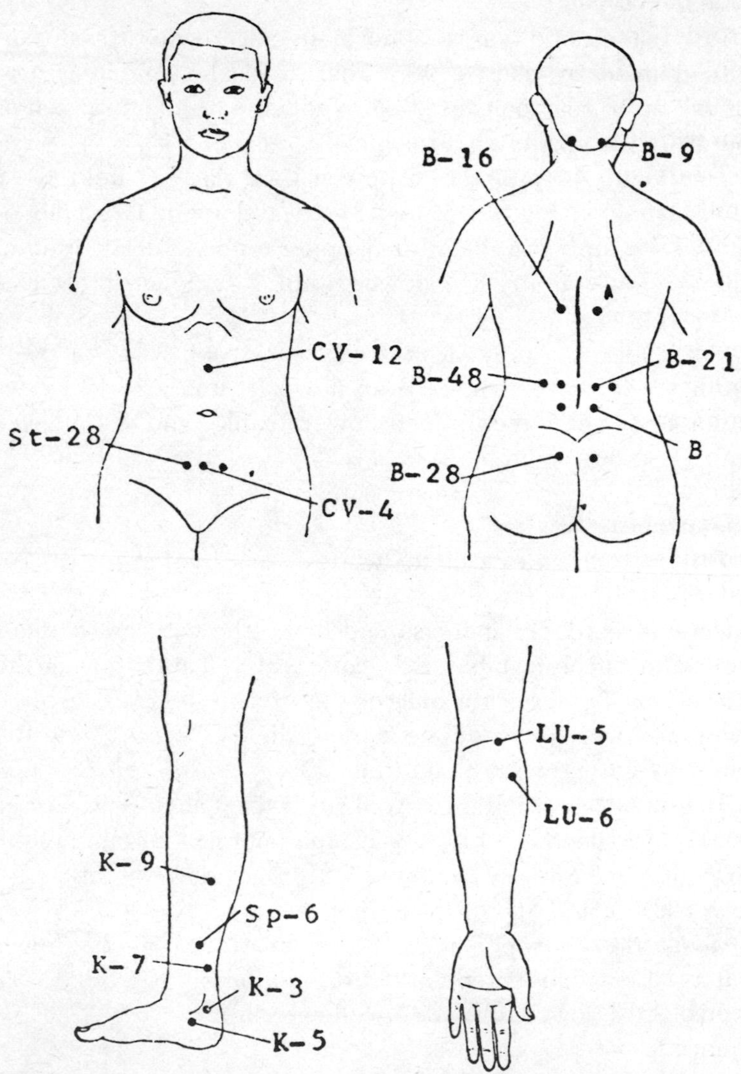

Vital points of treatment for Dysmenorrhea

no ill effects from the retroflexion of the womb. However, this disorder can create menstrual abnormalities, oppressive conditions of the bladder and rectum, pain in the lower abdomen and the lower back. It can lead to sterility, and occurs in combination with inflammation of the uterine lining or affiliated organs.

Treatment: Acupuncture: Apply at B–16 (back, B–21 (lower trunk), B–22 (lower trunk), B–29 (lower trunk), K–14 (abdomen), CV–4 (abdomen), K–9 (lower limb), St–40 (lower limb), and Lu–5 (upper limb).

Moxacautery: Apply at B–16 (back), B–21 (lower trunk), B–29 (lower trunk, CV–12 (abdomen), CV–4 (abdomen), St–28 (abdomen), LI–11 (upper limb) or T–4 (upper limb), St–36 (lower limb), and K–8 (lower limb).

Descended Uterus and Prolapsed Uterus

Descendus uteri is a disorder in which portea vaginalis uteri protrudes from the vaginal entrance. Prolapsus utori is a disorder in which portea vaginalis uteri protrudes outside the vaginal entrance. These disorders tend to happen to a person with loose muscle tension.

Treatment: It is permissible to follow the treatments given in the section of retroflexion of the womb. In particular, select the following locations for treatment.

Acupuncture and moxacautery: Apply at GV–19 (head), B–42 (back), CV–12 (abdomen), Li–8 (lower limb), Li–1 (lower limb), K–10 (lower limb) or K–2 (lower limb).

Endometritis

It is caused by gonococcal inflammation during childbirth, poor blood circulation of the entire body, poor hygiene, or an abnormal position of the uterus. In acute cases, this is accompanied by fever, puslike whites with bad odor and labor-like pain. In chronic cases there is a serous or puslike secretion, and the patient tends to have hypermenorrhea. The symptoms are melancholia, headache, lumbago, and menostasis.

Treatment: Acupuncture and moxacautery: Apply at B–16 (back), B–21 (lower trunk), B–48 (lower trunk), B–28 (lower trunk), CV–12 (abdomen), St–27 (abdomen), or GB–26 (abdomen), Sp–10 (lower limb), GB–33 (lower limb), K–3 (lower limb), and K–5 (lower limb).

Myoma Uteri

There are no recognizable subjective symptoms when myoma uteri is small. However, when the tumor is enlarged, there will be bleeding, pain (appearing as menostasis), and oppressiveness (tension and oppression of the lower abdominal region, dysuria, constipation, edema, and sciatica). Also, the patient can suffer functional disorder of the heart and sterility.

Treatment: Acupuncture and moxacautery: Apply at GV–7 (back), B–21 (lower trunk), B–22 (lower trunk), B–28 (lower trunk), St–25 (abdomen), CV–4 (abdomen), K–12 (abdomen), K–9 (lower limb), and Sp–6 (lower limb).

Sterility

Sterility is defined as the lack of impregnation when a couple want to have children. There is idiopathic (congenital) sterility and also secondary sterility which is caused by problems from a previous pregnancy. At times the sterility is caused due to inadequacies of the male sperm. Sterility on the part of a female can be due to abnormalities of the external genitals, vagina, the uterus, Fallopian tubes, and ovaries, or due to general body diseases such as obesity, diabetes, and chlorosis. Hysteria and frigidity can also cause sterility.

Pregnancy can be made possible through acupuncture and moxacautery treatments by correcting physical abnormalities if the sterility is caused by hypogenitalismus or abnormal positioning of the uterus, chills and other abnormalities of the constitution.

Treatment: Acupuncture and moxacautery: Apply at B–21 (lower trunk), B–23 (lower trunk), B–27 (lower trunk), B–49

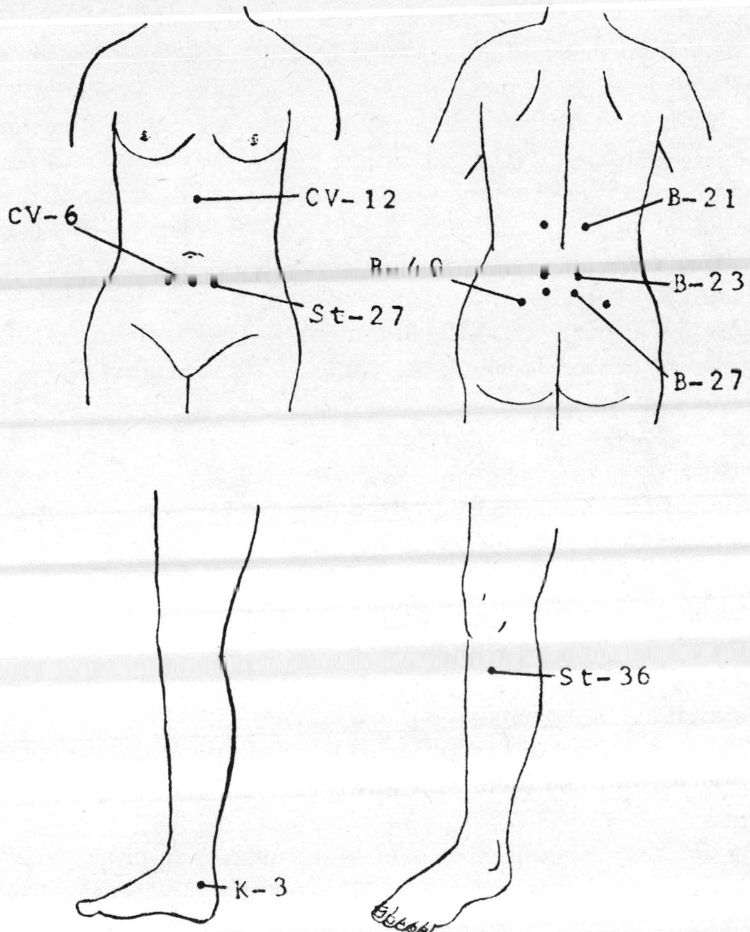

Vital points of treatment for Sterility

(lower trunk), CV–12 (abdomen), CV–6 (abdomen), or St–27 (abdomen), St–36 (lower limb), and K–3 (lower limb).

Frigidity

Frigidity refers to the condition in which a woman does not feel enjoyable sensations and cannot reach climax satisfactorily during intercourse. (A woman is said to be frigid if she has no sexual excitement.) This condition can be caused by the patient's mental and emotional state or also by disorders of the sexual organs. In many cases sterility will follow.

Treatment: Acupuncture and moxacautery: Apply at GV–11 (back), B–15 (back), B–21 (lower trunk), B–23 (lower trunk), B–28 (lower trunk), CV–12 (abdomen), K–12 (abdomen), CV–3 (abdomen), St–36 (lower limb), and Li–8 (lower limb) or Li–1 (lower limb).

Chills

In this condition, such localized areas as the patient's lower trunk, legs, and arms feel constantly and especially cold despite the wearing of warm clothing. This is due to obstructed circulation of the blood in the localized area and mostly occurs in anemic persons. In addition, the tendency to complain of cold is further increased if the blood circulation is congested in the pelvis. Because a woman has more subcutaneous fat around her hips and buttocks and the internal body temperature is unable to be transmitted, she is more susceptible to this coldness than a man.

Treatment: Acupuncture and moxacautery: Apply at B–18 (back), B–21 (lower trunk), B–22 (lower trunk), B–28 (lower trunk), B–49 (lower trunk) or B–50 (lower trunk), GV–3 (lower trunk), CV–4 (abdomen), CV–12 (abdomen), St–27 (abdomen), St–36 (lower limb), K–10 (lower limb), K–5 (lower limb), K–3 (lower limb) and St–43 (lower limb).

Menopausal Disorders

These disorders arise in women around the age of 48 years who have stopped menstruating. About 50 percent of these women suffer from some disorders. These are disorders of

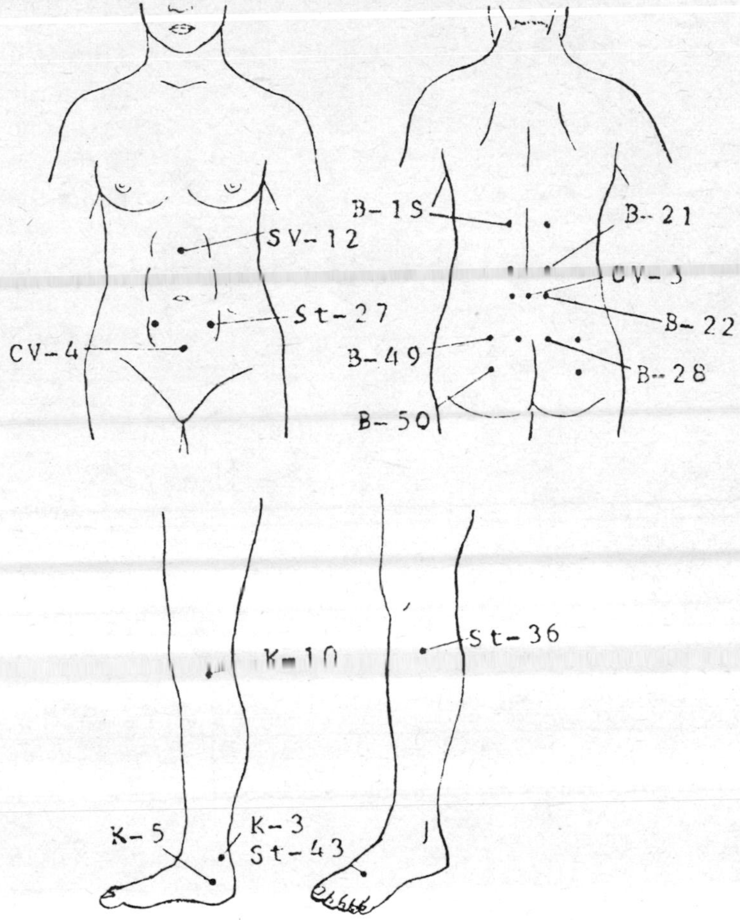

Vital points of treatment for Chills

vasomotor nerves (such as rush of blood to the head, hot flashes, heart palpitations, abnormal perspiration, and dizziness, disorders of mental capacity (such as loss of memory, insomnia, eye troubles, headaches, and depression).

Treatment: Acupuncture: Apply at B–9 (neck), B–11 (back), B–14 (back), B–21 (lower trunk), B–27 (lower trunk), CV–12

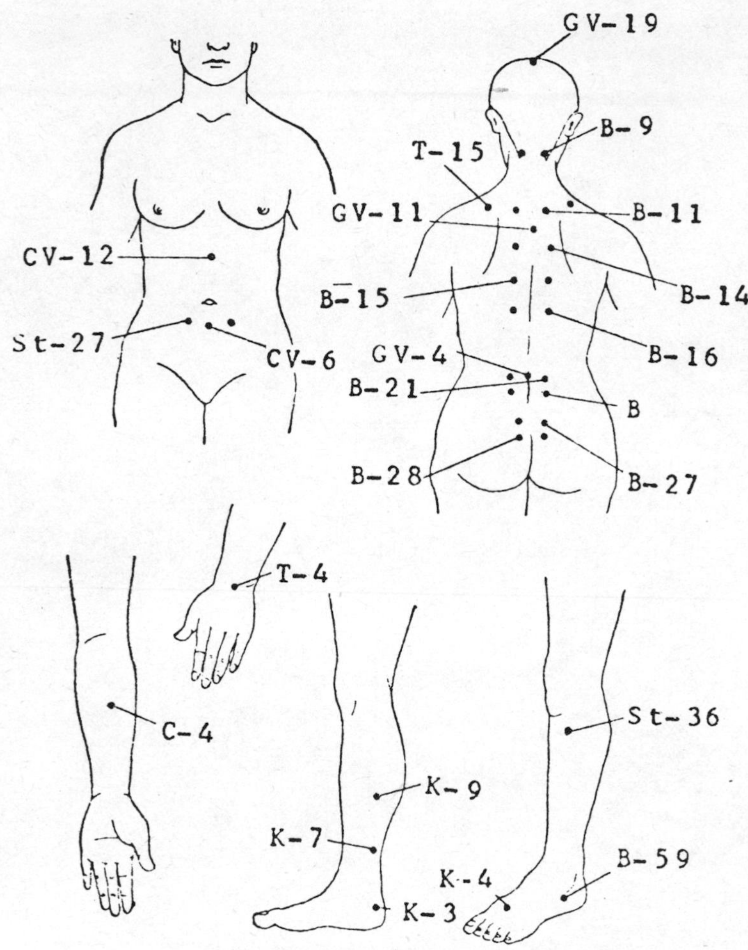

Vital points of treatment for Menopausal Disorders

(abdomen), CV–6 (abdomen), C–3 (upper limb), T–4 (upper limb) or K–7 (lower limb), Li–3 (lower limb), and B–59 (lower limb).

Moxacautery: Apply at GV–19 (head), T–15 (back), GV–11 (back), B–15 (back), B–21 (lower trunk) GV–4 (lower trunk),

B–28 (lower trunk), St–27 (abdomen), St–36 (lower limb), and K–7 (lower limb) or K–3 (lower limb).

CHAPTER XXXVI

Dermatology

Eczema

Eczema is the most frequent among all the skin diseases. It is said to be caused by various stimulations to the physical constitution. Eczema can develop in the various areas of the head, face, groin, the flexor side of the arms and legs, and elsewhere. In the beginning slight reddish blotches and papules appear and gradually form into blisters or pustules and become moist. Then scabs form and the scaly skin peels off. Finally it heals.

If the eczema becomes chronic, it tends to reappear and the skin becomes thick.

Treatment: Acupuncture and moxacautery: Apply at B–9 (neck), LI–15 (back), B–12 (back), B–18 (back), B–21 (lower trunk), CV–12 (abdomen), LI–11 (upper limb), St–36 (lower limb), and K–9 (lower limb).

Apply acupuncture and moxacautery around the affected area.

Pruritus

In this disease the patient experiences itching over the entire body day and night. It tends to develop in older persons. Fur-

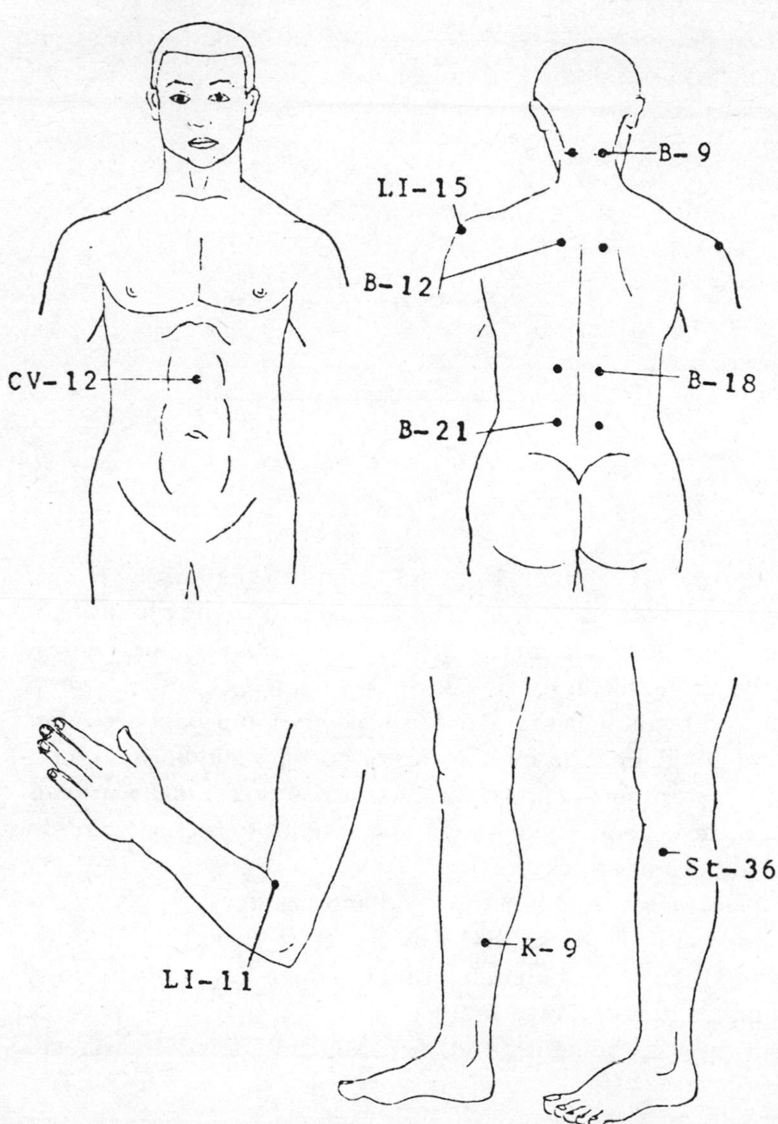

Vital points of treatment for Eczema

thermore, the climate has an important part to play in the condition of the patient. This disease may complicate tuberculosis, jaundice, diabetes, and kidney ailments. In women, this disease may be limited to the genital or anal area and be somewhat related with menstruation.

Treatment: Acupuncture: Apply at GB–21 (back), LI–15 (back), GV–11 (back), B–16 (back), B–18 (back), B–22 (lower trunk), CV–12 (abdomen), St–27 (abdomen), LI–10 (upper limb), Sp–6 (lower limb), and St–36 (lower limb).

Shingles (Herpes Zoster)

Shingles is a disorder which causes the skin to become red and form clusters of blisters about the size of a grain of millet in the area controlled by peripheral nerves. Neuralgia occurs in the area of eruption. Shingles tends to develop in the chest and abdominal areas or on the face. The blisters gradually turn turbid and become pustulous. Then they dry up, form scabs, and heal.

Treatment: For shingles which occur on the area of the chest, the same treatment is applicable here as is described in the section on intercostal neuralgia.

For shingles which occur in the face, apply acupuncture and moxacautery at GB–20 (neck), B–9 (neck), B–12 (back), GV–11 (back), and LI–11 (upper limb).

CHAPTER XXXVII

Opthalmic Diseases

Blepharitis ("Bleary Eyes")

The edge of the eyelid tends to become inflamed in scrofulous children more than others and tends to appear in combination with conjunctivitis, rhinitis, and eczema. There are various types of symptoms such as congestion of blood in the external canthus (corner of the eye), yellowish scaly scabs along the eyelid, ulcerous-looking pustules at the roots of the eyelashes, and eczema spread over the skin of the lid.

Treatment: Acupuncture and moxacautery: Apply at B–9 (neck), T–22 (face), GV–11 (back), B–11 (back), B–18 (back), and LI–11 (upper limb) or LI–4 (upper limb).

Acupuncture: Lightly apply at GB–14 (face), St–2 (face), and GB–1 (face).

Sty (Hordeolum)

Sties are a suppurative inflammation in the glands of the follicles of the eyelash. It produces hyperemia and hard lumps in the eyelid, and painful swelling. In 3 or 4 days, the sty drains of pus, but it will tend to reappear. Sometimes, it will reappear in a different part of the eyelid again and again.

Treatment: Acupuncture: Apply at GB–2 (face), and LI–4 (upper limb).

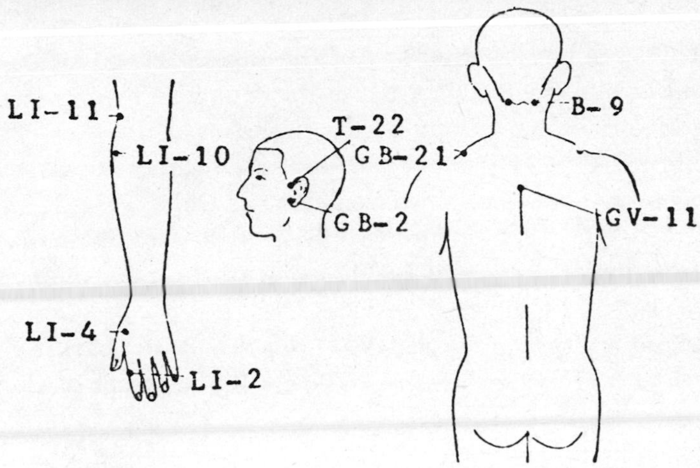

Vital points of treatment for Hardeolum

Moxacautery: Apply at B–9 (neck), T–22 (face), GB–21 (back), GV–11 (back), LI–10 (upper limb), and LI–11 (upper limb) and LI–2 (upper limb).

Blepharospasmus (Eyelid Spasms)

This is caused by spasms of the orbicularis oculi. There are two types of spasms; one is clonic with frequent blinking of the eyelid; the other is the tonic in which the eyelid remains closed for a while. This disorder can be caused by reflex action due to irritation of the eyeball and also by organic or functional nervous disorders. Other mental and emotional reactions such as hysteria may be involved.

Treatment: Acupuncture: Apply at GB–20 (neck), B–9 (neck), GB–21 (back), B–10 (back), B–2 (face), St–2 (face), GB–1 (face), GB–3 (face), T–17 (neck), and LI–11 (upper limb).

Moxacautery: Apply at GV–21 (head), B–9 (neck), T–17 (neck), and LI–11 (upper limb).

Blepharoptosis

This is caused by disorders of the muscle which raises the upper eyelid (oculomotor) and of the Mueller's Nerve (sympathetic nerve). Blepharoptosis in some cases can be congenital. Otherwise it will be brought about neurally (nerve disorder) or from myasthenia (muscular weakness) as well.

Treatment: Acupuncture: Apply at B–2 (face), St–2 (face), GB–3 (face), B–3 (face), GB–20 (neck), LI–4 (upper limb), and GV–11 (lower limb).

Moxacautery: Apply at GV–11 (back), B–10 (back), T–17 (neck), LI–11 (upper limb), Sp–6 (lower limb), and St–41 (lower limb).

Conjunctivitis

Conjunctivitis is caused by contagious bacteria or irritation due to dust, light, chemicals, and gases. Sometimes it accompa-

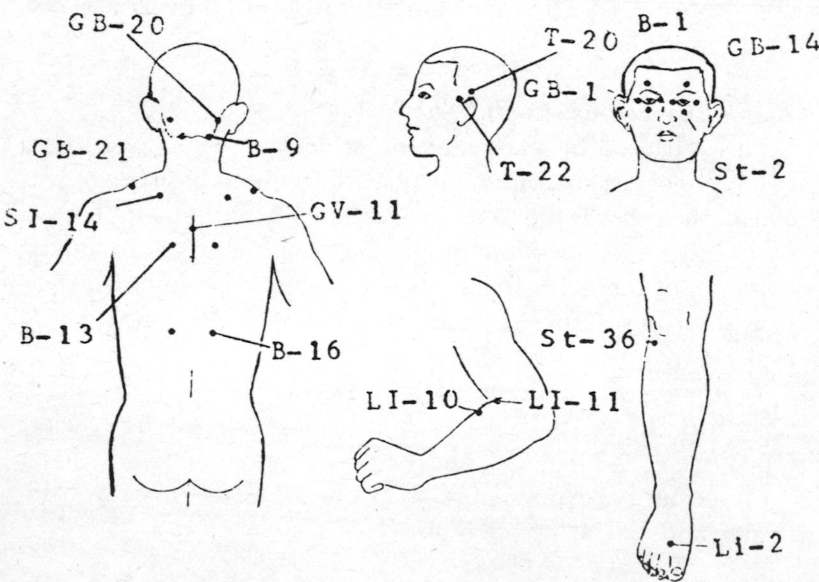

Vital points of treatment for Conjunctivitis

nies rhinitis and blepharitis. As a result some cases will be acute, semichronic, or chronic. Recognizable symptoms are irritating sensation of foreign matter in the eye, pain, and tears. The conjunctiva (back of the eyelid) is generally congested with blood and may develop swelling, edema, or hemorrhage. Furthermore, conjunctivitis tends to accompany superficial keratitis. In chronic cases the congestion is very light but there is a slight discharge in the eye.

Treatment: Acupuncture: Apply at B–1 (face), GB–1 (face), St–2 (face), T–20 (head), GB–14 (face), B–9 (neck), GB–21 (back), SI–14 (back), B–13 (back), B–16 (back), LI–10 (upper limb), LI–11 (upper limb), and Li–2 (lower limb).

Moxacautery: Apply at T–22 (face), B–9 (neck) or GB–20 (neck), GB–21 (lower trunk), GV–11 (lower trunk), B–13 (lower trunk), LI–10 (upper limb), and St–36 (lower limb).

Shallow applications of acupuncture at points around the eyes are very effective.

Vernal Conjunctivitis

This eye disease is considered to be caused by allergy. It occurs mostly in young people, becoming worse in spring and summer. It is shown to be generally accompanied by itchiness, photophobia, and tears. There are two types of vernal conjunctivitis. One type affects the eyelid; another mainly involves the eyeball. In the former case there is congestion of blood in the conjunctiva of the eyelid and slightly cloudy multi-angle projections are formed. As the number of projections increases, a stonewall pattern forms. This is mistaken for the granules of trachoma. In the latter case there are grayish or reddish projections like banks around the cornea. Relapses are frequent. This disease is difficult to cure.

Treatment: Follow the same treatment as that given in the section on conjunctivitis.

Phlyctena of the Cornea (Leucomatous Spots)

This disease is likely to occur more often in scrofulous children or to persons with exudative diathesis. Relapses are frequent. Around the edges of the cornea, small projections like blisters develop to the size of a grain of millet. Eventually they break and become ulcerous and finally heal. Many thin blood vessels are gathered around and enter the cornea. This disease is accompanied by photophobia (dazzling glare), tears, sensations of foreign matter in the eye, and discharges from the eye. This disease may develop inside of the cornea. In such cases a slight cloudiness remains in the cornea.

Treatment is the same as that described in the section on conjunctivitis.

Trachoma

Trachoma develops with the congestion of blood and cellular infiltration in the conjunctiva tissue, and forming small mamillae or granules. This disease is caused by a virus *(Chlamydozoon trachomatis)* and is contagious. The symptoms ease as the disease becomes chronic. Some symptoms are the sensations of foreign matter (irritation), dryness, discomfort, photophobia (dazzling glare), oppressiveness of the eyelid, and fatigue. There are frequent discharges from the eye.

At first the part of the conjunctiva adjacent to the eyelid (the back of the eyelid) turns red and turbid, and granules or mamillae develop inside. Eventually, the area heals and leaves white, smooth cicatrices. However, when the eyes are tired, the condition may be immediately worsened.

Then, in the upper region of the cornea a cloudy curtain forms which obstructs the vision. The thin blood vessels gather and enter the cornea. This is called trachoma pannus. The cornea is injured and the irritation becomes severe. This disease is likely to accompany various other diseases of the eyelid or in the lachrymal glands.

Treatment: Acupuncture and moxacautery: Apply at B–11

(back) or GV–15 (head), B–9 (neck), T–22 (face), GB–21 (back), B–16 (back), B–18 (back), CV–12 (abdomen), LI–11 (upper limb), LI–4 (upper limb), St–36 (lower limb), and Sp–6 (lower limb).

Keratosis of the Cornea ("Dry Eye")

This disease occurs in children who are fed artificial nutrition; therefore, the main cause is thought to be vitamin A deficiency. When babies are affected by this disease, the first symptom is dryness of the cornea. The conjunctiva (mucous membrane covering the anterior part of the eye) and the cornea lose their brightness; the cornea becomes dry and gradually turns turbid. Then the cornea softens and turns ulcerous in the central region; finally, a hole develops and the iris prolapses. In most cases the patients develop night-blindness.

Treatment: Acupuncture: Apply at GB–1 (face), B–1 (face), GB–14 (face), B–9 (neck), and LI–11 (upper limb). In addition, apply acupuncture of the skin (lightly) around the eyes and at the shoulders.

Moxacautery: Apply at T–22 (face), B–9 (neck), B–11 (back), GV–11 (back), B–12 (back), B–16 (back), LI–4 (upper limb), and St–36 (lower limb).

Keratitis Parenchymatosa

This is caused most frequently by syphilis (especially congenital syphilis); also, rarely, by tuberculosis. The parenchyma of the cornea is affected and the surface loses its brightness and turns opaque like frosted glass. The opacity starts in the area around the edges or from the center and gradually spreads out over the entire area. When the eye recovers, the opacity is gradually absorbed from the periphery. Generally it will take two months for recovery. In many instances the patient will be left with slightly obstructed eyesight. Usually, congestion of blood appears around the edges of the cornea accompanied by photophobia, tears, and sometimes pain.

Treatment: Acupuncture: Apply at B–2 (face), GB–14 (face), T–23 (face), GB–20 (neck), B–9 (neck), GB–21 (back), T–15 (back), B–12 (back), B–16 (back), and St–36 (lower limb).

Moxacautery: Apply at T–22 (face), GB–20 (neck), B–9 (neck), GV–11 (back), B–16 (back), CV–12 (abdomen), St–27 (abdomen), LI–11 (upper limb), LI–4 (upper limb), K–9 (lower limb), and St–36 (lower limb).

Also apply acupuncture around the eyes.

Dacryostenosis

This is a disease in which the duct (nasolacrimal duct) which opens to the inferior nasal meatus from the lower end of the lacrimal sac, is clogged or constricted. Tears flow freely, especially in a cold wind. It may be caused by such disorders as trachoma, rhinitis, or chronic dacryocystitis. Usually, the "bougie" method is attempted to expand the duct.

Treatment: Acupuncture: Apply at B–1 (face), GB–1 (face), St–3 (face), B–9 (neck), GB–20 (neck), GB–21 (back), B–11 (back), LI–11 (upper limb), and LI–4 (upper limb).

Moxacautery: Apply at GB–7 (head) or T–22 (face), GV–22 (head), B–9 (neck), St–14 (back), B–12 (back), GV–11 (back), B–21 (lower trunk), LI–11 (upper arm), and St–36 (lower limb).

Iritis

This disease causes inflammation of the dark brown region (iris) in the cornea, which enlarges or closes the pupil. In the beginning, the patient suffers obstructed vision, photophobia, and tears. In serious cases, there will be pain in the eyes and headache. Blood is congested around the cornea. The iris swells and changes color and the pupil shrinks. Deposits form in the back of the cornea and pus collects at the bottom. When the inflammation of the ciliary body is combined with iritis, the patient will generally lose his eyesight. The causes of this disease are thought to originate in syphilis, tuberculosis, rheumatism, and other general diseases of the body. This is because the internal body bacteria adhere to the blood vessels of the iris.

Treatment: Acupuncture: Apply at B–1 (face), GB–3 (face), GB–16 (head), or GB–17 (head), GB–20 (neck), B–9 (neck), B–12 (back), B–16 (back), CV–12 (abdomen), St–27 (lower limb), LI–11 (lower limb), and GB–33 (lower limb).

Cataracts

The human eye sees through a lens which corresponds to the lens of a camera. Cataracts cause vision to be obscured due to the opacity of the lens.

At the beginning, its symptoms are: images in the eye (like seeing small insects flying before the face), polyopia (multi-vision), night blindness or day blindness (poor vision due to strong light). Gradually the patient will lose his sight.

Cataracts can be of congenital nature, due to an external wound, and of a secondary nature, due to other diseases of the eye. In most cases, however, cataracts result from the aging process as in senile cataracts, or also result symptomatically from diabetes, such as diabetic cataract.

Treatment by acupuncture and moxacautery is only applicable in the last two cases. Even these types of cataracts are only treatable at the early stages and before the disease has advanced too far and visional interference has not occurred to a great degree.

Treatment: Acupuncture: Apply at B–1 (face), GB–14, (face), GB–1 (face), GB–19 (head), GB–20 (neck), B–9 (neck), B–10 (back), B–16 (back), LI–10 (upper limb), and GB–33 (lower limb) or St–6 (lower limb).

Moxacautery: Apply at T–22 (face), B–9 (neck), T–15 (back), B–16 (back), B–21 (lower trunk), CV–12 (abdomen), Li–13 (abdomen), LI–11 (upper limb), LI–4 (upper limb), St–36 (lower limb), and K–3 (lower limb).

Glaucoma

This disease is caused by increase in the contents of the eyeball which in turn increases pressure in the eyeball. The pupils are enlarged and appear bluish. Hence it is sometimes called "blue cataracts." The real cause of the increase is unknown; however, glaucoma will sometimes develop as a consequence of other eye diseases.

In the case of acute glaucoma, the eye will suddenly become painful; the head will ache on one side as in migraine; vomiting follows. The patient loses almost all his vision. The conjunctiva of the eye becomes congested with blood and frequently will swell. This occurs mostly to aged people. It can be accompanied by prodromes (headache, heavy-headedness, and rainbow vision). As the seizures recur, the disease gradually progresses.

Glaucoma can strike young people as well, but more gradually.

There is a type called simple glaucoma in which vision is slowly obstructed, the visual field becomes narrow. There is no

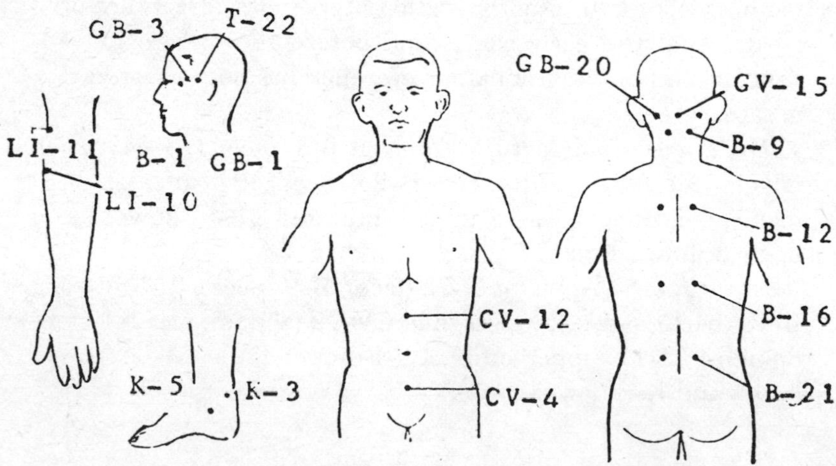

Vital points of treatment for Glaucoma

outward visible change in the region of the eyes; the pressure in the eye simply increases and is noticed.

Treatment: Acupuncture: Apply at GB–20 (neck), B–9 (neck), GB–3 (face), B–1 (face), and GB–1 (face).

Moxacautery: Apply at T–22 (neck), GV–15 (neck), GB–20 (neck), B–9 (neck), B–12 (neck), B–16 (back), K–21 (lower trunk), CV–12 (abdomen), CV–4 (abdomen), LI–11 (upper limb) or LI–10 (upper limb), and K–3 (lower limb) or K–5 (lower limb).

Central Retinitis

This disease is considered caused by syphilis, tuberculosis, and eye irritation from strong light. Frequently it will affect only one of the eyes. The external region of the eye indicates no changes, but vision is abstructed. This obstruction accompanies an apparent dark spot at the visional center and abnormal and apparent distortion of the size and shape of objects.

In many instances, the vision may be saved, but relapses will be frequent.

Treatment: Acupuncture: Apply at B–1 (face), GB–14 (face),

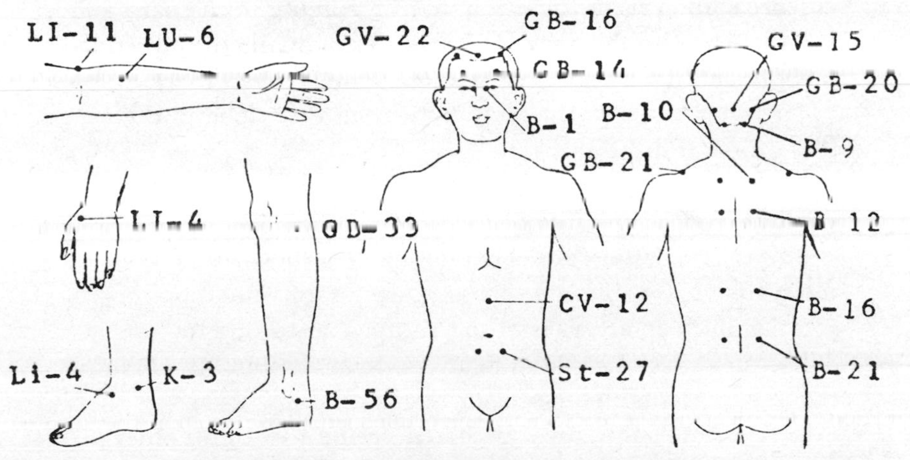

Vital points of treatment for Central Retinitis

GB–20 (neck), B–9 (neck), GB–21 (back), B–10 (back), B–12 (back), LI–11 (upper limb), Lu–6 (upper limb), B–56 (lower limb), and Li–4 (lower limb).

Moxacautery: Apply at GB–16 (head), or GV–22 (head), GV–15 (head), B–9 (neck), B–16 (back), B–21 (lower trunk), CV–12 (abdomen), St–27 (abdomen), LI–11 (upper limb) or LI–4 (upper limb), GB–33 (lower limb), and K–3 (lower limb).

Chronic Inflammation of the Optic Nerve Axis

In the past this disease was thought to be a type of amblyopia associated with beriberi, vitamin B_1 deficiency. Now, however, it is considered as an independent disease. It occurs more frequently in young persons rather than adults. It gradually obstructs the vision of both eyes and develops symptoms of neurasthenia.

In addition to such symptoms involving the eye as the apparent dark spot at the visional center, day-blindness (the vision weakens under strong light), and photophobia, the patient also complains of its affects over the whole body, such as headache, heavy-headedness, lack of concentration, emotional instability, dizziness upon rising, lack of appetite, ringing in the ears, and dry mouth. Also this may further be accompanied by pseudomyopia and disturbances of seeing capacity.

Treatment: Follow the same treatment described in the section on central retinitis.

Hemorrhage of the Eye Ground

This is a recurring retinal hemorrhage of the vitreous body at the retina. It is considered to be multiple inflammations of the arterial and venous walls of the retina due to tuberculosis.

Treatment is effective in many cases in stopping the hemorrhage or for complete recovery.

Treatment is the same as that described in the section for central retinitis.

Sclerosis of the Retinal Blood Vessels

It is necessary to treat the entire body for this disease, since the causes tend to stem from high blood pressure and arteriosclerosis.

For treatment, refer to the section on high blood pressure and arteriosclerosis.

Nephritis-Induced Retinitis

For treatment of this disease, follow the treatment described in the section on nephritis and atrophy of the kidney.

Diabetic Retinitis

For treatment of this disease, follow the treatment described in the section on diabetes.

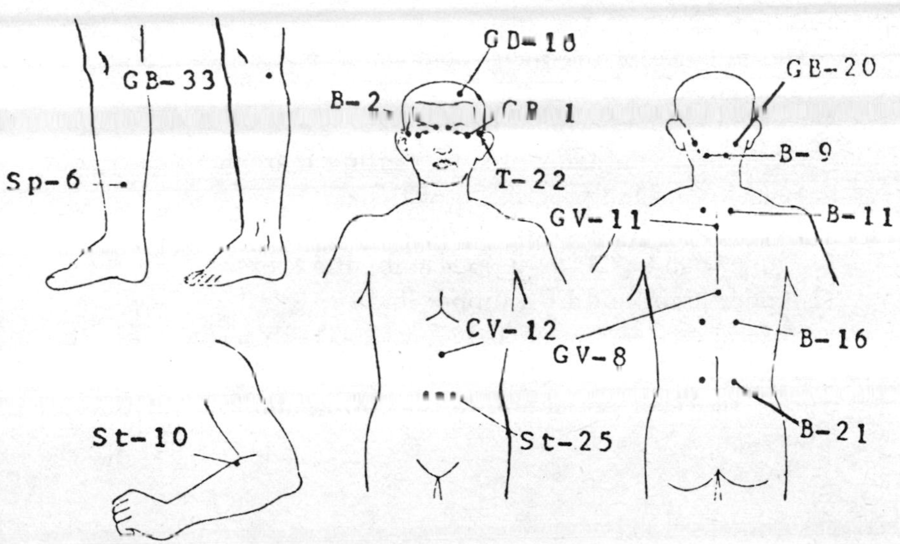

Vital points of treatment for Asthenopia

Asthenopia

After reading or precise or close work, the eyes usually become tired and vision blurs and produces pain in the eyes, headache, and general imbalance of the entire body. These symptoms occur due to maladjustment, dyplopia, and bad eyeglasses; additionally, it accompanies neurasthenia and hysteria. Sometimes these symptoms appear in the presence of other eye diseases.

Treatment: Acupuncture: Apply at B–2 (face), GB–1 (face), GB–16 (head), GB–20 (neck), B–9 (neck), B–11 (back), B–12 (back), LI–10 (upper limb), GB–33 (lower limb), and Sp–6 (lower limb).

Moxacautery: T–22 (face), GB–16 (head), B–9 (neck), GV–11 (back), GV–8 (back), B–16 (back), B–21 (lower trunk), CV–12 (abdomen), St–25 (abdomen), and GB–33 (lower limb).

Presbyopia

The distance of the focus point may be increased due to diminishing elasticity of the lens, causing farsightedness. The farsighted person becomes fatigued at close work. This condition is a part of the aging process, starting at around the age of forty-five years and progressing with age.

Treatment: Acupuncture: Apply at B–2 (face), GB–20 (neck), B–9 (upper limb), GB–21 (upper limb), B–12 (upper limb), LI–11 (upper limb), and LI–4 (upper limb).

Moxacautery: Apply at T–12 (face), GV–15 (head), GB–20 (neck), GB–21 (back), GV–11 (back), B–16 (back), B–21 (lower trunk), LI–11 (upper limb), St–36 (lower limb), and GB–35 (lower limb).

CHAPTER XXXVIII

Ear, Nose and Throat, and Dental Divisions

External Otitis

This is a disease in which the canal (external auditory canal) becomes inflamed and develops swelling and pus. External wounds and foreign matter provoke this disease, and thus, cause bacteria to be transmitted to the sebaceous glands and the cerumen glands and cause infection.

In the beginning the pain is severe, and the more the patient pulls the ear, the more the pain will increase. Redness and swelling develop all the way to the opening of the ear. Also, the swelling can spread to the eyelids, cheeks, or jaw. The formation of a large boil may disturb the patient's hearing, but once the pus is drained, the pain will disappear and the patient will recover.

Treatment: Acupuncture: Apply at GB–12 (head), T–17 (neck), SI–16 (neck), T–21 (face) or SI–19 (face), LI–11 (upper limb), and LI–4 (upper limb).

Moxacautery: Apply repeated applications of moxacauter at T–17 (neck), LI–11 (upper limb), and LI–4 (upper limb).

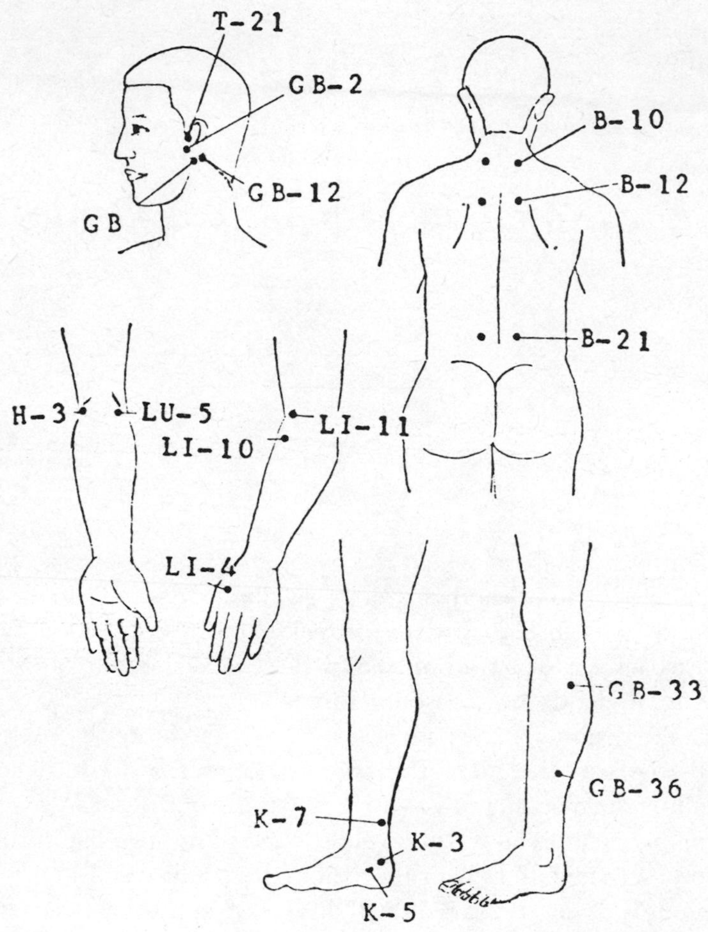

Vital points of treatment for Otitis Media

Otitis Media

This disease, in acute cases, often appears following an acute infectious disease or an acute infection in the nose or throat. The patient complains of internal ear pain, ringing in the ears and difficulty in hearing. This may also be accompanied by high fever, headache, and loss of appetite as well. The tympanic membrane turns red and swollen. The pain will be relieved if a hole is incised in the tympanic membrane and the pus drained. Acute mastoiditis is liable to accompany this disease. In addition, it can easily become chronic with pus running continuously from the protuberance of the tympanic membrane.

Treatment: Acupuncture: Apply at T–21 (face), GB–2 (face), GB–12 (head), T–17 (neck), B–10 (back), B–12 (back), B–21 (lower trunk), LI–11 (upper limb), Lu–5 (upper limb), LI–4 (upper limb), GB–33 (lower limb) or GB–36 (lower limb), and K–7 (lower limb).

Moxacautery: Apply at T–17 (neck), LI–10 (upper limb) or SI–8 (upper limb), LI–4 (upper limb), K–3 (lower limb) or K–5 (lower limb).

Earache

The cause, in most cases of spontaneous earache, stems from diseases in the hearing organ itself or from obstructions in the canals of nearby structures. For most severe earaches, the causes stem from furuncle of the ear, or acute suppurative otitis media.

Treatment. Acupuncture: Apply at T–17 (neck), T–21 (face), and GB–11 (head).

Moxacautery: Apply at T–17 (neck), SI–8 (upper limb), T–9 (upper limb), an K–3 (lower limb).

Occlusion of the Eustachian Tube

The nasopharyngeal cavity and the cavity of the middle ear are connected by the eustachian tube which adjusts the flow of air in the middle ear cavity. This disorder occurs when the eustachian tube is occluded and will tend to develop in conjunction with otitis media and accompanies rhinitis, pharyngitis, and diseases of the adenoids and paranasal sinuses.

The patient complains of such symptoms as the sensation of clogged ears, ringing in the ears, and difficulties in hearing.

Treatment: Acupuncture: Apply at GB–12 (head), T–17 (neck), SI–16 (neck), B–2 (face), LI–11 (upper limb), and Lu–5 (upper limb).

Moxacautery: Apply at GB–12 (head), GV–21 (head), B–11 (back), GV–11 (back), SI–8 (upper limb), LI–4 (upper limb), and K–5 (lower limb).

Tinnitus Aurium (Ringing in the Ear)

This symptom occurs when the auditory nerves are excited. Sometimes it will occur because the nerves perceive arterial noises around the ear. It can also occur from such causes as foreign matter in the external auditory canal, otitis media, auricular indurations, internal otitis, inflammation of the auditory nerve. Furthermore, it often accompanies such diseases as arteriosclerosis, cardiac diseases, gastrointestinal diseases, dire neurosis, and menopause. It is apt to be accompanied with dizziness.

Treatment: Acupuncture: Apply at GB–12 (head), T–21 (face) or SI–19 (face), GB–11 (lower limb). Furthermore, apply shallow acupuncture at the stiff regions of the neck, shoulders and back.

Moxacautery: GB–12 (head) or T–17 (neck), GB–20 (neck), B–21 (lower trunk), SI–8 (upper limb), K–3 (lower limb).

Acute Rhinitis

This is a disease in which the nasal membrane is congested with blood and swollen. Nasal mucus becomes watery and increased and nasal occlusion occurs. The patient sneezes and his voice becomes nasal. Eventually, the nasal mucus becomes thick and puslike. The patient tends to suffer headache and fever. This symptom is likely to occur at the early stages of a cold.

Treatment: Acupuncture: Apply at B–9 (neck), GB–20 (neck), St–19 (face), SI–8 (upper limb), and K–3 (lower limb).

Moxacautery: Apply at GV–21 (head) or GV–22 (head), GB–15 (head), B–11 (back), GV–11 (back), LI–10 (upper limb), LI–4 (upper limb), and St–36 (lower limb).

For excessive nasal mucus accompanied by decrease in the sense of smell, apply shallow acupuncture at LI–20 (face).

Chronic Rhinitis

This disease in most cases develops following the stage of acute rhinitis. This is always accompanied by nasal occlusion. Nasal discharge is either thick or puslike in nature. In one type of rhinitis (incrassational) the nasal mucous membrane thickens; and in the other type (simple), the blood vessels of mucous membrane become congested.

Treatment: Acupuncture: Apply at B–9 (neck), GB–20 (neck), B–2 (face), LI–20 (face), B–12 (back), LI–11 (upper limb), Lu–6 (upper limb), St–36 (lower limb), and Sp–6 (lower limb).

Moxacautery: Apply at B–9 (neck), GV–22 (head), GV–11 (back), B–11 (back), LI–11 (upper limb), and LI–4 (upper limb).

Sinusitis (Inflammation of the Accessory Nasal Sinuses)

Sinusitis is a disease in which pus accumulates in the sinuses of the bones around the nasal cavity (accessory nasal cavities). Most frequently, pus accumulates in the Sinus maxillaris and in the Sinus frontalis. Colds and rhinitis cause sinusitis. A large amount of yellowish puslike nasal mucus is discharged from the nasal cavity. The patient suffers nasal occlusion and headaches, and decrease in his powers of memory and concentration.

In general, this disease is likely to become chronic and is difficult to cure. However, treatment by acupuncture and moxacautery sometimes brings considerable relief.

Treatment: Acupuncture: Apply at B–9 (neck), GB–20 (neck), LI–20 (face), B–2 (face), SI–19 (face), GB–21 (back), B–12 (back), LI–11 (upper limb), Lu–5 (upper limb), and Sp–8 (lower limb).

Moxacautery: Apply at GV–22 (head), CV–21 (head) or GV–19 (head), GV–15 (head), B–9 (neck), GV–11 (back), B–11 (back) or B–12 (back), LI–11 (upper limb) or LI–10 (upper limb), SI–8 (upper limb), and St–36 (lower limb).

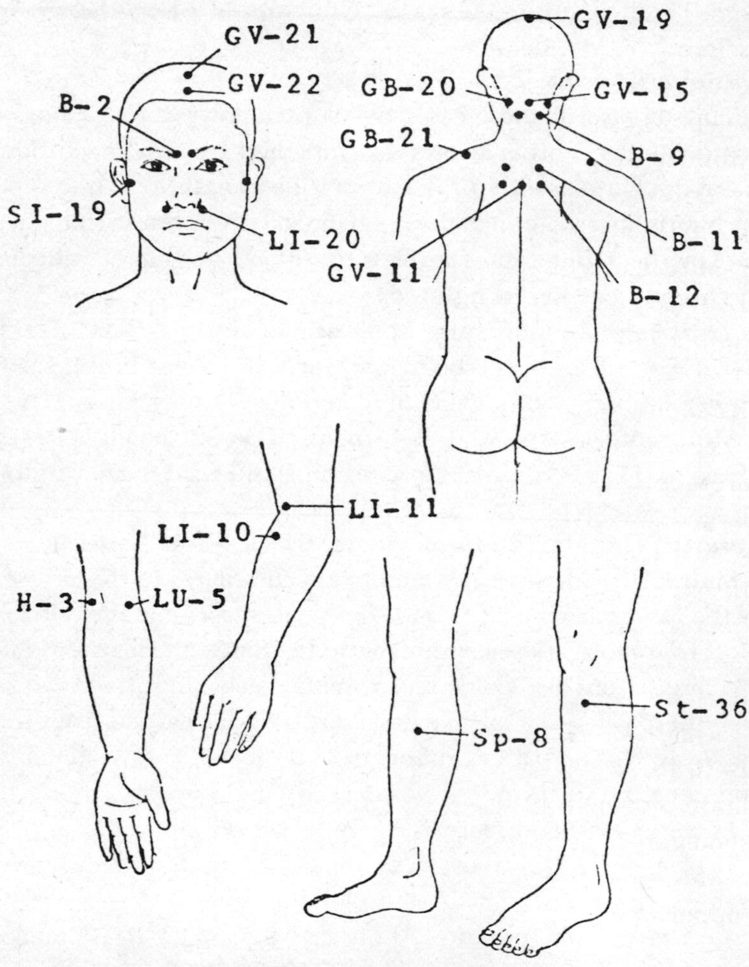

Vital points of treatment for Inflammation of the accessory nasal sinuses

Epistaxis (Nosebleed)

Epistaxis occurs when the blood vessels in the front region of the nasal septum are ruptured. Rupture can be caused by sneezing, flushing, inflammations and also by external wounds, etc. This happens more often to persons suffering from arteriosclerosis, cardiac ailments, and anemia. Also, it can be the direct cause of such disorders as nasal mucous membrane and of nasal polypus. It may also occur as compensatory bleeding in women.

Treatment: Acupuncture: Apply at GV–21 (head), B–9 (neck), B–12 (back), and Lu–6 (upper limb).

Moxacautery: Apply at GV–15 (head) or GV–22 (head), GV–13 (back) or GV–11 (Back), and LI–11 (upper limb) or LI–10 (upper limb).

Adenoids (Enlarged Glands)

This occurs when the pharyngeal tonsils located behind the area between the nasal cavity and the pharynx become enlarged. It will occur mostly to scrofulous children of elementary school age. Because of nasal blockage, the patient breathes through his mouth, snores, his sleep is uneven, and he frequently wakes up. Some patients even wet their beds. Patients generally decrease in their powers of memory and concentration. A student's grades will go down.

Treatment: Acupuncture: Apply at T–17 (neck), LI–18 (neck), B–10 (back), B–12 (back), LI–11 (upper limb) or LI–4 (upper limb); also apply shallow acupuncture in the region of the neck, shoulders, and back.

Moxacautery: Apply at GV–11 (back), B–11 (back), and LI–11 (upper limb) or Lu–6 (upper limb).

Pharyngitis and Laryngitis

Acute pharyngitis occurs due to exposure to the cold, irritating gases, and other direct irritations of the pharynx. The patient feels dryness, fever, irritability, and experiences sensations of foreign matter and itching accompanied by pain in the region of the pharynx. The pain increases whenever the patient

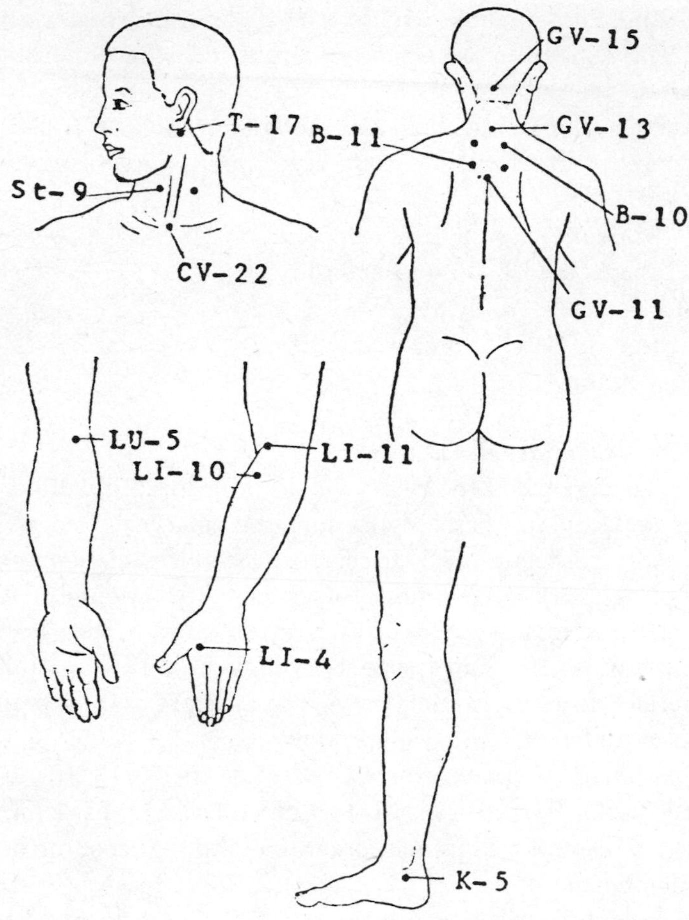

Vital points of treatment for Pharyngitis and Laryngitis

tries to swallow. The mucous membrane of the pharynx is congested with blood and becomes red throughout. Pharyngitis can easily become chronic and also be easily complicated with laryngitis. If a person is suffering from a chronic nasal ailment, acute pharyngitis will become chronic and the mucus on the mucous membrane increases. The patient must clear his throat frequently. Sometimes, granules form on the mucous membrane.

Treatment: Acupuncture: Apply at T–17 (neck), St–9 (neck), CV–22 (neck), GV–13 (back), B–11 (back), LI–10 (upper limb), and Lu–5 (upper limb).

Moxacautery: Apply at B–10 (back), GV–11 (back) GV–15 (head), LI–4 (upper limb), Lu–5 (upper limb), and K–5 (lower limb).

Acute Tonsillitis

This is a disease in which the tonsils (glands) swell due to bacterial infection. In many cases, it is usually caused by a cold. It usually occurs in scrofulous children. In the beginning there is pain in the pharynx and swallowing becomes painful. There is a sensation of dryness. The tonsils turn red and swell with pus-filled spots sometimes appearing. The patient sustains a fever and complains of fatigue throughout the entire body and of pain in the joints, lumbago, etc. The lymphatic glands of the mandibular region swell.

Treatment: Treatment for this disease may follow that described in the section on pharyngitis; however, it is important to pay special attention to the following treatment points.

Acupuncture: Apply at T–17 (neck) and SI–17 (neck).

Moxacautery: Apply at GV–11 (back), B–10 (back), and Lu–5 (upper limb).

Hypertrophy of the Tonsils

This ailment happens often in scrofulous children. The tonsils of the palate (glands) become enlarged and thus easily cause repeated tonsillitis. In many cases, there are complications with the adenoids. Generally, the patient is liable to snore and to catch cold easily.

Treatment: Acupuncture: Apply at T–17 (neck) and SI–17 (neck).

Moxacautery: Apply at GV–11 (back), B–10 (back), and Lu–5 (upper limb).

Toothache

If a disease originates in a tooth or in its surrounding tissues, an idiopathic toothache develops. In addition, rheumatism, pyrexia, menstruation, pregnancy, menopause, anemia, heart disease, hysteria, and neurasthenia can be very well complicated by toothache. Further, furuncles of the ear and otitis media can cause a radiating toothache. In addition, it can develop into neuralgic fit (trigeminal neuralgia of the teeth).

Through treatment by acupuncture and moxacautery toothaches may be temporarily relieved or completely cured.

Treatment: For toothache in the upper jaw, apply acupuncture at St–7 (face), St–3 (face), and St–44 (lower limb); moxacautery at B–13 (back) and St–44 (lower limb).

For toothache of the lower jaw, apply acupuncture at St–6

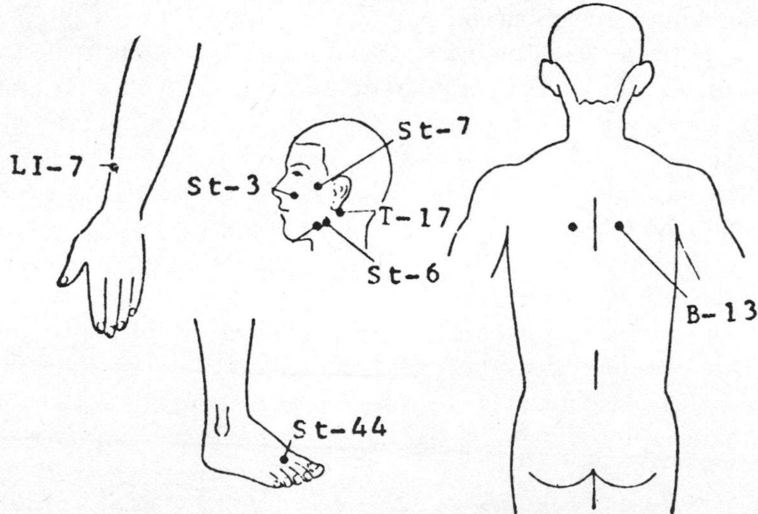

Vital points of treatment for Toothache

(face), St–5 (face), and T–17 (neck); moxacautery at T–17 (neck) and LI–7 (upper limb).

Treatment for the entire body: Apply acupuncture and moxacautery at GB–20 (neck), GB–21 (back), B–12 (back), LI–11 (upper limb), and St–36 (lower limb).

Alveolar Pyorrhea

In this disease pus issues from the gums and the alveolus around a tooth. The gum swells, turns purplish red and bleeds easily. Also, since the gum and the alveolar bone are destroyed, the teeth become loose. This disease is said to be caused by irritation from tartar on the teeth. However, overconsumption of animal products and chronic illness of the entire body are likely to provoke this disease.

Treatment: The following treatments of the whole body should be concurrently applied in addition to the symptomatic treatments referred to in the section on toothache.

Acupuncture and moxacautery: Apply at B–18 (back), B–21 (lower trunk), CV–12 (abdomen), B–9 (neck), Sp–8 (lower limb) and K–3 (lower limb).

CHAPTER XXXIX

Explanation of the 14 Meridians

1. ***The Lung Meridian (Yin Maximum)*** **(Abbreviations: Lu = Lung)**

The Lung Meridian originates at a location near the stomach, circles around the large intestines, turns up and joins the lungs. It further passes through the trachea and larynx; then, divides into two branches, one to the right and one to the left; and each branch passes through the respective armpits and from there through the outside of the anterior part of the arms and ends at the tip of the thumbs.

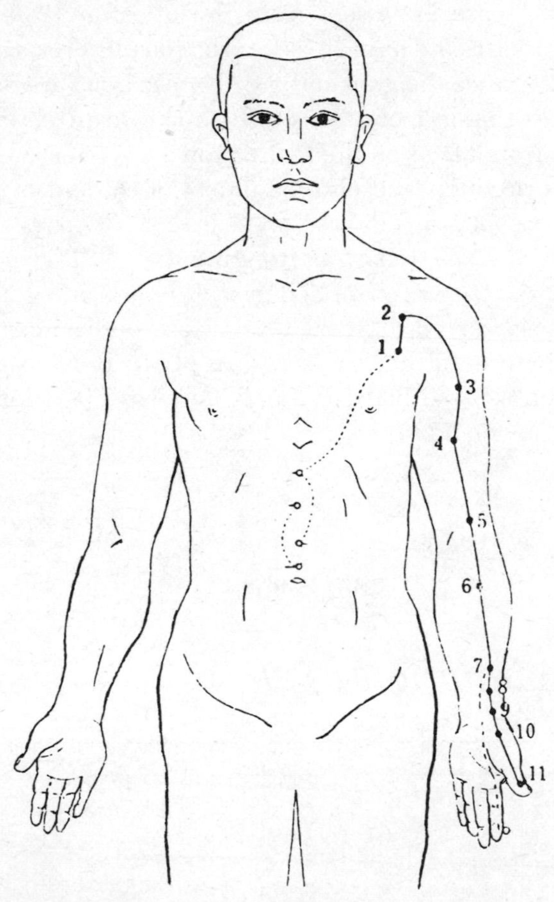

Lung Meridian
Lu–1 to Lu–11

2. *Large Intestine Meridian (Yang in Equilibrium)*

One branch of the Lung Meridian ends at the tip of the forefinger. At this point the Large Intestine Meridian originates and moves through the outside of the posterior surface of the arm and then extends through the shoulder to the back of the neck. It then enters the supraclavicular fossa. Here, the meridian branches out in two directions; one branch enters the lower teeth by way of the cheeks and exits again near the nostrils. The other branch enters the chest, coils around the lungs, passes through the diaphragm and ends at the large intestine.

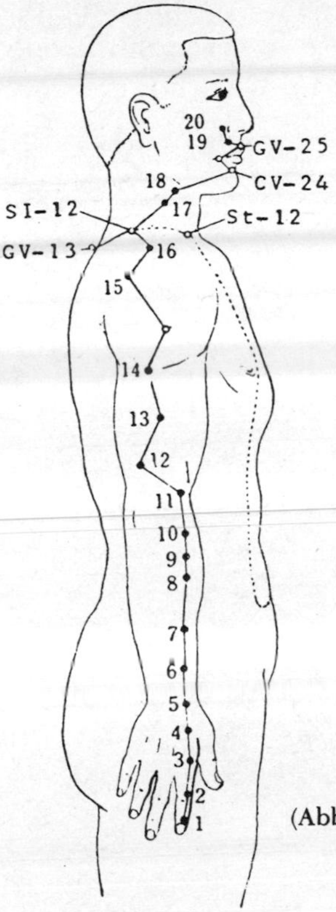

(Abbrev.: LI=Large Intestine)

Large Intestine Meridian
LI-1 to LI-20

3. *The Stomach Meridian (Yang in Equilibrium) of the Leg*

This meridian continues off the branch of the Large Intestine Meridian. The Stomach Meridian originates at the bridge of the nose, enters the upper teeth, circles the lips, and then extends behind the lower jaw. At this point it divides and one branch advances toward the forehead; another branch enters the supraclavicular fossa after following along the carotid artery and circling the larynx region. It passes the diaphragm, returns to the stomach and coils around the spleen. Yet another branch extends downward through the nipples, passing beside the navel; then moves down through the outside of the front surface of the legs and ends at the second toe of the foot.

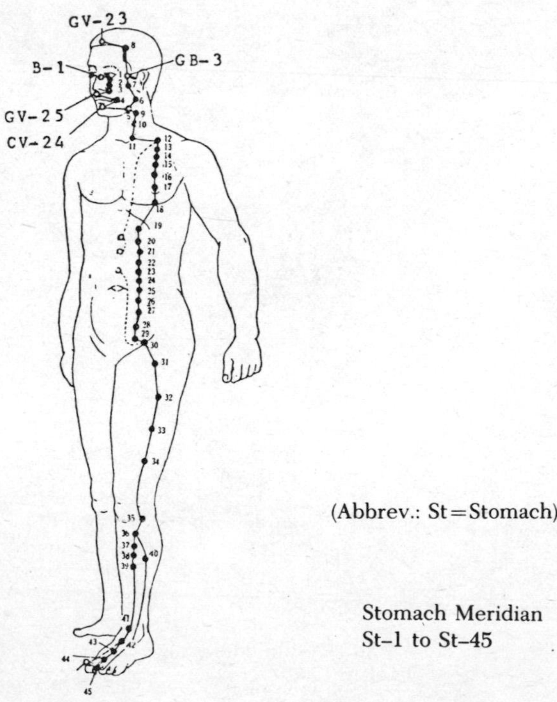

(Abbrev.: St=Stomach)

Stomach Meridian
St-1 to St-45

4. *The Spleen Meridian (Yin Maximum) of the Legs* (Abbrev: Sp = Spleen)

Succeeding the Stomach Meridian, the Spleen Meridian starts from the tip of the big toe, moves up the inner side of the front surface of the legs, enters the region of the abdomen, joins the spleen, and encircles the stomach. It further passes through the diaphragm, the pharynx, and reaches the tongue. A branch separates from the stomach area and extends to the region of the heart.

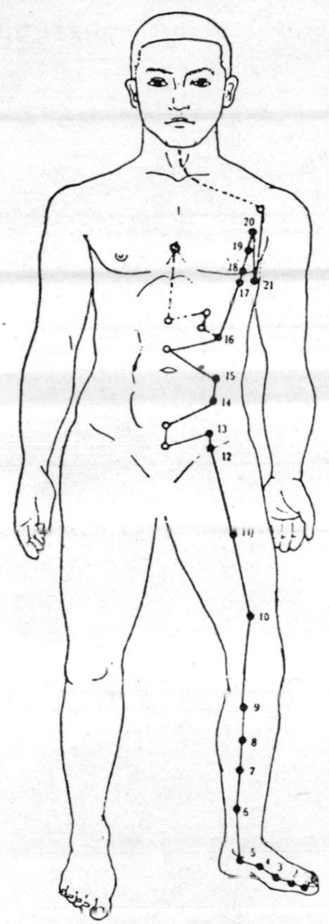

Spleen Meridian
Sp–1 to Sp–21

5. *The Heart Meridian (Yin Minimum) of the Arms* (Abbrev.: H = Heart)

The Heart Meridian starts from the Spleen Meridian in the region of the heart. It reaches the vicinity of the aorta and further extends down the abdomen and twines around the small intestine. One of its branches ascends from the vicinity of the aorta, passes through the pharynx, and reaches the deep region of the eyeball. Another branch moves up to the lung, passes through the armpit, the inner anterior surface of the arms and ends at the tip of the little finger (near the ring finger).

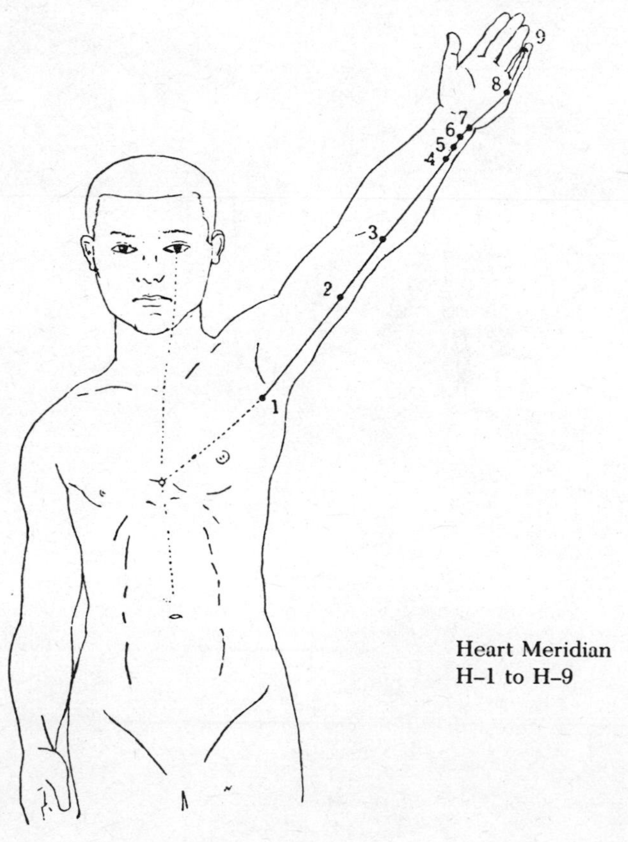

Heart Meridian
H-1 to H-9

6. *The Small Intestine Meridian (Yang Maximum) of the Arms*

The Small Intestine Meridian continues on from a branch of the Heart Meridian originating from the tip (outside) of the little finger, goes through the outside of the posterior surface of the arm to the shoulders. At this point, one branch descends to the front and enters the chest by way of the supraclavicular fossa. It then encircles the heart and extends toward the pharynx. It then descends through the diaphragm toward the stomach and joins the small intestines. Another branch moves up from the supraclavicular fossa to the cheek and advances from the outer edge of the eye to the inside of the ear. Yet another branch advances from the cheek to the lower eye region and then to the inner edge of the eye.

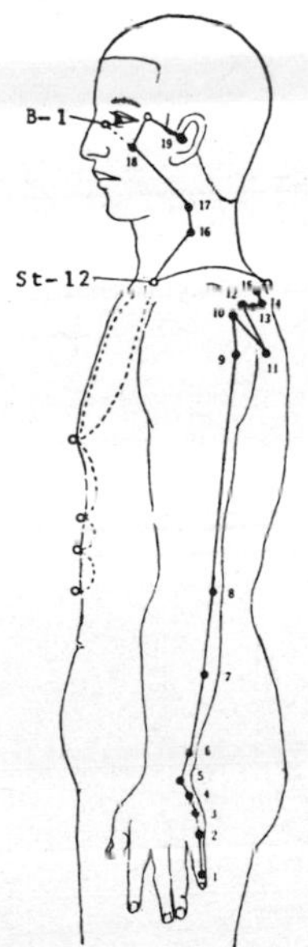

(Abbrev.: SI=Small Intestine)

Small Intestine
SI-1 to SI-10

7. *The Bladder Meridian (Yang Maximum) of the Legs* (Abbrev.: B = Bladder)

This Meridian follows from a branch of the Small Intestine Meridian starting from the eye, and extends up to the region of the head. (It enters from the top of the head and twines about the brain.) After circling the top of the head, it descends to the back of the neck and the back (on either side of the spine). It goes through the lumbar muscles, encircles the kidneys and joins at the bladder. Aside from this, another branch runs along the extreme outer edges of the spine and joins another branch which goes through from the lower back to the buttocks and then passes through the center of the back of the legs, ending at the outer edge of the little toe.

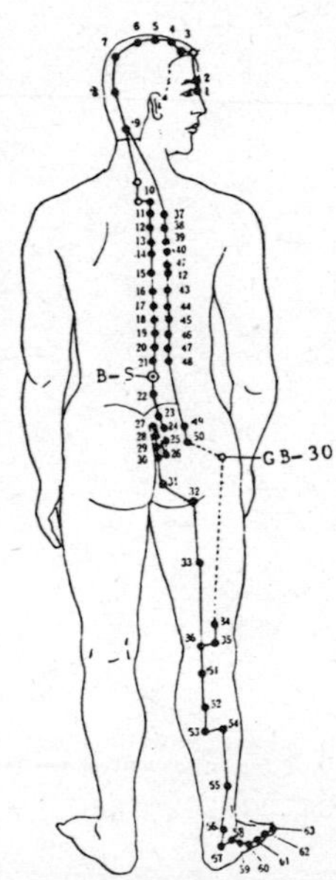

Bladder Meridian
B–1 to B–63

8. *The Kidney Meridian (Yin Minimum) of the Legs* (Abbrev.: K = Kidney)

This Meridian begins following the branch of the Bladder Meridian and originating from underneath the little toe. It goes through the bottom of the foot, then, moves up along the inside region of the leg, goes through the center of the back and joins the kidneys. It also encircles the bladder. One branch starts from the kidneys and passes through the liver and the diaphragm; it enters the lungs, passes the trachea, larynx, the base of the tongue. The other branch starts from the lungs, circles the heart and runs inside of the chest.

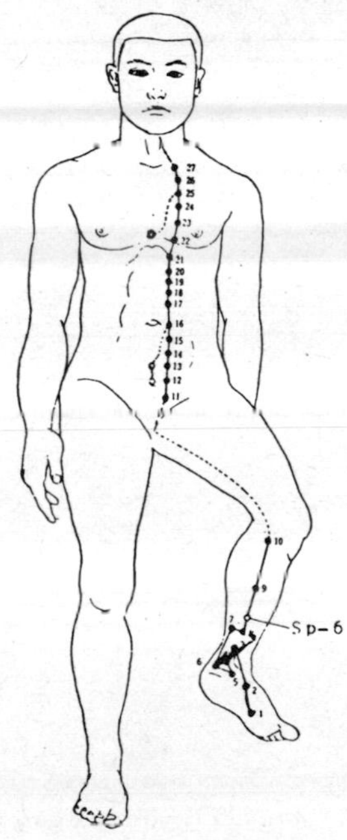

Kidney Meridian
K–1 to K–27

9. *The Circulation Meridian (Yin in Equilibrium) of the Arms*

This Meridian begins at the branch of the Kidney Meridian, starting inside of the chest and joins the pericardium. Then, it descends the diaphragm, enters inside the abdomen and circles the three warmers, one after the other. Furthermore, a branch starts from the center of the chest, extends to the side of the chest, passes through the center of the anterior surface of the arms, and ends at the tip of the middle finger.

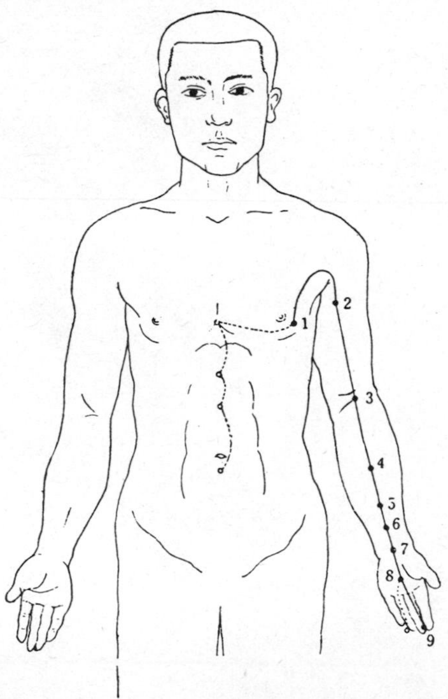

(Abbrev.: C=Circulation)

Circulation
Meridian
C–1 to C–9

10. ***The Triple Warmer Meridian (Yang Minimum) of the Hand***

This Meridian takes up the end of the branch of the Circulation Meridian at the tip of the ring finger. Starting from here it moves up along the middle of the posterior side of the arm, reaches the shoulder, moves around to the front, enters the supraclavicular fossa, is scattered in the area between the breasts, circles the pericardium, descends farther and returns to the Three Warmers.

A branch starts from a point between the breasts and goes through the supraclavicular fossa, moves up the back of the neck, reaches the back of the ear. From here, one part branches from the upper portion of the ear to the cheek, and then to the area below the eye. The other enters the ear, surfaces in the front of the ear, and, after passing through the cheek, ends at the outer edge of the eye.

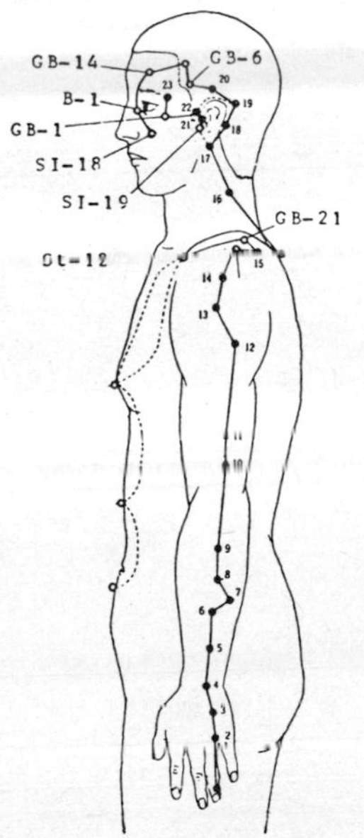

(Abbrev.: T=Triple Warmer

Triple Warmer
Meridian
T-1 to T-23

11. ***The Gallbladder Meridian (Yang Minimum) of the Legs***

This Meridian takes up at the branch of the Triple Warmer Meridian, starting up from the outer edge of the eye, and moving around the side of the head. From here, a branch enters the ear and emerges at the front of the body; another branch goes through the neck, descends to the shoulder and enters the supraclavicular fossa.

At this point the two branches join together. The Meridian then enters the chest and passes through the diaphragm, circles the liver, and returns to the gallbladder. There is another branch which starts from the shoulders, goes through the side of the chest and the hypochondriac region, and descends to the hip joint. These two branches join together here, and then descend through the middle of the outside of the leg and end at the tip of the fourth toe (near the fifth toe).

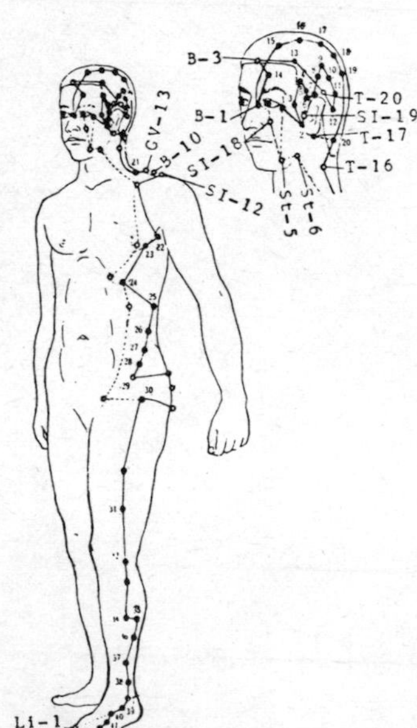

(Abbrev.: GB=Gallbladder)

Gallbladder
Meridian
GB-1 to GB-43

12. *The Liver Meridian (Yin in Equilibrium) of the Legs* (Abbrev.: Li = Liver)

A branch of the Bladder Meridian reaches the root of the nail of the big toe. This Meridian starts from here and moves up along the center of the inside of the leg and enters the groin. The Meridian then passes the lower abdomen, joins the liver, coils around the gallbladder, disperses in the side region of the chest, passes through the trachea and behind the larynx, reaches the eyeball, and exits at the top of the head. One branch starts from the eyeball, reaches around the cheek and the lips. The other branch moves up from the liver and enters the lungs. It then descends and ends at the vicinity of the stomach. (This point is the originating point of the Lung Meridian.)

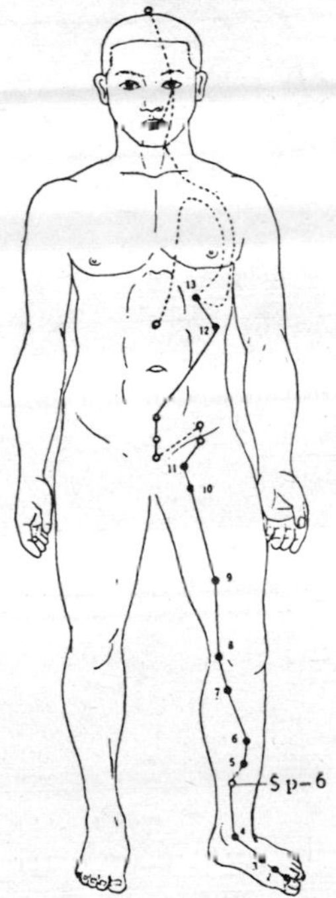

(Abbrev.: Li=Liver)

Livor Moridian
Li-1 to Li-13

13. *The Meridian of the Governing Vessel* (Abbrev.: GV = Governing Vessel)

This line originates in the perineal region and moves up along the center line of the back branching out at the left and right scapular region (intersecting with the Bladder Meridian).

These two branches join together at the back center line and continue up. The Meridian reaches the back of the neck to the top of the head along the center line, to the front of the head, ending at the roots of the upper teeth.

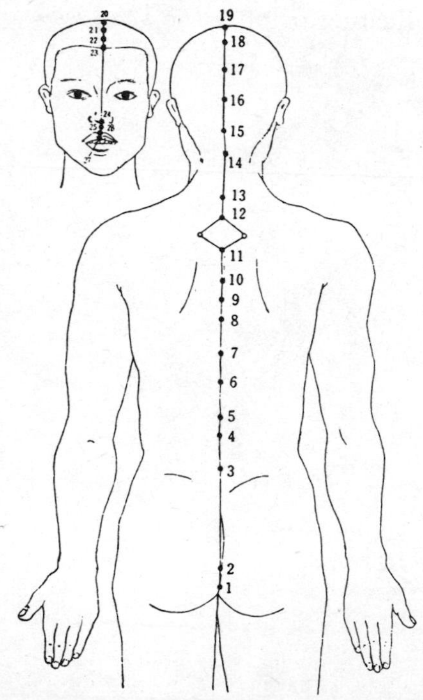

Meridian of the
Governing Vessel
GV–1 to GV–27

14. *The Meridian of the Vessel of Conception*

This Meridian originates at the perineal region, circles around the area of the external genitals, moves up along the pubic hair line, and further, along the center line of the abdomen, through the navel, until it reaches the larynx. From there, it comes to the face through the jaw, circles around the lips, then divides out into two branches, ending at the central lower region of the eyes. (Abbrev.: CV = Vessel of Conception)

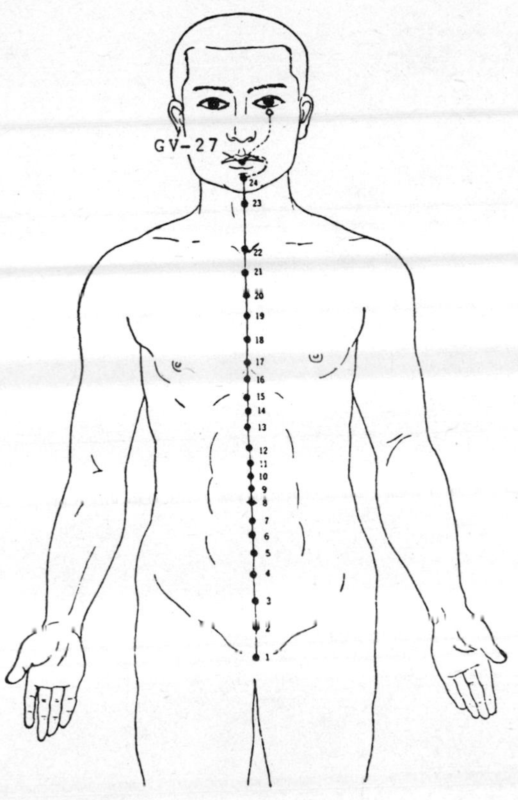

Meridian of the Vessel of Conception CV-1 to CV-24

Part II
Acupressure

For G.V.

I would like to extend a special note of appreciation to Walter Ian Fischman for his assistance in bringing this book to fruition.

I would also like to express my admiration for and obligation to the multitudes of physicians in previous centuries from whose experiences I have so liberally borrowed.

FZW

A few essential words about pain:

Pain is an alarm. It awakens you and your body to certain important facts. You might be near something dangerous, something either so hot or so cold that it hurts. Or you might be developing a disease, one symptom of which is pain. Or you might even be in the advanced stages of some illness where pain doesn't occur until the sickness is already established or in its late stages.

If the pain you are treating with the method in this book falls into one of the above categories, of course you won't get the best results. Even if you get some alleviation, it's not the best idea to continue to treat the pain by acupressure. In all cases of persistent pain without medical diagnosis, it is essential that you engage a physician to establish that diagnosis. And even with a diagnosis, a periodic recheck is not a bad idea, just in case the disease has changed its course. It is also very important to always double-check the possibility of pregnancy before giving any acupressure treatment. Do not use acupressure on a pregnant woman; it is fraught with the potential of setting off labor pains.

If you don't have a physician, your county or state medical society, whose number you can find in the telephone directory, will provide you with one. Under no circumstances or by no stretch of your imagination should you feel that this book is a substitute for a good practitioner of the healing arts, nor can the publisher, author or contributors to this volume be held responsible for all or any unpleasant consequences which may result from the faulty application of the methods described within.

The acupressure techniques described in this book are intended for the relief of minor discomforts or as a supplement to traditional medical treatment by a trained professional. The first-aid treatments have, for the most part, been in use for many years and are regarded as highly effective. However, they should be combined with conventional emergency techniques if there is any doubt about the problem, or if results are not forthcoming.

I hope that this volume, written both for the professional practitioner and for the personal use of the layman, will be of service and will assist in achieving better health for everyone.

IMPORTANT: The term "patient" as used throughout the book indicates a person who may need the help that acupressure can provide. Naturally, the same techniques are already in use by many practicing physicians.

ONE
FREEDOM FROM PAIN

Pain is something you already know about. It doesn't take too much effort to remember the dull, throbbing pulse of a toothache like the one that awakened you at 2 A.M. And nothing seemed to kill the pain as the hours dragged slowly toward morning.

Some people are all too familiar with migraine headaches. If you fit into this unhappy category, you well recall the blinding pain that gives daylight a searing quality and makes motion virtually impossible. Outside of medication, your only slight relief comes from a darkened room and a damp cloth on the forehead.

Trigeminal neuralgia? If you have acquired this unhappy malady, you know the hot, liquid flashes that seem to knife through an entire side of your face, a pain of such intensity that description reaches for new words.

But not everyone experiences suffering on such intense levels. Perhaps you just go on from day to day with the dull, constant ache of lumbosacral pain. Just every once in a while it escalates to the paralyzing level that increases with each muscle spasm. Even on good days, you know for sure in the back of your mind that you can still get that sudden "catch" and you won't be able to straighten up. Then it's bedrest, pain killers and maybe traction to keep the pain under control.

You can almost believe the philosophers who say that hell is right here.

But now there's a new way to deal with all these aches and pains. It's a little-known version of a technique that's centuries old. You see, although you may not be aware of it, you already possess an incredible power to heal. Within your hands is the ability to make headaches diminish, ease the pain of toothache, quiet an upset stomach, lighten or relieve the symptoms of a cold and alleviate all sorts of miscellaneous torments.

And that's just the start of a long, long list. Once you've mastered the information in this book, you may never suffer from stomach cramps again, without knowing how to obtain some immediate relief. Quite likely you can more easily face the unpleasant assortment of allergies and spend the rest of your life more sneeze-proof and itch-proof.

If insomnia is your problem, the treatment is right in your own hands. Within just a few weeks you can be dozing off gently and easily every single night, to awaken refreshed and full of energy in the morning. There are quite a few surprises on the list, too. For example, how would you like to have a simple drugless recipe for sunburn? Or a gentle, natural method for dealing with the emotional tension that seems to plague almost everyone these nervous-making days.

Motion sickness yields to treatment; so does the pain of arthritis, backache, muscle cramp, rheumatism and even tennis elbow.

What's the secret? It's a simple, nonmedicinal technique, a variation of acupuncture known as acu*pressure*.

Let's get the terms straight. Chances are, you already know something about acupuncture. It is the ancient Oriental healing art that uses long, slender needles precisely twirled into the human body to treat a wide range of illnesses.

The technique made front page news during Nixon's 1971 trip to China. *New York Times* columnist James Reston came down with appendicitis during the junket. His operation in the Peking hospital was standard, but afterward he developed the kind of pains that sometimes follow intestinal surgery. After consultation, the Chinese physicians used acupuncture to ease his discomfort. And as Reston told the rest of the world, it works . . . it really works.

In short order, acupuncture became a national fad. American doctors who were invited to visit China clamored to see acupuncture in everyday use. They watched in amazement as their Oriental colleagues sliced through muscle and bone to perform delicate open heart surgery. The only anesthetic—a few tiny needles in the patient's ear or forearm.

The visiting doctors saw entire hospitals where acupuncture treatment was employed. They learned about the "barefoot doctors" who used acupuncture to render simple medical aid to patients in the fields and factories of rural China. Most of all, they argued about what they saw. Many of them reluctantly admitted that there was something here. Not hypnotism, not fakery but clearly the utilization of forces outside the scope of their training and experience.

Back in the United States, acupuncture quickly became the number one medical subject. A whole host of Oriental practitioners working in the dim obscurity of Chinatown found hundreds of Westerners lining up for appointments. American doctors, taken completely by surprise, began to enroll in acupuncture courses specifically formed for members of the medical fraternity. Many of them took off for England, France, Italy, Hong Kong, Taiwan and other countries where acupuncture has long been a completely legitimate medical technique. Traditional doctors there, using nothing but long, thin needles, work side by side with Western-trained physicians.

Completely lost in the fever and excitement were a couple of rather interesting facts.

Despite appearances, acupuncture is vastly more complicated than it looks. Not the technique of inserting the needles; that's not much different from giving an injection. The hard part is knowing precisely *where* to insert the needles. There are over a thousand acupuncture "points" or needle sites. When used in combinations of four or five as required for most treatments, the possibilities mount up into numbers resembling the mileage between stars.

Also, acupuncture is by no means the only available technique. To a skilled and trained Oriental physician, it's just one of several treatment forms that he can employ to cure his patients. Acu*pressure* is considered to be almost as potent medicine as acupuncture. As a matter of fact, there are many conditions that respond better to acupressure massage than to needling, drugs or surgery.

Don't for one moment confuse acupressure with run-of-the mill massage: it's nothing like it at all. You see, standard generalized massage with its rubbing and kneading can't be considered a science. Not really. It's fine for working the kinks out of a stiff muscle or giving you some degree of relaxation. But that's about all.

On the other hand, acupressure makes use of the very precise points that have been in use for nearly five thousand years. By knowing the exact spot to press or rub, you can turn off many ailments just like flipping a switch. Pain will vanish in seconds. The proof, as well as the ability, is right in your own hands. Once you have learned just a few of the techniques in this book and tried them out, you will have no further doubts.

In many ways acupuncture and acupressure are really just two different ways of utilizing the exact same scientific principles. The main difference is that acupuncture, with its skin-piercing needle technique, is strictly for highly trained professionals. Acupressure is for everybody. As long as you observe the precautions spelled out in Chapter 3, you can gain the power to banish many simple pains and bring soothing relief to family and friends . . . and to yourself.

However, in order to utilize the full healing power of acupressure, you may have to free your mind from traditional thinking and take a couple of great leaps in logic. Incidentally, this idea applies to both acupuncture and acupressure.

For example, one of the most potent points for erasing the throbbing pain of a toothache is in the web of skin between your thumb and first finger. Another point that works is at the end of one finger just beside the nail.

Stiff neck? There's a highly effective point on your arm that can often bring relief in minutes. Just below your wrist there's a point that works wonders in easing the discomfort of a stiff shoulder joint. To relieve stomach distress, you may decide to apply finger pressure to a point on the side of your leg; to stop a toothache you may want to use a point between your second and third toes.

It's this strange use of points far removed from the seat of the actual pain that most people find so difficult to accept. And yet, these precise spots have proved to be effective for millions of people over thousands of years. Of course, not all points are distant from the trouble. Sometimes the proper point is close to the source of the discomfort. More often, you will use a combination of distant and close points to stop pain.

As a guide, it may help if you think of the acupressure points as "windows" into the body. According to the ancients who discovered the healing technique (as well as the professionals who practice it today), the points actually allow you to reach into the body and make contact with tissues and organs deep within the structure. Your fingers on the precise points can make profound changes, just as though there were really openings in the body.

How did it all get started? Nobody really knows, but we can make an educated guess. There's one theory concerning a warrior who was hit in the leg with an arrow during battle. Suddenly, he discovered that the arthritis that had been plaguing him a good part of his life magically vanished. Other soldiers had similar experiences with other complaints and other wounds.

It seems likely that a few early physicians became curious. They started to seek out additional spots on the body that might have similar effects. Gradually, they located quite a few sensitive areas and passed the word around. Other healers began to treat and to experiment. Slowly a healing art took shape.

While that might not seem to be a very scientific approach, it really has quite a few factors in its favor. If you recognize the fact that this experimentation took place over a period of thousands of years, multiply it by the hundreds of millions of Chinese who lived during that time, and multiply once more by the number of potential points, you'll wind up with a gigantic sample. By simple trial and error, using a pool of information this big, some pattern had to emerge.

What emerged was acupuncture and with it, acupressure.

For many people, the most difficult aspect of acupressure to accept is the fact that it is so very simple. You don't need instruments or years of training. Only three things are required. The first two are the strength you already have in your hands plus the information you will find in this book. The last item is equally important. It's the sincere desire to banish pain. You see, as you proceed, and before you have gained enough skill, you will be a less-than-perfect pupil. But if you want to know freedom from hurt you will keep working. Within a surprisingly short time, you will acquire a repertoire of points and pressures sufficient to deal with virtually any pain situation you find.

As you learn and as you work, it may help if you keep in mind the fact that acupressure is very closely linked to Oriental history, customs and beliefs. The Chinese in particular were masters at formulating great, celestial theories. But that's because they were very limited in what they could do with human beings. A set of very rigid religious rules made sure of that.

In order to get to heaven, people had to be buried intact; that is, with all the physical parts they had when they came into this world. And so autopsies were forbidden. Also taboo was any sort of research that mutilated a human body, even a dead one. Very few operations were permitted if the purpose was to remove any part of the human body, no matter how small or minor.

Because of this, Chinese doctors never got a chance to really look at the inside of a human body. As a result they had to formulate their concepts of anatomy by logical reasoning based on the few bits of actual information they possessed. Surprisingly enough, it turned out to be a pretty workable system. In much the same way that a blind person is supposed to develop superlative hearing by way of compensation, Oriental doctors were masters of diagnosing illness based on very simple factors, many of which their Western colleagues still ignore.

Chinese physicians always examined a patient's face very carefully to detect minute changes in coloring. They listened attentively to the sound of his voice, because this could be a clue to his illness. They did this while they felt the patient's wrists for twelve, yes twelve, pulses.

Modesty limited their options even more. A doctor was forbidden to see his female patients in any condition other than fully dressed. Except for this very elaborate system of taking the pulse, the doctor rarely touched a woman patient. He could of course ask questions, but even so it was considered bad form if they were of an extremely personal nature.

The stand-in for a female body was a carved ivory doll in the shape of a woman's figure. Using a crayon a woman patient would mark specific spots on the doll to show the doctor where the painful spots were located. This was as close as he ever came to making a physical examination.

And yet despite such limitations that would completely stymie a Western doctor, the Chinese physicians developed a system of medicine that is regarded by many as being at least as sophisticated and effective as the Western variety. The anatomical charts they produced thousands of years ago, although based on the slenderest threads of concrete knowledge, are not too different from the diagrams we use today.

It is important to keep this picture in mind because it's a clue to understanding why acupressure could only have developed in the Orient. Physicians there were basically concerned with practical considerations: If a system of healing worked, fine. If not, let's find something else. And once they did latch onto a medical system that produced results, they could use logical thought to extend it into many different directions. They did this with acupuncture and they did the same with acupressure.

Let's return for a moment to the story about the warrior who was hit in the arm with an arrow only to find that his arthritis vanished. A similar situation exists with acupressure. Quite likely, without ever thinking about it, you may have discovered it for yourself.

At some time in the past, you must have hit that bony protuberance at the end of your elbow that many people refer to as the "funny bone." What happened? You instinctively reached out with your other hand to rub your elbow in an attempt to ease the pain.

Similarly with a stubbed toe. Odds are good that you rubbed it gently and then firmly so that it would stop hurting. Without knowing anything about acupressure, you utilized what is called a Local Point; that is, one right at the site of the problem.

But in the very same way, you may have learned about the use of Distant Points. Let's say you had a headache. For a while you tried rubbing the spot where it hurt but that didn't do much good. After a bit you may have continued rubbing but shifted to a different locale. Perhaps you applied pressure to the bottom of the two bony protuberances at the base of your skull. As you pressed, the pain gradually disappeared. A miraculous cure? Not at all. A simple acupressure treatment!

This is a very simple introduction to a healing technique that takes in more territory than you ever imagined. For example, it's a highly effective way to pinpoint and identify different illnesses. Here's how it works: Quite often when you are ill, a point on your skin quite far away from the actual site of the malady becomes tender to the touch. Oriental doctors use this fact to confirm their diagnoses. They sometimes seek out these points and press them firmly to see if the spot is tender. If so, it frequently proves that they are on the right track. In this book you will learn how to do this for yourself. You'll learn where the points are and which one corresponds to each specific problem.

There are at least sixteen theories as to why acupuncture and acupressure work, but none of them provides a complete answer. As you might expect, there are two main divisions: Eastern and Western, and you can pretty well take your choice.

The idea that follows traditional Oriental thinking says there is a force or energy that flows through the body called "chi." Sometimes this force becomes unbalanced or impeded. Either acupuncture needles or acupressure applied to the proper point adjusts the flow by "unblocking" it. Since a body in which the chi is balanced and moving freely is a healthy body, the disease or pain is automatically taken care of.

Western doctors, of course, view the process in an entirely different light. According to one school of thought, the needles or the pressure in some way act upon one aspect of the nervous system called the autonomic nerves. Other theories exist with other explanations.

As you can well understand, scientists in these two different worlds have a great deal of trouble communicating with each other. All of which is rather odd because, no matter what the reason why the procedure works, the important fact is that it *does* work.

As a matter of fact, this is not at all unique in the annals of medicine. The same reasoning applies to aspirin. To this day, nobody really knows how or why it works. There are lots of theories and lots of guesses, but no definitive answers. However, one basic truth remains: Aspirin is a highly effective medication for a wide variety of ailments, and it seems to do the job with an absolute minimum of side effects. For this reason, it is the most widely prescribed and sold medication in the world today. The same applies to anesthetics, the chemicals that put you to sleep. They work, but we don't know why.

Certainly, the Chinese have proved that they will go along with anything that works. Today, their medical schools are divided into two categories: traditional and Western. Graduates of both systems work together at hospitals. Both are considered equally valuable and both techniques are regarded as perfectly normal medical procedures to be utilized for the patient's benefit.

What's more, acupuncture and acupressure are still expanding and growing today. New points are discovered on the same basis of "when I do this, here's what happens." Then, as the next step, researchers find out if the newly discovered point works all the time and if it will work for other scientists. If so, another point takes its place in the roster of available treatments.

Not all of the new discoveries these days are coming out of China. There are reports of new points for acupuncture and acupressure from Czechoslovakia, England, France, the Soviet Union, Japan, Korea and to some extent virtually every country in the world. Even in the United States, medical researchers are turning up their share of new points and new findings and are coming up with more ways to utilize the existing collection.

Currently, there are well over a thousand known points. But don't get discouraged. Only a few of these are of the powerhouse variety known to be highly effective for one or more conditions. These are called major points. And so when you practice acupressure, there are really only a few precise spots that you have to find and treat. Also, since most of these points are used for more than one ailment, you will be able to handle a wide range of maladies.

Keep one important fact in mind. In many cases, much of your acupressure treatment, using only your hands, will be just as effective as the needling technique of acupuncture. As proof, I'll let you in on a secret. Because they use acupuncture needles and because patients come to them for this treatment, doctors are often locked into this technique. But they all know a good many "emergency points" and they are taught to use needles, ball point pens, fingers or almost anything to stimulate these points in an emergency. And what is more of an emergency than pain? And so, even when they use acupressure to treat a condition, doctors will sometimes insert a few needles into "tonic" points that don't have much to do with the basic problem, but "tone" the patient generally.

In many emergencies, it's the acupressure that did the job. The needles are supplementary. The same is true for nonemergencies in many instances. Happily, because the only healing you will do is with your hands, you won't be forced into any subterfuges. And yet, the treatments you give will be fully effective.

Using your hands instead of an acupuncture needle has several advantages. Primarily, it's easier to find the point. After all, you are working with the flat, broad surface of your thumb and fingers. They cover a lot more territory than a tiny acupuncture needle and the search is simpler.

The type of acupressure that you will learn in this book is actually a combination of three different types or schools of treatment.

1. *Chinese Acupressure*. This is the healing art that developed along side of acupuncture down through the centuries. This book will offer a selection of the most effective points and techniques.
2. *Japanese Shiatsu.* This is the Japanese version of healing hands. Like a tea ceremony, it can get very ornate. I have selected parts of this method and simplified the complex ritual.
3. *Judo Revival Points*. Originally designed to bring an opponent back into consciousness after he'd been clobbered in this ancient martial art, the same points can be utilized for nonbelligerent health care.

And now, it's time to get to work!

TWO
PAINS YOU CAN EASE WITH ACUPRESSURE

You will probably have to prove it for yourself. The list of human miseries you can ease with acupressure is so long and so all-encompassing that you may be tempted to doubt. It just sounds too good. The ills are so varied and the treatment so simple.

That's fine. I'll be quite pleased to have you remain skeptical until you have convinced yourself just how effective acupressure can be. To guide your thinking, here's a partial list of the physical maladies whose symptoms can be materially eased or significantly improved through the proper use of acupressure.

1. Allergies (including runny nose, watering eyes, sneezing and all the other manifestations of this problem)
2. Arthritis (including the stiffness, the ache and the agony)
3. Asthma (relief of acute attacks and general alleviation of the condition)
4. Backache (upper, lower and midback pains, stiffness and sprains)
5. Bronchitis (the pain and the hacking)
6. Bruises (the pain and the discoloration)
7. Bursitis (mobility again with little or no pain)
8. Colds (the stomach upset eased, tearing eyes and running nose alleviated)
9. Constipation (regularity without drugs)

10. Coughs (no more hacking—although you may also have to give up smoking)
11. Diarrhea (your body will resume normal bowel movements)
12. Facial pain (from simple muscular aches to trigeminal neuralgia)
13. Fatigue (tiredness can hurt but you can ease the pain)
14. Gastritis (no more upset)
15. Golfer's calf (plus other pulled muscles)
16. Gout (it's still around but can be considerably relieved)
17. Hay fever (reduce itching nose, watering eyes, sneezing no matter how high the pollent count)
18. Headache (the simple type due to tension, upset stomach, etc.)
19. Insomnia (peaceful sleep without thrashing or wide awake sessions late at night)
20. Joint pains (ease ache in arms, legs, hands, etc.)
21. Lumbago (even long-standing conditions often yield to treatment)
22. Menstrual cramps (almost all of the pain can be relieved)
23. Menstrual irregularity (gradually periods will occur on more regular schedule)
24. Mental tension (fear, worry and the hectic pace at which we live all takes a toll, but the effect can be eased)
25. Migraine headache (the blinding, searing pain can be largely or completely alleviated)
26. Motion sickness (car, boat or plane, there's no reason to be ill)
27. Muscle cramp (the well-known charley horse will yield to treatment)
28. Muscle pain (too much exercise or not enough, suffering can be reduced)
29. Nasal congestion (stuffed nose, blocked nose, swollen nose all respond to treatment)
30. Neuralgia (cut down the dosage of pain killers or even eliminate them after a course of treatments)
31. Nosebleed (it's messy, painful and unnecessary)
32. Rheumatism (the misery and the ache don't have to be a part of your life any longer)
33. Rheumatoid arthritis (proper treatment can keep the pain from becoming worse)
34. Sacroiliac pain (even the recurring type can be helped)
35. Sciatica (results may not be quick but the condition can be eased with a regular course of treatment)
36. Sexual dysfunction (obstacles to achieving a more fulfilling sex life can be overcome)
37. Sinusitis (as long as the condition is not caused by a structural problem, the trouble can be eased)
38. Sprains (your hands can give fast, emergency relief)
39. Stiff neck (full mobility and no pain)

40. Stomach ache (overeating, nervous tension, etc. cause the condition that you can eliminate almost completely)
41. Stomach cramps (those "knots" in your stomach will also yield to treatment)
42. Sunburn (this may be a surprise item on the list but your hands can ameliorate Old Sol's souvenir)
43. Tennis elbow (you can be back in play after only a few treatments although it's a much better idea to rest the affected arm)
44. Tonsillitis (mild conditions can often be completely subdued; pain relief only for more severe cases)
45. Toothache (virtually complete relief for steady and throbbing pain until the dentist can take action)
46. Whiplash injuries (the pain and the headache can be toned down to a merciful extent)

Of course, there's another side to this same picture; here is a list of conditions that will not respond to acupressure treatment. Even more important, some of them can actually be made much worse through the use of hand manipulation. Accept these maladies as being completely in the hands-off department. Even if you don't directly do harm, you can still cause damage by keeping a patient from getting competent medical care.

1. Contagious diseases such as whooping cough, measles, malaria, osteomyelitis, etc.
2. Internal disorders involving such organs as heart, liver, kidneys, lungs, etc.
3. Beware of patients susceptible to internal bleeding that can be triggered by external forces; conditions such as stomach ulcers, duodenal ulcers, hemophilia, etc.
4. Cancer of *any* type
5. Broken bones.

Obviously all of these conditions are far beyond the capabilities of hand manipulation and should be treated only by a professional medical practitioner.

THREE

HOW TO APPLY THE FORCE OF ACUPRESSURE

Stripped down to its simplest form, there are really only three things you have to know in order to give successful acupressure treatments:

1. *What point to use for each specific condition*
2. *How to find the point*
3. *How to apply pressure*

Each one of these is a key element. Without it, the treatment will not be effective. Happily, each of them is relatively simple. Follow the instructions exactly, however, with no variations of your own devising . . . until you have racked up quite a bit of experience.

In this chapter, I want to detail the various ways in which to apply acupressure and also give you some of the basic thinking behind this healing technique. If you understand what you are doing, you'll be better at it.

The main idea is to use your hands in a very precise way. Most of the time you will apply pressure with your thumbs. Do not use the end of your thumb or your thumbnails. That's reserved for first-aid manipulation as described in Chapter 7.

Instead, apply pressure with the ball of your thumb. Keep in mind that the key element is pressure. You don't punch, jab or poke. Think of your thumb as an extension of your arm, your shoulder and the entire rest of your body. It's as if the healing force is flowing in a smooth motion out from your body.

And so, much of the time, your thumb will remain rigid while you adjust the pressure with your hand, arm, etc. Also, it is a gradual type of pressure.

At first just touch the ball of your thumb to the proper spot. Then begin to press gradually. Slowly increase the pressure. Watch your patient carefully and stay in contact. Ask, "Does that hurt? Are you comfortable? What are you feeling? Does that hurt now?"

To give a fully effective acupressure treatment, you need to apply as much pressure as your patient can take. The force you exert with your thumbs should be almost, but not quite, painful.

There's a very delicate balance between just enough pressure and too much. The best guideline is the tolerance of your patient. If the patient flinches, squirms, winces or yipes in complaint, ease up on the pressure. However, do press hard enough to get some response first before modifying the force. The only way you can tell is to push until you get a reaction. For this reason, it's usually a good idea to explain that there may be a little bit of pain, but that's normal and won't do any harm. Anything beyond this is too much, however. It's a very thin line but you will get the knack of it after just a few practice sessions. But that's why you need the full cooperation and help of your patient. He's the final judge of whether you have reached that critical point approaching—but not crossing—the threshold of pain.

Naturally, certain parts of the body will require a lot less force to reach this limit than others. Along the spine, for example, you can only indulge in modest pressure before eliciting an "ouch" from your patient. In the muscles of the back, legs, thigh, etc. the body can probably take all the pressure you can generate.

Use your index and middle fingers in much the same way. Again, it's the ball of the finger that does the work. As with your thumb, keep the digits rigid and let the force flow from the rest of your body.

It's as if you are holding your arm stiff with your finger extended and leaning toward a wall. Only your finger touches the wall and keeps you from losing your balance. So all the force from your entire body is being channeled through your finger. To increase the force, you merely lean harder. This is the technique for acupressure.

Because your middle and index fingers do not have the same strength as your thumb, you may have to vary the method slightly to transmit heavy pressure. Rest your index finger on the point and place you middle finger on top of the index digit. With the fingers stacked in this manner, you will be able to exert considerably more pressure.

Do not rush. This is no place for haste. Instead, all motions should be slow and extremely smooth. If you get impatient, you may very well induce muscular spasms in your patient and wind up doing more harm than good.

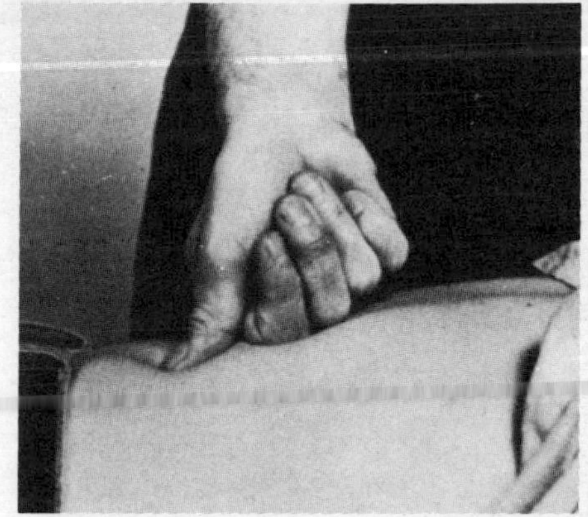

1. Most of the time you will probably apply pressure with the force of your thumb, as shown.

2. It's difficult to apply as much pressure with the index finger as with the thumb. By doubling up with your middle finger on top of your index finger, you'll wind up with a surprising amount of force.

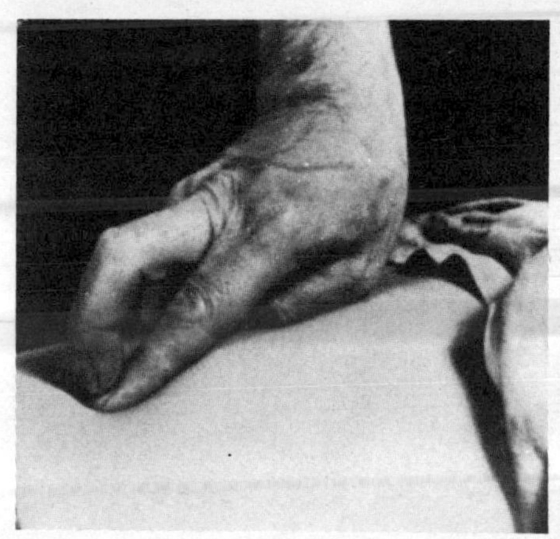

So take your time.

After first pressing your finger or thumb to the skin and gradually applying more and more pressure, you will gradually reach the point where the pleasure of the pressure is about to turn into pain.

Stop right there. Without releasing the pressure, hold that force for seven seconds. Then very gradually release the pressure until you are again just resting your digits on the skin. Wait about five seconds and then repeat the pressure build up once more until you have achieved the maximum limit. Then slowly, slowly ease off again. Follow this same procedure for a third time and then move on to another point.

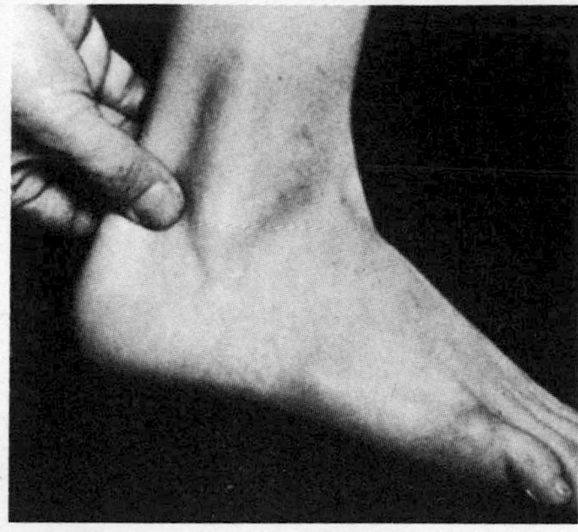

3. In some areas of the body, you will find it's easier to apply pressure with a sort of pinching motion, as shown here.

4. Because there is some stretching and flexibility to the skin, you will be able to rotate your thumb in a small back-and-forth arc while still pressing down. For certain points (as noted in the treatment section) this gives better results.

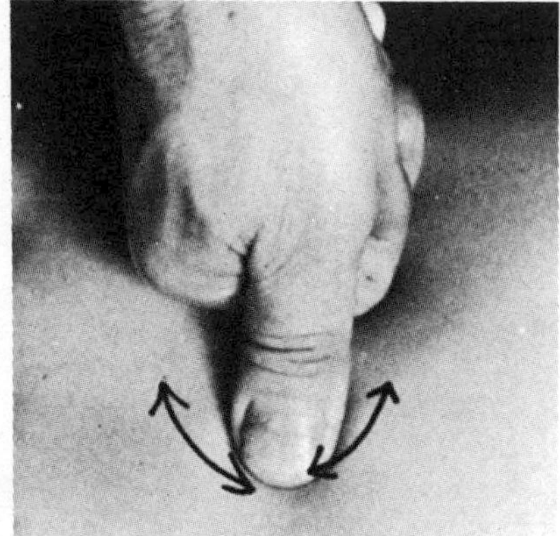

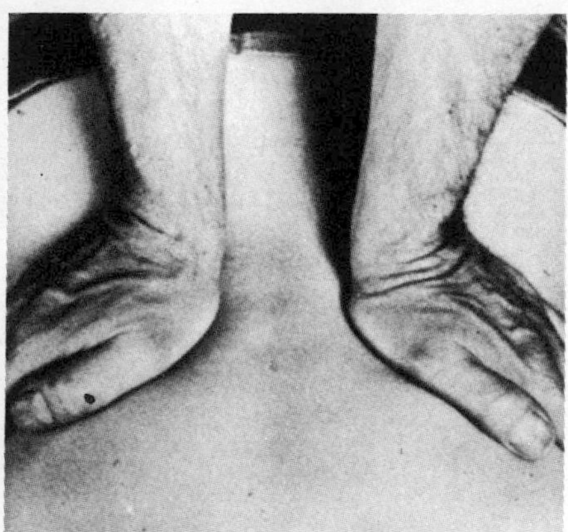

5. Sometimes pain will be so acute that it's impossible to apply enough force to help the condition. In such cases, press down with the heel of your hand using firm, steady pressure. Very gradually and slowly, release the pressure. Quite likely, you can follow this treatment with standard thumb or finger acupressure.

Do you have that timing and sequence straight?

1. Place your digit on the point.
2. Gradually press with increasing force. It may take as long as ten seconds before you are at maximum.
3. Hold the full pressure for exactly seven seconds.
4. Release the pressure as slowly as you applied it; if necessary, take up to ten seconds.
5. Wait about five seconds with your digit finger resting on the point and then reapply pressure.

The full treatment for any one point consists of three pressure applications, with waiting periods in between.

There are body areas where it's impossible to follow the straight pressure method I have outlined. In these instances, you will have to vary your technique.

A modified pinching motion can be quite effective. For example, let's say that you are working on the point located in back of your ankle bone. The easiest technique is merely to apply the pressure between your thumb on one side and your index and middle fingers on the other side of the ankle.

This method will still concentrate the force right over the point where it will be effective. In other areas, you may have to use only your thumb and index finger to apply pressure. In general, save the pinching method for points where straight pressure is not practical.

Note that all these maneuvers are concerned only with pressure. There's no kneading, no rubbing, no movement at all except for straight downward force. After you have used acupressure effectively a few times, you may want to incorporate one variation. You can utilize a bit of finger rotation.

When you have achieved full pressure, hold the force at that level while you slowly revolve your thumb or finger back and forth. Only move as much as the skin will permit; in other words, don't shift your thumb on the surface. There is always a little "give" to the skin that will allow you to rotate your thumb back and forth within a small arc.

In some cases, this slight movement can make a treatment much more effective. However, always try straight pressure first. Introduce partial rotation if the regular method is not doing the entire job.

There is one other technique you should add to your repertoire in special cases. Occasionally, you may find a patient who is so tense or is in such pain that even gentle pressure is enough to send his muscles into spasm. You have to quiet the muscle tension before you can do any work.

To soothe spasm, use pressure applied with the heel of your hand. Place this pad of your hand directly over the painful spot. Apply pressure very gradually. You'll find that the patient can probably tolerate more force than he imagined because it is spread out over a larger area than that covered by your thumb.

Do keep in mind that full pressure will take much more time to reach in this technique than by using your fingers. Don't worry if you take as long as half a minute from the time you start to apply force until you have reached the maximum. The important thing is to work so gradually that the patient's body accepts the pressure.

If you try to rush this technique, you will merely cause a muscle spasm and that's the very thing you are trying to remove. When you have reached peak force, you will probably be pressing with the full weight of your body.

Hold that force. Hold it, if necessary, for one to three minutes. Then, as slowly as you applied the pressure, ease off. Again, take several minutes if necessary to achieve a smooth withdrawal of force. If you have done your work properly, the muscle will accept the force and will be free of spasm when you release the pressure.

Allow the muscle to relax. Don't attempt to follow up the treatment with any immediate acupressure. Keep the skin warm by covering with a towel or blanket and move on to treat another area of the body. After you have eased pain and tension in other spots, return to the first area and begin treatment.

It's important to use the proper treatment surface for your patients. Allow the patient to stretch out on a bed if that's the only available surface. A sofa is probably better because it tends to be a little firmer.

But best of all is the floor on which you have spread a one- or two-inch thick foam pad, or some firm cushions. You will probably find it's also easier to work on the floor because you can utilize the force of your body weight much more effectively.

Acupressure for other points may require sitting, kneeling, leaning, etc. Follow the instructions given for each individual point. The aim is always to make the patient as comfortable as possible while allowing you to exert the maximum amount of pressure.

In many instances you can be both patient and healer. You can reach quite a few of the points and thus treat yourself. You don't even have to schedule any formal sessions. Say you are driving in the car and notice that a shoulder is getting stiff. At the next traffic light, merely apply pressure in the proper spots to get back full mobility.

Once you become aware of your body, you can follow this on-the-spot treatment technique whenever an ache or pain develops. Most discomforts are quite simple to banish if treatment is started before the misery escalates. Zap the small aches and the big ones will never get a chance to build up.

FOUR
HOW TO LOCATE ACUPRESSURE POINTS

Almost all bodies are in proportion. You may find that difficult to believe as you look about you and see thin people, tall people, fat and short people. Also, there are people with long legs and short waists as well as individuals built in the exact reverse fashion.

And yet, almost everyone is subject to the same rules of relative proportion. For example, you may have seen a tiny puppy with huge, disproportionate paws. As you smiled at the baby dog stumbling over his own feet, you may have remarked, "He's going to grow up to be a big dog." You knew that the puppy would grow until his feet were in proportion to the rest of his body.

The same relation applies to people, and there are a series of amazingly intricate proportions that we all fit. What's more, the measuring tape is built right into us. The basic unit is called an *acu-inch,* and here's how to find it.

Ask the patient to form a circle with the tip of his middle finger just touching the tip of his thumb. This maneuver forms two creases on the middle finger, which mark off an acu-inch for *that specific person only*. This dimension varies from person to person.

Using a simple compass, measure off the distance between the outer edges of the two creases. You now have an individual acu-inch for that person.

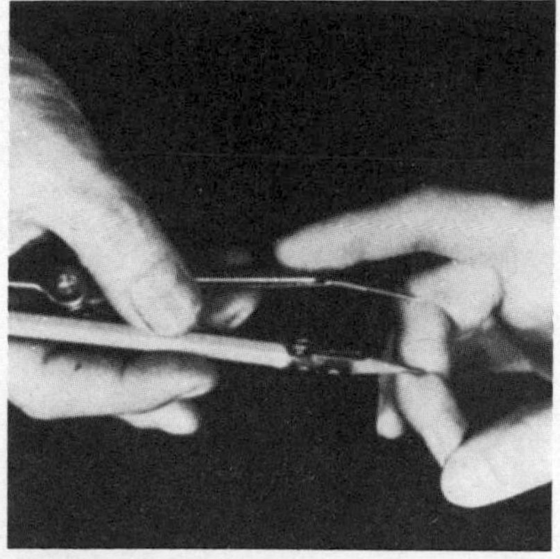

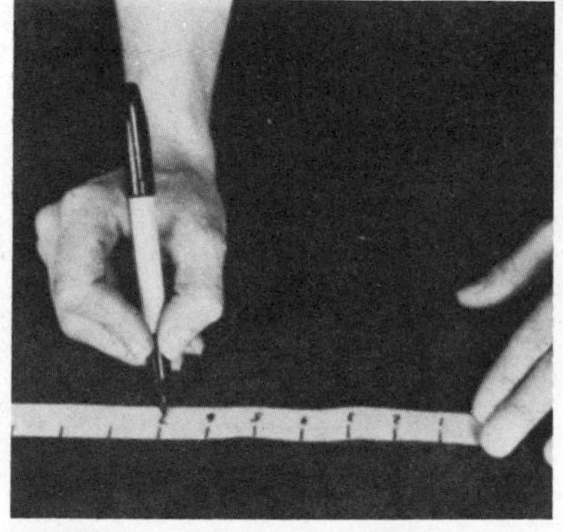

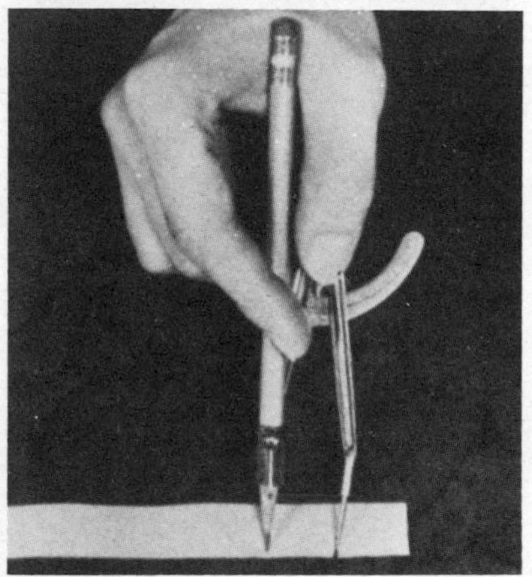

1. Have the patient touch the tip of his middle finger to the thumb. With a compass, measure the distance between the two finger-joint creases that are formed by this maneuver. The resulting setting represents an acu-inch for that specific individual.
2. "Walk" the compass down a length of tape and mark off the acu-inches to create a 10- or 12 acu-inch tape.
3. Use an indelible pen to darken the pencil marks and mark off the units.

Using this measurement, mark off a length of tape to make a flexible ruler. "Walk" the compass down the length of tape starting at one end until you have 15 acu-inches marked off. Use ball point pen or fine tipped felt marker to indicate the separations. At the same time, include the 1 to 15 acu-inch notations. Also, write the patient's name on the tape.

The best tape for the purpose is a dressmaking tape, if you can find one that is blank on the back surface. A tape of this type is flexible and yet has absolutely no stretch that might throw your measurements off. Many types of ribbon will do. Just make sure that the type you select won't stretch when you yank on it, or your measurements will soon be thrown off kilter.

At this point you have a homemade tape measure that doesn't seem to match any ruler or yardstick you can find. What's it good for? Well, you have just created a highly efficient measuring tool that will enable you to locate a vast series of very precise acupressure points.

You see, because the body is in proportion, many points are located an exact distance from certain body landmarks. The distances are measured in acu-inches.

The number of acu-inches from landmark to point is the same for every single person. It's the length of the acu-inch that varies from one individual to another. That's why the made-to-order tape measure that you construct will only work with that one individual. For each patient that you treat, you will have to make another tape measure, but since the process is easy, it's no problem.

Just for fun, you might want to check the accuracy of the tape measures that you make. Try these tests:

1. The width of four fingers measured across the knuckles as shown is 3 acu-inches.
2. Flex your hand upward and mark off the main skin crease at the wrist with a felt pen. Bend you elbow to form an acute angle and mark off the outer end of the elbow crease. The distance between these two marked points is 12 acu-inches.
3. Mark off the upper end of the crease formed between your arm and shoulder. The distance between this mark and the one at your elbow is 9 acu-inches.
4. The distance from the highest point of your ankle bone on the outside of your foot to the bottom of your heel is 3 acu-inches.
5. The distance from the point midway between your eyebrows and the middle of the natural hairline (or where it once was) is 3 acu-inches.

Keep this last measurement in mind. Some points are located precise distances away from the natural hairline. If your patient is bald, you can merely measure up 3 acu-inches from a spot midway between his eyebrows and you will have located his natural hairline. Mark this spot and use it as a basis for the additional location measurements you need.

There are literally hundreds of measurements just like these that you can use in order to find the precise location of acupressure points. It's a simple, yet amazingly accurate method.

Once you have accumulated some experience in acupressure, you may be able to locate a great many points merely by eye. But until you develop this skill, always use the acu-inch tape measure. Also, don't hesitate to mark the point on the patient's skin once you have located it. Ball point pens work well, as do many types of felt tip markers. In any event, it will all come out in the wash.

Also, stay alert for the "ouch" response mentioned in Chapter 3 when you feel for the proper acupressure point. There's a reason for this. Many of the

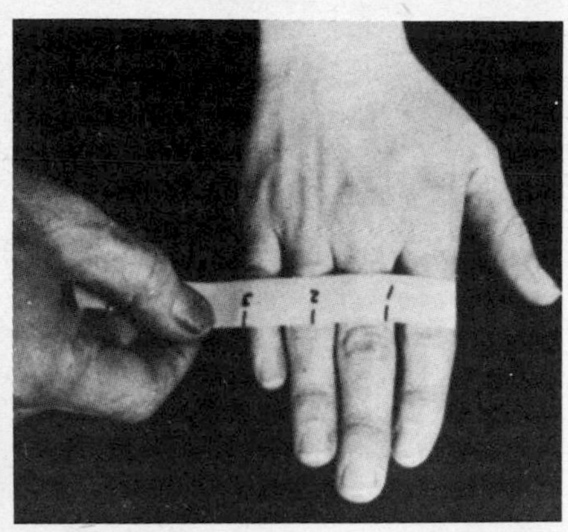

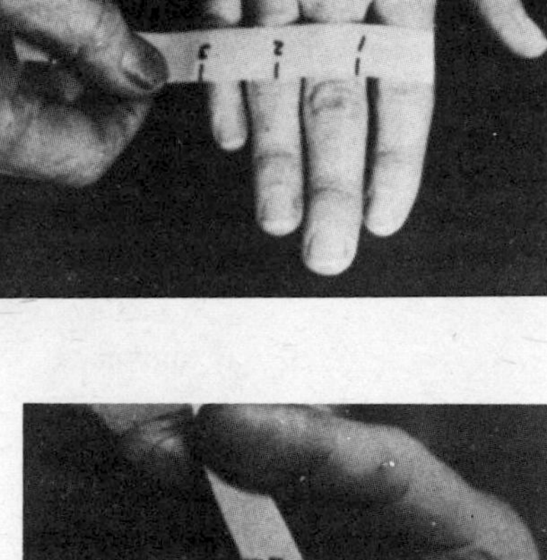

4. Check the accuracy of the acu-inch tape. Four finger widths measured as shown should equal 3 acu-inches.

5. The furthest wrist fold to elbow fold should measure 12 acu-inches.

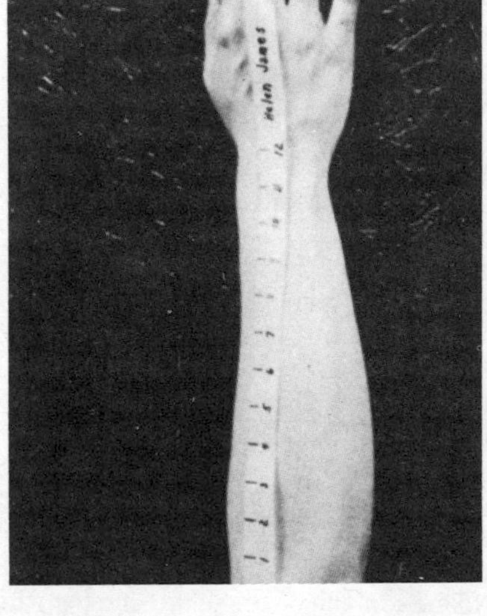

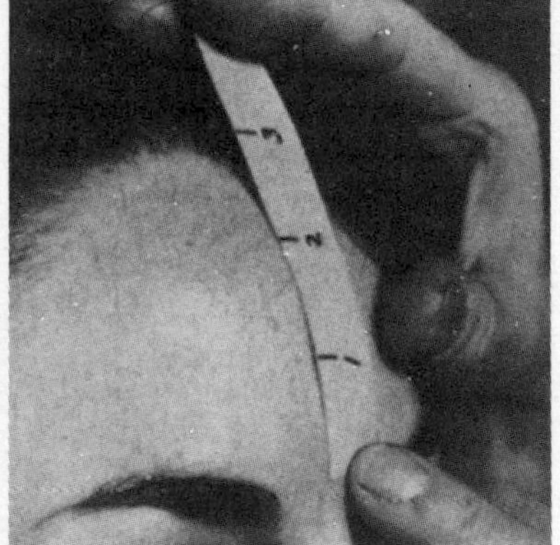

6. The distance from the midpoint of the eyebrow to the hairline should equal 3 acu-inches.

points listed as effective for the treatment of a condition actually get quite tender if the malady is present. And so, just finding the tender or "ouch" spots is an effective guide to the point.

In most cases, the point will be tender only if the malady is present. In the absence of sickness, the point will probably not be sensitive to pressure.

Most of the acupressure points are the same ones that are used for acupuncture. Down through the years, several methods of identifying points have been developed.

Because the points are arranged along a series of lines called meridians that crisscross the body, many systems refer to the name of the meridian and then the number of the position that the point occupies along it. For example, one point might be called Triple Warmer #7, the next point along the meridian would be Triple Warmer #8 and so on.

It sounds simple except that there's some disagreement as to the digits. In some numbering methods, when a new point is discovered (and new developments are occurring even these days), the meridian is renumbered to accommodate the addition.

Happily, there is a convenient way out of this confusion. Each point also has a Chinese name and that never does change. And so in this book, I will be using the English translation of the Chinese name for each acupressure point.

Actually, it's kind of fun because the names are rather colorful. The original purpose might have been to help students and physicians remember them. Some names accurately describe the spot on the body where they are located. Others go off in quite poetic fashion. And so when you go to work on a point known as Cheek Chariot, one called Terrestrial Granary, Head Support or Listening Palace, do realize that you are in very good company, with nomenclature that may date back several thousand years.

The world of medicine has developed some very precise terminology to describe parts of the body as well as various functions, conditions and the like. Medical dictionaries are fully as hefty as the tome recommended for high school and college students.

But I'm not going to use any of the technical language contained in a medical dictionary. For most of the anatomical landmarks that you have to locate, there are common, well-known names that are probably quite familiar to you. These will do nicely.

Since many of these body landmarks are fairly large, the distances are measured from a specific spot in that area. For example, if you are told to measure a certain distance up the leg from the ankle bone, we're talking about the highest point on the ankle bone; that is, where it sticks out the furthest. Take a look at your own ankle and you will note that you can identify this spot quite easily. Other instructions may ask you to measure from the uppermost part or the lower edge. It's all very easy. Just take an extra moment to follow the directions carefully.

Finally, note that many of the points are bilateral. That is, they occur in pairs, with one on each side of the body. Where indicated, treat both sides. Other points are along a center line down the front or back of the body. In these cases, there is just one point to treat.

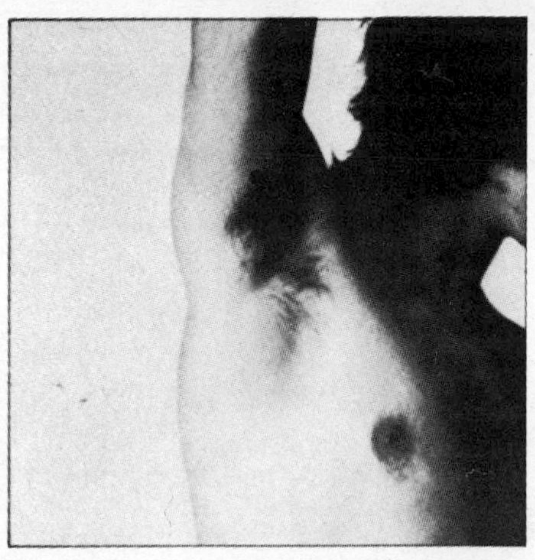

POINT: Extreme Spring
LANDMARK: arm-shoulder fold
DISTANCE FROM LANDMARK: right at fold
LOCATION: in the armpit, in the center of the crease (treat both arms)
POSITION: seated or flat on back
TYPE OF PRESSURE: pulsed with thumb or fingers
AMOUNT OF PRESSURE: as much as patient can take

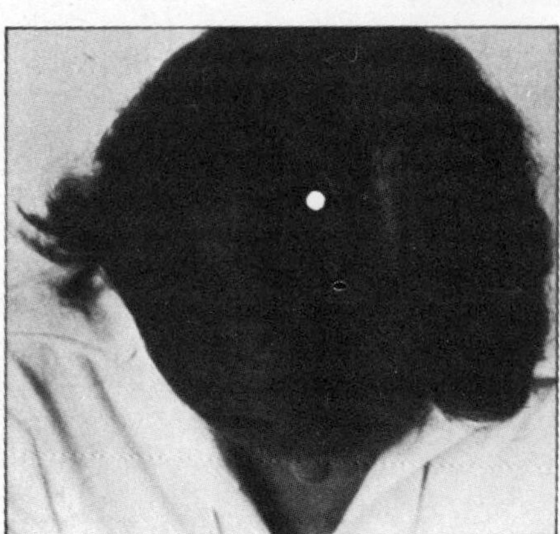

POINT: Anterior Vertex
LANDMARK: natural hairline at forehead
DISTANCE FROM LANDMARK: 3½ acu-inches behind the natural hairline
LOCATION: on top of head, along front-to-back center line of head
POSITION: seated
TYPE OF PRESSURE: pulsed with thumb
AMOUNT OF PRESSURE: as much as patient can take

FIVE
LANDMARKS

There's an easy way to locate most of the acupressure points. Merely measure from a known, easy-to-find anatomical landmark. That's the method used in this book. Along with the description of the various points, you will also find a series of landmarks together with the road-map directions to the point.

Use these body landmarks as starting points. From here, it's easy to find your way. But do take a few moments to familiarize yourself with these essential signposts.

Here's a list of the landmarks, the names given to them and a brief description of where they are . . . just to make certain we are all on the same highway.

1 KNEECAP
2 NAVEL
3 NIPPLES
4 INNER ANKLE BONE: Most measurements from this landmark are figured from the point where the bone sticks out the furthest (the high point). It's usually about in the middle of the bone.
5 OUTER ANKLE BONE: See above.
6 BUTTOCKS FOLD: Mark the spot where the back of the upper thigh joins the buttocks. Mark the fold line.

7 SPINE KNOB AT NECK (VERTEBRA): With the head tilted forward (chin on chest) feel along the spine at the neck for the first knob or vertebra that protrudes out further than the others in that immediate area. Mark the spot carefully.
8 INNER ELBOW FOLD: Bend the arm upward 45 degrees or more and mark the end of the crease at the elbow fold.
9 OUTER ELBOW FOLD: See above.
10 BACK OF KNEE FOLD: Bend the knee and mark the fold.
11 ARM-SHOULDER FOLD
12 NOSE-CHEEK FOLDS: Note the natural lines in the face at the outer edges of the nostrils running down to the outer edges of the mouth.
13 REAR HEAD BONES: Feel for the two bones or knobs at the rear of the skull just at the point where the neck joins the head. There is one bone on either side of the head. Identify them.
14 THIGH-STOMACH FOLD: Raise the leg up at a sharp angle and mark the natural fold that forms along the leg-stomach line.
15 FRONT HIP BONE: Feel for the sharp upper points of the hip bones.
16 TOE KNUCKLE: Corresponds to finger knuckles. Locate and mark.
17 LOWER JAWBONE ANGLE: With your fingers, trace the jawbone back until the point where it forms a sharp angle just under the ear. Mark the spot.
18 UPPER JAWBONE: This is the cheekbone. Find it and feel along it to the point where it joins the lower jawbone just in front of the ear. Mark the spot.
19 INNER WRIST FOLD: Drop the hand and mark the fold at the wrist.
20 OUTER WRIST FOLD: Bend hand upward and mark the fold line.
21 THROAT NOTCH: Feel along the collar bone at the base of the throat. In the middle of this bone there is a pronounced notch. Mark the spot.
22 NATURAL HAIRLINE—FOREHEAD: If the patient has a full complement of hair, this is your guide. If the patient is bald or partially so, measure 3 acu-inches up from a line joining the inside corners of the eyebrows to calculate where the hairline should be.
23 NATURAL HAIRLINE—BACK OF HEAD: This one exists for everyone.

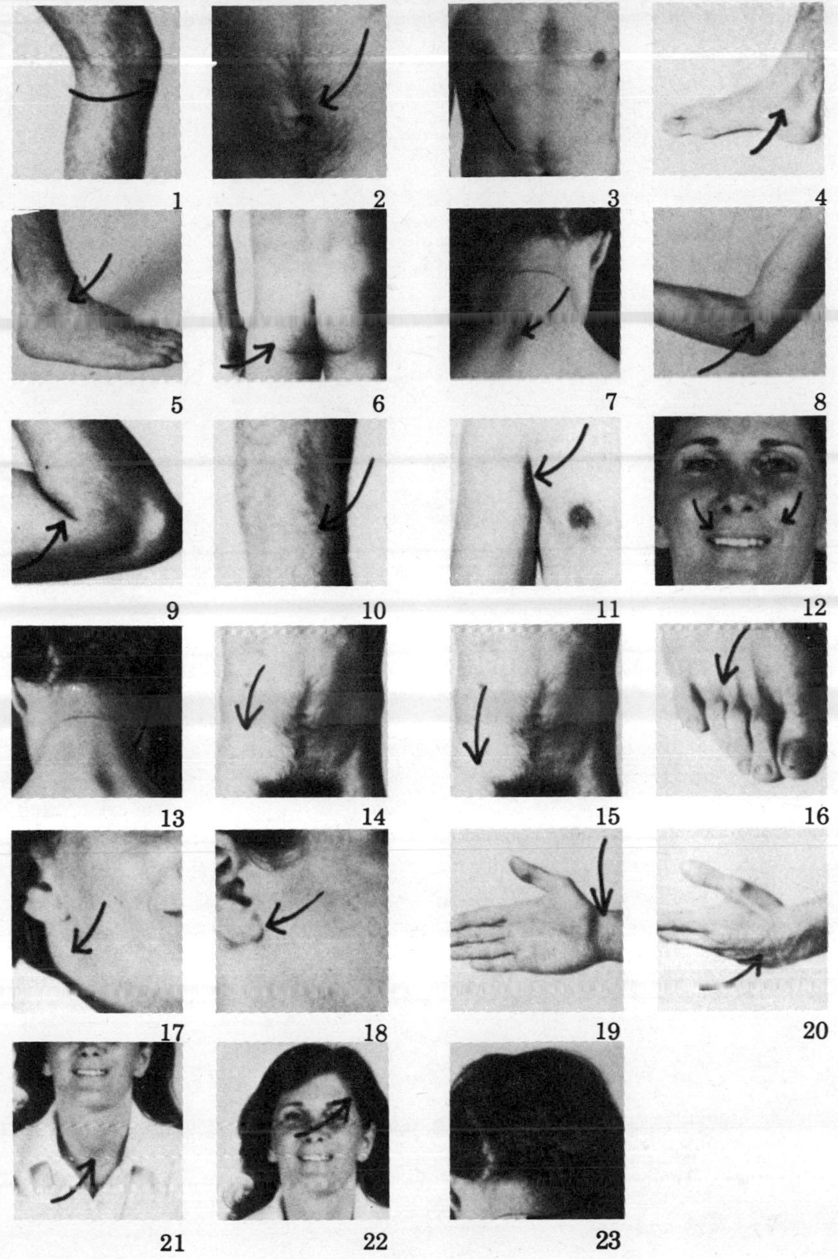
1
2
3
4
5
6
7
8
9
10
11
12
13
14
15
16
17
18
19
20
21
22
23

SIX

ACUPRESSURE TREATMENT

This section tells you how to treat the large number of pains, maladies and discomforts that acupressure can relieve. Use these simple step-by-step procedures in the following way:

1. Look up the malady you wish to treat
2. Find the landmark (as described in Chapter 5)
3. Using the acu-inch measure (as described in Chapter 4), find the correct point (or points, as most are bilateral) by following distance and location directions.
4. Apply the type and amount of pressure recommended

Remember, acupressure promises no miracles. But these points have proven effective in thousands of cases, and all are worth a try. You have nothing to lose but pain!

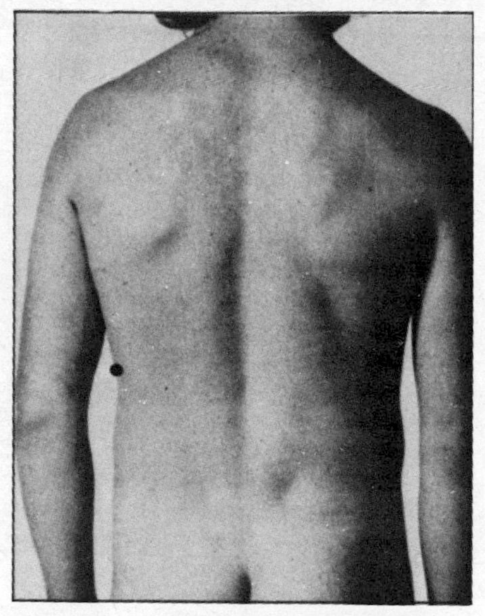

POINT: Broad Door
LANDMARK: lowest rib on chest
DISTANCE FROM LANDMARK: just below
LOCATION: 3 acu-inches toward the center, measuring from the side of the body (treat both sides)
POSITION: face down
TYPE OF PRESSURE: pulsed with thumb or fingers
AMOUNT OF PRESSURE: as much as patient can take

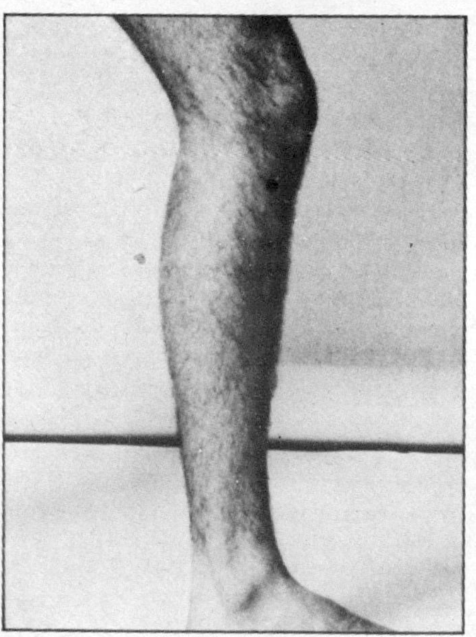

POINT: Walking Three Miles
LANDMARK: kneecap
DISTANCE FROM LANDMARK: 3 acu-inches below (in the depression)
LOCATION: 1 acu-inch toward the outside of the leg (treat both legs)
POSITION: seated in chair or flat on back
TYPE OF PRESSURE: pulsed with thumb (or pinching motion)
AMOUNT OF PRESSURE: quite firm

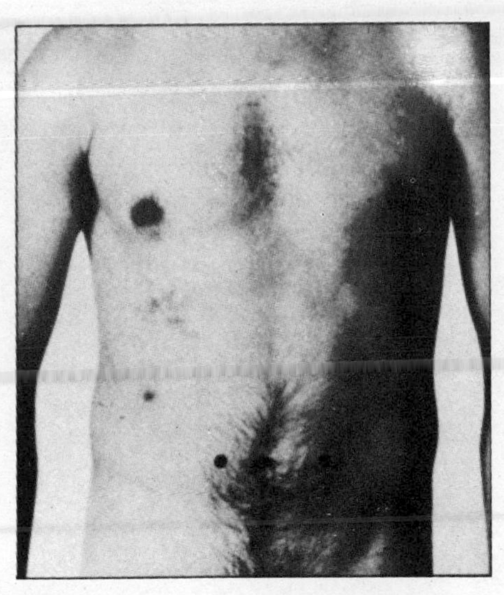

POINT: Celestial Pivot
LANDMARK: navel
DISTANCE FROM LANDMARK: right at the landmark
LOCATION: 2 acu-inches on either side of navel (treat both sides)
POSITION: flat on back
TYPE OF PRESSURE: pulsed with thumb or fingers
AMOUNT OF PRESSURE: as much as patient can take

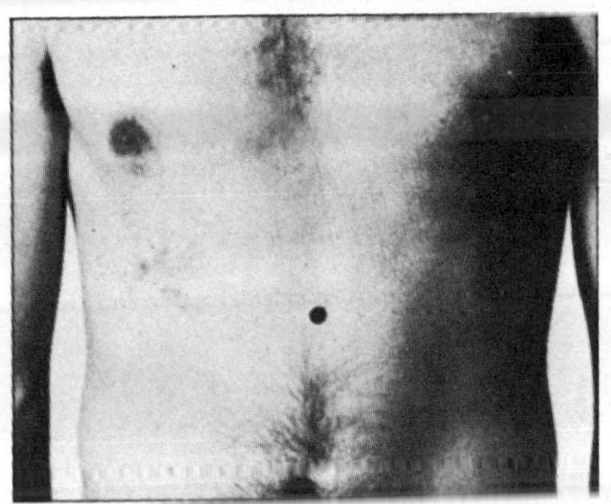

POINT: Middle Epigastrium
LANDMARK: navel
DISTANCE FROM LANDMARK: 4 acu-inches above
POSITION: flat on back
TYPE OF PRESSURE: pulsed with thumb
AMOUNT OF PRESSURE: as much as patient can take

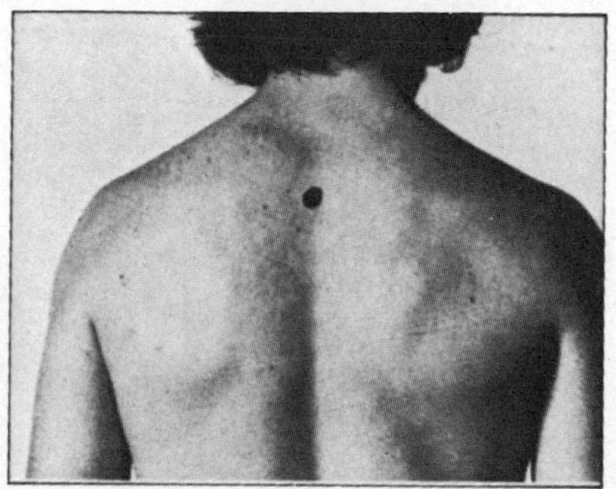

POINT: Seeking Path
LANDMARK: spine knob at neck
DISTANCE FROM LANDMARK: between landmark and next knob down the spine
LOCATION: right on spine
POSITION: on stomach
TYPE OF PRESSURE: pulsed with thumb
AMOUNT OF PRESSURE: quite firm

POINT: Welcome Fragrance
LANDMARK: nose-cheek fold
DISTANCE FROM LANDMARK: within the fold
LOCATION: ½ acu-inch up from the bottom of the nose on the cheeks (treat both sides)
POSITION: flat on back
TYPE OF PRESSURE: pulsed with thumb or fingers
AMOUNT OF PRESSURE: as much as patient can take

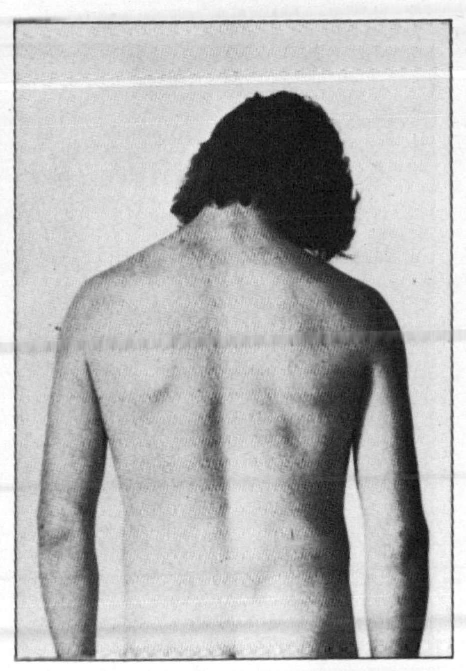

POINT: Celestial Pillar
LANDMARK: natural hairline at the back of neck
DISTANCE FROM LANDMARK: right on landmark
LOCATION: right on the hairline and 1 acu-inch on either side of the front-to-back center line of the head (treat both sides)
POSITION: seated or flat on back
TYPE OF PRESSURE: pulsed with thumb
AMOUNT OF PRESSURE: gently, then gradually increasing to maximum that patient can tolerate

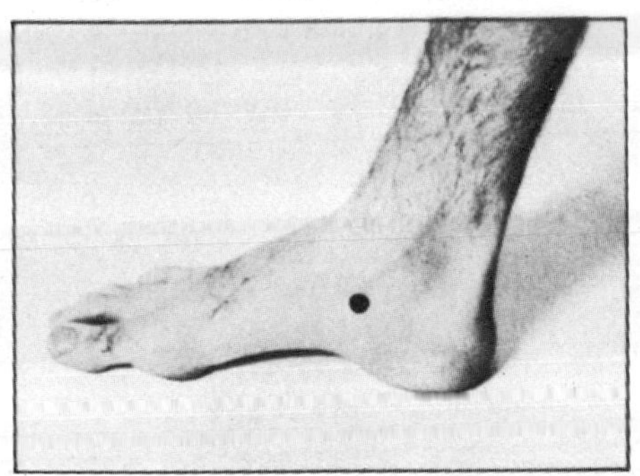

POINT: Shine To Sea
LANDMARK: inner ankle bone
DISTANCE FROM LANDMARK: immediately below
LOCATION: hollow space just below (treat both legs)
POSITION: seated or flat on back
TYPE OF PRESSURE: pulsed with thumb, pinching motion
AMOUNT OF PRESSURE: as much as patient can take

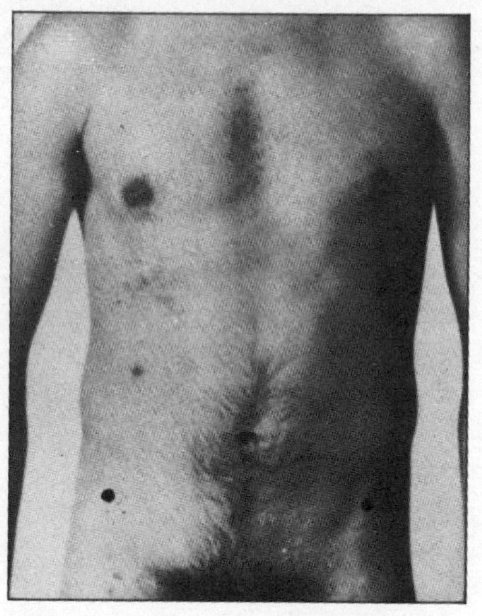

POINT: Five Pivots
LANDMARK: hip bone
DISTANCE FROM LANDMARK: 1 acu-inch toward center of body and just below hip bone
LOCATION: lower abdomen (treat both sides)
POSITION: flat on back
TYPE OF PRESSURE: pulsed with thumb, pinching motion
AMOUNT OF PRESSURE: as much as patient can take

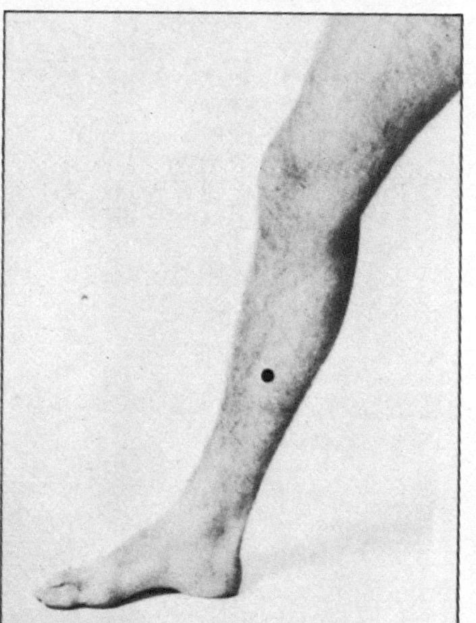

POINT: Leaking Valley
LANDMARK: inner ankle bone
DISTANCE FROM LANDMARK: 7 acu-inches above
LOCATION: inside of lower leg (treat both legs)
POSITION: seated or flat on back
TYPE OF PRESSURE: pulsed with thumb, pinching motion
AMOUNT OF PRESSURE: as much as patient can take

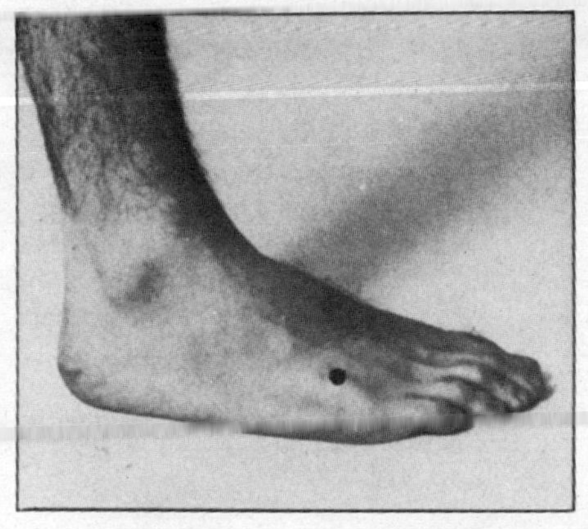

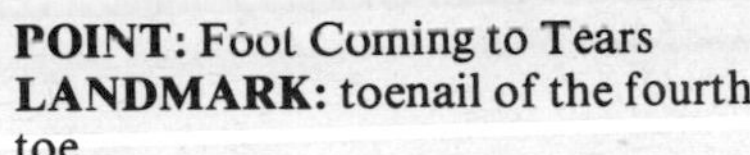

POINT: Foot Coming to Tears
LANDMARK: toenail of the fourth toe
DISTANCE FROM LANDMARK: right at landmark
LOCATION: at the intersection of a line drawn along the little-toe side of the nail and a horizontal line across the top of the nail (treat both feet)
POSITION: flat on back
TYPE OF PRESSURE: pulsed with thumb, pinching motion; repeat as needed
AMOUNT OF PRESSURE: as much as patient can take

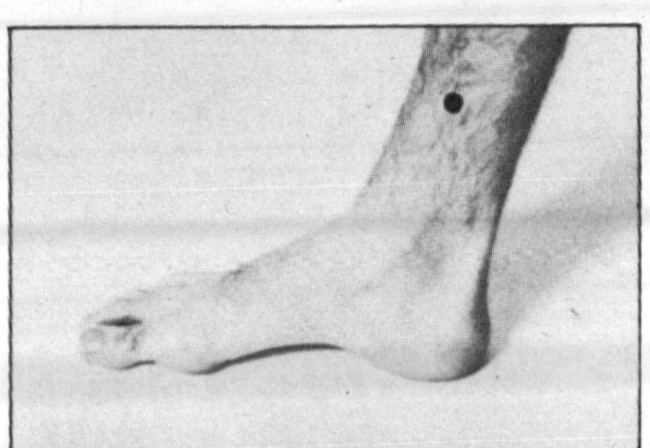

POINT: Crossroad of Three Yins
LANDMARK: inner ankle bone
DISTANCE FROM LANDMARK: 3 acu-inches above
LOCATION: inside of lower leg (treat both legs)
POSITION: seated or flat on back
TYPE OF PRESSURE: pulsed with thumb, pinching motion
AMOUNT OF PRESSURE: as much as patient can take

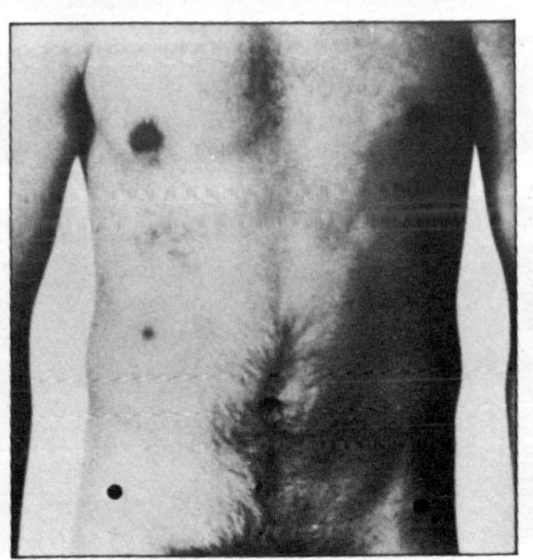

POINT: Protecting Path
LANDMARK: hip bone
DISTANCE FROM LANDMARK: 3 acu-inches directly below
LOCATION: lower abdomen (treat both sides)
POSITION. flat on back
TYPE OF PRESSURE: pulsed with thumb or fingers
AMOUNT OF PRESSURE: as much as patient can take

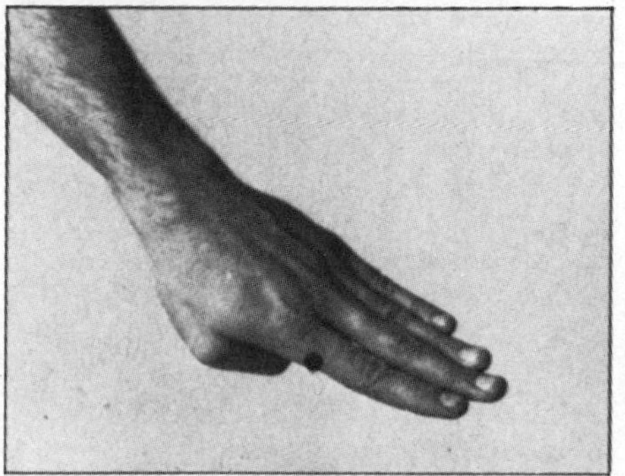

POINT: Two Intervals
LANDMARK: knuckles
DISTANCE FROM LANDMARK: just below the knuckle of the index finger
LOCATION: on the side of the index finger toward the thumb (treat both hands)
POSITION: seated
TYPE OF PRESSURE: pulsed or pinching motion
AMOUNT OF PRESSURE: as much as patient can take

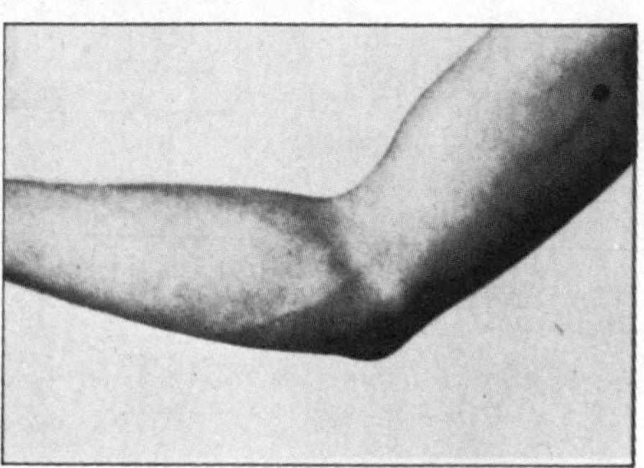

POINT: Celestial Spring
LANDMARK: inner elbow fold
DISTANCE FROM LANDMARK: 7 acu-inches up from elbow fold and 1 acu-inch in from the inner edge of the arm
LOCATION: upper arm (treat both arms)
POSITION: seated or flat on back
TYPE OF PRESSURE: pulsed with thumb
AMOUNT OF PRESSURE: as much as patient can take

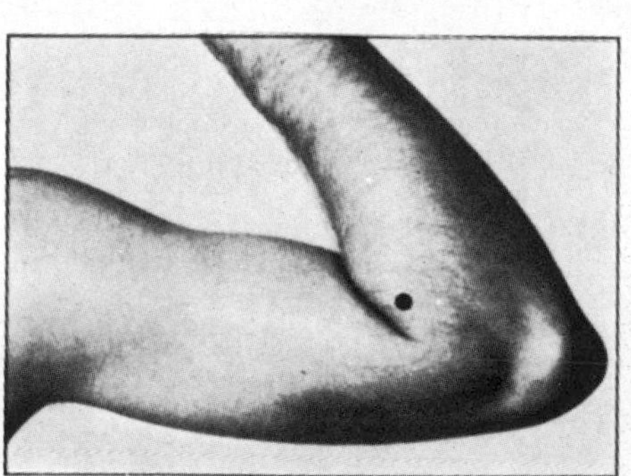

POINT: Bent Pond
LANDMARK: outer elbow fold
DISTANCE FROM LANDMARK: right at the end of the fold
LOCATION: elbow (treat both arms)
POSITION: seated or flat on back
TYPE OF PRESSURE: pulsed with thumb, pinching motion
AMOUNT OF PRESSURE: as much as patient can take

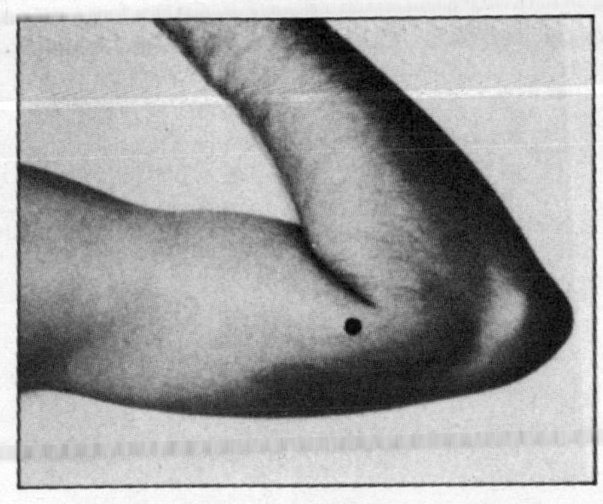

POINT: Elbow Bone
LANDMARK: outer elbow fold
DISTANCE FROM LANDMARK: 1 acu-inch above crease and just over the end of it
LOCATION: elbow (treat both arms)
POSITION: seated or flat on back
TYPE OF PRESSURE: pulsed with thumb, pinching motion
AMOUNT OF PRESSURE: as much as patient can take

ARTHRITIS (GEN WHOLE BODY)

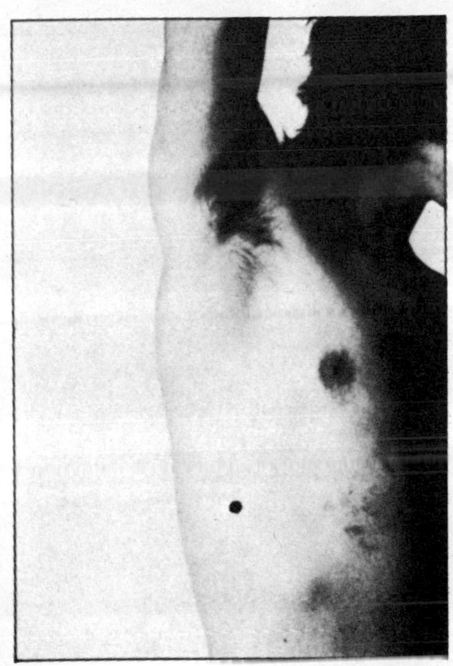

POINT: Great Bundle
LANDMARK: arm-shoulder fold
DISTANCE FROM LANDMARK: 6 acu-inches down
LOCATION: on the side of the body along the ribs (treat both sides)
POSITION: flat on back
TYPE OF PRESSURE: pulsed with thumb or fingers
AMOUNT OF PRESSURE: as much as patient can take

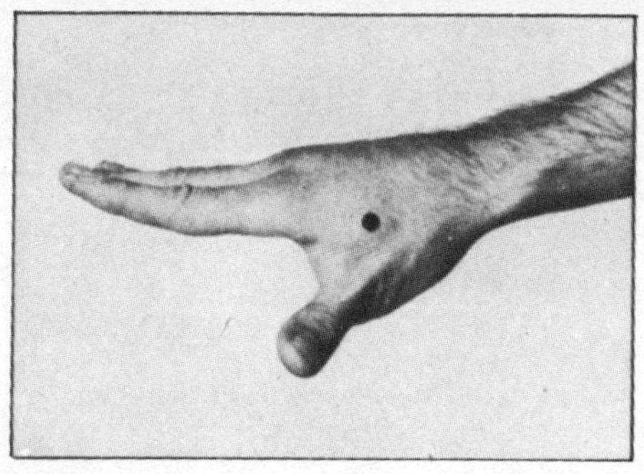

POINT: Connecting the Valleys
LANDMARK: back of hand
DISTANCE FROM LANDMARK: 1 acu-inch down from the point where bones of thumb and index finger meet
LOCATION: on the back of the hand (treat both hands)
POSITION: seated
TYPE OF PRESSURE: pulsed with thumb, pinching motion
AMOUNT OF PRESSURE: as much as patient can take

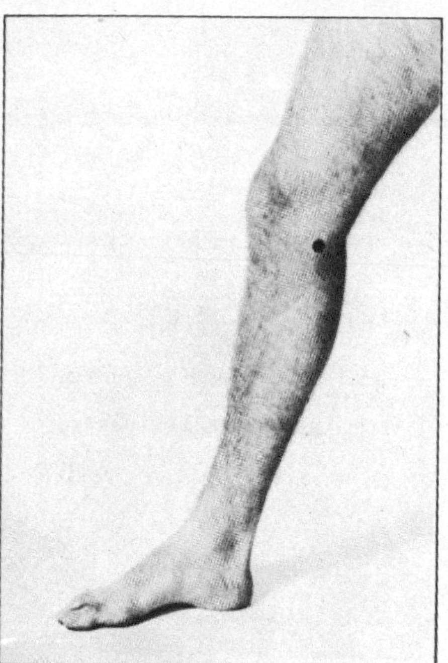

POINT: Knee Pass
LANDMARK: back of knee fold
DISTANCE FROM LANDMARK: 3 acu-inches down from knee fold
LOCATION: inner surface of calf, in the center (treat both legs)
POSITION: seated or flat on back
TYPE OF PRESSURE: pulsed with thumb, pinching motion
AMOUNT OF PRESSURE: as much as patient can take

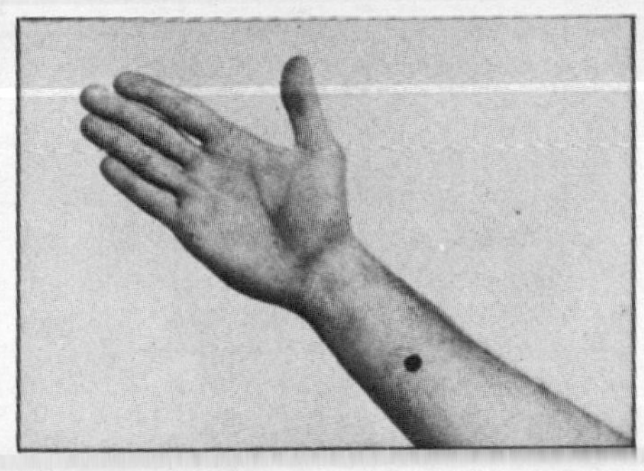

POINT: Inner Pass
LANDMARK: inner wrist fold
DISTANCE FROM LANDMARK: 2 acu-inches up
LOCATION: on the inner surface of the forearm (treat both sides)
POSITION: seated or flat on back
TYPE OF PRESSURE: pulsed with thumb, pinching motion
AMOUNT OF PRESSURE: as much as patient can take

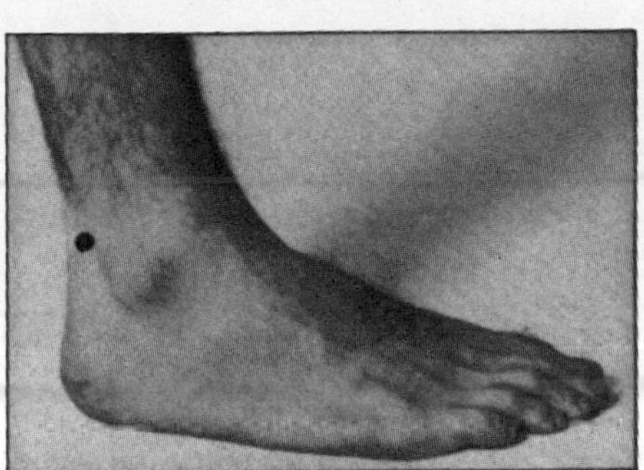

POINT: K'un Lun Mountains
LANDMARK: outer ankle bone
DISTANCE FROM LANDMARK: just in back
LOCATION: in the depression behind outer ankle bone (treat both feet)
POSITION: flat on back
TYPE OF PRESSURE: pulsed with thumb, pinching motion
AMOUNT OF PRESSURE: as much as patient can take

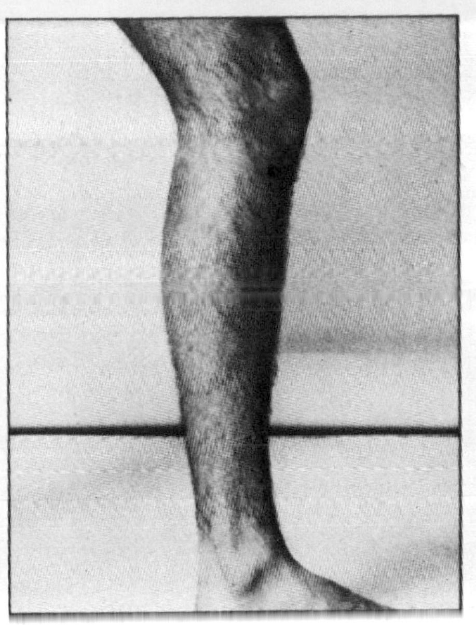

POINT: Walking Three Miles
LANDMARK: kneecap
DISTANCE FROM LANDMARK: 3 acu-inches below (in the depression)
LOCATION: 1 acu-inch toward the outside of the leg (treat both legs)
POSITION: seated in chair or flat on back
TYPE OF PRESSURE: pulsed with thumb (or pinching motion)
AMOUNT OF PRESSURE: quite firm

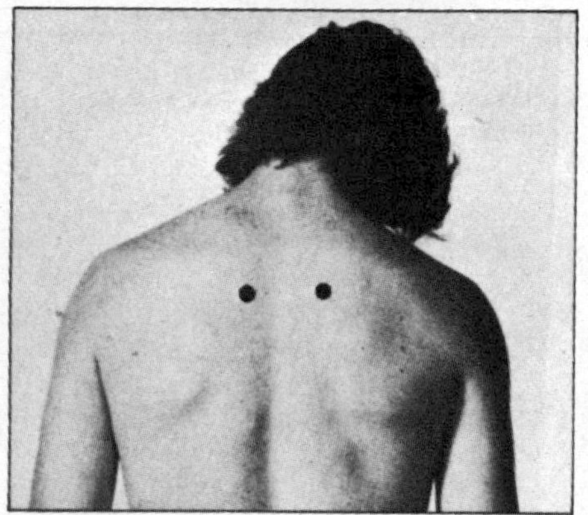

POINT: Lung Locus
LANDMARK: spine knob at neck
DISTANCE FROM LANDMARK: 2nd spine knob (vertebra) down
LOCATION: on the back, 1½ acu-inches on either side of the spine (treat both sides)
POSITION: on stomach
TYPE OF PRESSURE: pulsed with thumb
AMOUNT OF PRESSURE: as much as patient can take

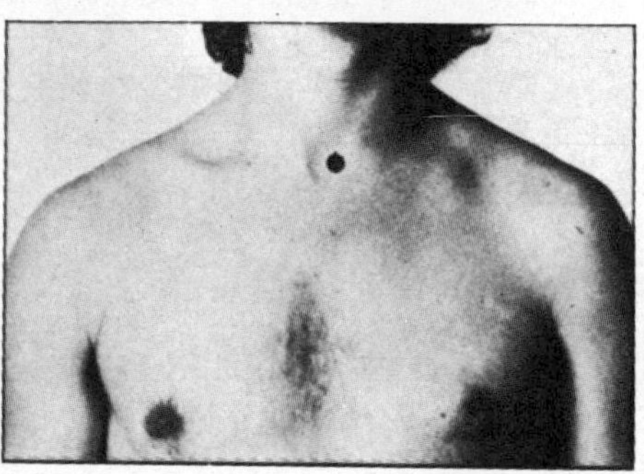

POINT: Sky Prominence
LANDMARK: throat notch
DISTANCE FROM LANDMARK: right on the spot
LOCATION: on throat, just above uppermost chest bone
POSITION: flat on back
TYPE OF PRESSURE: insert finger pressing inward and downward
AMOUNT OF PRESSURE: gently at first, then increased force with pulsed pressure to the extent that patient can take

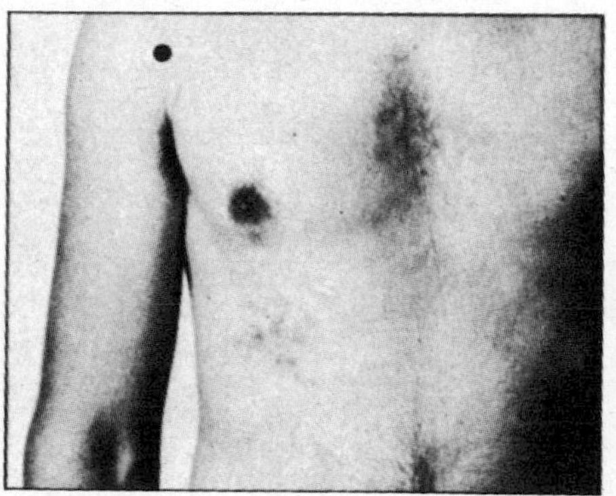

POINT: Central Perfecture
LANDMARK: arm-shoulder fold
DISTANCE FROM LANDMARK: 4 acu-inches up
LOCATION: on shoulder, 6 acu-inches on either side of centerline of chest (treat both sides of body)
POSITION: flat on back
TYPE OF PRESSURE: pulsed with thumb or fingers
AMOUNT OF PRESSURE: as much as patient can take

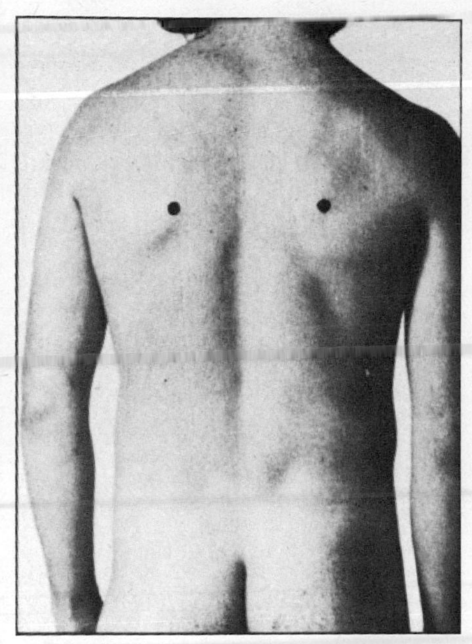

POINT: Superficial Tortuosity
LANDMARK: spine knob at neck
DISTANCE FROM LANDMARK: 4th spine knob (vertebra) down
LOCATION: on the back, 3 acu-inches on either side of the spine (treat both sides)
POSITION: on stomach
TYPE OF PRESSURE: pulsed with thumb
AMOUNT OF PRESSURE: as much as patient can take

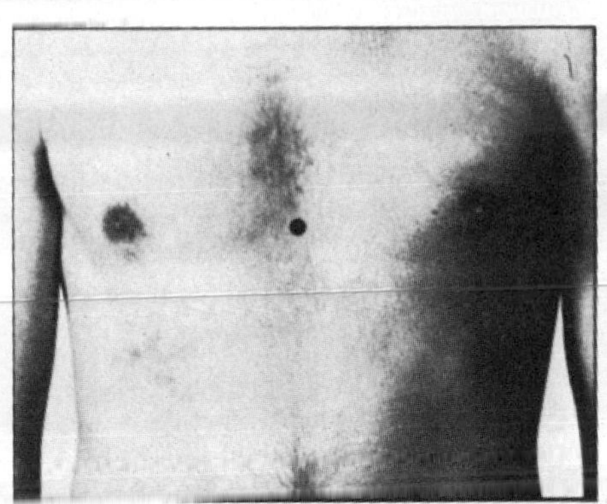

POINT: Upper Epigastrium
LANDMARK: nipples
DISTANCE FROM LANDMARK: midway between
LOCATION: on the chest, at the midpoint of a line drawn between the two nipples
POSITION: flat on back
TYPE OF PRESSURE: pulsed with thumb or fingers
AMOUNT OF PRESSURE: as much as patient can take

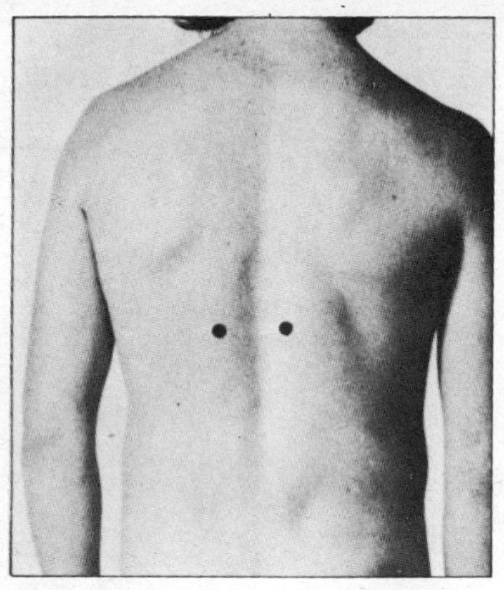

POINT: Diaphragm Locus
LANDMARK: spine knob at neck
DISTANCE FROM LANDMARK: 6th spine knob (vertebra) down
LOCATION: on back, 1½ acu-inches on either side of spine (treat both sides)
POSITION: on stomach
TYPE OF PRESSURE: pulsed with thumb
AMOUNT OF PRESSURE: as much as patient can take

BRONCHITIS

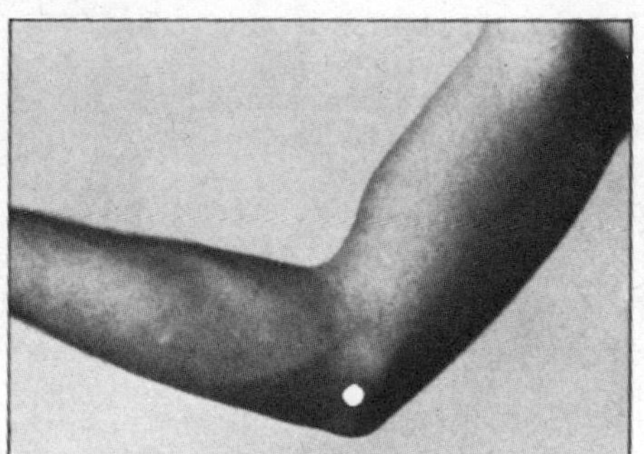

POINT: Young Sea
LANDMARK: inner elbow fold
DISTANCE FROM LANDMARK: at the body-side edge of the fold, when elbow is bent
LOCATION: elbow (treat both arms)
POSITION: seated or flat on back
TYPE OF PRESSURE: pulsed with thumb, pinching motion
AMOUNT OF PRESSURE: as much as patient can take

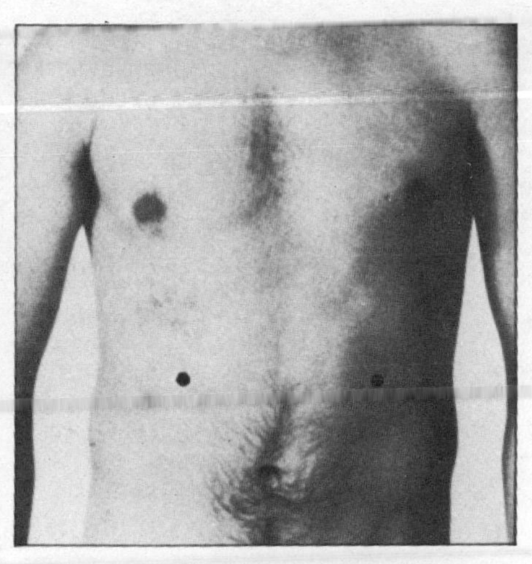

POINT: Sorrow Belly
LANDMARK: navel
DISTANCE FROM LANDMARK: 3 acu-inches above the navel
LOCATION: on the chest, 3½ acu-inches on either side of the center line of the body (treat both sides)
POSITION: flat on back
TYPE OF PRESSURE: pulsed with thumb or fingers
AMOUNT OF PRESSURE: gently, then as much as patient can tolerate

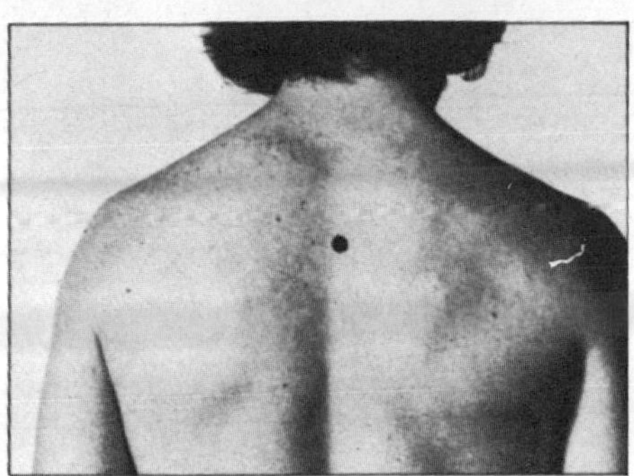

POINT: Pillar of Body
LANDMARK: spine knob at neck
DISTANCE FROM LANDMARK: 2nd spine knob (vertebra) below
LOCATION: on the back, at the spine
POSITION: on stomach
TYPE OF PRESSURE: pulsed with thumb or fingers
AMOUNT OF PRESSURE: as much as patient can take

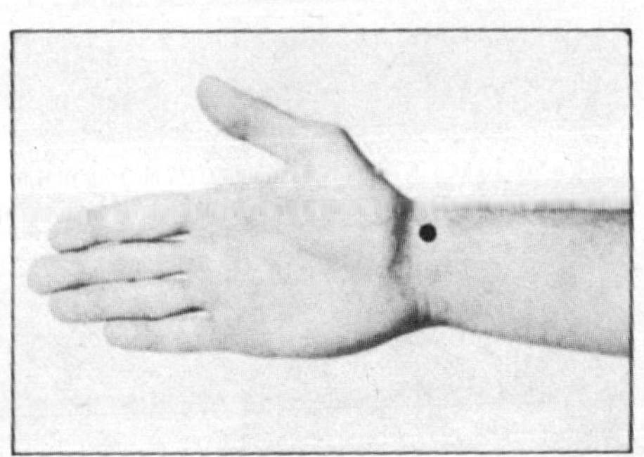

POINT: Meridian Gutter
LANDMARK: inner wrist fold
DISTANCE FROM LANDMARK: 1 acu-inch above
LOCATION: on the inside of the wrist, approximately where the pulse is taken (treat both wrists)
POSITION: flat on back or seated
TYPE OF PRESSURE: pulsed with thumb, pinching motion
AMOUNT OF PRESSURE: as much as patient can take

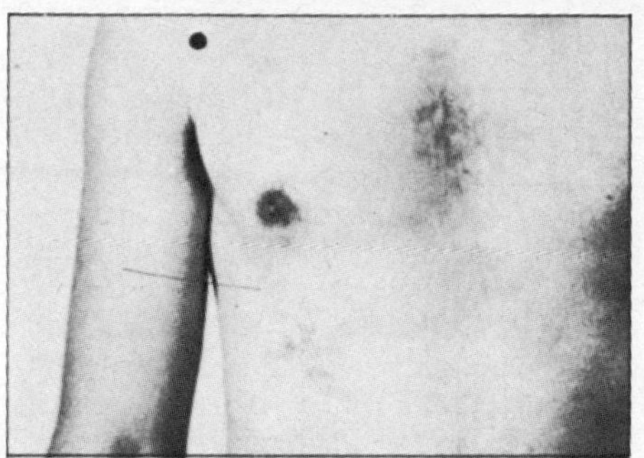

POINT: Central Perfecture
LANDMARK: arm-shoulder fold
DISTANCE FROM LANDMARK: 4 acu-inches up
LOCATION: on shoulder, 6 acu-inches on either side of centerline of chest (treat both sides of body)
POSITION: flat on back
TYPE OF PRESSURE: pulsed with thumb or fingers
AMOUNT OF PRESSURE: as much as patient can take

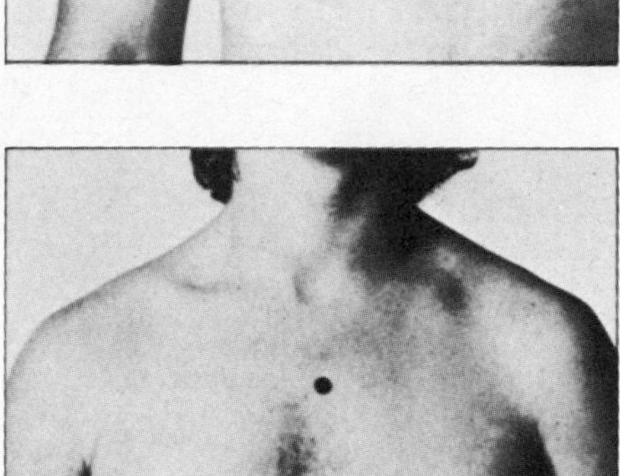

POINT: Rotating Machine
LANDMARK: throat notch
DISTANCE FROM LANDMARK: 1 acu-inch below
LOCATION: middle line of the chest
POSITION: flat on back
TYPE OF PRESSURE: pulsed with fingers
AMOUNT OF PRESSURE: gently at first; when tolerance is reached, use pulsed pressure to the extent that patient can take

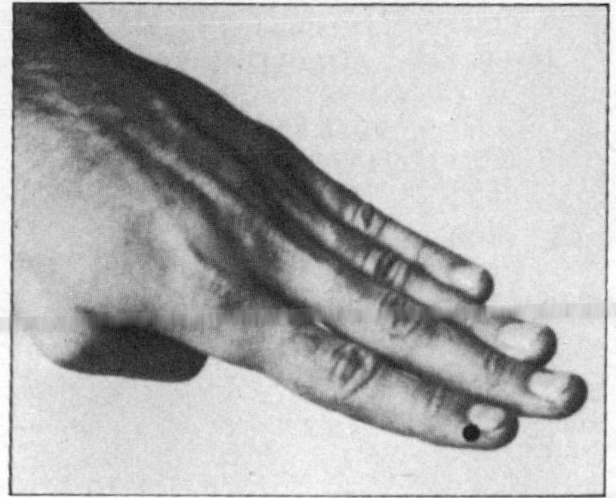

POINT: Tradesman Yang
LANDMARK: fingernail of index finger
DISTANCE FROM LANDMARK: close to the landmark
LOCATION: at the intersection of a line drawn along the thumb-side edge of the nail and a horizontal line across the base of the nail (treat both fingers)
POSITION: seated
TYPE OF PRESSURE: pulsed with thumb, pinching motion
AMOUNT OF PRESSURE: as much as patient can take

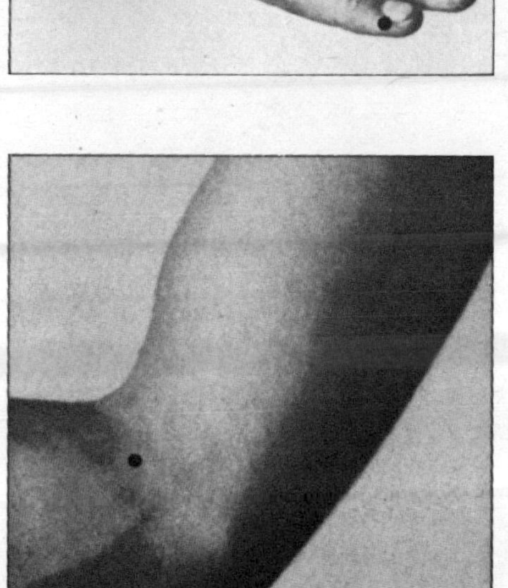

POINT: Crooked Pond
LANDMARK: inner elbow fold
DISTANCE FROM LANDMARK: along the body-side edge of fold, when elbow is bent
LOCATION: elbow (treat both arms)
POSITION: seated or flat on back
TYPE OF PRESSURE: pulsed with thumb, pinching motion
AMOUNT OF PRESSURE: as much as patient can take

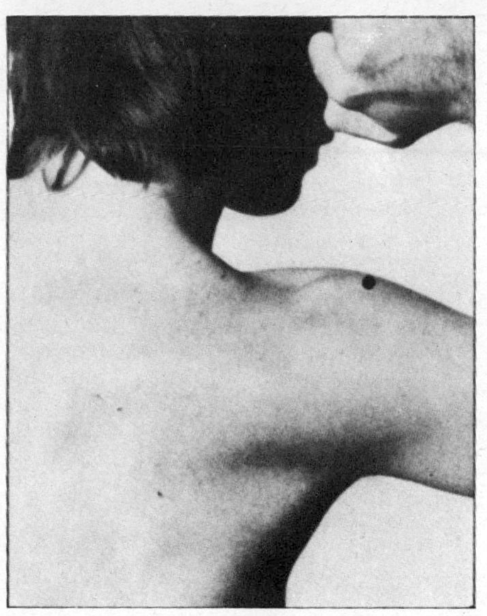

POINT: Huge Bone
LANDMARK: arm-shoulder fold
DISTANCE FROM LANDMARK: in a line directly below
LOCATION: on the shoulder at the top; feel for the spot where the collar bone meets the arm—slight hollow (treat both shoulders)
POSITION: seated or flat on back
TYPE OF PRESSURE: pulsed with thumb
AMOUNT OF PRESSURE: as much as patient can take

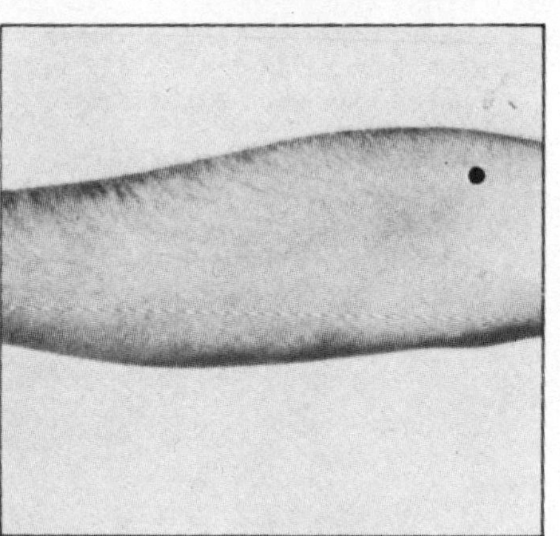

POINT: Short Narrow Marsh
LANDMARK: inner elbow fold
DISTANCE FROM LANDMARK: 1 acu-inch in from the bodyside edge of the arm
LOCATION: right on the crease (treat both arms)
POSITION: seated or flat on back
TYPE OF PRESSURE: pulsed with thumb, pinching motion
AMOUNT OF PRESSURE: as much as patient can take

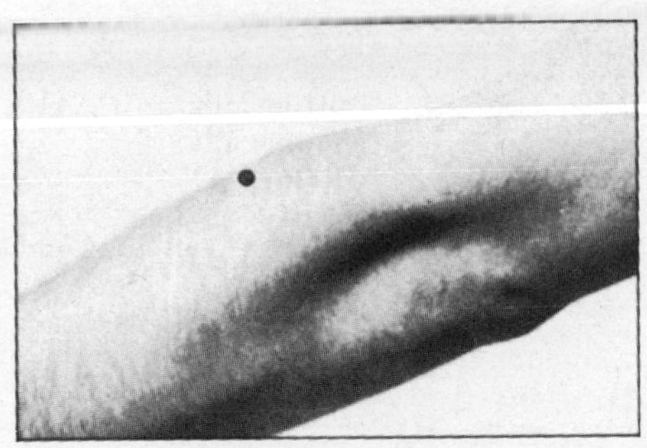

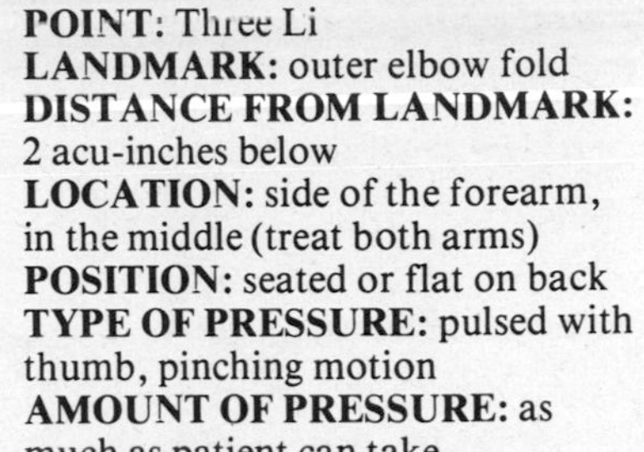

POINT: Three Li
LANDMARK: outer elbow fold
DISTANCE FROM LANDMARK: 2 acu-inches below
LOCATION: side of the forearm, in the middle (treat both arms)
POSITION: seated or flat on back
TYPE OF PRESSURE: pulsed with thumb, pinching motion
AMOUNT OF PRESSURE: as much as patient can take

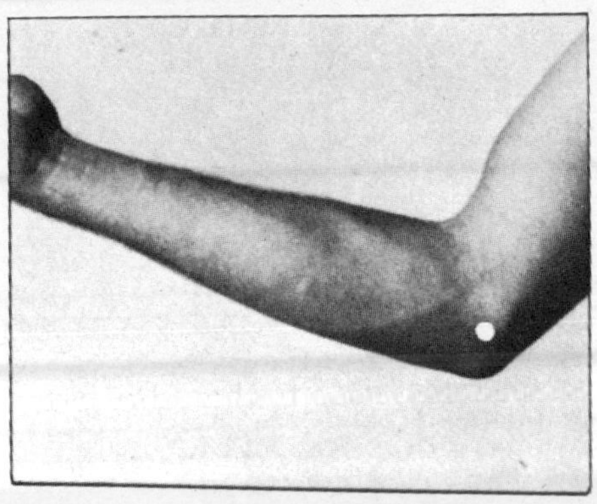

POINT: Young Sea
LANDMARK: inner elbow fold
DISTANCE FROM LANDMARK: at the body-side edge of the fold, when elbow is bent
LOCATION: elbow (treat both arms)
POSITION: seated or flat on back
TYPE OF PRESSURE: pulsed with thumb, pinching motion
AMOUNT OF PRESSURE: as much as patient can take

CALF PAIN

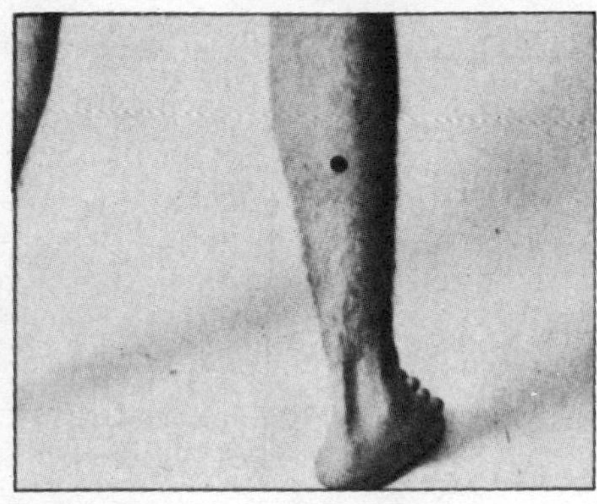

POINT: Supporting Hill
LANDMARK: outer ankle bone
DISTANCE FROM LANDMARK: 8 acu-inches up
LOCATION: back of calf, in the muscle hollow when the toes are stretched out (treat both legs)
POSITION: face down
TYPE OF PRESSURE: pulsed with thumb
AMOUNT OF PRESSURE: as much as patient can take

CALF SPASM

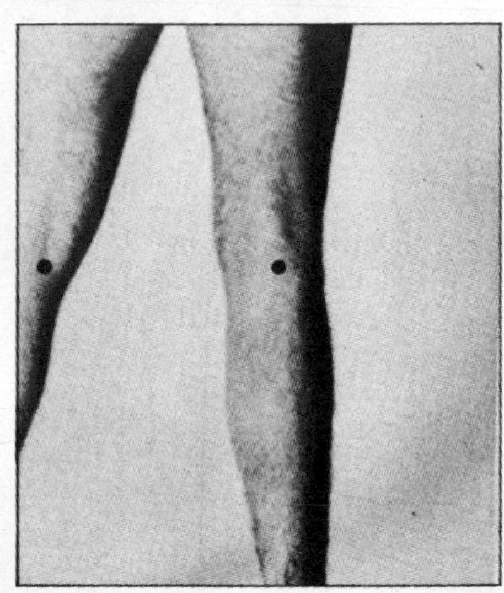

POINT: Orderly Edge
LANDMARK: back of knee fold
DISTANCE FROM LANDMARK: right in fold
LOCATION: back of knee, in the center of fold (treat both legs)
POSITION: face down
TYPE OF PRESSURE: pulsed with thumb
AMOUNT OF PRESSURE: as much as patient can take

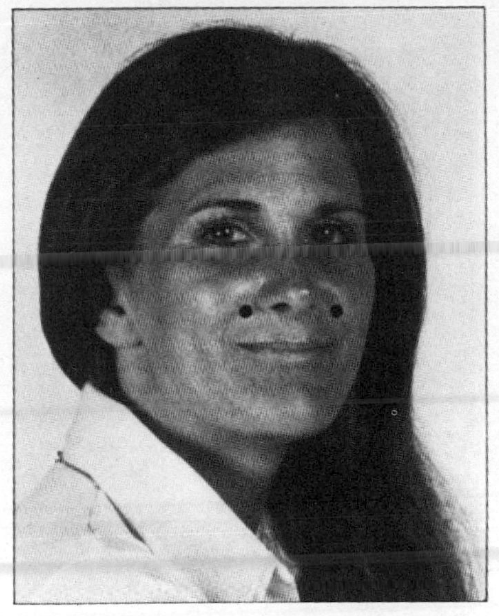

POINT: Welcome Fragrance
LANDMARK: nose-cheek fold
DISTANCE FROM LANDMARK: right on the fold
LOCATION: ½ acu-inch up from the bottom of the nose on the cheeks (treat both sides)
POSITION: flat on back
TYPE OF PRESSURE: pulsed with thumb or fingers
AMOUNT OF PRESSURE: as much as patient can take

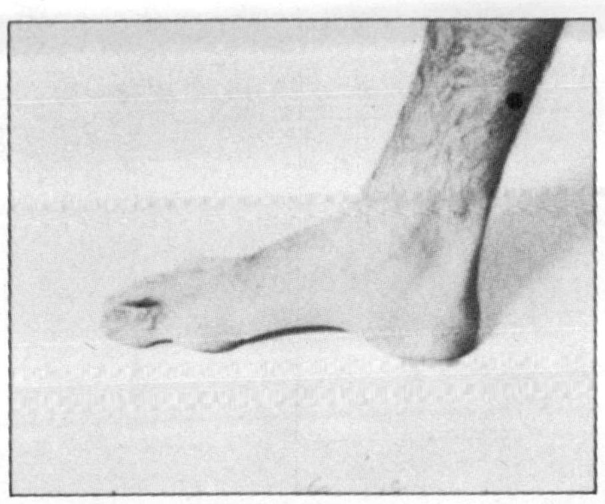

POINT: Repeating Stagnant
LANDMARK: inner ankle bone
DISTANCE FROM LANDMARK: 3 acu-inches above and 1 acu-inch behind
LOCATION: back of lower leg (treat both legs)
POSITION: seated or flat on back
TYPE OF PRESSURE: pulsed with thumb, pinching motion
AMOUNT OF PRESSURE: as much as patient can take

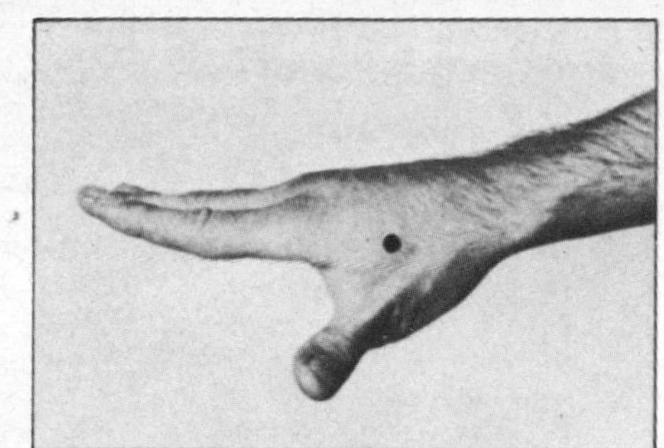

POINT: Connecting the Valleys
LANDMARK: back of hand
DISTANCE FROM LANDMARK: 1 acu-inch down from the point where bones of thumb and index finger meet
LOCATION: on the back of the hand (treat both hands)
POSITION: seated
TYPE OF PRESSURE: pulsed with thumb, pinching motion
AMOUNT OF PRESSURE: as much as patient can take

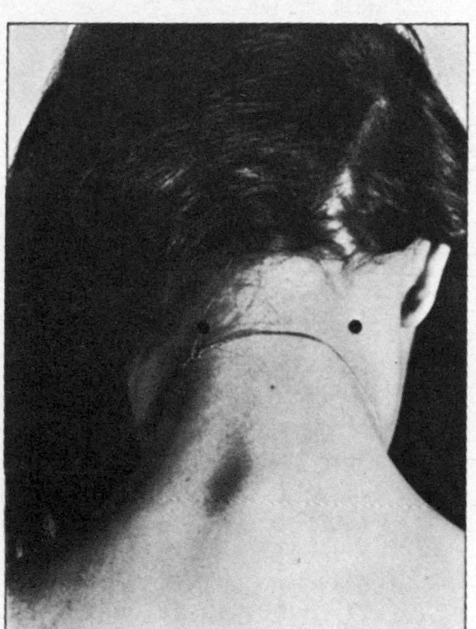

POINT: Wind Pond
LANDMARK: rear head bones
DISTANCE FROM LANDMARK: immediately below
LOCATION: feel for a depression or groove on each side just below the landmark (treat both sides)
POSITION: seated or face down
TYPE OF PRESSURE: pulsed with thumbs or fingers
AMOUNT OF PRESSURE: as much as patient can take
NOTE: if patient is sitting up, stand in front of him and rest his head against your chest; exert pressure with your fingers

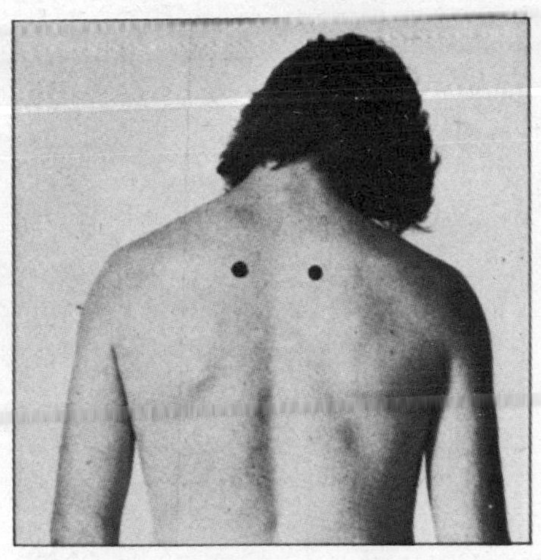

POINT: Windy Door
LANDMARK: spine knob at neck
DISTANCE FROM LANDMARK: 2nd spine knob (vertebra) down
LOCATION: on back, 1½ acu-inches on either side of spine (treat both sides)
POSITION: face down
TYPE OF PRESSURE: pulsed with thumb
AMOUNT OF PRESSURE: as much as patient can take

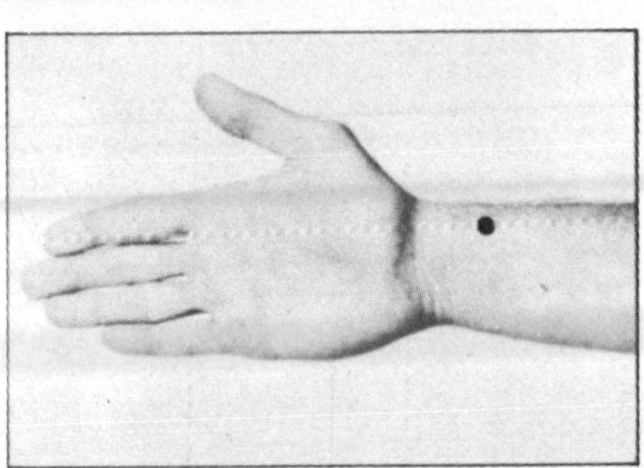

POINT: Extreme Shortcoming
LANDMARK: inner wrist fold
DISTANCE FROM LANDMARK: 2 acu-inches above
POSITION: on the inside of the wrist near the pulse (treat both arms)
TYPE OF PRESSURE: pulsed with thumb, pinching motion
AMOUNT OF PRESSURE: as much as patient can take

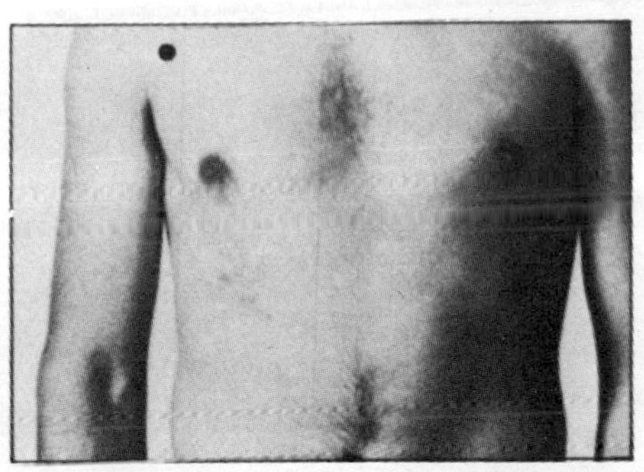

POINT: Central Perfecture
LANDMARK: arm-shoulder fold
DISTANCE FROM LANDMARK: 4 acu-inches up
LOCATION: on shoulder, 6 acu-inches on either side of centerline of chest (treat both sides of body)
POSITION: flat on back
TYPE OF PRESSURE: pulsed with thumb or fingers
AMOUNT OF PRESSURE: as much as patient can take

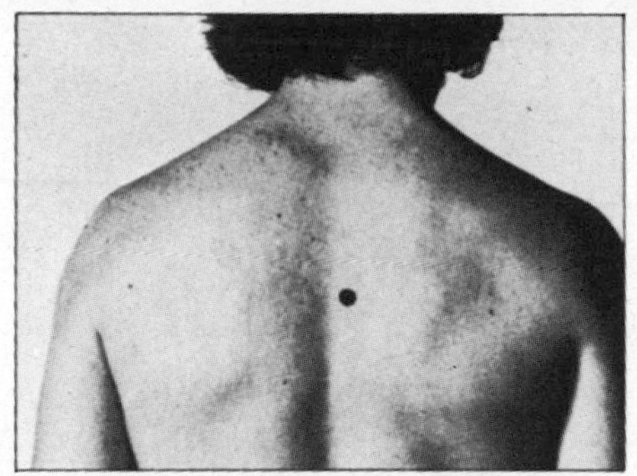

POINT: God's Path
LANDMARK: spine knob at neck
DISTANCE FROM LANDMARK: 5th spine knob (vertebra) down
LOCATION: right on the spine
POSITION: on stomach
TYPE OF PRESSURE: pulsed with thumb or fingers
AMOUNT OF PRESSURE: gently at first to establish tolerance, then as much as patient can take

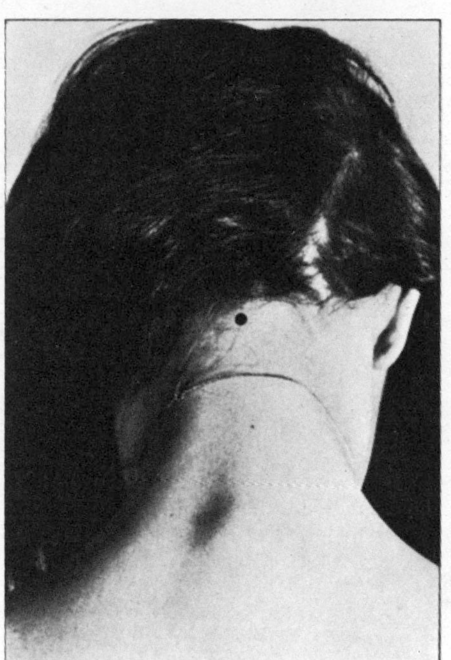

POINT: Dumb Gate
LANDMARK: natural hairline at back of head
DISTANCE FROM LANDMARK: right on the hairline
LOCATION: middle of hairline at back of head (at spine)
POSITION: face down
TYPE OF PRESSURE: pulsed with thumb or fingers
AMOUNT OF PRESSURE: gently at first to establish tolerance, then as much as patient can take

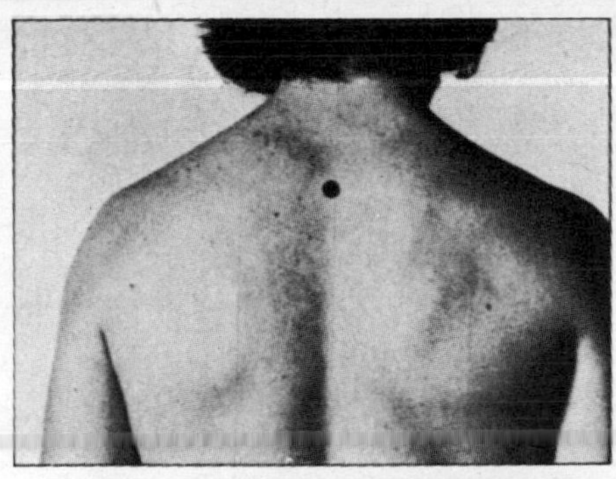

POINT: Seeking Path
LANDMARK: spine knob at neck
DISTANCE FROM LANDMARK: between landmark and next knob down the spine
LOCATION: right on spine
POSITION: on stomach
TYPE OF PRESSURE: pulsed with thumb
AMOUNT OF PRESSURE: quite firm

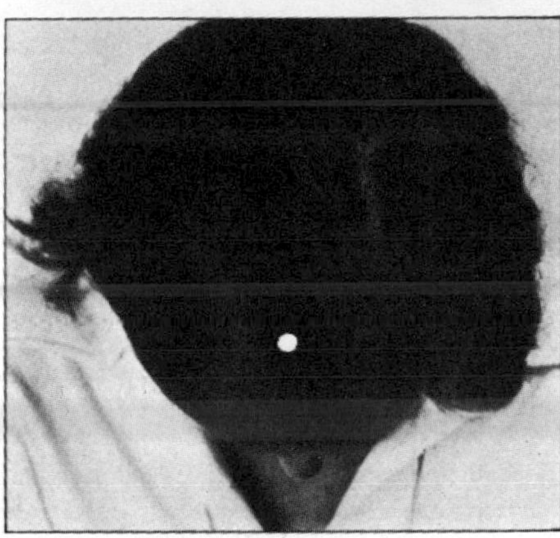

POINT: Fontanelle Meet
LANDMARK: natural hairline at forehead
DISTANCE FROM LANDMARK: 2 acu-inches above
LOCATION: at the center line of the head
POSITION: seated or flat on back
TYPE OF PRESSURE: pulsed with thumb
AMOUNT OF PRESSURE: as much as patient can take

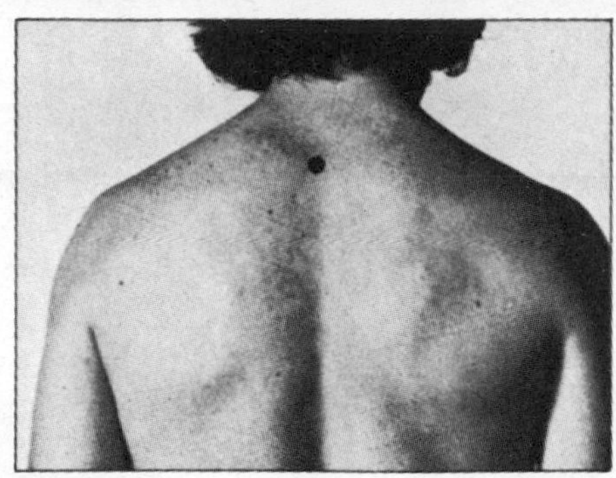

POINT: Big Vertebra
LANDMARK: natural hairline at back of head
DISTANCE FROM LANDMARK: 3 acu-inches down
LOCATION: upper back, right on the spine
POSITION: face down
TYPE OF PRESSURE: pulsed with thumb
AMOUNT OF PRESSURE: as much as patient can take

COLITIS

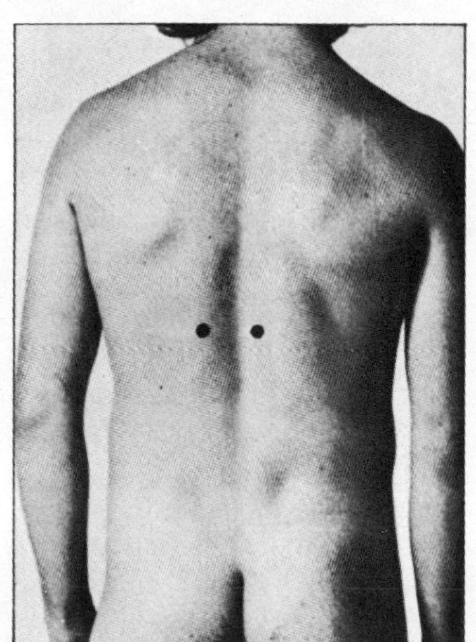

POINT: Spleen Locus
LANDMARK: spine knob at neck
DISTANCE FROM LANDMARK: 11th spine knob (vertebra) below
LOCATION: 1½ acu-inches on either side of the spine (treat both sides)
POSITION: face down
TYPE OF PRESSURE: pulsed with thumb
AMOUNT OF PRESSURE: as much as patient can take

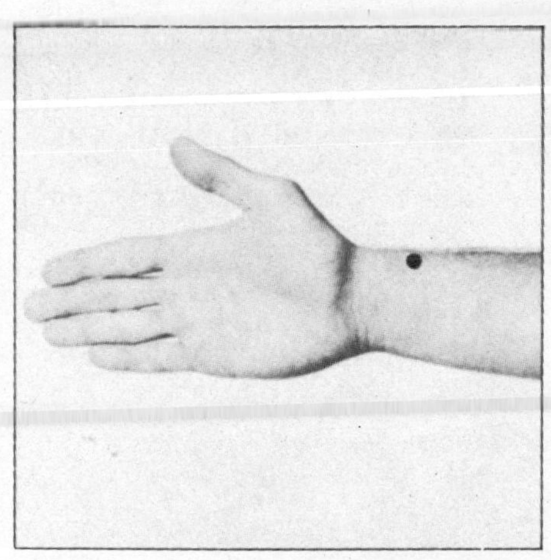

POINT: Extreme Shortcoming
LANDMARK: inner wrist fold
DISTANCE FROM LANDMARK:
2 acu-inches above
POSITION: on the inside of the wrist near the pulse (treat both arms)
TYPE OF PRESSURE: pulsed with thumb, pinching motion
AMOUNT OF PRESSURE: as much as patient can take

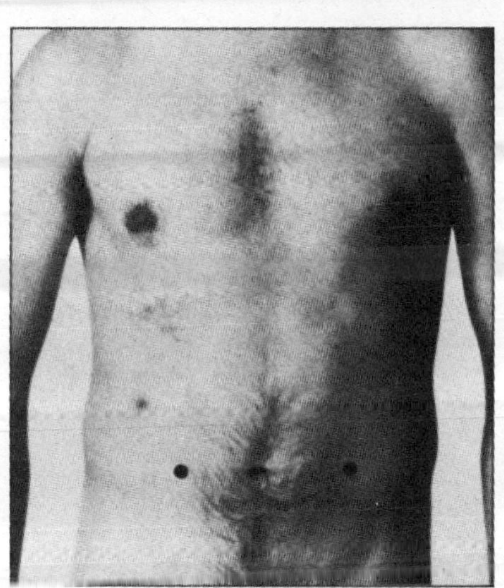

POINT: Great Cross
LANDMARK: navel
DISTANCE FROM LANDMARK:
at the same level as the navel and 3½ to 4 acu-inches on either side
LOCATION: on the stomach (treat both sides)
POSITION: flat on back
TYPE OF PRESSURE: pulsed with thumb or fingers
AMOUNT OF PRESSURE: as much as patient can take

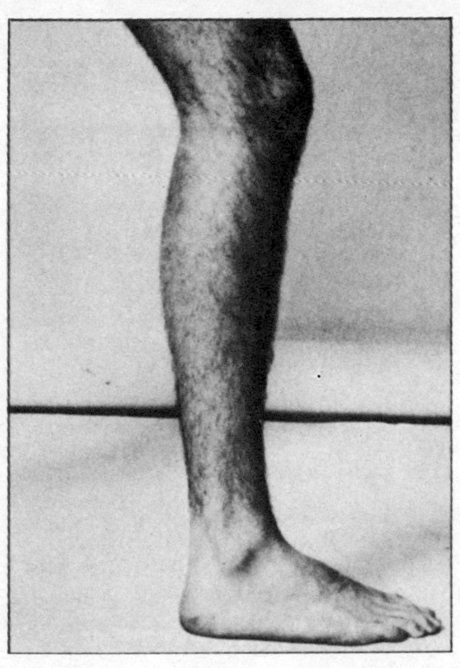

POINT: Super Great Void
LANDMARK: kneecap
DISTANCE FROM LANDMARK: 6 acu-inches below
LOCATION: right alongside the shin bone toward the outer edge of the leg (treat both legs)
POSITION: flat on back
TYPE OF PRESSURE: pulsed with thumb
AMOUNT OF PRESSURE: as much as patient can take

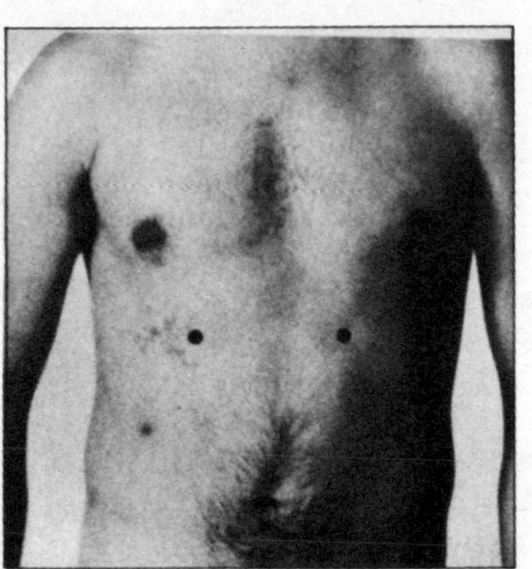

POINT: Beam Gate
LANDMARK: navel
DISTANCE FROM LANDMARK: 4 acu-inches above
LOCATION: on the chest, 2 acu-inches on either side of the center line of the chest (treat both sides)
POSITION: flat on back
TYPE OF PRESSURE: pulsed with thumb
AMOUNT OF PRESSURE: as much as patient can take

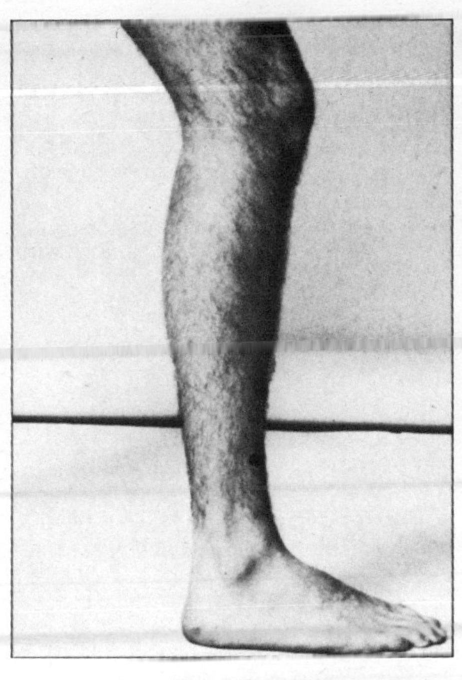

POINT: Inferior Great Void
LANDMARK: kneecap
DISTANCE FROM LANDMARK: 9 acu-inches below
LOCATION: right alongside the shin bone toward the outer edge of the leg (treat both legs)
POSITION: flat on back
TYPE OF PRESSURE: pulsed with thumb
AMOUNT OF PRESSURE: as much as patient can take

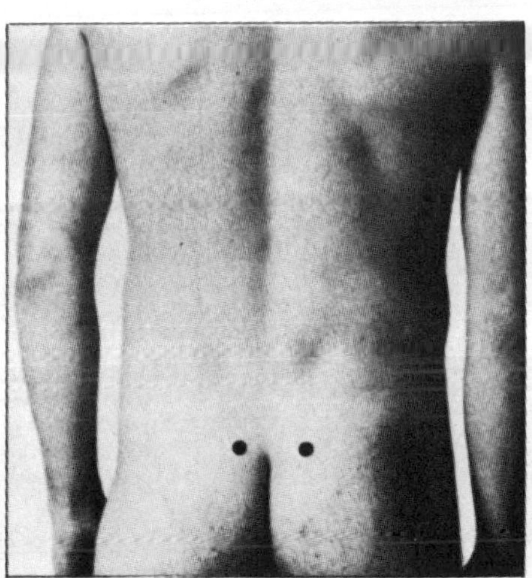

POINT: Small Intestine Locus
LANDMARK: buttocks
DISTANCE FROM LANDMARK: immediately above
LOCATION: just above the swell of the buttocks and 1½ acu-inches on either side of spine (treat both sides)
POSITION: face down
TYPE OF PRESSURE: pulsed with thumb
AMOUNT OF PRESSURE: as much as patient can take

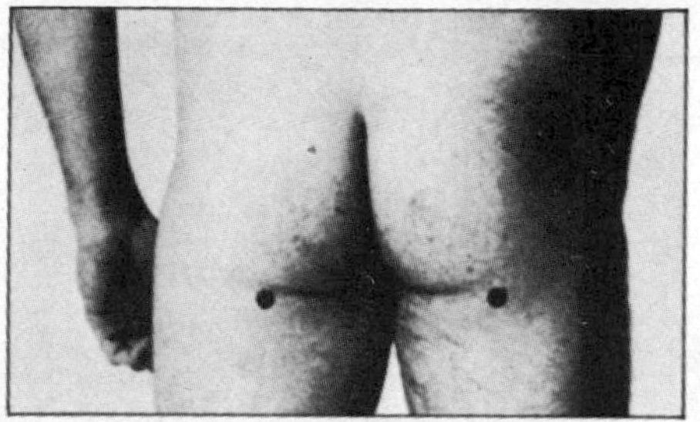

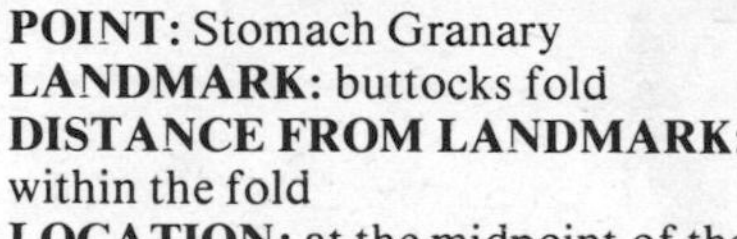

POINT: Stomach Granary
LANDMARK: buttocks fold
DISTANCE FROM LANDMARK: within the fold
LOCATION: at the midpoint of the fold line (treat both legs)
POSITION: face down
TYPE OF PRESSURE: pulsed with thumb
AMOUNT OF PRESSURE: as much as possible

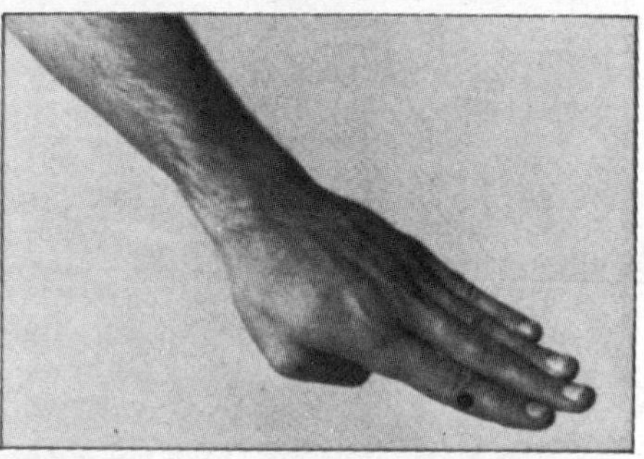

POINT: Two Intervals
LANDMARK: knuckles
DISTANCE FROM LANDMARK: just below the knuckle of the index finger
LOCATION: on the side of the index finger toward the thumb (treat both hands)
POSITION: seated
TYPE OF PRESSURE: pulsed or pinching motion
AMOUNT OF PRESSURE: as much as patient cn an take

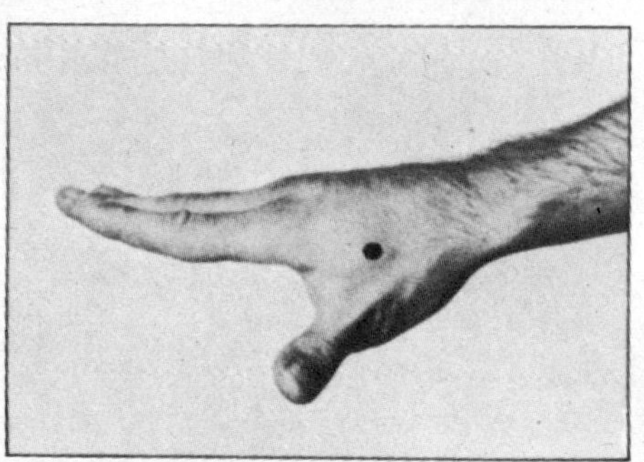

POINT: Connecting the Valleys
LANDMARK: back of hand
DISTANCE FROM LANDMARK: 1 acu-inch down from the point where bones of thumb and index finger meet
LOCATION: on the back of the hand (treat both hands)
POSITION: seated
TYPE OF PRESSURE: pulsed with thumb, pinching motion
AMOUNT OF PRESSURE: as much as patient can take

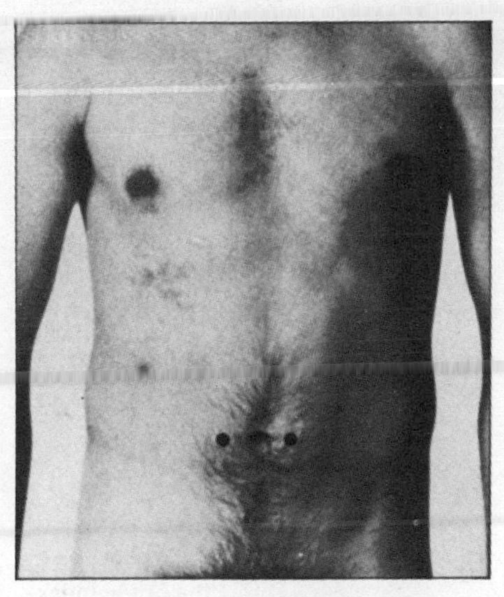

POINT: Mang Locus
LANDMARK: navel
DISTANCE FROM LANDMARK: ½ acu-inch on either side
LOCATION: at the level of the navel (treat both sides)
POSITION: flat on back
TYPE OF PRESSURE: pulsed with thumb
AMOUNT OF PRESSURE: as much as patient can take

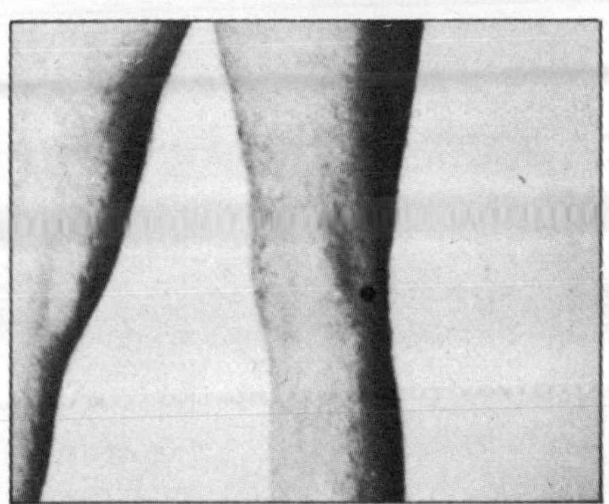

POINT: Room of Determination
LANDMARK: back of knee fold
DISTANCE FROM LANDMARK: 1 acu-inch above the fold
LOCATION: 1 acu-inch from outer edge of knee fold (treat both legs)
POSITION: face down
TYPE OF PRESSURE: pulsed with thumb
AMOUNT OF PRESSURE: as much as patient can take

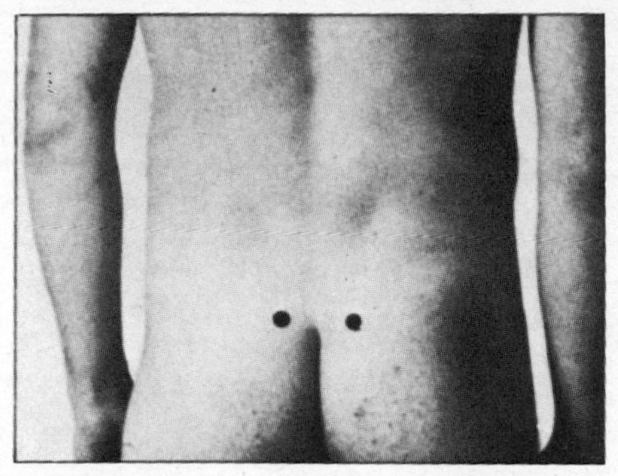

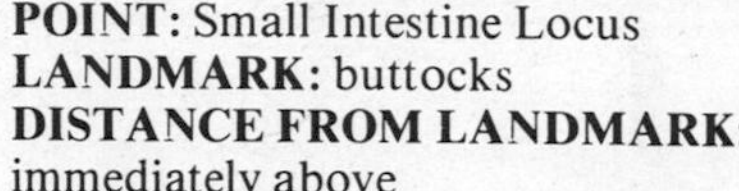

POINT: Small Intestine Locus
LANDMARK: buttocks
DISTANCE FROM LANDMARK: immediately above
LOCATION: just above the swell of the buttocks and 1½ acu-inches on either side of spine (treat both sides)
POSITION: face down
TYPE OF PRESSURE: pulsed with thumb
AMOUNT OF PRESSURE: as much as patient can take

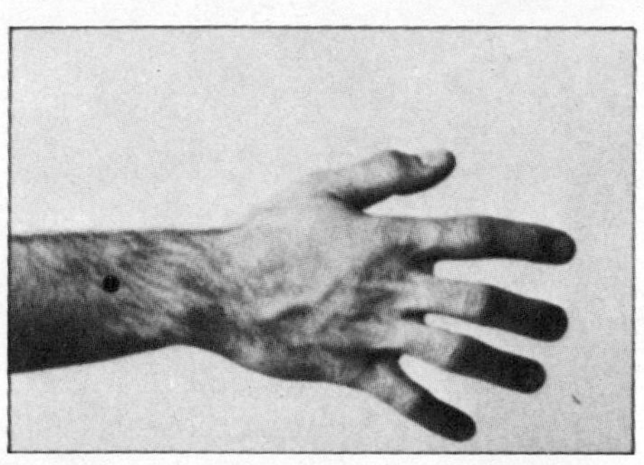

POINT: Branching Ditch
LANDMARK: wrist fold
DISTANCE FROM LANDMARK: 3 acu-inches above
LOCATION: on the back of the forearm, in the middle (treat both arms)
POSITION: seated or flat on back
TYPE OF PRESSURE: pulsed with thumb, pinching motion
AMOUNT OF PRESSURE: as much as patient can take

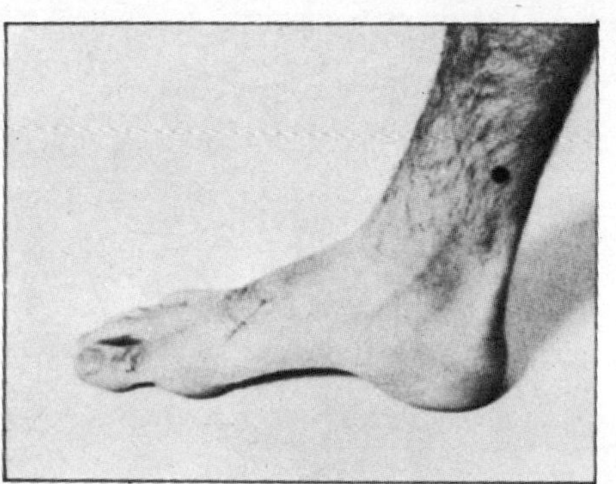

POINT: Delivering Message
LANDMARK: inner ankle bone
DISTANCE FROM LANDMARK: 3 acu-inches above
LOCATION: in the middle of the leg (treat both legs)
POSITION: flat on back
TYPE OF PRESSURE: pulsed with thumb, pinching motion
AMOUNT OF PRESSURE: as much as patient can take

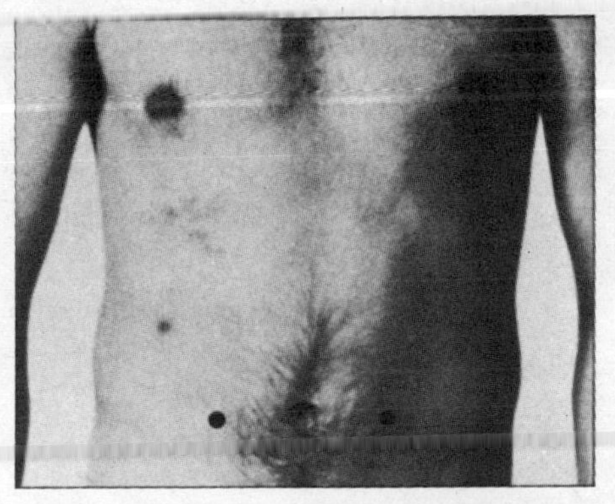

POINT: Great Cross
LANDMARK: navel
DISTANCE FROM LANDMARK: at the same level as the navel and 3½ to 4 acu-inches on either side
LOCATION: on the stomach (treat both sides)
POSITION: flat on back
TYPE OF PRESSURE: pulsed with thumb or fingers
AMOUNT OF PRESSURE: as much as patient can take

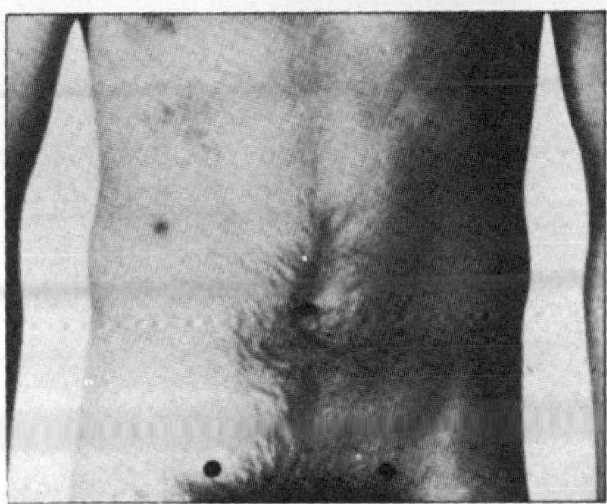

POINT: Perfecture House
LANDMARK: thigh-stomach fold, navel
DISTANCE FROM LANDMARK: in the fold at a point 3 acu-inches down from the navel
LOCATION: lower stomach (treat both sides)
POSITION: flat on back
TYPE OF PRESSURE: pulsed with thumb
AMOUNT OF PRESSURE: as much as patient can take

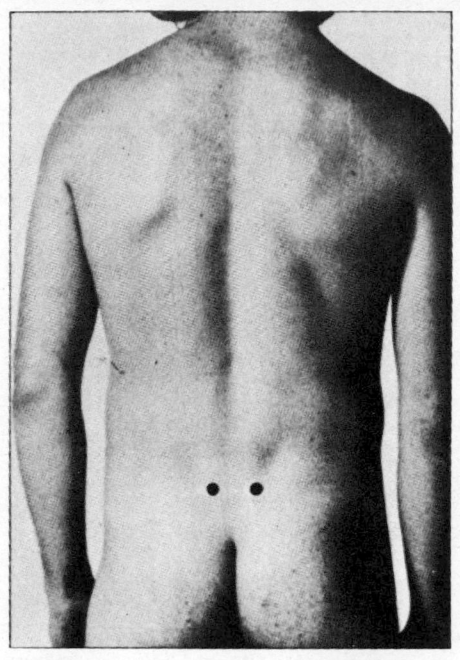

POINT: Large Intestine Locus
LANDMARK: spine knob at neck
DISTANCE FROM LANDMARK: 16th spine knob (vertebra) below
LOCATION: 1½ acu-inches on either side of the spine (treat both sides)
POSITION: face down
TYPE OF PRESSURE: pulsed with thumb
AMOUNT OF PRESSURE: as much as patient can take

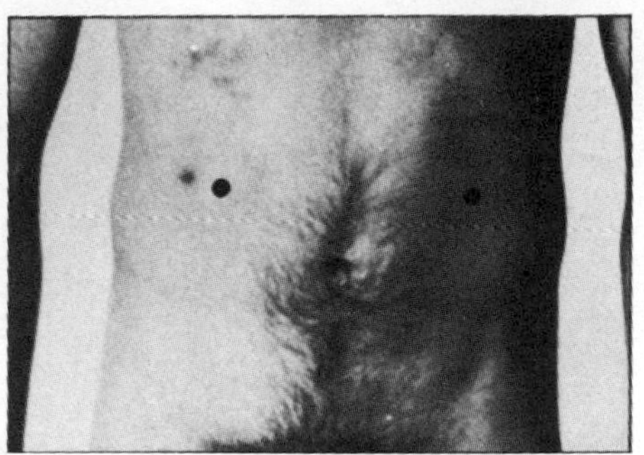

POINT: Sorrow Belly
LANDMARK: navel
DISTANCE FROM LANDMARK: 3 acu-inches above the navel
LOCATION: on the chest, 3½ acu-inches on either side of the center line of the body (treat both sides)
POSITION: flat on back
TYPE OF PRESSURE: pulsed with thumb or fingers
AMOUNT OF PRESSURE: gently, then as much as patient can tolerate

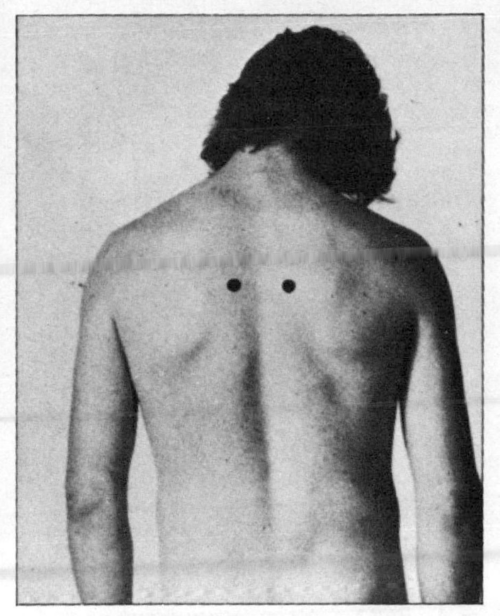

POINT: Lung Locus
LANDMARK: spine knob at neck
DISTANCE FROM LANDMARK: 2nd spine knob (vertebra) down
LOCATION: on the back, 1½ acu-inches on either side of the spine (treat both sides)
POSITION: on stomach
TYPE OF PRESSURE: pulsed with thumb
AMOUNT OF PRESSURE: as much as patient can take

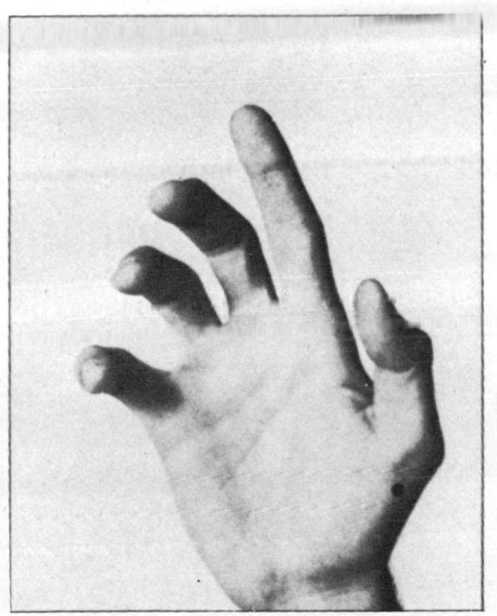

POINT: Fish Seam
LANDMARK: thumb fold in palm of hand
DISTANCE FROM LANDMARK: 1 acu-inch above
LOCATION: on the palm side of the hand; apply pressure right on top of the thumb bone (treat both hands)
POSITION: seated
TYPE OF PRESSURE: pulsed with thumb, pinching motion
AMOUNT OF PRESSURE: as much as patient can take

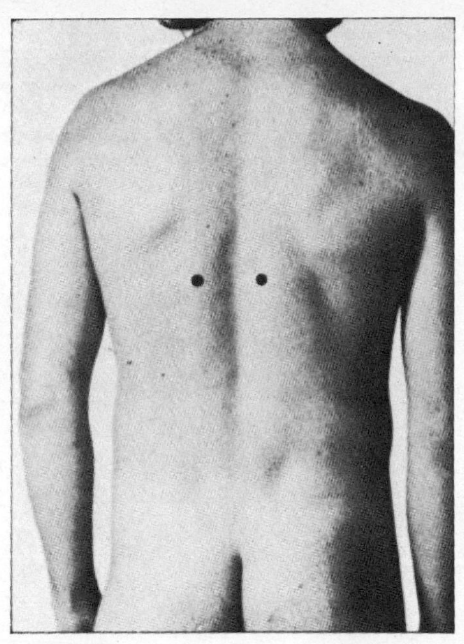

POINT: Diaphragm Locus
LANDMARK: spine knob at neck
DISTANCE FROM LANDMARK: 6th spine knob (vertebra) down
LOCATION: on back, 1½ acu-inches on either side of spine (treat both sides)
POSITION: on stomach
TYPE OF PRESSURE: pulsed with thumb
AMOUNT OF PRESSURE: as much as patient can take

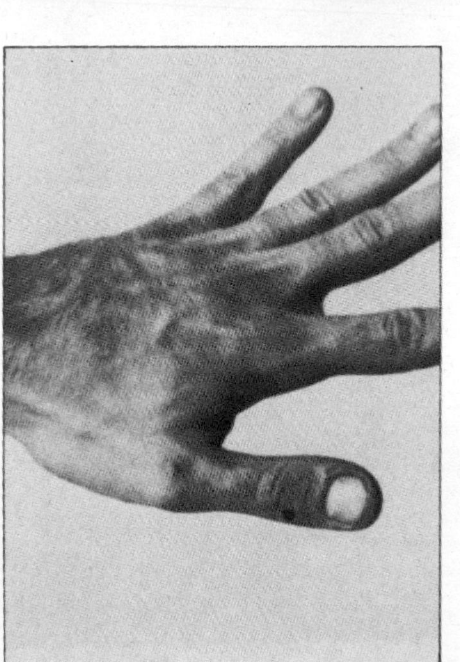

POINT: Yang Tradesman
LANDMARK: thumbnail
DISTANCE FROM LANDMARK: close to landmark
LOCATION: at the intersection of a line drawn along the outer edge of nail and a horizontal line across the base of the nail (treat both thumbs)
POSITION: seated
TYPE OF PRESSURE: pulsed with thumb, pinching motion
AMOUNT OF PRESSURE: as much as patient can take

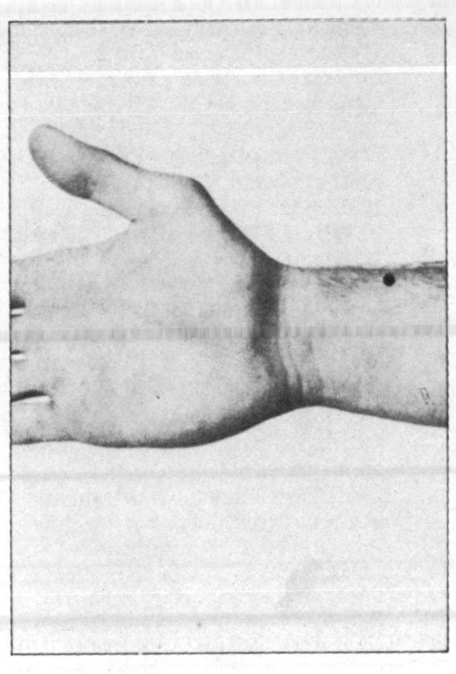

POINT: Extreme Shortcoming
LANDMARK: inner wrist fold
DISTANCE FROM LANDMARK: 2 acu-inches above
POSITION: on the inside of the wrist near the pulse (treat both arms)
TYPE OF PRESSURE: pulsed with thumb, pinching motion
AMOUNT OF PRESSURE: as much as patient can take

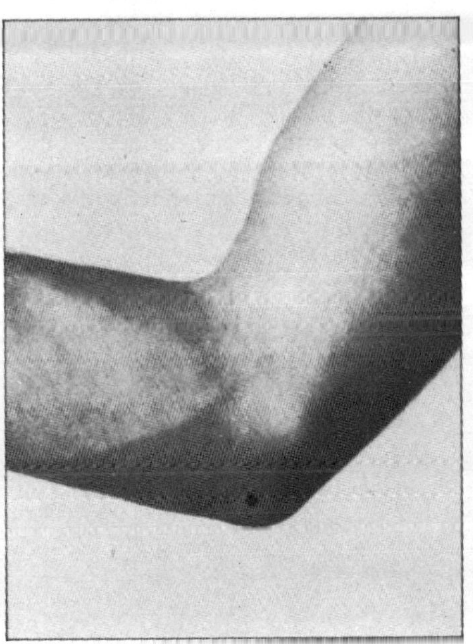

POINT: Young Sea
LANDMARK: inner elbow fold
DISTANCE FROM LANDMARK: at the body-side edge of the fold, when elbow is bent
LOCATION: elbow (treat both arms)
POSITION: seated or flat on back
TYPE OF PRESSURE: pulsed with thumb, pinching motion
AMOUNT OF PRESSURE: as much as patient can take

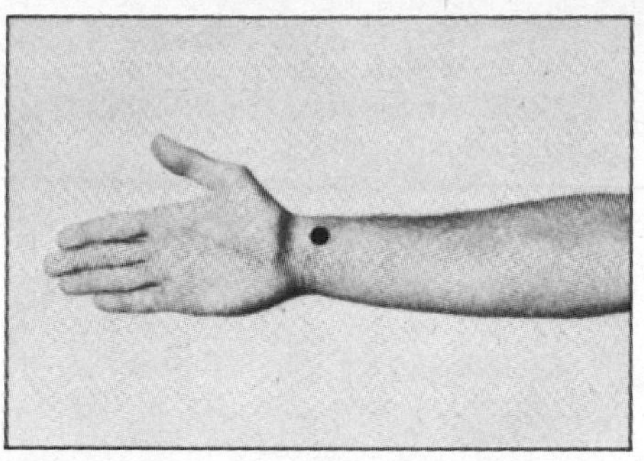

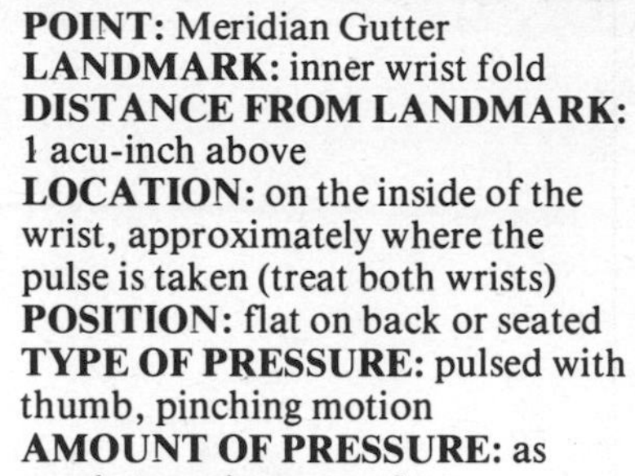

POINT: Meridian Gutter
LANDMARK: inner wrist fold
DISTANCE FROM LANDMARK: 1 acu-inch above
LOCATION: on the inside of the wrist, approximately where the pulse is taken (treat both wrists)
POSITION: flat on back or seated
TYPE OF PRESSURE: pulsed with thumb, pinching motion
AMOUNT OF PRESSURE: as much as patient can take

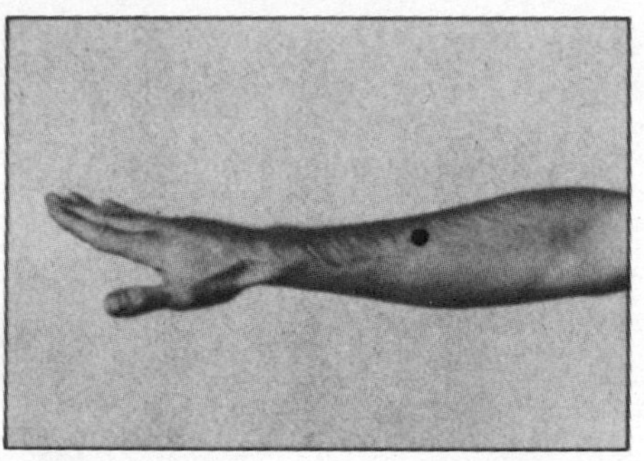

POINT: Supreme Cave
LANDMARK: inner elbow fold
DISTANCE FROM LANDMARK: 5 acu-inches down
LOCATION: on the inner surface of the forearm, 1 acu-inch in from the outer edge (treat both arms)
POSITION: seated or flat on back
TYPE OF PRESSURE: pulsed with thumb, pinching motion
AMOUNT OF PRESSURE: as much as patient can take

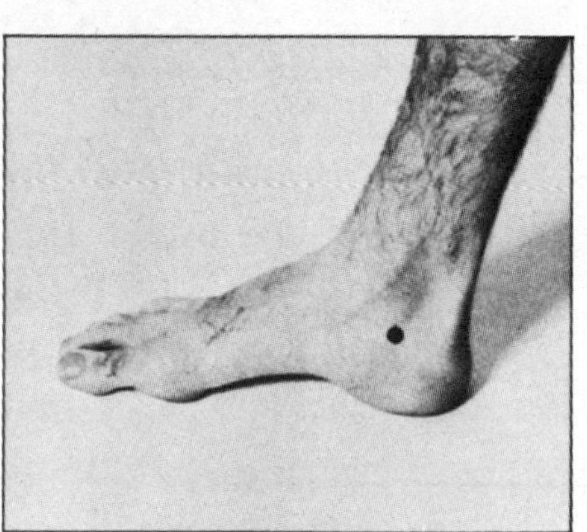

POINT: Great Brook
LANDMARK: inner ankle bone
DISTANCE FROM LANDMARK: just in back of ankle bone
LOCATION: in the depression that you can feel at this spot (treat both legs)
POSITION: flat on back
TYPE OF PRESSURE: pulsed with thumb, pinching motion
AMOUNT OF PRESSURE: as much as patient can take

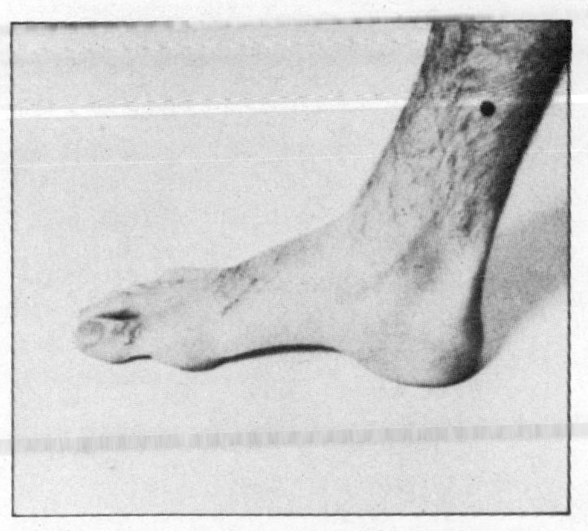

POINT: Delivering Message
LANDMARK: inner ankle bone
DISTANCE FROM LANDMARK: 3 acu-inches above
LOCATION: in the middle of the leg (treat both legs)
POSITION: flat on back
TYPE OF PRESSURE: pulsed with thumb, pinching motion
AMOUNT OF PRESSURE: as much as patient can take

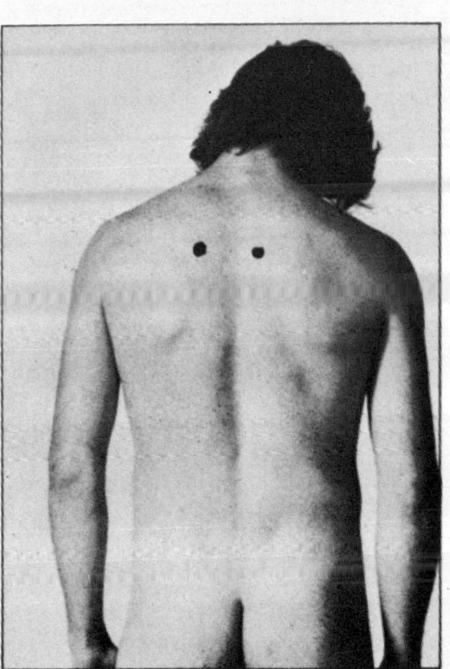

POINT: Windy Door
LANDMARK: spine knob at neck
DISTANCE FROM LANDMARK: 2nd spine knob (vertebra) down
LOCATION: on back, 1½ acu-inches on either side of spine (treat both sides)
POSITION: face down
TYPE OF PRESSURE: pulsed with thumb
AMOUNT OF PRESSURE: as much as patient can take

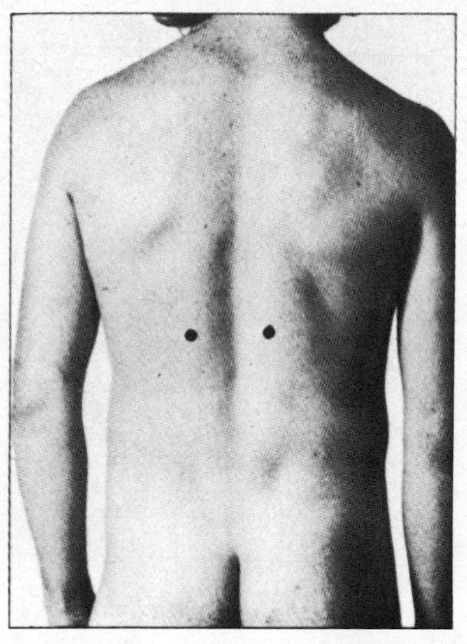

POINT: Gallbladder Locus
LANDMARK: spine knob at neck
DISTANCE FROM LANDMARK: 10th spine knob (vertebra) below
LOCATION: on the back, 1½ acu-inches from spine (treat both sides)
POSITION: on stomach
TYPE OF PRESSURE: pulsed with thumb
AMOUNT OF PRESSURE: gently at first, then as much as patient can take

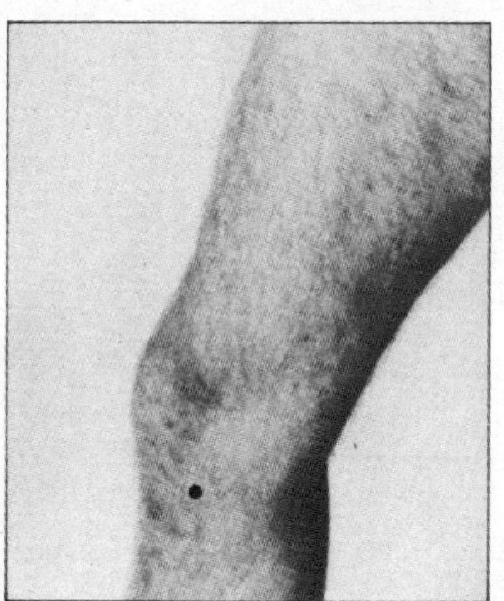

POINT: Spring in Shady Mound
LANDMARK: back of knee fold
DISTANCE FROM LANDMARK: 2 acu-inches below
LOCATION: on the inner surface of the leg, in the approximate center (treat both legs)
POSITION: flat on back or seated
TYPE OF PRESSURE: pulsed with thumb
AMOUNT OF PRESSURE: as much as patient can take

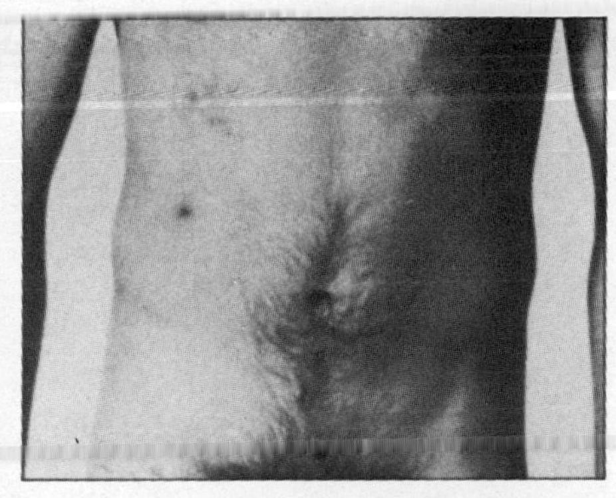

POINT: Crooked Bone
LANDMARK: navel
DISTANCE FROM LANDMARK: 5 acu-inches directly below
LOCATION: on the lower abdomen
POSITION: flat on back
TYPE OF PRESSURE: pulsed with thumb
AMOUNT OF PRESSURE: as much as patient can take

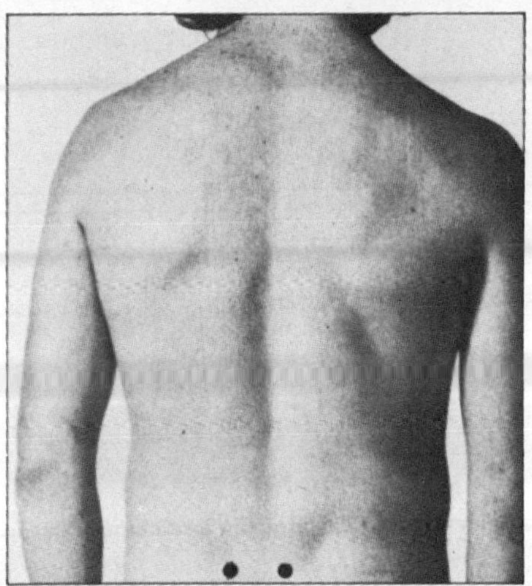

POINT: Large Intestine Locus
LANDMARK: spine knob at neck
DISTANCE FROM LANDMARK: 16th spine knob (vertebra) below
LOCATION: 1½ acu-inches on either side of the spine (treat both sides)
POSITION: face down
TYPE OF PRESSURE: pulsed with thumb
AMOUNT OF PRESSURE: as much as patient can take

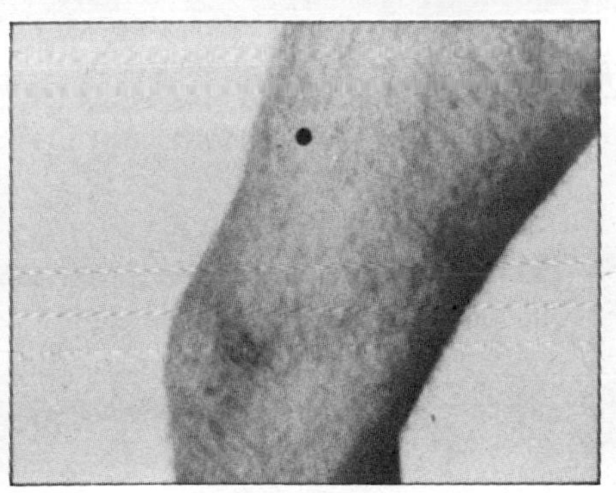

POINT: Sea of Blood
LANDMARK: back of knee fold
DISTANCE FROM LANDMARK: 3 acu-inches above
LOCATION: inner surface of thigh, approximately 2 acu-inches forward of the back surface (treat both legs)
POSITION: flat on back
TYPE OF PRESSURE: pulsed with thumb
AMOUNT OF PRESSURE: as much as patient can take

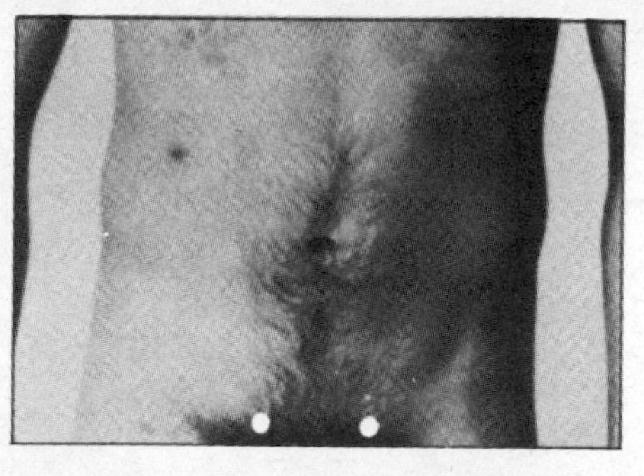

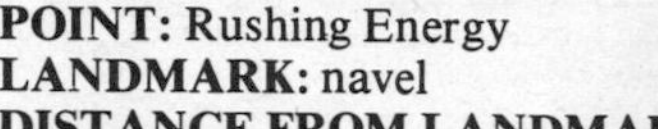

POINT: Rushing Energy
LANDMARK: navel
DISTANCE FROM LANDMARK: 5 acu-inches below
LOCATION: 2½ acu-inches to either side of stomach center line (treat both sides)
POSITION: flat on back
TYPE OF PRESSURE: pulsed with thumb
AMOUNT OF PRESSURE: as much as patient can take

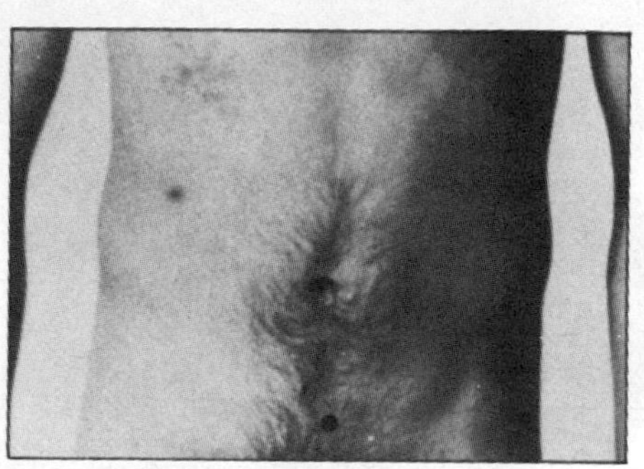

POINT: Middle Extreme
LANDMARK: navel
DISTANCE FROM LANDMARK: 5 acu-inches directly below
LOCATION: on lower adbomen
POSITION: flat on back
TYPE OF PRESSURE: pulsed with thumb
AMOUNT OF PRESSURE: as much as patient can take

DENTAL PAIN

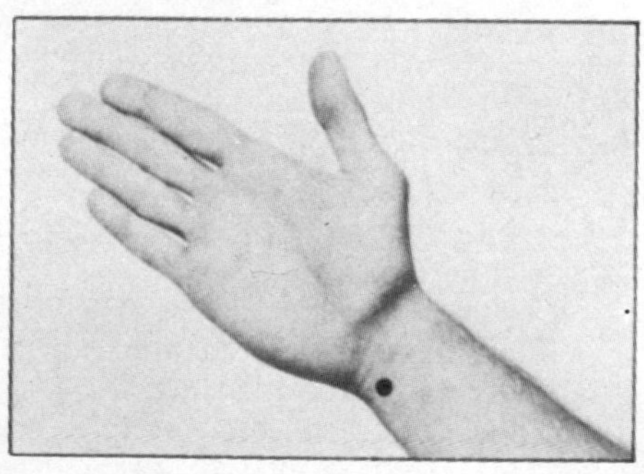

POINT: God's Door
LANDMARK: inner wrist fold
DISTANCE FROM LANDMARK: right on the fold
LOCATION: 1 acu-inch in from outer edge (side with little finger) of arm, on the inner surface of the forearm (treat both arms)
POSITION: seated
TYPE OF PRESSURE: pulsed with thumb
AMOUNT OF PRESSURE: as much as patient can take

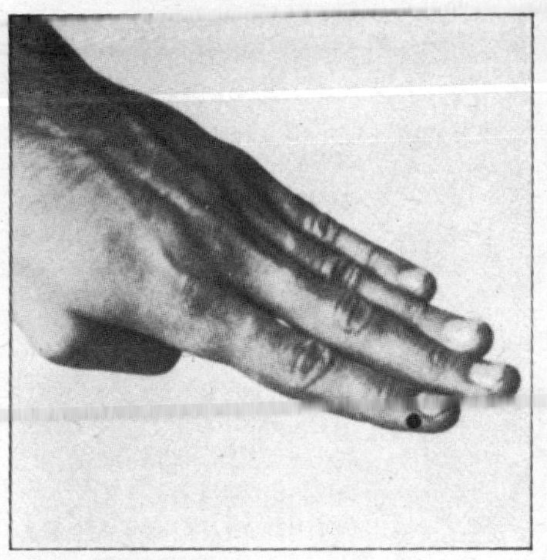

POINT: Tradesman Yang
LANDMARK: fingernail of index finger
DISTANCE FROM LANDMARK: close to the landmark
LOCATION: at the intersection of a line drawn along the thumb-side edge of the nail and a horizontal line across the base of the nail (treat both fingers)
POSITION: seated
TYPE OF PRESSURE: pulsed with thumb, pinching motion
AMOUNT OF PRESSURE: as much as patient can take

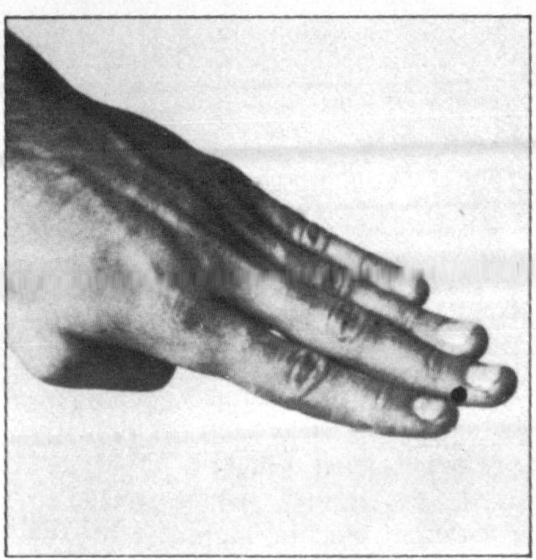

POINT: Middle Flush
LANDMARK: middle fingernail
DISTANCE FROM LANDMARK: close to the landmark
LOCATION: at the intersection of a line along the thumb-side edge of the nail and a horizontal line across the base of the nail (treat both hands)
POSITION: seated
TYPE OF PRESSURE: pulsed with thumb, pinching motion
AMOUNT OF PRESSURE: as much as patient can take

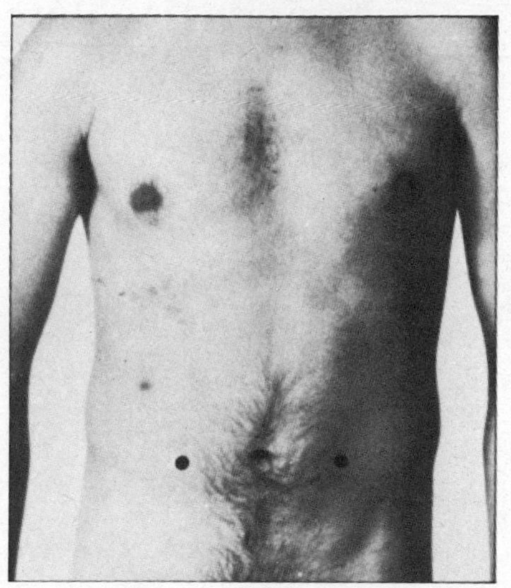

POINT: Great Cross
LANDMARK: navel
DISTANCE FROM LANDMARK: at the same level as the navel and 3½ to 4 acu-inches on either side
LOCATION: on the stomach (treat both sides)
POSITION: flat on back
TYPE OF PRESSURE: pulsed with thumb or fingers
AMOUNT OF PRESSURE: as much as patient can take

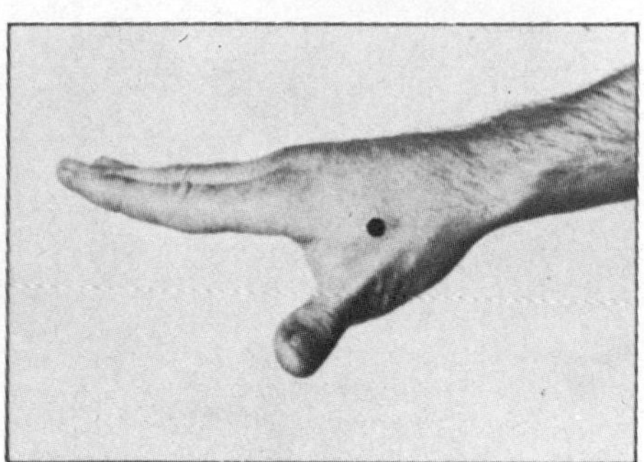

POINT: Connecting the Valleys
LANDMARK: back of hand
DISTANCE FROM LANDMARK: 1 acu-inch down from the point where bones of thumb and index finger meet
LOCATION: on the back of the hand (treat both hands)
POSITION: seated
TYPE OF PRESSURE: pulsed with thumb, pinching motion
AMOUNT OF PRESSURE: as much as patient can take

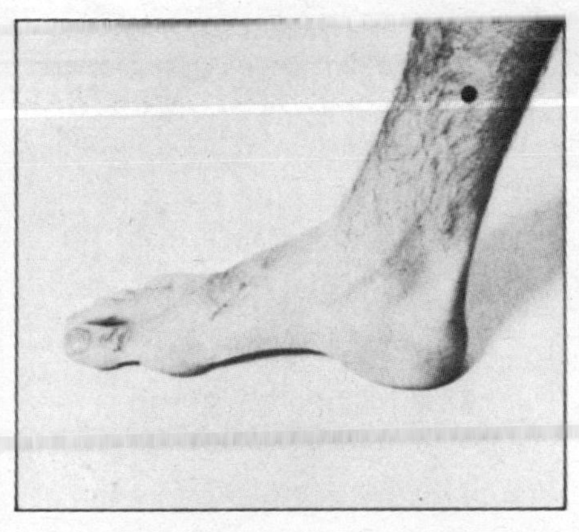

POINT: Crossroad of Three Yins
LANDMARK: inner ankle bone
DISTANCE FROM LANDMARK: 3 acu-inches above
LOCATION: inside of lower leg (treat both legs)
POSITION: seated or flat on back
TYPE OF PRESSURE: pulsed with thumb, pinching motion
AMOUNT OF PRESSURE: as much as patient can take

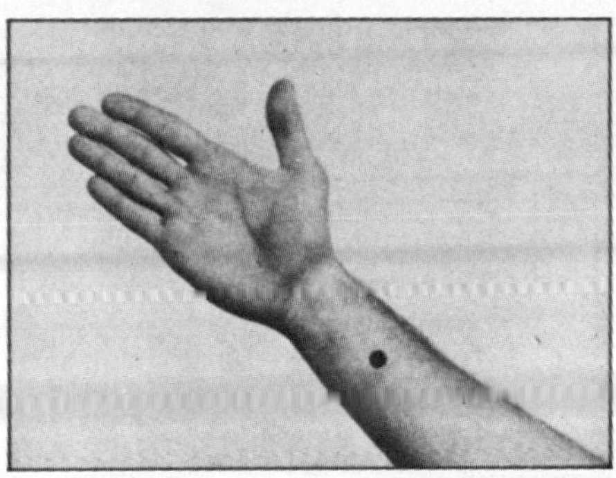

POINT: Inner Pass
LANDMARK: inner wrist fold
DISTANCE FROM LANDMARK: 2 acu-inches up
LOCATION: on the inner surface of the forearm (treat both sides)
POSITION: seated or flat on back
TYPE OF PRESSURE: pulsed with thumb, pinching motion
AMOUNT OF PRESSURE: as much as patient can take

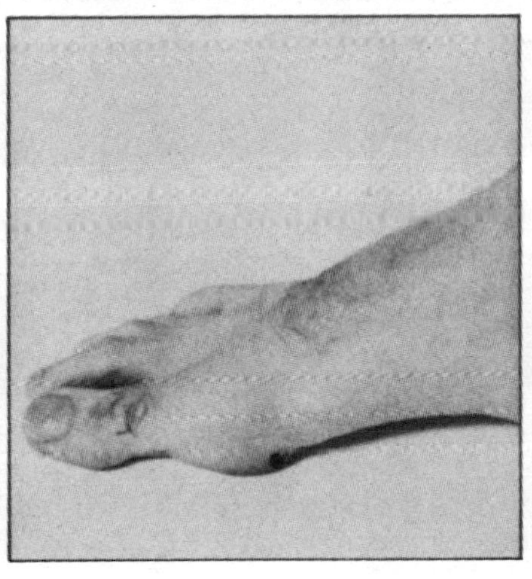

POINT: Too White
LANDMARK: toe knuckle of big toe
DISTANCE FROM LANDMARK: immediately back (toward the ankle)
LOCATION: inner edge of foot (treat both feet)
POSITION: flat on back
TYPE OF PRESSURE: pulsed with thumb, pinching motion
AMOUNT OF PRESSURE: as much as patient can take

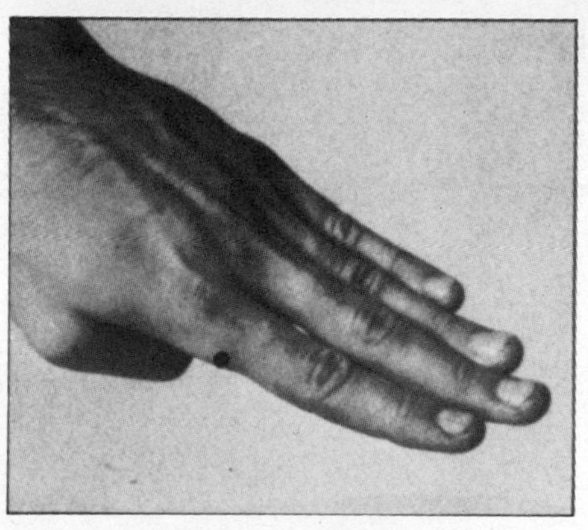

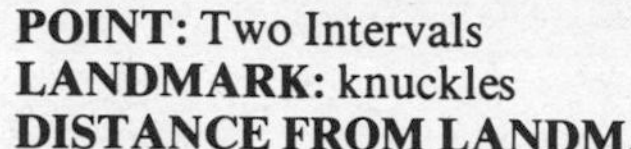

POINT: Two Intervals
LANDMARK: knuckles
DISTANCE FROM LANDMARK: just below the knuckle of the index finger
LOCATION: on the side of the index finger toward the thumb (treat both hands)
POSITION: seated
TYPE OF PRESSURE: pulsed or pinching motion
AMOUNT OF PRESSURE: as much as patient can take

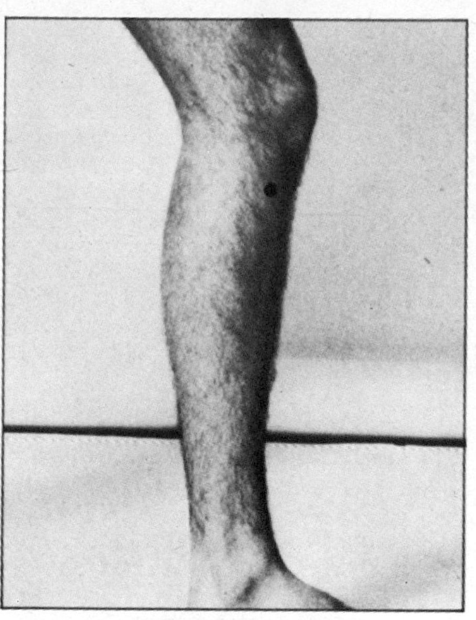

POINT: Walking Three Miles
LANDMARK: kneecap
DISTANCE FROM LANDMARK: 3 acu-inches below (in the depression)
LOCATION: 1 acu-inch toward the outside of the leg (treat both legs)
POSITION: seated in chair or flat on back
TYPE OF PRESSURE: pulsed with thumb (or pinching motion)
AMOUNT OF PRESSURE: quite firm

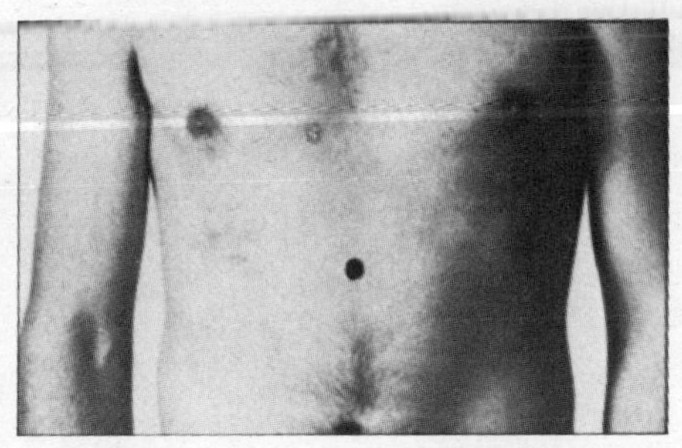

POINT: Middle Epigastrium
LANDMARK: navel
DISTANCE FROM LANDMARK: 4 acu-inches above
POSITION: flat on back
TYPE OF PRESSURE: pulsed with thumb
AMOUNT OF PRESSURE: as much as patient can take

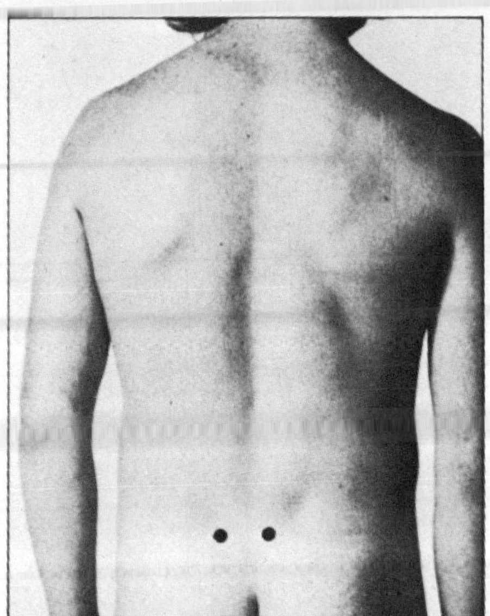

POINT: Large Intestine Locus
LANDMARK: spine knob at neck
DISTANCE FROM LANDMARK: 16th spine knob (vertebra) below
LOCATION: 1½ acu-inches on either side of the spine (treat both sides)
POSITION: face down
TYPE OF PRESSURE: pulsed with thumb
AMOUNT OF PRESSURE: as much as patient can take

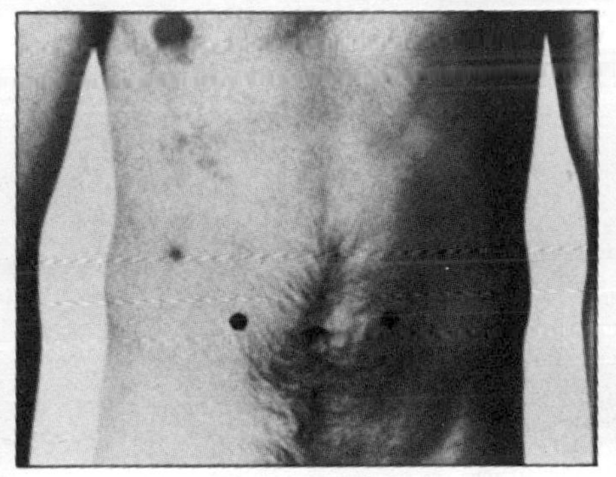

POINT: Celestial Pivot
LANDMARK: navel
DISTANCE FROM LANDMARK: right at the landmark
LOCATION: 2 acu-inches on either side of navel (treat both sides)
POSITION: flat on back
TYPE OF PRESSURE: pulsed with thumb or fingers
AMOUNT OF PRESSURE: as much as patient can take

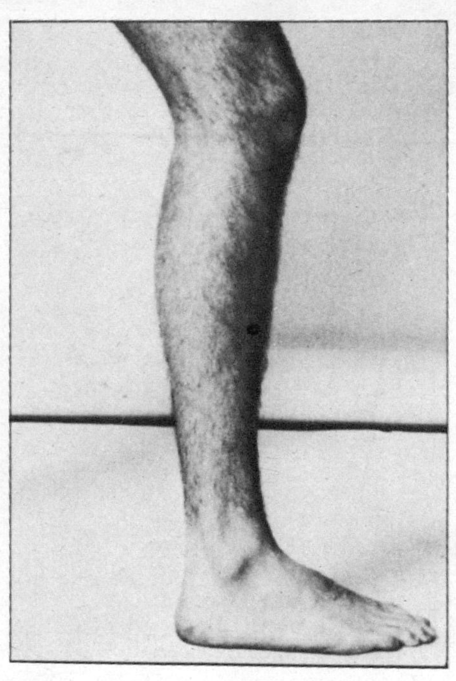

POINT: Super Great Void
LANDMARK: kneecap
DISTANCE FROM LANDMARK: 6 acu-inches below
LOCATION: right alongside the shin bone toward the outer edge of the leg (treat both legs)
POSITION: flat on back
TYPE OF PRESSURE: pulsed with thumb
AMOUNT OF PRESSURE: as much as patient can take

DIZZINESS

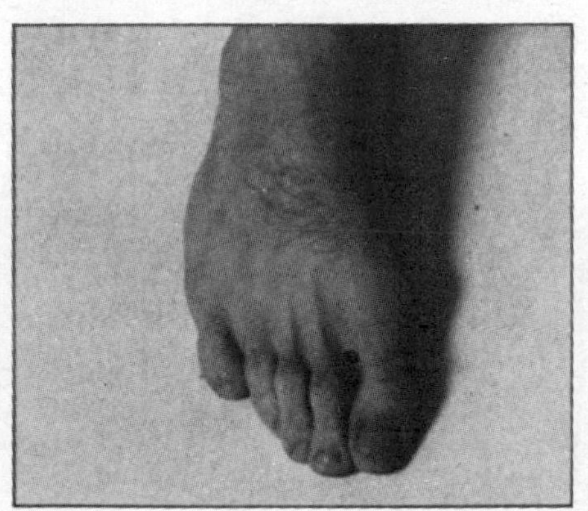

POINT: Between Columns
LANDMARK: toe knuckles
DISTANCE FROM LANDMARK: 1½ acu-inch forward (toward toes)
LOCATION: in the web of skin between the big toe and the second toe (treat both feet)
POSITION: flat on back or seated
TYPE OF PRESSURE: pulsed with thumb, pinching motion
AMOUNT OF PRESSURE: as much as patient can take

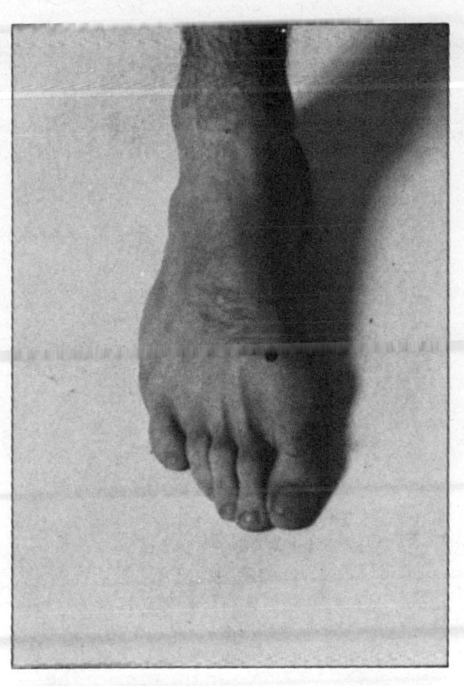

POINT: Great Flush
LANDMARK: toe knuckles
DISTANCE FROM LANDMARK: 1 acu-inch back (toward ankle)
LOCATION: on upper surface of foot between first and second toes (treat both feet)
POSITION: flat on back or seated
TYPE OF PRESSURE: pulsed with thumb, pinching motion
AMOUNT OF PRESSURE: as much as patient can take

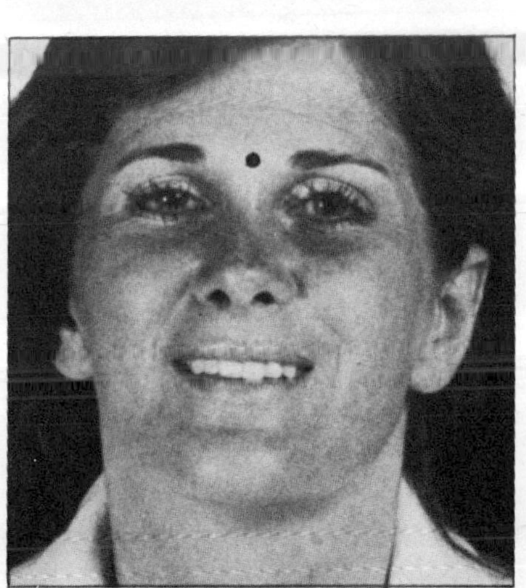

POINT: New Point
LANDMARK: eyebrows
DISTANCE FROM LANDMARK: at the landmark
LOCATION: between the eyebrows
POSITION: flat on back or seated
TYPE OF PRESSURE: use pinching motion between thumb and index finger
AMOUNT OF PRESSURE: as much as patient can take

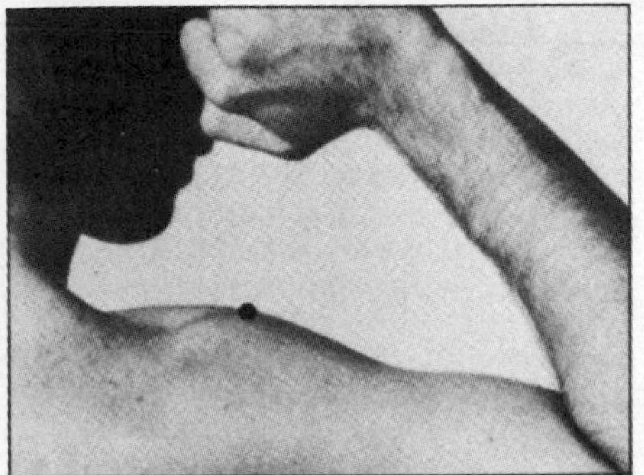

POINT: Huge Bone
LANDMARK: arm-shoulder fold
DISTANCE FROM LANDMARK: in a line directly below
LOCATION: on the shoulder at the top; feel for the spot where the collar bone meets the arm—slight hollow (treat both shoulders)
POSITION: seated or flat on back
TYPE OF PRESSURE: pulsed with thumb
AMOUNT OF PRESSURE: as much as patient can take

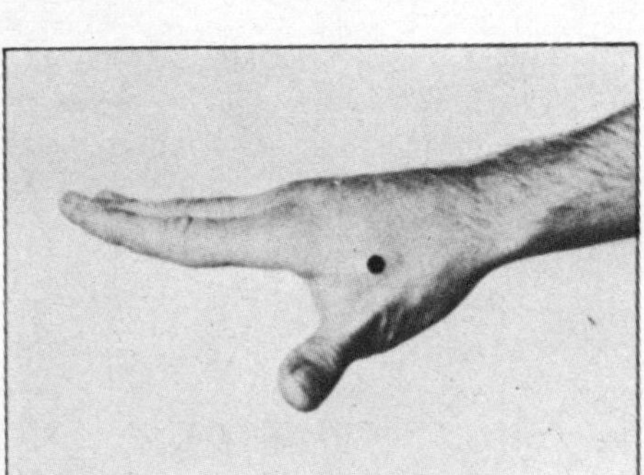

POINT: Connecting the Valleys
LANDMARK: back of hand
DISTANCE FROM LANDMARK: 1 acu-inch down from the point where bones of thumb and index finger meet
LOCATION: on the back of the hand (treat both hands)
POSITION: seated
TYPE OF PRESSURE: pulsed with thumb, pinching motion
AMOUNT OF PRESSURE: as much as patient can take

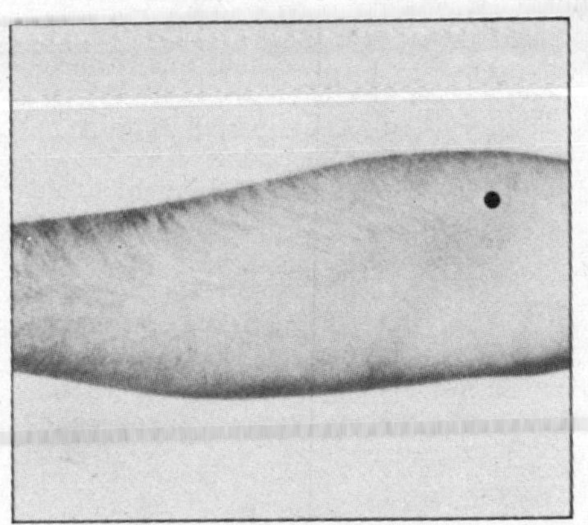

POINT: Short Narrow Marsh
LANDMARK: outer elbow fold
DISTANCE FROM LANDMARK: 1 acu-inch in from the body-side edge of the arm
LOCATION: right on the crease (treat both arms)
POSITION: seated or flat on back
TYPE OF PRESSURE: pulsed with thumb, pinching motion
AMOUNT OF PRESSURE: as much as patient can take

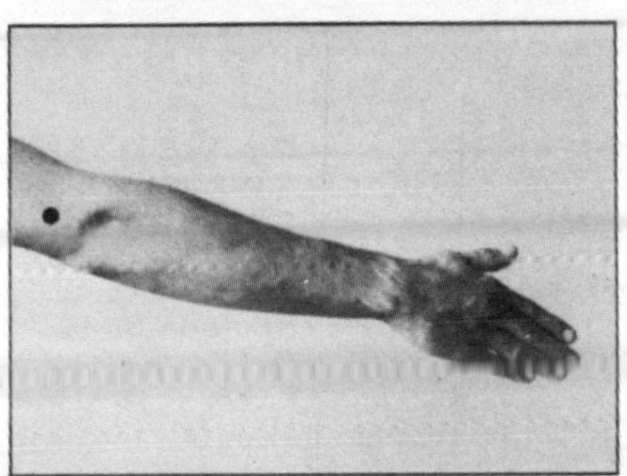

POINT: Bitter Cold Abyss
LANDMARK: outer elbow fold
DISTANCE FROM LANDMARK: 1½ acu-inches above end of fold
LOCATION: back of arm, in a line up from the elbow when arm is straight (treat both arms)
POSITION: seated
TYPE OF PRESSURE: pulsed with thumb, pinching motion
AMOUNT OF PRESSURE: as much as patient can take

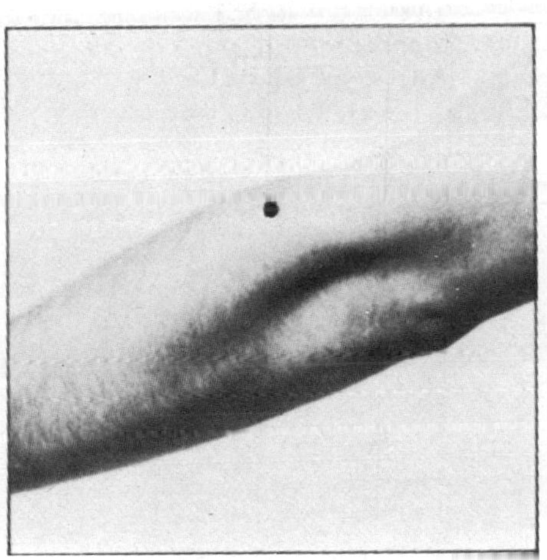

POINT: Bent Pond
LANDMARK: outer elbow fold
DISTANCE FROM LANDMARK: right at the end of the fold
LOCATION: elbow (treat both arms)
POSITION: seated or flat on back
TYPE OF PRESSURE: pulsed with thumb, pinching motion
AMOUNT OF PRESSURE: as much as patient can take

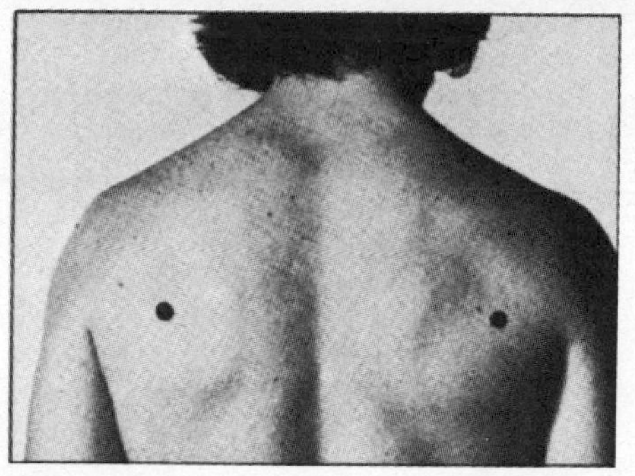

POINT: Celestial Ancestor
LANDMARK: spine knob at neck
DISTANCE FROM LANDMARK: 4th spine knob (vertebra) down
LOCATION: on a level with 4th spine knob, and 5 acu-inches on either side of center of back (treat both sides)
POSITION: on stomach
TYPE OF PRESSURE: pulsed with thumb
AMOUNT OF PRESSURE: gently to establish tolerance, then as much as patient can take

EXHAUSTION

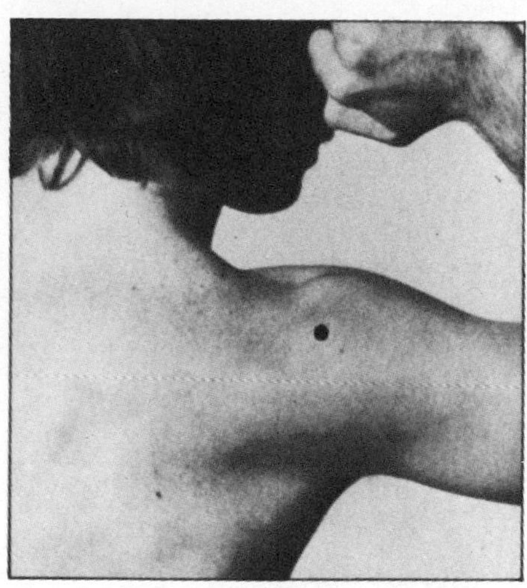

POINT: Shoulder Bone II
LANDMARK: extreme edge of shoulder
DISTANCE FROM LANDMARK: right at the landmark
LOCATION: on the back surface of the shoulder, about 1 acu-inch back from the highest point in the hollow formed when the arm is raised (treat both arms)
POSITION: seated
TYPE OF PRESSURE: pulsed with thumb, pinching motion
AMOUNT OF PRESSURE: gently, then as much as patient can take

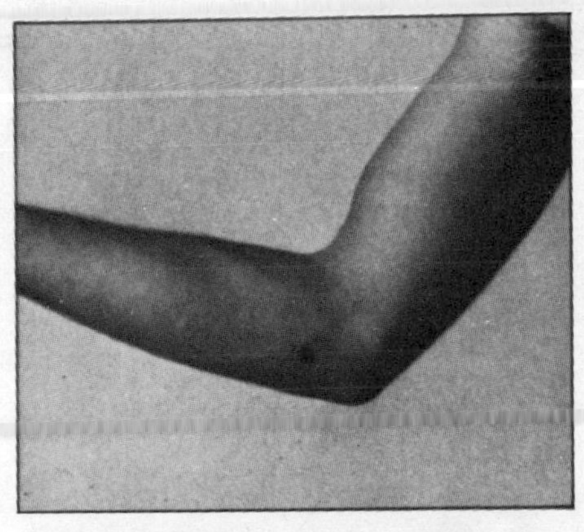

POINT: Young Sea
LANDMARK: inner elbow fold
DISTANCE FROM LANDMARK: at the body-side edge of the fold, when elbow is bent
LOCATION: elbow (treat both arms)
POSITION: seated or flat on back
TYPE OF PRESSURE: pulsed with thumb, pinching motion
AMOUNT OF PRESSURE: as much as patient can take

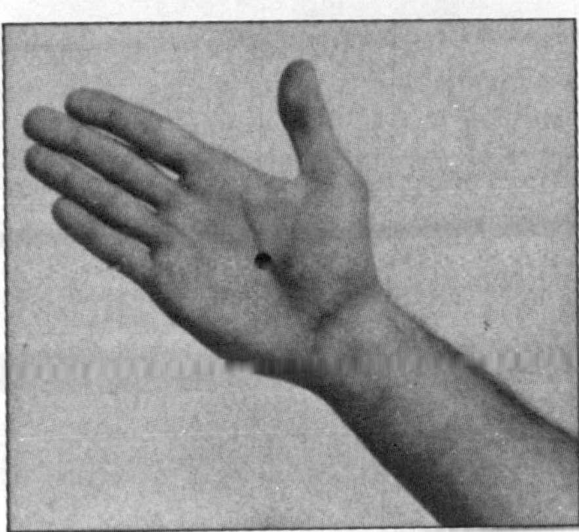

POINT: Labored Palace
LANDMARK: hand
DISTANCE FROM LANDMARK: close to the landmark
LOCATION: clench fist and mark the point where the tip of the middle finger meets the palm (treat both hands)
POSITION: seated
TYPE OF PRESSURE: pulsed with thumb, pinching motion
AMOUNT OF PRESSURE: as much as patient can take

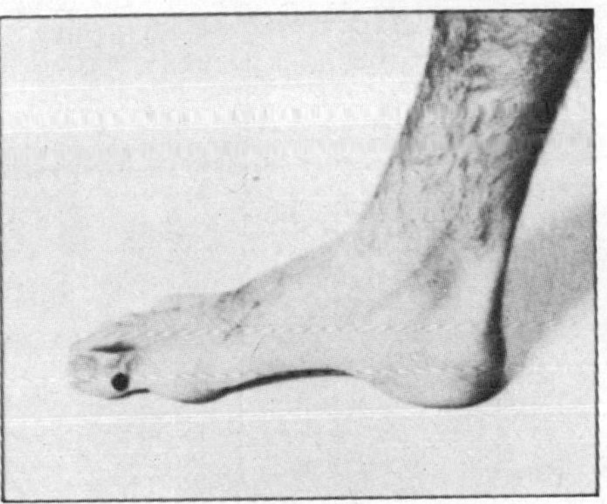

POINT: Great Metropolis
LANDMARK: toe knuckle of big toe
DISTANCE FROM LANDMARK: just in front of toe knuckle
LOCATION: outer side of big toe (treat both feet)
POSITION: seated or flat on back
TYPE OF PRESSURE: pulsed with thumb, pinching motion
AMOUNT OF PRESSURE: as much as patient can take

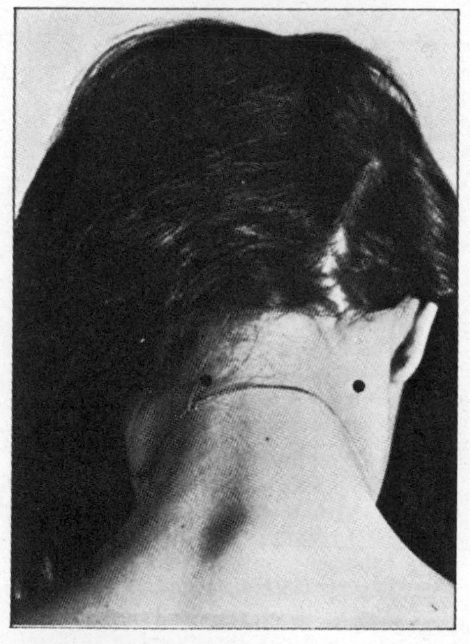

POINT: Wind Pond
LANDMARK: lower jawbone angle
DISTANCE FROM LANDMARK: immediately below
LOCATION: feel for a depression or groove on each side just below the landmark (treat both sides)
POSITION: seated or face down
TYPE OF PRESSURE: pulsed with thumbs or fingers
AMOUNT OF PRESSURE: as much as patient can take
NOTE: if patient is sitting up, stand in front of him and rest his head against your chest; exert pressure with your fingers

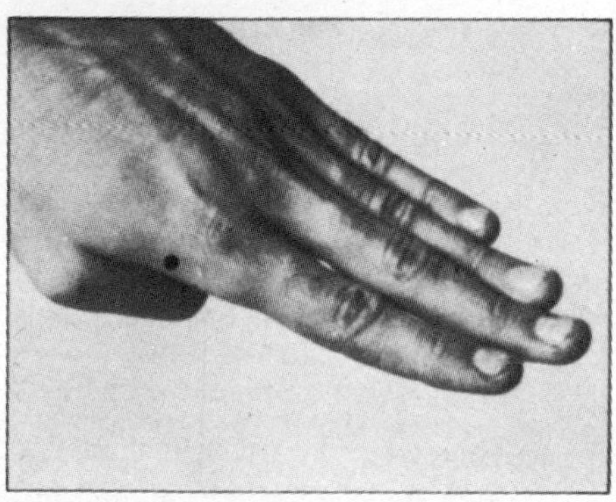

POINT: Three Intervals
LANDMARK: knuckle of index finger
DISTANCE FROM LANDMARK: immediately in front
LOCATION: on the thumb-side edge of the index finger (treat both hands)
POSITION: seated
TYPE OF PRESSURE: pulsed with thumb, pinching motion
AMOUNT OF PRESSURE: as much as patient can take

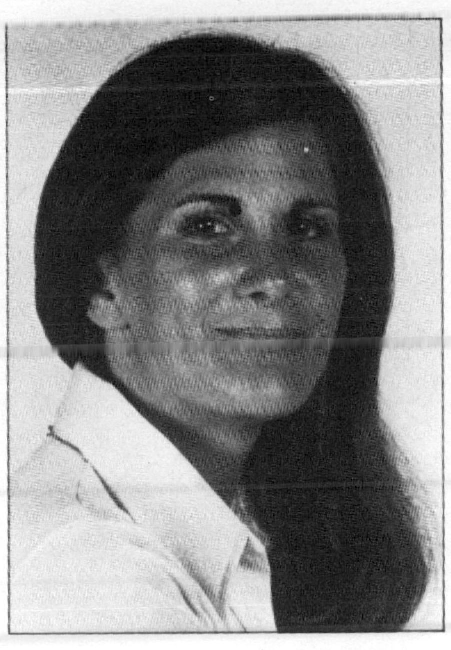

POINT: Drilling Bamboo
LANDMARK: eyebrow
DISTANCE FROM LANDMARK: right on eyebrow
LOCATION: at the inside end (toward nose) of the eyebrows (treat both eyebrows)
POSITION: seated or flat on back
TYPE OF PRESSURE: pulsed with thumb or fingers
AMOUNT OF PRESSURE: treat both at one time, with maximum pressure that patient can stand

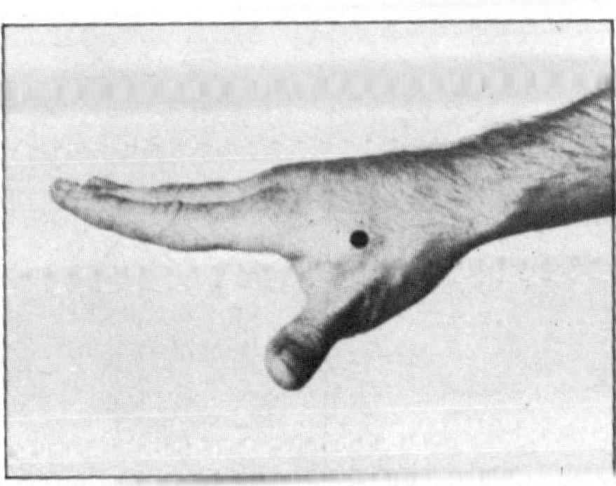

POINT: Connecting the Valleys
LANDMARK: back of hand
DISTANCE FROM LANDMARK: 1 acu-inch down from the point where bones of thumb and index finger meet
LOCATION: on the back of the hand (treat both hands)
POSITION: seated
TYPE OF PRESSURE: pulsed with thumb, pinching motion
AMOUNT OF PRESSURE: as much as patient can take

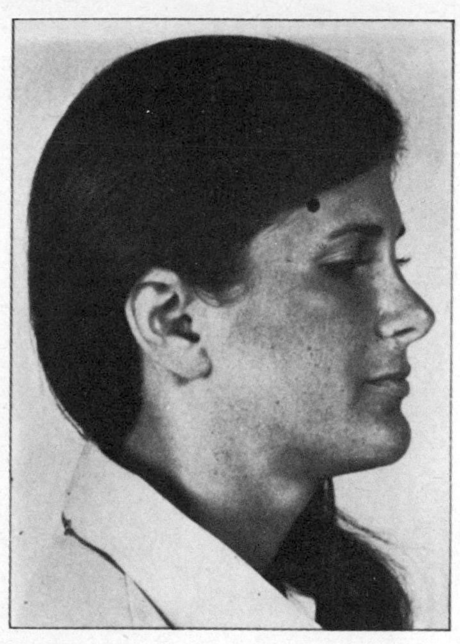

POINT: Head Support
LANDMARK: natural hairline of the forehead
DISTANCE FROM LANDMARK: right on the hairline
LOCATION: at the point where the side of the hairline joins the upper section of the sideburns (treat both sides of head)
POSITION: seated or flat on back
TYPE OF PRESSURE: pulsed with thumb or fingers
AMOUNT OF PRESSURE: as much as patient can take

FACIAL PAIN

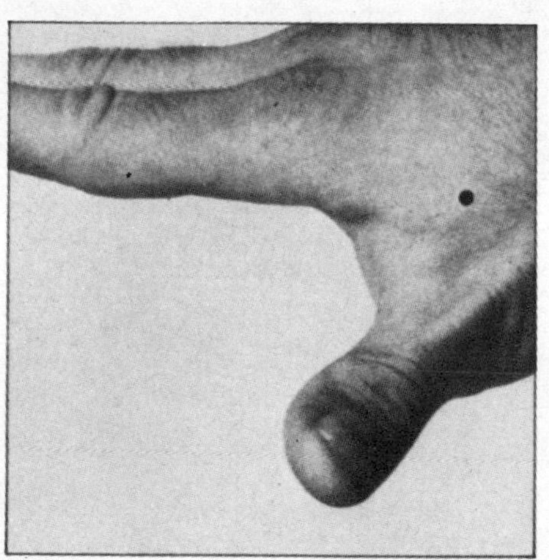

POINT: Connecting the Valleys
LANDMARK: back of hand
DISTANCE FROM LANDMARK: 1 acu-inch down from the point where bones of thumb and index finger meet
LOCATION: on the back of the hand (treat both hands)
POSITION: seated
TYPE OF PRESSURE: pulsed with thumb, pinching motion
AMOUNT OF PRESSURE: as much as patient can take

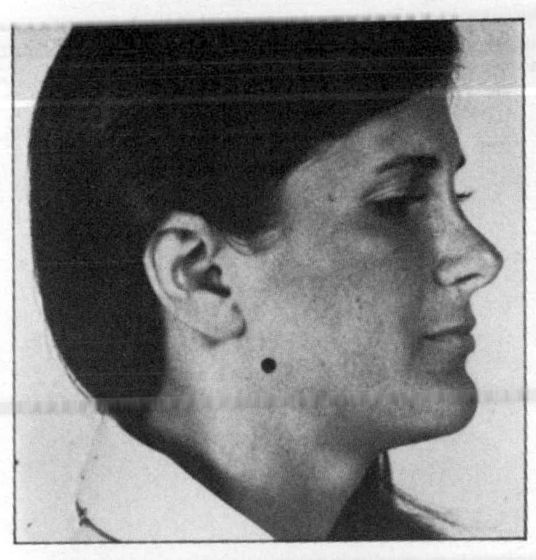

POINT: Cheek Charlot
LANDMARK: lower jawbone angle
DISTANCE FROM LANDMARK: about ½ acu-inch forward
LOCATION: feel lower jawline and locate a depression at the point (treat both sides of face)
POSITION: seated
TYPE OF PRESSURE: pulsed with fingers
AMOUNT OF PRESSURE: as much as patient can take

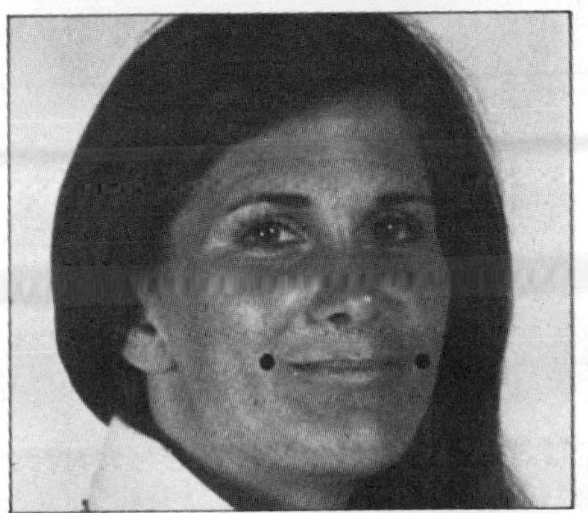

POINT: Terrestrial Granary
LANDMARK: corner of mouth
DISTANCE FROM LANDMARK: ½ acu-inch on either side of mouth
LOCATION: on a horizontal line with mouth corner on either side of face (treat both sides)
POSITION: seated
TYPE OF PRESSURE: pulsed with thumb and forefinger used together
AMOUNT OF PRESSURE: as much as patient can take

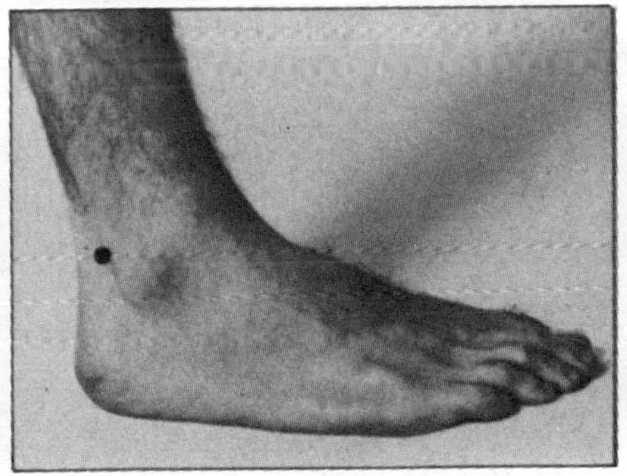

POINT: K'un Lun Mountains
LANDMARK: outer ankle bone
DISTANCE FROM LANDMARK: just in back
LOCATION: in the depression behind outer ankle bone (treat both feet)
POSITION: flat on back
TYPE OF PRESSURE: pulsed with thumb, pinching motion
AMOUNT OF PRESSURE: as much as patient can take

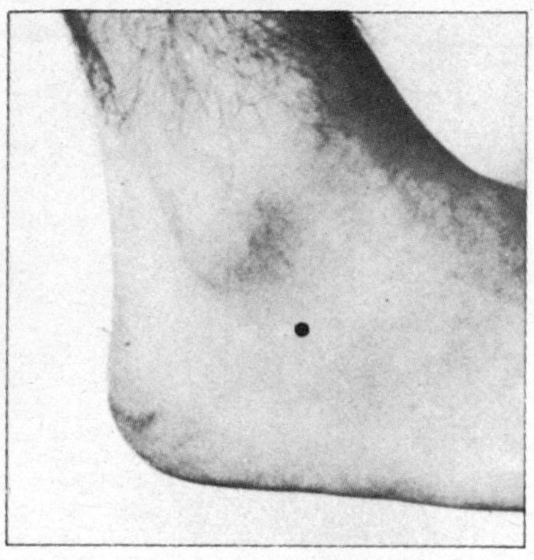

POINT: Great Cemetery
LANDMARK: outer ankle bone
DISTANCE FROM LANDMARK: immediately in front of and slightly below
LOCATION: on the outer surface of the foot (treat both feet)
POSITION: flat on back
TYPE OF PRESSURE: pulsed with thumb, pinching motion
AMOUNT OF PRESSURE: as much as patient can take

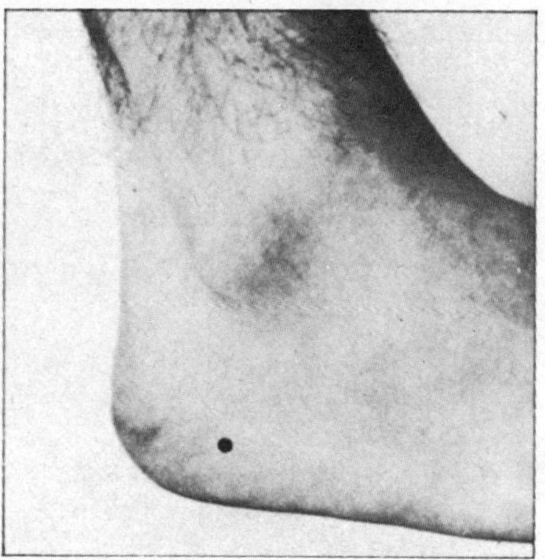

POINT: Stretching Vessel
LANDMARK: outer ankle bone
DISTANCE FROM LANDMARK: immediately below
LOCATION: in the depression behind outer ankle bone (treat both feet)
POSITION: flat on back
TYPE OF PRESSURE: pulsed with thumb, pinching motion
AMOUNT OF PRESSURE: as much as patient can take

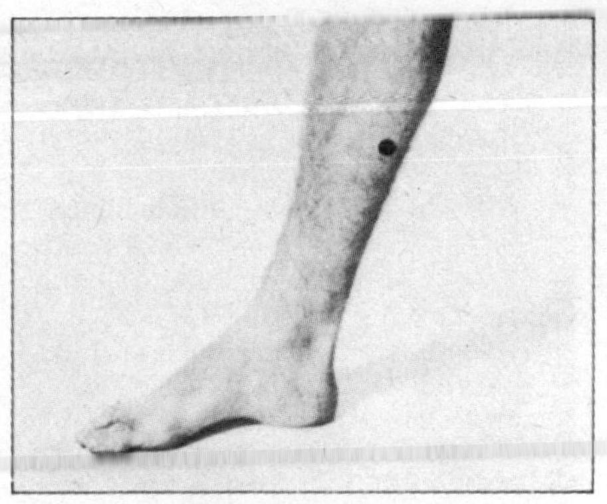

POINT: Building for Guest
LANDMARK: inner ankle bone
DISTANCE FROM LANDMARK: 5 acu-inches above the back side
LOCATION: back of lower leg; feel for the muscle when the toes are firmly extended, and locate the central depression of this muscle (treat both feet)
POSITION: on stomach
TYPE OF PRESSURE: pulsed with thumb
AMOUNT OF PRESSURE: as much as patient can take

GALLBLADDER PAIN

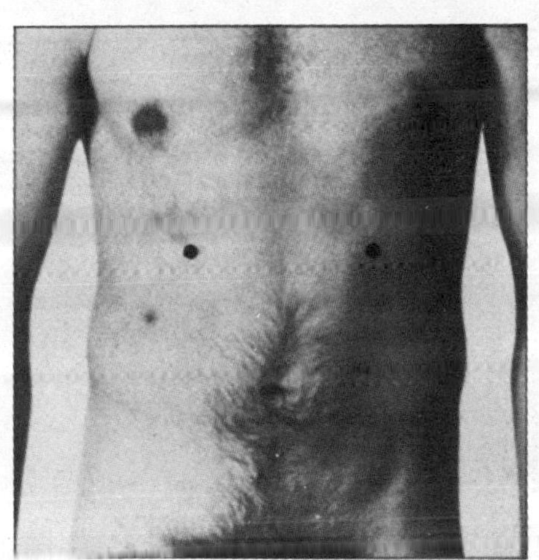

POINT: Sun Moon
LANDMARK: nipple
DISTANCE FROM LANDMARK: 7 acu-inches below
LOCATION: on the chest in a direct line below each nipple (treat both sides of chest)
POSITION: flat on back
TYPE OF PRESSURE: pulsed with fingers
AMOUNT OF PRESSURE: gently, then with increased pressure

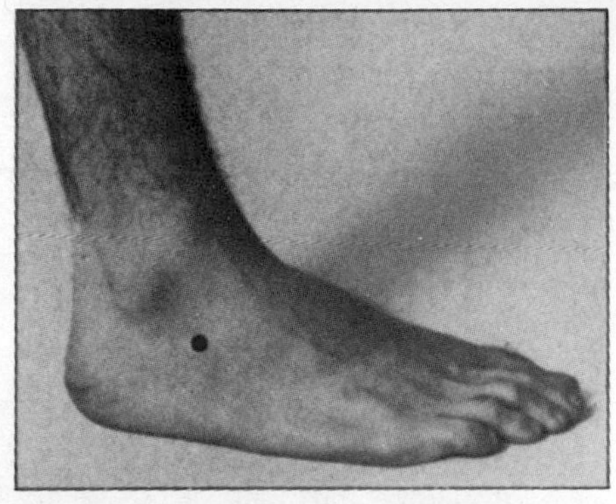

POINT: Great Cemetery
LANDMARK: outer ankle bone
DISTANCE FROM LANDMARK: immediately in front of and slightly below
LOCATION: on the outer surface of the foot (treat both feet)
POSITION: flat on back
TYPE OF PRESSURE: pulsed with thumb, pinching motion
AMOUNT OF PRESSURE: as much as patient can take

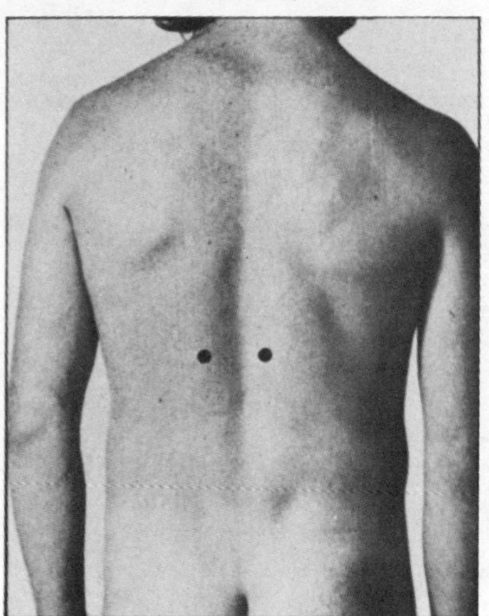

POINT: Gallbladder Locus
LANDMARK: spine knob at neck
DISTANCE FROM LANDMARK: 10th spine knob (vertebra) below
LOCATION: on the back, 1½ acu-inches from spine (treat both sides)
POSITION: on stomach
TYPE OF PRESSURE: pulsed with thumb
AMOUNT OF PRESSURE: gently at first, then as much as patient can take

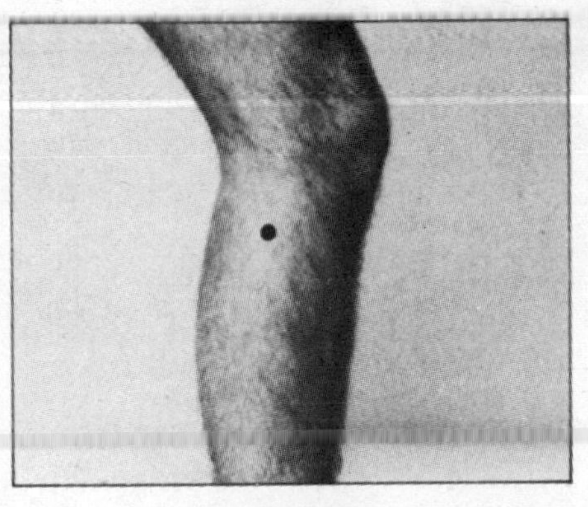

POINT: Spring in the Sunny Hill
LANDMARK: back of knee fold
DISTANCE FROM LANDMARK: 3 acu-inches down
LOCATION: on the outer side of the leg (feel for small long bone underneath) (treat both legs)
POSITION: seated or lying on side
TYPE OF PRESSURE: pulsed with thumb
AMOUNT OF PRESSURE: as much as patient can take

GASTRITIS

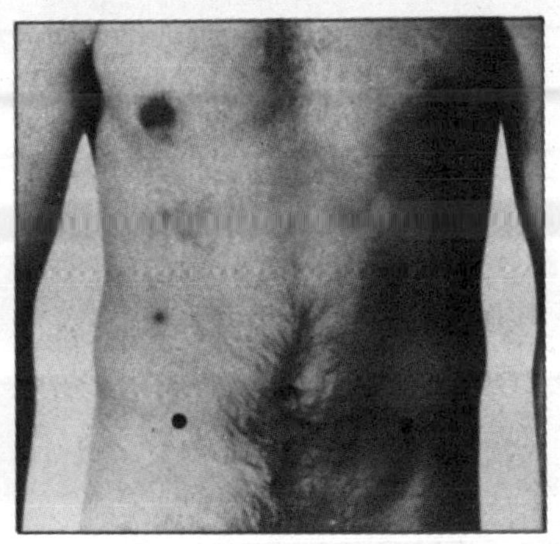

POINT: Sorrow Belly
LANDMARK: navel
DISTANCE FROM LANDMARK: 3 acu-inches above the navel
LOCATION: on the chest, 3½ acu-inches on either side of the center line of the body (treat both sides)
POSITION: flat on back
TYPE OF PRESSURE: pulsed with thumb or fingers
AMOUNT OF PRESSURE: gently, then as much as patient can tolerate

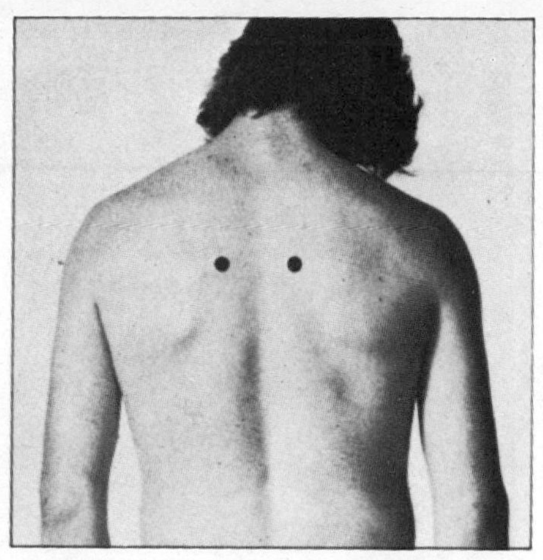

POINT: Lung Locus
LANDMARK: spine knob at neck
DISTANCE FROM LANDMARK: 2nd spine knob (vertebra) down
LOCATION: on the back, 1½ acu-inches on either side of the spine (treat both sides)
POSITION: on stomach
TYPE OF PRESSURE: pulsed with thumb
AMOUNT OF PRESSURE: as much as patient can take

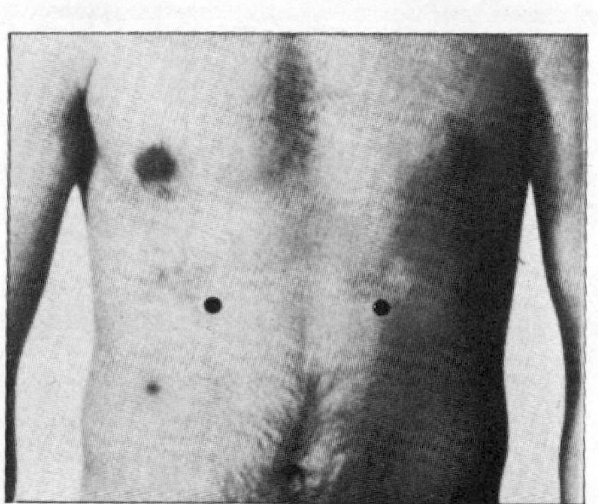

POINT: Beam Gate
LANDMARK: navel
DISTANCE FROM LANDMARK: 4 acu-inches above
LOCATION: on the chest, 2 acu-inches on either side of the center line of the chest (treat both sides)
POSITION: flat on back
TYPE OF PRESSURE: pulsed with thumb
AMOUNT OF PRESSURE: as much as patient can take

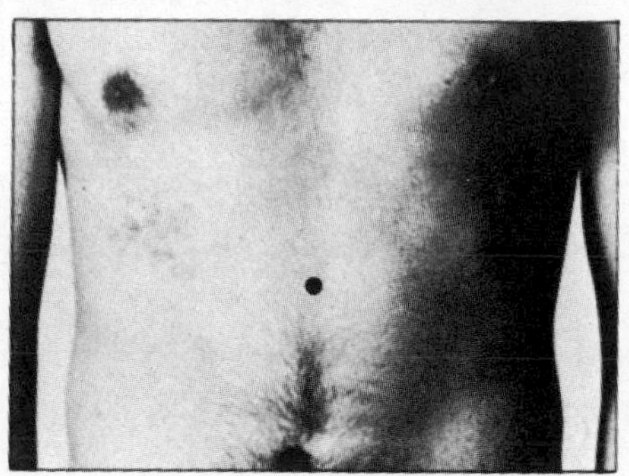

POINT: Middle Epigastrium
LANDMARK: navel
DISTANCE FROM LANDMARK: 4 acu-inches above
POSITION: flat on back
TYPE OF PRESSURE: pulsed with thumb
AMOUNT OF PRESSURE: as much as patient can take

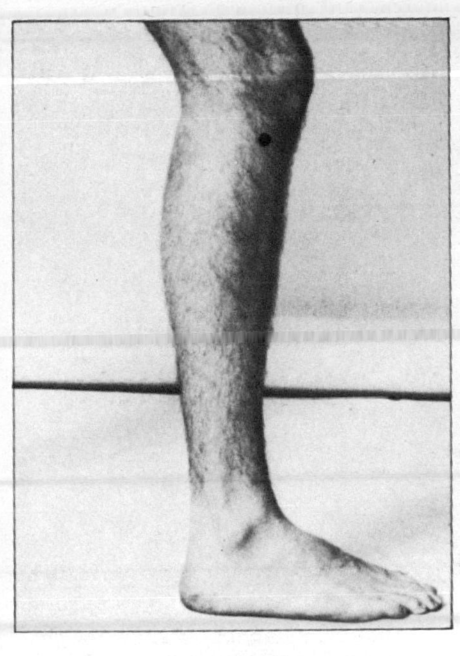

POINT: Walking Three Miles
LANDMARK: kneecap
DISTANCE FROM LANDMARK: 3 acu-inches below (in the depression)
LOCATION: 1 acu-inch toward the outside of the leg (treat both legs)
POSITION: seated in chair or flat on back
TYPE OF PRESSURE: pulsed with thumb (or pinching motion)
AMOUNT OF PRESSURE: quite firm

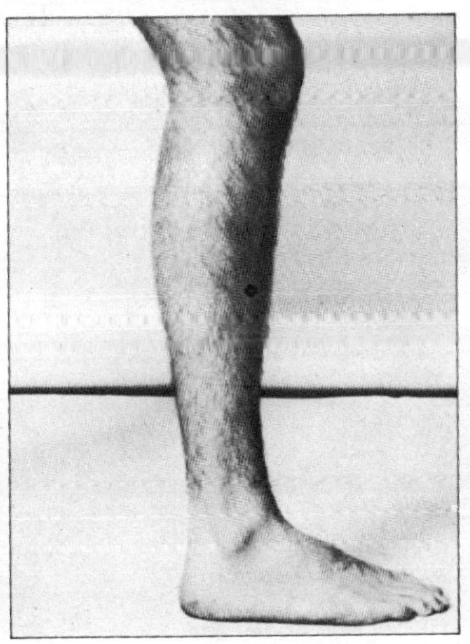

POINT: Super Great Void
LANDMARK: kneecap
DISTANCE FROM LANDMARK: 6 acu-inches below
LOCATION: right alongside the shin bone toward the outer edge of the leg (treat both legs)
POSITION: flat on back
TYPE OF PRESSURE: pulsed with thumb
AMOUNT OF PRESSURE: as much as patient can take

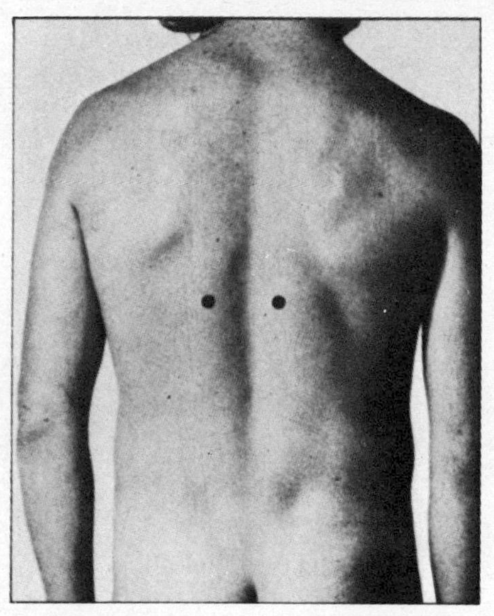

POINT: Diaphragm Locus
LANDMARK: spine knob at neck
DISTANCE FROM LANDMARK: 6th spine knob (vertebra) down
LOCATION: on back, 1½ acu-inches on either side of spine (treat both sides)
POSITION: on stomach
TYPE OF PRESSURE: pulsed with thumb
AMOUNT OF PRESSURE: as much as patient can take

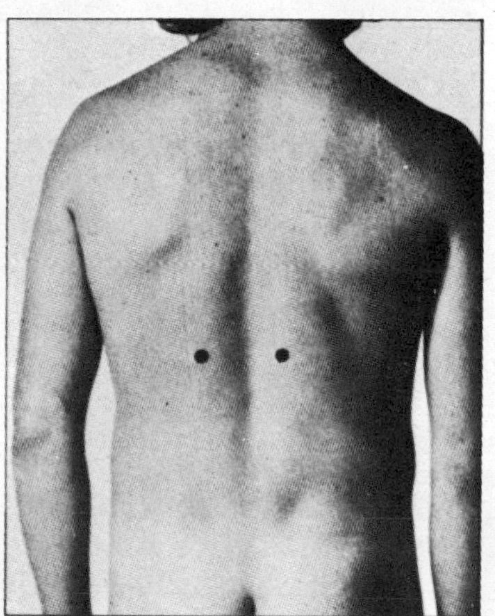

POINT: Spleen Locus
LANDMARK: spine knob at neck
DISTANCE FROM LANDMARK: 11th spine knob (vertebra) below
LOCATION: 1½ acu-inches on either side of the spine (treat both sides)
POSITION: face down
TYPE OF PRESSURE: pulsed with thumb
AMOUNT OF PRESSURE: as much as patient can take

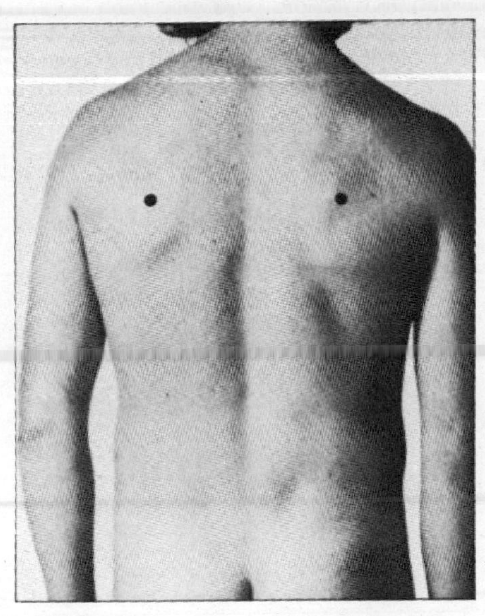

POINT: Great Gate
LANDMARK: spine knob at neck
DISTANCE FROM LANDMARK: 3rd spine knob (vertebra) below
LOCATION: 3 acu-inches on either side of spine (treat both sides)
POSITION: face down
TYPE OF PRESSURE: pulsed with thumb or fingers
AMOUNT OF PRESSURE: as much as patient can take

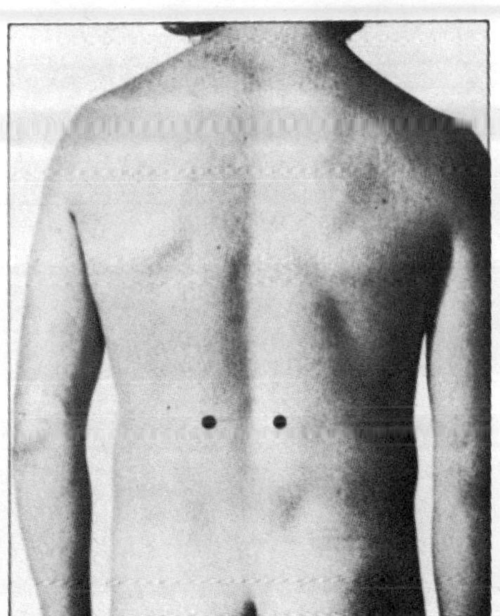

POINT: Stomach Locus
LANDMARK: spine knob at neck
DISTANCE FROM LANDMARK: 12th spine knob (vertebra) below
LOCATION: 1½ acu-inches on either side of spine (treat both sides)
POSITION: face down
TYPE OF PRESSURE: pulsed with thumb
AMOUNT OF PRESSURE: gently, then firm

POINT: Terrestrial Granary
LANDMARK: corner of mouth
DISTANCE FROM LANDMARK: ½ acu-inch on either side of mouth
LOCATION: on a horizontal line with mouth corner on either side of face (treat both sides)
POSITION: seated
TYPE OF PRESSURE: pulsed with thumb and forefinger used together
AMOUNT OF PRESSURE: as much as patient can take

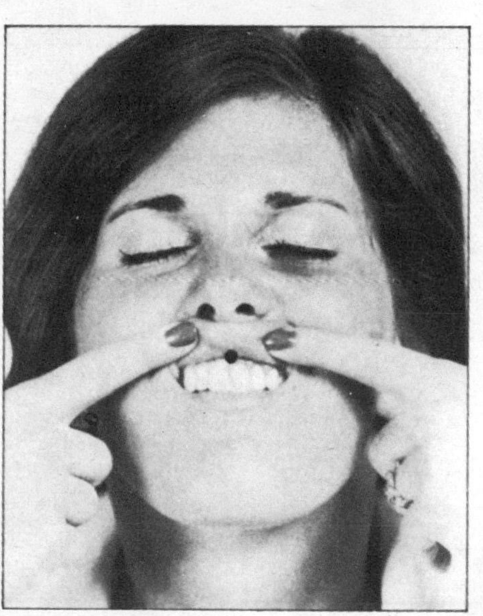

POINT: Gum Crossing
LANDMARK: gums
DISTANCE FROM LANDMARK: at the landmark
LOCATION: midpoint between the inner surface of the upper lip and the upper gums
POSITION: seated
TYPE OF PRESSURE: pulsed, or steady pressure with thumb-pinching motion
AMOUNT OF PRESSURE: as much as patient can take

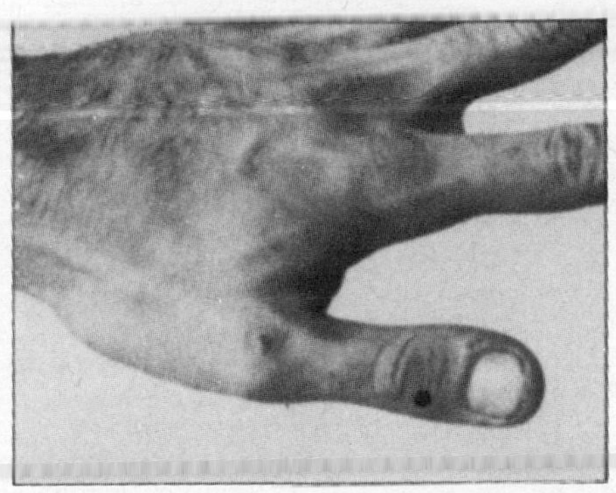

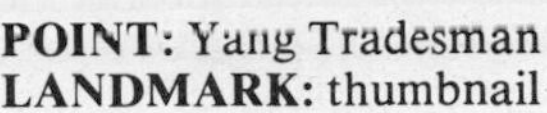

POINT: Yang Tradesman
LANDMARK: thumbnail
DISTANCE FROM LANDMARK: close to landmark
LOCATION: at the intersection of a line drawn along the outer edge of nail and a horizontal line across the base of the nail (treat both thumbs)
POSITION: seated
TYPE OF PRESSURE: pulsed with thumb, pinching motion
AMOUNT OF PRESSURE: as much as patient can take

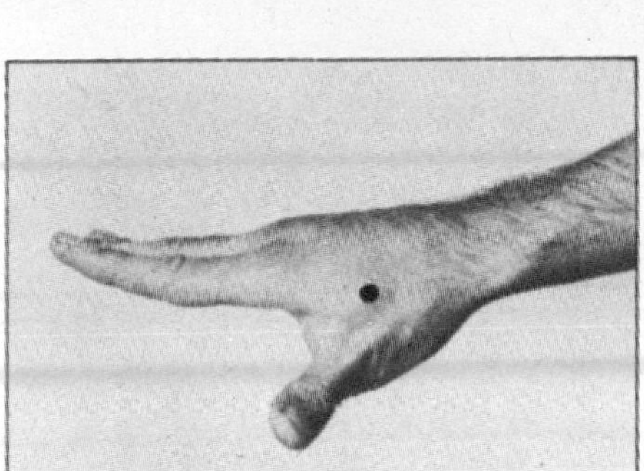

POINT: Connecting the Valleys
LANDMARK: back of hand
DISTANCE FROM LANDMARK: 1 acu-inch down from the point where bones of thumb and index finger meet
LOCATION: on the back of the hand (treat both hands)
POSITION: seated
TYPE OF PRESSURE: pulsed with thumb, pinching motion
AMOUNT OF PRESSURE: as much as patient can take

GOUT

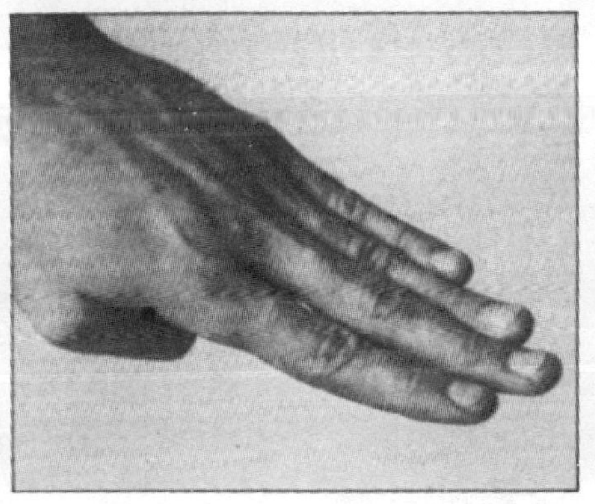

POINT: Three Intervals
LANDMARK: knuckle of index finger
DISTANCE FROM LANDMARK: immediately in front
LOCATION: on the thumb-side edge of the index finger (treat both hands)
POSITION: seated
TYPE OF PRESSURE: pulsed with thumb, pinching motion
AMOUNT OF PRESSURE: as much as patient can take

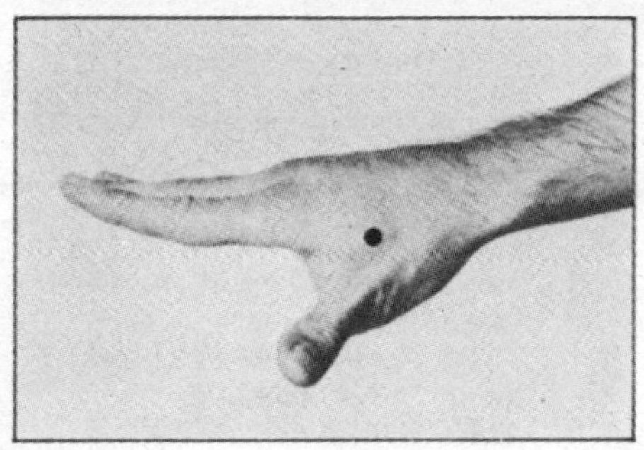

POINT: Connecting the Valleys
LANDMARK: back of hand
DISTANCE FROM LANDMARK: 1 acu-inch down from the point where bones of thumb and index finger meet
LOCATION: on the back of the hand (treat both hands)
POSITION: seated
TYPE OF PRESSURE: pulsed with thumb, pinching motion
AMOUNT OF PRESSURE: as much as patient can take

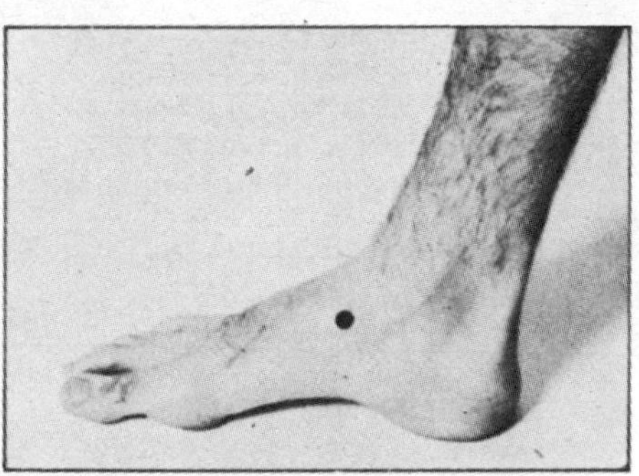

POINT: Trades Hill
LANDMARK: inner ankle bone
DISTANCE FROM LANDMARK: just in front
LOCATION: in the depression just below and in front of the ankle bone, on the inner surface of the leg (treat both legs)
POSITION: seated or flat on back
TYPE OF PRESSURE: pulsed with thumb, pinching motion
AMOUNT OF PRESSURE: as much as patient can take

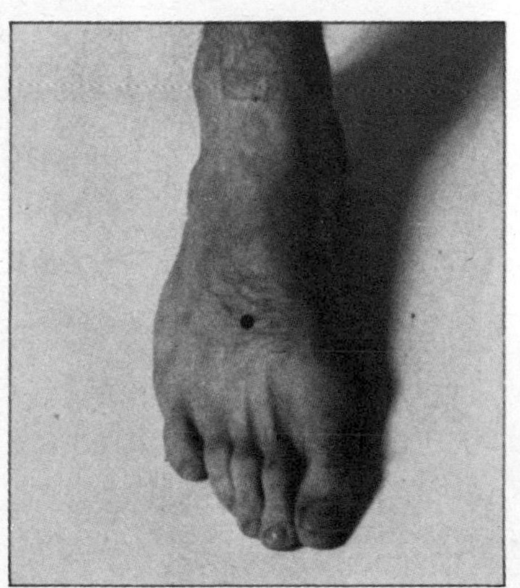

POINT: Sinking Valley
LANDMARK: toe knuckles
DISTANCE FROM LANDMARK: just behind (toward ankle)
LOCATION: on the foot, between the bones of the second and third toes (treat both feet)
POSITION: seated or flat on back
TYPE OF PRESSURE: pulsed with thumb, or thumb-pinching motion
AMOUNT OF PRESSURE: very gently at first, then as much as patient can take

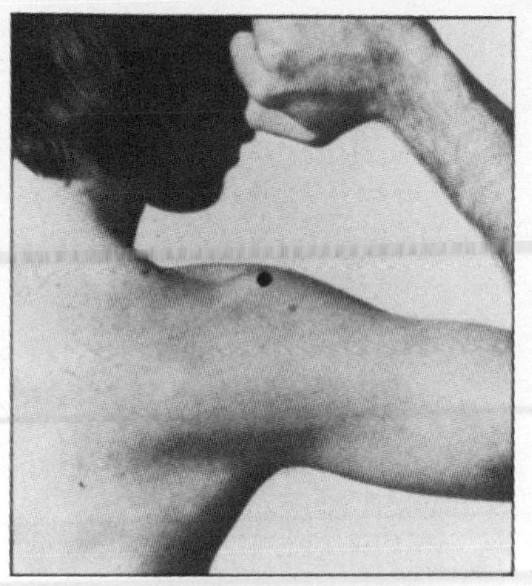

POINT: Shoulder Bone I
LANDMARK: extreme edge of shoulder
DISTANCE FROM LANDMARK: right at the landmark
LOCATION: on the shoulder, in the hollow formed when the arm is raised (treat both arms)
POSITION: seated
TYPE OF PRESSURE: pulsed with thumb
AMOUNT OF PRESSURE: gently, then as much as patient can take

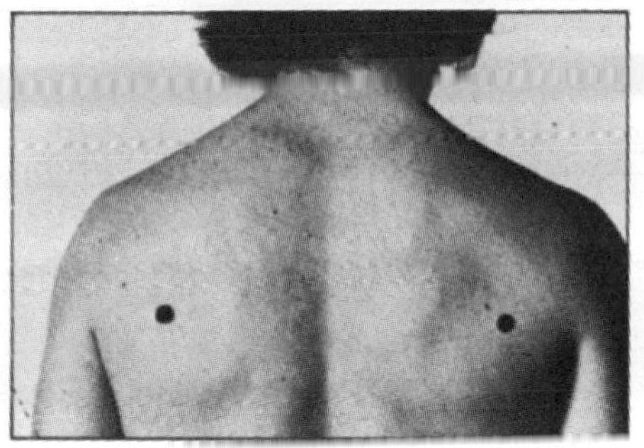

POINT: Celestial Ancestor
LANDMARK: spine knob at neck
DISTANCE FROM LANDMARK: 4th spine knob (vertebra) down
LOCATION: on a level with 4th spine knob, and 5 acu-inches on either side of center of back (treat both sides)
POSITION: on stomach
TYPE OF PRESSURE: pulsed with thumb
AMOUNT OF PRESSURE: gently to establish tolerance, then as much as patient can take

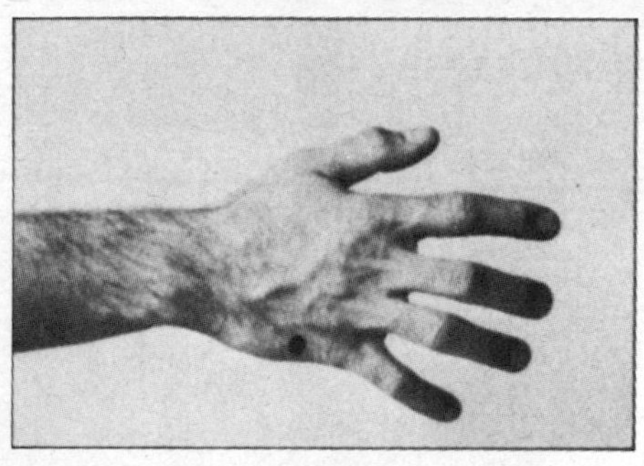

POINT: Back Stream
LANDMARK: knuckle of little finger
DISTANCE FROM LANDMARK: immediately above (toward the wrist)
LOCATION: on the side of the hand, just above little finger knuckle (treat both hands)
POSITION: seated
TYPE OF PRESSURE: pulsed with thumb, pinching motion
AMOUNT OF PRESSURE: as much as patient can take

HAYFEVER

POINT: Stalk Bone
LANDMARK: nose
DISTANCE FROM LANDMARK: immediately below
LOCATION: directly below each nostril and centered under the nostril (treat both points at once)
POSITION: seated or flat on back
TYPE OF PRESSURE: pulsed with thumb and forefinger at one time
AMOUNT OF PRESSURE: as much as patient can take

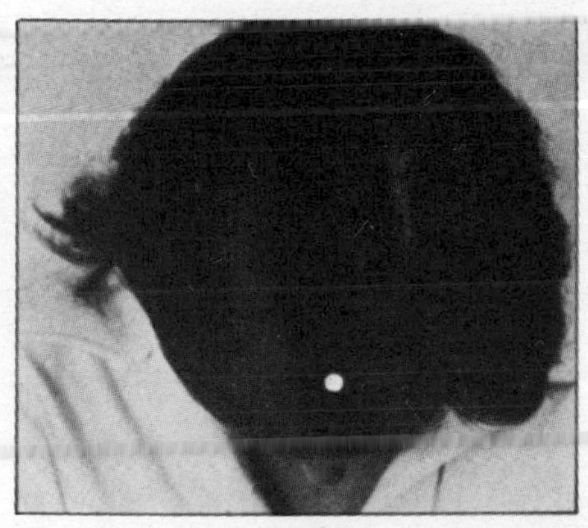

POINT: Super Star
LANDMARK: natural hairline at forehead
DISTANCE FROM LANDMARK: 1 acu-inch above
LOCATION: on the midline of the head
POSITION: seated or flat on back
TYPE OF PRESSURE: pulsed with thumb
AMOUNT OF PRESSURE: as much as patient can take

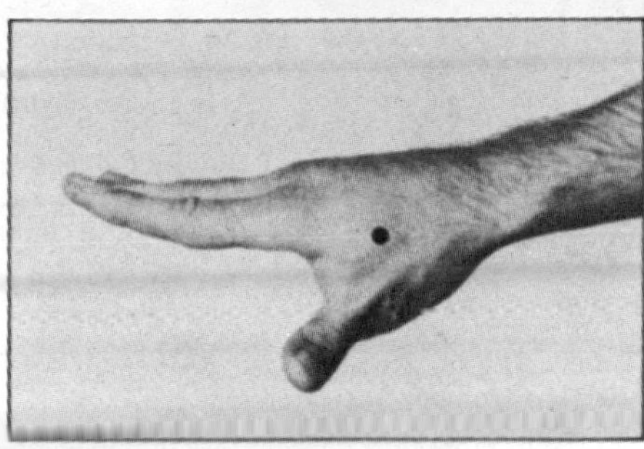

POINT: Connecting the Valleys
LANDMARK: back of hand
DISTANCE FROM LANDMARK: 1 acu-inch down from the point where bones of thumb and index finger meet
LOCATION: on the back of the hand (treat both hands)
POSITION: seated
TYPE OF PRESSURE: pulsed with thumb, pinching motion
AMOUNT OF PRESSURE: as much as patient can take

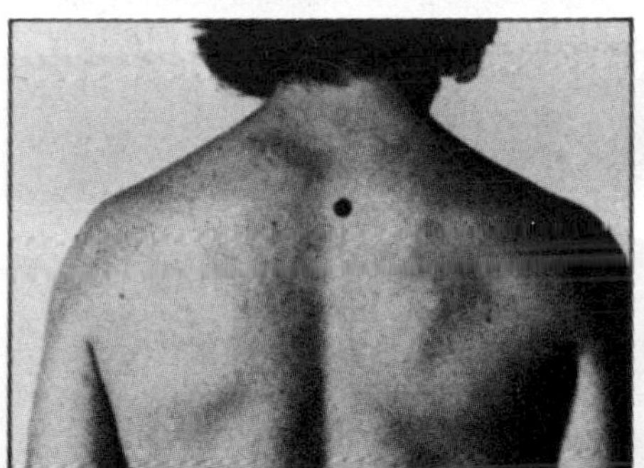

POINT: Seeking Path
LANDMARK: spine knob at neck
DISTANCE FROM LANDMARK: between landmark and next knob down the spine
LOCATION: right on spine
POSITION: on stomach
TYPE OF PRESSURE: pulsed with thumb
AMOUNT OF PRESSURE: quite firm

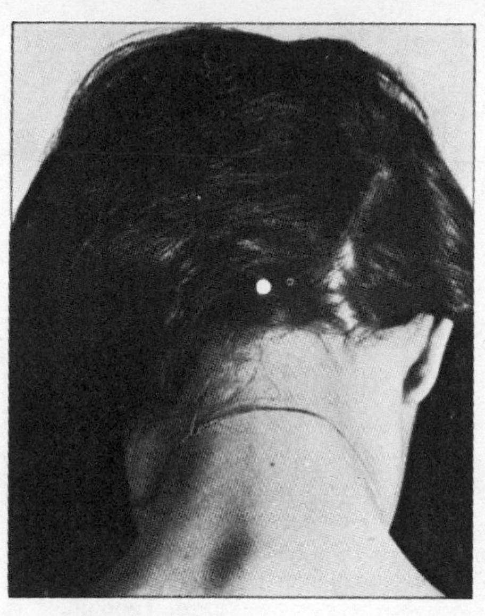

POINT: Windy Prefecture
LANDMARK: natural hairline at back of head
DISTANCE FROM LANDMARK: 1 acu-inch above
LOCATION: on top of head, along front-to-back center line of head
POSITION: seated or face down
TYPE OF PRESSURE: pulsed with thumb
AMOUNT OF PRESSURE: as much as patient can take

HEADACHE

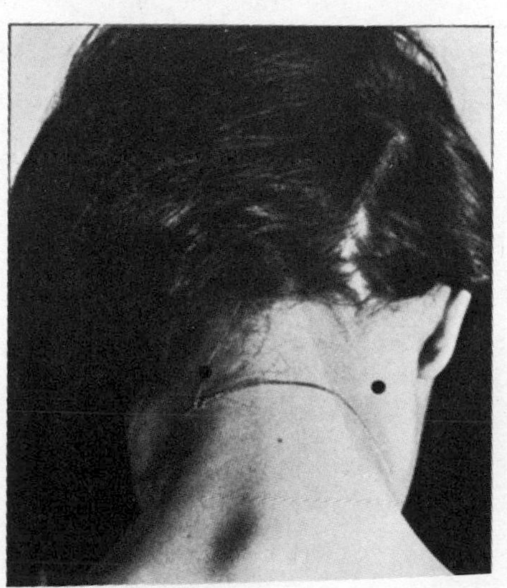

POINT: Wind Pond
LANDMARK: rear head bones
DISTANCE FROM LANDMARK: immediately below
LOCATION: feel for a depression or groove on each side just below the landmark (treat both sides)
POSITION: seated or face down
TYPE OF PRESSURE: pulsed with thumbs or fingers
AMOUNT OF PRESSURE: as much as patient can take
NOTE: if patient is sitting up, stand in front of him and rest his head against your chest; exert pressure with your fingers

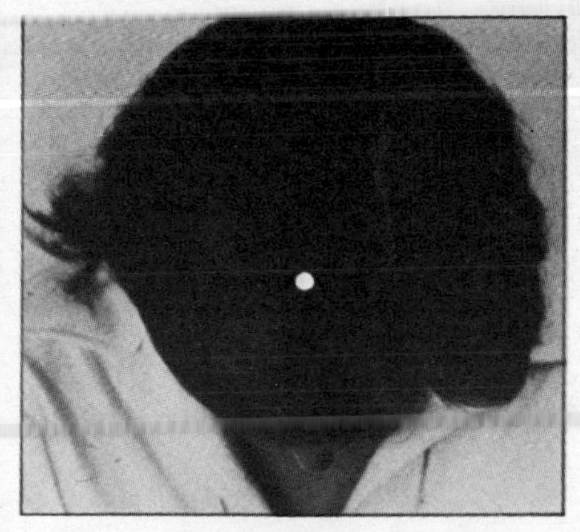

POINT: Fontanelle Meet
LANDMARK: natural hairline at forehead
DISTANCE FROM LANDMARK: 2 acu-inches above
LOCATION: at the center line of the head
POSITION: seated or flat on back
TYPE OF PRESSURE: pulsed with thumb
AMOUNT OF PRESSURE: as much as patient can take

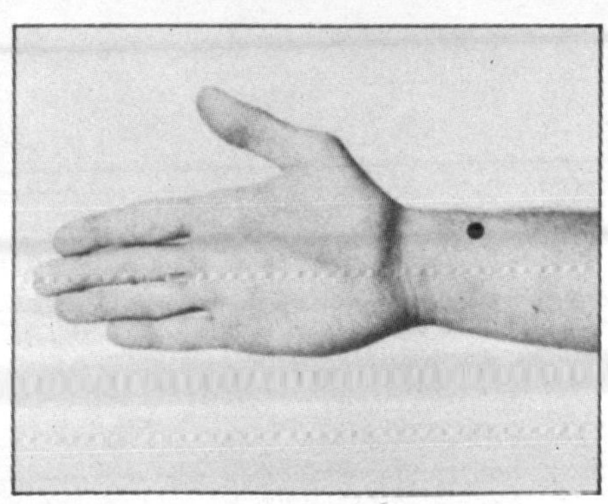

POINT: Extreme Shortcoming
LANDMARK: inner wrist fold
DISTANCE FROM LANDMARK: 2 acu-inches above
POSITION: on the inside of the wrist near the pulse (treat both arms)
TYPE OF PRESSURE: pulsed with thumb, pinching motion
AMOUNT OF PRESSURE: as much as patient can take

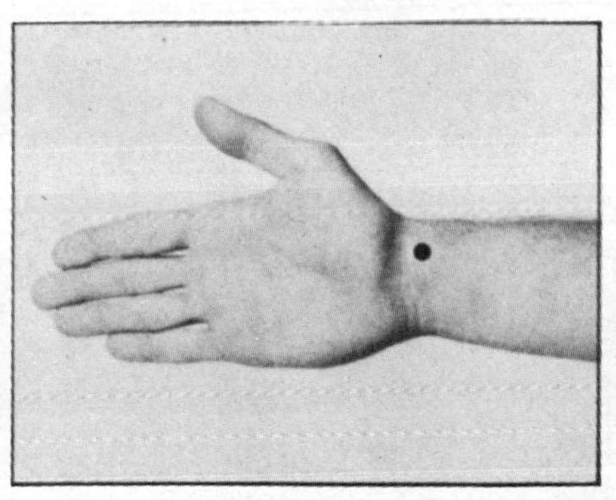

POINT: Meridian Gutter
LANDMARK: inner wrist fold
DISTANCE FROM LANDMARK: 1 acu-inch above
LOCATION: on the inside of the wrist, approximately where the pulse is taken (treat both wrists)
POSITION: flat on back or seated
TYPE OF PRESSURE: pulsed with thumb, pinching motion
AMOUNT OF PRESSURE: as much as patient can take

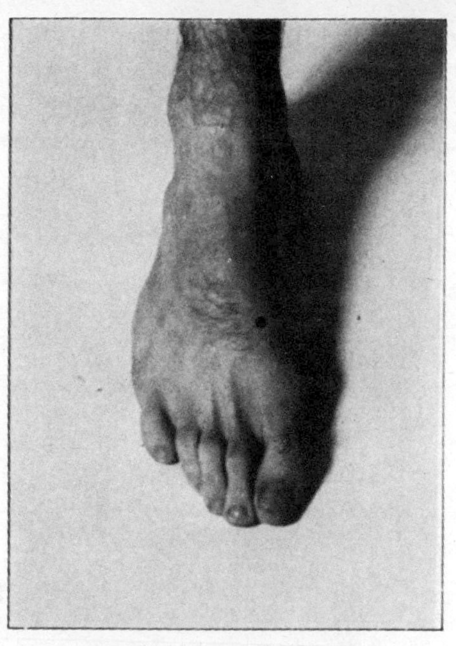

POINT: Great Flush
LANDMARK: toe knuckles
DISTANCE FROM LANDMARK: 1 acu-inch back (toward ankle)
LOCATION: on upper surface of foot between first and second toes (treat both feet)
POSITION: flat on back or seated
TYPE OF PRESSURE: pulsed with thumb, pinching motion
AMOUNT OF PRESSURE: as much as patient can take

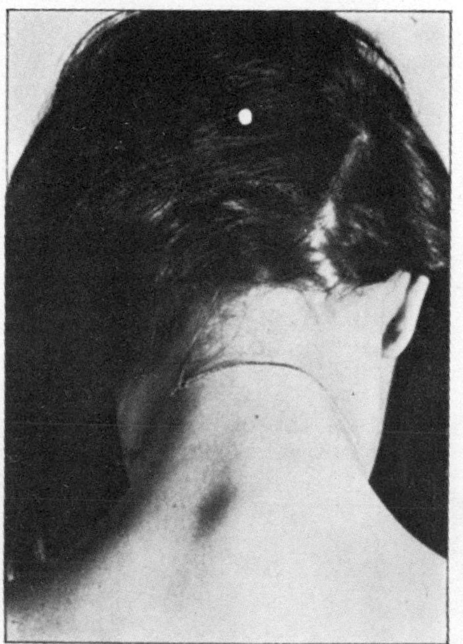

POINT: Strong Connections
LANDMARK: natural hairline at forehead
DISTANCE FROM LANDMARK: 8 acu-inches in back of natural hairline
LOCATION: on top of head, along front-to-back center line of head
POSITION: flat on back or seated
TYPE OF PRESSURE: pulsed with thumb
AMOUNT OF PRESSURE: as much as patient can take

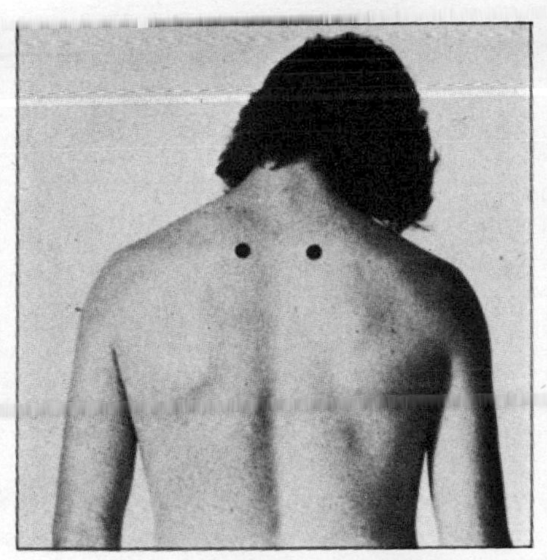

POINT: Great Slaughter
LANDMARK: spine knob at neck
DISTANCE FROM LANDMARK: 1st spine knob (vertebra) below
LOCATION: 1½ acu-inches on either side of spine (treat both sides)
POSITION: face down
TYPE OF PRESSURE: pulsed with thumb
AMOUNT OF PRESSURE: as much as patient can take

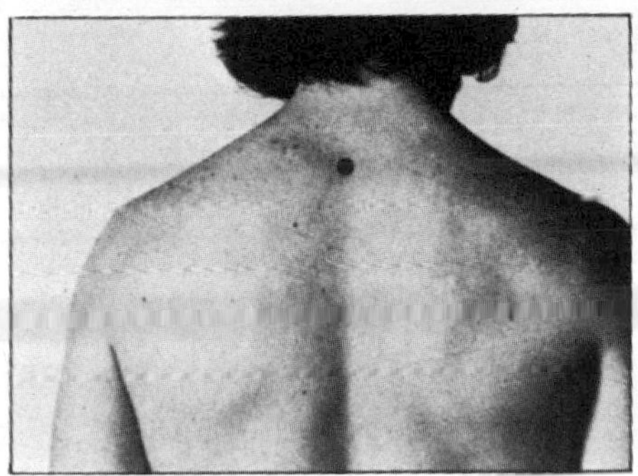

POINT: Big Vertebra
LANDMARK: natural hairline at back of head
DISTANCE FROM LANDMARK: 3 acu-inches down
LOCATION: upper back, right on the spine
POSITION: face down
TYPE OF PRESSURE: pulsed with thumb
AMOUNT OF PRESSURE: as much as patient can take

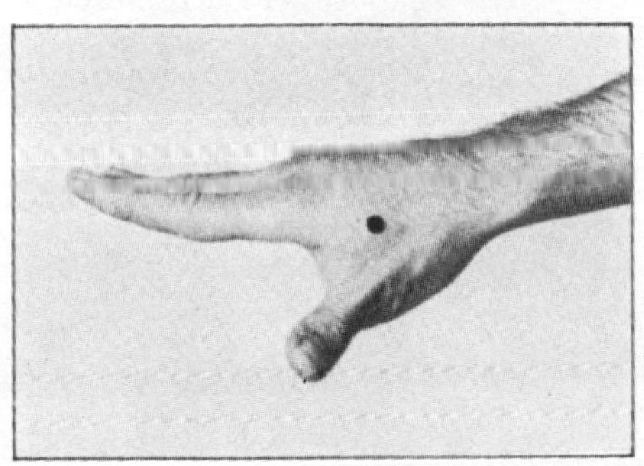

POINT: Connecting the Valleys
LANDMARK: back of hand
DISTANCE FROM LANDMARK: 1 acu-inch down from the point where bones of thumb and index finger meet
LOCATION: on the back of the hand (treat both hands)
POSITION: seated
TYPE OF PRESSURE: pulsed with thumb, pinching motion
AMOUNT OF PRESSURE: as much as patient can take

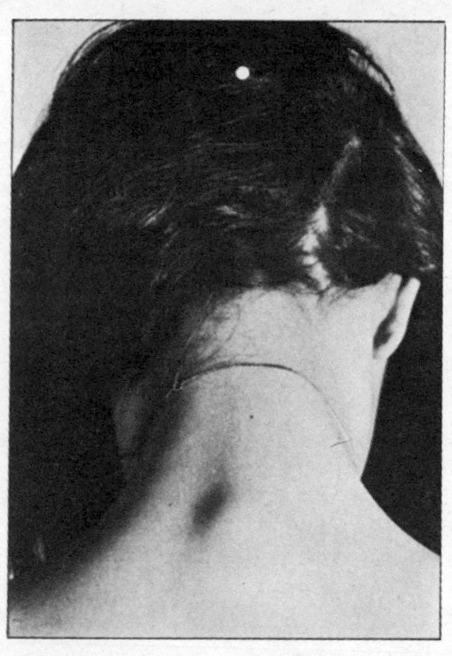

POINT: Posterior Vertex
LANDMARK: natural hairline at forehead
DISTANCE FROM LANDMARK: 6½ acu-inches in back of natural hairline
LOCATION: on top of head, along center line of head
POSITION: seated
TYPE OF PRESSURE: pulsed with thumb
AMOUNT OF PRESSURE: as much as patient can take

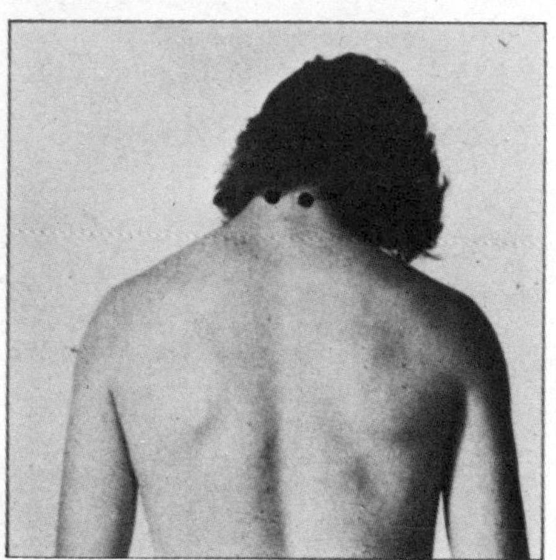

POINT: Celestial Pillar
LANDMARK: natural hairline at the back of neck
DISTANCE FROM LANDMARK: right on landmark
LOCATION: right on the hairline and 1 acu-inch on either side of the front-to-back center line of the head (treat both sides)
POSITION: seated or flat on back
TYPE OF PRESSURE: pulsed with thumb
AMOUNT OF PRESSURE: gently, then gradually increasing to maximum that patient can tolerate

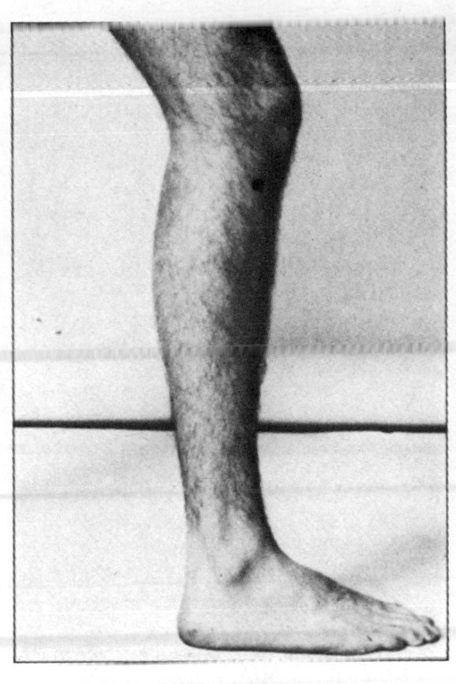

POINT: Walking Three Miles
LANDMARK: kneecap
DISTANCE FROM LANDMARK: 3 acu-inches below (in the depression)
LOCATION: 1 acu-inch toward the outside of the leg (treat both legs)
POSITION: seated in chair or flat on back
TYPE OF PRESSURE: pulsed with thumb (or pinching motion)
AMOUNT OF PRESSURE: quite firm

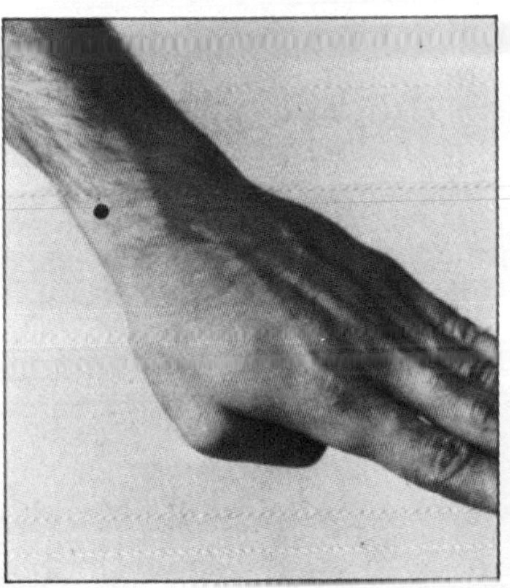

POINT: Sunny Stream
LANDMARK: outer wrist fold
DISTANCE FROM LANDMARK: right on fold
LOCATION: top of hand; feel for hollow at base of thumb (treat both hands)
POSITION: seated
TYPE OF PRESSURE: pulsed with thumb, or thumb-pinching motion
AMOUNT OF PRESSURE: as much as patient can take

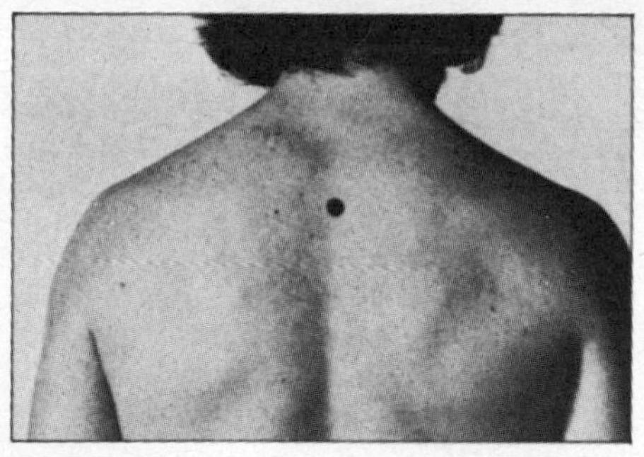

POINT: Seeking Path
LANDMARK: spine knob at neck
DISTANCE FROM LANDMARK: between landmark and next knob down the spine
LOCATION: right on spine
POSITION: on stomach
TYPE OF PRESSURE: pulsed with thumb
AMOUNT OF PRESSURE: quite firm

HICCUPS

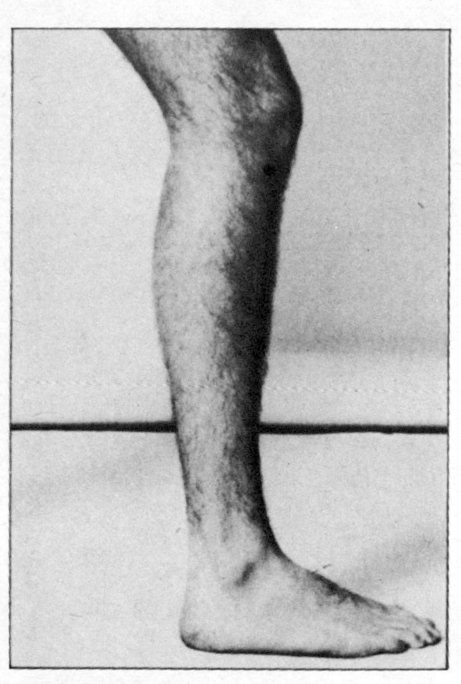

POINT: Walking Three Miles
LANDMARK: kneecap
DISTANCE FROM LANDMARK: 3 acu-inches below (in the depression)
LOCATION: 1 acu-inch toward the outside of the leg (treat both legs)
POSITION: seated in chair or flat on back
TYPE OF PRESSURE: pulsed with thumb (or pinching motion)
AMOUNT OF PRESSURE: quite firm

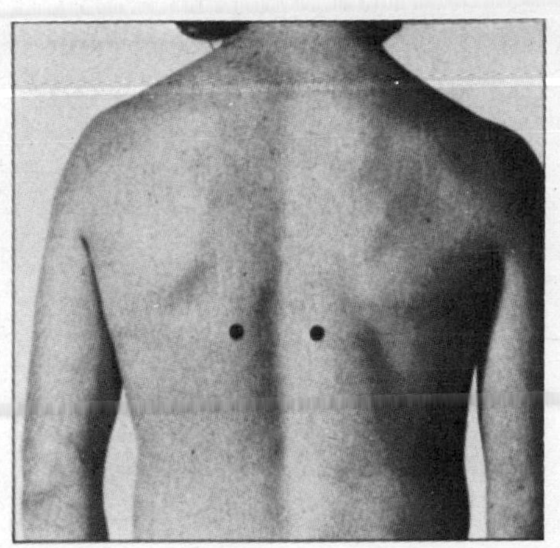

POINT: Diaphragm Locus
LANDMARK: spine knob at neck
DISTANCE FROM LANDMARK: 6th spine knob (vertebra) down
LOCATION: on back, 1½ acu-inches on either side of spine (treat both sides)
POSITION: on stomach
TYPE OF PRESSURE: pulsed with thumb
AMOUNT OF PRESSURE: as much as patient can take

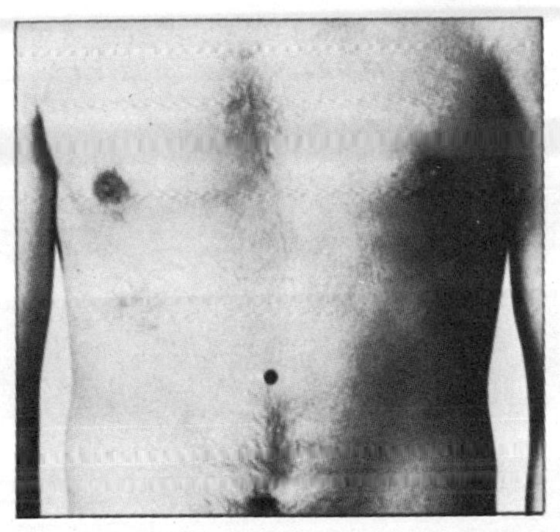

POINT: Middle Epigastrium
LANDMARK: navel
DISTANCE FROM LANDMARK: 4 acu-inches above
POSITION: flat on back
TYPE OF PRESSURE: pulsed with thumb
AMOUNT OF PRESSURE: as much as patient can take

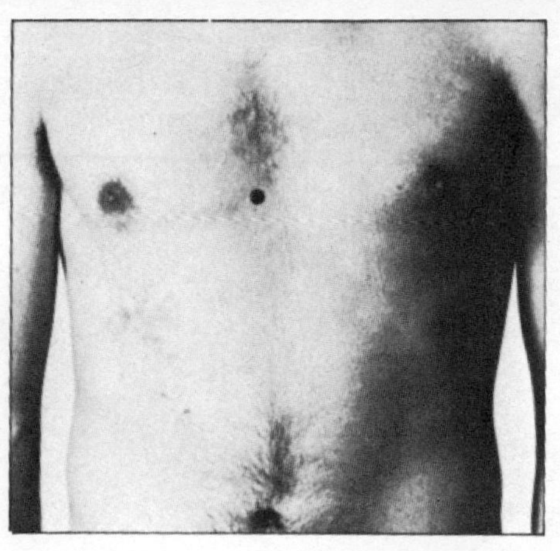

POINT: Upper Epigastrium
LANDMARK: nipples
DISTANCE FROM LANDMARK: midway between
LOCATION: on the chest, at the midpoint of a line drawn between the two nipples
POSITION: flat on back
TYPE OF PRESSURE: pulsed with thumb or fingers
AMOUNT OF PRESSURE: as much as patient can take

HIGH BLOOD PRESSURE

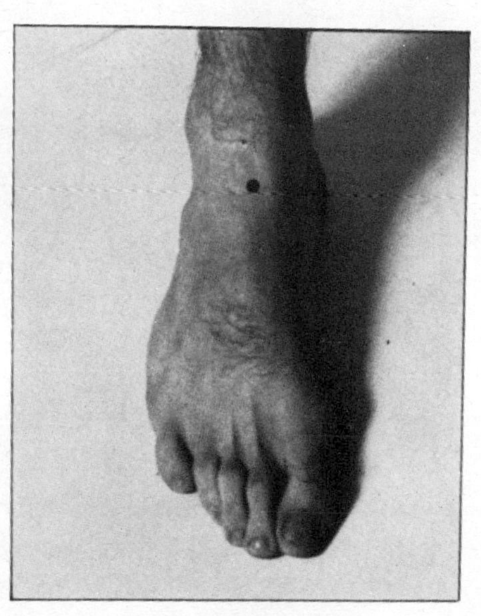

POINT: Great Flush
LANDMARK: toe knuckles
DISTANCE FROM LANDMARK: 1 acu-inch back (toward ankle)
LOCATION: on upper surface of foot between first and second toes (treat both feet)
POSITION: flat on back or seated
TYPE OF PRESSURE: pulsed with thumb, pinching motion
AMOUNT OF PRESSURE: as much as patient can take

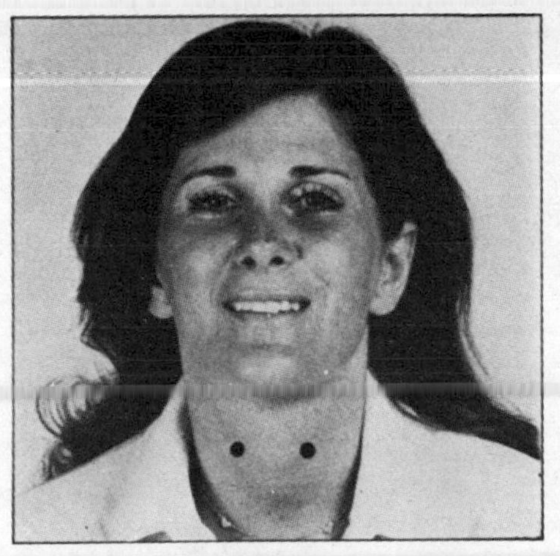

POINT: Welcomed by Man
LANDMARK: Adam's apple
DISTANCE FROM LANDMARK: 1 acu-inch on either side
LOCATION: on the throat, at the same level or slightly below the Adam's apple (treat both sides)
POSITION: flat on back or seated
TYPE OF PRESSURE: pulsed with thumb or fingers
AMOUNT OF PRESSURE: gently at first, then as much as patient can take

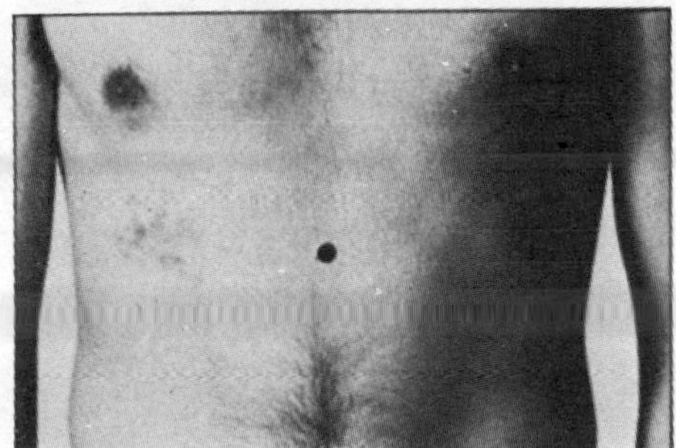

POINT: Middle Epigastrium
LANDMARK: navel
DISTANCE FROM LANDMARK: 4 acu-inches above
POSITION: flat on back
TYPE OF PRESSURE: pulsed with thumb
AMOUNT OF PRESSURE: as much as patient can take

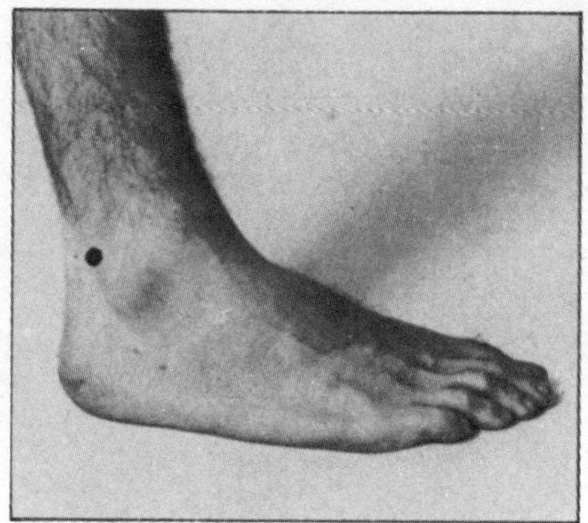

POINT: K'un Lun Mountains
LANDMARK: outer ankle bone
DISTANCE FROM LANDMARK: just in back
LOCATION: in the depression behind outer ankle bone (treat both feet)
POSITION: flat on back
TYPE OF PRESSURE: pulsed with thumb, pinching motion
AMOUNT OF PRESSURE: as much as patient can take

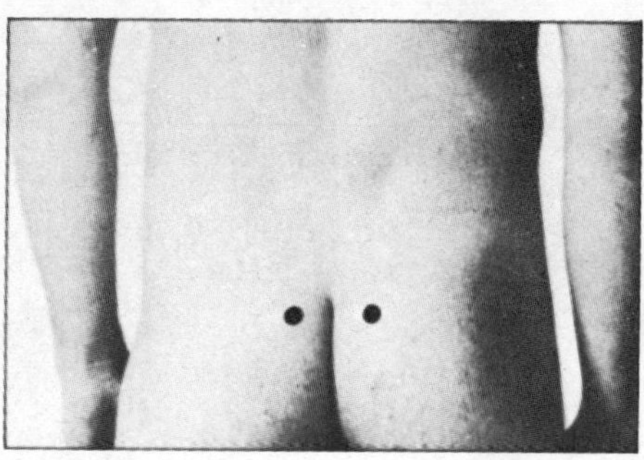

POINT: Small Intestine Locus
LANDMARK: buttocks
DISTANCE FROM LANDMARK: immediately above
LOCATION: just above the swell of the buttocks and 1½ acu-inches on either side of spine (treat both sides)
POSITION: face down
TYPE OF PRESSURE: pulsed with thumb
AMOUNT OF PRESSURE: as much as patient can take

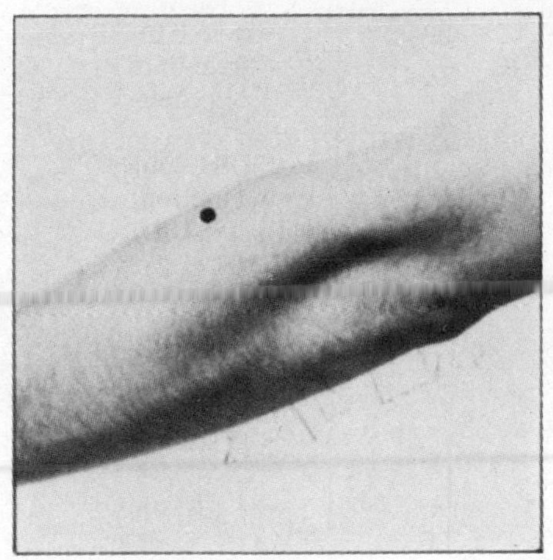

POINT: Three Li
LANDMARK: outer elbow fold
DISTANCE FROM LANDMARK: 2 acu-inches below
LOCATION: side of the forearm, in the middle (treat both arms)
POSITION: seated or flat on back
TYPE OF PRESSURE: pulsed with thumb, pinching motion
AMOUNT OF PRESSURE: as much as patient can take

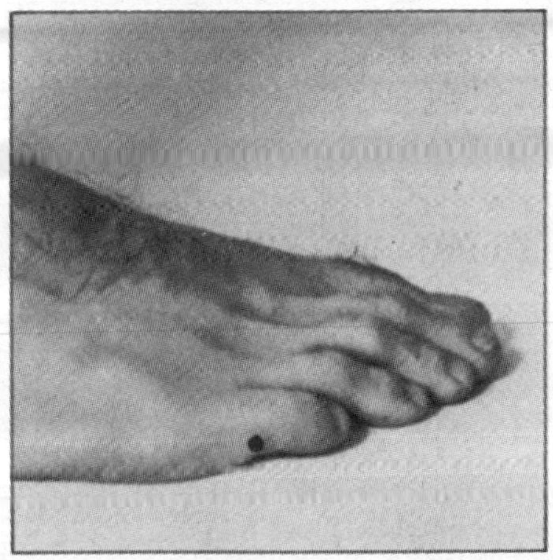

POINT: Communicating the Valleys
LANDMARK: toe knuckle of little toe
DISTANCE FROM LANDMARK: close to the landmark
LOCATION: on the outer edge of the foot, just in front of toe knuckle (treat both feet)
POSITION: seated or flat on back
TYPE OF PRESSURE: pulsed with thumb
AMOUNT OF PRESSURE: as much as patient can take; repeat as needed

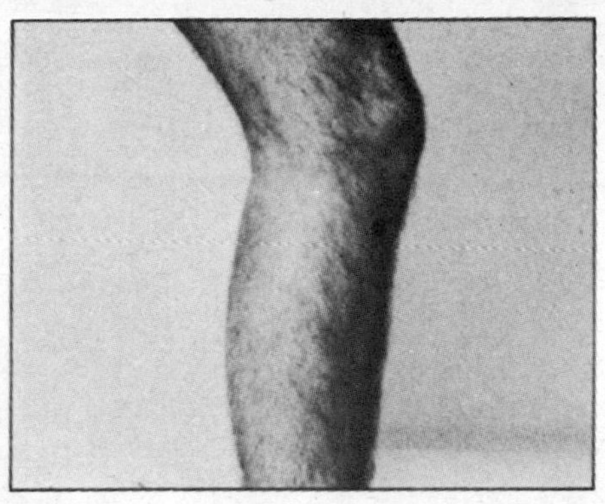

POINT: Walking Three Miles
LANDMARK: kneecap
DISTANCE FROM LANDMARK: 3 acu-inches below (in the depression)
LOCATION: 1 acu-inch toward the outside of the leg (treat both legs)
POSITION: seated in chair or flat on back
TYPE OF PRESSURE: pulsed with thumb (or pinching motion)
AMOUNT OF PRESSURE: quite firm

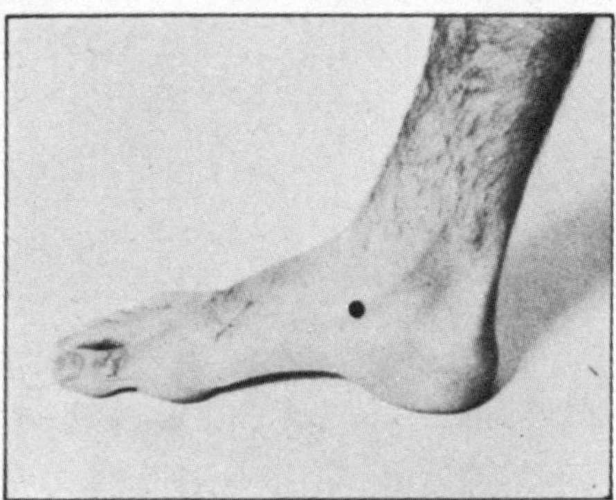

POINT: Trades Hill
LANDMARK: inner ankle bone
DISTANCE FROM LANDMARK: just in front
LOCATION: in the depression just below and in front of the ankle bone, on the inner surface of the leg (treat both legs)
POSITION: seated or flat on back
TYPE OF PRESSURE: pulsed with thumb, pinching motion
AMOUNT OF PRESSURE: as much as patient can take

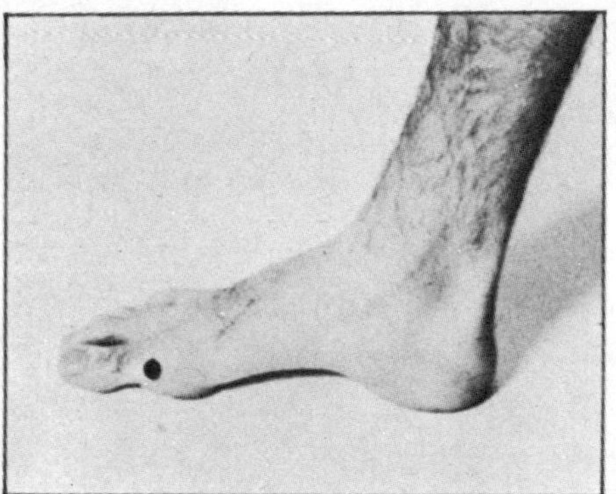

POINT: Great Metropolis
LANDMARK: toe knuckle of big toe
DISTANCE FROM LANDMARK: just in front of toe knuckle
LOCATION: outer side of big toe (treat both feet)
POSITION: seated or flat on back
TYPE OF PRESSURE: pulsed with thumb, pinching motion
AMOUNT OF PRESSURE: as much as patient can take

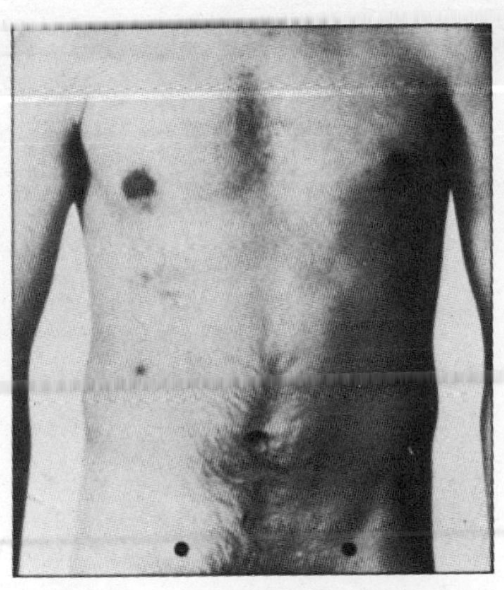

POINT: Perfecture House
LANDMARK: thigh-stomach fold, navel
DISTANCE FROM LANDMARK: in the fold at a point 3 acu-inches down from the navel
LOCATION: lower stomach (treat both sides)
POSITION: flat on back
TYPE OF PRESSURE: pulsed with thumb
AMOUNT OF PRESSURE: as much as patient can take

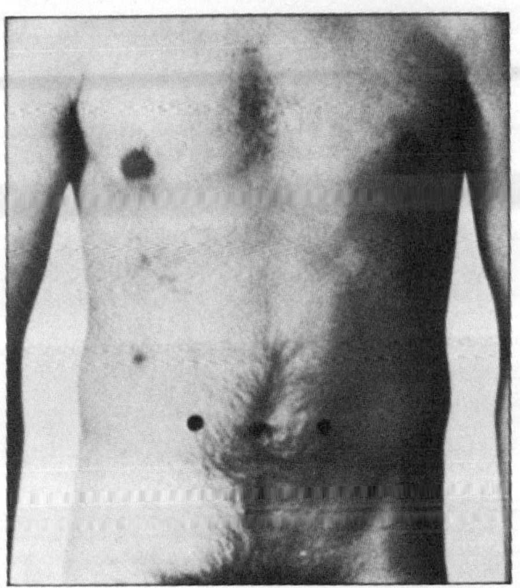

POINT: Celestial Pivot
LANDMARK: navel
DISTANCE FROM LANDMARK: right at the landmark
LOCATION: 2 acu-inches on either side of navel (treat both sides)
POSITION: flat on back
TYPE OF PRESSURE: pulsed with thumb or fingers
AMOUNT OF PRESSURE: as much as patient can take

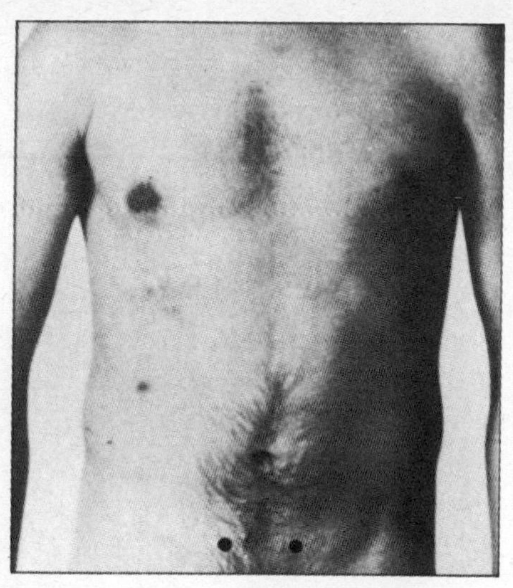

POINT: Four Full
LANDMARK: navel
DISTANCE FROM LANDMARK: 2 acu-inches below
LOCATION: on lower abdomen, 1 acu-inch on either side of center line of stomach (treat both sides)
POSITION: flat on back
TYPE OF PRESSURE: pulsed with thumb
AMOUNT OF PRESSURE: as much as patient can take

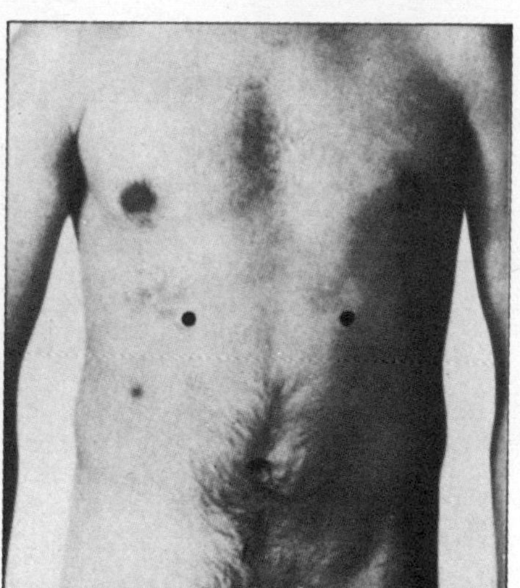

POINT: Beam Gate
LANDMARK: navel
DISTANCE FROM LANDMARK: 4 acu-inches above
LOCATION: on the chest, 2 acu-inches on either side of the center line of the chest (treat both sides)
POSITION: flat on back
TYPE OF PRESSURE: pulsed with thumb
AMOUNT OF PRESSURE: as much as patient can take

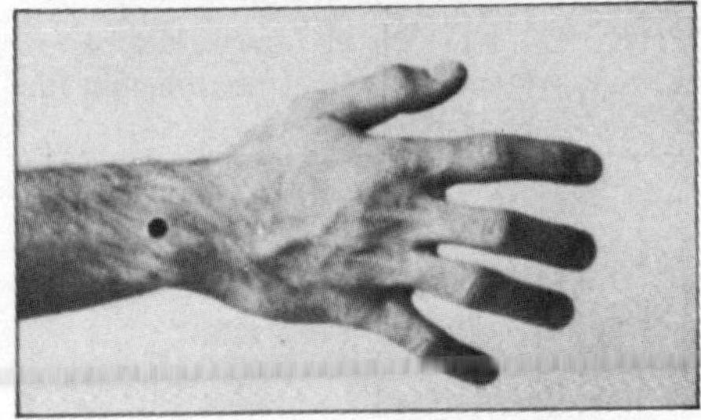

POINT: Outer Pass
LANDMARK: outer wrist fold
DISTANCE FROM LANDMARK: 2 acu-inches above
LOCATION: on back surface of wrist, in the center (treat both arms)
POSITION: seated or flat on back
TYPE OF PRESSURE: pulsed with thumb, pinching motion repeat often
AMOUNT OF PRESSURE: as much as patient can take

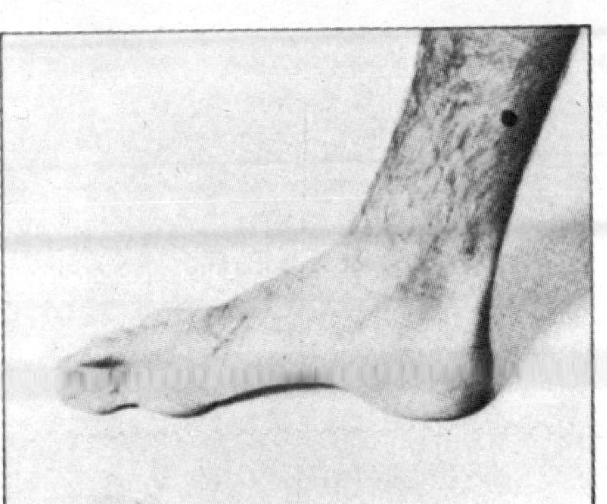

POINT: Delivering Message
LANDMARK: inner ankle bone
DISTANCE FROM LANDMARK: 3 acu-inches above
LOCATION: in the middle of the leg (treat both legs)
POSITION: flat on back
TYPE OF PRESSURE: pulsed with thumb, pinching motion
AMOUNT OF PRESSURE: as much as patient can take

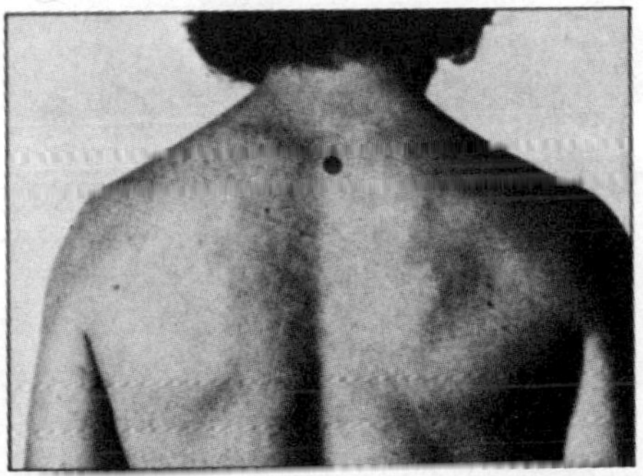

POINT: Big Vertebra
LANDMARK: natural hairline at back of head
DISTANCE FROM LANDMARK: 3 acu-inches down
LOCATION: upper back, right on the spine
POSITION: face down
TYPE OF PRESSURE: pulsed with thumb
AMOUNT OF PRESSURE: as much as patient can take

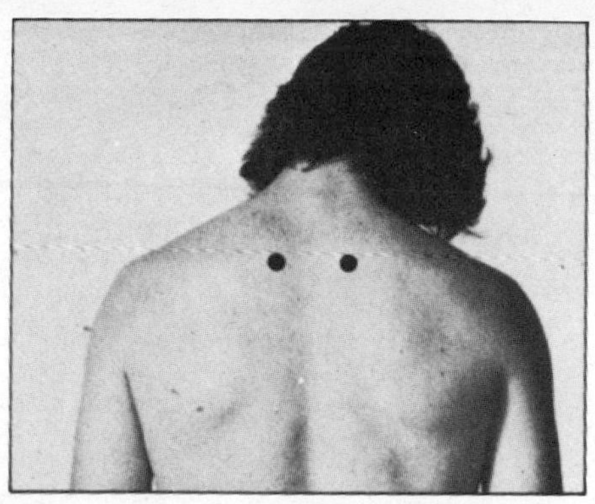

POINT: Great Slaughter
LANDMARK: spine knob at neck
DISTANCE FROM LANDMARK: 1st spine knob (vertebra) below
LOCATION: 1½ acu-inches on either side of the spine (treat both sides)
POSITION: face down
TYPE OF PRESSURE: pulsed with thumb
AMOUNT OF PRESSURE: as much as patient can take

INSOMNIA

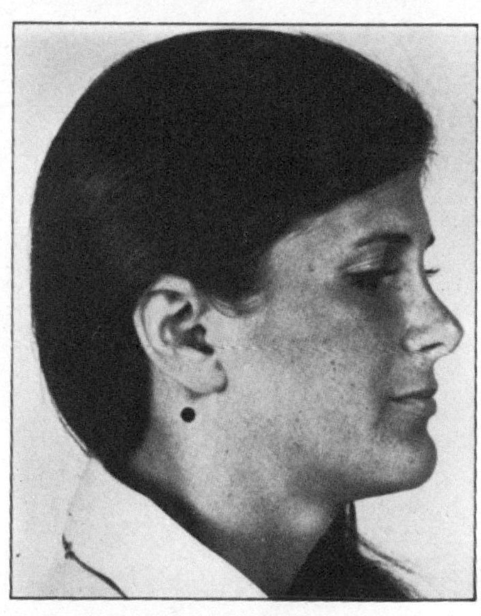

POINT: New Point
LANDMARK: ear lobe
DISTANCE FROM LANDMARK: 1 acu-inch behind bottom edge of ear lobe
LOCATION: on side of head behind the ear (treat both sides)
POSITION: seated or flat, lying on side
TYPE OF PRESSURE: pulsed with thumb or fingers
AMOUNT OF PRESSURE: gently at first, then as much as patient can take

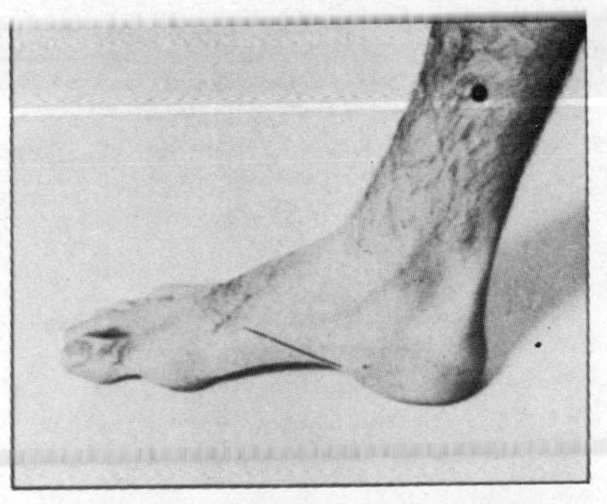

POINT: Crossroad of Three Yins
LANDMARK: inner ankle bone
DISTANCE FROM LANDMARK: 3 acu-inches above
LOCATION: inside of lower leg (treat both legs)
POSITION: seated or flat on back
TYPE OF PRESSURE: pulsed with thumb, pinching motion
AMOUNT OF PRESSURE: as much as patient can take

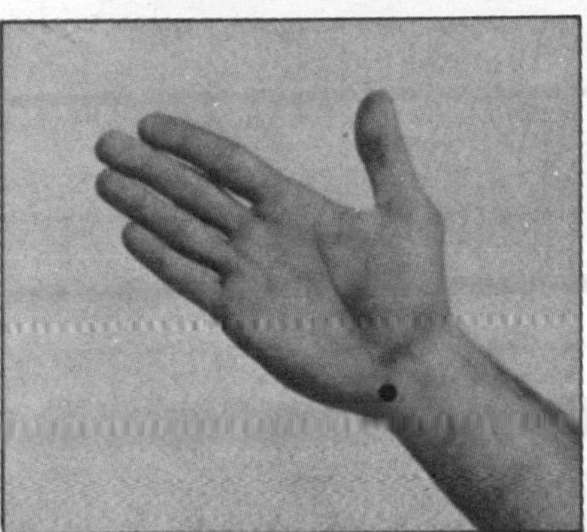

POINT: God's Door
LANDMARK: inner wrist fold
DISTANCE FROM LANDMARK: right on the fold
LOCATION: 1 acu-inch in from outer edge (side with little finger) of arm, on the inner surface of the forearm (treat both arms)
POSITION: seated
TYPE OF PRESSURE: pulsed with thumb
AMOUNT OF PRESSURE: as much as patient can take

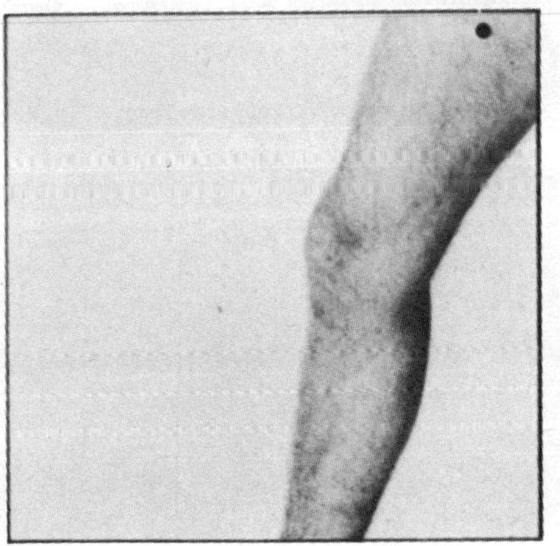

POINT: Five Miles
LANDMARK: thigh-stomach fold
DISTANCE FROM LANDMARK: 1 acu-inch above
LOCATION: on the lower abdomen, 4 acu-inches away from center line of body (treat both sides)
POSITION: flat on back
TYPE OF PRESSURE: pulsed with thumb or fingers
AMOUNT OF PRESSURE: gently, then with firm pressure

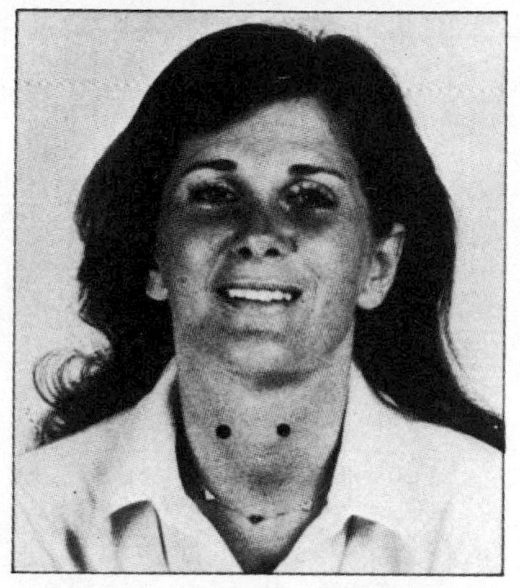

POINT: Welcomed by Man
LANDMARK: Adam's apple
DISTANCE FROM LANDMARK: 1 acu-inch on either side
LOCATION: on the throat, at the same level or slightly below the Adam's apple (treat both sides)
POSITION: flat on back or seated
TYPE OF PRESSURE: pulsed with thumb or fingers
AMOUNT OF PRESSURE: gently at first, then as much as patient can take

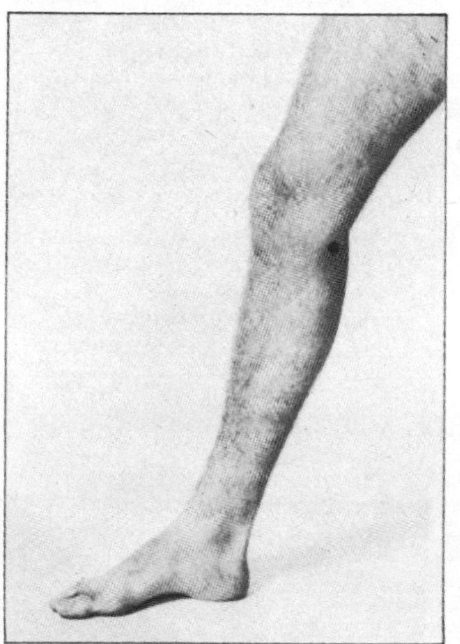

POINT: Great Brook
LANDMARK: back of knee fold
DISTANCE FROM LANDMARK: right on the fold
LOCATION: back of knee, at the inner end of the fold (treat both legs)
POSITION: face down
TYPE OF PRESSURE: pulsed with thumb
AMOUNT OF PRESSURE: gently at first, then as much as patient can take

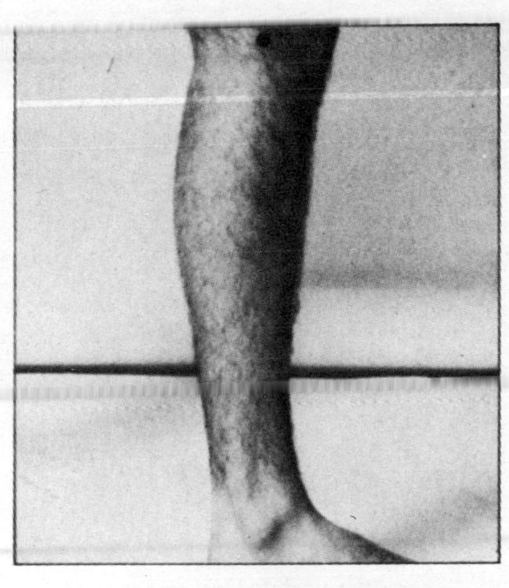

POINT: Knee Yang Pass
LANDMARK: back of knee fold
DISTANCE FROM LANDMARK: right at the fold
LOCATION: center of the outer surface of the leg at the knee (treat both legs)
POSITION: seated or lying on side
TYPE OF PRESSURE: pulsed with thumb or fingers
AMOUNT OF PRESSURE: as much as patient can take

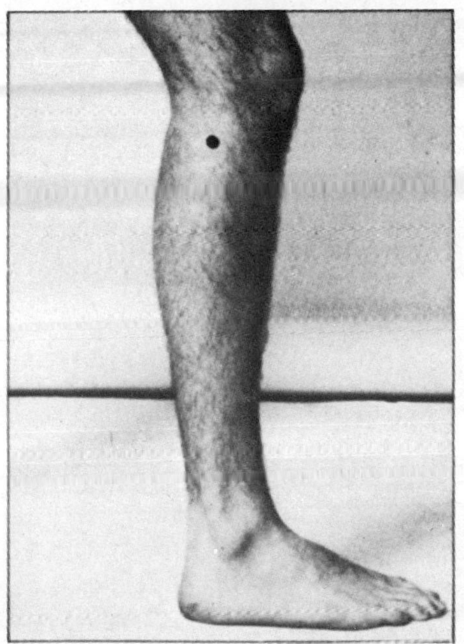

POINT: Spring in the Sunny Hill
LANDMARK: back of knee fold
DISTANCE FROM LANDMARK: 3 acu-inches down
LOCATION: on the outer side of the leg (feel for small long bone underneath) (treat both legs)
POSITION: seated or lying on side
TYPE OF PRESSURE: pulsed with thumb
AMOUNT OF PRESSURE: as much as patient can take

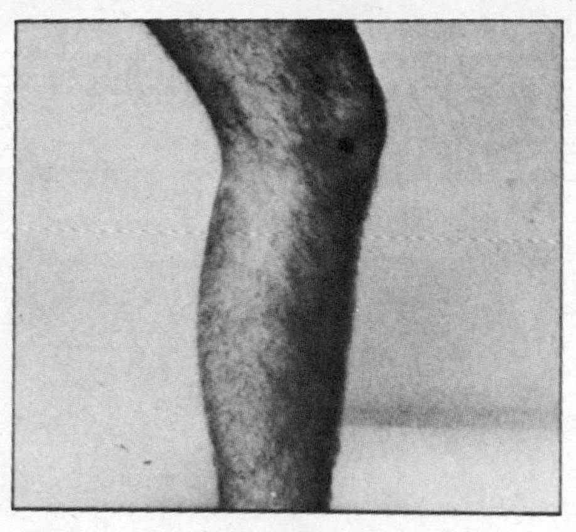

POINT: Nose of Calf
LANDMARK: kneecap
DISTANCE FROM LANDMARK: just below
LOCATION: feel for depression on knee, slightly toward the outer edge of kneecap (treat both legs)
POSITION: seated or flat on back
TYPE OF PRESSURE: pulsed with thumb
AMOUNT OF PRESSURE: as much as patient can take

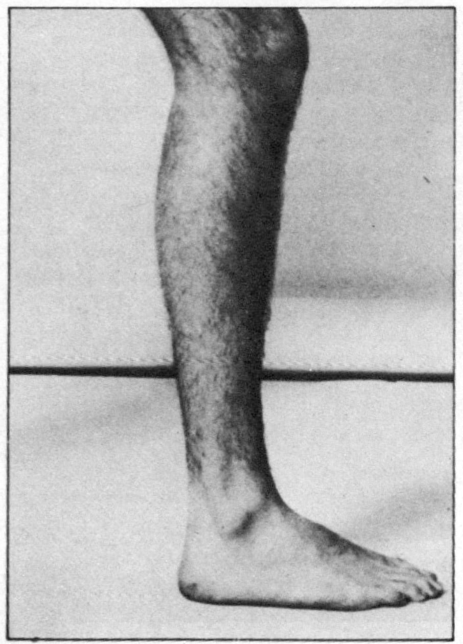

POINT: Walking Three Miles
LANDMARK: kneecap
DISTANCE FROM LANDMARK: 3 acu-inches below (in the depression)
LOCATION: 1 acu-inch toward the outside of the leg (treat both legs)
POSITION: seated in chair or flat on back
TYPE OF PRESSURE: pulsed with thumb (or pinching motion)
AMOUNT OF PRESSURE: quite firm

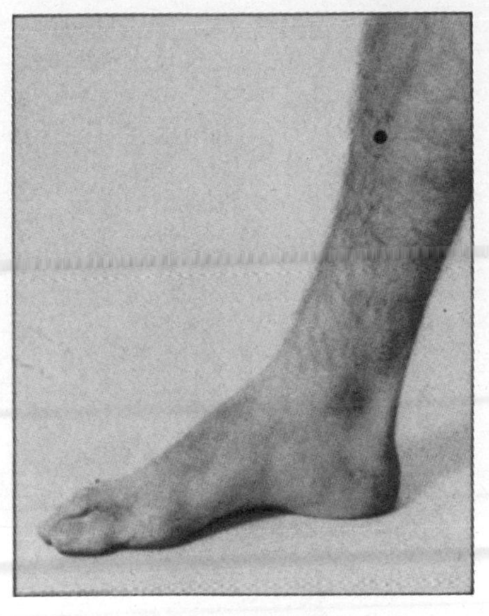

POINT: Isolated Harshness
LANDMARK: inner ankle bone
DISTANCE FROM LANDMARK: 7 acu-inches above
LOCATION: on the inner surface of the leg, just behind the shin bone (treat both legs)
POSITION: seated or flat on back
TYPE OF PRESSURE: pulsed with thumb, pinching motion
AMOUNT OF PRESSURE: as much as patient can tolerate

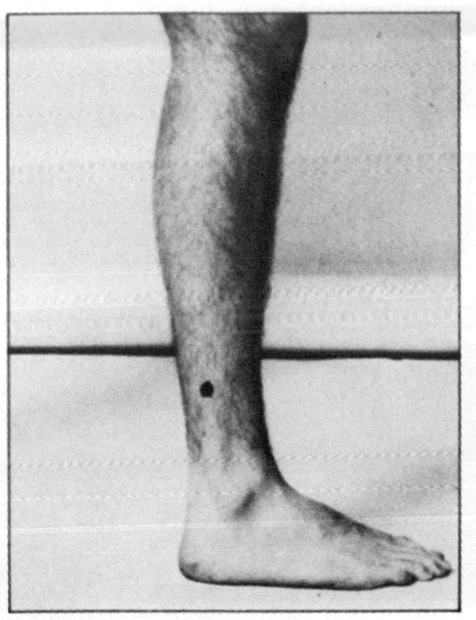

POINT: Suspended Bell
LANDMARK: outer ankle bone
DISTANCE FROM LANDMARK: 3 acu-inches above
LOCATION: on the outer surface of the leg, in the middle (treat both legs)
POSITION: seated or flat on back
TYPE OF PRESSURE: pulsed with thumb, pinching motion
AMOUNT OF PRESSURE: as much as patient can take

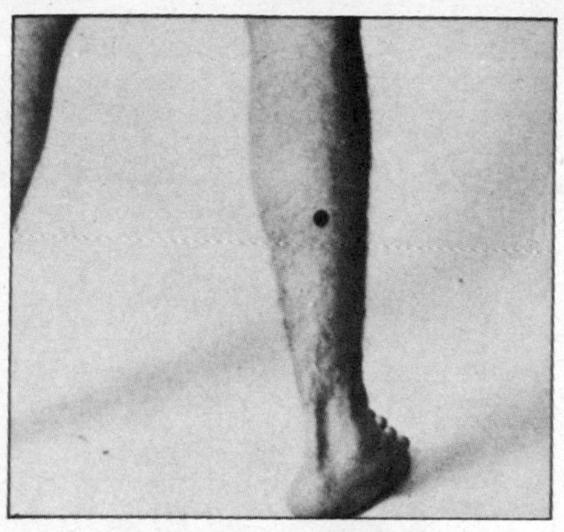

POINT: Supporting Hill
LANDMARK: outer ankle bone
DISTANCE FROM LANDMARK: 8 acu-inches up
LOCATION: back of calf, in the muscle hollow when the toes are stretched out (treat both legs)
POSITION: face down
TYPE OF PRESSURE: pulsed with thumb
AMOUNT OF PRESSURE: as much as patient can take

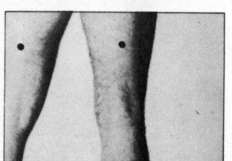

POINT: Organ Gate
LANDMARK: buttocks fold
DISTANCE FROM LANDMARK: 6 acu-inches below buttocks fold
LOCATION: on the back of the thigh, in the middle (treat both legs)
POSITION: face down
TYPE OF PRESSURE: pulsed with thumb
AMOUNT OF PRESSURE: as much as possible

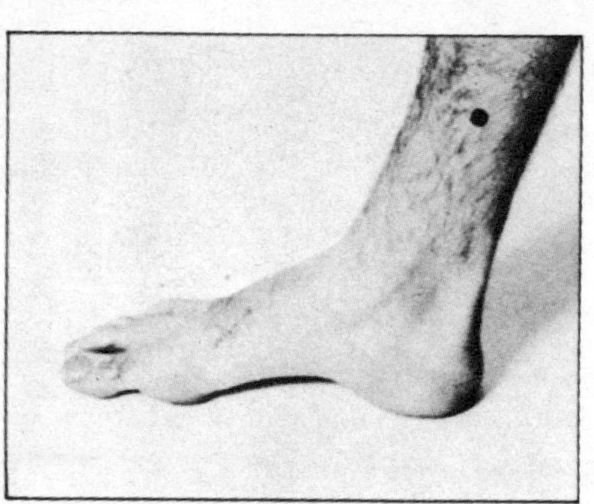

POINT: Crossroad of Three Yins
LANDMARK: inner ankle bone
DISTANCE FROM LANDMARK: 3 acu-inches above
LOCATION: inside of lower leg (treat both legs)
POSITION: seated or flat on back
TYPE OF PRESSURE: pulsed with thumb, pinching motion
AMOUNT OF PRESSURE: as much as patient can take

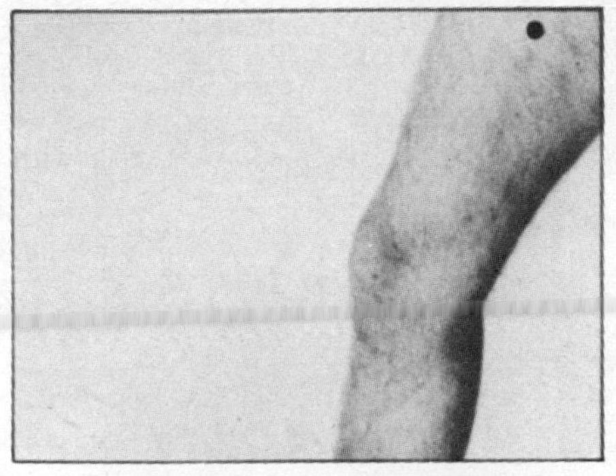

POINT: Five Miles
LANDMARK: thigh-stomach fold
DISTANCE FROM LANDMARK: 1 acu-inch above
LOCATION: on the lower abdomen, 4 acu-inches away from center line of body (treat both sides)
POSITION: flat on back
TYPE OF PRESSURE: pulsed with thumb or fingers
AMOUNT OF PRESSURE: gently, then with firm pressure

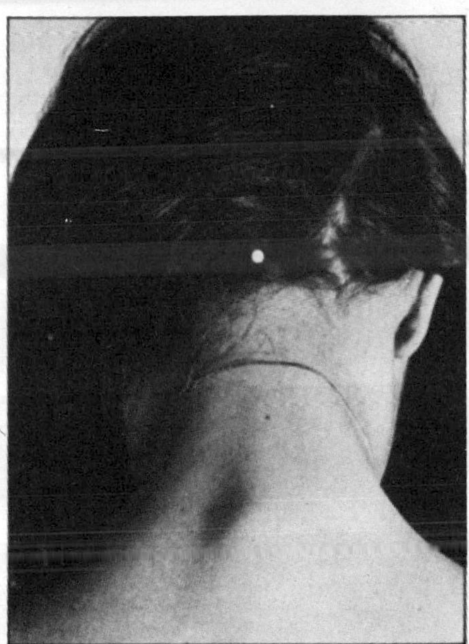

POINT: Windy Prefecture
LANDMARK: natural hairline at back of head
DISTANCE FROM LANDMARK: 1 acu-inch above
LOCATION: on top of head, along front-to-back center line of head
POSITION: seated or face down
TYPE OF PRESSURE: pulsed with thumb
AMOUNT OF PRESSURE: as much as patient can take

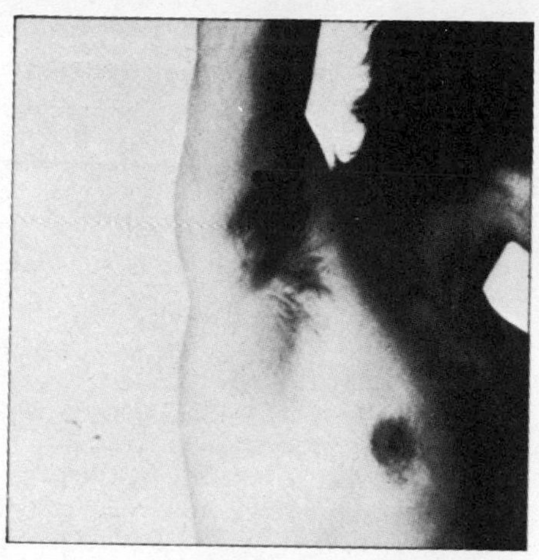

POINT: Extreme Spring
LANDMARK: arm-shoulder fold
DISTANCE FROM LANDMARK: right at fold
LOCATION: in the armpit, in the center of the crease (treat both arms)
POSITION: seated or flat on back
TYPE OF PRESSURE: pulsed with thumb or fingers
AMOUNT OF PRESSURE: as much as patient can take

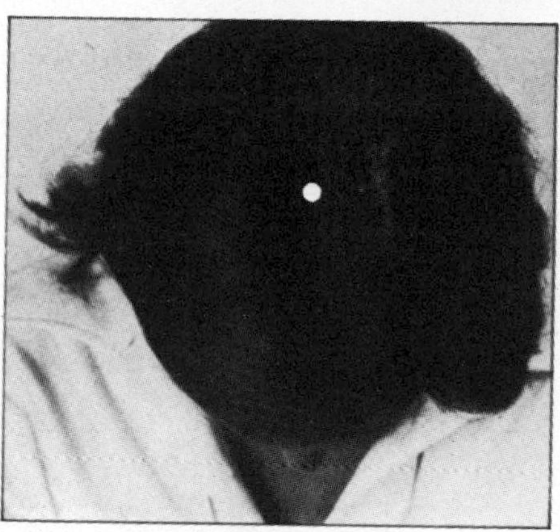

POINT: Anterior Vertex
LANDMARK: natural hairline at forehead
DISTANCE FROM LANDMARK: 3½ acu-inches behind the natural hairline
LOCATION: on top of head, along front-to-back center line of head
POSITION: seated
TYPE OF PRESSURE: pulsed with thumb
AMOUNT OF PRESSURE: as much as patient can take

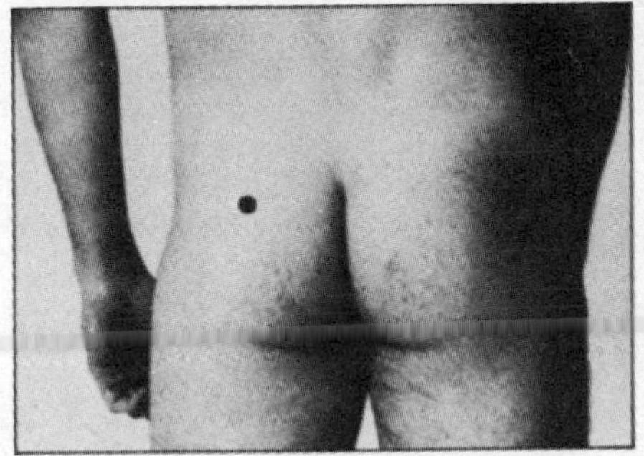

POINT: Circular Jump
LANDMARK: buttocks fold
DISTANCE FROM LANDMARK: 5 acu-inches up
LOCATION: on the side of the buttocks, approximately 3 acu-inches from the center line of the buttocks toward the rear (treat both sides)
POSITION: face down
TYPE OF PRESSURE: pulsed with thumb
AMOUNT OF PRESSURE: as much as patient can take

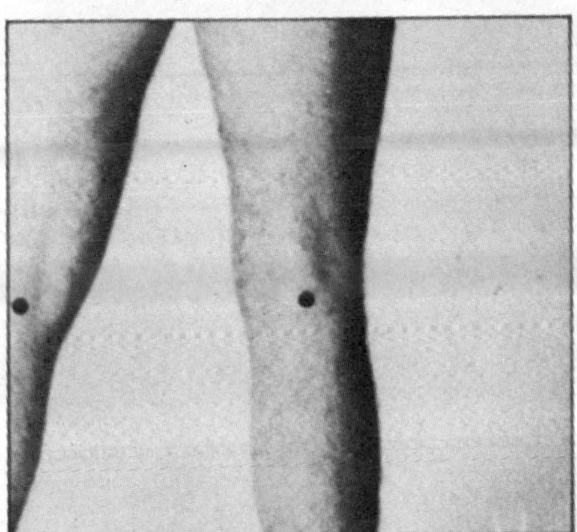

POINT: Orderly Edge
LANDMARK: back of knee fold
DISTANCE FROM LANDMARK: right in fold
LOCATION: back of knee, in the center of fold (treat both legs)
POSITION: face down
TYPE OF PRESSURE: pulsed with thumb
AMOUNT OF PRESSURE: as much as patient can take

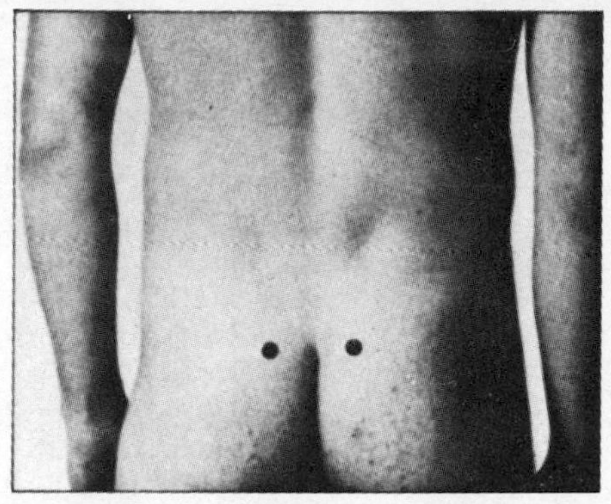

POINT: Small Intestine Locus
LANDMARK: buttocks
DISTANCE FROM LANDMARK: immediately above
LOCATION: just above the swell of the buttocks and 1½ acu-inches on either side of spine (treat both sides)
POSITION: face down
TYPE OF PRESSURE: pulsed with thumb
AMOUNT OF PRESSURE: as much as patient can take

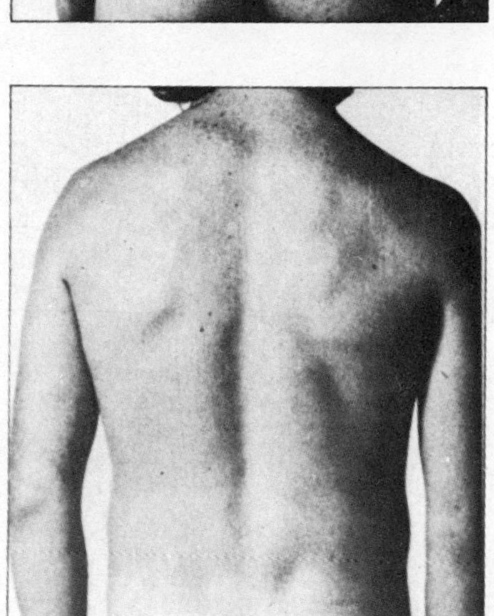

POINT: Large Intestine Locus
LANDMARK: spine knob at neck
DISTANCE FROM LANDMARK: 16th spine knob (vertebra) below
LOCATION: 1½ acu-inches on either side of the spine (treat both sides)
POSITION: face down
TYPE OF PRESSURE: pulsed with thumb
AMOUNT OF PRESSURE: as much as patient can take

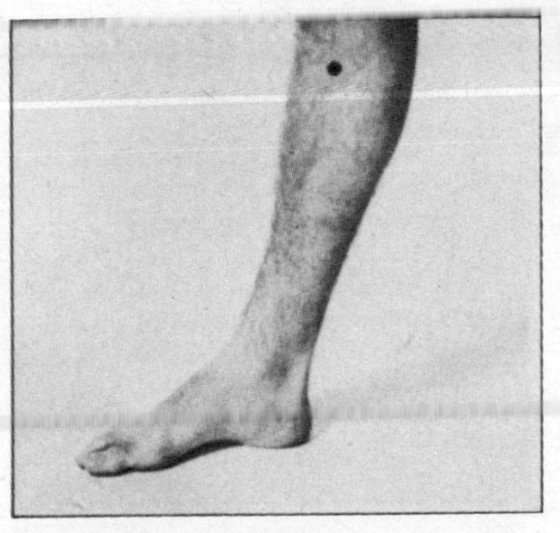

POINT: Terrestrial Machine
LANDMARK: inner ankle bone
DISTANCE FROM LANDMARK: 10 acu-inches above
LOCATION: on the inner surface of the leg, in the approximate center (treat both legs)
POSITION: seated or flat on back
TYPE OF PRESSURE: pulsed with thumb, pinching motion
AMOUNT OF PRESSURE: as much as patient can take

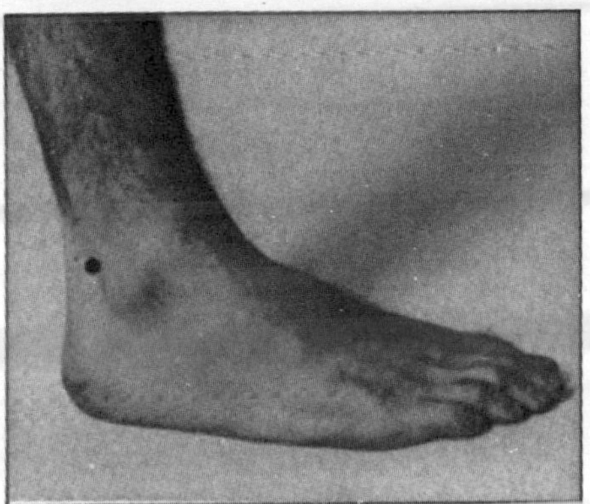

POINT: K'un Lun Mountains
LANDMARK: outer ankle bone
DISTANCE FROM LANDMARK: just in back
LOCATION: in the depression behind outer ankle bone (treat both feet)
POSITION: flat on back
TYPE OF PRESSURE: pulsed with thumb, pinching motion
AMOUNT OF PRESSURE: as much as patient can take

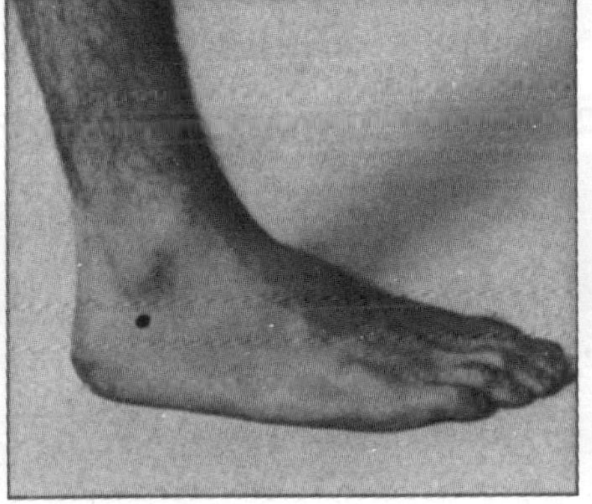

POINT: Stretching Vessel
LANDMARK: outer ankle bone
DISTANCE FROM LANDMARK: immediately below
LOCATION: in the depression behind outer ankle bone (treat both feet)
POSITION: flat on back
TYPE OF PRESSURE: pulsed with thumb, pinching motion
AMOUNT OF PRESSURE: as much as patient can take

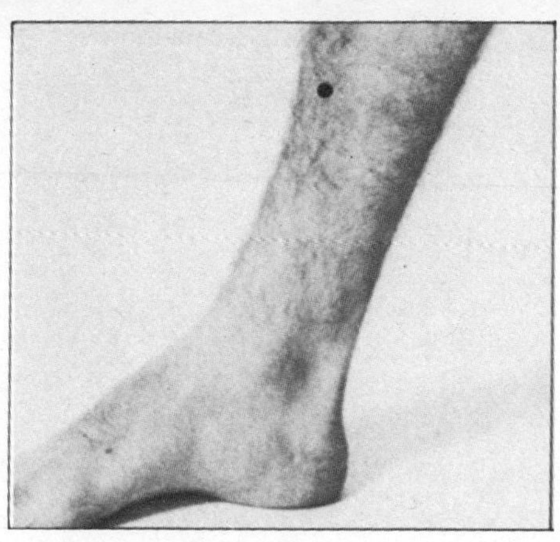

POINT: Insect Gutter
LANDMARK: inner ankle bone
DISTANCE FROM LANDMARK: 5 acu-inches above
LOCATION: on the inner surface of the leg just behind the edge of the shin bone (treat both legs)
POSITION: flat on back or seated
TYPE OF PRESSURE: pulsed with thumb, pinching motion
AMOUNT OF PRESSURE: as much as patient can take

LUMBAR PAINS

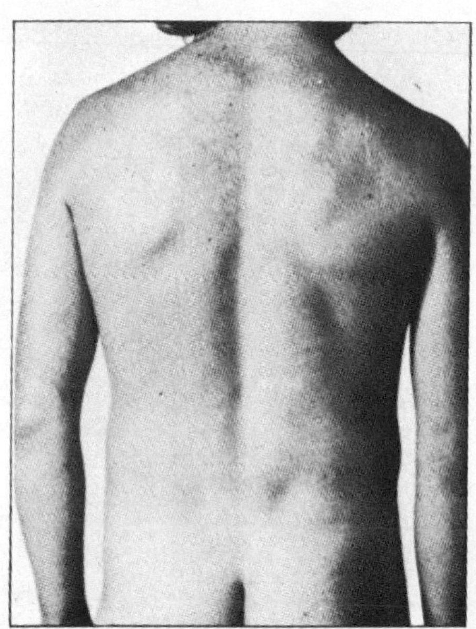

POINT: Series of spine points
LANDMARK: lower end of spine
DISTANCE FROM LANDMARK: 1½ acu-inches on either side of spine
LOCATION: lower back; treat at the level of each spinal knob in the lower half of the back (treat both sides)
POSITION: face down
TYPE OF PRESSURE: pulsed with thumb or fingers
AMOUNT OF PRESSURE: gently first, then as much as patient can take

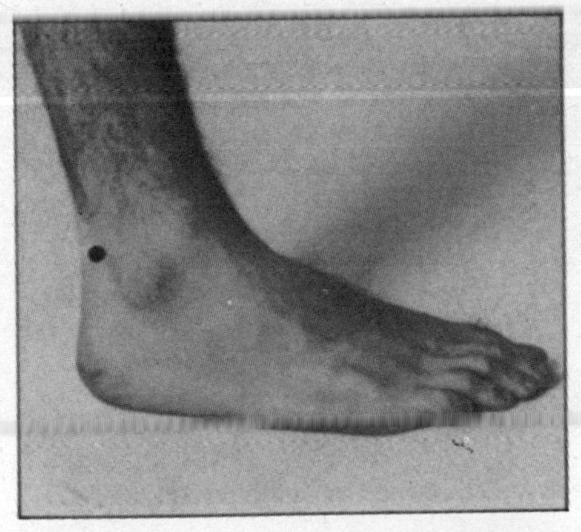

POINT: K'un Lun Mountains
LANDMARK: outer ankle bone
DISTANCE FROM LANDMARK: just in back
LOCATION: in the depression behind outer ankle bone (treat both feet)
POSITION: flat on back
TYPE OF PRESSURE: pulsed with thumb, pinching motion
AMOUNT OF PRESSURE: as much as patient can take

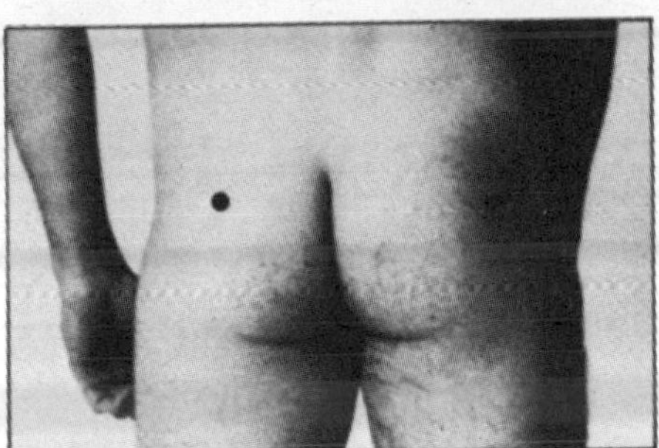

POINT: Circular Jump
LANDMARK: buttocks fold
DISTANCE FROM LANDMARK: 5 acu-inches up
LOCATION: on the side of the buttocks, approximately 3 acu-inches from the center line of the buttocks toward the rear (treat both sides)
POSITION: face down
TYPE OF PRESSURE: pulsed with thumb
AMOUNT OF PRESSURE: as much as patient can take

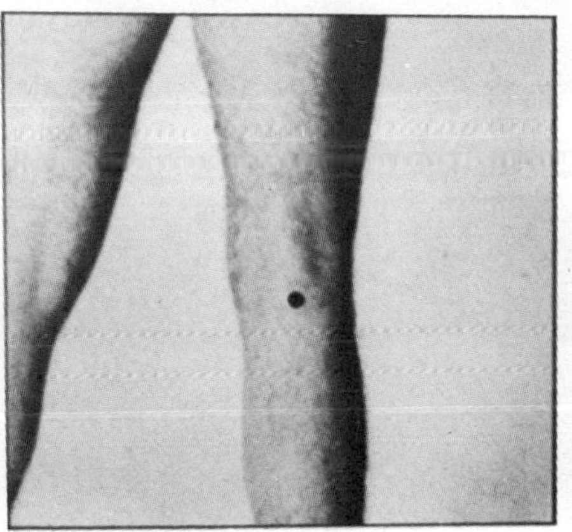

POINT: Orderly Edge
LANDMARK: back of knee fold
DISTANCE FROM LANDMARK: right in fold
LOCATION: back of knee, in the center of fold (treat both legs)
POSITION: face down
TYPE OF PRESSURE: pulsed with thumb
AMOUNT OF PRESSURE: as much as patient can take

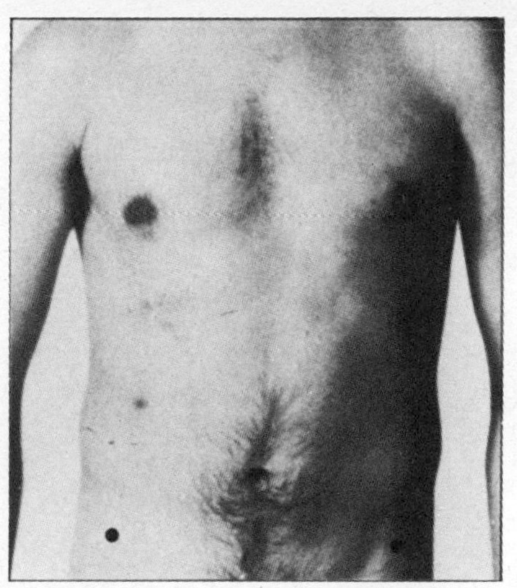

POINT: Five Pivots
LANDMARK: hip bone
DISTANCE FROM LANDMARK: 1 acu-inch toward center of body and just below hip bone
LOCATION: lower abdomen (treat both sides)
POSITION: flat on back
TYPE OF PRESSURE: pulsed with thumb, pinching motion
AMOUNT OF PRESSURE: as much as patient can take

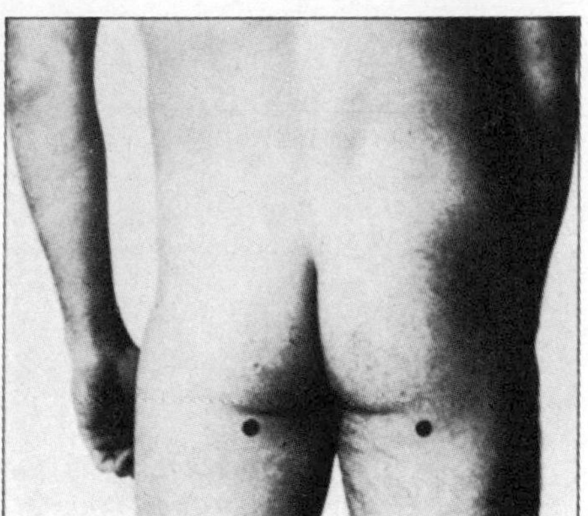

POINT: Stomach Granary
LANDMARK: buttocks fold
DISTANCE FROM LANDMARK: within the fold
LOCATION: at the midpoint of the fold line (treat both legs)
POSITION: face down
TYPE OF PRESSURE: pulsed with thumb
AMOUNT OF PRESSURE: as much as possible

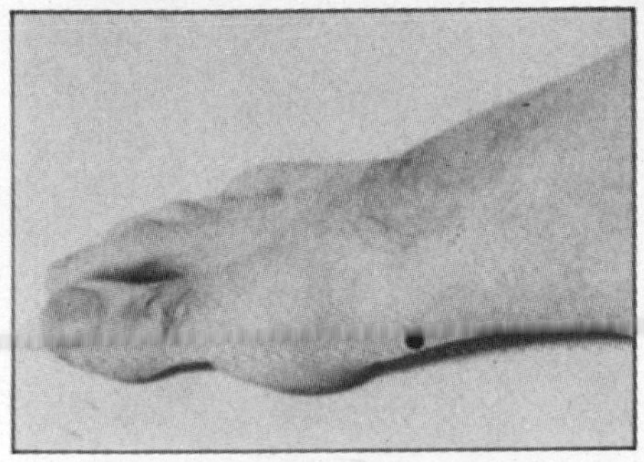

POINT: Generation Gap
LANDMARK: big toe joint
DISTANCE FROM LANDMARK: 1 acu-inch back (toward ankle) from big toe joint
LOCATION: on the inner edge of the foot (treat both feet)
POSITION: flat on back
TYPE OF PRESSURE: pulsed with thumb or percussion (jab with thumb)
AMOUNT OF PRESSURE: as much as patient can take

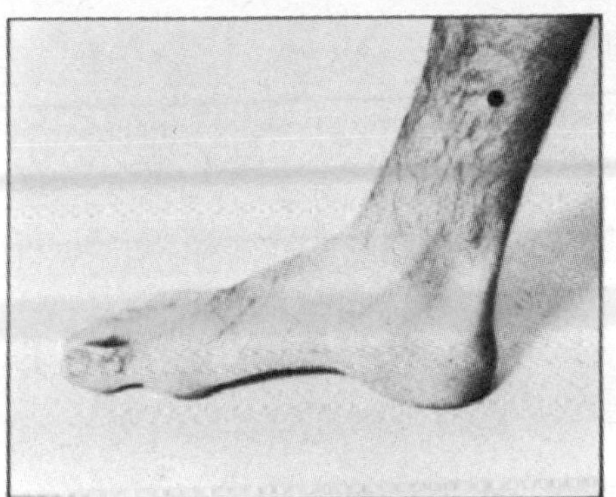

POINT: Crossroad of Three Yins
LANDMARK: inner ankle bone
DISTANCE FROM LANDMARK: 3 acu-inches above
LOCATION: inside of lower leg (treat both legs)
POSITION: seated or flat on back
TYPE OF PRESSURE: pulsed with thumb, pinching motion
AMOUNT OF PRESSURE: as much as patient can take

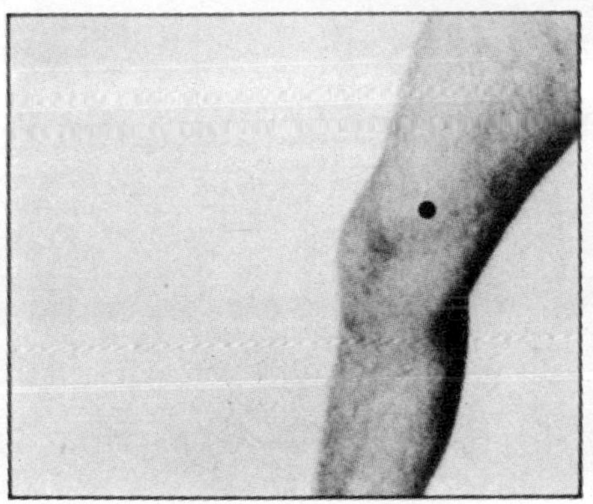

POINT: Sea of Blood
LANDMARK: back of knee fold
DISTANCE FROM LANDMARK: 3 acu-inches above
LOCATION: inner surface of thigh, approximately 2 acu-inches forward of the back surface (treat both legs)
POSITION: flat on back
TYPE OF PRESSURE: pulsed with thumb
AMOUNT OF PRESSURE: as much as patient can take

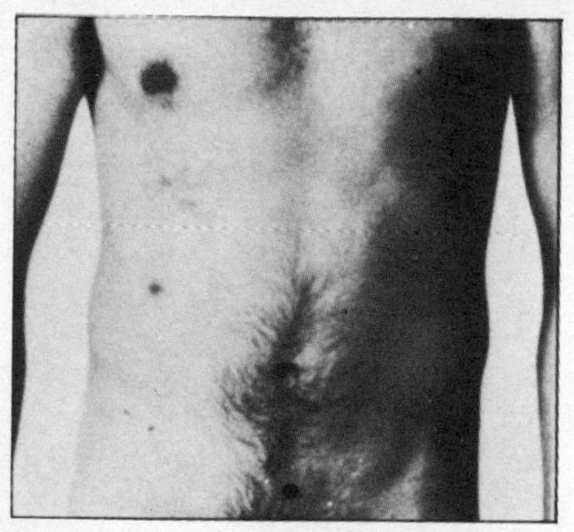

POINT: Middle Extreme
LANDMARK: navel
DISTANCE FROM LANDMARK: 5 acu-inches directly below
LOCATION: on lower adbomen
POSITION: flat on back
TYPE OF PRESSURE: pulsed with thumb
AMOUNT OF PRESSURE: as much as patient can take

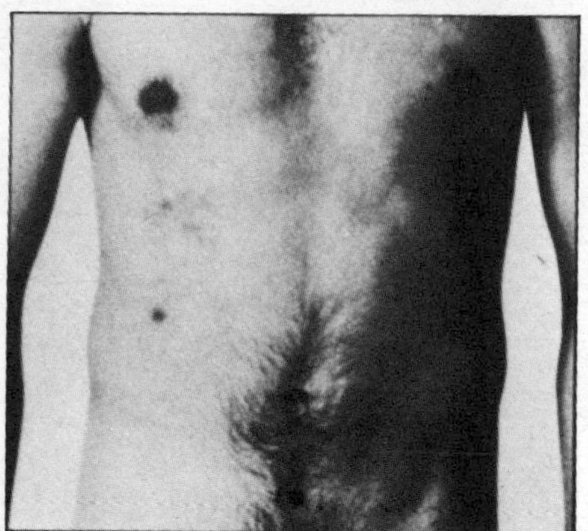

POINT: Pass Origin
LANDMARK: navel
DISTANCE FROM LANDMARK: 3 acu-inches below
LOCATION: on lower abdomen in a line directly below navel
POSITION: flat on back
TYPE OF PRESSURE: pulsed with thumb
AMOUNT OF PRESSURE: as much as patient can take

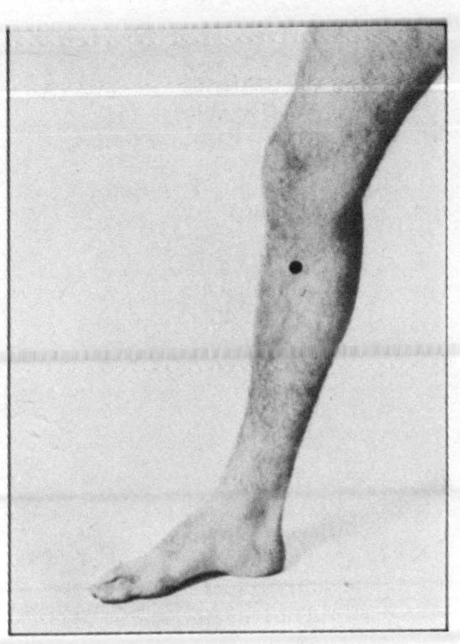

POINT: Terrestrial Machine
LANDMARK: inner ankle bone
DISTANCE FROM LANDMARK: 10 acu-inches above
LOCATION: on the inner surface of the leg, in the approximate center (treat both legs)
POSITION: seated or flat on back
TYPE OF PRESSURE: pulsed with thumb, pinching motion
AMOUNT OF PRESSURE: as much as patient can take

MENSTRUAL PAIN

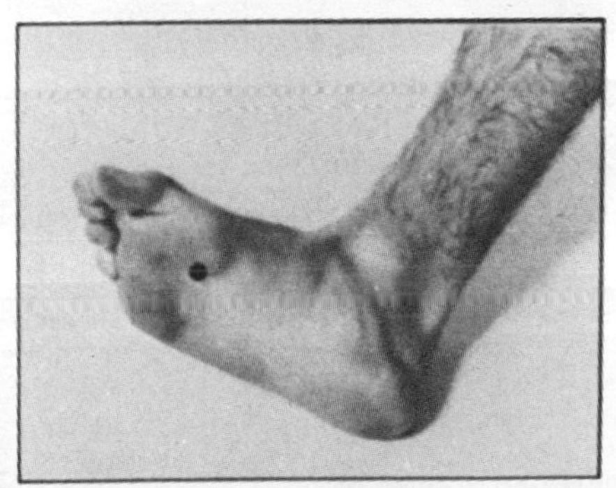

POINT: Pouring Spring
LANDMARK: bottom of foot
DISTANCE FROM LANDMARK: within landmark
LOCATION: on the bottom of the foot, in the depression just in back of the ball when the foot is raised (treat both feet)
POSITION: flat on back
TYPE OF PRESSURE: alternating pulsed and steady with thumb
AMOUNT OF PRESSURE: as much as patient can take

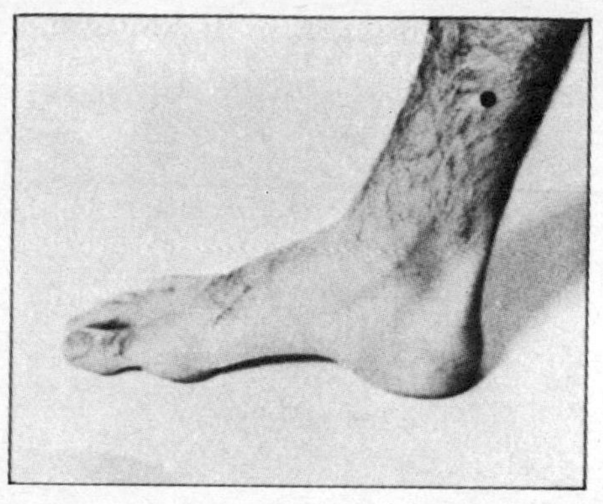

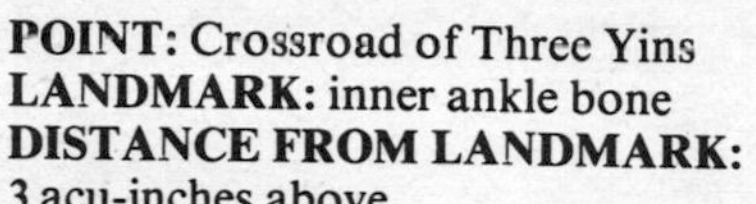

POINT: Crossroad of Three Yins
LANDMARK: inner ankle bone
DISTANCE FROM LANDMARK: 3 acu-inches above
LOCATION: inside of lower leg (treat both legs)
POSITION: seated or flat on back
TYPE OF PRESSURE: pulsed with thumb, pinching motion
AMOUNT OF PRESSURE: as much as patient can take

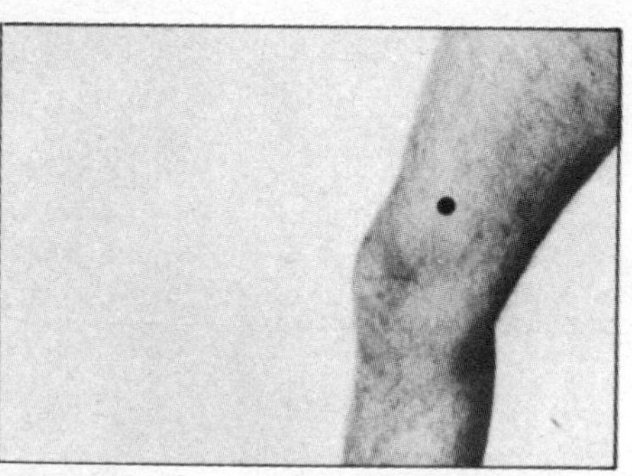

POINT: Sea of Blood
LANDMARK: back of knee fold
DISTANCE FROM LANDMARK: 3 acu-inches above
LOCATION: inner surface of thigh, approximately 2 acu-inches forward of the back surface (treat both legs)
POSITION: flat on back
TYPE OF PRESSURE: pulsed with thumb
AMOUNT OF PRESSURE: as much as patient can take

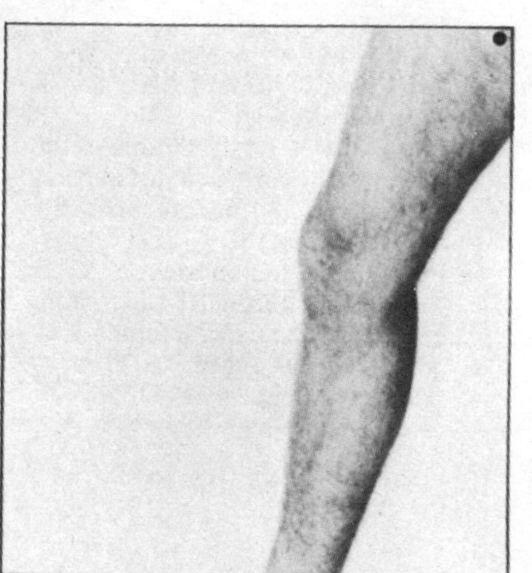

POINT: Yin Screen
LANDMARK: thigh-stomach fold
DISTANCE FROM LANDMARK: 1 acu-inch below
LOCATION: on upper thigh, 3 acu-inches on either side of center line of body (treat both sides)
POSITION: flat on back
TYPE OF PRESSURE: pulsed with thumb or fingers
AMOUNT OF PRESSURE: gently, then as much as patient can take

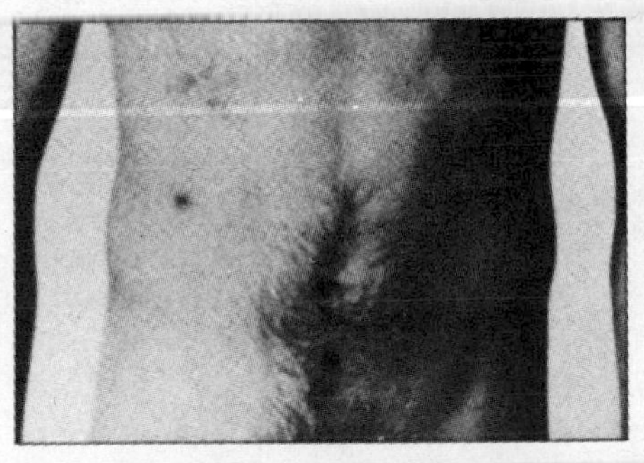

POINT: Pass Origin
LANDMARK: navel
DISTANCE FROM LANDMARK: 3 acu-inches below
LOCATION: on lower abdomen in a line directly below navel
POSITION: flat on back
TYPE OF PRESSURE: pulsed with thumb
AMOUNT OF PRESSURE: as much as patient can take

MENTAL TENSION AND ANXIETY

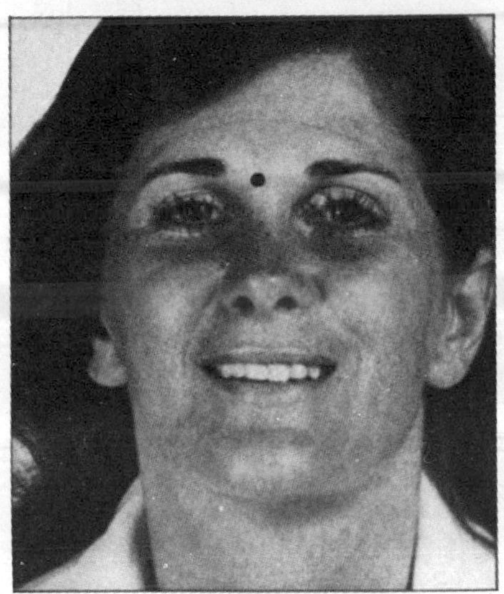

POINT: New Point
LANDMARK: eyebrows
DISTANCE FROM LANDMARK: point midway between the eyebrows
LOCATION: on a line joining the inside ends of the eyebrows
POSITION: seated or flat on back
TYPE OF PRESSURE: pinching motion with thumb and forefinger while also pressing in firmly
AMOUNT OF PRESSURE: as much as patient can take

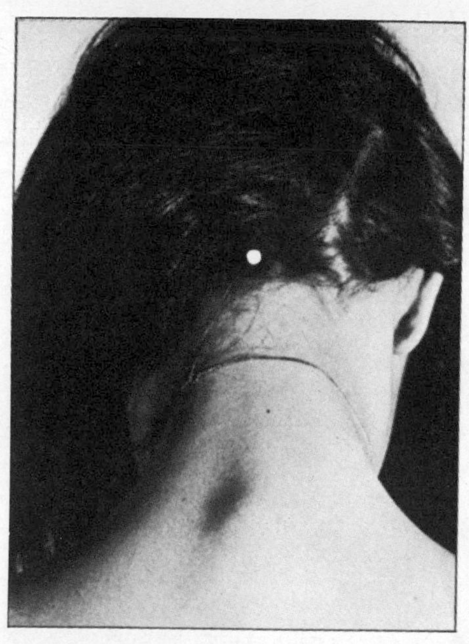

POINT: Windy Prefecture
LANDMARK: natural hairline at back of head
DISTANCE FROM LANDMARK: 1 acu-inch above
LOCATION: on top of head, along front-to-back center line of head
POSITION: seated or face down
TYPE OF PRESSURE: pulsed with thumb
AMOUNT OF PRESSURE: as much as patient can take

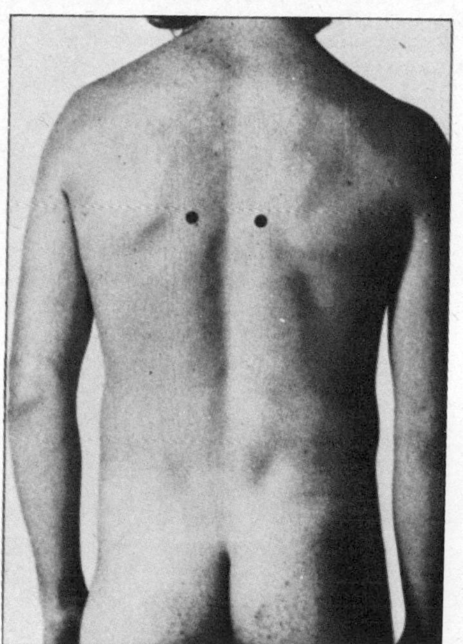

POINT: Heart Locus
LANDMARK: spine knob at neck
DISTANCE FROM LANDMARK: 6th spine knob (vertebra) below
LOCATION: 1½ acu-inch on either side of the spine (treat both sides)
POSITION: face down
TYPE OF PRESSURE: pulsed with thumb or fingers
AMOUNT OF PRESSURE: quite firm; repeat 2-3 times if necessary

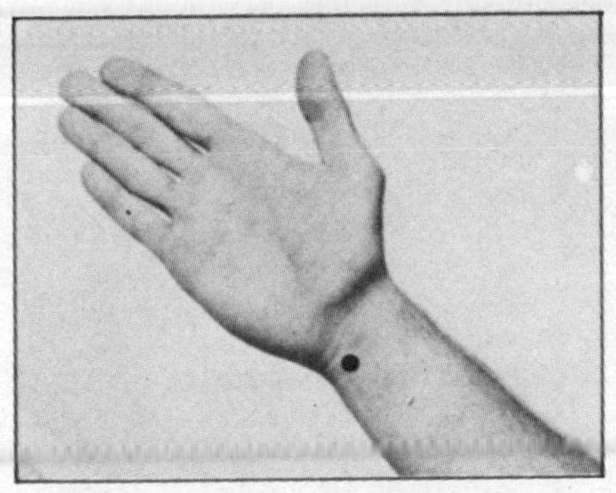

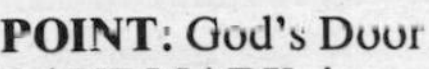

POINT: God's Door
LANDMARK: inner wrist fold
DISTANCE FROM LANDMARK: right on the fold
LOCATION: 1 acu-inch in from outer edge (side with little finger) of arm, on the inner surface of the forearm (treat both arms)
POSITION: seated
TYPE OF PRESSURE: pulsed with thumb
AMOUNT OF PRESSURE: as much as patient can take

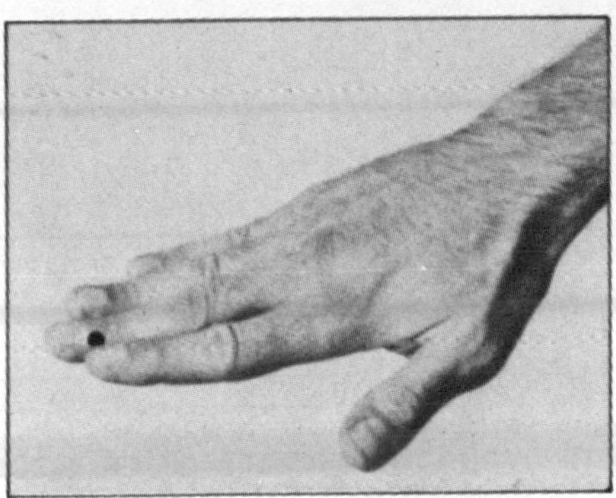

POINT: Middle Flush
LANDMARK: fingernail of middle finger
DISTANCE FROM LANDMARK: close to the landmark
LOCATION: on the middle finger, at the intersection of a line drawn along the thumb-side edge of the nail and a horizontal line drawn across the base of the nail (treat both fingers)
POSITION: seated
TYPE OF PRESSURE: pulsed with thumb, pinching motion
AMOUNT OF PRESSURE: as much as patient can take

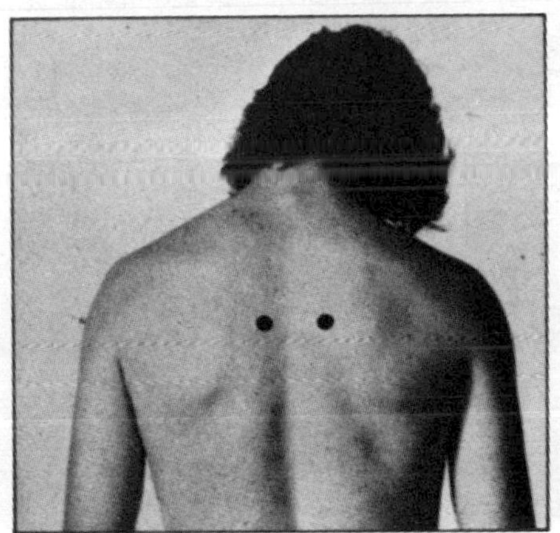

POINT: Lung Locus
LANDMARK: spine knob at neck
DISTANCE FROM LANDMARK: 2nd spine knob (vertebra) down
LOCATION: on the back, 1½ acu-inches on either side of the spine (treat both sides)
POSITION: on stomach
TYPE OF PRESSURE: pulsed with thumb
AMOUNT OF PRESSURE: as much as patient can take

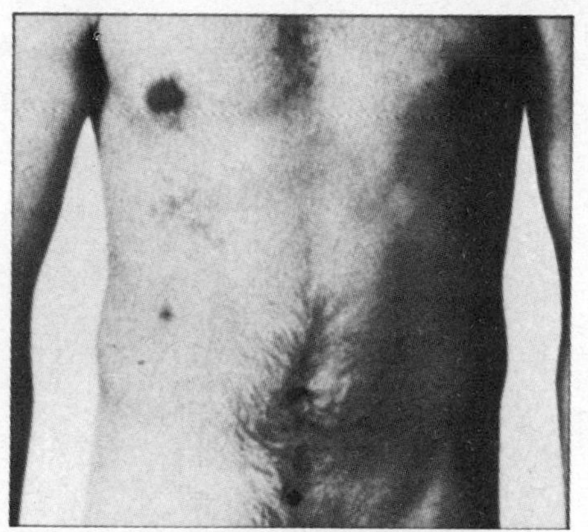

POINT: Pass Origin
LANDMARK: navel
DISTANCE FROM LANDMARK: 3 acu-inches below
LOCATION: on lower abdomen in a line directly below navel
POSITION: flat on back
TYPE OF PRESSURE: pulsed with thumb
AMOUNT OF PRESSURE: as much as patient can take

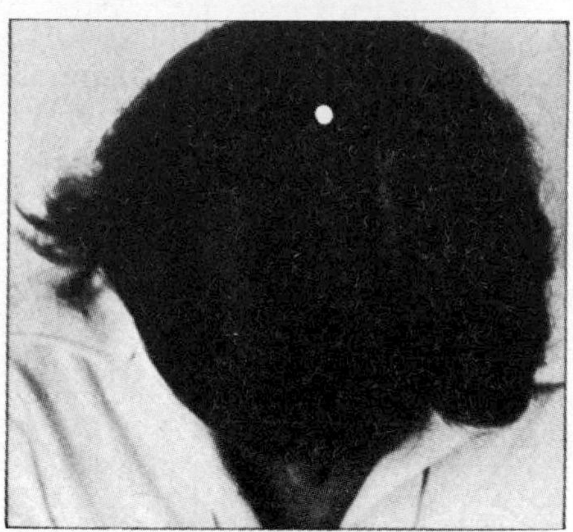

POINT: Hundred Meetings
LANDMARK: natural hairline at forehead
DISTANCE FROM LANDMARK: 5 acu-inches above
LOCATION: on top of head, right on front-to-back center line of head
POSITION: seated or flat on back
TYPE OF PRESSURE: pulsed with thumb or fingers
AMOUNT OF PRESSURE: as much as patient can take; repeat as needed

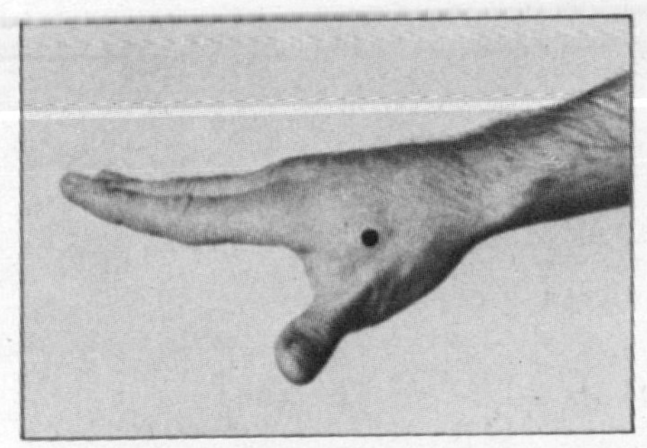

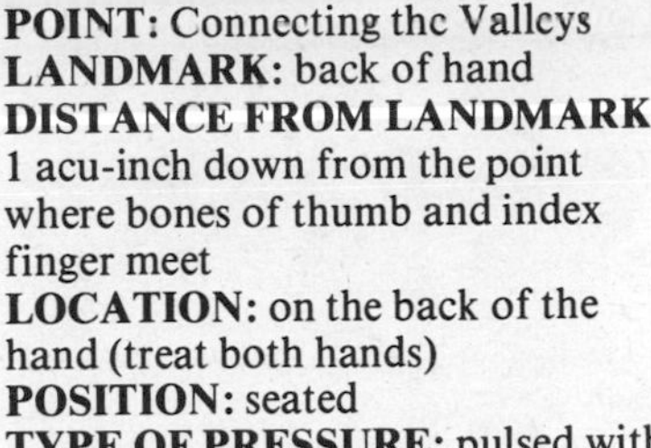

POINT: Connecting the Valleys
LANDMARK: back of hand
DISTANCE FROM LANDMARK: 1 acu-inch down from the point where bones of thumb and index finger meet
LOCATION: on the back of the hand (treat both hands)
POSITION: seated
TYPE OF PRESSURE: pulsed with thumb, pinching motion
AMOUNT OF PRESSURE: as much as patient can take

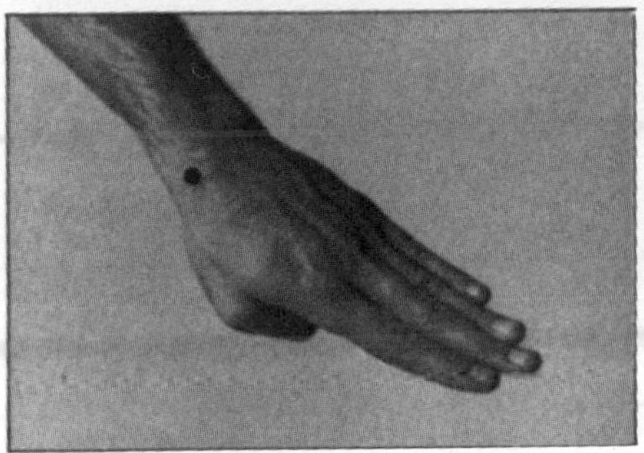

POINT: Sunny Stream
LANDMARK: outer wrist fold
DISTANCE FROM LANDMARK: right on fold
LOCATION: top of hand; feel for hollow at base of thumb (treat both hands)
POSITION: seated
TYPE OF PRESSURE: pulsed with thumb, or thumbpinching motion
AMOUNT OF PRESSURE: as much as patient can take

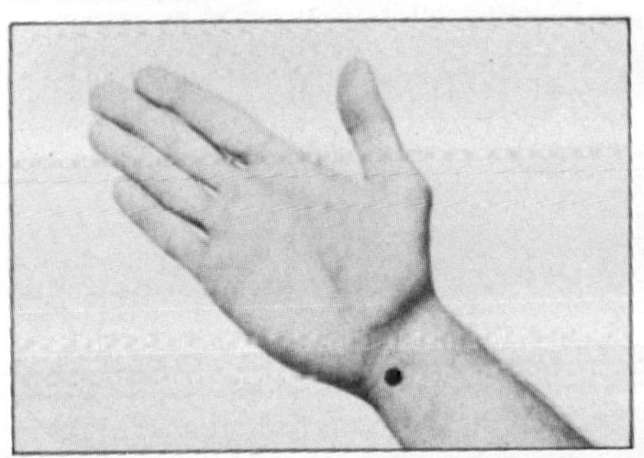

POINT: God's Door
LANDMARK: inner wrist fold
DISTANCE FROM LANDMARK: right on the fold
LOCATION: 1 acu-inch in from outer edge (side with little finger) of arm, on the inner surface of the forearm (treat both arms)
POSITION: seated
TYPE OF PRESSURE: pulsed with thumb
AMOUNT OF PRESSURE: as much as patient can take

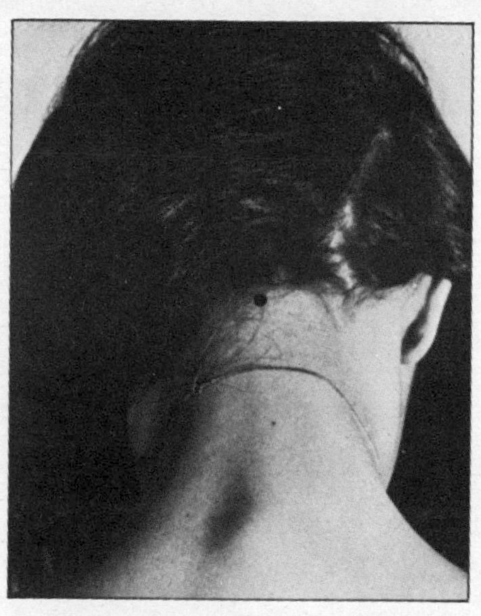

POINT: Dumb Gate
LANDMARK: natural hairline at back of head
DISTANCE FROM LANDMARK: right on the hairline
LOCATION: middle of hairline at back of head (at spine)
POSITION: face down
TYPE OF PRESSURE: pulsed with thumb or fingers
AMOUNT OF PRESSURE: gently at first to establish tolerance, then as much as patient can take

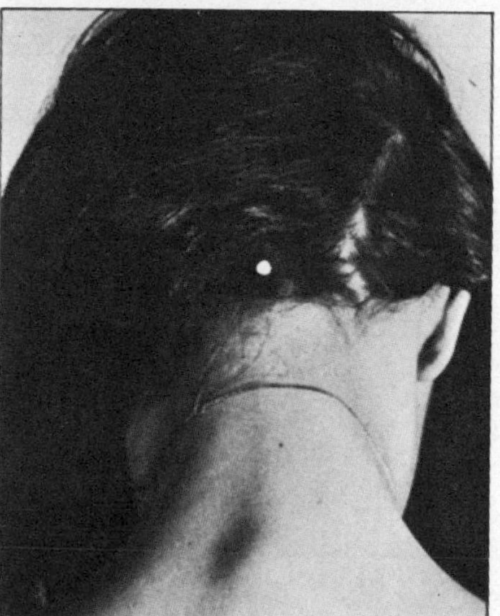

POINT: Windy Prefecture
LANDMARK: natural hairline at back of head
DISTANCE FROM LANDMARK: 1 acu-inch above
LOCATION: on top of head, along front-to-back center line of head
POSITION: seated or face down
TYPE OF PRESSURE: pulsed with thumb
AMOUNT OF PRESSURE: as much as patient can take

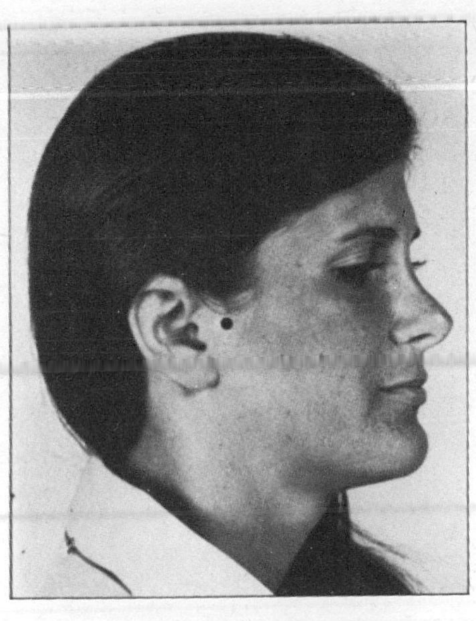

POINT: Upper Pass
LANDMARK: ear
DISTANCE FROM LANDMARK: ½ acu-inch in front of ear
LOCATION: feel for arched bone in front of ear; point is just under the arch (treat both sides of face)
POSITION: seated or flat on back
TYPE OF PRESSURE: pulsed with thumb or fingers
AMOUNT OF PRESSURE: as much as patient can take; repeat as needed

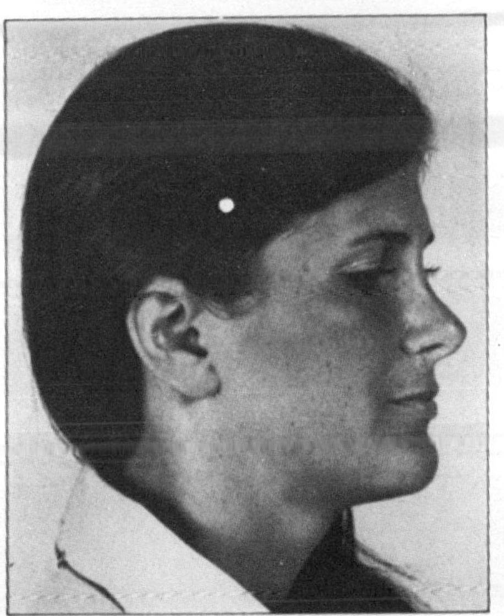

POINT: Jaw Hated
LANDMARK: forward line of natural sideburns and ear
DISTANCE FROM LANDMARK: 3½ acu-inches up from upper edge of ear
LOCATION: right on the line of the sideburn (treat both sides of face)
POSITION: seated or flat on back
TYPE OF PRESSURE: pulsed with thumb or fingers
AMOUNT OF PRESSURE: as much as patient can take; repeat as needed

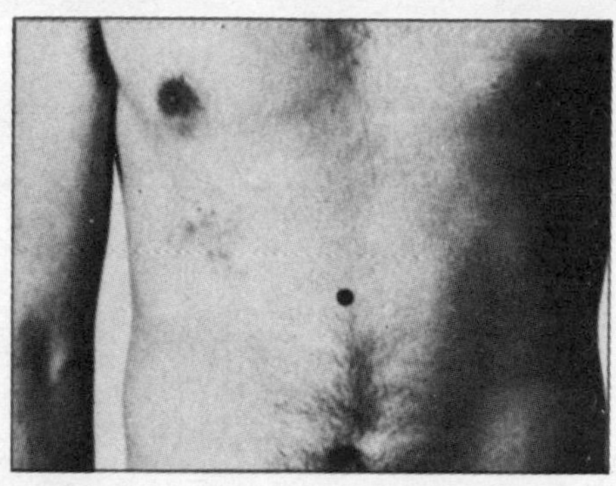

POINT: Middle Epigastrium
LANDMARK: navel
DISTANCE FROM LANDMARK: 4 acu-inches above
POSITION: flat on back
TYPE OF PRESSURE: pulsed with thumb
AMOUNT OF PRESSURE: as much as patient can take

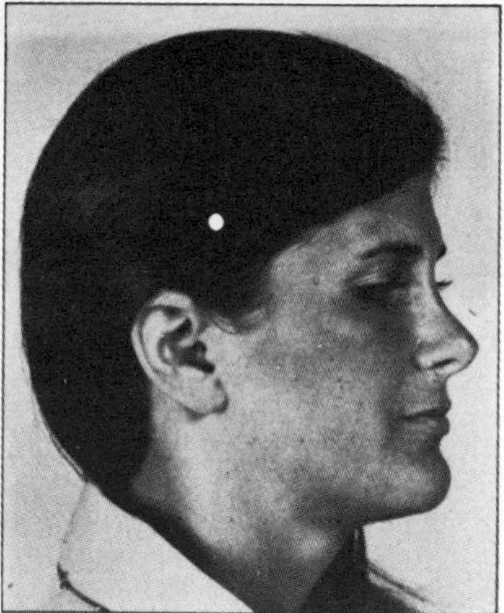

POINT: Skull in Suspension
LANDMARK: natural line of sideburns and ear
DISTANCE FROM LANDMARK: 2½ acu-inches up from upper tip of ear
LOCATION: right along line of natural sideburn (treat both sides of face)
POSITION: seated or flat on back
TYPE OF PRESSURE: pulsed with thumb or fingers
AMOUNT OF PRESSURE: as much as patient can take; repeat as needed

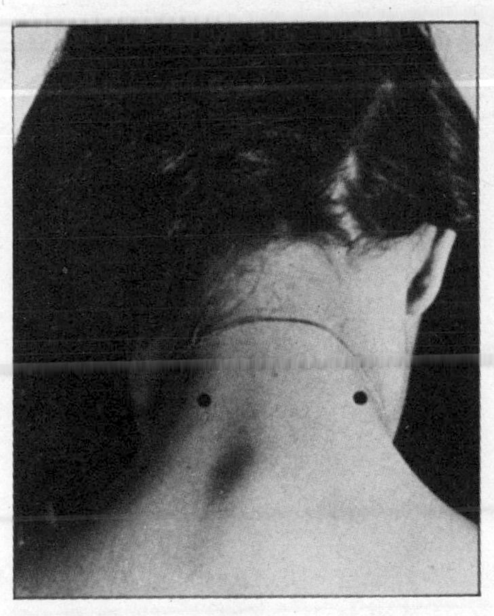

POINT: Wind Pond
LANDMARK: rear head bones
DISTANCE FROM LANDMARK: immediately below
LOCATION: feel for a depression or groove on each side just below the landmark (treat both sides)
POSITION: seated or face down
TYPE OF PRESSURE: pulsed with thumbs or fingers
AMOUNT OF PRESSURE: as much as patient can take
NOTE: if patient is sitting up, stand in front of him and rest his head against your chest; exert pressure with your fingers

MOTION SICKNESS

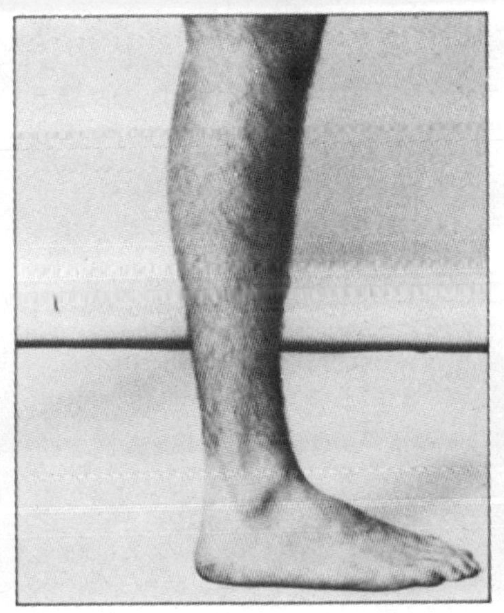

POINT: Walking Three Miles
LANDMARK: kneecap
DISTANCE FROM LANDMARK: 3 acu-inches below (in the depression)
LOCATION: 1 acu-inch toward the outside of the leg (treat both legs)
POSITION: seated in chair or flat on back
TYPE OF PRESSURE: pulsed with thumb (or pinching motion)
AMOUNT OF PRESSURE: quite firm

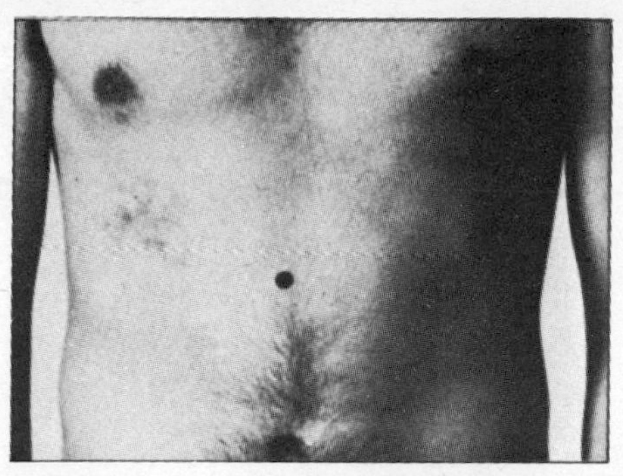

POINT: Middle Epigastrium
LANDMARK: navel
DISTANCE FROM LANDMARK: 4 acu-inches above
POSITION: flat on back
TYPE OF PRESSURE: pulsed with thumb
AMOUNT OF PRESSURE: as much as patient can take

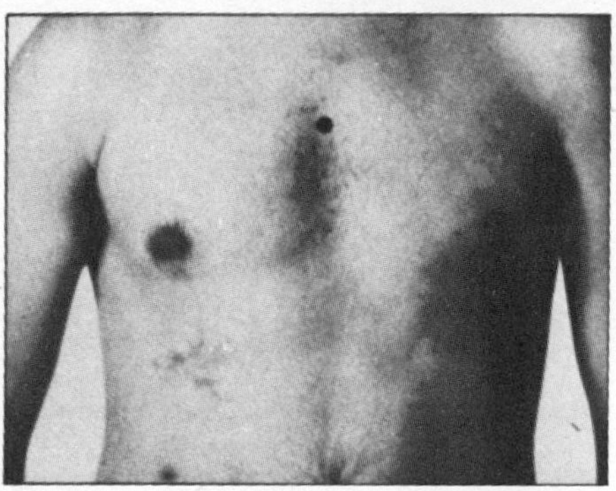

POINT: Purple Palace
LANDMARK: navel
DISTANCE FROM LANDMARK: 15 acu-inches up
LOCATION: on center line of chest directly above navel
POSITION: flat on back
TYPE OF PRESSURE: pulsed with thumb or fingers
AMOUNT OF PRESSURE: as much as patient can take

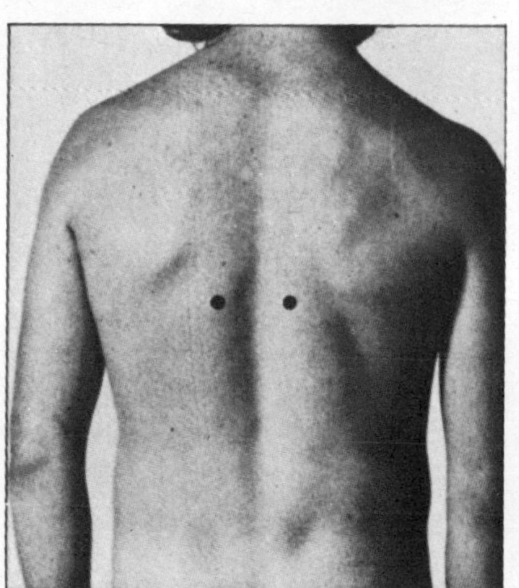

POINT: Liver Locus
LANDMARK: spine knob at neck
DISTANCE FROM LANDMARK: 9th spine knob (vertebra) below
LOCATION: on the back, 1½ acu-inches on either side of the spine (treat both sides)
POSITION: face down
TYPE OF PRESSURE: pulsed with thumb or fingers
AMOUNT OF PRESSURE: as much as patient can take

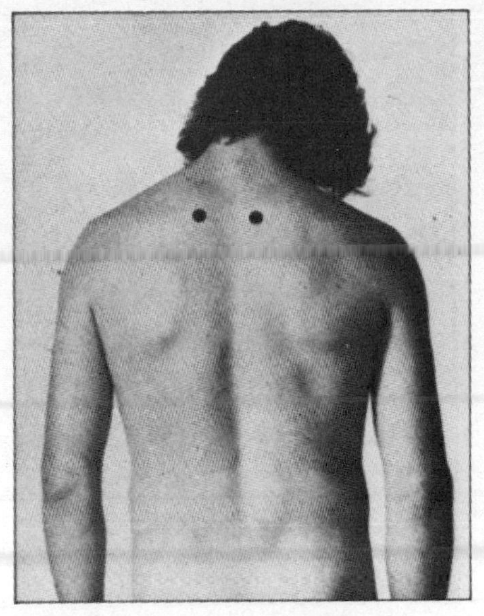

POINT: Great Slaughter
LANDMARK: spine knob at neck
DISTANCE FROM LANDMARK: 1st spine knob (vertebra) below
LOCATION: 1½ acu-inches on either side of spine (treat both sides)
POSITION: face down
TYPE OF PRESSURE: pulsed with thumb
AMOUNT OF PRESSURE: as much as patient can take

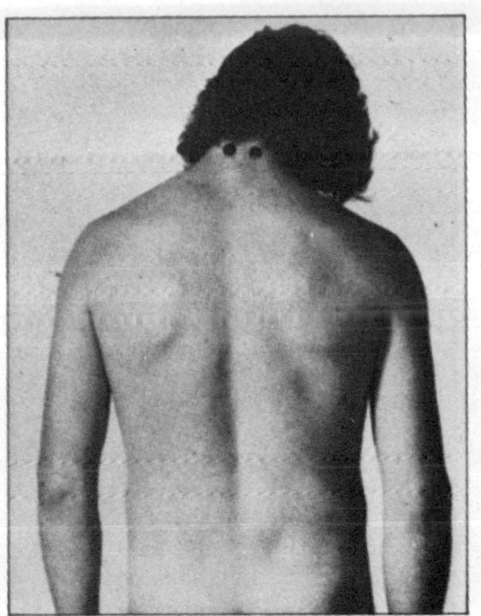

POINT: Celestial Pillar
LANDMARK: natural hairline at the back of neck
DISTANCE FROM LANDMARK: right on landmark
LOCATION: right on the hairline and 1 acu-inch on either side of the front-to-back center line of the head (treat both sides)
POSITION: seated or flat on back
TYPE OF PRESSURE: pulsed with thumb
AMOUNT OF PRESSURE: gently, then gradually increasing to maximum that patient can tolerate

POINT: Welcome Fragrance
LANDMARK: nose-cheek fold
DISTANCE FROM LANDMARK: right in the fold
LOCATION: ½ acu-inch up from the bottom of the nose on the cheeks (treat both sides)
POSITION: flat on back
TYPE OF PRESSURE: pulsed with thumb or fingers
AMOUNT OF PRESSURE: as much as patient can take

POINT: New Point
LANDMARK: eyebrows
DISTANCE FROM LANDMARK: point midway between the eyebrows
LOCATION: on a line joining the inside ends of the eyebrows
POSITION: seated or flat on back
TYPE OF PRESSURE: pinching motion with thumb and forefinger while also pressing in firmly
AMOUNT OF PRESSURE: as much as patient can take

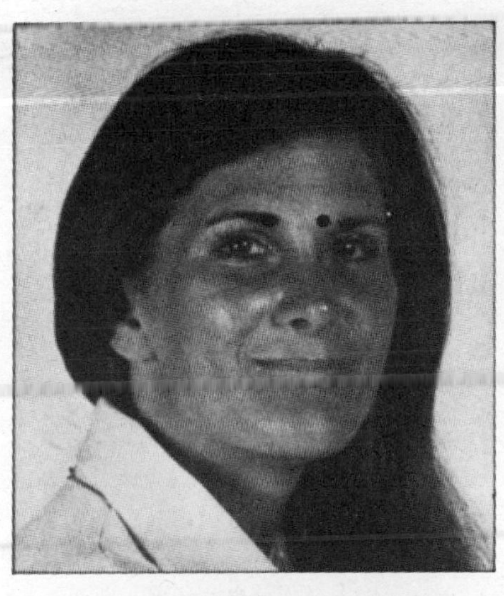

POINT: Drilling Bamboo
LANDMARK: eyebrow
DISTANCE FROM LANDMARK: right on eyebrow
LOCATION: at the inside end (toward nose) of the eyebrows (treat both eyebrows)
POSITION: seated or flat on back
TYPE OF PRESSURE: pulsed with thumb or fingers
AMOUNT OF PRESSURE: treat both at one time, with maximum pressure that patient can stand

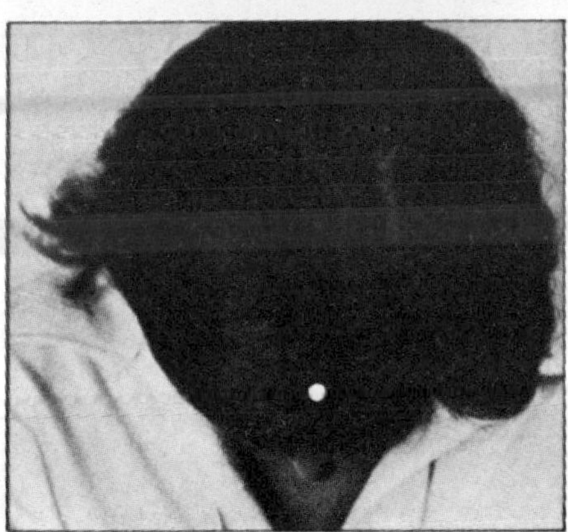

POINT: Super Star
LANDMARK: natural hairline at forehead
DISTANCE FROM LANDMARK: 1 acu-inch above
LOCATION: on the midline of the head
POSITION: seated or flat on back
TYPE OF PRESSURE: pulsed with thumb
AMOUNT OF PRESSURE: as much as patient can take

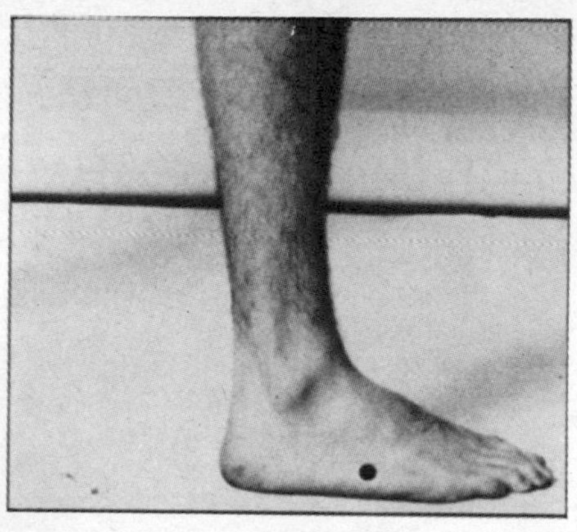

POINT: Capital Bone
LANDMARK: toe knuckle of little toe
DISTANCE FROM LANDMARK: close to the landmark
LOCATION: feel back (toward the ankle) along the outer edge of the foot to a bump about 2 acu-inches from landmark; point is just in back of and under this bump (treat both feet)
POSITION: seated or flat on back
TYPE OF PRESSURE: pulsed with thumb
AMOUNT OF PRESSURE: as much as patient can take

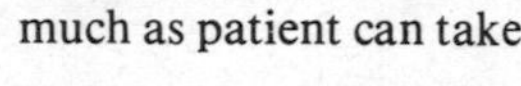

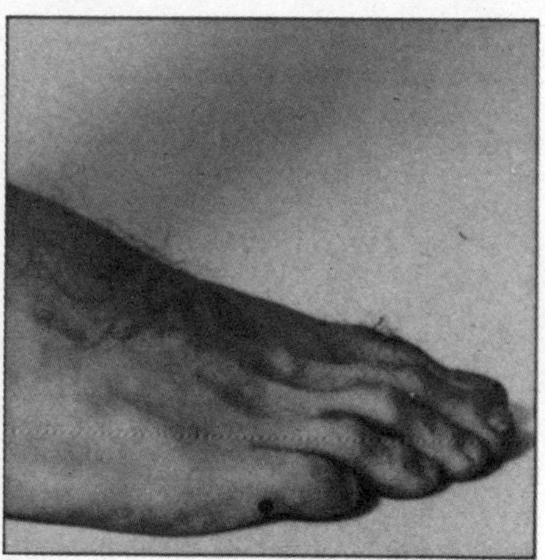

POINT: Communicating the Valleys
LANDMARK: toe knuckle of little toe
DISTANCE FROM LANDMARK: close to the landmark
LOCATION: on the outer edge of the foot, just in front of toe knuckle (treat both feet)
POSITION: seated or flat on back
TYPE OF PRESSURE: pulsed with thumb
AMOUNT OF PRESSURE: as much as patient can take; repeat as needed

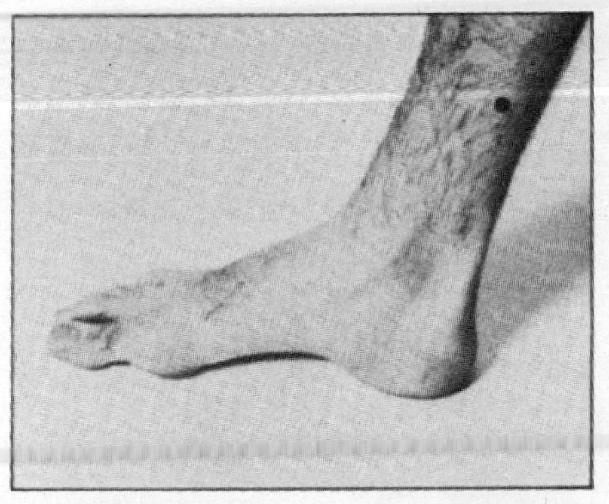

POINT: Delivering Message
LANDMARK: inner ankle bone
DISTANCE FROM LANDMARK: 3 acu-inches above
LOCATION: in the middle of the leg (treat both legs)
POSITION: flat on back
TYPE OF PRESSURE: pulsed with thumb pinching movement
AMOUNT OF PRESSURE: as much as patient can take

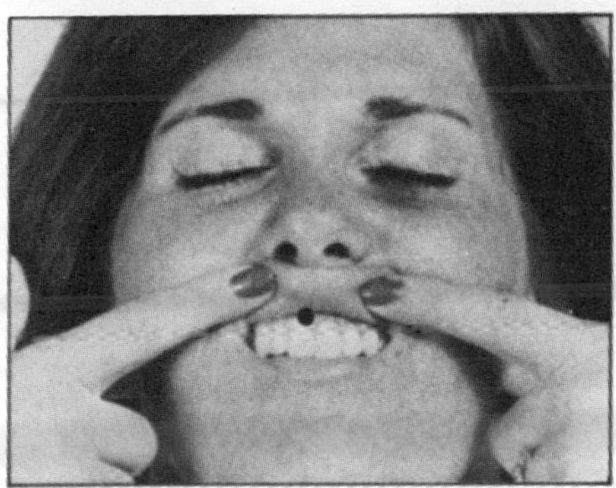

POINT: Gum Crossing
LANDMARK: gums
DISTANCE FROM LANDMARK: at the landmark
LOCATION: midpoint between the inner surface of the upper lip and the upper gums
POSITION: seated
TYPE OF PRESSURE: pulsed, or steady pressure with thumb-pinching motion
AMOUNT OF PRESSURE: as much as patient can take

NAUSEA

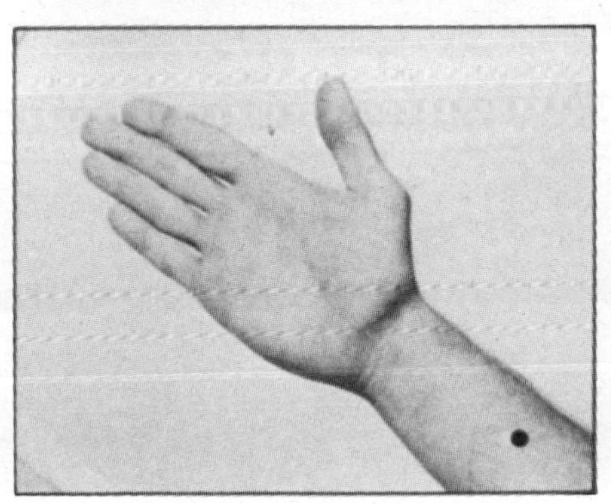

POINT: Inner Pass
LANDMARK: inner wrist fold
DISTANCE FROM LANDMARK: 2 acu-inches up
LOCATION: on the inner surface of the forearm (treat both sides)
POSITION: seated or flat on back
TYPE OF PRESSURE: pulsed with thumb, pinching motion
AMOUNT OF PRESSURE: as much as patient can take

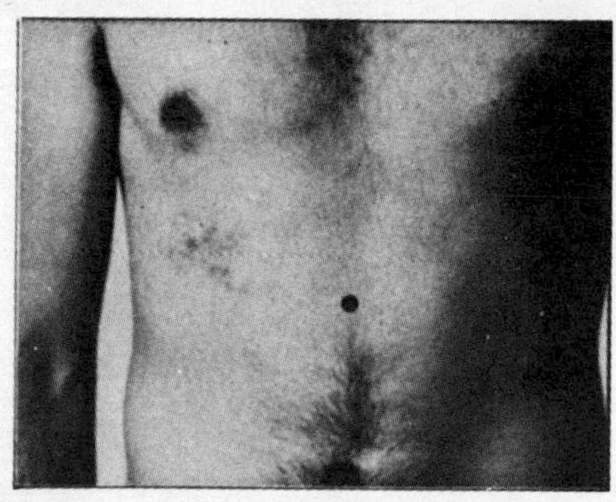

POINT: Middle Epigastrium
LANDMARK: navel
DISTANCE FROM LANDMARK: 4 acu-inches above
POSITION: flat on back
TYPE OF PRESSURE: pulsed with thumb
AMOUNT OF PRESSURE: as much as patient can take

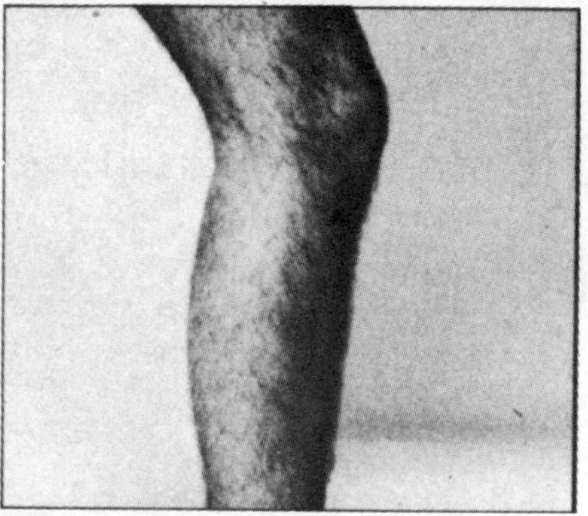

POINT: Walking Three Miles
LANDMARK: kneecap
DISTANCE FROM LANDMARK: 3 acu-inches below (in the depression)
LOCATION: 1 acu-inch toward the outside of the leg (treat both legs)
POSITION: seated in chair or flat on back
TYPE OF PRESSURE: pulsed with thumb (or pinching motion)
AMOUNT OF PRESSURE: quite firm

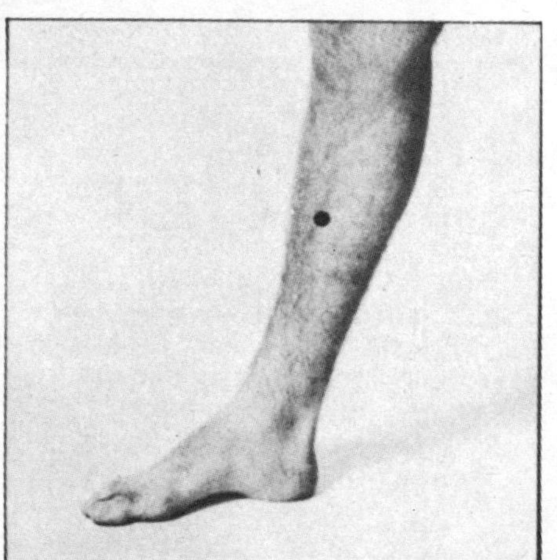

POINT: Leaking Valley
LANDMARK: inner ankle bone
DISTANCE FROM LANDMARK: 7 acu-inches above
LOCATION: inside of lower leg (treat both legs)
POSITION: seated or flat on back
TYPE OF PRESSURE: pulsed with thumb, pinching motion
AMOUNT OF PRESSURE: as much as patient can take

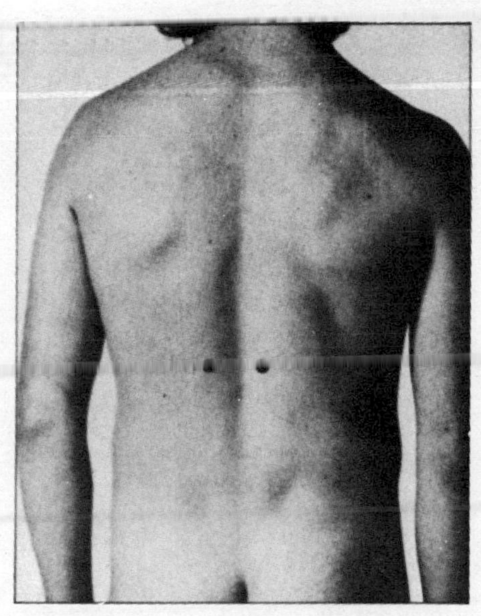

POINT: Spleen Locus
LANDMARK: spine knob at neck
DISTANCE FROM LANDMARK: 11th spine knob (vertebra) below
LOCATION: 1½ acu-inches on either side of the spine (treat both sides)
POSITION: face down
TYPE OF PRESSURE: pulsed with thumb
AMOUNT OF PRESSURE: as much as patient can take

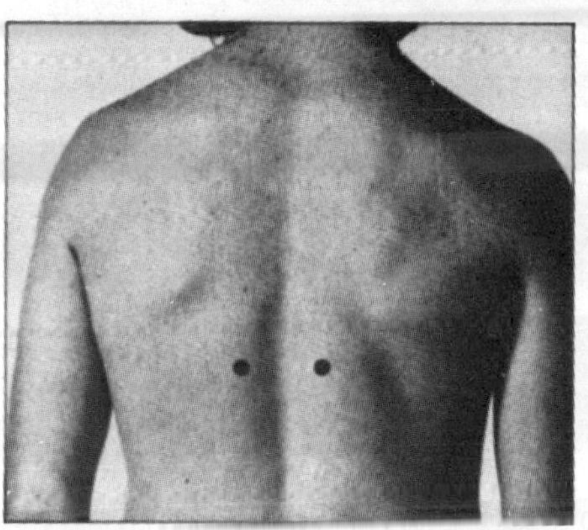

POINT: Diaphragm Locus
LANDMARK: spine knob at neck
DISTANCE FROM LANDMARK: 6th spine knob (vertebra) below
LOCATION: on back, 1½ acu-inches on either side of spine (treat both sides)
POSITION: on stomach
TYPE OF PRESSURE: pulsed with thumb
AMOUNT OF PRESSURE: as much as patient can take

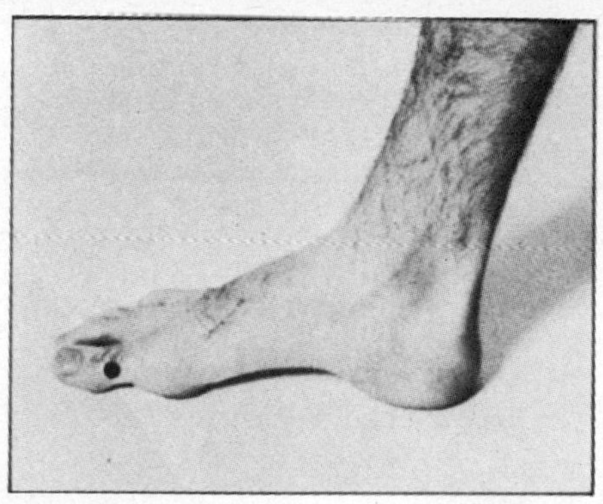

POINT: Great Metropolis
LANDMARK: toe knuckle of big toe
DISTANCE FROM LANDMARK: just in front of toe knuckle
LOCATION: outer side of big toe (treat both feet)
POSITION: seated or flat on back
TYPE OF PRESSURE: pulsed with thumb, pinching motion
AMOUNT OF PRESSURE: as much as patient can take

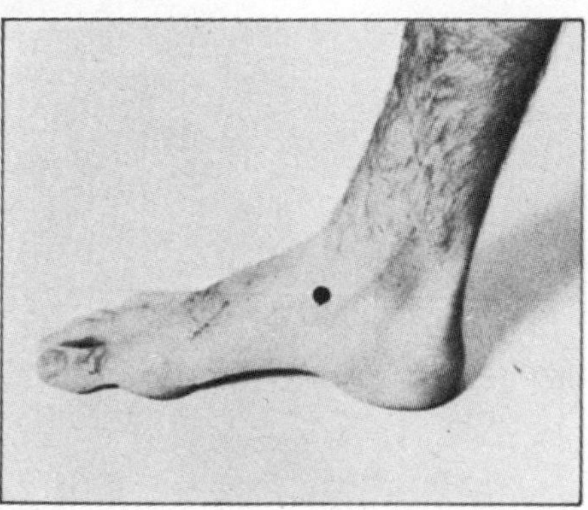

POINT: Trades Hill
LANDMARK: inner ankle bone
DISTANCE FROM LANDMARK: just in front
LOCATION: in the depression just below and in front of the ankle bone, on the inner surface of the leg (treat both legs)
POSITION: seated or flat on back
TYPE OF PRESSURE: pulsed with thumb, pinching motion
AMOUNT OF PRESSURE: as much as patient can take

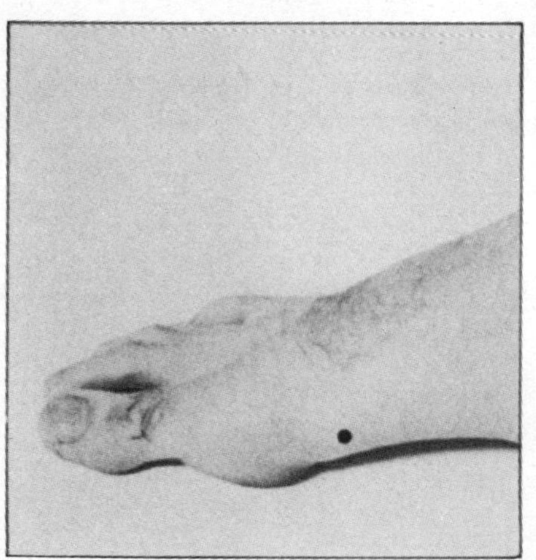

POINT: Generation Gap
LANDMARK: big toe joint
DISTANCE FROM LANDMARK: 1 acu-inch back (toward ankle) from big toe joint
LOCATION: on the inner edge of the foot (treat both feet)
POSITION: flat on back
TYPE OF PRESSURE: pulsed with thumb or percussion (jab with thumb)
AMOUNT OF PRESSURE: as much as patient can take

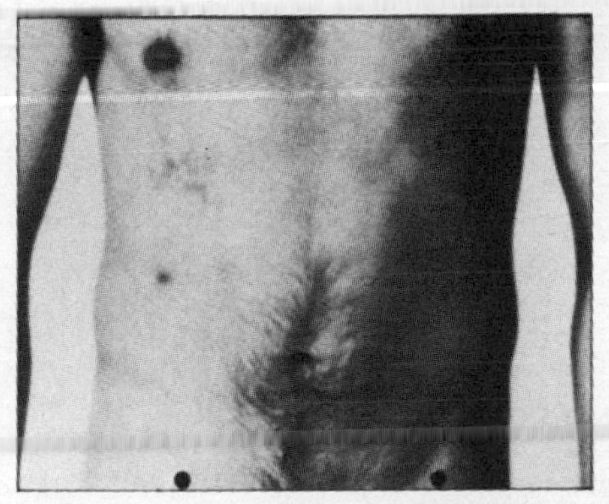

POINT: Perfecture House
LANDMARK: thigh-stomach fold, navel
DISTANCE FROM LANDMARK: in the fold at a point 3 acu-inches down from the navel
LOCATION: lower stomach (treat both sides)
POSITION: flat on back
TYPE OF PRESSURE: pulsed with thumb
AMOUNT OF PRESSURE: as much as patient can take

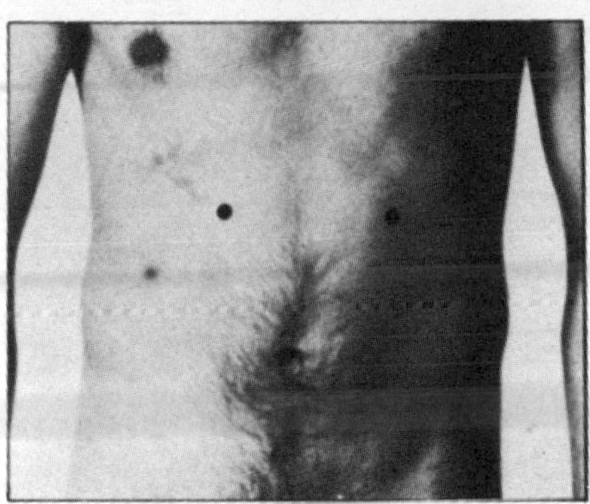

POINT: Beam Gate
LANDMARK: navel
DISTANCE FROM LANDMARK: 4 acu-inches above
LOCATION: on the chest, 2 acu-inches on either side of the center line of the chest (treat both sides)
POSITION: flat on back
TYPE OF PRESSURE: pulsed with thumb
AMOUNT OF PRESSURE: as much as patient can take

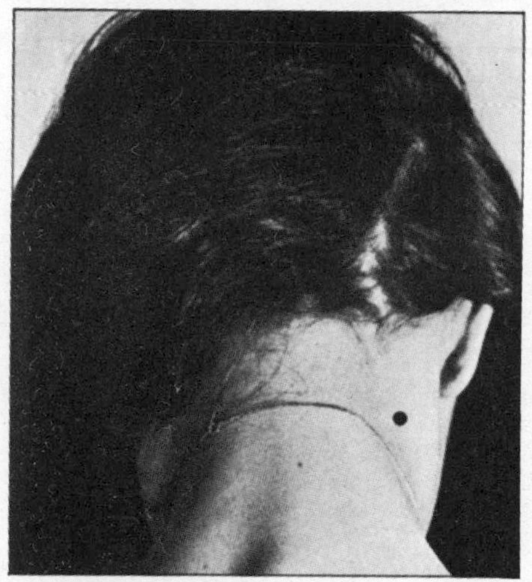

POINT: Celestial Window
LANDMARK: natural hairline on neck and ear
DISTANCE FROM LANDMARK: right on natural hairline, at a point intersected by a horizontal line drawn underneath the ear (the point where the ear, *not* the lobe, attaches to the head)
LOCATION: back of neck (treat both sides)
POSITION: seated or face down
TYPE OF PRESSURE: pulsed with thumb or fingers
AMOUNT OF PRESSURE: as much as patient can take

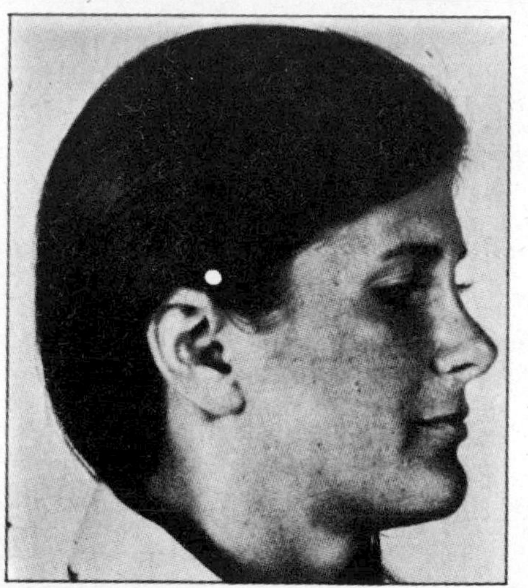

POINT: Tortuous Sideburn
LANDMARK: natural hairline of sideburns and ear
DISTANCE FROM LANDMARK: right on sideburn and about 1 acu-inch above outer line of ear
LOCATION: on the temple (treat both sides)
POSITION: seated or flat on back
TYPE OF PRESSURE: pulsed with thumb or fingers
AMOUNT OF PRESSURE: as much as patient can take

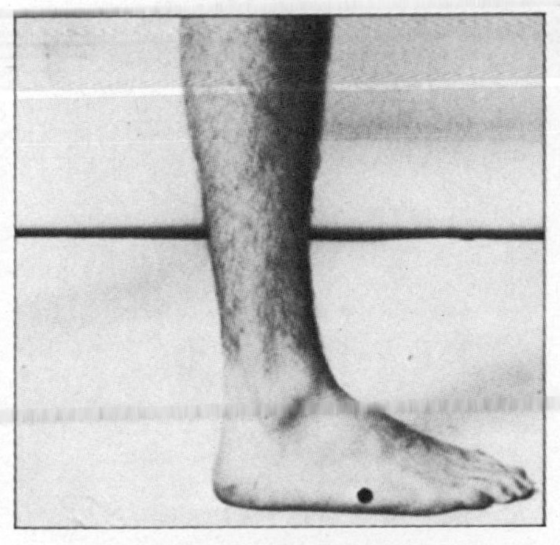

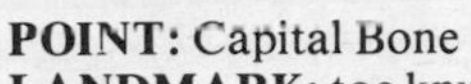

POINT: Capital Bone
LANDMARK: toe knuckle of little toe
DISTANCE FROM LANDMARK: close to the landmark
LOCATION: feel back (toward the ankle) along the outer edge of the foot to a bump about 2 acu-inches from landmark; point is just in back of and under this bump (treat both feet)
POSITION: seated or flat on back
TYPE OF PRESSURE: pulsed with thumb
AMOUNT OF PRESSURE: as much as patient can take

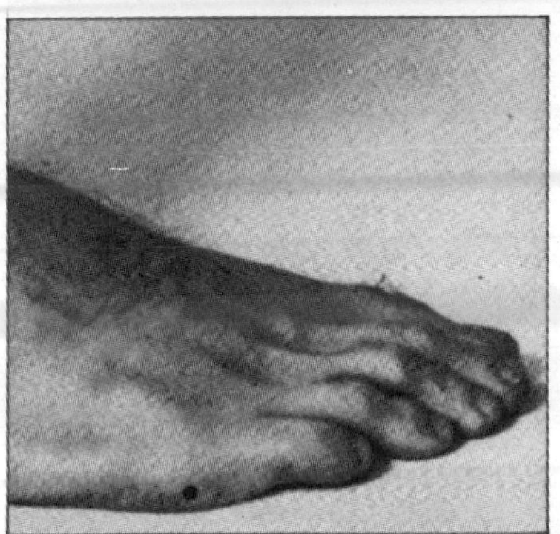

POINT: Restrict Bone
LANDMARK: toe knuckle of little toe
DISTANCE FROM LANDMARK: close to the landmark
LOCATION: on the outer edge of the foot, just behind toe knuckle (treat both feet)
POSITION: seated or flat on back
TYPE OF PRESSURE: pulsed with thumb
AMOUNT OF PRESSURE: as much as patient can take; repeat as needed

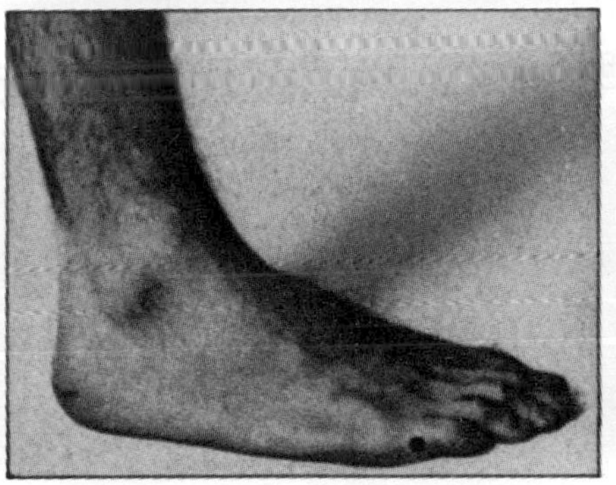

POINT: Communicating the Valleys
LANDMARK: toe knuckle of little toe
DISTANCE FROM LANDMARK: close to the landmark
LOCATION: on the outer edge of the foot, just in front of toe knuckle (treat both feet)
POSITION: seated or flat on back
TYPE OF PRESSURE: pulsed with thumb
AMOUNT OF PRESSURE: as much as patient can take; repeat as needed

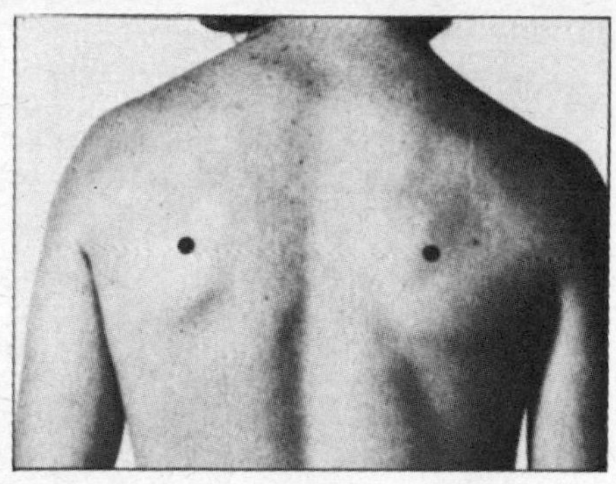

POINT: Great Gate
LANDMARK: spine knob at neck
DISTANCE FROM LANDMARK: 3rd spine knob (vertebra) below
LOCATION: 3 acu-inches on either side of spine (treat both sides)
POSITION: face down
TYPE OF PRESSURE: pulsed with thumb or fingers
AMOUNT OF PRESSURE: as much as patient can take

NEURALGIA, GENERAL

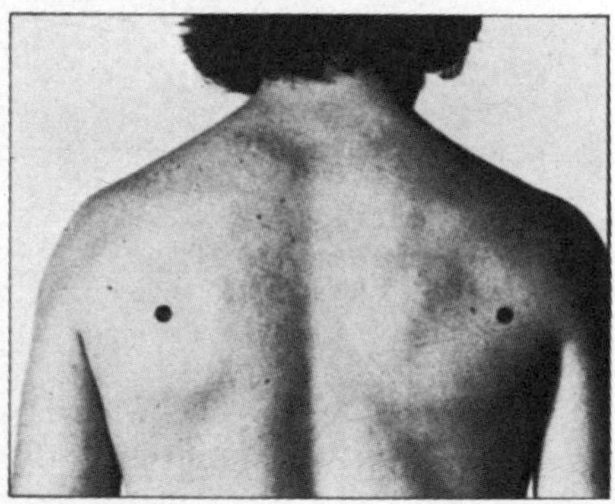

POINT: Celestial Ancestor
LANDMARK: spine knob at neck
DISTANCE FROM LANDMARK: 4th spine knob (vertebra) down
LOCATION: on a level with 4th spine knob, and 5 acu-inches on either side of center of back (treat both sides)
POSITION: on stomach
TYPE OF PRESSURE: pulsed with thumb
AMOUNT OF PRESSURE: gently to establish tolerance, then as much as patient can take

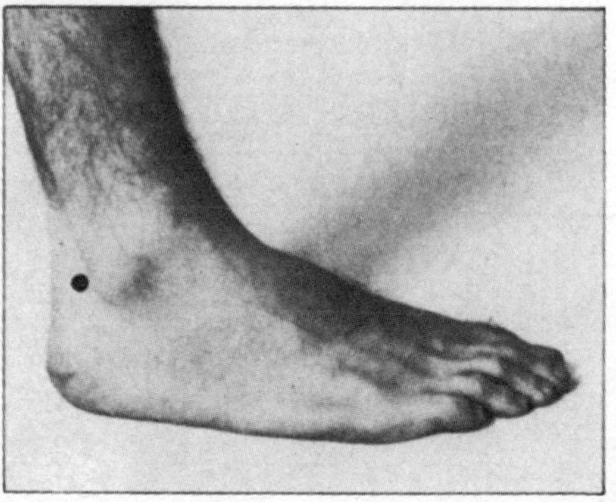

POINT: K'un Lun Mountains
LANDMARK: outer ankle bone
DISTANCE FROM LANDMARK: just in back
LOCATION: in the depression behind outer ankle bone (treat both feet)
POSITION: flat on back
TYPE OF PRESSURE: pulsed with thumb, pinching motion
AMOUNT OF PRESSURE: as much as patient can take

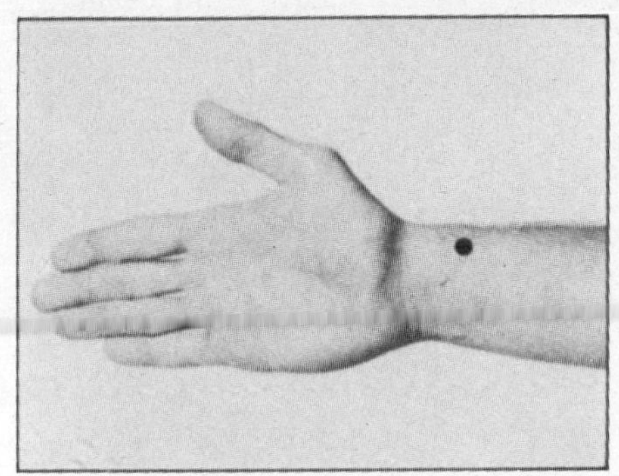

POINT: Extreme Shortcoming
LANDMARK: inner wrist fold
DISTANCE FROM LANDMARK: 2 acu-inches above
POSITION: on the inside of the wrist near the pulse (treat both arms)
TYPE OF PRESSURE: pulsed with thumb, pinching motion
AMOUNT OF PRESSURE: as much as patient can take

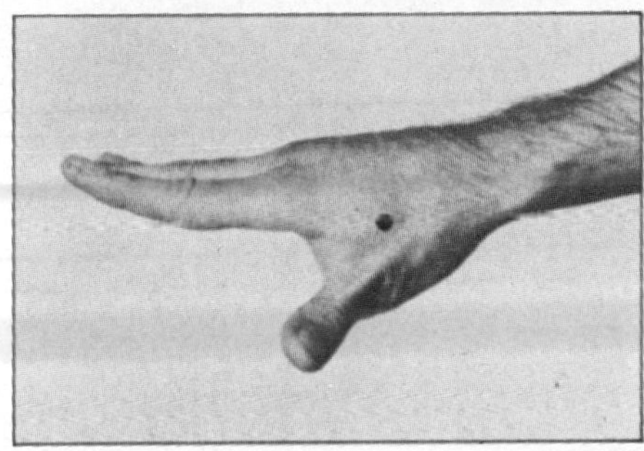

POINT: Connecting the Valleys
LANDMARK: back of hand
DISTANCE FROM LANDMARK: 1 acu-inch down from the point where bones of thumb and index finger meet
LOCATION: on the back of the hand (treat both hands)
POSITION: seated
TYPE OF PRESSURE: pulsed with thumb, pinching motion
AMOUNT OF PRESSURE: as much as patient can take

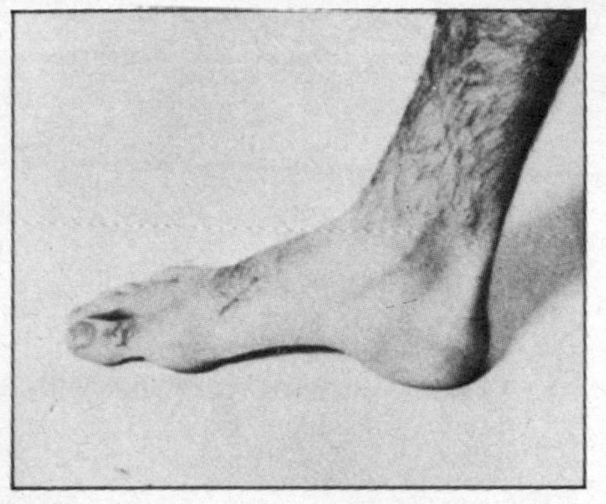

POINT: Repeating Stagnant
LANDMARK: inner ankle bone
DISTANCE FROM LANDMARK: 3 acu-inches above and 1 acu-inch behind
LOCATION: back of lower leg (treat both legs)
POSITION: seated or flat on back
TYPE OF PRESSURE: pulsed with thumb, pinching motion
AMOUNT OF PRESSURE: as much as patient can take

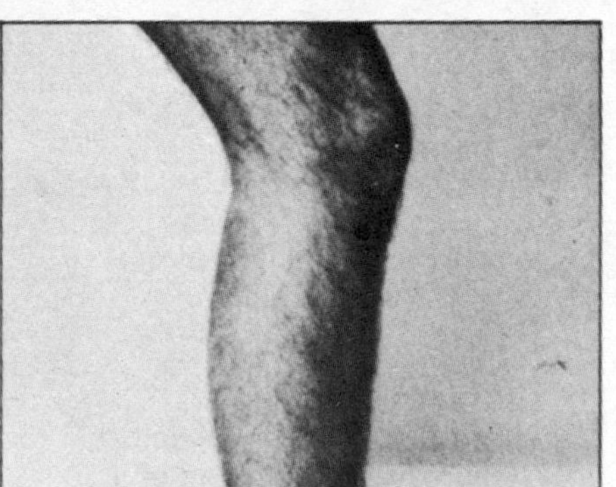

POINT: Walking Three Miles
LANDMARK: kneecap
DISTANCE FROM LANDMARK: 3 acu-inches below (in the depression)
LOCATION: 1 acu-inch toward the outside of the leg (treat both legs)
POSITION: seated in chair or flat on back
TYPE OF PRESSURE: pulsed with thumb (or pinching motion)
AMOUNT OF PRESSURE: quite firm

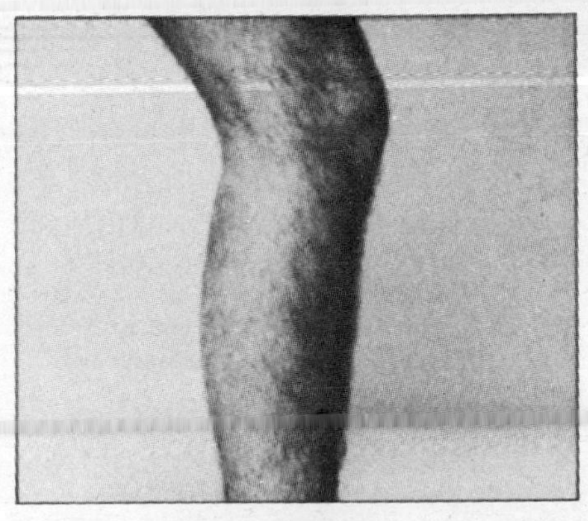

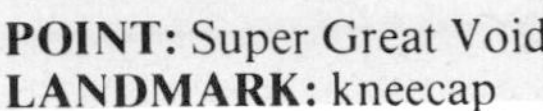

POINT: Super Great Void
LANDMARK: kneecap
DISTANCE FROM LANDMARK: 6 acu-inches below
LOCATION: right alongside the shin bone toward the outer edge of the leg (treat both legs)
POSITION: flat on back
TYPE OF PRESSURE: pulsed with thumb
AMOUNT OF PRESSURE: as much as patient can take

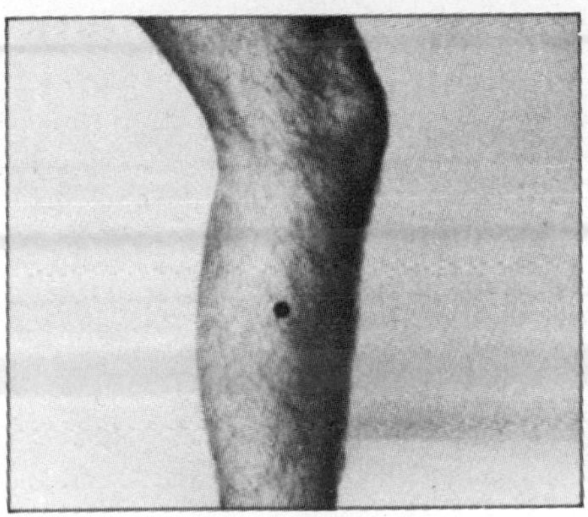

POINT: Rich and Prosperous
LANDMARK: outer ankle bone
DISTANCE FROM LANDMARK: 8 acu-inches above the upper edge of outer ankle bone
LOCATION: on the side of the leg, 1 acu-inch to the side (toward the outside of the leg) of the shin bone (treat both legs)
POSITION: seated or flat on back
TYPE OF PRESSURE: pulsed with thumb, pinching motion
AMOUNT OF PRESSURE: as much as patient can take

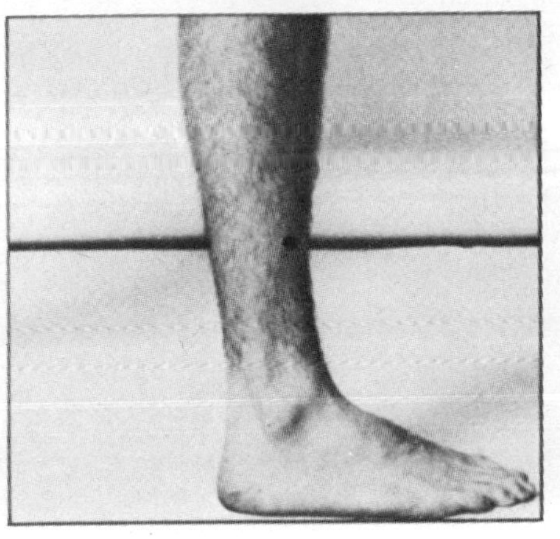

POINT: Inferior Great Void
LANDMARK: kneecap
DISTANCE FROM LANDMARK: 9 acu-inches below
LOCATION: right alongside the shin bone toward the outer edge of the leg (treat both legs)
POSITION: flat on back
TYPE OF PRESSURE: pulsed with thumb
AMOUNT OF PRESSURE: as much as patient can take

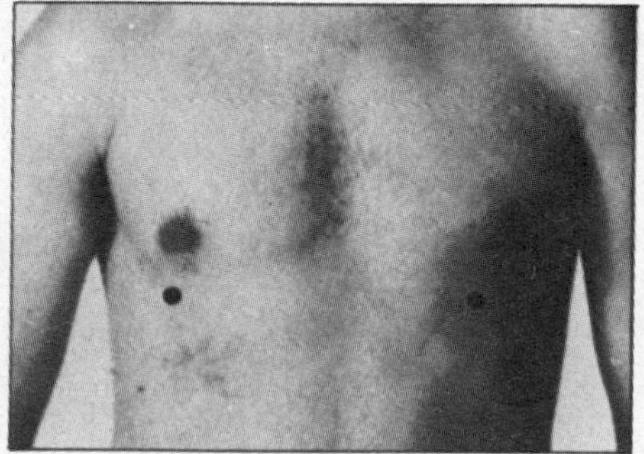

POINT: Time Door
LANDMARK: nipples
DISTANCE FROM LANDMARK: 2nd rib down, below each nipple
LOCATION: on the chest, in the space between the ribs and directly underneath the nipple (treat both sides of chest)
POSITION: flat on back
TYPE OF PRESSURE: pulsed with fingers
AMOUNT OF PRESSURE: first gently, then with as much force as patient can take

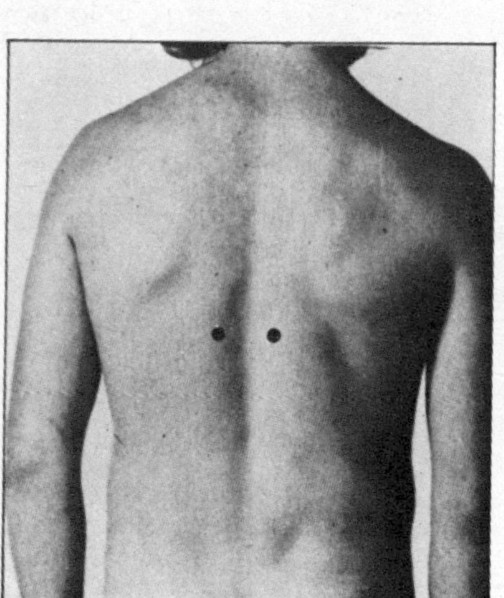

POINT: Diaphragm Locus
LANDMARK: spine knob at neck
DISTANCE FROM LANDMARK: 6th spine knob (vertebra) down
LOCATION: on back, 1½ acu-inches on either side of spine (treat both sides)
POSITION: on stomach
TYPE OF PRESSURE: pulsed with thumb
AMOUNT OF PRESSURE: as much as patient can take

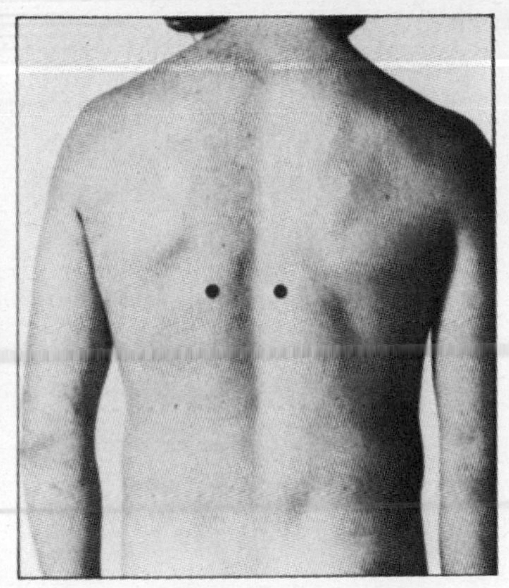

POINT: Liver Locus
LANDMARK: spine knob at neck
DISTANCE FROM LANDMARK: 9th spine knob (vertebra) below
LOCATION: on the back, 1½ acu-inches on either side of the spine (treat both sides)
POSITION: face down
TYPE OF PRESSURE: pulsed with thumb or fingers
AMOUNT OF PRESSURE: as much as patient can take

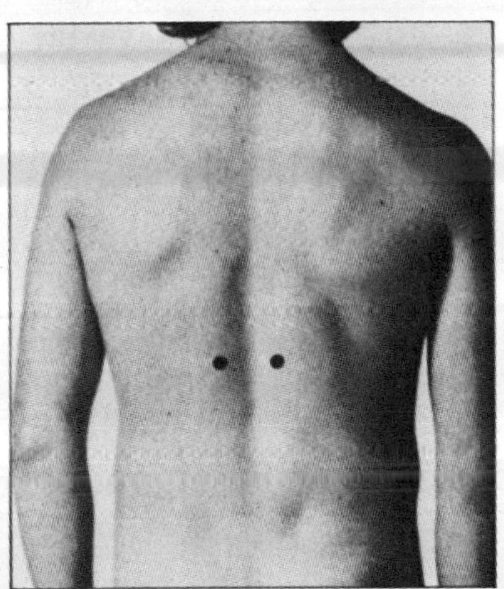

POINT: Gallbladder Locus
LANDMARK: spine knob at neck
DISTANCE FROM LANDMARK: 10th spine knob (vertebra) below
LOCATION: on the back, 1½ acu-inches from spine (treat both sides)
POSITION: on stomach
TYPE OF PRESSURE: pulsed with thumb
AMOUNT OF PRESSURE: gently at first, then as much as patient can take

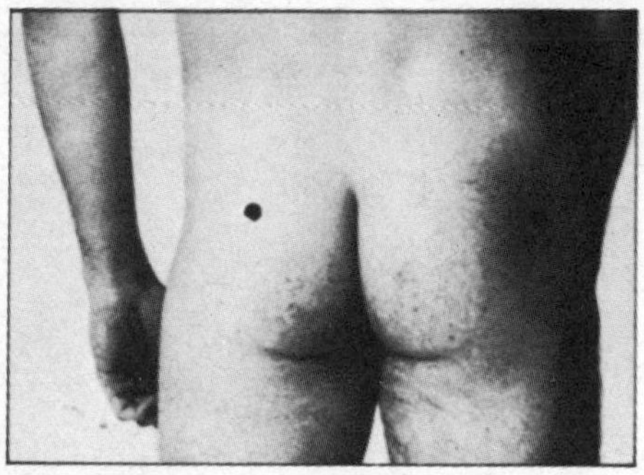

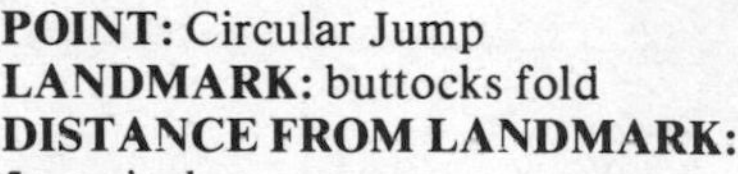

POINT: Circular Jump
LANDMARK: buttocks fold
DISTANCE FROM LANDMARK: 5 acu-inches up
LOCATION: on the side of the buttocks, approximately 3 acu-inches from the center line of the buttocks toward the rear (treat both sides)
POSITION: face down
TYPE OF PRESSURE: pulsed with thumb
AMOUNT OF PRESSURE: as much as patient can take

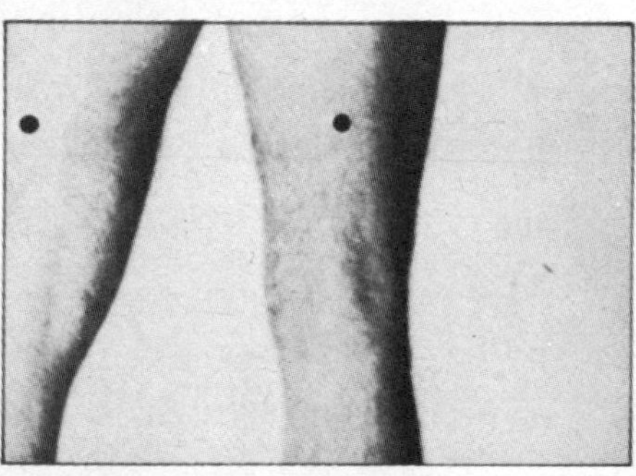

POINT: Organ Gate
LANDMARK: buttocks fold
DISTANCE FROM LANDMARK: 6 acu-inches below buttocks fold
LOCATION: on the back of the thigh, in the middle (treat both legs)
POSITION: face down
TYPE OF PRESSURE: pulsed with thumb
AMOUNT OF PRESSURE: as much as possible

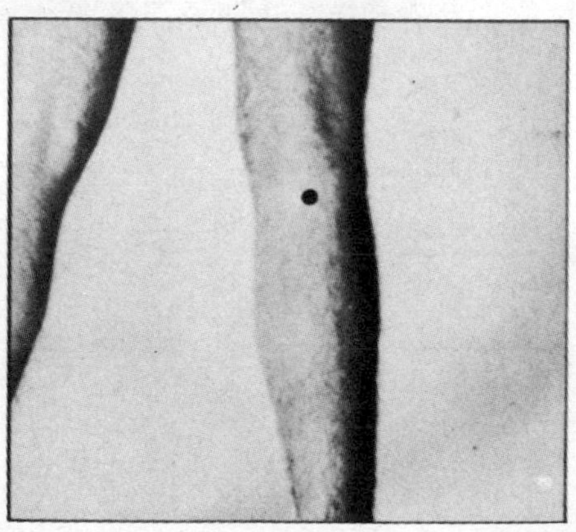

POINT: Orderly Edge
LANDMARK: back of knee fold
DISTANCE FROM LANDMARK: right in fold
LOCATION: back of knee, in the center of fold (treat both legs)
POSITION: face down
TYPE OF PRESSURE: pulsed with thumb
AMOUNT OF PRESSURE: as much as patient can take

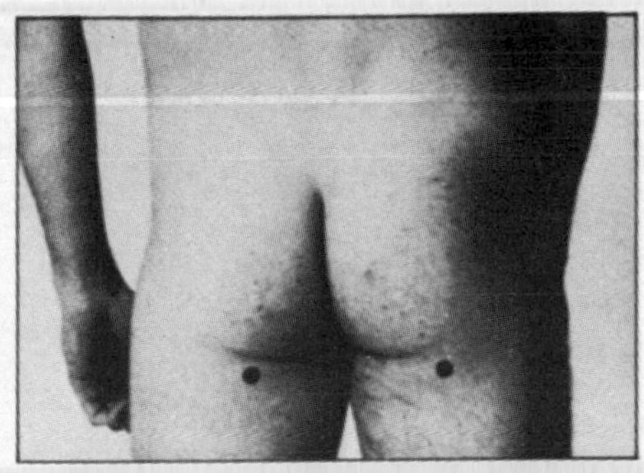

POINT: Stomach Granary
LANDMARK: buttocks fold
DISTANCE FROM LANDMARK: within the fold
LOCATION: at the midpoint of the fold line (treat both legs)
POSITION: face down
TYPE OF PRESSURE: pulsed with thumb
AMOUNT OF PRESSURE: as much as possible

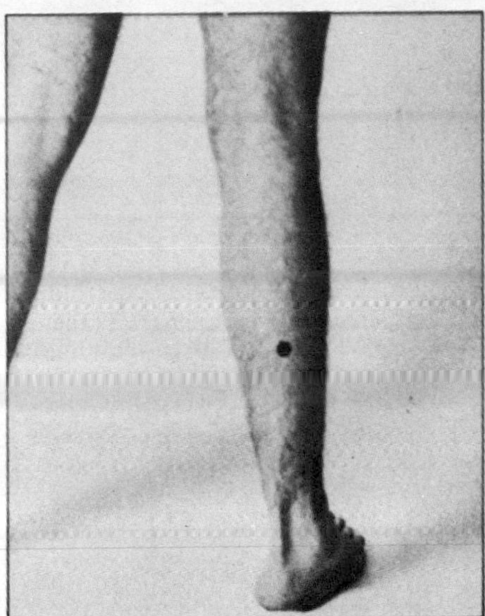

POINT: Supporting Hill
LANDMARK: outer ankle bone
DISTANCE FROM LANDMARK: 8 acu-inches up
LOCATION: back of calf, in the muscle hollow when the toes are stretched out (treat both legs)
POSITION: face down
TYPE OF PRESSURE: pulsed with thumb
AMOUNT OF PRESSURE: as much as patient can take

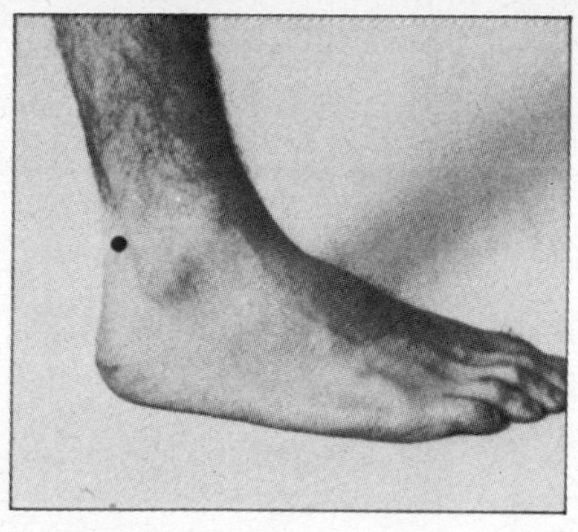

POINT: K'un Lun Mountains
LANDMARK: outer ankle bone
DISTANCE FROM LANDMARK: just in back
LOCATION: in the depression behind outer ankle bone (treat both feet)
POSITION: flat on back
TYPE OF PRESSURE: pulsed with thumb, pinching motion
AMOUNT OF PRESSURE: as much as patient can take

SHOULDER PAIN

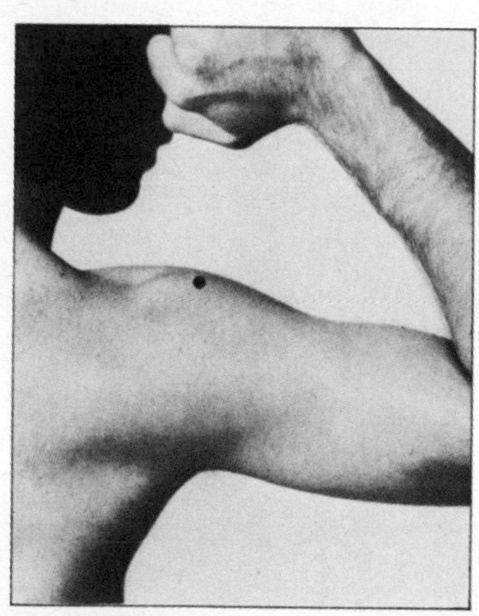

POINT: Shoulder Bone I
LANDMARK: extreme edge of shoulder
DISTANCE FROM LANDMARK: right at the landmark
LOCATION: on the shoulder, in the hollow formed when the arm is raised (treat both arms)
POSITION: seated
TYPE OF PRESSURE: pulsed with thumb
AMOUNT OF PRESSURE: gently, then as much as patient can take

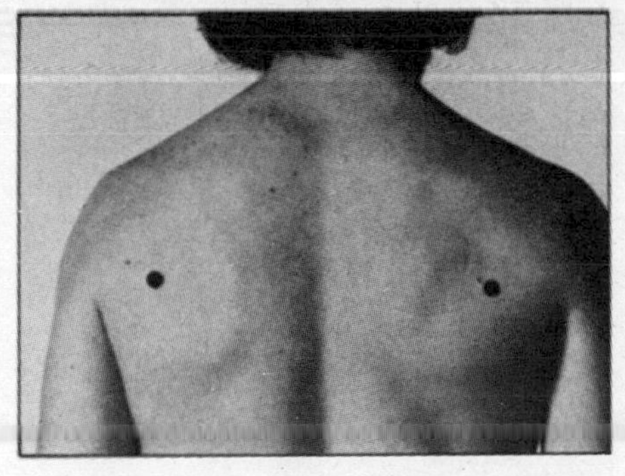

POINT: Celestial Ancestor
LANDMARK: spine knob at neck
DISTANCE FROM LANDMARK: 4th spine knob (vertebra) down
LOCATION: on a level with 4th spine knob, and 5 acu-inches on either side of center of back (treat both sides)
POSITION: on stomach
TYPE OF PRESSURE: pulsed with thumb
AMOUNT OF PRESSURE: gently to establish tolerance, then as much as patient can take

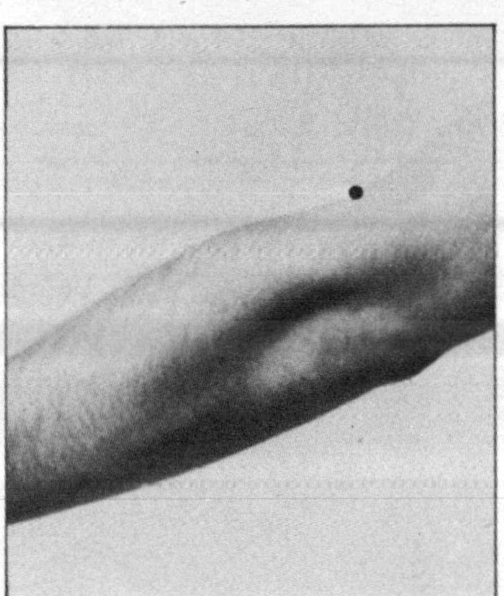

POINT: Elbow Bone
LANDMARK: outer elbow fold
DISTANCE FROM LANDMARK: 1 acu-inch above crease and just over the end of it
LOCATION: elbow (treat both arms)
POSITION: seated or flat on back
TYPE OF PRESSURE: pulsed with thumb, pinching motion
AMOUNT OF PRESSURE: as much as patient can take

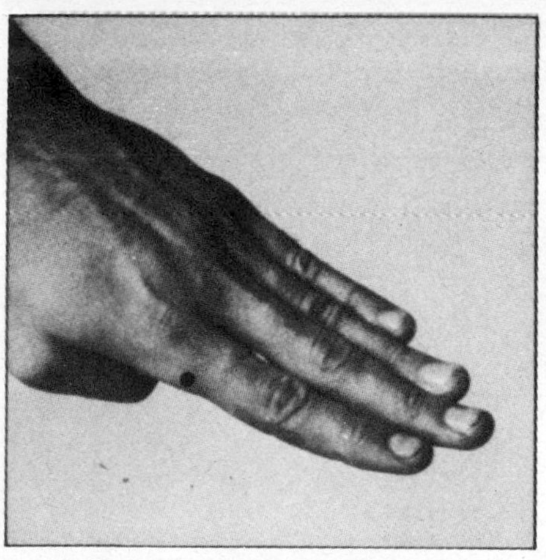

POINT: Two Intervals
LANDMARK: knuckles
DISTANCE FROM LANDMARK: just below the knuckle of the index finger
LOCATION: on the side of the index finger toward the thumb (treat both hands)
POSITION: seated
TYPE OF PRESSURE: pulsed or pinching motion
AMOUNT OF PRESSURE: as much as patient can take

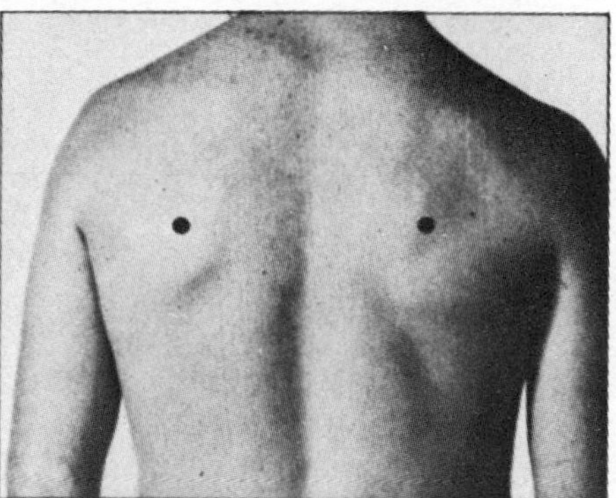

POINT: Great Gate
LANDMARK: spine knob at neck
DISTANCE FROM LANDMARK: 3rd spine knob (vertebra) below
LOCATION: 3 acu-inches on either side of spine (treat both sides)
POSITION: face down
TYPE OF PRESSURE: pulsed with thumb or fingers
AMOUNT OF PRESSURE: as much as patient can take

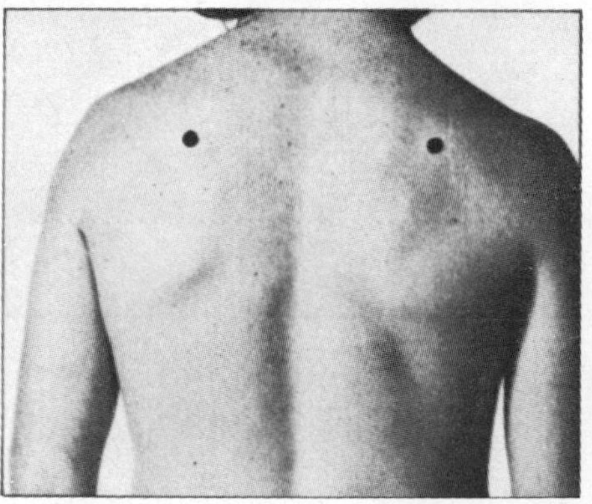

POINT: Support
LANDMARK: spine knob at neck
DISTANCE FROM LANDMARK: 2nd spine knob (vertebra) down
LOCATION: 3 acu-inches on either side of spine (treat both sides)
POSITION: face down
TYPE OF PRESSURE: pulsed with thumb; repeat as needed
AMOUNT OF PRESSURE: gently at first, increasing to maximum tolerance

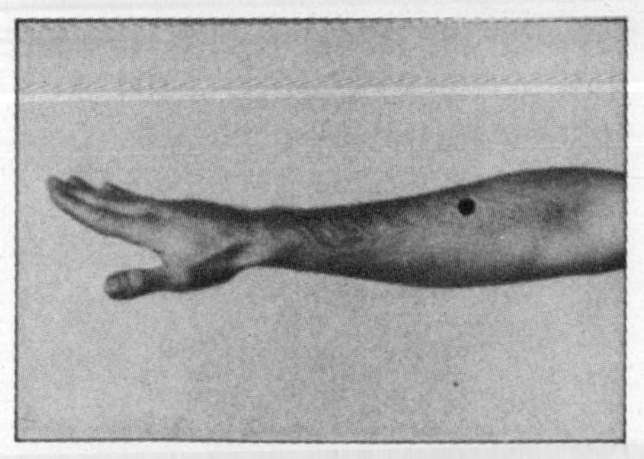

POINT: Supreme Cave
LANDMARK: inner elbow fold
DISTANCE FROM LANDMARK: 5 acu-inches down
LOCATION: on the inner surface of the forearm, 1 acu-inch in from the outer edge (treat both arms)
POSITION: seated or flat on back
TYPE OF PRESSURE: pulsed with thumb, pinching motion
AMOUNT OF PRESSURE: as much as patient can take

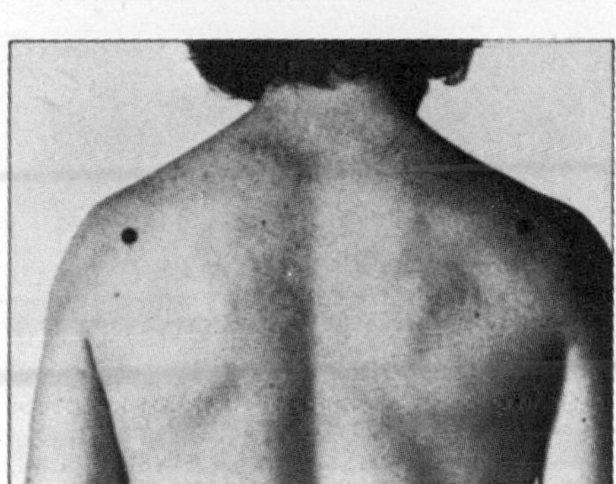

POINT: Shoulder Bone II
LANDMARK: extreme edge of shoulder
DISTANCE FROM LANDMARK: right at the landmark
LOCATION: on the back surface of the shoulder, about 1 acu-inch back from the highest point in the hollow formed when the arm is raised (treat both arms)
POSITION: seated
TYPE OF PRESSURE: pulsed with thumb, pinching motion
AMOUNT OF PRESSURE: gently, then as much as patient can take

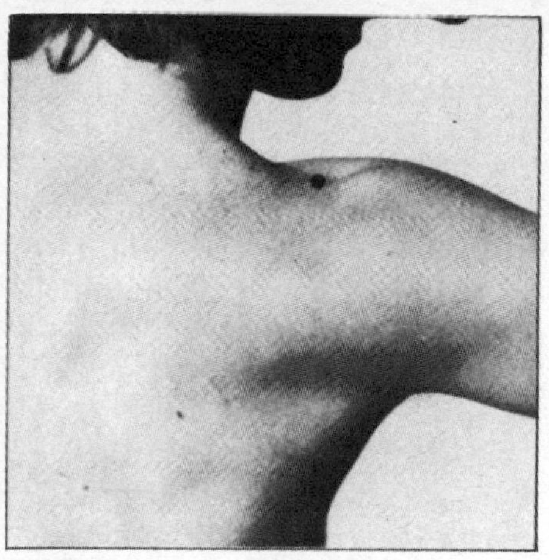

POINT: Shoulder Well
LANDMARK: base of neck
DISTANCE FROM LANDMARK: in the general area
LOCATION: in the hollow at the base of the neck (at the shoulder) formed when the arm is raised (treat both shoulders)
POSITION: seated
TYPE OF PRESSURE: pulsed with thumb, pinching motion
AMOUNT OF PRESSURE: gently, then as much as patient can take

SINUS

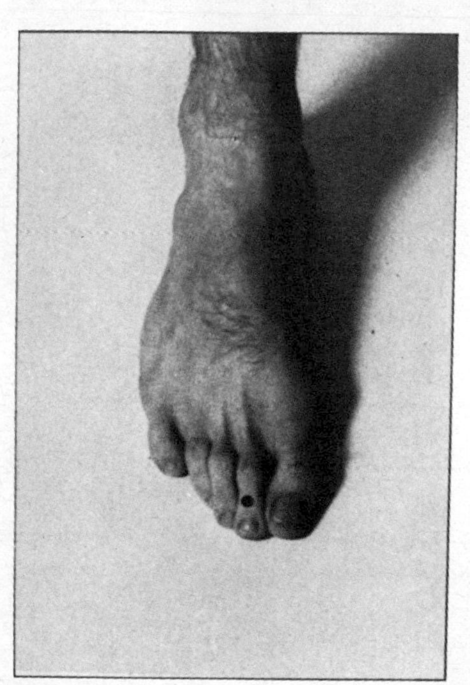

POINT: Strict Exchange
LANDMARK: toenail of the second toe
DISTANCE FROM LANDMARK: right on landmark
LOCATION: at the intersection of a line drawn along the little-toe side of the nail and a horizontal line across the top of the nail (treat both feet)
POSITION: flat on back
TYPE OF PRESSURE: pulsed with thumb, pinching motion
AMOUNT OF PRESSURE: as much as patient can take

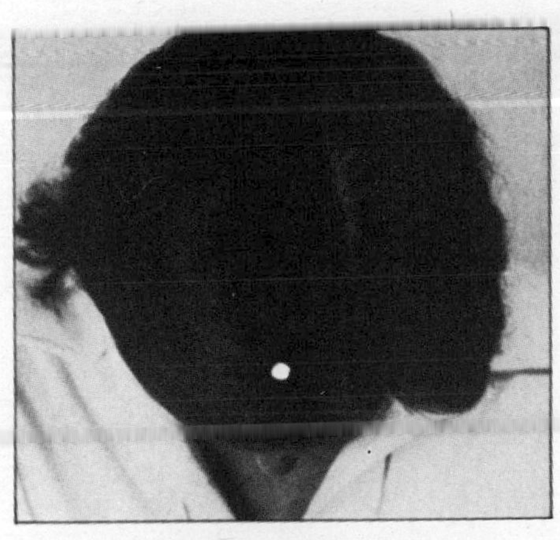

POINT: Super Star
LANDMARK: natural hairline at forehead
DISTANCE FROM LANDMARK: 1 acu-inch above
LOCATION: on the midline of the head
POSITION: seated or flat on back
TYPE OF PRESSURE: pulsed with thumb
AMOUNT OF PRESSURE: as much as patient can take

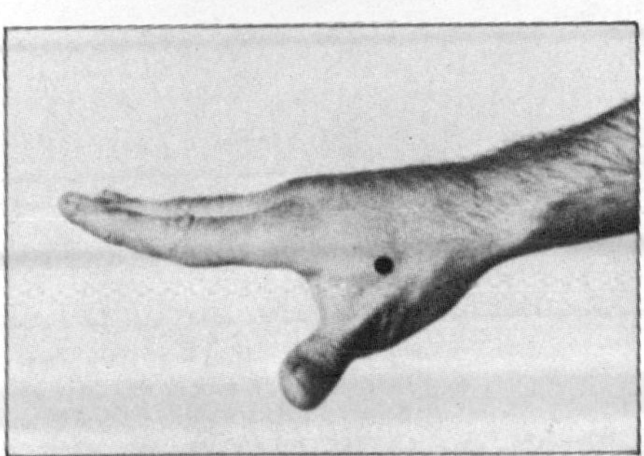

POINT: Connecting the Valleys
LANDMARK: back of hand
DISTANCE FROM LANDMARK: 1 acu-inch down from the point where bones of thumb and index finger meet
LOCATION: on the back of the hand (treat both hands)
POSITION: seated
TYPE OF PRESSURE: pulsed with thumb, pinching motion
AMOUNT OF PRESSURE: as much as patient can take

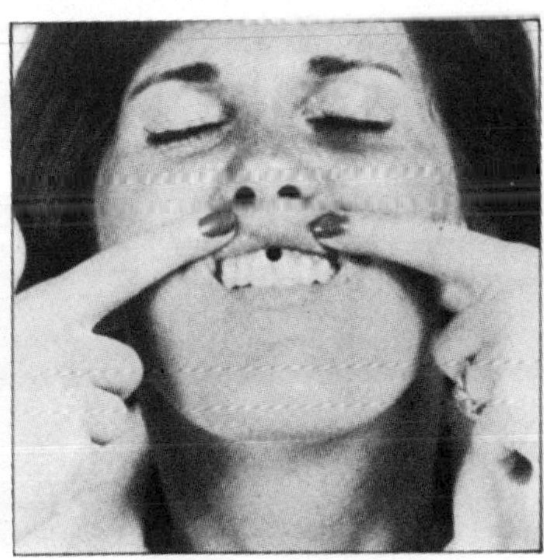

POINT: Gum Crossing
LANDMARK: gums
DISTANCE FROM LANDMARK: at the landmark
LOCATION: midpoint between the inner surface of the upper lip and the upper gums
POSITION: seated
TYPE OF PRESSURE: pulsed, or steady pressure with thumb-pinching motion
AMOUNT OF PRESSURE: as much as patient can take

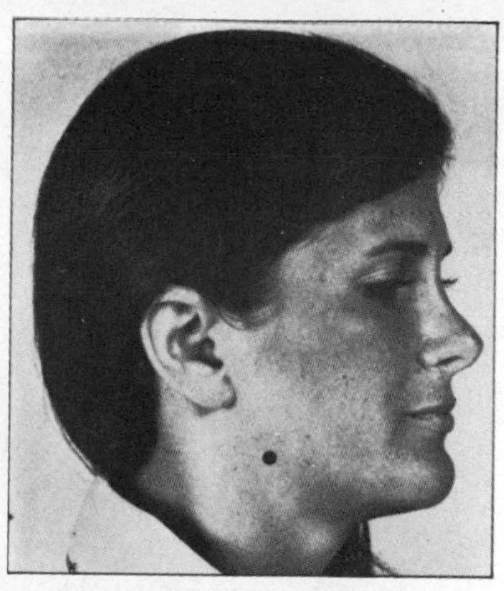

POINT: Cheek Chariot
LANDMARK: lower jawbone angle
DISTANCE FROM LANDMARK: about ½ acu-inch forward
LOCATION: feel lower jawline and locate a depression at the point (treat both sides of face)
POSITION: seated
TYPE OF PRESSURE: pulsed with fingers
AMOUNT OF PRESSURE: as much as patient can take

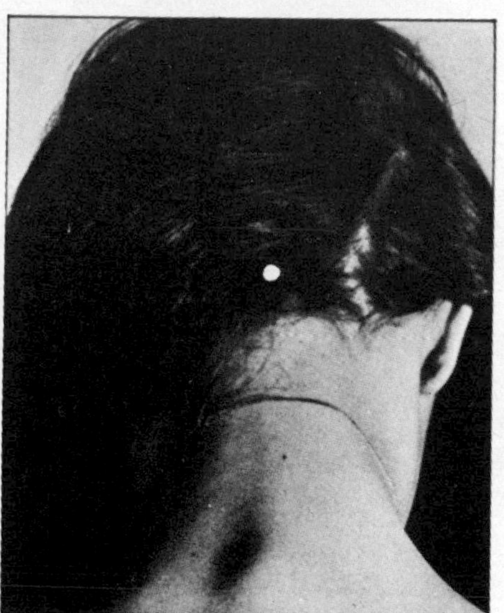

POINT: Windy Prefecture
LANDMARK: natural hairline at back of head
DISTANCE FROM LANDMARK: 1 acu-inch above
LOCATION: on top of head, along front-to-back center line of head
POSITION: seated or face down
TYPE OF PRESSURE: pulsed with thumb
AMOUNT OF PRESSURE: as much as patient can take

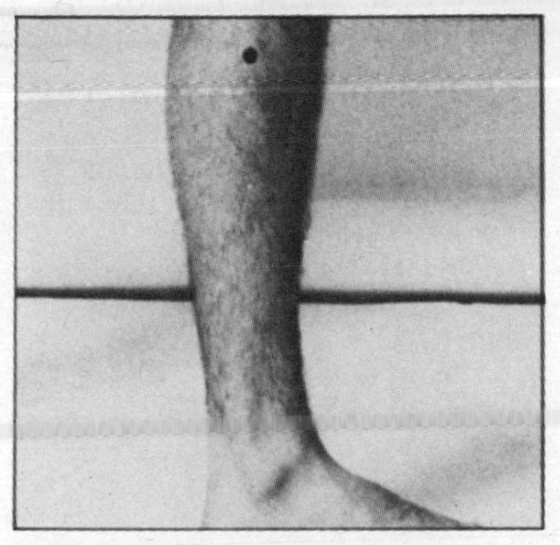

POINT: Rich and Prosperous
LANDMARK: outer ankle bone
DISTANCE FROM LANDMARK: 8 acu-inches above the upper edge of outer ankle bone
LOCATION: on the side of the leg, 1 acu-inch to the side (toward the outside of the leg) of the shin bone (treat both legs)
POSITION: seated or flat on back
TYPE OF PRESSURE: pulsed with thumb, pinching motion
AMOUNT OF PRESSURE: as much as patient can take

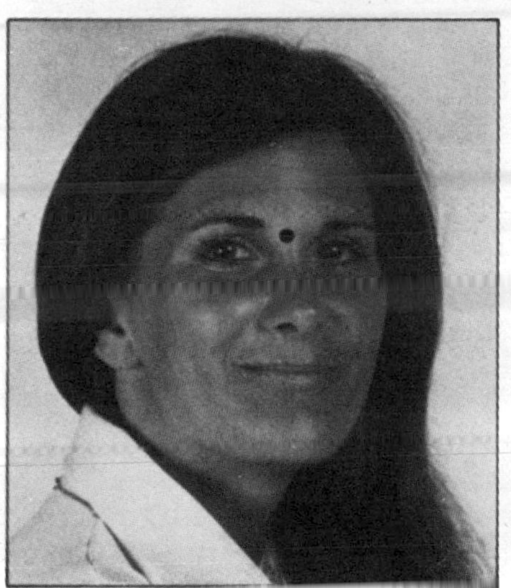

POINT: New Point
LANDMARK: eyebrows
DISTANCE FROM LANDMARK: point midway between the eyebrows
LOCATION: on a line joining the inside ends of the eyebrows
POSITION: seated or flat on back
TYPE OF PRESSURE: pinching motion with thumb and forefinger while also pressing in firmly
AMOUNT OF PRESSURE: as much as patient can take

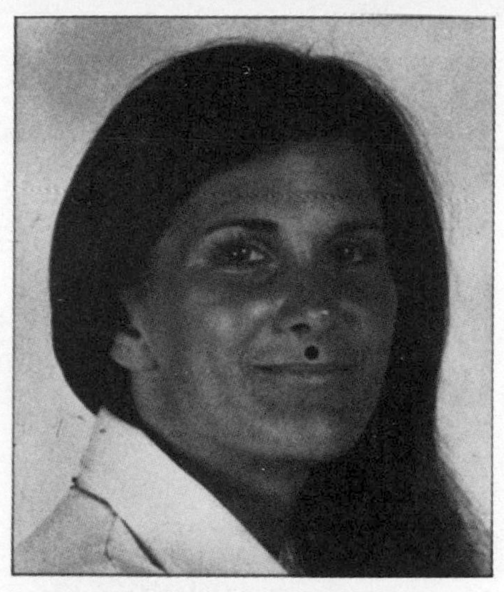

POINT: Middle of Man
LANDMARK: nose
DISTANCE FROM LANDMARK: just under landmark
LOCATION: directly under the center of the nose, on the upper lip
POSITION: flat on back
TYPE OF PRESSURE: alternating pulsed and steady pressure with thumb or fingers
AMOUNT OF PRESSURE: as much as patient can take

POINT: Welcome Fragrance
LANDMARK: nose-cheek fold
DISTANCE FROM LANDMARK: right in the fold
LOCATION: ½ acu-inch up from the bottom of the nose on the cheeks (treat both sides)
POSITION: flat on back
TYPE OF PRESSURE: pulsed with thumb or fingers
AMOUNT OF PRESSURE: as much as patient can take

POINT: Drilling Bamboo
LANDMARK: eyebrow
DISTANCE FROM LANDMARK: right on eyebrow
LOCATION: at the inside end (toward nose) of the eyebrows (treat both eyebrows)
POSITION: seated or flat on back
TYPE OF PRESSURE: pulsed with thumb or fingers
AMOUNT OF PRESSURE: treat both at one time, with maximum pressure that patient can stand

SORE THROAT

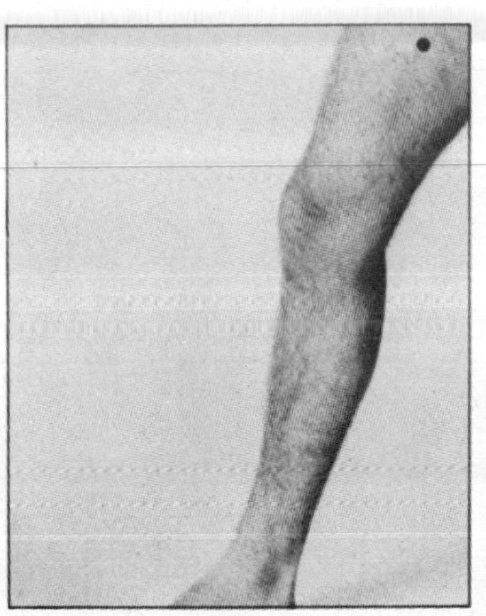

POINT: Five Miles
LANDMARK: thigh-stomach fold
DISTANCE FROM LANDMARK: 1 acu-inch above
LOCATION: on the lower abdomen, 4 acu-inches away from center line of body (treat both sides)
POSITION: flat on back
TYPE OF PRESSURE: pulsed with thumb or fingers
AMOUNT OF PRESSURE: gently, then with firm pressure

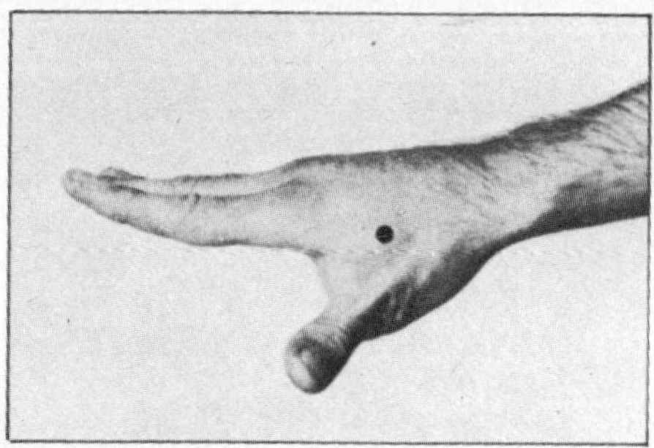

POINT: Connecting the Valleys
LANDMARK: back of hand
DISTANCE FROM LANDMARK: 1 acu-inch down from the point where bones of thumb and index finger meet
LOCATION: on thc back of the hand (treat both hands)
POSITION: seated
TYPE OF PRESSURE: pulsed with thumb, pinching motion
AMOUNT OF PRESSURE: as much as patient can take

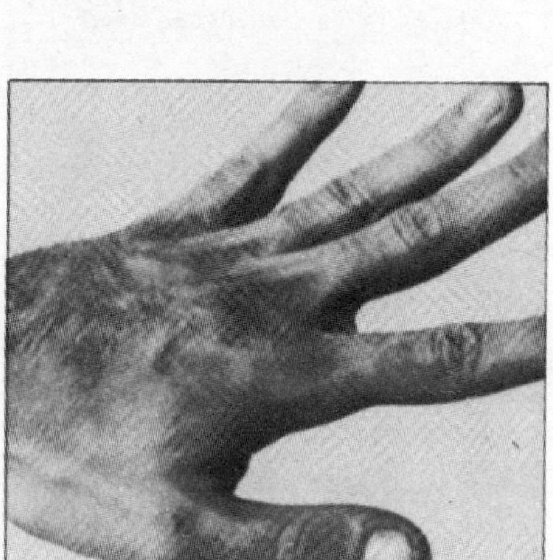

POINT: Yang Tradesman
LANDMARK: thumbnail
DISTANCE FROM LANDMARK: close to landmark
LOCATION: at the intersection of a line drawn along the outer edge of nail and a horizontal line across the base of the nail (treat both thumbs)
POSITION: seated
TYPE OF PRESSURE: pulsed with thumb, pinching motion
AMOUNT OF PRESSURE: as much as patient can take

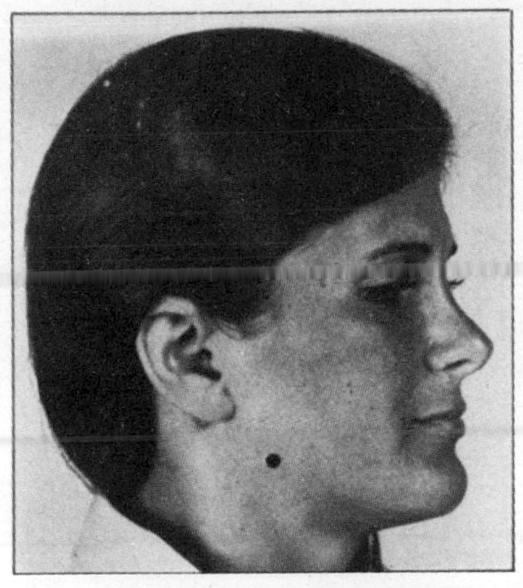

POINT: Cheek Chariot
LANDMARK: lower jawbone angle
DISTANCE FROM LANDMARK: about ½ acu-inch forward
LOCATION: feel lower jawline and locate a depression at the point (treat both sides of face)
POSITION: seated
TYPE OF PRESSURE: pulsed with fingers
AMOUNT OF PRESSURE: as much as patient can take

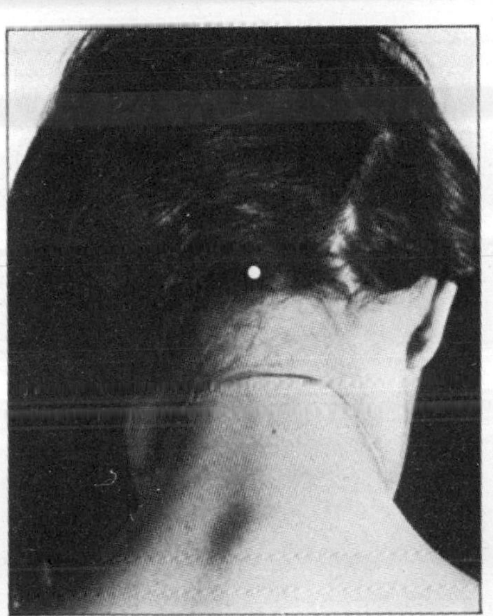

POINT: Windy Prefecture
LANDMARK: natural hairline at back of head
DISTANCE FROM LANDMARK: 1 acu-inch above
LOCATION: on top of head, along front-to-back center line of head
POSITION: seated or face down
TYPE OF PRESSURE: pulsed with thumb
AMOUNT OF PRESSURE: as much as patient can take

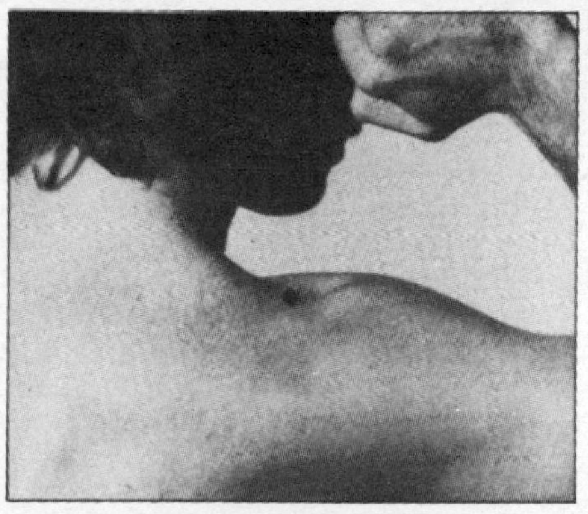

POINT: Shoulder Well
LANDMARK: base of neck
DISTANCE FROM LANDMARK: in the general area
LOCATION: in the hollow at the base of the neck (at the shoulder) formed when the arm is raised (treat both shoulders)
POSITION: seated
TYPE OF PRESSURE: pulsed with thumb, pinching motion
AMOUNT OF PRESSURE: gently, then as much as patient can take

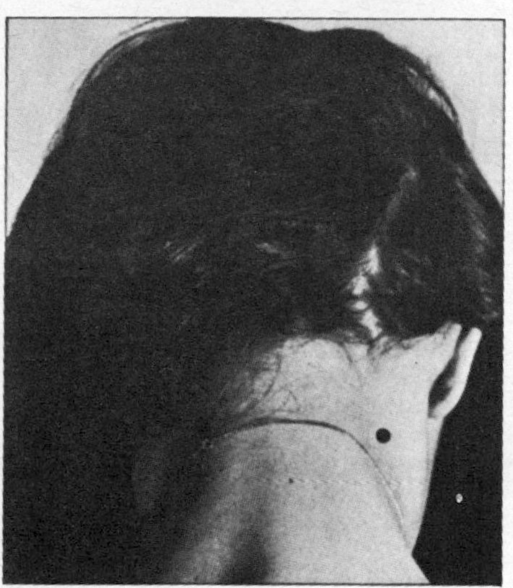

POINT: Wind Pond
LANDMARK: rear head bones
DISTANCE FROM LANDMARK: immediately below
LOCATION: feel for a depression or groove on each side just below the landmark (treat both sides)
POSITION: seated or face down
TYPE OF PRESSURE: pulsed with thumbs or fingers
AMOUNT OF PRESSURE: as much as patient can take
NOTE: if patient is sitting up, stand in front of him and rest his head against your chest; exert pressure with your fingers

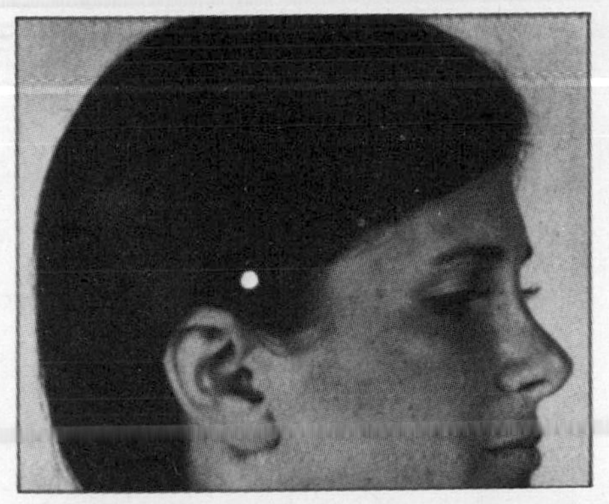

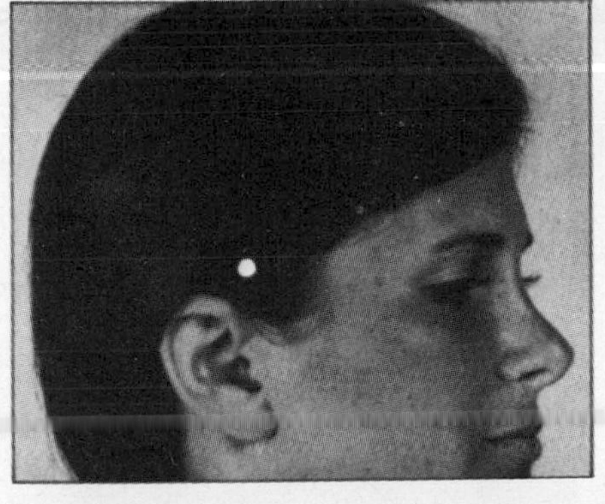

POINT: Tortuous Sideburn
LANDMARK: natural hairline of sideburns and ear
DISTANCE FROM LANDMARK: right on sideburn and about 1 acu-inch above outer line of ear
LOCATION: on the temple (treat both sides)
POSITION: seated or flat on back
TYPE OF PRESSURE: pulsed with thumb or fingers
AMOUNT OF PRESSURE: as much as patient can take

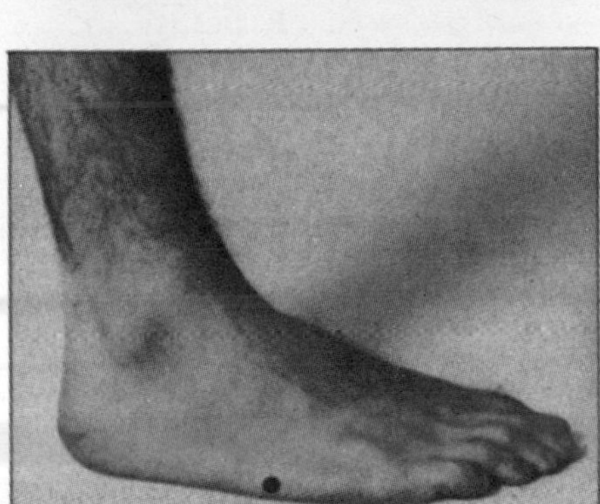

POINT: Capital Bone
LANDMARK: toe knuckle of little toe
DISTANCE FROM LANDMARK: close to the landmark
LOCATION: feel back (toward the ankle) along the outer edge of the foot to a bump about 2 acu-inches from landmark; point is just in back of and under this bump (treat both feet)
POSITION: seated or flat on back
TYPE OF PRESSURE: pulsed with thumb
AMOUNT OF PRESSURE: as much as patient can take

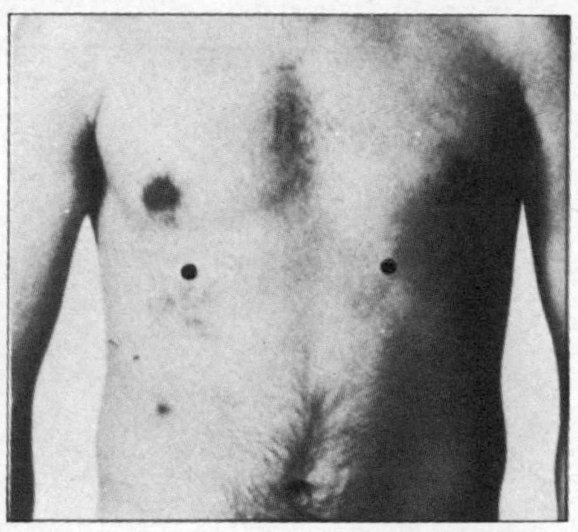

POINT: Beam Gate
LANDMARK: navel
DISTANCE FROM LANDMARK: 4 acu-inches above
LOCATION: on the chest, 2 acu-inches on either side of the center line of the chest (treat both sides)
POSITION: flat on back
TYPE OF PRESSURE: pulsed with thumb
AMOUNT OF PRESSURE: as much as patient can take

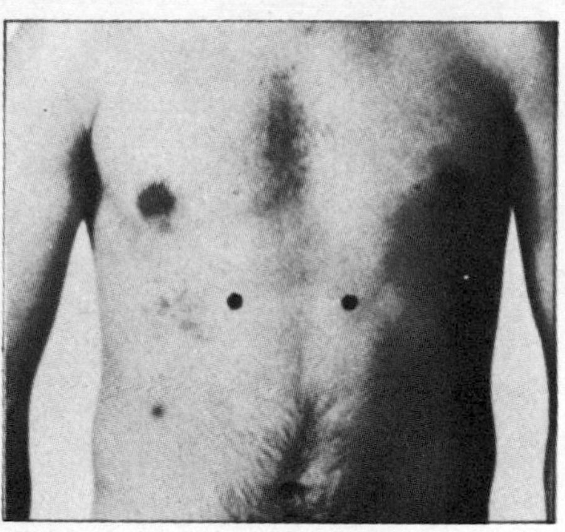

POINT: Reaching Valley
LANDMARK: navel
DISTANCE FROM LANDMARK: 5 acu-inches above
LOCATION: 1 acu-inch on either side of center line of stomach (treat both sides)
POSITION: flat on back
TYPE OF PRESSURE: pulsed with fingers
AMOUNT OF PRESSURE: as much as patient can take

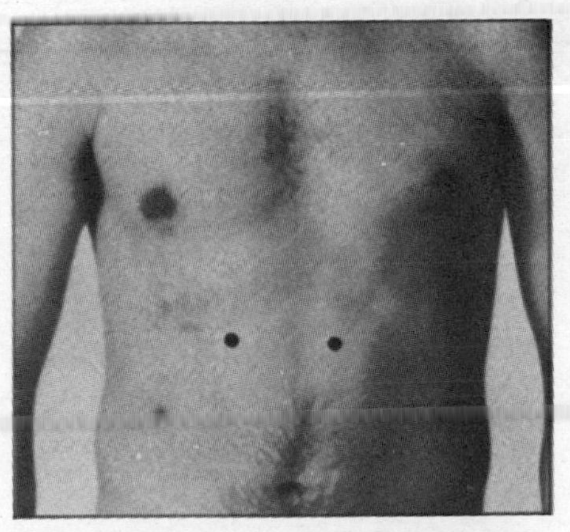

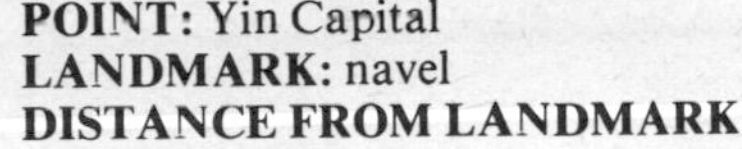

POINT: Yin Capital
LANDMARK: navel
DISTANCE FROM LANDMARK: 4 acu-inches above
LOCATION: 1 acu-inch on either side of center line of stomach (treat both sides)
POSITION: flat on back
TYPE OF PRESSURE: pulsed with fingers
AMOUNT OF PRESSURE: gently at first, then quite firmly

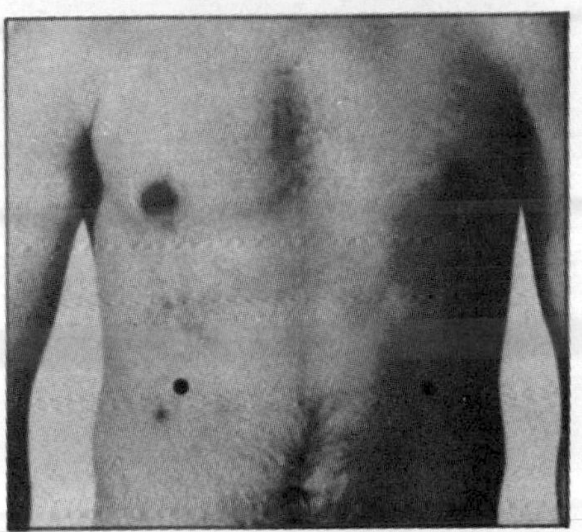

POINT: Sorrow Belly
LANDMARK: navel
DISTANCE FROM LANDMARK: 3 acu-inches above the navel
LOCATION: on the chest, 3½ acu-inches on either side of the center line of the body (treat both sides)
POSITION: flat on back
TYPE OF PRESSURE: pulsed with thumb or fingers
AMOUNT OF PRESSURE: gently, then as much as patient can tolerate

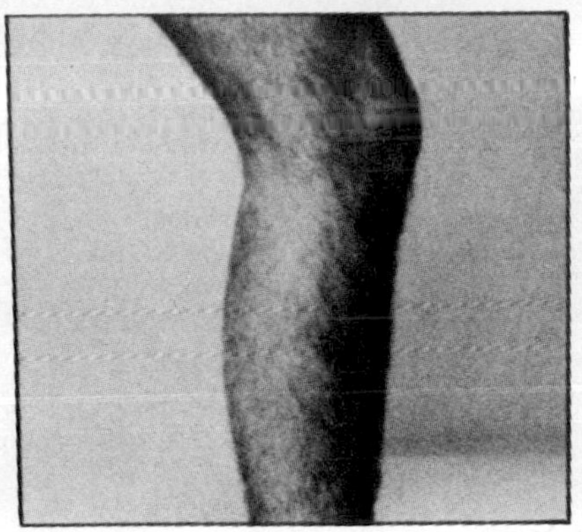

POINT: Walking Three Miles
LANDMARK: kneecap
DISTANCE FROM LANDMARK: 3 acu-inches below (in the depression)
LOCATION: 1 acu-inch toward the outside of the leg (treat both legs)
POSITION: seated in chair or flat on back
TYPE OF PRESSURE: pulsed with thumb (or pinching motion)
AMOUNT OF PRESSURE: quite firm

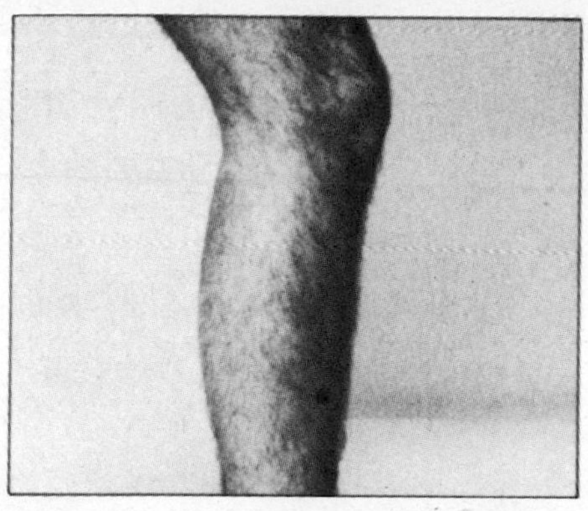

POINT: Super Great Void
LANDMARK: kneecap
DISTANCE FROM LANDMARK: 6 acu-inches below
LOCATION: right alongside the shin bone toward the outer edge of the leg (treat both legs)
POSITION: flat on back
TYPE OF PRESSURE: pulsed with thumb
AMOUNT OF PRESSURE: as much as patient can take

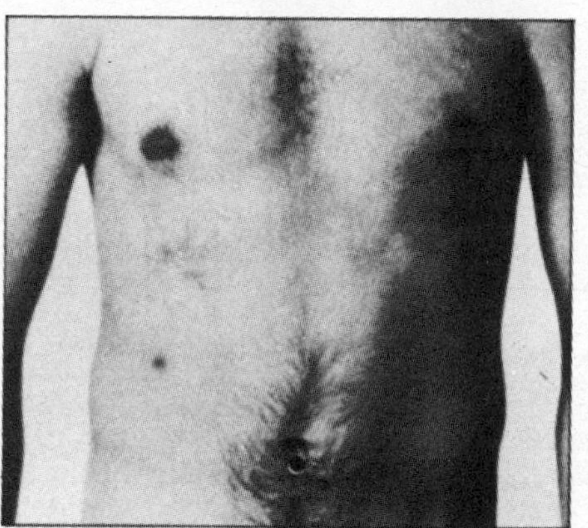

POINT: Vapor Sea
LANDMARK: navel
DISTANCE FROM LANDMARK: 1½ acu-inch below navel
LOCATION: on lower abdomen directly below navel
POSITION: flat on back
TYPE OF PRESSURE: pulsed with thumb or fingers
AMOUNT OF PRESSURE: gently, then more firmly according to tolerance of the patient

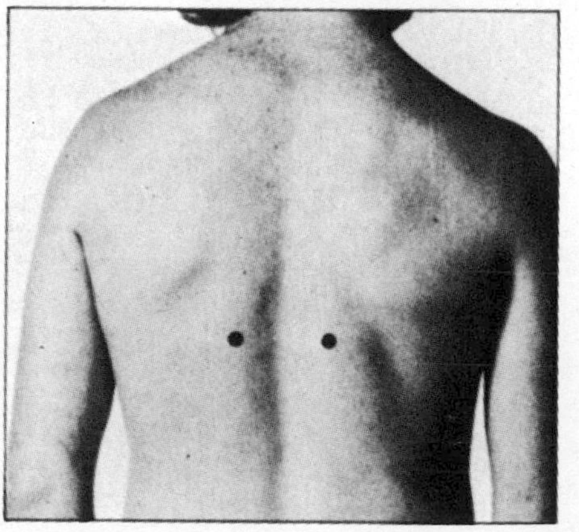

POINT: Diaphragm Locus
LANDMARK: spine knob at neck
DISTANCE FROM LANDMARK: 6th spine knob (vertebra) below
LOCATION: on back, 1½ acu-inches on either side of spine (treat both sides)
POSITION: on stomach
TYPE OF PRESSURE: pulsed with thumb
AMOUNT OF PRESSURE: as much as patient can take

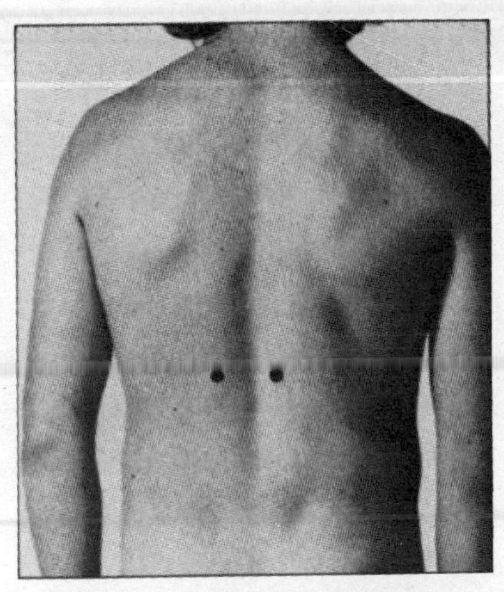

POINT: Spleen Locus
LANDMARK: spine knob at neck
DISTANCE FROM LANDMARK: 11th spine knob (vertebra) below
LOCATION: 1½ acu-inches on either side of the spine (treat both sides)
POSITION: face down
TYPE OF PRESSURE: pulsed with thumb
AMOUNT OF PRESSURE: as much as patient can take

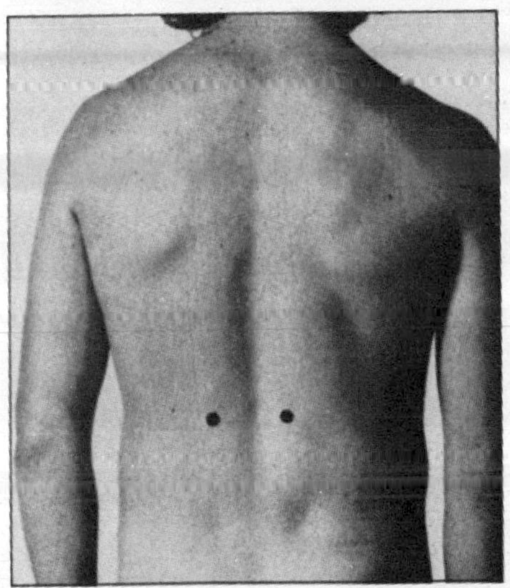

POINT: Stomach Locus
LANDMARK: spine knob at neck
DISTANCE FROM LANDMARK: 12th spine knob (vertebra) below
LOCATION: 1½ acu-inches on either side of spine (treat both sides)
POSITION: face down
TYPE OF PRESSURE: pulsed with thumb
AMOUNT OF PRESSURE: gently, then firm

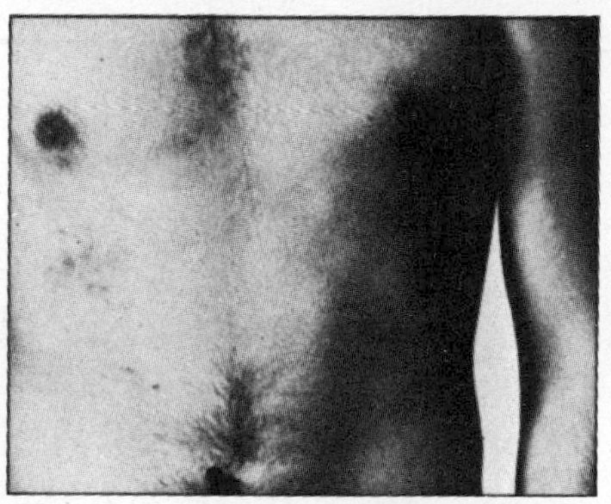

POINT: Spiritual Shrine
LANDMARK: navel
DISTANCE FROM LANDMARK: at the landmark
LOCATION: right in the navel
POSITION: flat on back
TYPE OF PRESSURE: pulsed, with fingers
AMOUNT OF PRESSURE: gently, then more firmly according to tolerance

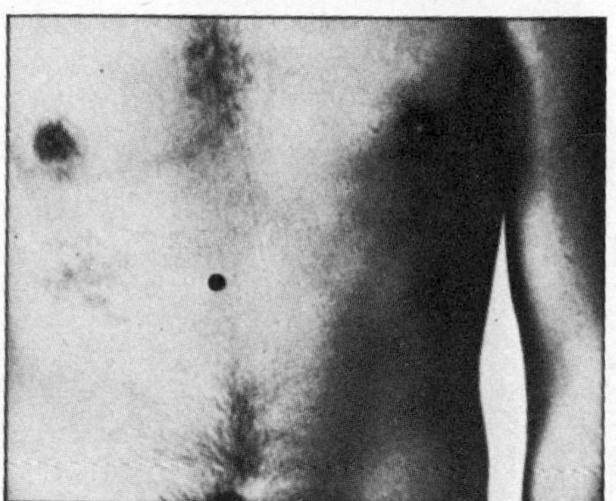

POINT: Great Temple
LANDMARK: navel
DISTANCE FROM LANDMARK: 6 acu-inches above
LOCATION: on the chest, directly above the navel
POSITION: flat on back
TYPE OF PRESSURE: pulsed with thumb or fingers
AMOUNT OF PRESSURE: as much as patient can tolerate

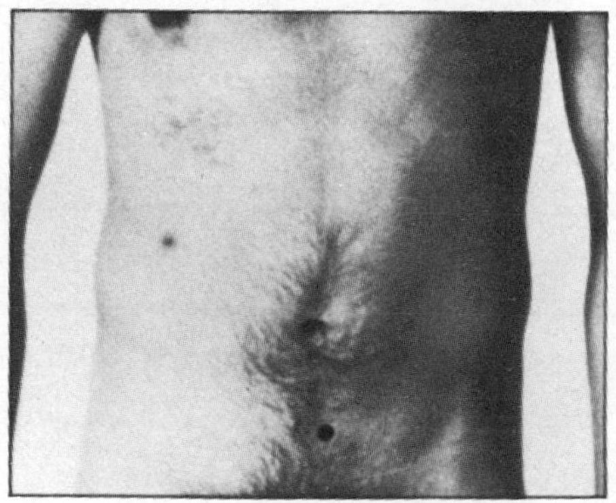

POINT: Pass Origin
LANDMARK: navel
DISTANCE FROM LANDMARK: 3 acu-inches below
LOCATION: on lower abdomen in a line directly below navel
POSITION: flat on back
TYPE OF PRESSURE: pulsed with thumb
AMOUNT OF PRESSURE: as much as patient can take

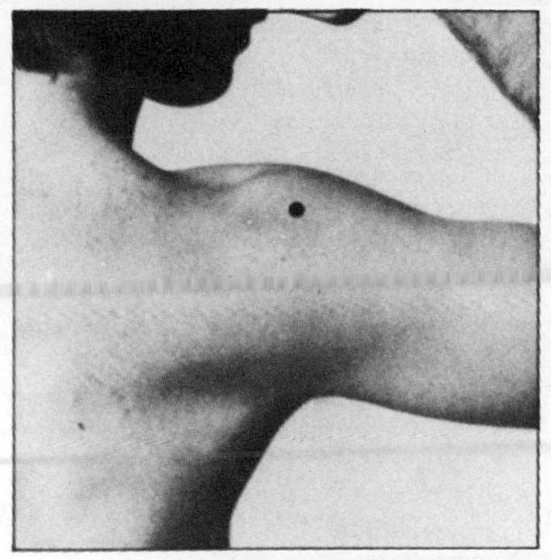

POINT: Shoulder Bone II
LANDMARK: extreme edge of shoulder
DISTANCE FROM LANDMARK: right at the landmark
LOCATION: on the back surface of the shoulder, about 1 acu-inch back from the highest point in the hollow formed when the arm is raised (treat both arms)
POSITION: seated
TYPE OF PRESSURE: pulsed with thumb, pinching motion
AMOUNT OF PRESSURE: gently, then as much as patient can take

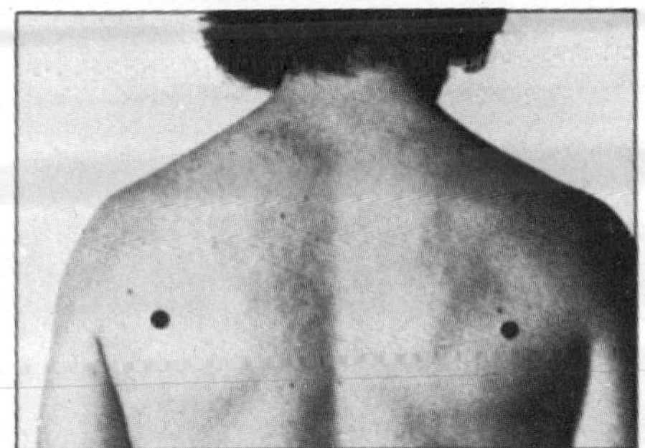

POINT: Celestial Ancestor
LANDMARK: spine knob at neck
DISTANCE FROM LANDMARK: 4th spine knob (vertebra) down
LOCATION: on a level with 4th spine knob and 5 acu-inches on either side of center of back (treat both sides)
POSITION: on stomach
TYPE OF PRESSURE: pulsed with thumb
AMOUNT OF PRESSURE: gently to establish tolerance, then as much as patient can take

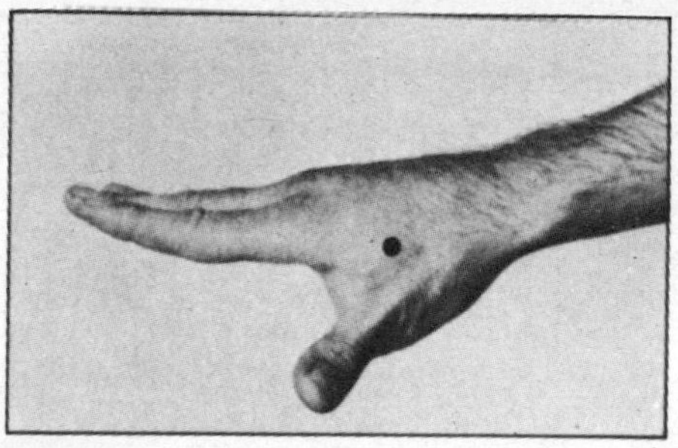

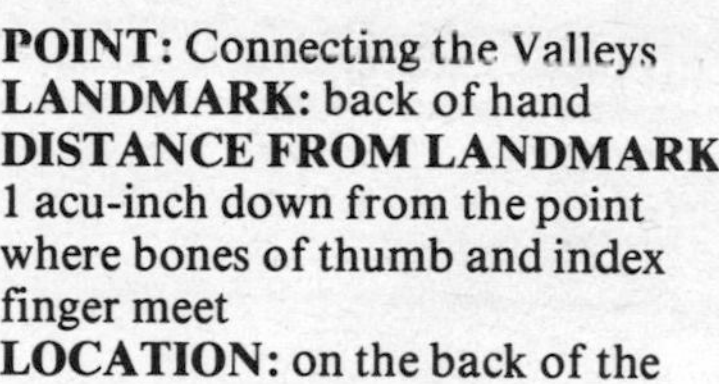

POINT: Connecting the Valleys
LANDMARK: back of hand
DISTANCE FROM LANDMARK: 1 acu-inch down from the point where bones of thumb and index finger meet
LOCATION: on the back of the hand (treat both hands)
POSITION: seated
TYPE OF PRESSURE: pulsed with thumb, pinching motion
AMOUNT OF PRESSURE: as much as patient can take

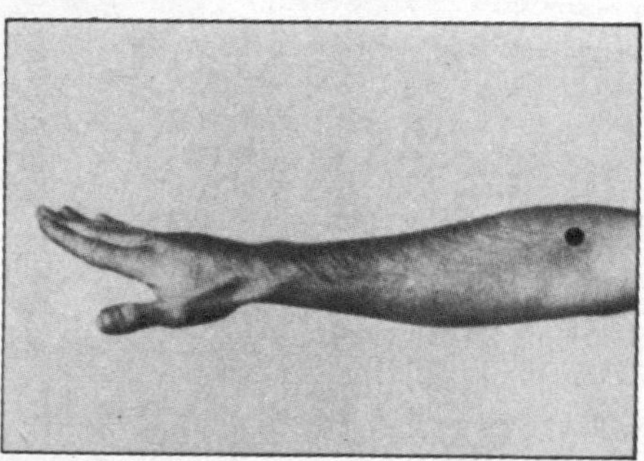

POINT: Short Narrow Marsh
LANDMARK: inner elbow fold
DISTANCE FROM LANDMARK: 1 acu-inch in from the body-side edge of the arm
LOCATION: right on the crease (treat both arms)
POSITION: seated or flat on back
TYPE OF PRESSURE: pulsed with thumb, pinching motion
AMOUNT OF PRESSURE: as much as patient can take

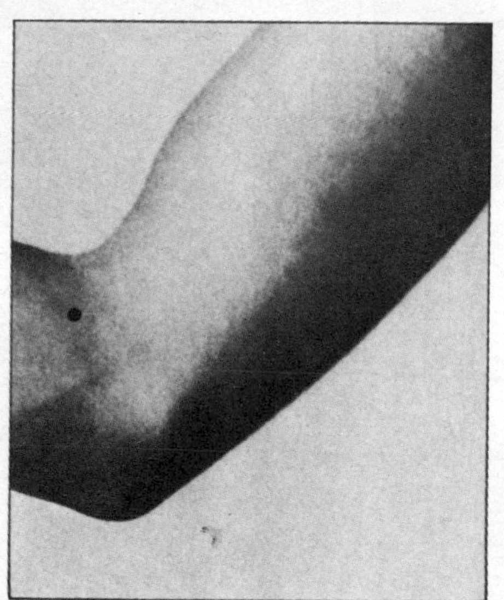

POINT: Crooked Pond
LANDMARK: inner elbow fold
DISTANCE FROM LANDMARK: right at the body-side edge of fold, when elbow is bent
LOCATION: elbow (treat both arms)
POSITION: seated or flat on back
TYPE OF PRESSURE: pulsed with thumb, pinching motion
AMOUNT OF PRESSURE: as much as patient can take

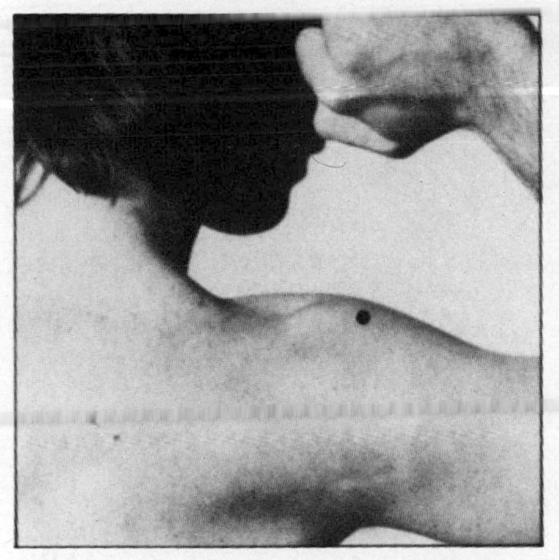

POINT: Huge Bone
LANDMARK: arm-shoulder fold
DISTANCE FROM LANDMARK: in a line directly below
LOCATION: on the shoulder at the top; feel for the spot where the collar bone meets the arm—slight hollow (treat both shoulders)
POSITION: seated or flat on back
TYPE OF PRESSURE: pulsed with thumb
AMOUNT OF PRESSURE: as much as patient can take

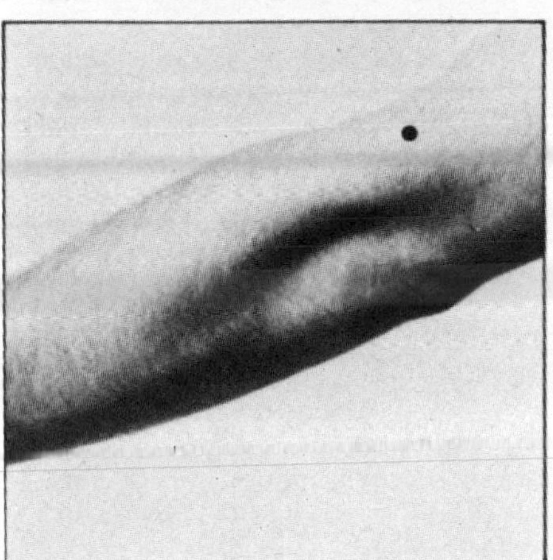

POINT: Elbow Bone
LANDMARK: outer elbow fold
DISTANCE FROM LANDMARK: 1 acu-inch above crease and just over the end of it
LOCATION: elbow (treat both arms)
POSITION: seated or flat on back
TYPE OF PRESSURE: pulsed with thumb, pinching motion
AMOUNT OF PRESSURE: as much as patient can take

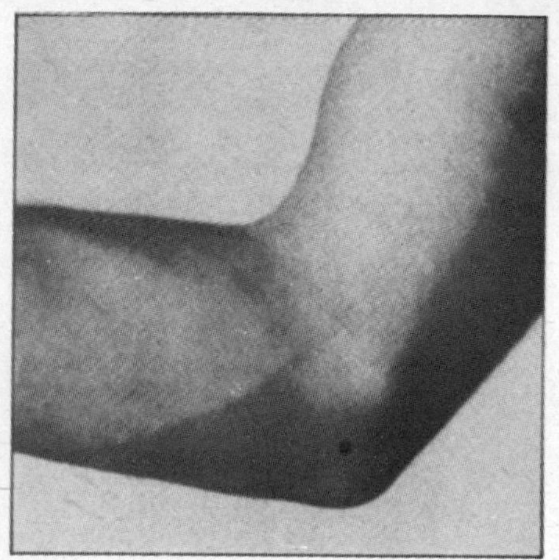

POINT: Young Sea
LANDMARK: inner elbow fold
DISTANCE FROM LANDMARK: at the body-side edge of the fold, when elbow is bent
LOCATION: elbow (treat both arms)
POSITION: seated or flat on back
TYPE OF PRESSURE: pulsed with thumb, pinching motion
AMOUNT OF PRESSURE: as much as patient can take

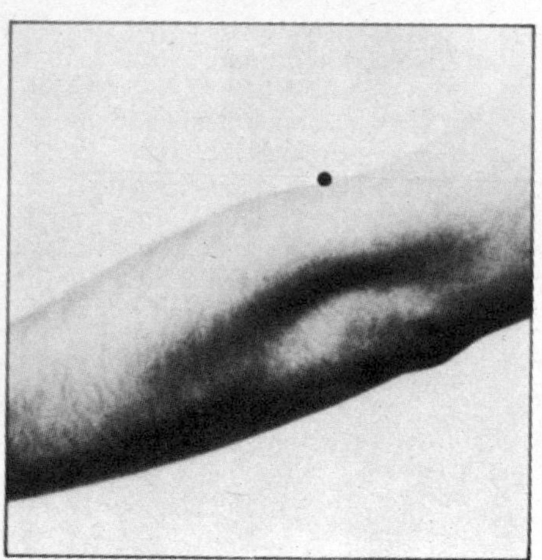

POINT: Bent Pond
LANDMARK: outer elbow fold
DISTANCE FROM LANDMARK: right at the end of the fold
LOCATION: elbow (treat both arms)
POSITION: seated or flat on back
TYPE OF PRESSURE: pulsed with thumb, pinching motion
AMOUNT OF PRESSURE: as much as patient can take

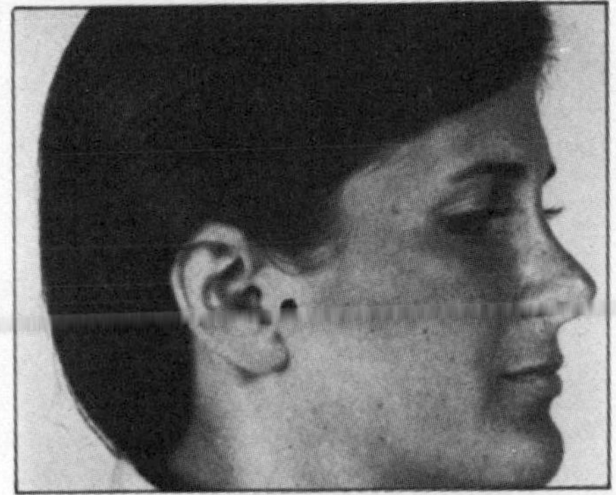

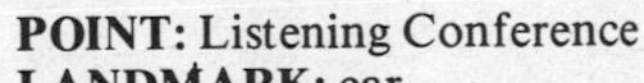

POINT: Listening Conference
LANDMARK: ear
DISTANCE FROM LANDMARK: directly in front
LOCATION: in the hollow in front of the ear that is formed when the mouth is opened wide (treat both sides of face)
POSITION: seated or flat on back
TYPE OF PRESSURE: pulsed with thumb or fingers
AMOUNT OF PRESSURE: as much as patient can tolerate

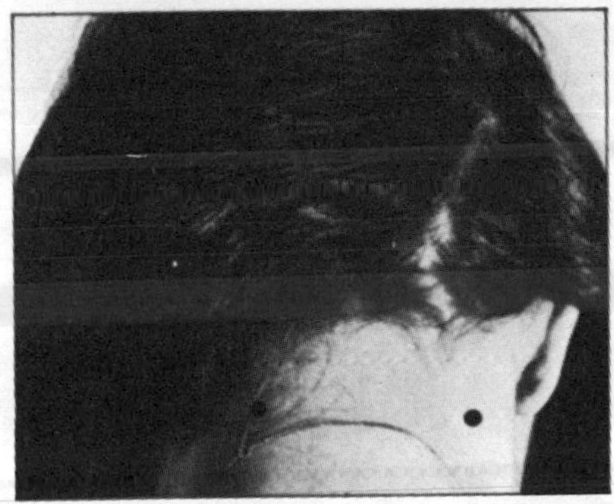

POINT: Wind Pond
LANDMARK: rear head bones
DISTANCE FROM LANDMARK: immediately below
LOCATION: feel for a depression or groove on each side just below the landmark (treat both sides)
POSITION: seated or face down
TYPE OF PRESSURE: pulsed with thumbs or fingers
AMOUNT OF PRESSURE: as much as patient can take
NOTE: if patient is sitting up, stand in front of him and rest his head against your chest; exert pressure with your fingers

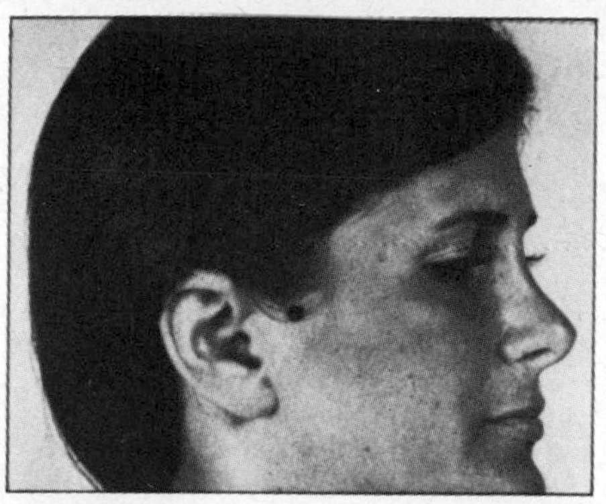

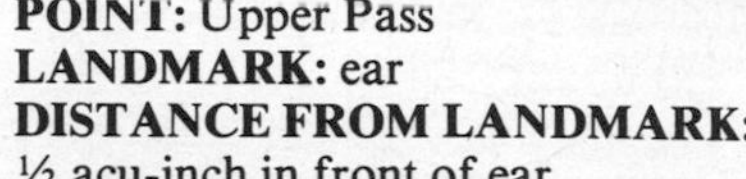

POINT: Upper Pass
LANDMARK: ear
DISTANCE FROM LANDMARK: ½ acu-inch in front of ear
LOCATION: feel for arched bone in front of ear; point is just under the arch (treat both sides of face)
POSITION: seated or flat on back
TYPE OF PRESSURE: pulsed with thumb or fingers
AMOUNT OF PRESSURE: as much as patient can take; repeat as needed

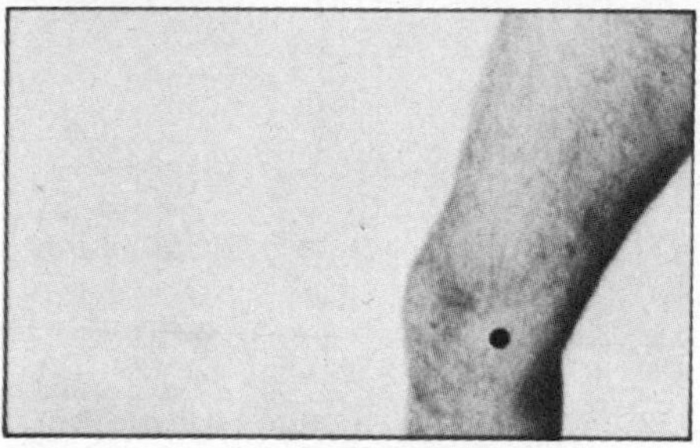

POINT: Knee Pass
LANDMARK: back of knee fold
DISTANCE FROM LANDMARK: 3 acu-inches down from knee fold
LOCATION: inner surface of calf, in the center (treat both legs)
POSITION: seated or flat on back
TYPE OF PRESSURE: pulsed with thumb, pinching motion
AMOUNT OF PRESSURE: as much as patient can take

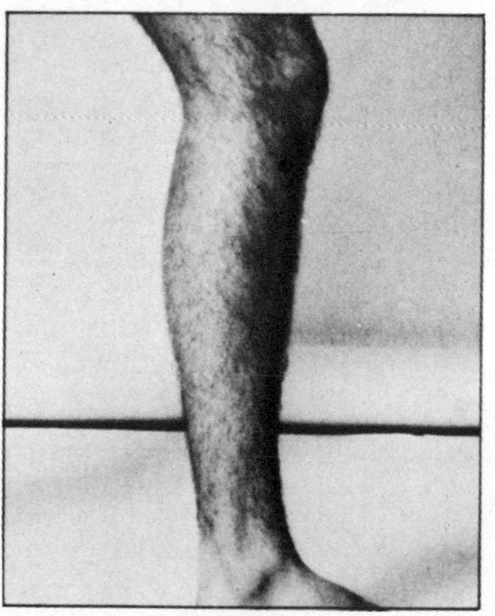

POINT: Walking Three Miles
LANDMARK: kneecap
DISTANCE FROM LANDMARK: 3 acu-inches below (in the depression)
LOCATION: 1 acu-inch toward the outside of the leg (treat both legs)
POSITION: seated in chair or flat on back
TYPE OF PRESSURE: pulsed with thumb (or pinching motion)
AMOUNT OF PRESSURE: quite firm

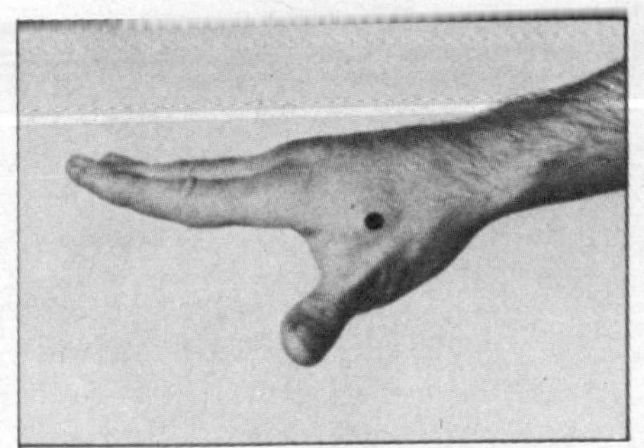

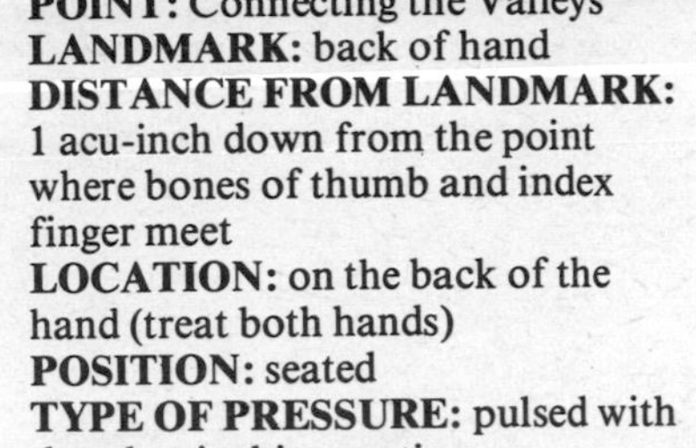

POINT: Connecting the Valleys
LANDMARK: back of hand
DISTANCE FROM LANDMARK: 1 acu-inch down from the point where bones of thumb and index finger meet
LOCATION: on the back of the hand (treat both hands)
POSITION: seated
TYPE OF PRESSURE: pulsed with thumb, pinching motion
AMOUNT OF PRESSURE: as much as patient can take

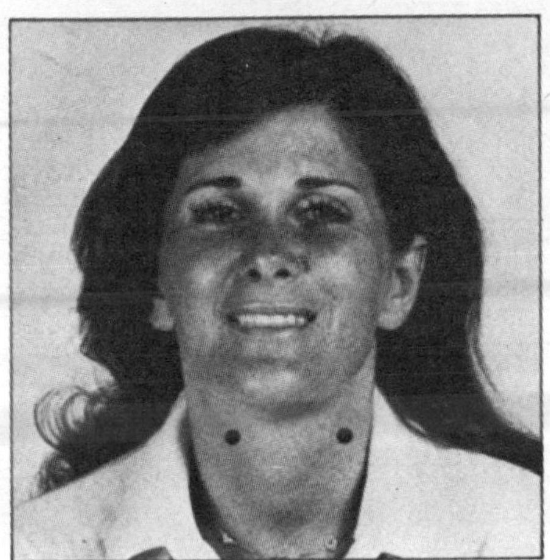

POINT: Celestial Window
LANDMARK: Adam's apple
DISTANCE FROM LANDMARK: right at the level of the Adam's apple
LOCATION: on the neck, 3½ acu-inches on either side of the vertical center line in the front of the neck (treat both sides)
POSITION: flat on back
TYPE OF PRESSURE: pulsed with fingers
AMOUNT OF PRESSURE: as much as patient can take

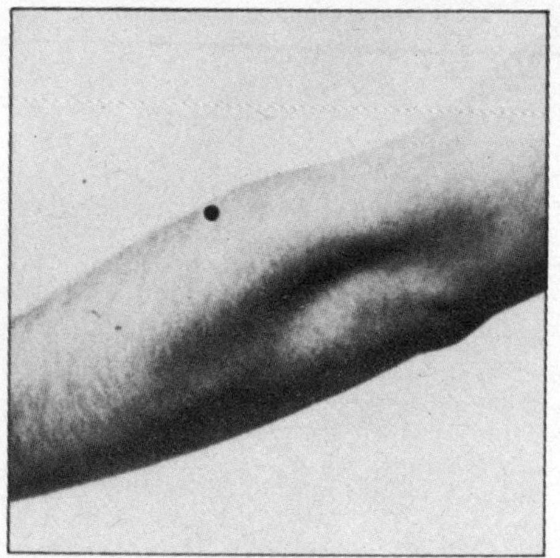

POINT: Three Li
LANDMARK: outer elbow fold
DISTANCE FROM LANDMARK: 2 acu-inches below
LOCATION: side of the forearm, in the middle (treat both arms)
POSITION: seated or flat on back
TYPE OF PRESSURE: pulsed with thumb, pinching motion
AMOUNT OF PRESSURE: as much as patient can take

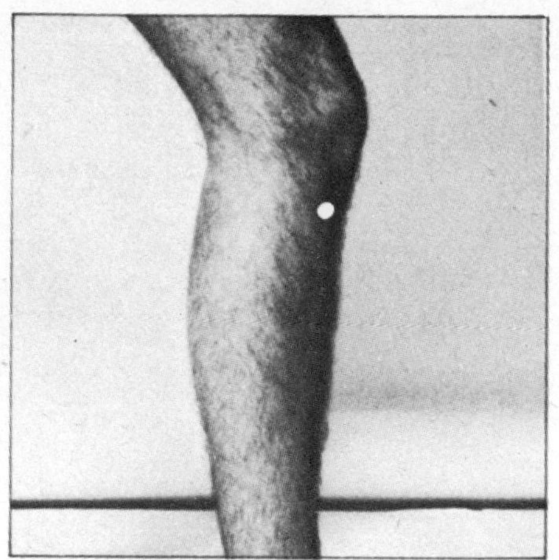

POINT: Walking Three Miles
LANDMARK: kneecap
DISTANCE FROM LANDMARK: 3 acu-inches below (in the depression)
LOCATION: 1 acu-inch toward the outside of the leg (treat both legs)
POSITION: seated in chair or flat on back
TYPE OF PRESSURE: pulsed with thumb (or pinching motion)
AMOUNT OF PRESSURE: quite firm

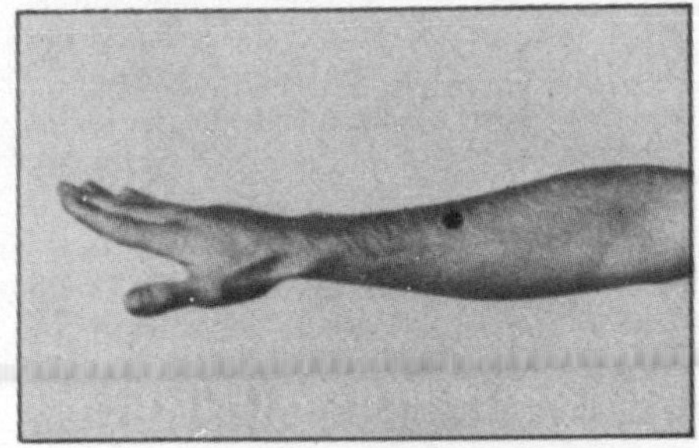

POINT: Supreme Cave
LANDMARK: inner elbow fold
DISTANCE FROM LANDMARK: 5 acu-inches down
LOCATION: on the inside surface of the forearm, 1 acu-inch in from the outer edge (treat both arms)
POSITION: seated or flat on back
TYPE OF PRESSURE: pulsed with thumb, pinching motion
AMOUNT OF PRESSURE: as much as patient can take

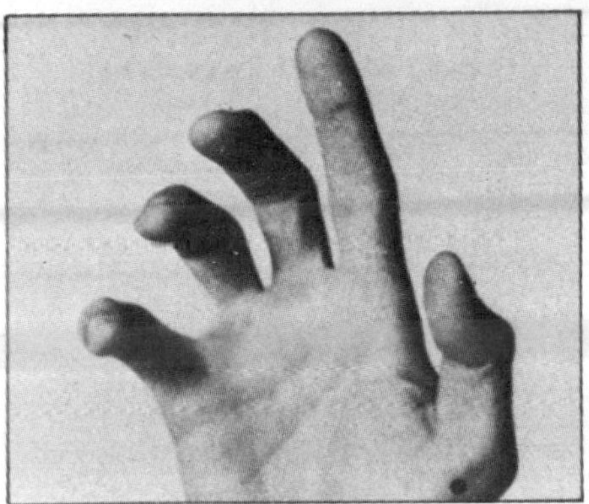

POINT: Fish Seam
LANDMARK: thumb fold in palm of hand
DISTANCE FROM LANDMARK: 1 acu-inch above thumb crease
LOCATION: on the palm side of the hand; apply pressure right on top of the thumb bone (treat both hands)
POSITION: seated
TYPE OF PRESSURE: pulsed with thumb, pinching movement
AMOUNT OF PRESSURE: as much as patient can take

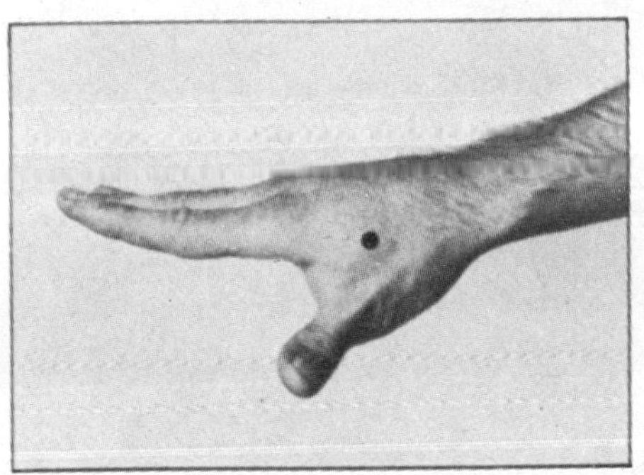

POINT: Connecting the Valleys
LANDMARK: back of hand
DISTANCE FROM LANDMARK: 1 acu-inch down from the point where bones of thumb and index finger meet
LOCATION: on the back of the hand (treat both hands)
POSITION: seated
TYPE OF PRESSURE: pulsed with thumb, pinching motion
AMOUNT OF PRESSURE: as much as patient can take

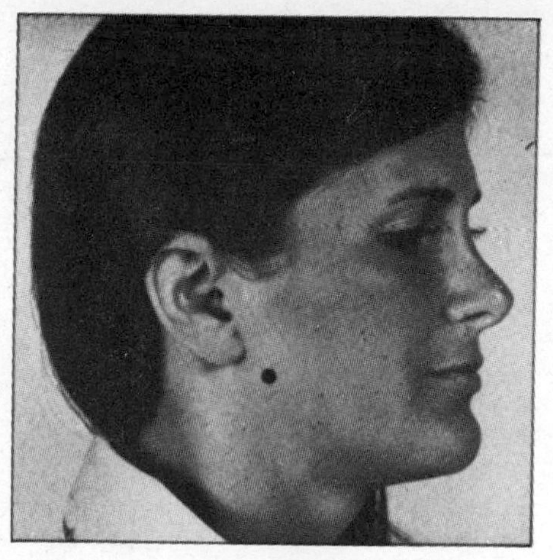

POINT: Celestial Acceptance
LANDMARK: lower jawbone angle
DISTANCE FROM LANDMARK: right on landmark
LOCATION: feel the sharp angle of the jawbone at the back of the cheek; the point is in the muscle of the neck just in the back of the angle (treat both sides of jaw)
POSITION: seated or flat on back
TYPE OF PRESSURE: pulsed with thumb or fingers
AMOUNT OF PRESSURE: gently, then as much as patient can tolerate

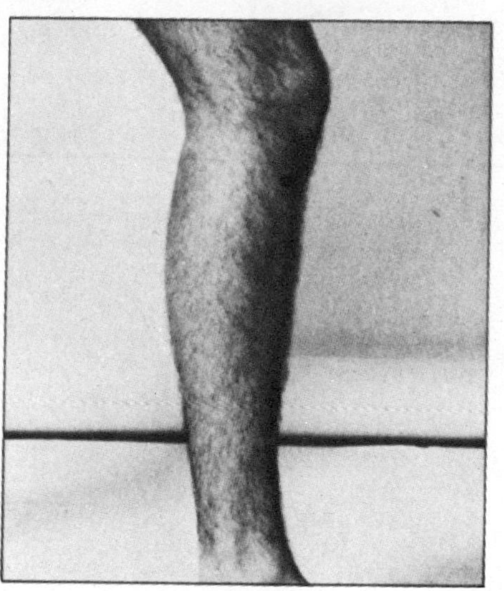

POINT: Walking Three Miles
LANDMARK: kneecap
DISTANCE FROM LANDMARK: 3 acu-inches below (in the depression)
LOCATION: 1 acu-inch toward the outside of the leg (treat both legs)
POSITION: seated in chair or flat on back
TYPE OF PRESSURE: pulsed with thumb (or pinching motion)
AMOUNT OF PRESSURE: quite firm

TOOTHACHE

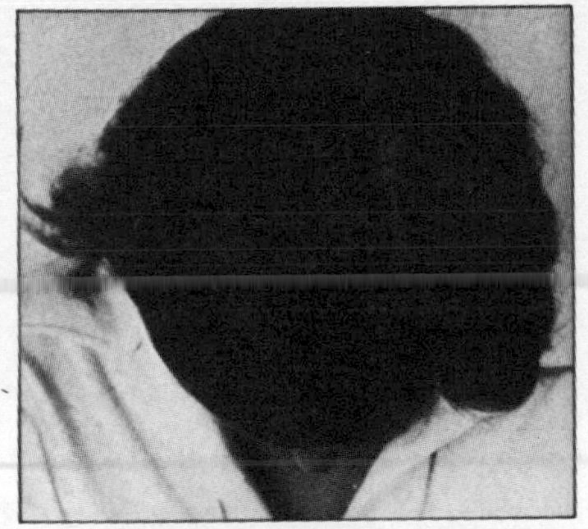

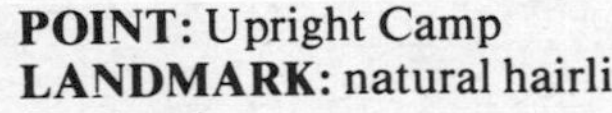

POINT: Upright Camp
LANDMARK: natural hairline at forehead
DISTANCE FROM LANDMARK: 7 acu-inches above natural hairline
LOCATION: on top of head, 1 acu-inch on either side of the front-to back center line of the head (treat both sides)
POSITION: seated or flat on back
TYPE OF PRESSURE: pulsed with thumb
AMOUNT OF PRESSURE: as much as patient can tolerate

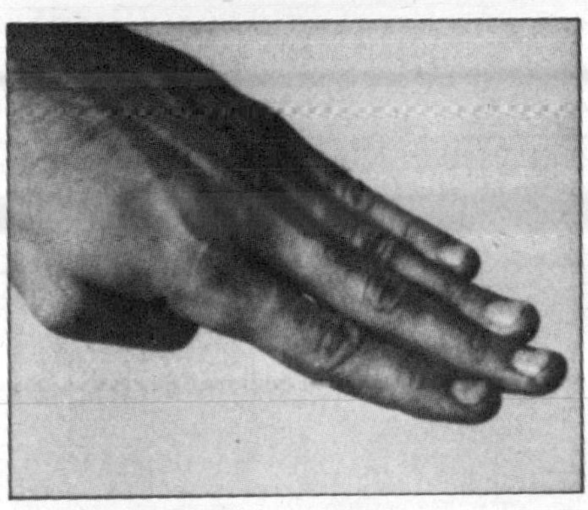

POINT: Three Intervals
LANDMARK: knuckle of index finger
DISTANCE FROM LANDMARK: immediately in front
LOCATION: on the thumb-side edge of the index finger (treat both hands)
POSITION: seated
TYPE OF PRESSURE: pulsed with thumb, pinching motion
AMOUNT OF PRESSURE: as much as patient can take

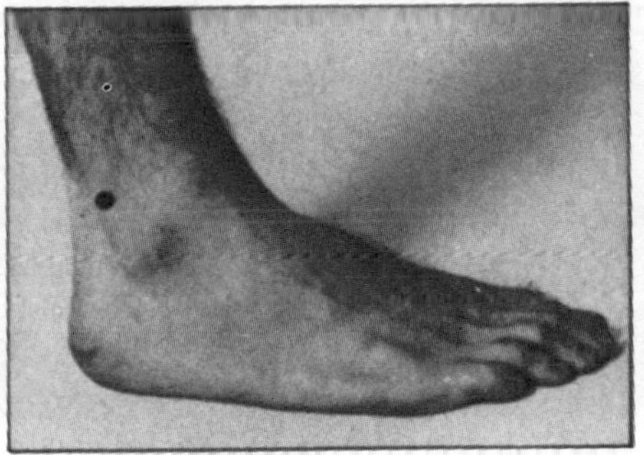

POINT: K'un Lun Mountains
LANDMARK: outer ankle bone
DISTANCE FROM LANDMARK: just in back
LOCATION: in the depression behind outer ankle bone (treat both feet)
POSITION: flat on back
TYPE OF PRESSURE: pulsed with thumb, pinching motion
AMOUNT OF PRESSURE: as much as patient can take

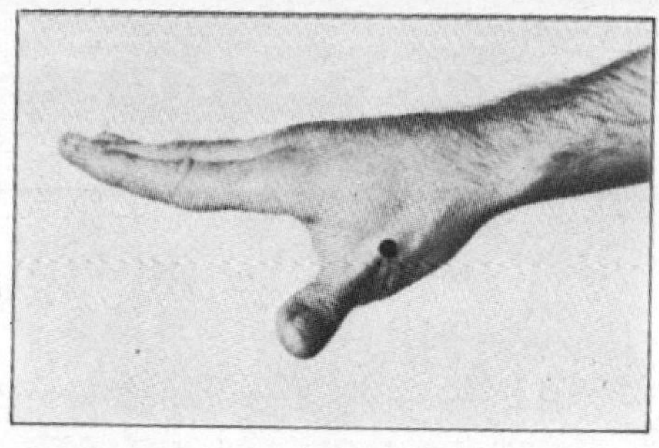

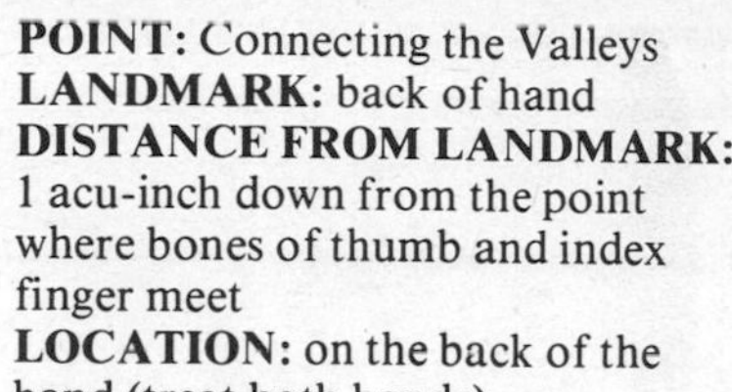

POINT: Connecting the Valleys
LANDMARK: back of hand
DISTANCE FROM LANDMARK: 1 acu-inch down from the point where bones of thumb and index finger meet
LOCATION: on the back of the hand (treat both hands)
POSITION: seated
TYPE OF PRESSURE: pulsed with thumb, pinching motion
AMOUNT OF PRESSURE: as much as patient can take

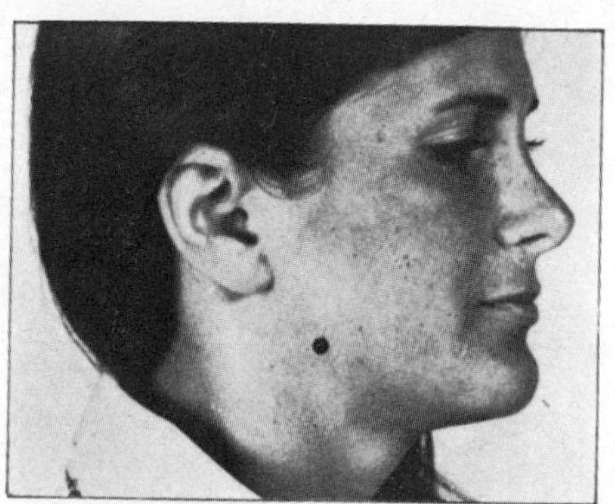

POINT: Cheek Chariot
LANDMARK: lower jawbone angle
DISTANCE FROM LANDMARK: about ½ acu-inch forward
LOCATION: feel lower jawline and locate a depression at the point (treat both sides of face)
POSITION: seated
TYPE OF PRESSURE: pulsed with fingers
AMOUNT OF PRESSURE: as much as patient can take

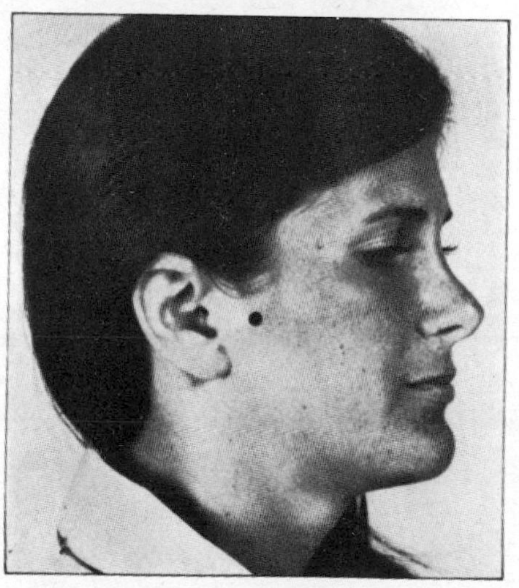

POINT: Lower Pass
LANDMARK: upper jawbone and ear
DISTANCE FROM LANDMARK: just under jawbone and in front of ear
LOCATION: on the cheek; feel for the horizontal jawbone and then feel for the hollow under it, just in front of the ear (treat both sides)
POSITION: seated or flat on back
TYPE OF PRESSURE: pulsed with thumb or fingers
AMOUNT OF PRESSURE: gently at first, then as much as can be tolerated

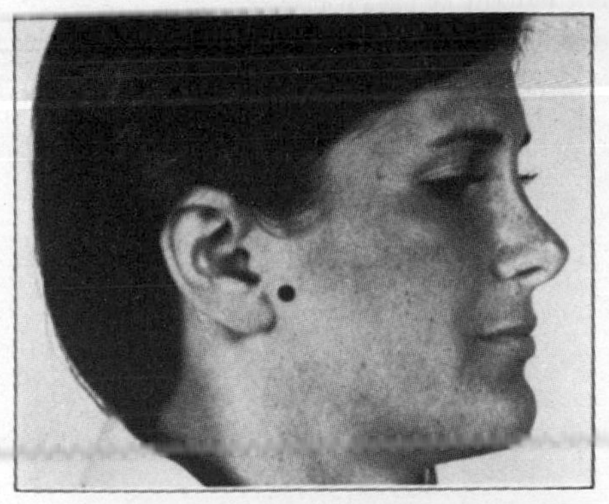

POINT: Listening Conference
LANDMARK: ear
DISTANCE FROM LANDMARK: directly in front
LOCATION: in the hollow in front of the ear that is formed when the mouth is opened wide (treat both sides of face)
POSITION: seated or flat on back
TYPE OF PRESSURE: pulsed with thumb or fingers
AMOUNT OF PRESSURE: as much as patient can tolerate

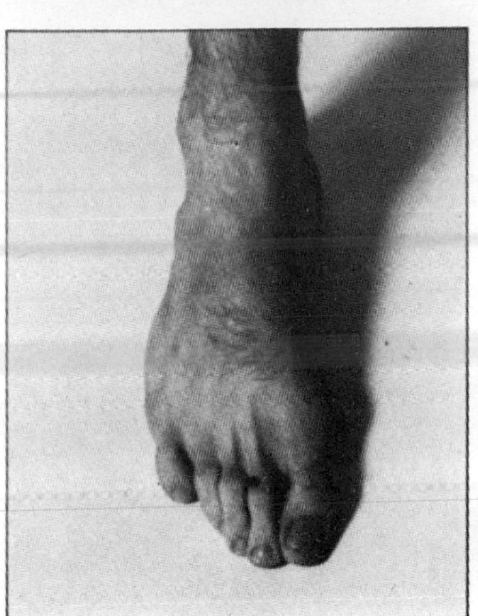

POINT: Inner Court
LANDMARK: toe knuckles
DISTANCE FROM LANDMARK: just behind (toward ankle)
LOCATION: in the web of skin between the 2nd and 3rd toes (treat both feet)
POSITION: seated or flat on back
TYPE OF PRESSURE: pulsed with thumb, pinching motion
AMOUNT OF PRESSURE: as much as can be tolerated; repeat as needed

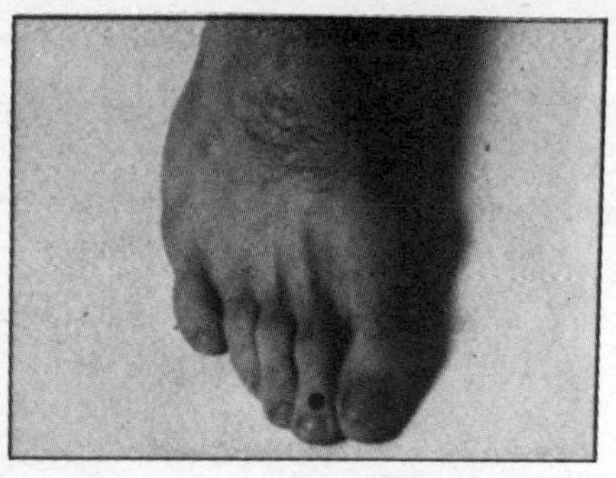

POINT: Strict Exchange
LANDMARK: toenail of the second toe
DISTANCE FROM LANDMARK: right on landmark
LOCATION: at the intersection of a line drawn along the little-toe side of the nail and a horizontal line across the top of the nail (treat both feet)
POSITION: flat on back
TYPE OF PRESSURE: pulsed with thumb, pinching motion
AMOUNT OF PRESSURE: as much as patient can take

WHIPLASH

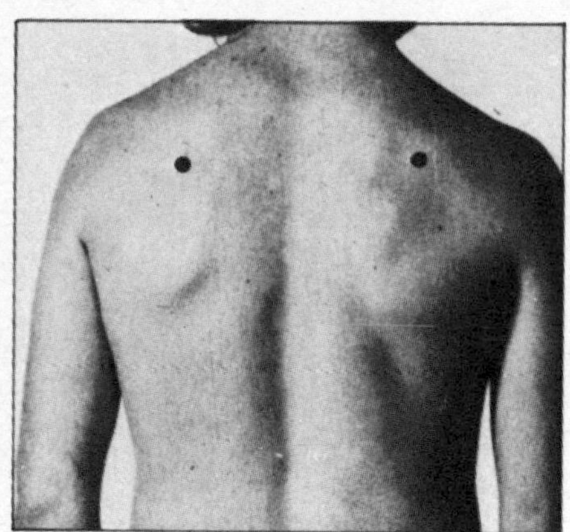

POINT: Support
LANDMARK: spine knob at neck
DISTANCE FROM LANDMARK: 2nd spine knob (vertebra) down
LOCATION: 3 acu-inches on either side of spine (treat both sides)
POSITION: face down
TYPE OF PRESSURE: pulsed with thumb; repeat as needed
AMOUNT OF PRESSURE: gently at first, increasing to maximum tolerance

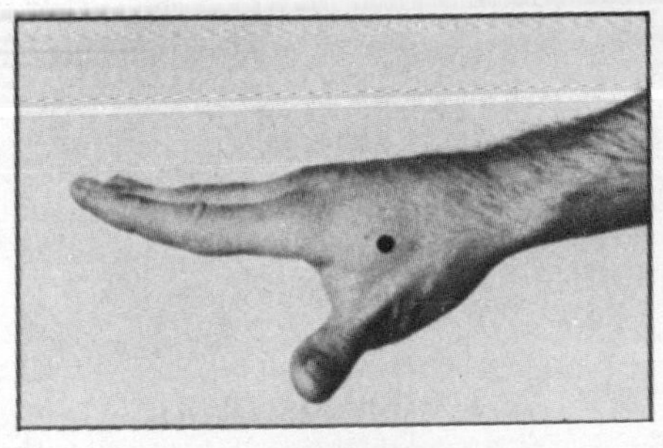

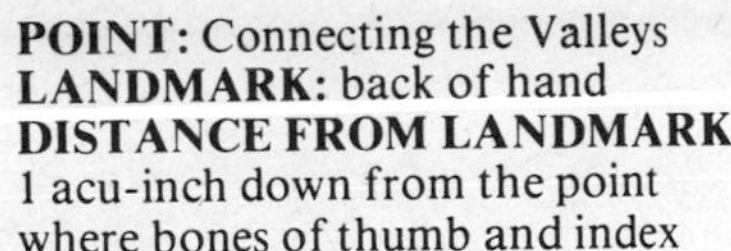

POINT: Connecting the Valleys
LANDMARK: back of hand
DISTANCE FROM LANDMARK: 1 acu-inch down from the point where bones of thumb and index finger meet
LOCATION: on the back of the hand (treat both hands)
POSITION: seated
TYPE OF PRESSURE: pulsed with thumb, pinching motion
AMOUNT OF PRESSURE: as much as patient can take

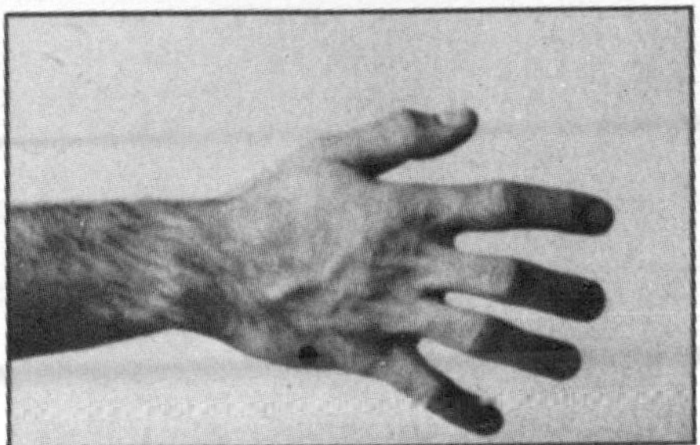

POINT: Back Stream
LANDMARK: knuckle of little finger
DISTANCE FROM LANDMARK: immediately above (toward the wrist)
LOCATION: on the side of the hand, just above little finger knuckle (treat both hands)
POSITION: seated
TYPE OF PRESSURE: pulsed with thumb, pinching motion
AMOUNT OF PRESSURE: as much as patient can take

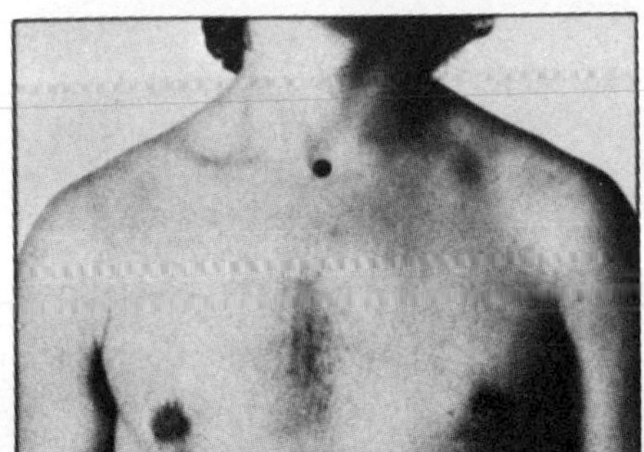

POINT: Sky Prominence
LANDMARK: throat notch
DISTANCE FROM LANDMARK: right on the spot
LOCATION: on throat, just above uppermost chest bone
POSITION: flat on back
TYPE OF PRESSURE: insert finger pressing inward and downward
AMOUNT OF PRESSURE: gently at first, then increased force with pulsed pressure to the extent that patient can take

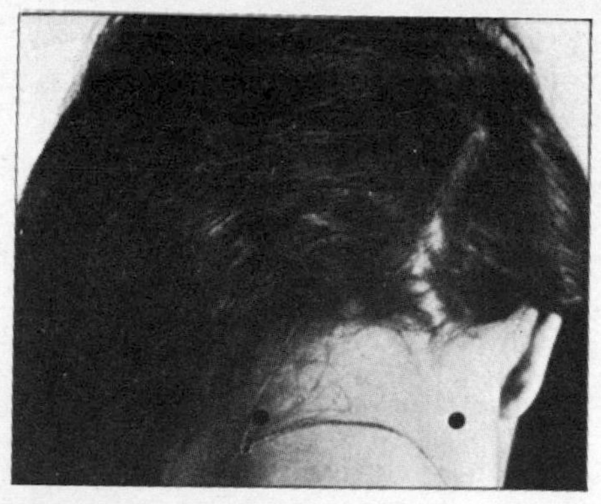

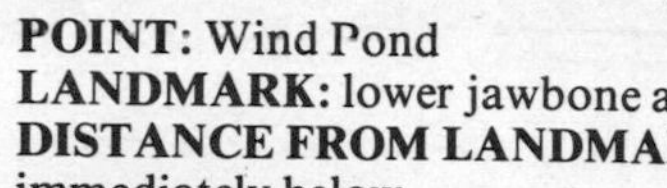

POINT: Wind Pond
LANDMARK: lower jawbone angle
DISTANCE FROM LANDMARK: immediately below
LOCATION: feel for a depression or groove on each side just below the landmark (treat both sides)
POSITION: seated or face down
TYPE OF PRESSURE: pulsed with thumbs or fingers
AMOUNT OF PRESSURE: as much as patient can take
NOTE: if patient is sitting up, stand in front of him and rest his head against your chest; exert pressure with your fingers

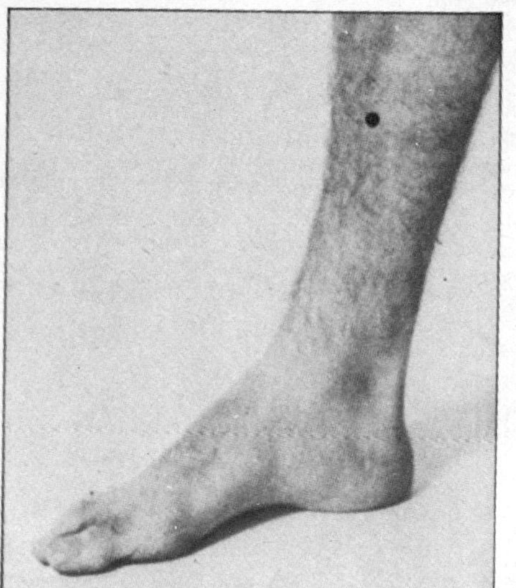

POINT: Insect Gutter
LANDMARK: inner ankle bone
DISTANCE FROM LANDMARK: 5 acu-inches above
LOCATION: on the inner surface of the leg just behind the edge of the shin bone (treat both legs)
POSITION: flat on back or seated
TYPE OF PRESSURE: pulsed with thumb, pinching motion
AMOUNT OF PRESSURE: as much as patient can take

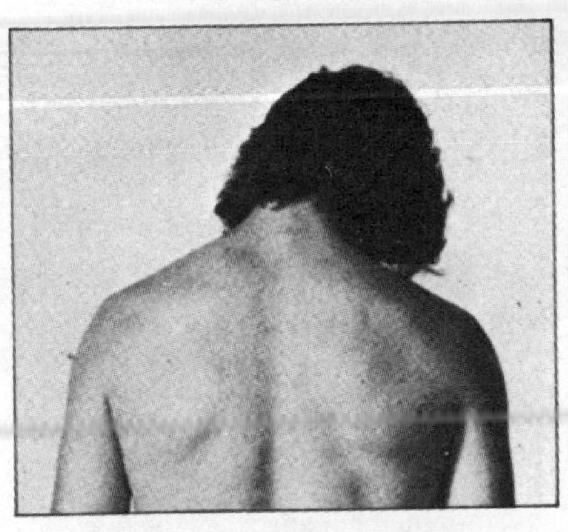

POINT: Celestial Pillar
LANDMARK: natural hairline at the back of neck
DISTANCE FROM LANDMARK: right on landmark
LOCATION: right on the hairline and 1 acu-inch on either side of the front-to-back center line of the head (treat both sides)
POSITION: seated or flat on back
TYPE OF PRESSURE: pulsed with thumb
AMOUNT OF PRESSURE: gently, then gradually increasing to maximum that patient can tolerate

WRITER'S CRAMP

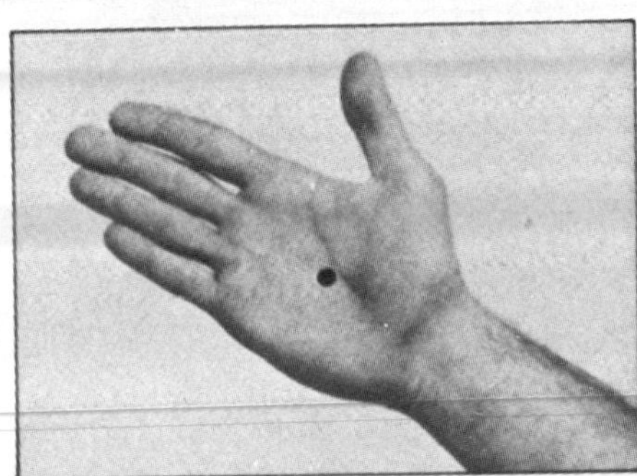

POINT: Labored Palace
LANDMARK: hand
DISTANCE FROM LANDMARK: close to the landmark
LOCATION: clench fist and mark the point where the tip of the middle finger meets the palm (treat both hands)
POSITION: seated
TYPE OF PRESSURE: pulsed with thumb, pinching motion
AMOUNT OF PRESSURE: as much as patient can take

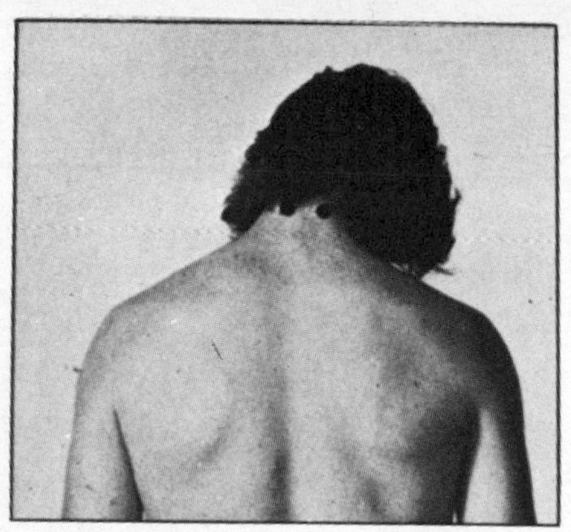

POINT: Celestial Pillar
LANDMARK: natural hairline at the back of neck
DISTANCE FROM LANDMARK: right on landmark
LOCATION: right on the hairline and 1 acu-inch on either side of the front-to-back center line of the head (treat both sides)
POSITION: seated or flat on back
TYPE OF PRESSURE: pulsed with thumb
AMOUNT OF PRESSURE: gently, then gradually increasing to maximum that patient can tolerate

SEVEN
FIRST-AID ACUPRESSURE

One of the most valuable and immediate benefits of acupressure is in first-aid treatment. There are three main types of first-aid situations with which you will deal:

1. while awaiting professional medical attention
2. in treating minor discomforts that do not require a doctor's care
3. in handling good Samaritan situations

The first group includes pain-relief techniques to make the patient more comfortable until a doctor arrives. Bear in mind that in all cases of injury there is no substitute for professional medical care; in these cases acupressure therapy begins *after* you have sent for a doctor, and a preliminary diagnosis has been made. The second group comprises such conditions as insect bites and sunburn. Again, always keep in mind that any unusual or severe reaction requires immediate medical attention. A typical example of the third case would be at some remote location—in the mountains, on a beach—where there is no means of communication to summon professional help. In this instance your knowledge of acupressure may actually save someone's life.

With acupressure, you need never feel like a helpless bystander—you can always achieve some on-the-spot results that can bring relief and comfort.

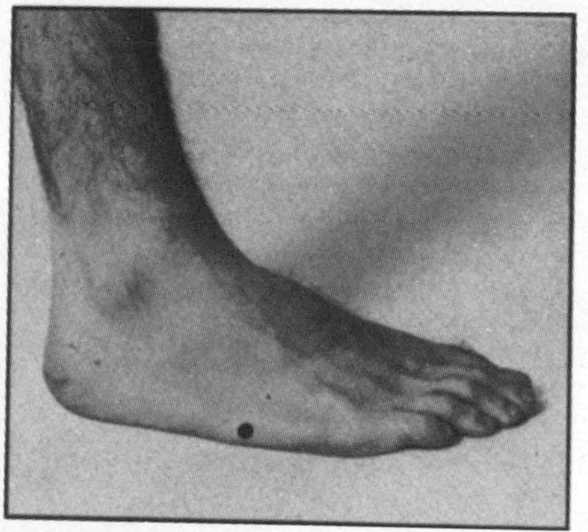

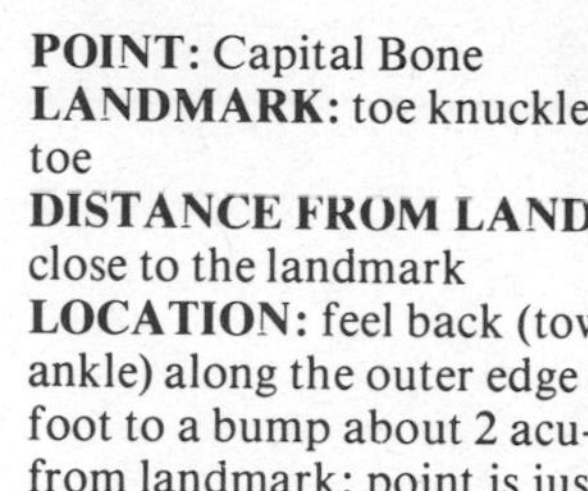

POINT: Capital Bone
LANDMARK: toe knuckle of little toe
DISTANCE FROM LANDMARK: close to the landmark
LOCATION: feel back (toward the ankle) along the outer edge of the foot to a bump about 2 acu-inches from landmark; point is just in back of and under this bump (treat both feet)
POSITION: seated or flat on back
TYPE OF PRESSURE: pulsed with thumb
AMOUNT OF PRESSURE: as much as patient can take

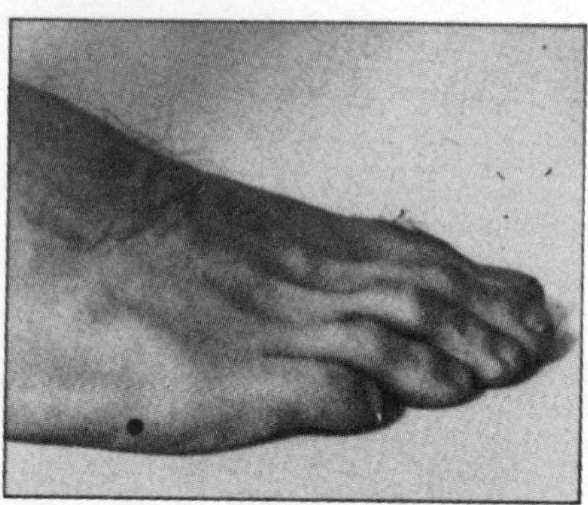

POINT: Restrict Bone
LANDMARK: toe knuckle of little toe
DISTANCE FROM LANDMARK: close to the landmark
LOCATION: on the outer edge of the foot, just behind toe knuckle (treat both feet)
POSITION: seated or flat on back
TYPE OF PRESSURE: pulsed with thumb
AMOUNT OF PRESSURE: as much as patient can take; repeat as needed

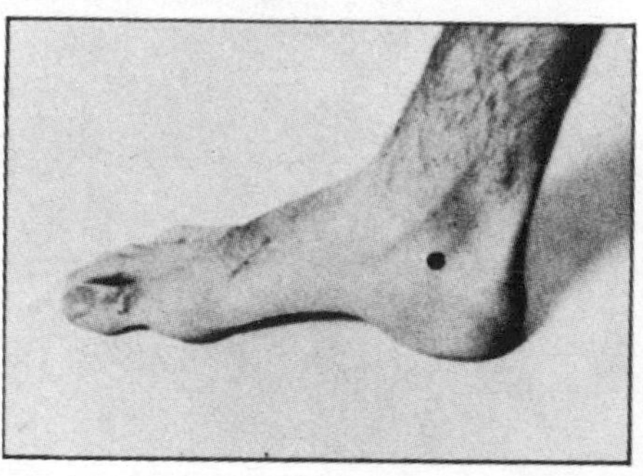

POINT: Shine To Sea
LANDMARK: inner ankle bone
DISTANCE FROM LANDMARK: immediately below
LOCATION: hollow space just below (treat both legs)
POSITION: seated or flat on back
TYPE OF PRESSURE: pulsed with thumb, pinching motion
AMOUNT OF PRESSURE: as much as patient can take

BRUISES

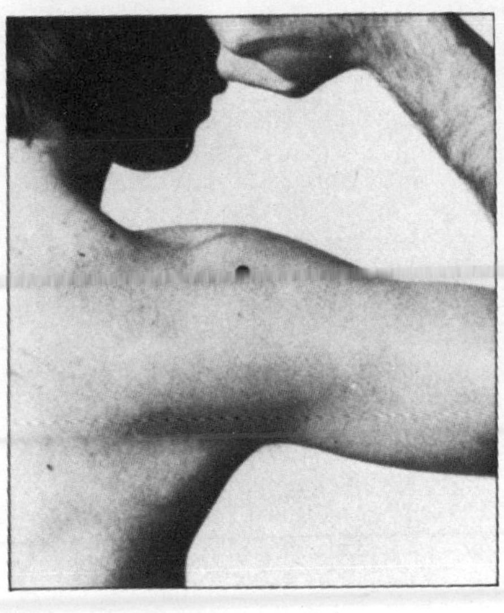

POINT: Shoulder Bone II
LANDMARK: extreme edge of shoulder
DISTANCE FROM LANDMARK: right at the landmark
LOCATION: on the back surface of the shoulder, about 1 acu-inch back from the highest point in the hollow formed when the arm is raised (treat both arms)
POSITION: seated
TYPE OF PRESSURE: pulsed with thumb, pinching motion
AMOUNT OF PRESSURE: gently, then as much as patient can take

BURNS AND SCALDS

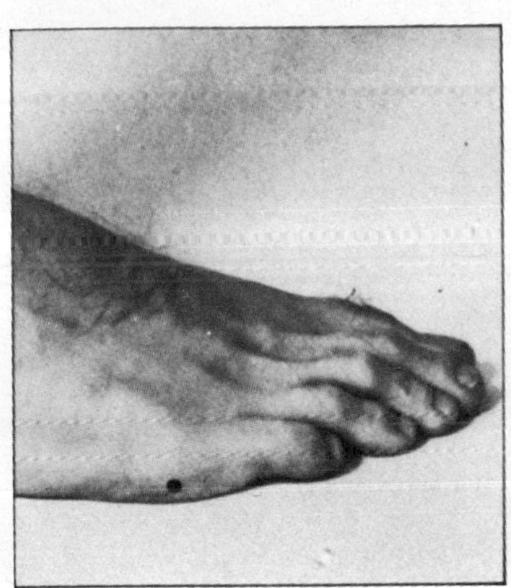

POINT: Restrict Bone
LANDMARK: toe knuckle of little toe
DISTANCE FROM LANDMARK: close to the landmark
LOCATION: on the outer edge of the foot, just behind toe knuckle (treat both feet)
POSITION: seated or flat on back
TYPE OF PRESSURE: pulsed with thumb
AMOUNT OF PRESSURE: as much as patient can take; repeat as needed

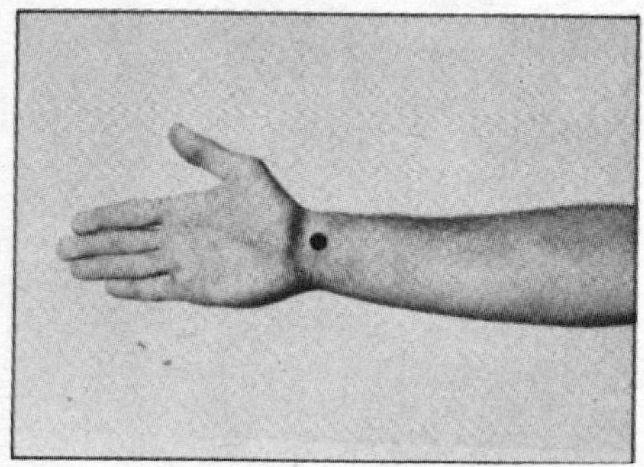

POINT: Great Gulf
LANDMARK: inner wrist fold
DISTANCE FROM LANDMARK: right on landmark
LOCATION: on the thumb-side edge, right where the pulse is taken (treat both hands)
POSITION: seated or flat on back
TYPE OF PRESSURE: pulsed with thumb, pinching motion
AMOUNT OF PRESSURE: as much as patient can take

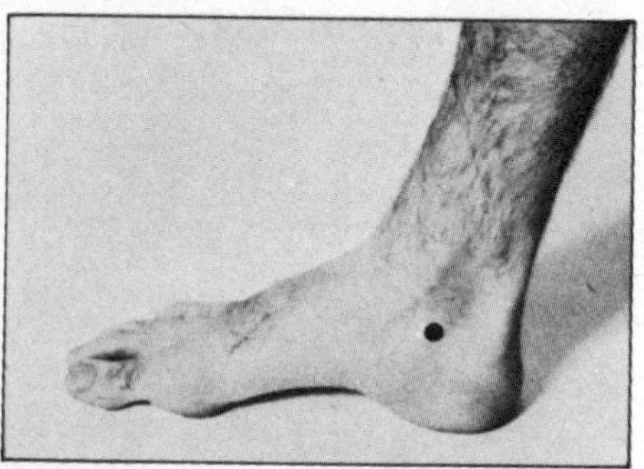

POINT: Shine To Sea
LANDMARK: inner ankle bone
DISTANCE FROM LANDMARK: immediately below
LOCATION: hollow space just below (treat both legs)
POSITION: seated or flat on back
TYPE OF PRESSURE: pulsed with thumb, pinching motion
AMOUNT OF PRESSURE: as much as patient can take

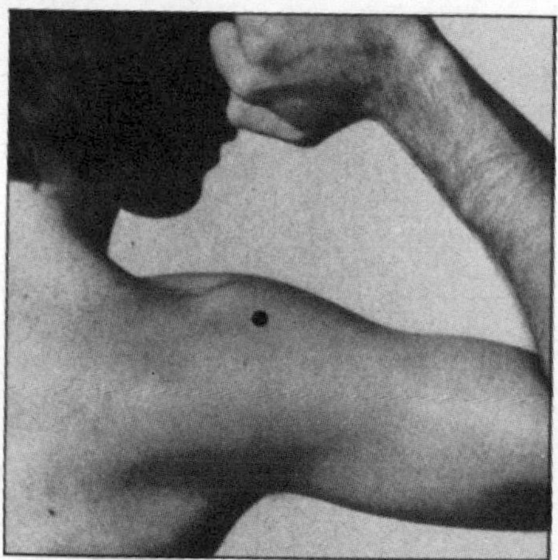

POINT: Shoulder Bone II
LANDMARK: extreme edge of shoulder
DISTANCE FROM LANDMARK: right at the landmark
LOCATION: on the back surface of the shoulder, about 1 acu-inch back from the highest point in the hollow formed when the arm is raised (treat both arms)
POSITION: seated
TYPE OF PRESSURE: pulsed with thumb, pinching motion
AMOUNT OF PRESSURE: gently, then as much as patient can take

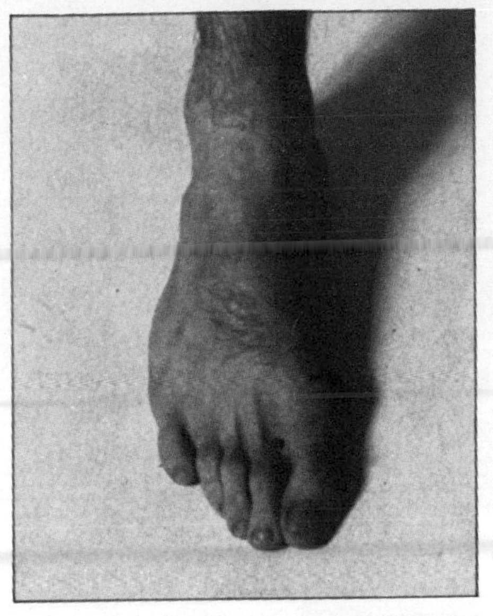

POINT: Between Columns
LANDMARK: toe knuckles
DISTANCE FROM LANDMARK: 1½ acu-inch forward (toward toes)
LOCATION: in the web of skin between the big toe and the second toe (treat both feet)
POSITION: flat on back or seated
TYPE OF PRESSURE: pulsed with thumb, pinching motion
AMOUNT OF PRESSURE: as much as patient can take

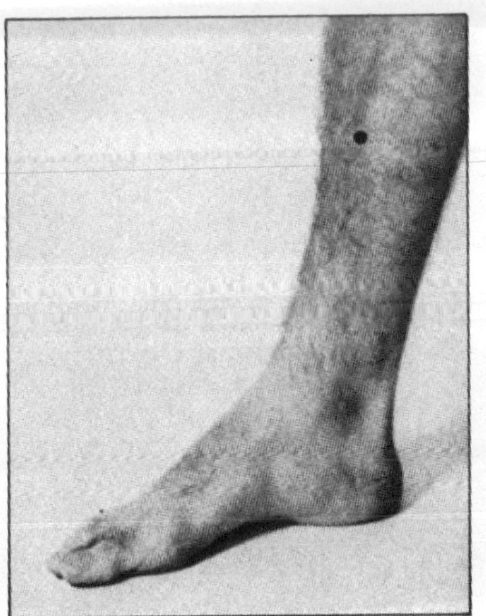

POINT: Insect Gutter
LANDMARK: inner ankle bone
DISTANCE FROM LANDMARK: 5 acu-inches above
LOCATION: on the inner surface of the leg just behind the edge of the shin bone (treat both legs)
POSITION: flat on back or seated
TYPE OF PRESSURE: pulsed with thumb, pinching motion
AMOUNT OF PRESSURE: as much as patient can take

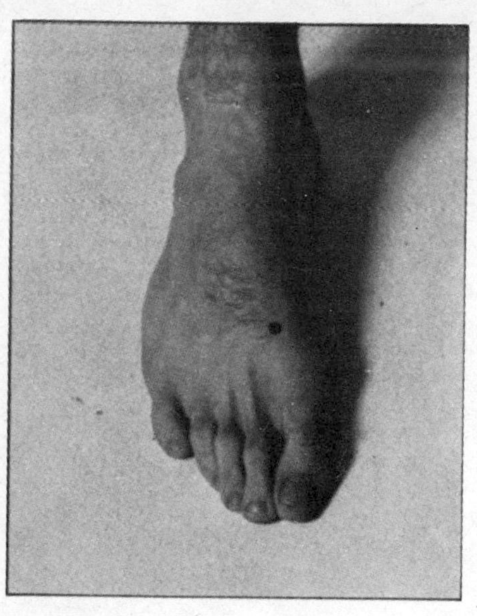

POINT: Great Flush
LANDMARK: toe knuckles
DISTANCE FROM LANDMARK: 1 acu-inch back (toward ankle)
LOCATION: on upper surface of foot between first and second toes (treat both feet)
POSITION: flat on back or seated
TYPE OF PRESSURE: pulsed with thumb, pinching motion
AMOUNT OF PRESSURE: as much as patient can take

EARACHE

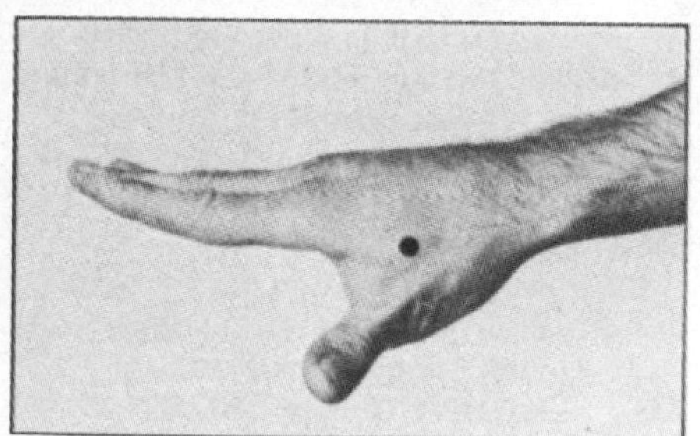

POINT: Connecting the Valleys
LANDMARK: back of hand
DISTANCE FROM LANDMARK: 1 acu-inch down from the point where bones of thumb and index finger meet
LOCATION: on the back of the hand (treat both hands)
POSITION: seated
TYPE OF PRESSURE: pulsed with thumb, pinching motion
AMOUNT OF PRESSURE: as much as patient can take

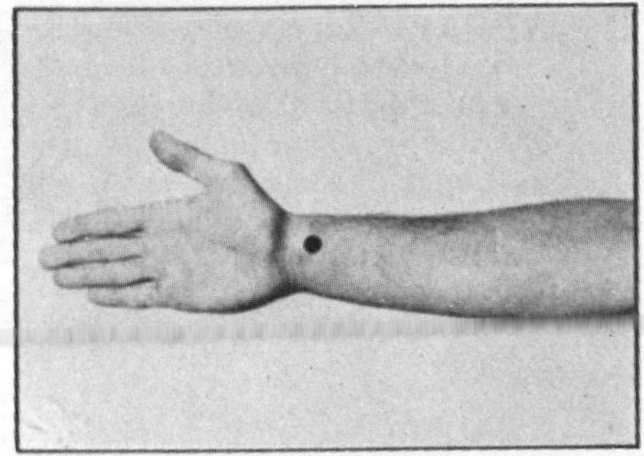

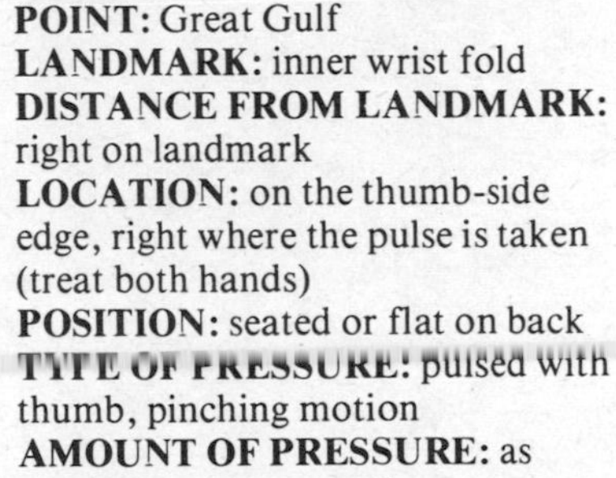

POINT: Great Gulf
LANDMARK: inner wrist fold
DISTANCE FROM LANDMARK: right on landmark
LOCATION: on the thumb-side edge, right where the pulse is taken (treat both hands)
POSITION: seated or flat on back
TYPE OF PRESSURE: pulsed with thumb, pinching motion
AMOUNT OF PRESSURE: as much as patient can take

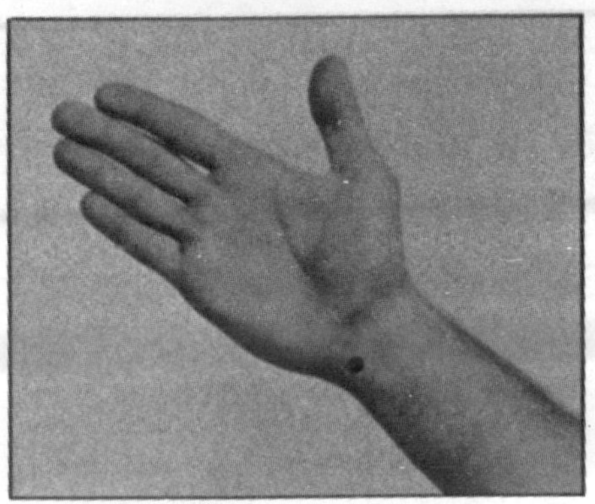

POINT: God's Door
LANDMARK: inner wrist fold
DISTANCE FROM LANDMARK: right on the fold
LOCATION: 1 acu-inch in from outer edge (side with little finger) of arm, on the inner surface of the forearm (treat both arms)
POSITION: seated
TYPE OF PRESSURE: pulsed with thumb
AMOUNT OF PRESSURE: as much as patient can take

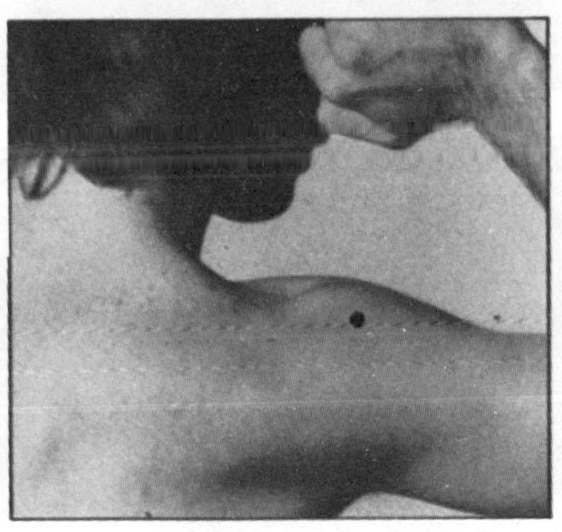

POINT: Shoulder Bone II
LANDMARK: extreme edge of shoulder
DISTANCE FROM LANDMARK: right at the landmark
LOCATION: on the back surface of the shoulder, about 1 acu-inch back from the highest point in the hollow formed when the arm is raised (treat both arms)
POSITION: seated
TYPE OF PRESSURE: pulsed with thumb, pinching motion
AMOUNT OF PRESSURE: gently, then as much as patient can take

POINT: Simple Bone
LANDMARK: nose
DISTANCE FROM LANDMARK: right on landmark
LOCATION: the tip of the nose
POSITION: sitting or flat on back
TYPE OF PRESSURE: pinch the tip of the nose with thumbnail pressure; alternate pulsed and steady pressure
AMOUNT OF PRESSURE: as much as patient can take

POINT: Middle of Man
LANDMARK: nose
DISTANCE FROM LANDMARK: just under landmark
LOCATION: directly under the center of the nose, on the upper lip
POSITION: flat on back
TYPE OF PRESSURE: alternating pulsed and steady pressure with thumb or fingers
AMOUNT OF PRESSURE: as much as patient can take

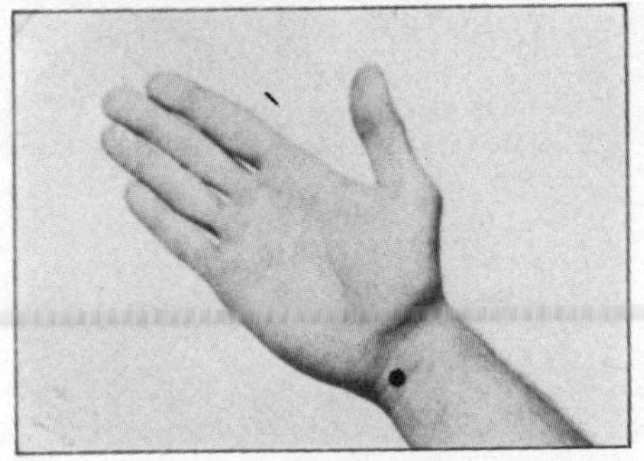

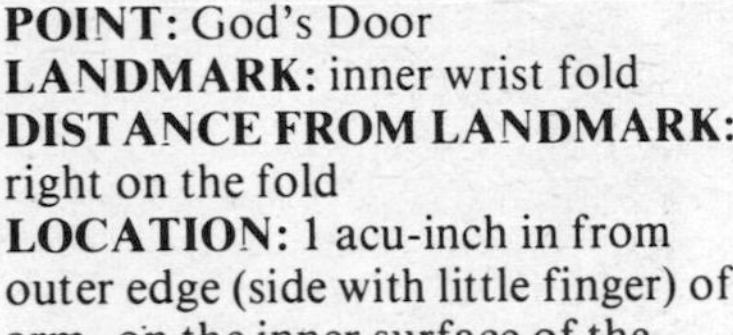

POINT: God's Door
LANDMARK: inner wrist fold
DISTANCE FROM LANDMARK: right on the fold
LOCATION: 1 acu-inch in from outer edge (side with little finger) of arm, on the inner surface of the forearm (treat both arms)
POSITION: seated
TYPE OF PRESSURE: pulsed with thumb
AMOUNT OF PRESSURE: as much as patient can take

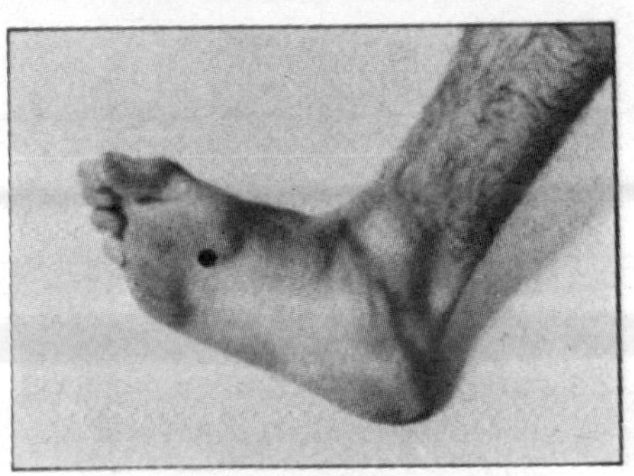

POINT: Pouring Spring
LANDMARK: bottom of foot
DISTANCE FROM LANDMARK: within landmark
LOCATION: on the bottom of the foot, in the depression just in back of the ball when the foot is raised (treat both feet)
POSITION: flat on back
TYPE OF PRESSURE: alternating pulsed and steady with thumb
AMOUNT OF PRESSURE: as much as patient can take

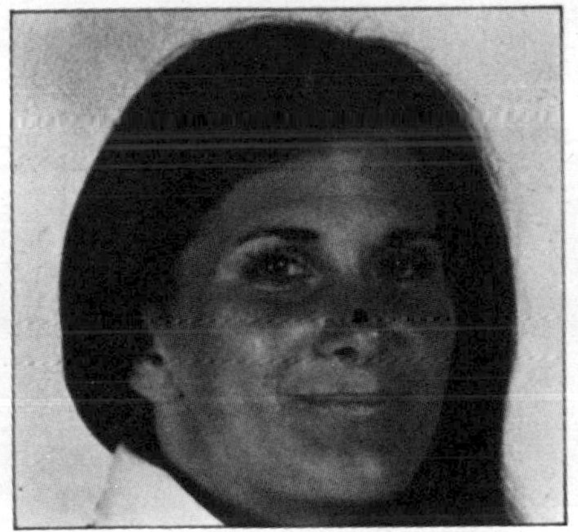

POINT: Simple Bone
LANDMARK: nose
DISTANCE FROM LANDMARK: right on landmark
LOCATION: the tip of the nose
POSITION: seated or flat on back
TYPE OF PRESSURE: pinch the tip of the nose with thumbnail pressure; alternate pulsed and steady pressure
AMOUNT OF PRESSURE: as much as patient can take

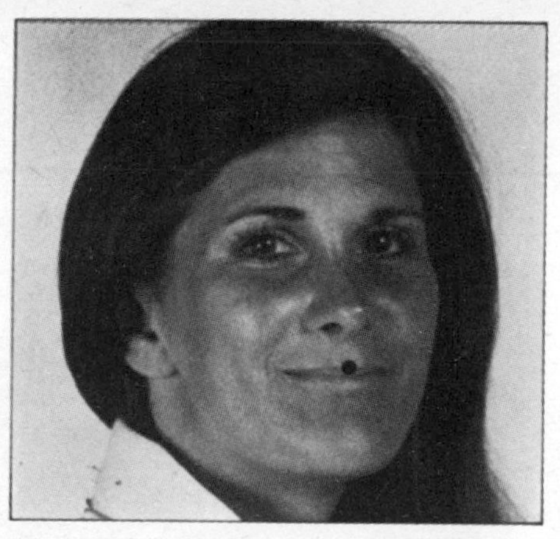

POINT: Middle of Man
LANDMARK: nose
DISTANCE FROM LANDMARK: just under landmark
LOCATION: directly under the center of the nose, on the upper lip
POSITION: flat on back
TYPE OF PRESSURE: alternating pulsed and steady pressure with thumb or fingers
AMOUNT OF PRESSURE: as much as patient can take

FROSTBITE

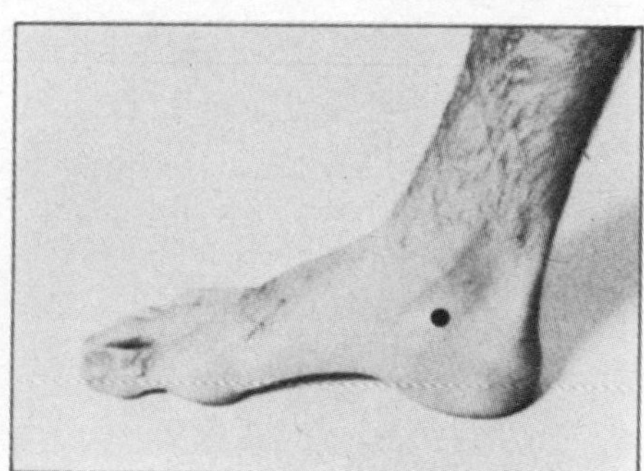

POINT: Shine To Sea
LANDMARK: inner ankle bone
DISTANCE FROM LANDMARK: immediately below
LOCATION: hollow space just below (treat both legs)
POSITION: seated or flat on back
TYPE OF PRESSURE: pulsed with thumb, pinching motion
AMOUNT OF PRESSURE: as much as patient can take

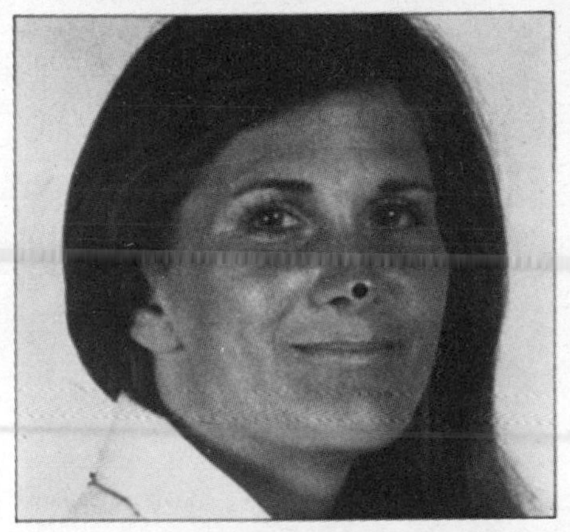

POINT: Simple Bone
LANDMARK: nose
DISTANCE FROM LANDMARK: right on landmark
LOCATION: the tip of the nose
POSITION: seated or flat on back
TYPE OF PRESSURE: pinch the tip of the nose with thumbnail pressure; alternate pulsed and steady pressure
AMOUNT OF PRESSURE: as much as patient can take

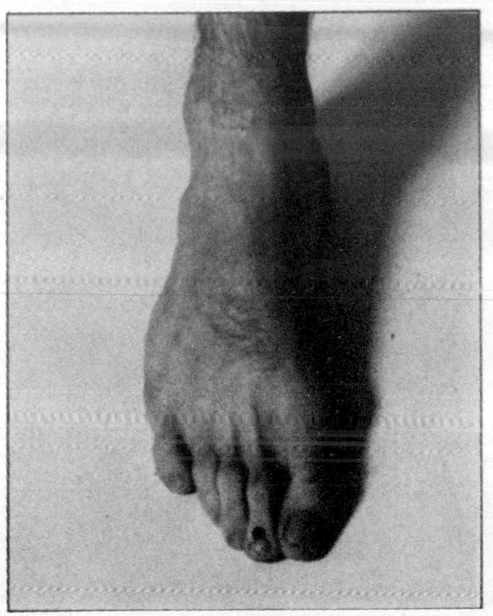

POINT: Strict Exchange
LANDMARK: toenail of the second toe
DISTANCE FROM LANDMARK: right on landmark
LOCATION: at the intersection of a line drawn along the little-toe side of the nail and a horizontal line across the top of the nail (treat both feet)
POSITION: flat on back
TYPE OF PRESSURE: pulsed with thumb, pinching motion
AMOUNT OF PRESSURE: as much as patient can take

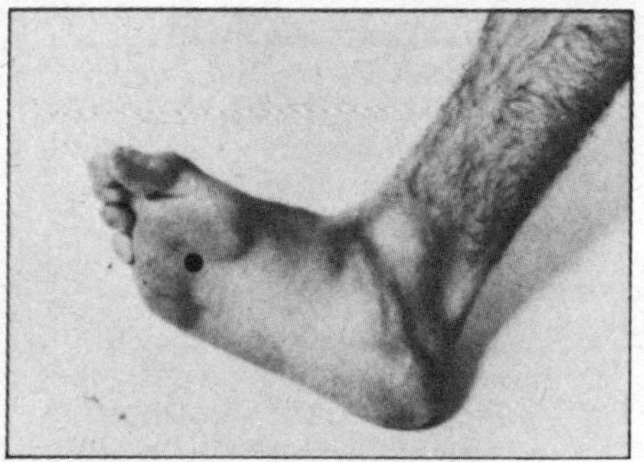

POINT: Pouring Spring
LANDMARK: bottom of foot
DISTANCE FROM LANDMARK: within landmark
LOCATION: on the bottom of the foot, in the depression just in back of the ball when the foot is raised (treat both feet)
POSITION: flat on back
TYPE OF PRESSURE: alternating pulsed and steady with thumb
AMOUNT OF PRESSURE: as much as patient can take

POINT: Middle of Man
LANDMARK: nose
DISTANCE FROM LANDMARK: just under landmark
LOCATION: directly under the center of the nose, on the upper lip
POSITION: flat on back
TYPE OF PRESSURE: alternating pulsed and steady pressure with thumb or fingers
AMOUNT OF PRESSURE: as much as patient can take

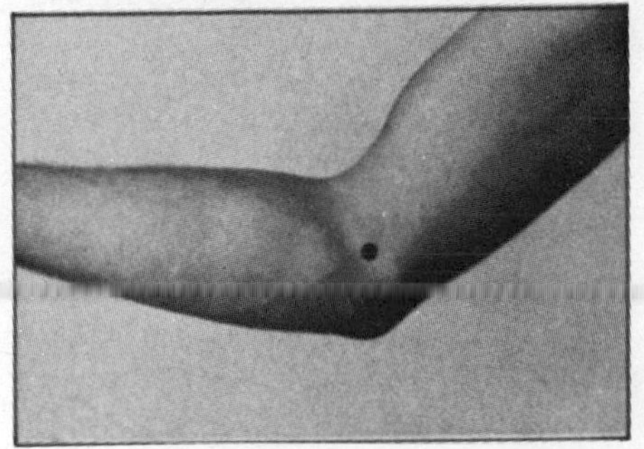

POINT: Crooked Pond
LANDMARK: inner elbow fold
DISTANCE FROM LANDMARK: right at the body-side edge of fold, when elbow is bent
LOCATION: elbow (treat both arms)
POSITION: seated or flat on back
TYPE OF PRESSURE: pulsed with thumb, pinching motion
AMOUNT OF PRESSURE: as much as patient can take

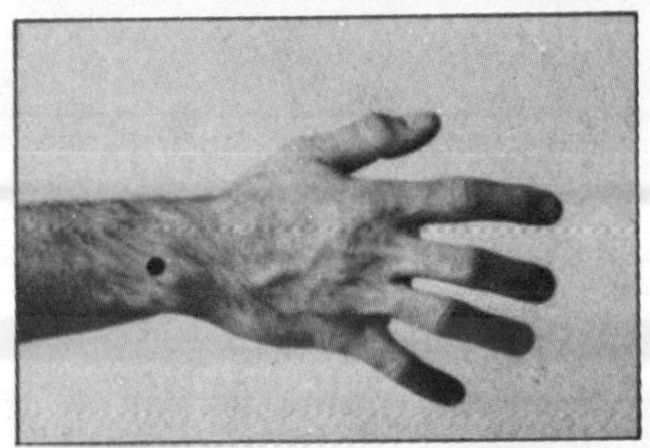

POINT: Outer Pass
LANDMARK: outer wrist fold
DISTANCE FROM LANDMARK: 2 acu-inches above
LOCATION: on back surface of wrist, in the center (treat both arms)
POSITION: seated or flat on back
TYPE OF PRESSURE: pulsed with thumb, pinching motion—repeat often
AMOUNT OF PRESSURE: as much as patient can take

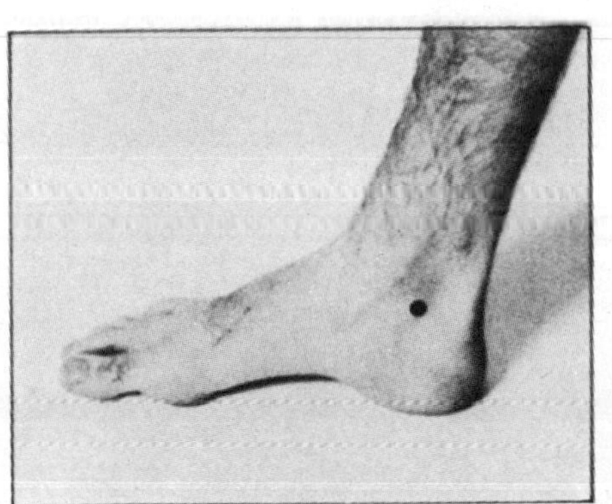

POINT: Shine To Sea
LANDMARK: inner ankle bone
DISTANCE FROM LANDMARK: immediately below
LOCATION: hollow space just below (treat both legs)
POSITION: seated or flat on back
TYPE OF PRESSURE: pulsed with thumb, pinching motion
AMOUNT OF PRESSURE: as much as patient can take

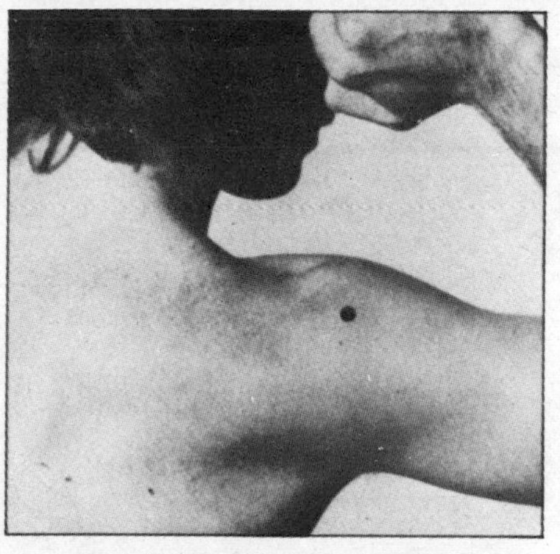

POINT: Shoulder Bone II
LANDMARK: extreme edge of shoulder
DISTANCE FROM LANDMARK: right at the landmark
LOCATION: on the back surface of the shoulder, about 1 acu-inch back from the highest point in the hollow formed when the arm is raised (treat both arms)
POSITION: seated
TYPE OF PRESSURE: pulsed with thumb, pinching motion
AMOUNT OF PRESSURE: gently, then as much as patient can take

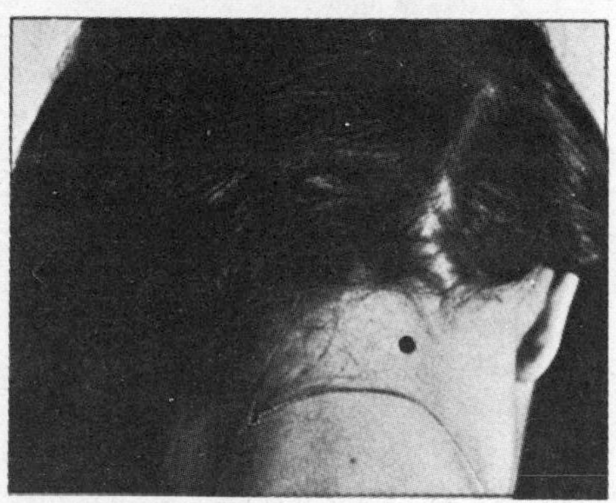

POINT: Celestial Pillar
LANDMARK: natural hairline at the back of neck
DISTANCE FROM LANDMARK: right on landmark
LOCATION: right on the hairline and 1 acu-inch on either side of the front-to-back center line of the head (treat both sides)
POSITION: seated or flat on back
TYPE OF PRESSURE: pulsed with thumb
AMOUNT OF PRESSURE: gently, then gradually increasing to maximum that patient can tolerate

INSECT BITES

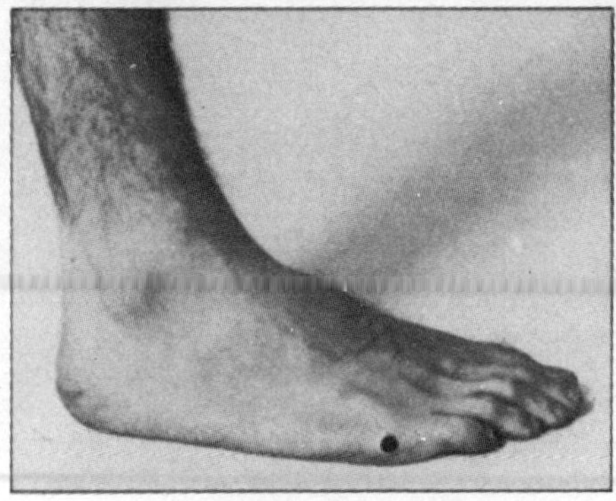

POINT: Restrict Bone
LANDMARK: toe knuckle of little toe
DISTANCE FROM LANDMARK: close to the landmark
LOCATION: on the outer edge of the foot, just behind toe knuckle (treat both feet)
POSITION: seated or flat on back
TYPE OF PRESSURE: pulsed with thumb
AMOUNT OF PRESSURE: as much as patient can take; repeat as needed

NOSEBLEED

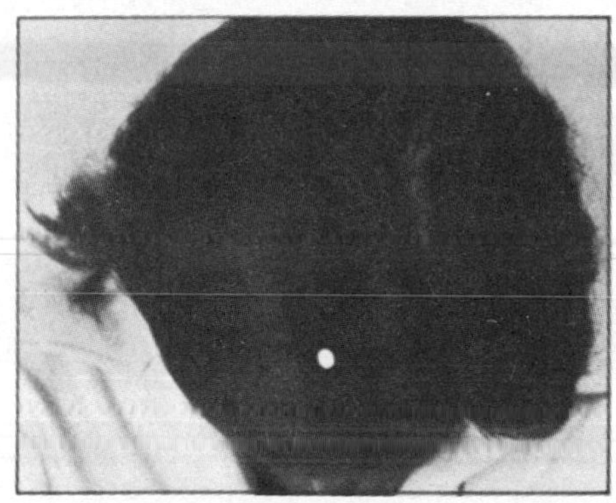

POINT: Fontanelle Meet
LANDMARK: natural hairline at forehead
DISTANCE FROM LANDMARK: 2 acu-inches above
LOCATION: at the center line of the head
POSITION: seated or flat on back
TYPE OF PRESSURE: pulsed with thumb
AMOUNT OF PRESSURE: as much as patient can take

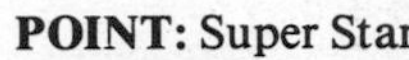

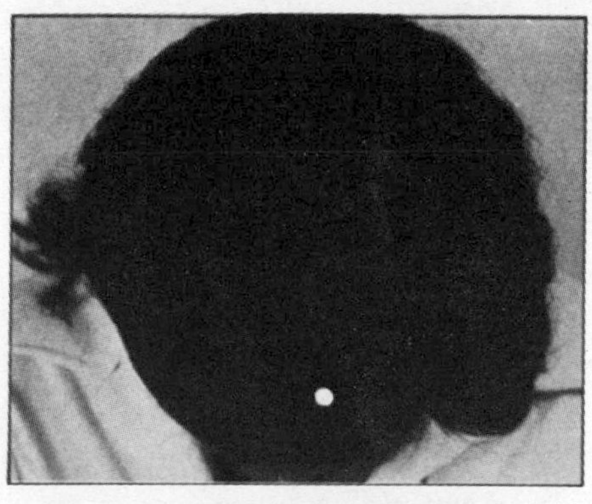

POINT: Super Star
LANDMARK: natural hairline at forehead
DISTANCE FROM LANDMARK: 1 acu-inch above
LOCATION: on the midline of the head
POSITION: seated or flat on back
TYPE OF PRESSURE: pulsed with thumb
AMOUNT OF PRESSURE: as much as patient can take

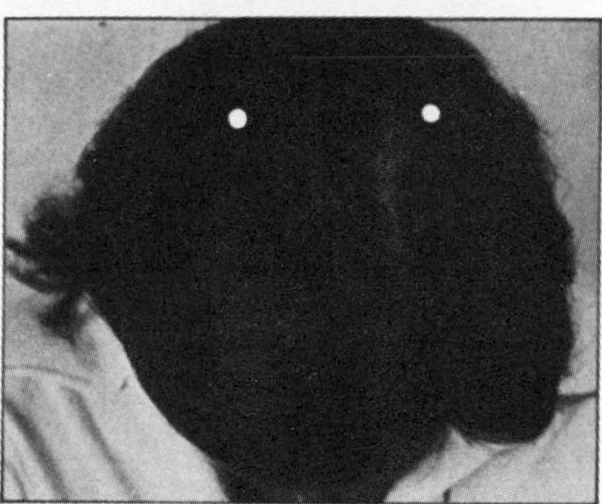

POINT: Discard Refute
LANDMARK: natural hairline at forehead
DISTANCE FROM LANDMARK: 5½ acu-inches above natural hairline
LOCATION: on top of the head near the back, and 1½ acu-inches on either side of front-to-back center line of head (treat both sides)
POSITION: seated
TYPE OF PRESSURE: pulsed with thumb or fingers
AMOUNT OF PRESSURE: as much as patient can take

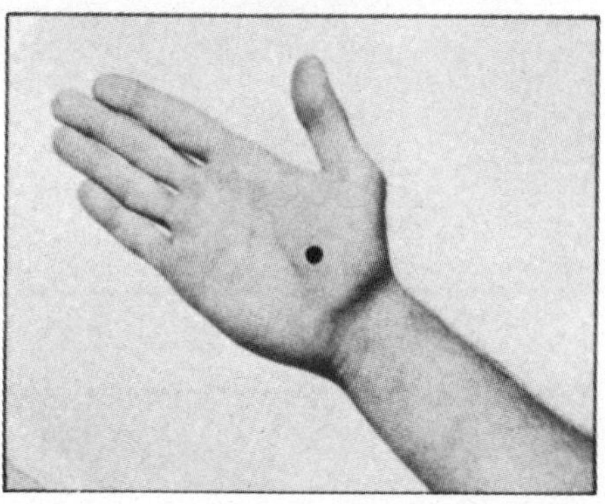

POINT: Labored Palace
LANDMARK: hand
DISTANCE FROM LANDMARK: close to the landmark
LOCATION: clench fist and mark the point where the tip of the middle finger meets the palm (treat both hands)
POSITION: seated
TYPE OF PRESSURE: pulsed with thumb, pinching motion
AMOUNT OF PRESSURE: as much as patient can take

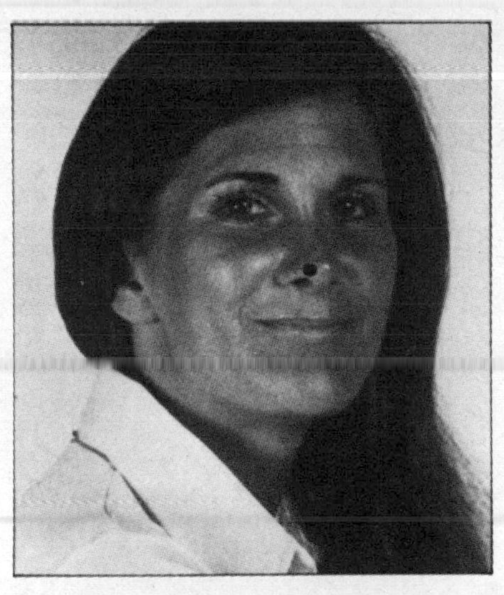

POINT: Simple Bone
LANDMARK: nose
DISTANCE FROM LANDMARK: right on landmark
LOCATION: the tip of the nose
POSITION: seated or flat on back
TYPE OF PRESSURE: pinch the tip of the nose with thumbnail pressure; alternate pulsed and steady pressure
AMOUNT OF PRESSURE: as much as patient can take

POINT: Stalk Bone
LANDMARK: nose
DISTANCE FROM LANDMARK: immediately below
LOCATION: directly below each nostril and centered under the nostril (treat both points at once)
POSITION: seated or flat on back
TYPE OF PRESSURE: pulsed with thumb and forefinger at one time
AMOUNT OF PRESSURE: as much as patient can take

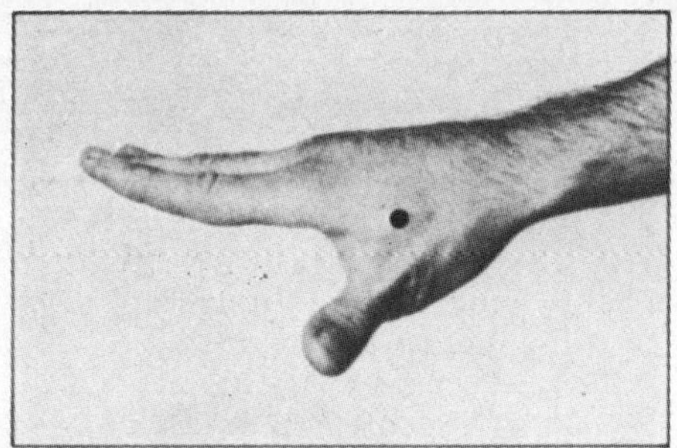

POINT: Connecting the Valleys
LANDMARK: back of hand
DISTANCE FROM LANDMARK: 1 acu-inch down from the point where bones of thumb and index finger meet
LOCATION: on the back of the hand (treat both hands)
POSITION: seated
TYPE OF PRESSURE: pulsed with thumb, pinching motion
AMOUNT OF PRESSURE: as much as patient can take

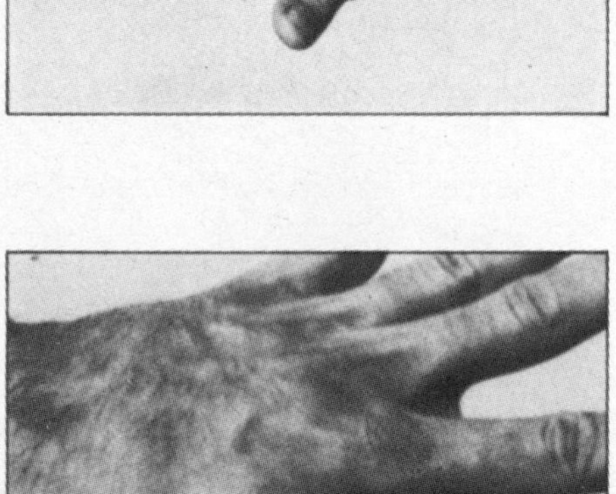

POINT: Yang Tradesman
LANDMARK: thumbnail
DISTANCE FROM LANDMARK: close to landmark
LOCATION: at the intersection of a line drawn along the outer edge of nail and a horizontal line across the base of the nail (treat both thumbs)
POSITION: seated
TYPE OF PRESSURE: pulsed with thumb, pinching movement
AMOUNT OF PRESSURE: as much as patient can take

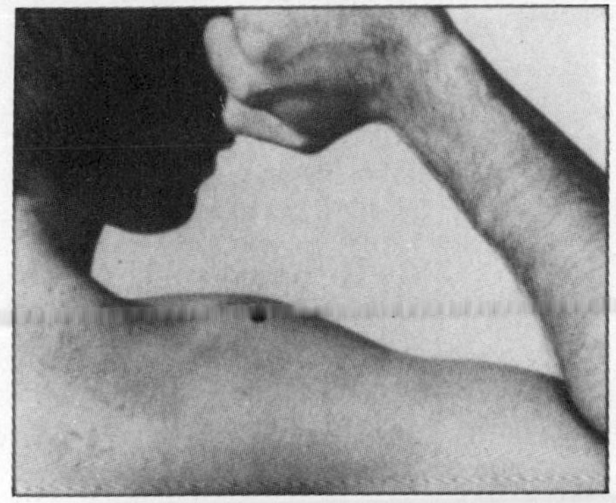

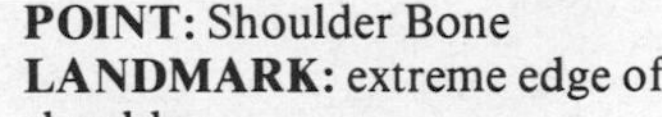

POINT: Shoulder Bone
LANDMARK: extreme edge of shoulder
DISTANCE FROM LANDMARK: right at the landmark
LOCATION: on the shoulder, in the hollow formed when the arm is raised (treat both arms)
POSITION: seated
TYPE OF PRESSURE: pulsed with thumb
AMOUNT OF PRESSURE: gently, then as much as patient can take

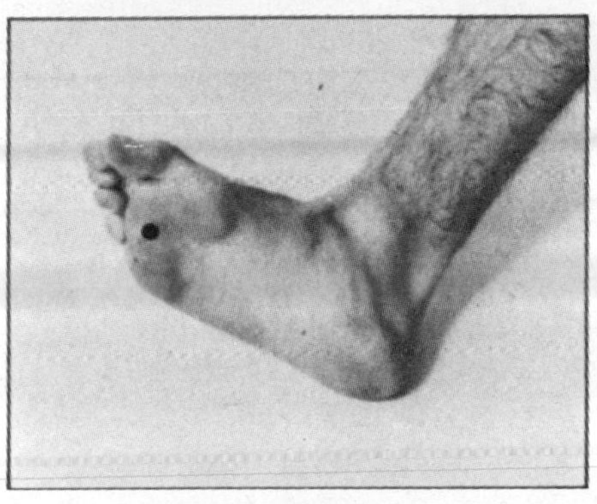

POINT: Pouring Spring
LANDMARK: bottom of foot
DISTANCE FROM LANDMARK: within landmark
LOCATION: on the bottom of the foot, in the depression just in back of the ball when the foot is raised (treat both feet)
POSITION: flat on back
TYPE OF PRESSURE: alternating pulsed and steady with thumb
AMOUNT OF PRESSURE: as much as patient can take

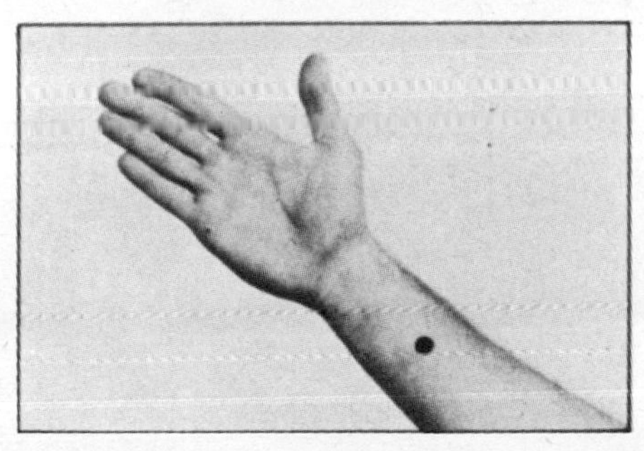

POINT: Inner Pass
LANDMARK: inner wrist fold
DISTANCE FROM LANDMARK: 2 acu-inches up
LOCATION: on the inner surface of the forearm (treat both sides)
POSITION: seated or flat on back
TYPE OF PRESSURE: pulsed with thumb, pinching motion
AMOUNT OF PRESSURE: as much as patient can take

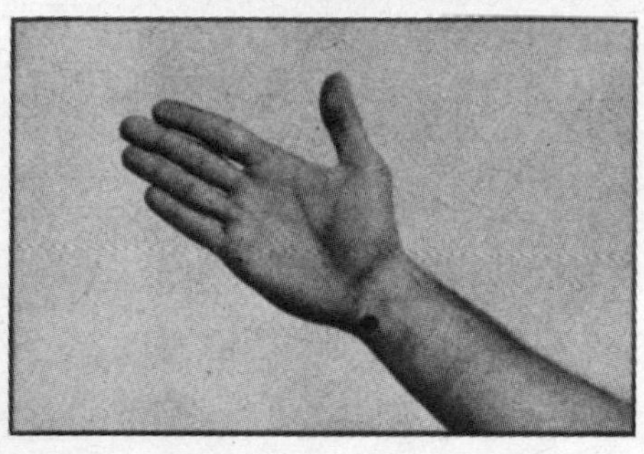

POINT: God's Door
LANDMARK: inner wrist fold
DISTANCE FROM LANDMARK: right on the fold
LOCATION: 1 acu-inch in from outer edge (side with little finger) of arm, on the inner surface of the forearm (treat both arms)
POSITION: seated
TYPE OF PRESSURE: pulsed with thumb
AMOUNT OF PRESSURE: as much as patient can take

SNAKE BITES

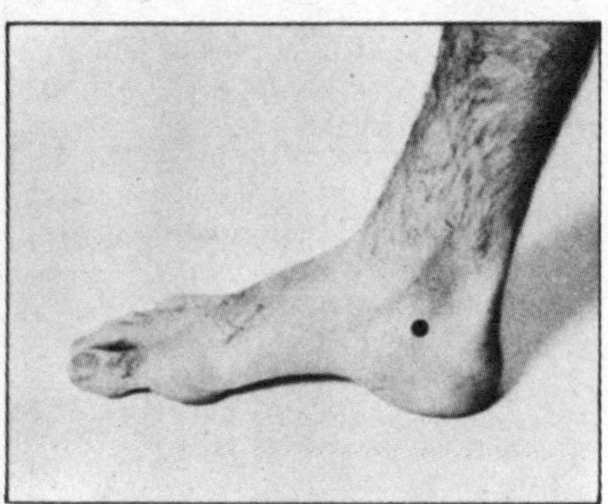

POINT: Shine To Sea
LANDMARK: inner ankle bone
DISTANCE FROM LANDMARK: immediately below
LOCATION: hollow space just below (treat both legs)
POSITION: seated or flat on back
TYPE OF PRESSURE: pulsed with thumb, pinching motion
AMOUNT OF PRESSURE: as much as patient can take

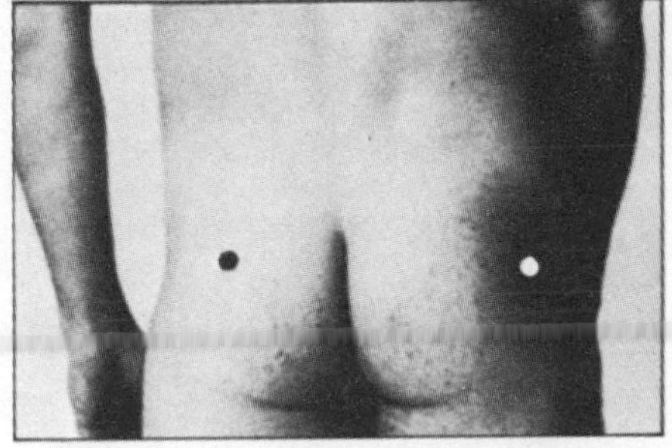

POINT: Circular Jump
LANDMARK: buttocks fold
DISTANCE FROM LANDMARK: 5 acu-inches up
LOCATION: on the side of the buttocks, approximately 3 acu-inches from the center line of the buttocks toward the rear (treat both sides)
POSITION: face down
TYPE OF PRESSURE: pulsed with thumb
AMOUNT OF PRESSURE: as much as patient can take

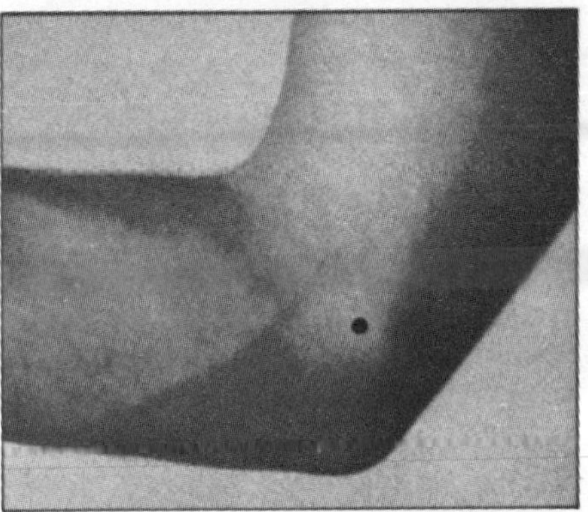

POINT: Crooked Pond
LANDMARK: inner elbow fold
DISTANCE FROM LANDMARK: right at the body-side edge of fold, when elbow is bent
LOCATION: elbow (treat both arms)
POSITION: seated or flat on back
TYPE OF PRESSURE: pulsed with thumb, pinching motion
AMOUNT OF PRESSURE: as much as patient can take

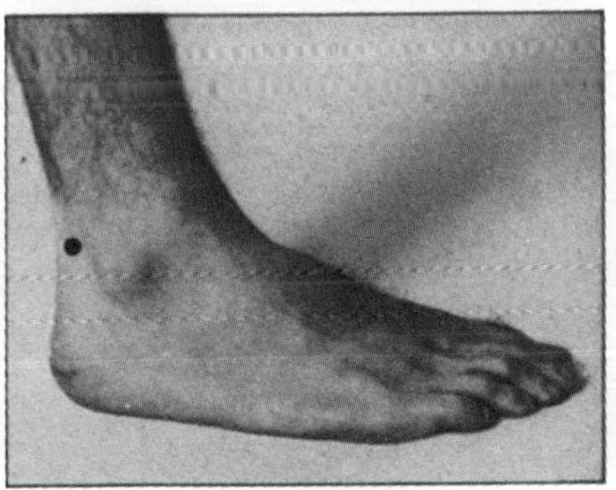

POINT: K'un Lun Mountains
LANDMARK: outer ankle bone
DISTANCE FROM LANDMARK: just in back
LOCATION: in the depression behind outer ankle bone (treat both feet)
POSITION: flat on back
TYPE OF PRESSURE: pulsed with thumb, pinching motion
AMOUNT OF PRESSURE: as much as patient can take

SUNBURN

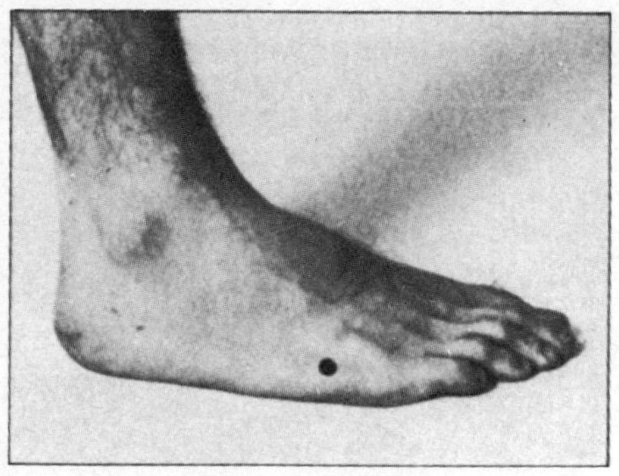

POINT: Restrict Bone
LANDMARK: toe knuckle of little toe
DISTANCE FROM LANDMARK: close to the landmark
LOCATION: on the outer edge of the foot, just behind toe knuckle (treat both feet)
POSITION: seated or flat on back
TYPE OF PRESSURE: pulsed with thumb
AMOUNT OF PRESSURE: as much as patient can take; repeat as needed

SUN STROKE

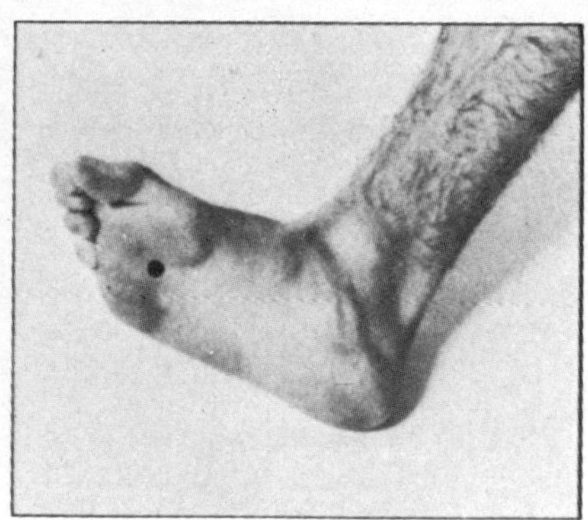

POINT: Pouring Spring
LANDMARK: bottom of foot
DISTANCE FROM LANDMARK: within landmark
LOCATION: on the bottom of the foot, in the depression just in back of the ball when the foot is raised (treat both feet)
POSITION: flat on back
TYPE OF PRESSURE: alternating pulsed and steady with thumb
AMOUNT OF PRESSURE: as much as patient can take

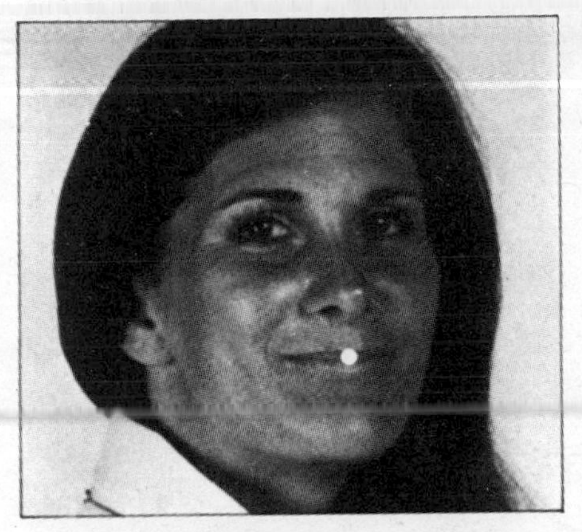

POINT: Middle of Man
LANDMARK: nose
DISTANCE FROM LANDMARK: just under landmark
LOCATION: directly under the center of the nose, on the upper lip
POSITION: flat on back
TYPE OF PRESSURE: alternating pulsed and steady pressure with thumb or fingers
AMOUNT OF PRESSURE: as much as patient can take

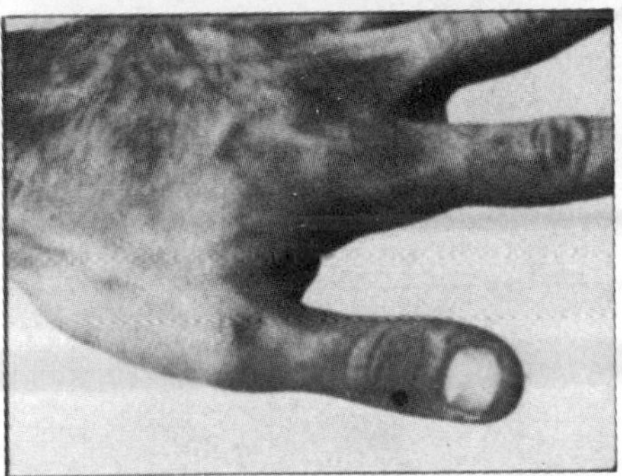

POINT: Yang Tradesman
LANDMARK: thumbnail
DISTANCE FROM LANDMARK: close to landmark
LOCATION: at the intersection of a line drawn along the outer edge of nail and a horizontal line across the base of the nail (treat both thumbs)
POSITION: seated
TYPE OF PRESSURE: pulsed with thumb, pinching motion
AMOUNT OF PRESSURE: as much as patient can take

SUFFOCATION

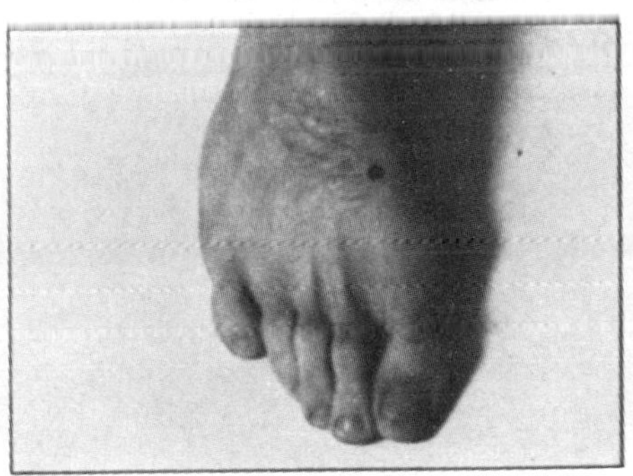

POINT: Great Flush
LANDMARK: toe knuckles
DISTANCE FROM LANDMARK: 1 acu-inch back (toward ankle)
LOCATION: on upper surface of foot between first and second toes (treat both feet)
POSITION: flat on back or seated
TYPE OF PRESSURE: pulsed with thumb, pinching motion
AMOUNT OF PRESSURE: as much as patient can take

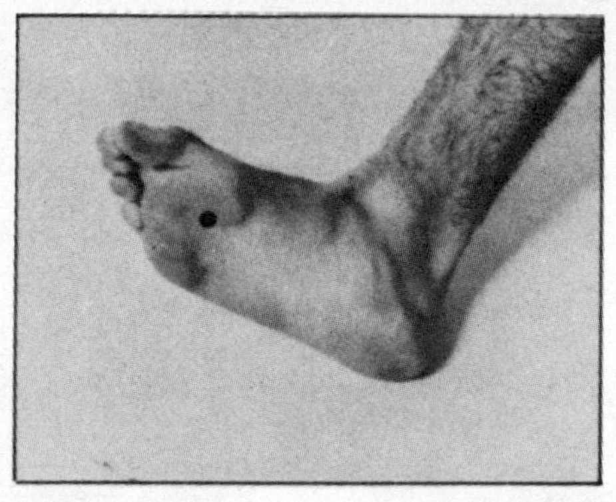

POINT: Pouring Spring
LANDMARK: bottom of foot
DISTANCE FROM LANDMARK: within landmark
LOCATION: on the bottom of the foot, in the depression just in back of the ball when the foot is raised (treat both feet)
POSITION: flat on back
TYPE OF PRESSURE: alternating pulsed and steady with thumb
AMOUNT OF PRESSURE: as much as patient can take

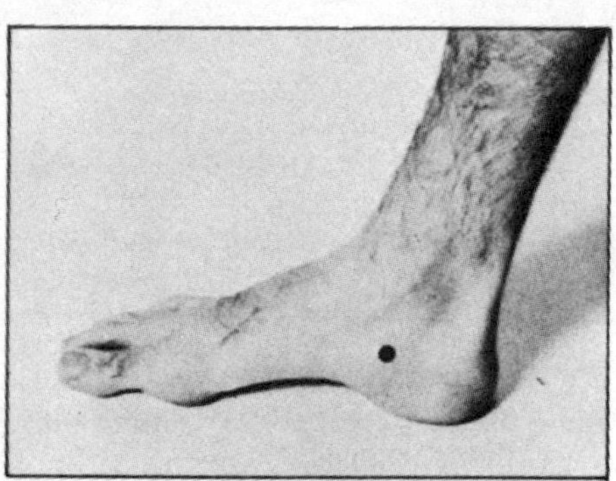

POINT: Great Brook
LANDMARK: inner ankle bone
DISTANCE FROM LANDMARK: just in back of ankle bone
LOCATION: in the depression that you can feel at this spot (treat both legs)
POSITION: flat on back
TYPE OF PRESSURE: pulsed with thumb, pinching motion
AMOUNT OF PRESSURE: as much as patient can take

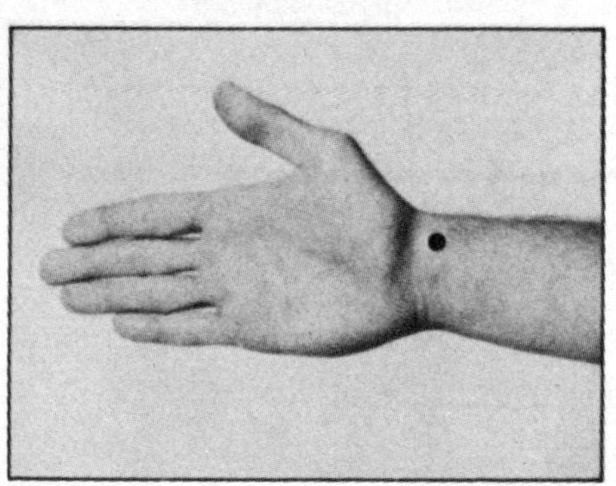

POINT: Great Gulf
LANDMARK: inner wrist fold
DISTANCE FROM LANDMARK: right on landmark
LOCATION: on the thumb-side edge, right where the pulse is taken (treat both hands)
POSITION: seated or flat on back
TYPE OF PRESSURE: pulsed with thumb, pinching motion
AMOUNT OF PRESSURE: as much as patient can take

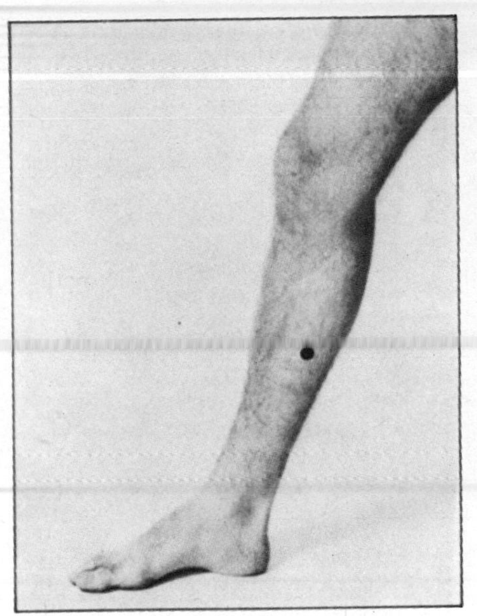

POINT: Building for Guest
LANDMARK: inner ankle bone
DISTANCE FROM LANDMARK: 5 acu-inches above the back side
LOCATION: back of lower leg; feel for the muscle when the toes are firmly extended, and locate the central depression of this muscle (treat both feet)
POSITION: on stomach
TYPE OF PRESSURE: pulsed with thumb
AMOUNT OF PRESSURE: as much as patient can take

TESTICLE INJURY OR PAIN

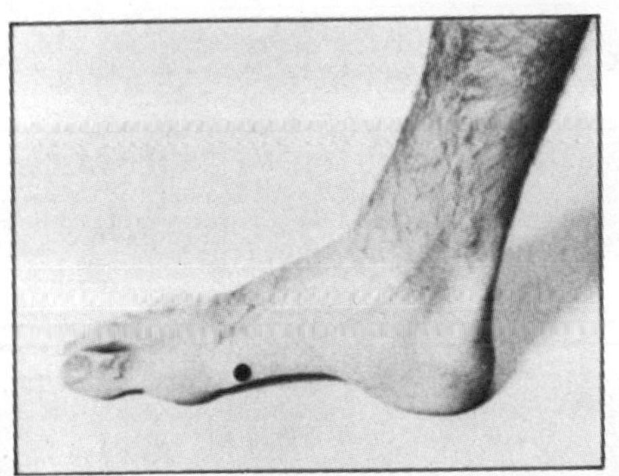

POINT: Generation Gap
LANDMARK: big toe joint
DISTANCE FROM LANDMARK: 1 acu-inch back (toward ankle) from big toe joint
LOCATION: on the inner edge of the foot (treat both feet)
POSITION: flat on back
TYPE OF PRESSURE: pulsed with thumb or percussion (jab with thumb)
AMOUNT OF PRESSURE: as much as patient can take

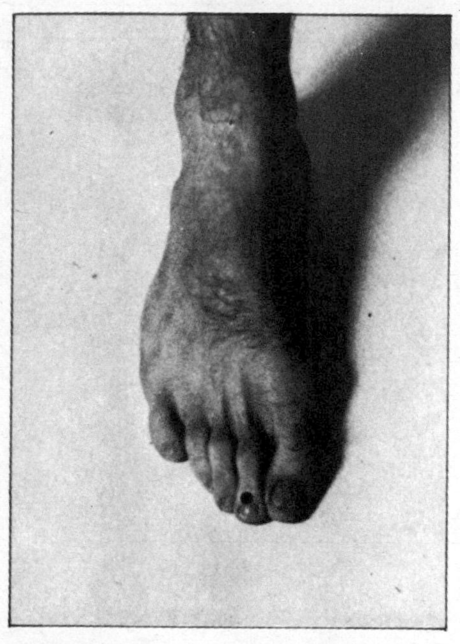

POINT: Strict Exchange
LANDMARK: toenail of the second toe
DISTANCE FROM LANDMARK: right on landmark
LOCATION: at the intersection of a line drawn along the little-toe side of the nail and a horizontal line across the top of the nail (treat both feet)
POSITION: flat on back
TYPE OF PRESSURE: pulsed with thumb, pinching motion
AMOUNT OF PRESSURE: as much as patient can take

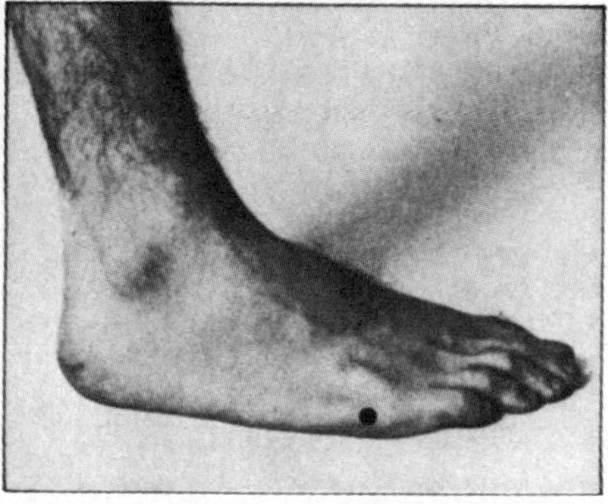

POINT: Restrict Bone
LANDMARK: toe knuckle of little toe
DISTANCE FROM LANDMARK: close to the landmark
LOCATION: on the outer edge of the foot, just behind toe knuckle (treat both feet)
POSITION: seated or flat on back
TYPE OF PRESSURE: pulsed with thumb
AMOUNT OF PRESSURE: as much as patient can take; repeat as needed

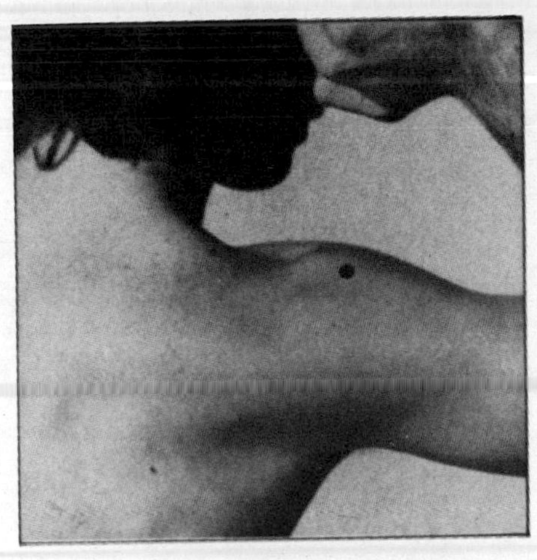

POINT: Shoulder Bone I
LANDMARK: extreme edge of shoulder
DISTANCE FROM LANDMARK: right at the landmark
LOCATION: on the shoulder, in the hollow formed when the arm is raised (treat both arms)
POSITION: seated
TYPE OF PRESSURE: pulsed with thumb
AMOUNT OF PRESSURE: gently, then as much as patient can take

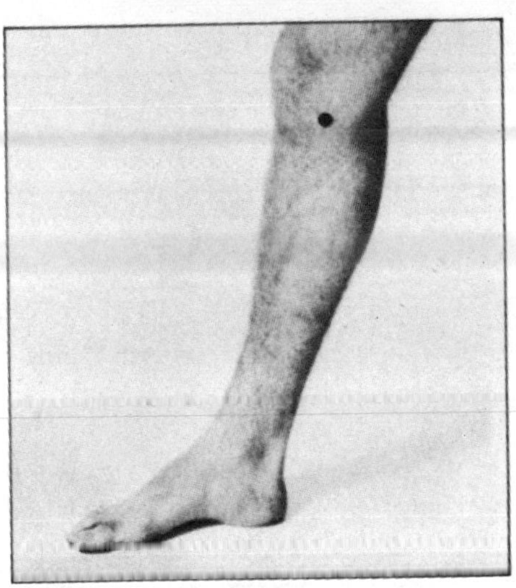

POINT: Spring in Shady Mound
LANDMARK: back of knee fold
DISTANCE FROM LANDMARK: 2 acu-inches below
LOCATION: on the inner surface of the leg, in the approximate center (treat both legs)
POSITION: flat on back or seated
TYPE OF PRESSURE: pulsed with thumb
AMOUNT OF PRESSURE: as much as patient can take

EIGHT
SEXUAL ACUPRESSURE

Sexual dysfunction. Just the term itself can evoke some chilling fears for quite a few people. And yet, the path to fuller, richer sexual experience may lie through the simple use of the same acupressure techniques that you have already learned. Many of the same points used to treat common discomforts and maladies can be highly effective for more prevalent types of sexual inadequacy.

Do not expect miracles. To a large extent sexual competence is within your own head. Also, do not think the techniques in this chapter will transform you overnight into a satyr or sex goddess. It won't.

However, within the limits of reason you may find you have perked up your sexual interest, extended your capacity to enjoy, and heightened your receptivity to sexual sensation. What does this mean in everyday terms?

Just this. Quite possibly, your sexual activities will turn out to be considerably more fun, your pleasure sessions will last longer, and the impact of orgasm will be more profound. At least so we are told by the Oriental practitioners, who use acupressure to correct dysfunction and stimulate sexual appetite.

This does not mean that you will immediately take on the role of a sexual athlete able to sustain intercourse with anyone you please for as long as you like. The fact remains that it's virtually impossible to have rewarding sex with someone you are not sexually attracted to—that's the first step. In fact, many trained professionals are available if your problem is deep seated. You are strongly advised to seek their help in cases of severe sexual dysfunction. However, the acupressure techniques detailed in this chapter, must be allowed enough time for an extended course of treatment in order to give you a boost of a magnitude to vanquish many doubts concerning effectiveness. It may take a month or so until the results become evident. If successful, it's a small price to pay for a new outlook on your sexual life.

Also, don't be afraid to experiment a bit with different points taken from the roster given here. When you find a combination that seems to be especially effective for your condition, stay with it.

You may find it most effective to utilize the maintenance procedure that many people follow. They regard sexual acupressure as a daily routine. That's sound thinking. After all, if you want to keep your body slim and limber, there's no better insurance than daily calesthenics. A similar regime using sexual acupressure every day can help maintain your vigor, interest, and capacity.

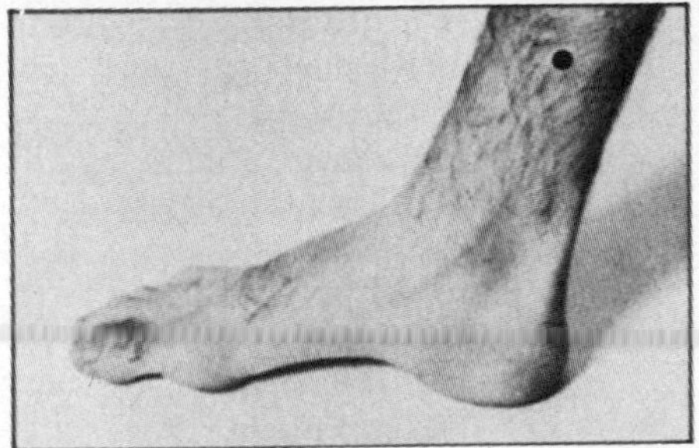

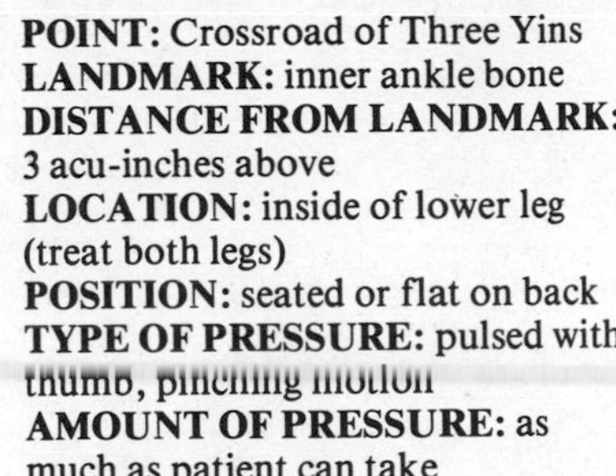

POINT: Crossroad of Three Yins
LANDMARK: inner ankle bone
DISTANCE FROM LANDMARK: 3 acu-inches above
LOCATION: inside of lower leg (treat both legs)
POSITION: seated or flat on back
TYPE OF PRESSURE: pulsed with thumb, pinching motion
AMOUNT OF PRESSURE: as much as patient can take

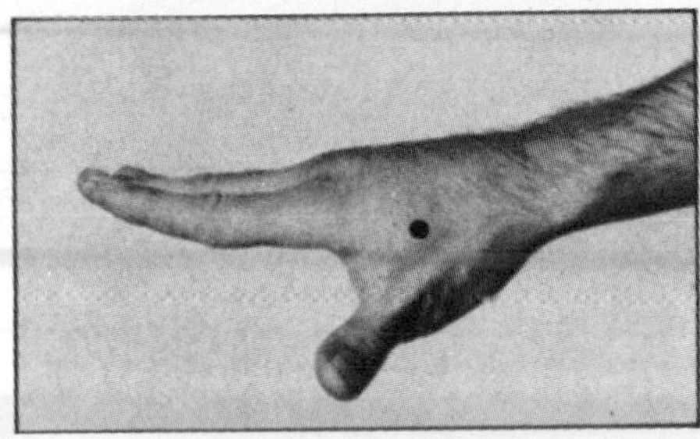

POINT: Connecting the Valleys
LANDMARK: back of hand
DISTANCE FROM LANDMARK: 1 acu-inch down from the point where bones of thumb and index finger meet
LOCATION: on the back of the hand (treat both hands)
POSITION: seated
TYPE OF PRESSURE: pulsed with thumb, pinching motion
AMOUNT OF PRESSURE: as much as patient can take

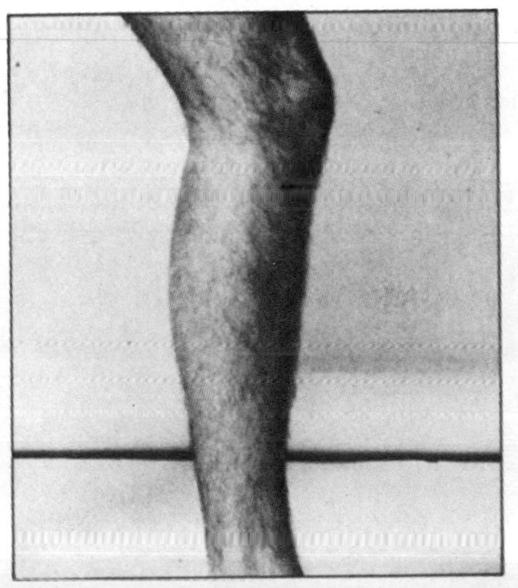

POINT: Walking Three Miles
LANDMARK: kneecap
DISTANCE FROM LANDMARK: 3 acu-inches below (in the depression)
LOCATION: 1 acu inch toward the outside of the leg (treat both legs)
POSITION: seated in chair or flat on back
TYPE OF PRESSURE: pulsed with thumb (or pinching motion)
AMOUNT OF PRESSURE: quite firm

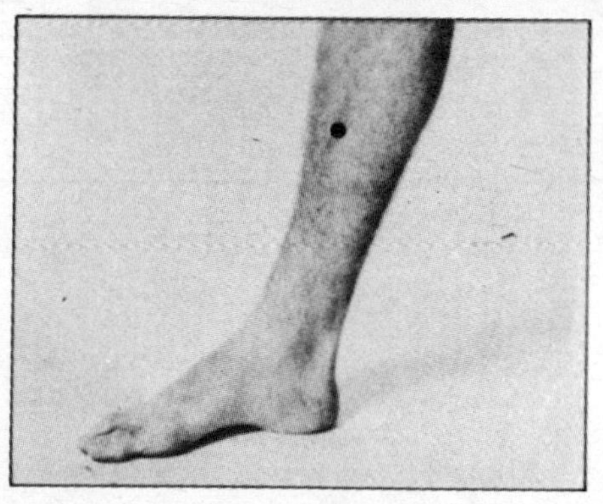

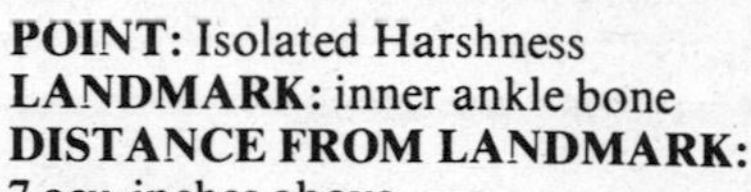

POINT: Isolated Harshness
LANDMARK: inner ankle bone
DISTANCE FROM LANDMARK: 7 acu-inches above
LOCATION: on the inner surface of the leg, just behind the shin bone (treat both legs)
POSITION: seated or flat on back
TYPE OF PRESSURE: pulsed with thumb, pinching motion
AMOUNT OF PRESSURE: as much as patient can tolerate

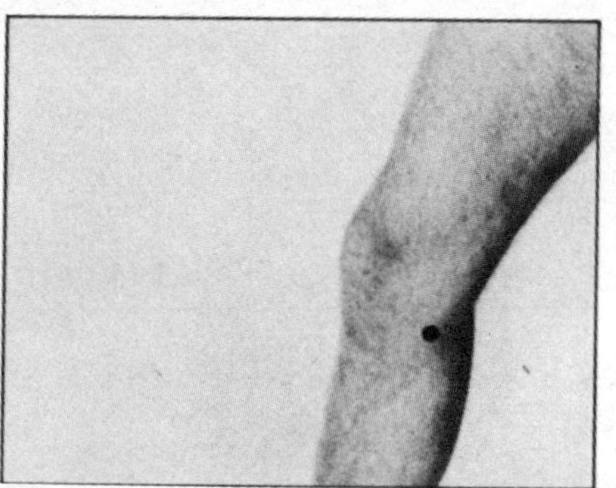

POINT: Knee Pass
LANDMARK: back of knee fold
DISTANCE FROM LANDMARK: 3 acu-inches down from knee fold
LOCATION: inner surface of calf, in the center (treat both legs)
POSITION: seated or flat on back
TYPE OF PRESSURE: pulsed with thumb, pinching motion
AMOUNT OF PRESSURE: as much as patient can take

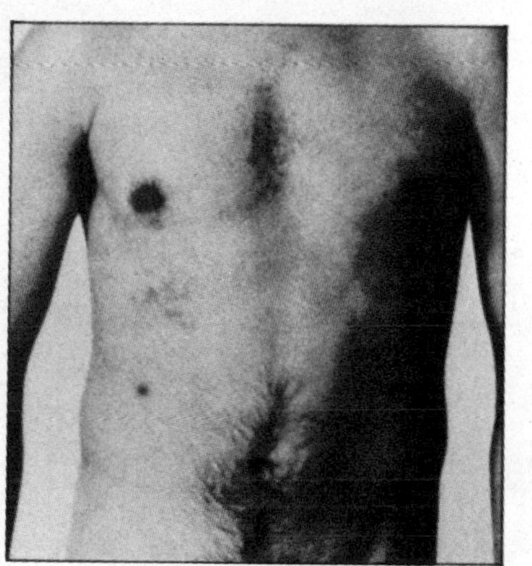

POINT: Pass Origin
LANDMARK: navel
DISTANCE FROM LANDMARK: 3 acu-inches below
LOCATION: on lower abdomen in a line directly below navel
POSITION: flat on back
TYPE OF PRESSURE: pulsed with thumb
AMOUNT OF PRESSURE: as much as patient can take

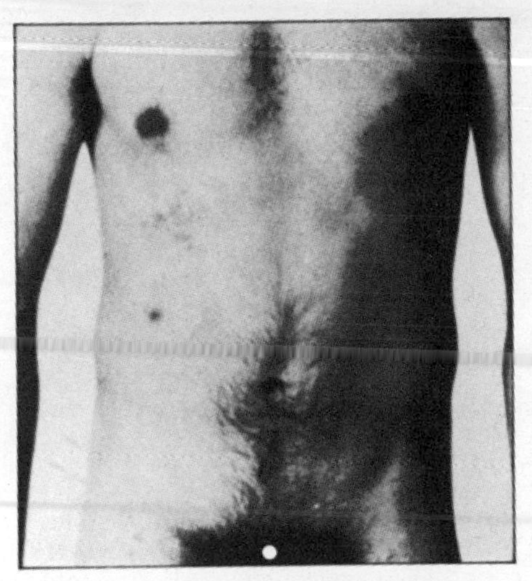

POINT: Crooked Bone
LANDMARK: navel
DISTANCE FROM LANDMARK: 5 acu-inches directly below
LOCATION: on the lower abdomen
POSITION: flat on back
TYPE OF PRESSURE: pulsed with thumb
AMOUNT OF PRESSURE: as much as patient can take

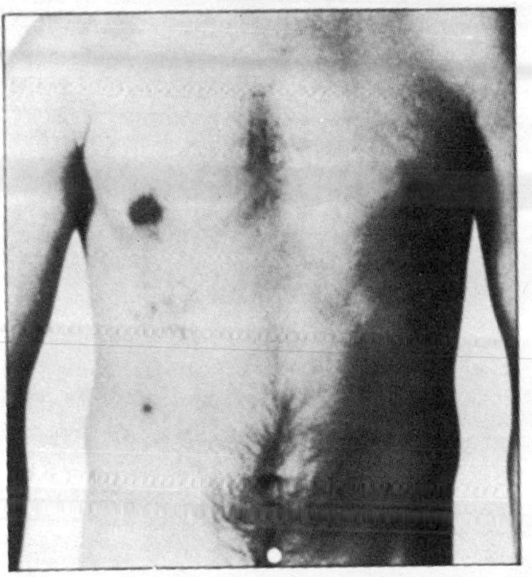

POINT: Middle Extreme
LANDMARK: navel
DISTANCE FROM LANDMARK: 4 acu-inches directly below
LOCATION: on lower abdomen
POSITION: flat on back
TYPE OF PRESSURE: pulsed with thumb
AMOUNT OF PRESSURE: as much as patient can take

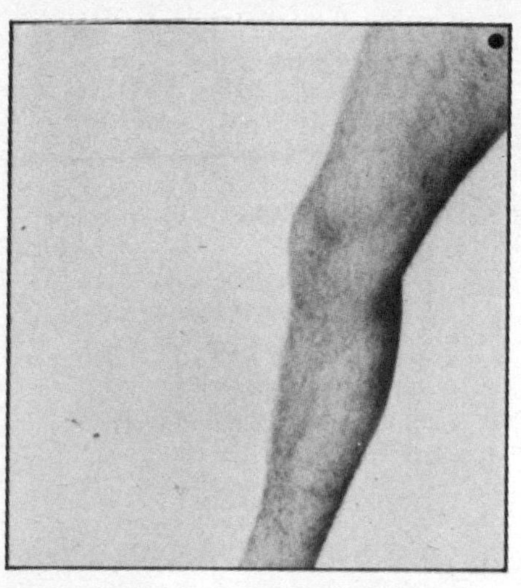

POINT: Yin Screen
LANDMARK: thigh-stomach fold
DISTANCE FROM LANDMARK: 1 acu-inch below
LOCATION: on upper thigh, 3 acu-inches on either side of center line of body (treat both sides)
POSITION: flat on back
TYPE OF PRESSURE: pulsed with thumb or fingers
AMOUNT OF PRESSURE: gently, then as much as patient can take

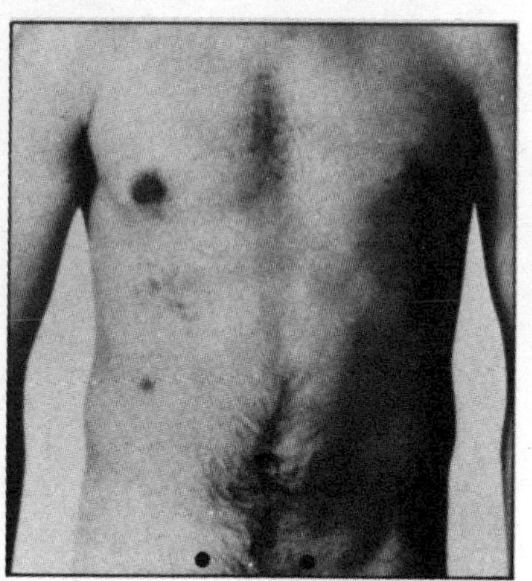

POINT: Great Threat
LANDMARK: navel
DISTANCE FROM LANDMARK: 4 acu-inches below
LOCATION: on the lower abdomen, 1½ acu-inches to either side of an up-and-down center line of the body (treat both sides)
POSITION: flat on back
TYPE OF PRESSURE: pulsed with thumb or fingers
AMOUNT OF PRESSURE: as much as patient can take

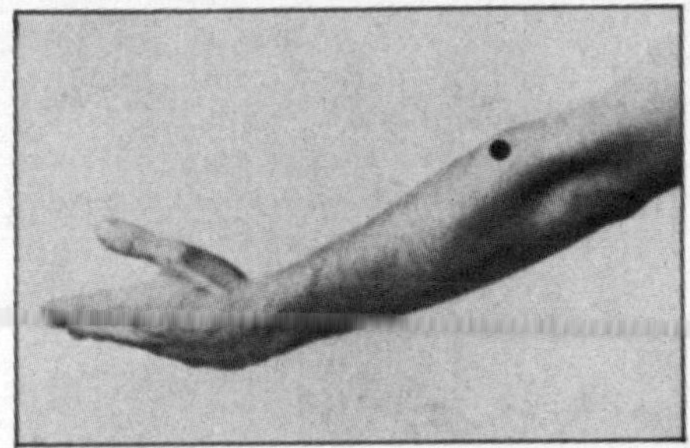

POINT: Three Li
LANDMARK: outer elbow fold
DISTANCE FROM LANDMARK: 2 acu-inches below
LOCATION: side of the forearm, in the middle (treat both arms)
POSITION: seated or flat on back
TYPE OF PRESSURE: pulsed with thumb, pinching motion
AMOUNT OF PRESSURE: as much as patient can take

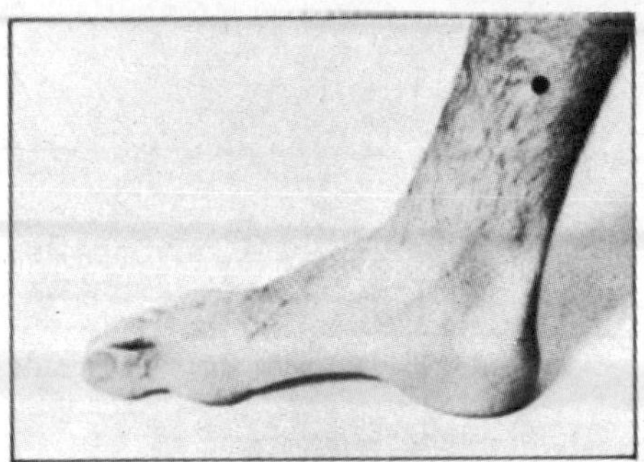

POINT: Crossroad of Three Yins
LANDMARK: inner ankle bone
DISTANCE FROM LANDMARK: 3 acu-inches above
LOCATION: inside of lower leg (treat both legs)
POSITION: seated or flat on back
TYPE OF PRESSURE: pulsed with thumb, pinching motion
AMOUNT OF PRESSURE: as much as patient can take

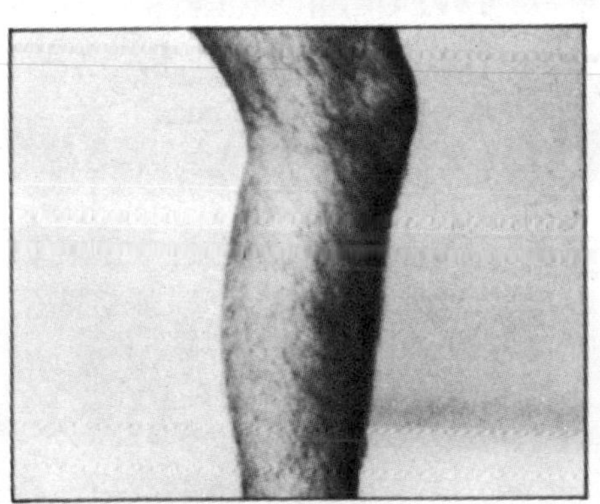

POINT: Walking Three Miles
LANDMARK: kneecap
DISTANCE FROM LANDMARK: 3 acu-inches below (in the depression)
LOCATION: 1 acu-inch toward the outside of the leg (treat both legs)
POSITION: seated in chair or flat on back
TYPE OF PRESSURE: pulsed with thumb (or pinching motion)
AMOUNT OF PRESSURE: quite firm

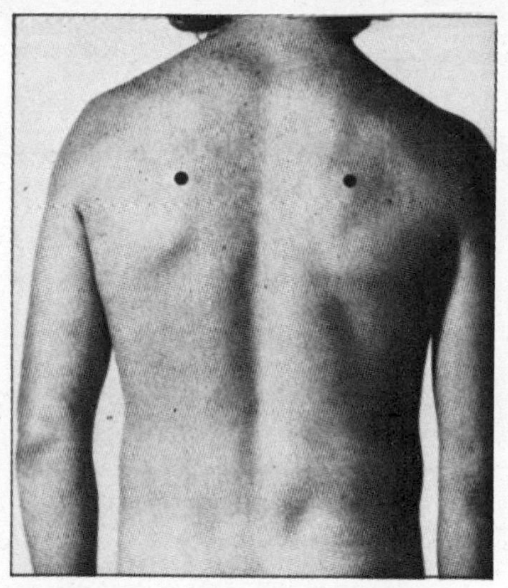

POINT: Superficial Tortuosity
LANDMARK: spine knob at neck
DISTANCE FROM LANDMARK: 4th spine knob (vertebra) down
LOCATION: on the back, 3 acu-inches on either side of the spine (treat both sides)
POSITION: on stomach
TYPE OF PRESSURE: pulsed with thumb
AMOUNT OF PRESSURE: as much as patient can take

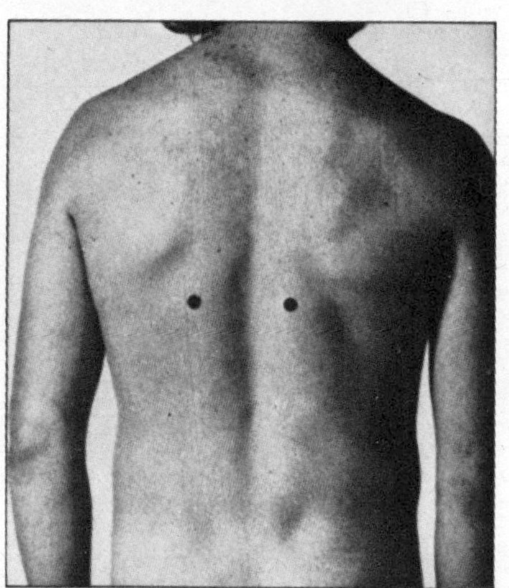

POINT: Liver Locus
LANDMARK: spine knob at neck
DISTANCE FROM LANDMARK: 9th spine knob (vertebra) below
LOCATION: on the back, 1½ acu-inches on either side of the spine (treat both sides)
POSITION: face down
TYPE OF PRESSURE: pulsed with thumb or fingers
AMOUNT OF PRESSURE: as much as patient can take

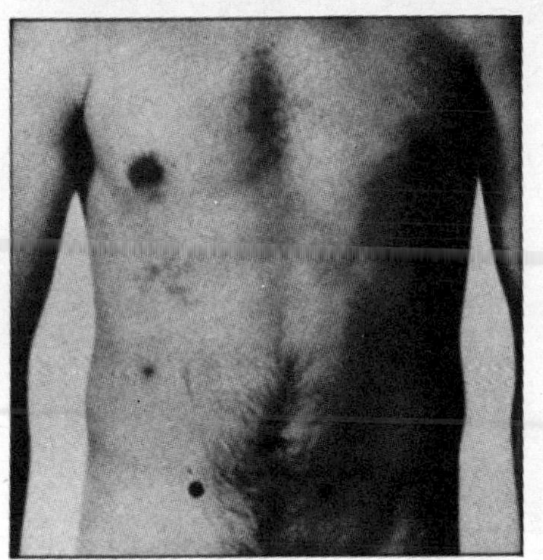

POINT: New Point
LANDMARK: hip bone
DISTANCE FROM LANDMARK: at the level of the landmark
LOCATION: on the abdomen, 3 acu-inches from the upper tip of the hip bone measured toward the center of the body (treat both sides)
POSITION: flat on back
TYPE OF PRESSURE: pulsed with thumb or fingers
AMOUNT OF PRESSURE: as much as patient can take

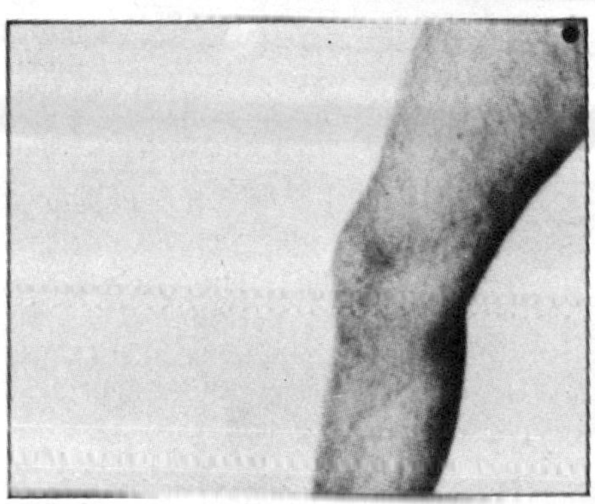

POINT: Yin Screen
LANDMARK: thigh-stomach fold
DISTANCE FROM LANDMARK: 1 acu-inch below
LOCATION: on upper thigh, 3 acu-inches on either side of center line of body (treat both sides)
POSITION: flat on back
TYPE OF PRESSURE: pulsed with thumb or fingers
AMOUNT OF PRESSURE: gently, then as much as patient can take

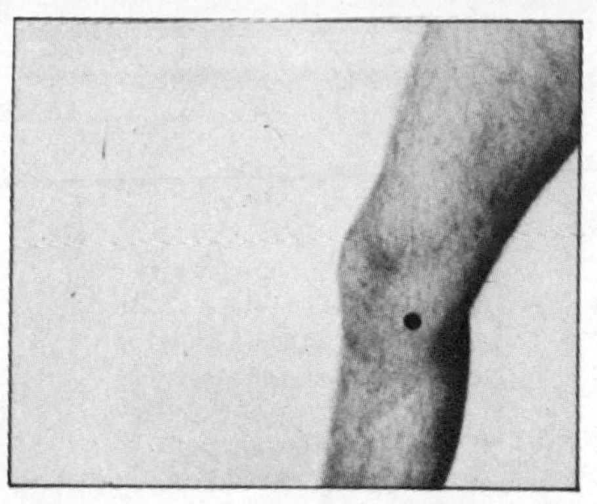

POINT: Knee Pass
LANDMARK: back of knee fold
DISTANCE FROM LANDMARK: 3 acu-inches down from knee fold
LOCATION: inner surface of calf, in the center (treat both legs)
POSITION: seated or flat on back
TYPE OF PRESSURE: pulsed with thumb, pinching motion
AMOUNT OF PRESSURE: as much as patient can take

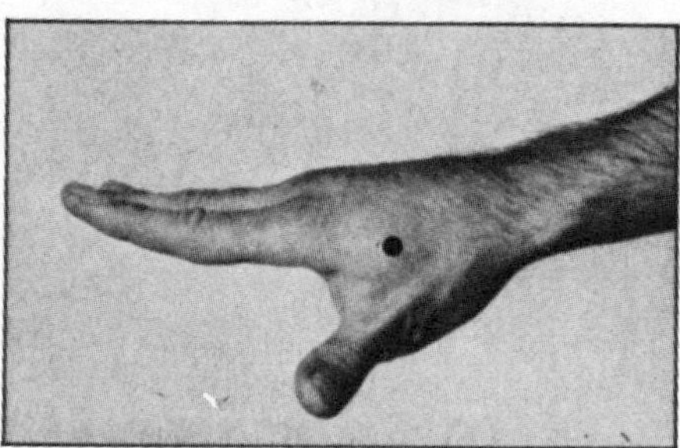

POINT: Connecting the Valleys
LANDMARK: back of hand
DISTANCE FROM LANDMARK: 1 acu-inch down from the point where bones of thumb and index finger meet
LOCATION: on the back of the hand (treat both hands)
POSITION: seated
TYPE OF PRESSURE: pulsed with thumb, pinching motion
AMOUNT OF PRESSURE: as much as patient can take

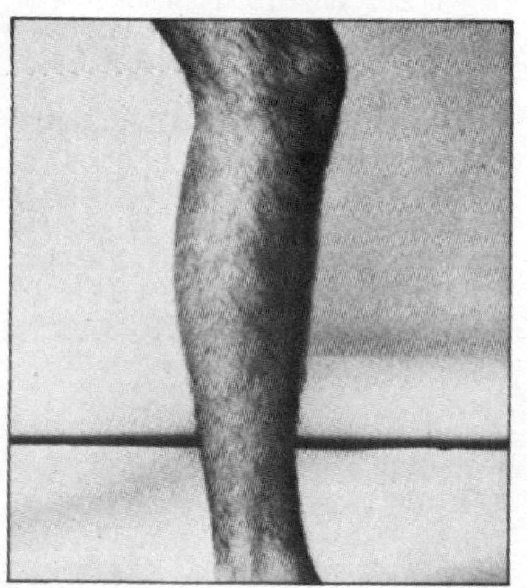

POINT: Walking Three Miles
LANDMARK: kneecap
DISTANCE FROM LANDMARK: 3 acu-inches below (in the depression)
LOCATION: 1 acu-inch toward the outside of the leg (treat both legs)
POSITION: seated in chair or flat on back
TYPE OF PRESSURE: pulsed with thumb (or pinching motion)
AMOUNT OF PRESSURE: quite firm

NINE
CASE HISTORIES

The use of acupressure in the practice of medicine is more widespread than most people are aware. Here are some typical case histories from four ethical, licensed medical practitioners (M.D.s) who use acupressure daily. That is not to say that they use only acupressure, but rather that when indicated they find it a powerful adjunct to their practice.

ROBERT M. GILLER, M.D.

Name:	George F.
Age:	37
Symptoms:	Mr. F. had the hiccups for three weeks; they had started suddenly after a big meal. None of the "family cures"—holding his breath, sugar, and the like—had brought any relief. His family physician determined that there was no serious cause for the hiccups; but, as they continued, Mr. F. lost weight, fatigued easily, and became increasingly ill-tempered.
Treatment:	Gentle acupressure at a point in the middle of the forehead slowed the hiccups considerably; complete control was effected with a single acupuncture treatment in the midback area (Diaphragm Locus).

Name: Steven S.
Age: 11
Symptoms: Steven suffered from occasional nosebleeds (repeated nosebleeds should lead to an examination for blood deficiencies). He did not respond to the folk remedies his mother used.
Treatment: As the child sat with his head back, acupressure was applied to both nostrils for at least five minutes. He was instructed to breathe through his mouth, as the pressure should be strong enough to prevent forced breathing through the nose. In addition, massage was applied to the hollow at the base of the skull (Wind Pond). This first-aid treatment proved most effective.

Name: Allen R.
Age: 14
Symptoms: Allen persistently got car sick. At first it was a lightheaded feeling, then general discomfort followed by nausea and vomiting. Motion-sickness medication was only somewhat effective.
Treatment: The family was instructed on massage of the appropriate acupressure points (Between Columns, Connecting the Valleys). Allen has experienced no further symptoms.

Name: Roberta S.
Age: 57
Symptoms: Mrs. S. first experienced shoulder pain after helping an elderly patient during a volunteer visit to the hospital. In the beginning several aspirins relieved the pain; the pain grew more persistent, and was accompanied by restricted movement of the left arm. Her family physician diagnosed bursitis and prescribed stronger pain relievers. An orthopedist confirmed the diagnosis, and despite several cortisone injections Mrs. S. continued to suffer pain and limited motion.
Treatment: After two acupuncture treatments pain was reduced by 50 percent. Acupressure massage to the tender areas of the shoulder and upper back was performed before treatment with the needles (Shoulder Well, Tortuous Wall, Support, Huge Bone, Shoulder Bone, Wind Pond). After another treatment full motion of the arm was restored.

Name: Michael G.
Age: 47
Symptoms: Mr. G. had a history of periodic low back pain, but never anything serious. After some household exertion, Mr. G. experienced more pain in his lower back than usual; the following morning the pain was so great that he could not get out of bed. Pain killers offered little relief. After several days in bed the pain subsided enough for Mr. G. to go to the hospital, and X-rays showed nothing abnormal.
Treatment: Mr. G.'s lower back muscles were in a state of spasm. The sensitive area was warmed, then acupressure massage applied. At first there was an increase in pain, but after thirty minutes of massage pain was cut in half. Acupuncture treatment was also used, as well as home massage of the back, hips, and legs (Kidney Locus, Circular Jump, Stomach Granary, Spring in the Sunny Hill). After one week he was back at work.

Name: Rose G.
Age: 28
Symptoms: Miss G. was involved in an automobile accident. At the moment of impact she had felt a "snap" in her neck; later she complained of a stiff neck, as well as headaches, nausea, occasional shoulder pain, and difficulties in memory and concentration. X-rays were normal and Miss G.'s problems, which seemed to be worsening, were attributed to "post-whiplash syndrome."
Treatment: Miss G. had severe spasms of her neck and shoulder muscles. Massage first exacerbated the symptoms, then brought relief. Acupuncture was then used, and she was given a program of points to treat at home (Wind Pond, Celestial Pillar, Great Slaughter). In less than a month she was without pain or limited neck movement.

Name: Helen M.
Age: 52
Symptoms: Mrs. M. had been confined to her home due to intense neuralgia of the toes, so that walking was extremely painful.
Treatment: Examination revealed tender areas in the anterior part of the foot, and in the calf. Acupuncture needles and deep massage were applied. (Dissolving Brook, Great Cemetery, Stretching Vessel) Relief was achieved in three treatments.

Name: Stuart D.
Age: 34
Symptoms: Mr. D. suffered intermittently from constipation, which was generally brought on by stress and nervous tension. Laxatives did not work well; when constipation became severe, Mr. D. would also suffer a dull ache in his lower back.
Treatment: Tender areas in the abdomen and lower back became evident during examination; a program of acupuncture, acupressure and home massage was begun for these regions (Bladder Locus, Celestial Pivot). No further episodes of constipation have been reported.

Name: Elizabeth R.
Age: 31
Symptoms: Miss R. experienced extremely difficult menstrual periods, characterized by severe headaches, cramps, and general discomfort. Various specialists and numerous pain-killers produced no success.
Treatment: Miss R. arrived during her period, in considerable pain. Examination revealed tenderness along the inner surface of her legs and in her lower back. Acupressure massage brought immediate relief (Spring in Shady Mound, Terrestrial Machine, Repeating Stagnant). She now treats herself regularly with massage before her period, and continues to be nearly free from headaches and cramps.

Name: Barbara Z.
Age: 43
Symptoms: Mrs. Z. had recurrent pains on one side of her head. This was initially diagnosed as migraine, but numerous medications brought only partial relief. Associated with the pain was irritability and depression. A diagnosis of low blood sugar was made, but a special diet failed to afford relief. During her headaches her scalp became tender and she could barely move her head because of tightening of the neck muscles.
Treatment: Acupuncture and acupressure massage have reduced the frequency and severity of her headaches. Whenever Mrs. Z. feels tension building in her head, she methodically locates the tender spots and applies rotating pressure until the tenderness—and pain—is relieved (Connecting the Valleys, K'un Lun Mountains, Suspended Bell, Great Flush).

Most headaches respond to this treatment: locate the associated tender areas in head, neck, and face, and apply gentle rotating pressure until tenderness is relieved.

Name: Inez C.
Age: 39
Symptoms: Mrs. C. began experiencing periodic heartburn and stomach pain, as a result of pressure on the job. As the pains became more severe, she consulted a physician, who told her she was too tense, and would develop a stomach ulcer. Tranquilizers were prescribed, but her symptoms continued.
Treatment: A general massage program was initiated to promote relaxation (Connecting the Valleys, Shoulder Well, Great Flush, Water Spring). At each visit another part of the body was massaged. After three treatments there was a noticeable improvement, and after six visits she was symptom-free.

FRED S. GRUNWALD, M.D., F.I.C.S., F.A.C.A.

Name: Lila J.
Age: 41
Symptoms: Ache in arms after helping neighbor load cartons into station wagon in preparation for opening summer cabin.
Treatment: Bent Pont, Elbow Bone, Celestial Spring. Condition gradually subsidied. Pain was largely eased the day after the first treatment and completely gone after the second treatment.

Name: Jenny D.
Age: 14
Symptoms: History of asthma in varying degrees of severity. Began when she was approximately ten. Seems to bear relationship to such airborne elements as smoke, etc. Neighbor burning leaves triggered the attack that prompted search for medical treatment.
Treatment: Upper Epigastrium and Lung Locus. Then Superficial Tortuosity alternating with Sky Prominence. Symptoms gradually subsided.

Name: Harold P.
Age: 48
Symptoms: Patient had been painting interior rooms of apartment with paint roller. Work occupied most of the weekend. On Monday, patient reported severe pain in upper arm and shoulder upon even slight movement. Condition was diagnosed as bursitis.
Treatment: Acupuncture was combined with acupressure using Three Li, Huge Bone, Short Narrow Marsh. Immediate pain was relieved so that patient could resume normal activities; the basic condition was gradually relieved using a combination of acupuncture and acupressure over the course of five additional treatments.

Name: Janice L.
Age: 26
Symptoms: Worked in advertising agency with high level of nervous tension. Suffered from chronic constipation since coming to New York and entering present line of work.
Treatment: Over series of six treatments using Spleen Locus, Large Intestine Locus, Branching Ditch, Rich and Prosperous, the condition gradually eased until patient resumed normal bowel movements.

Name: Norman K.
Age: 33
Symptoms: Winter cold that lingered. After cold gone, cough remained and resisted all remedies.
Treatment: Supreme Cave, Fish Seam, Yang Tradesman. Acute symptoms alleviated in two treatments. After three more treatments, remaining discomfort gone.

Name: Jacqueline H.
Age: 51
Symptoms: Severe pain in right elbow after digging in garden during first spring weekend.
Treatment: Bitter Cold Abyss, Huge Bone, Bent Pond, Short Narrow Marsh. One treatment eased most of the discomfort, remainder gone after two more treatments.

Name: Vincent L.
Age: 63
Symptoms: Patient complained of extreme fatigue when traveling on long trips with children and grandchildren.

Treatment: Since it was impractical to stop for rest, patient was instructed to have someone apply acupressure to Great Metropolis and Young Sea whenever the condition occurred. This eased the fatigue and gave patient an extra boost of energy.

Name: Peter H.
Age: 58
Symptoms: In extremely cold weather, patient complained of severe facial pains that lingered even after entering warm shelter.
Treatment: Patient was instructed to apply acupressure to Terrestrial Granary, Connecting the Valleys, Cheek Chariot whenever the pains appeared, and to repeat the acupressure until the discomfort had subsided.

Name: Agnes R.
Age: 27
Symptoms: Patient was referred by dentist who was undertaking a program of gum prophelaxis over an extended period of time. In the interim, the patient complained of continual gum discomfort.
Treatment: Patient was treated twice with good response and instructed on the points to self-treat whenever the pain became severe. Points used were Gum Crossing, Terrestrial Granary, Yin Screen.

Name: Clarice B.
Age: 34
Symptoms: Patient complained of recurrent episodes of stomach upset and indigestion. Nervous tension due to life style.
Treatment: Points used were Four Full, Trades Hill, Perfecture House and Beam Gate. Significant relief after five treatments.

Name: Henry H.
Age: 21
Symptoms: Patient complained of nasal congestion that was only partially relieved by decongestants. Series of desensitizing injections was only of moderate help.
Treatment: Patient was instructed to apply pressure to Welcome Fragrance and the New Point midway between the eyebrows whenever the nasal occlusion became too acute for comfort. Combination of professional treatment with self-ministrations kept the discomfort level within tolerance.

Name: Maybelle L.
Age: 41
Symptoms: Patient suffered from virtually constant sore throat (most probably as a result of cigarette smoking, which she refused to give up).
Treatment: A series of four treatments on Connecting the Valleys, Five Miles and Yang Tradesman eased the pain considerably. Permanent alleviation of pain will require the patient to give up smoking. Without this, sore throat will undoubtedly return.

Name: Nancy Y.
Age: 29
Symptoms: Upon learning of the death of a close friend, patient fainted.
Treatment: She was immediately treated by being placed in a prone position with her feet raised on several pillows. Acupressure was applied to Pouring Spring and Middle of Man. She revived swiftly as a result of the acupressure treatment.

HOWARD D. KURLAND, M.D.

Including acupressure as part of a total medical treatment program for headache relief, Dr. Kurland helps patients eliminate pain medication.

Name: Vera M.
Age: 36
Symptoms: Mrs. M. suffered from migraine headaches of major severity. The prime causes of these headaches, emotional and physical, were being treated: psychotherapy and antidepressive medication for the former, anticonvulsant drugs and diet modifications for the latter. Although several varieties of headache disappeared and others were substantially improved, Mrs. M. was still subject to such intense headache pain that she would have to retire to bed.
Treatment: The patient was taught how to administer acupressure stimulation to relieve vascular and tension headaches. She also taught her husband acupressure technique, so that when she felt unable to help herself she requested assist-

ance from him. Over a two-year period, Mrs. M. required only occasional and minimal use of aspirin-like medication, in addition to acupressure, for headache relief.

Name: Joseph G.
Age: 38
Symptoms: Mr. G. had a history of migraine headaches spanning over thirty years. For the last fifteen years the headaches had occurred in clusters, coming daily for five to seven consecutive days. The throbbing pain was accompanied by severe nausea and profuse sweating. Medical consultants recommended numerous preventive medicines, which were only partially successful; a heavy dependence on pain relievers had developed.
Treatment: The patient received three acupuncture treatments, each of which significantly reduced the pain and nausea. Mr. G. was taught how to stimulate the appropriate points with fingernail pressure. He reported good relief from headaches, and within a short period of time discontinued use of migraine preventatives and pain relievers. A follow-up visit two years later revealed that the headache cycles had been significantly reduced in frequency. The patient reported being infinitely more pain-free with acupressure than with analgesics.

Name: Florence M.
Age: 50
Symptoms: Mrs. M. had severe, throbbing frontal headaches, which frequently lasted several days. A diabetic, she sometimes experienced hypoglycemia (low blood sugar) despite daily insulin treatments and careful attention to diet. Often, these hypoglycemic episodes caused a headache to begin.
Treatment: Mrs. M. was instructed never to ignore the hypoglycemic symptoms preceding a headache, and to use acupressure for headache relief only after treating the hypoglycemia. Since her past suffering from headaches was so great, it took Mrs. M. nearly a year to overcome her dependence on narcotic pain killers. However, she was eventually able to liberate herself from these, and use acupressure exclusively and successfully to control headache pain.

Name: Frieda Y.
Age: 38
Symptoms: Mrs. Y. suffered from severe headache pain; usually

frontal, but occasionally beginning in the back of the head and producing a crushing sensation. The headaches often begin just prior to, or during, her menstrual period. In addition, electroencephalography revealed a seizure disorder which commonly produces headache. Further symptoms included dejection and despondency, which were intensified during the menstrual period but which remained throughout the month.

Treatment: Anticonvulsant and antidepressive medications were prescribed, as well as individual psychotherapy. Despite these treatments, intensified emotional stress sometimes produced severe headaches. She was taught acupressure for both frontal and top-of-the-head headaches. Most of these responded to acupressure, eliminating the need for further pain medication.

Editor's Note: Common points used by physicians for cases in this category include: Wind Pond, Extreme Shortcoming, Connecting the Valleys, and T'ai Yang.

INDEX